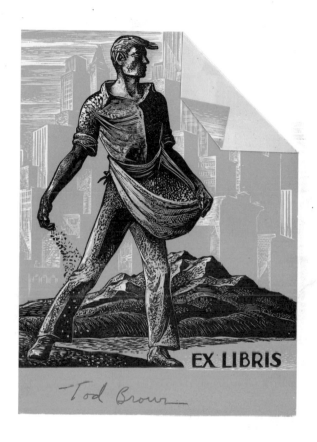

EX LIBRIS

Tod Brown

THE NEW TESTAMENT

THE
New Testament

Rendered From the Original Greek
With Explanatory Notes

PART ONE

The Four Gospels

TRANSLATED BY JAMES A. KLEIST, S.J.

PART TWO

Acts of the Apostles
Epistles and Apocalypse

TRANSLATED BY JOSEPH L. LILLY, C.M.

THE BRUCE PUBLISHING COMPANY
MILWAUKEE

IMPRIMI POTEST:
    Leo J. Burns, S.J.
    Vice-Provincial, Missouri Province

IMPRIMI POTEST:
    James W. Stakelum, C.M.
    Visitor

NIHIL OBSTAT:
    Robert G. Boucher, C.Ss.R., S.T.L., S.S.L.
    Censor deputatus

IMPRIMATUR:
    ✠ Moyses E. Kiley
    Archiepiscopus Milwauchiensis
October 22, 1952

Library of Congress Catalog Card Number: 54–7889

GENERAL FOREWORD

In presenting this new translation of the Gospel, a word must be said to justify the choice of a medium of expression quite different from that of the Douay-Challoner version.

The latter, indeed, was an honest attempt at rendering the Latin Vulgate into the English current at the time, and as such must remain a revered document of great historic worth. But new times create new interests. We find, therefore, a widespread feeling that the Bible should disclose its secrets in a diction that keeps pace with modern developments in the English language.

The distinctiveness of the present translation consists in the fact that it is directly derived from the Greek. This fact should obviously justify in every mind the appearance of the present book as a version definitely called for. But there is a still more direct reason which we find most clearly implied in a rather recent utterance of the Holy See.

For centuries, Catholic biblical scholars have been wide awake to the limited extent of their resources in the study of the Greek originals available today, but, says Pius XII, "for the last fifty years the conditions of biblical studies and their subsidiaries have greatly changed."[1] As was to be expected, "much light has been derived from these explorations for the more correct and fuller understanding of the Sacred Books." In particular it would be difficult to overestimate the advance made in the elucidation of that special development of ancient Greek which was actually spoken throughout the Mediterranean world at the time of Christ. This progress of biblical science in modern times clearly points the way to the Catholic scholar: "It is the *duty* of the exegete to lay hold, *with*

---

[1] *Divino Afflante Spiritu*, Encyclical Letter of Pope Pius XII on Promotion of Biblical Studies. National Catholic Welfare Conference, Washington, D. C., 1943.

the greatest care and reverence, of the very least expressions[2] which, under the inspiration of the Divine Spirit have flowed from the pen of the sacred writer, so as to arrive at a deeper and fuller knowledge of his meaning."[3]

If such, then, is the duty of the exegete, it surely would seem to follow that the translator's duty, in turn, must be to make these findings of biblical scholarship available to the general public by means of suitable renderings, based upon the Greek originals. That this attempt is full of risks we are well aware. A modern version, deviating from the one familiar to us from childhood and stamped, moreover, with the seal of literary allusions, has its own pitfalls. In the teeth of such initial difficulties, a translator then has no plain sailing. All he can hope for is that his version may have merit enough to convince its reader that it is not a hasty piece of work, but that it truly represents the fruit of conscientious labor and honest endeavor.

Accordingly, my principal object in this new translation of the Gospels has been to render the Greek into such modern English[4] as I felt would approve itself to American Catholics. In other words, I have aimed at doing what, after all, every Catholic priest is actually doing in the pulpit Sunday after Sunday. First, namely, he reads the pertinent passage from the official Douay-Challoner version. Next he lays down the book and launches forth into an exposition of its contents in language "understanded of the people." On this principle, then, I have avoided obsolescent words and expressions, such as "thou," "thee," "ye," as well as words which, though listed in dictionaries as "biblical," would not be readily understood by the

[2] See, for instance, "An Important Principle in the Rendering of the Gospels into Modern English," *American Ecclesiastical Review*, CX, 6 (1944), 435 ff., and "Emotion in the Gospels," *ibid.*, CXI, 1 (1944), 330 ff.

[3] See James A. Kleist, *The Gospel of St. Mark* (Milwaukee: Bruce, 1936), 137–180.

[4] Strictly "modern English" is all very well in its rightful place; but when the term is applied to a *translation*, particularly of an *ancient* writer, it needs to be modified so as to leave room for overcoming the inevitable weakness inherent in the very nature of translation. Just as the mentalities of two different persons may have much in common, yet must in their most characteristic properties be different, so the most characteristic features of one language — its "idioms" — cannot be "translated" so as to be characteristic of another. What is native to one language is generally alien to another. Consequently, it is enough for a translator to limit the peculiar flavor of the original to a minimum. Even the best translation is a hybrid.

average reader of today. The same purpose, moreover, called for a change in the word order or sentence structure of the original whenever it seemed that the requirements of current English usage or of clearness itself would be served by so doing.

Least of all was it my intention to produce a slavishly literal rendering of word for word; rather, my purpose has been to express, so far as possible, the exact meaning of the original text. It thus seemed necessary at times to use several words to convey the connotations of a single word in the Greek. Such liberties, in fact, belong to the recognized stock-in-trade of every classical scholar. Indeed, it must be borne in mind that the Greek New Testament is itself an ancient classic and should be treated as such. Thus, for instance, one notable feature of the ancient languages is their dearth of nouns and verbs, as compared with the truly exuberant wealth of modern English. The result is that ancient writers often were compelled to strain their vocabulary and to convey their meaning by an almost fatiguing repetition of the same Greek or Latin word. On the other hand, it is a distinct trend in modern English to be as specific as possible and vary the expression. But here, once more, caution is needed; for it may well be that the repetition of the same word adds a special charm and force to the original, such as should not be lost in the translation. A translator is a literary balancer.[5]

Where a Greek word or phrase is actually capable of more than one interpretation, the correct alternative generally is indicated in the notes. In the latter I have tried to do no more than help the reader to an *immediate* or *preliminary* *understanding* of obscure words or passages, supposing that he will look for further enlightenment from our standard biblical commentaries. The Greek text followed in this translation is that of Joseph M. Bover, S.J., in his *Novi Testamenti Biblia Graeca et Latina* (Madrid, 1943).

I am sure that no reader will find fault with my general object of presenting the Gospels in a modern dress. Of course, my personal manner of executing this object is a different matter. For obvious blemishes, however, should such be pointed out, whether in the interpretation of the Greek or in the verbal expression, there is an

---

[5] See Msgr. Knox's instructive paper, "Farewell to Machabees," *The Clergy Review*, XXX, 4 (1948), 217–231.

easy remedy. As for matters of taste, I can claim no more than tolerance, and may, perhaps, find comfort in a word of the psalmist
(118:96), who knew life and its trials: "Omnis perfectionis vidi
esse terminum!" That is, "All perfection — I have seen — is limited!"
There is a touch of sadness in the choice of omnis and, especially,
of vidi, implying: "by sad experience I have found this out."

I should like to close this Foreword with an admonition by Pius
XII: "Let all the other sons of the Church bear in mind that the
efforts of these resolute laborers in the vineyard of the Lord should
be judged not only with equity and justice, but also with the greatest
charity; all, moreover, should abhor that intemperate zeal which
imagines that whatever is new should, for that very reason, be
opposed or suspected."[6]

JAMES A. KLEIST, S.J.

Christmas, 1948

-----

[6] The following up-to-date helps to Bible study are within easy reach of the
general reader:

W. Dowd, S.J., The Gospel Guide (Milwaukee: The Bruce Publishing Co.,
1932).

A Commentary on the New Testament, prepared by the Catholic Biblical
Association (Washington, D. C., 1942).

John E. Steinmueller, S.T.D., and Kathryn Sullivan, R.S.C.J., A Companion
to the New Testament (New York: Joseph F. Wagner, 1945).

John E. Steinmueller, S.T.D., A Companion to Scripture Studies; I, General
Introduction to the Bible (New York: Joseph F. Wagner, 1941).

The two most useful commentaries on the Gospel according to St. John are
Évangile sélon saint Jean, by M.-J. Lagrange (5th ed.; Paris, 1936) and Das
Johannesevangelium, by Fritz Tillmann (4th ed.; Bonn, 1931).

The professional biblical scholar need not be told where to find an answer
to the numerous questions posed by biblical criticism. It is here enough to say
that Lagrange's treatment is a conservative and critical discussion of all problems
involved.

PREFACE

A word of explanation is needed here by way of introduction to this unusually important work — a rendition of the New Testament from ancient Greek into the English of our day. For the authentic sources of this book, we must go back to the very period immediately following our Savior's life on earth, and there hearken to his words as duly recorded by the men then still close to the apostolic age or living at that very time. It thus answers alike the most exacting demands of modern scholarship and no less the spiritual needs of millions of potential readers, in whatever walk of life, who speak one common English tongue.

The rendition of the Four Gospels is due to the Reverend James A. Kleist, S.J., who has left us this translation as a culmination of his long lifework in the field of ancient Greek. Particularly significant in relation to the present work, was his rendition of writings by the Apostolic Fathers, translated from ancient Greek into our own tongue. As his bequest to his fellow man, Father Kleist has left his translation of the Sacred Gospels from the ancient Greek into an accurate, literary, and yet highly popular and readily intelligible English.*

Notes for the Four Gospels were largely composed by the Rev. Henry Willmering, S.J., to whom particular credit must be given.

Following upon Father Kleist's admirable rendering of the Gospels, a similar translation is offered of all the remaining sections of the New Testament, equally rendered from the same reliable source. Included in Part II, as prepared by the Reverend Joseph L. Lilly, C.M., and admirably matching Father Kleist's rendi-

---

* Fr. Kleist, according to his own explanation, had definitely limited himself to providing "an immediate or preliminary understanding of obscure words or passages."

tion of the Gospels, will be found a careful and well-worded translation of the Acts of the Apostles, of the numerous Epistles that follow next in order, and finally of the Apocalypse with which the New Testament closes.

Scholarly introductions have been provided by the translator. They are offered, not merely for the Acts of the Apostles and the Apocalypse, but for each New Testament Epistle. Considering that these Epistles alone number no fewer than twenty-one, we can realize the extent of the labor implied in these excellently and carefully compiled aids for the reader. Moreover, Father Lilly has also supplied the notes for his section.

Combined, the two sections present us with the invaluable treasure of a truly modern version of the entire New Testament as rendered out of the original Greek text into our own modern vernacular. There is no reason, however, why these two works may nonetheless be considered as separate undertakings, each complete in its own distinctive field.

JOSEPH HUSSLEIN, S.J., PH.D.

General Editor, Science and Culture Series

St. Louis University

CONTENTS

PART ONE

THE FOUR GOSPELS

PART TWO

ACTS OF THE APOSTLES; EPISTLES AND APOCALYPSE

xi

CONTENTS

MAPS

LISTS OF ABBREVIATION

THE BOOKS OF THE NEW TESTAMENT

Mt.	The Gospel according to St. Matthew
Mk.	The Gospel according to St. Mark
Lk.	The Gospel according to St. Luke
Jn.	The Gospel according to St. John
Acts.	The Acts of the Apostles
Rom.	The Epistle to the Romans
1 Cor. . . .	The First Epistle to the Corinthians
2 Cor. . . .	The Second Epistle to the Corinthians
Gal.	The Epistle to the Galatians
Eph.	The Epistle to the Ephesians
Phil.	The Epistle to the Philippians
Col.	The Epistle to the Colossians
1 Thess. . . .	The First Epistle to the Thessalonians
2 Thess. . . .	The Second Epistle to the Thessalonians
1 Tim. . . .	The First Epistle to Timothy
2 Tim. . . .	The Second Epistle to Timothy
Tit.	The Epistle to Titus
Philemon . . .	The Epistle to Philemon
Hebr.	The Epistle to the Hebrews
James	The Epistle of St. James
1 Pet.	The First Epistle of St. Peter
2 Pet.	The Second Epistle of St. Peter
1 Jn.	The First Epistle of St. John
2 Jn.	The Second Epistle of St. John
3 Jn.	The Third Epistle of St. John
Jude	The Epistle of St. Jude
Apoc.	The Apocalypse (also called Revelations)

THE BOOKS OF THE OLD TESTAMENT

Gen.	The Book of Genesis
Exod. . . .	The Book of Exodus
Lev.	The Book of Leviticus
Num.	The Book of Numbers
Deut.	The Book of Deuteronomy
Jos.	The Book of Josue (also called Joshua)
Judges	The Book of Judges
Ruth	The Book of Ruth
1 Kings . . .	The First Book of Kings (also called 1 Samuel)
2 Kings . . .	The Second Book of Kings (also called 2 Samuel)
3 Kings . . .	The Third Book of Kings (also called 1 Kings)
4 Kings . . .	The Fourth Book of Kings (also called 2 Kings)
1 Par.	The First Book of Paralipomenon (also called 1 Chronicles)
2 Par.	The Second Book of Paralipomenon (also called 2 Chronicles)
Esdras	The Book of Esdras (also called Ezra)
Neh.	The Book of Nehemias (also called 2 Esdras, or Ezra)

1

LIST OF ABBREVIATIONS

Tob. . . . . The Book of Tobias (also called Tobit)
Jud. . . . . The Book of Judith
Esth. . . . . The Book of Esther
Job . . . . . The Book of Job
Ps. . . . . . The Book of Psalms (numbered according to the Vulgate)
Prov. . . . . The Book of Proverbs
Eccles. . . . . The Book of Ecclesiastes (also called Koheleth)
Cant. . . . . The Canticles of Canticles (also called Song of Songs)
Wisd. . . . . The Book of Wisdom (also called the Wisdom of Solomon)
Ecclus. . . . The Book of Ecclesiasticus (also called Sirach)
Isa. . . . . . The Book of Isaias (or Isaiah)
Jer. . . . . . The Book of Jeremias (or Jeremiah)
Lam. . . . . The Book of Lamentations (also called Threni)
Bar. . . . . The Book of Baruch
Ezech. . . . . The Book of Ezechiel
Dan. . . . . The Book of Daniel
Osee . . . . The Book of Osee (also called Hosea)
Joel . . . . The Book of Joel
Amos . . . . The Book of Amos
Abdias . . . . The Book of Abdias (also called Obadiah)
Jonas . . . . The Book of Jonas (or Jonah)
Mich. . . . . The Book of Micheas (also called Micah)
Nah. . . . . The Book of Nahum
Habacuc . . . The Book of Habacuc (or Habakkuk)
Sophonias . . . The Book of Sophonias (also called Zephaniah)
Agg. . . . . The Book of Aggeus (also called Haggai)
Zach. . . . . The Book of Zacharias (or Zachary, or Zechariah)
Mal. . . . . The Book of Malachias (or Malachy)
1 Mach. . . . The First Book of Machabees
2 Mach. . . . The Second Book of Machabees

OTHER ABBREVIATIONS

M. T. . . . . The Massoretic Text — the Hebrew text
LXX . . . . The Septuagint: a pre-Christian translation in Greek

OTHER NOTATIONS

Mt. 1:2 . . . Signifies: the Gospel of St. Matthew, Chapter 1, verse 2.
Isa. 35:5; 61:1 . In a series like this, the numbers refer to chapter and verse of the last preceding name; here: Isaias.
Mt. 7:6–11 . . Refers to St. Matthew, Chapter 7, verses 6 to 11.
9:6 . . . . . When numbers are given without any further qualification, these refer to chapter and verse of the same book in which the reference is made.
f., ff. . . . . Signifies the following verse, the following verses.
Ps. 81(82):6 . In quoting a psalm, when a number is given in parentheses, the first number refers to the Vulgate numbering of the psalms, and the number in parentheses refers to the Hebrew numbering of the same psalm.
parallel account . This means the account of the same incident which is found in another of the Gospels.

2

PART ONE

The Four Gospels

TRANSLATED BY JAMES A. KLEIST, S.J.

THE GOSPELS

Introductory Note

On opening the New Testament we come first upon the accounts of the life and teachings of Jesus Christ, called the Gospels. The general subject is the same in all four narratives; but since each evangelist writes from his own point of view, we speak of the Gospel according to St. Matthew, the Gospel according to St. Mark, the Gospel according to St. Luke, and the Gospel according to St. John the Evangelist.

In the popular mind, our word "Gospel" is a combination of *God* and *Spel*, the latter word signifying "news," "tidings," etc., and both together being taken to mean: "the word of God." In reality, however, it is a corruption not of *God spel* but of *good spel*, and thus really means: "good news," "glad tidings," "message of salvation." These words, then, would seem to express exactly the English equivalent.

But here an awkwardness arises. To a modern reader, the word "Gospel" immediately suggests, not the Baptist's or Christ's preaching of the kingdom of God (as in Mk. 1:14 or Mt. 4:23), but any one, or all, of the four particular concrete written forms in which this preaching was crystallized some decades after the Ascension. Obviously, the term "good news," on the lips of the Baptist or Christ, was less specific and more inclusive than our word "Gospel." To avoid this awkwardness, it has seemed advisable to use the expression "good news" or "the message of salvation" whenever the wider or more original sense of the word *Evangelium* was intended by the sacred writer, and reserve the word "Gospel" for passages where there is an approach to the modern term (see, for instance, 2 Tim. 2:8 or Mk. 1:1).

5

Since the first three accounts very frequently overlap in recording the deeds and sayings of Jesus, it is convenient, for the sake of comparison and more intimate study, to arrange them in parallel columns. Such an arrangement is called "synopsis," and the three evangelists, whose coincidences and divergences are thus seen "at a glance," are therefore spoken of as "Synoptics."

It may be asked how it is possible that the Synoptics, though telling essentially the same story, should nevertheless show so many divergencies in the choice and arrangement of subject matter and in their mode of expression. The problem concerned with the solution of this complicated question is called the "Synoptic Problem." That a clear-cut answer is practically beyond reach, should be evident from the outset. If we ourselves had been followers of Christ, and seen everything he ever did, and heard everything he ever said and had moreover entered fully into his mind, and, finally, had a perfect memory at our command, we should, no doubt, have one well-defined impression of his life and teaching. In fact, however, not one of the evangelists was in a position to fulfill all the conditions necessary for such an achievement. Consequently, they were compelled to rely on oral tradition in order that they might fill in such details as lay beyond their immediate observation. Besides, allowance must be made for differences arising out of individual qualifications for writing, not to mention personal tastes, and we must further also bear in mind that the ancients in general were more concerned with the sense of what was said on any given occasion than with the verbal expression of this sense.

It is obvious, moreover, that once one of the Gospels was put in circulation, every subsequent writer would feel free to select from the account what suited his own purpose in writing, or to modify its expression.

So, then, this bare recital of the difficulties under which the evangelists were laboring is enough to convince us that a perfect solution of the Synoptic Problem is beyond the reach of the keenest mind. Fortunately, however, we have the assurance, guaranteed by the Church's commission "to teach all nations" and by Christ's promise to be with the Church "as long as the world shall last," that all the four Gospels, whatever their dissimilarities may be, are the inspired word of God. Quite apart from this consideration, their actual agreement on all essential points is truly astonishing.

The following suggestions may help the reader to draw as much profit from the Gospels as possible.

First, all ancient compositions were intended by their authors to be read aloud, even when one was reading to himself. By "reading aloud" the ancients meant reading with an audible voice, slowly and meditatively, with frequent pauses even within the limits of the same sentence, and trying to capture the emotion of the narrator or the speaker, as the case may be. *It is for this reason that certain portions of the Gospels are presented colometrically* in the text offered here, that is, in short sense lines or thought units. This manner of presentation was very common in the classical schools of the Roman Empire at the time of St. Jerome, who, as he tells us, followed the common practice that had obtained in the writing of the Vulgate.

Second, it is well to begin by reading each Gospel as a whole from beginning to end on successive occasions, as opportunity serves. Each evangelist had one dominating object in view in selecting and arranging the material in hand. This object is best seen by continuous reading.

Third, since we read the Gospels in order to draw spiritual profit from them and enrich our daily lives, it is well to heed a warning given by our Lord himself in describing the several ways in which the divine seed is received: "Those described by the words, 'sown in the right kind of soil,' are such as listen to the message in the right and proper spirit, and therefore hold it fast and patiently bear fruit" (Lk. 8:15). Is not this warning needed as much today as it was nineteen centuries ago? The Chosen People had lamentably wandered away from the ideals held out to them in the Mosaic Law. It is, therefore, significant that Christ opened his preaching with the statement: "Do penance, for the kingdom of heaven is close at hand." To bring his people back to God was the immediate purpose of his divine mission.

Obviously, then, it would be disastrous for us today to treat the Gospels as literature of no more than antiquarian interest. Yet millions and millions of men read the Gospels today, and we seem to hear Christ say to them: "You have the Gospels at your finger ends . . . but you do not care to come to me in order to have *life*."

7

Let us heed his warning: "Give ear! Use your understanding!" The world at large is un-Christian and even anti-Christian. There is but one way of bringing it back to Christ, and that is through the Gospels. They solve all the vital problems that vex men's minds today.

The Gospels are not mere narratives of events distant in time and place; to the Christian they are a book of devotion. And here is where the reader's own initiative must impel him to mine the quarry that lies before him. The notes merely provide a rapid understanding of the context. But beneath the surface there are treasures which only devout meditation can unearth. In particular, Christ's utterances about himself are like "the wonders" which the psalmist found hidden in "the Law":

> "Open my eyes,
> and I will scan the wonders of your Law" (118:18).

Another conspicuous trait of the Gospels consists in the numerous parables used by our Lord to illustrate a truth or a rule of life. But here it is needful to add that the parable style of exhortation does not require every small detail of the illustration to have a counterpart in the application.

The Gospels are but fragmentary records of the life and teaching of Jesus Christ. St. Matthew's account is fullest in details; yet a comparison shows that he omitted much that is told by the other writers. St. Luke states (Acts 1:3) that after the Resurrection, Jesus spoke to the disciples about "the kingdom of God," that is, the Church; but he does not satisfy our curiosity regarding the content of these conversations. As to St. Mark, the fragmentary character of his narrative is at once evident, and we happen to know from Papias, the bishop of Hierapolis, that the disciples of St. John were painfully aware of this "shortcoming" of the Second Gospel.

Regarding, finally, the Gospel according to St. John, we have the testimony of some of his immediate disciples that the world could not hold all the volumes that would have to be written if all that Jesus did were faithfully recorded. This is a loss, no doubt; but the loss is not alarming. Much of this unwritten wealth of information found its way into the consciousness of the Church. There is, perhaps, a hint of this fact in Christ's parting words addressed to his disciples: "Teach them to observe all the commandments which I have given you" (Mt. 28:20). After all, it is the living Church that puts the Bible into our hands; it is she that guarantees its canonicity or inspirational character. The result is consoling: there can never be a clash or conflict between the Bible and the teaching of the Church. In this way, our loss of records is not absolute.

The customary order or sequence of the Gospels — Matthew, Mark, Luke, John — is attested by the Old Prologue of the Gospels and the Muratorian Fragment, and was by far the most commonly accepted one in the early Church. In particular, there is overwhelming evidence in favor of the view that the Gospel according to St. Matthew comes first in the order of time.

The Gospels were written in the ordinary everyday Greek of the time, and none of the writers makes any pretense to literary merit. Nonetheless, it would be easy to fill pages with what should be called gems of presentation found in them. There are phrases or passages in every Gospel which reflect the deep-felt emotion of the speaker or narrator, and lift the Christian reader into regions that lie beyond the natural circumference of the words as such. When Christ says, "I am the Way, and the Truth, and the Life," his words are part of everyone's vocabulary; but the Christian reader knows that they put him face to face with the Divinity.

In Christian art it is customary to characterize each of the evangelists by a significant symbol, in allusion to Ezech. 1:5 ff. and Apoc. 4:6. Thus, St. Matthew is symbolized by a human being, because he begins his Gospel with the genealogy of Christ; St. Mark, by a lion, because he opens his account with the preaching of John the Baptist, that voice ringing out in the desert; St. Luke, by an ox, suggested by the sacrifice of Zachary; St. John, by an eagle, because in his prologue he soars like an eagle and, with an eagle's eye, sees Christ in his pre-existent life.

In the present series of translations, each Gospel will be referred to by some distinctive variation of the Latin word Evangelium: The Good Message (Matthew); The Good News (Mark); The Good Tidings (Luke); The Good Word (John).

SAINT MATTHEW

Very little is known as certain about the person and life of the author of our First Gospel. He was one of the twelve Apostles. His Grecized name was Matthew (Mt. 9:9; 10:3; Mk. 3:18; Lk. 6:15; Acts 1:13). According to tradition and the evidence of the Gospels, he is identical with the man named Levi in Mk. 2:14; Lk. 5:27 and 29. He was the son of Alpheus, though not of the father of James, who bore the same name.

By profession, Matthew was a tax collector (Mt. 10:3; Mk. 2:14; Lk. 5:27), that is, one employed by the so-called publicans or men who collected the taxes imposed upon the Jews by the Roman government. Because of their business, which exposed them to frequent opportunities for greed and deception (Lk. 3:12–13), these men were detested by the Jews, to whom their co-operation with the foreign pagan masters was an abomination. Hence the frequent bracketing in the Synoptics of "sinners and tax collectors."

Obscure, too, and only sparingly lit up by tradition, is the later career of this Apostle. No doubt, he began his missionary work in Jewish communities, and it was perhaps this contact with the Jewish mind that induced him to prove that Christ was in reality the long-expected Messias. It is surmised that Arabia, Ethiopia, and Persia became his special fields of labor. An inference from Apoc. 18:20 and 21:14 seems to indicate that he died a martyr. His feast is kept on September 21.

The Gospel according to St. Matthew is a work of outstanding merit. It is well organized and systematically built up, not on chronological order — except, of course, in the broadest sense — but on an order suggested to him by the topics which he chose to present. According to tradition, he wrote his Gospel in the Aramaic language, which was common in Palestine at the time of Christ

11

and was similar to Hebrew. The Greek Gospel which has come down to us is, perhaps, a free translation of the Aramaic original, in the sense that, in translating it (perhaps with the Gospel according to St. Mark before him), St. Matthew was free to change his own original by additions and stylistic modifications. We need not suppose that all Jews at the time of Christ were bilingual; but, at any rate, a tax collector at Capharnaum, that busy trading center, could not carry on his business without being able to express himself in Greek.

The date of this Gospel is not certain. There are reasons for the view that it was written after the year 50 and before the destruction of Jerusalem, in the year 70.

St. Matthew makes a special point of convincing the Jews that Jesus Christ was the promised Messias. This is evident from his numerous references to the fulfillment of the ancient prophecies. It is also significant that, in fullness of detail, his version of the Sermon on the Mount far exceeds that of St. Luke. It is here, particularly, that he shows the fulfillment of the Law in Christ. He alone has preserved our Lord's important statement: "Do not think it is my mission to annul, but to fulfill." In later literature, none of the Gospels is so frequently quoted as that according to St. Matthew.

The life and teachings of Christ are presented in three great tableaux:

I. The Public Ministry in Galilee (4:12–18:35) preceded by an account of preliminary events. This section shows Jesus as a Teacher (4:12–7:29); as a Wonderworker (8:1–9:34); as engaged in conflict with the Jews (9:35–13:58); as instructing the disciples (14:1–18:35).

II. Christ's Ministry in Judea and Jerusalem (19:1–25:46).

III. The Passion, the Death, and the Resurrection of Jesus (26:1–28:20).

In reading this Gospel, it is interesting to watch the growth of attention given to Christ, that is, to see how his personality looms larger and larger, both in the impression he made on his hearers and in the increasing hostility of his enemies. It is a long way from his conception to his Ascension; and, as the mustard seed "is the tiniest of all seeds," yet grows and eventually becomes a tree, so the human and divine qualities of Christ stand out more and more conspicuously until the last five verses reveal the fullness of his splendor. Thus, endowed "with absolute authority in heaven and on earth," he commissions his Apostles to go into the world and "initiate all the nations into discipleship." Where, moreover, is the earthly monarch that has ever spoken to his subjects as Christ spoke to his followers: "And mark: I am with you at all times as long as the world shall last"?

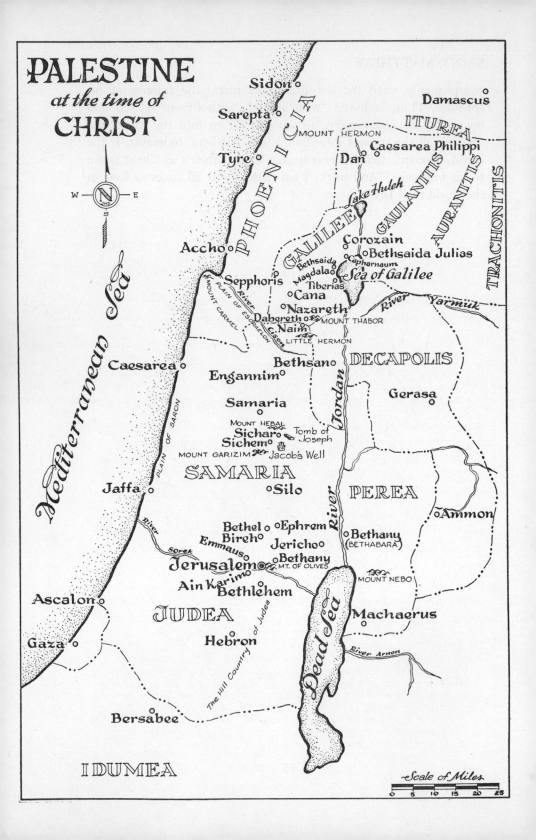

THE HOLY GOSPEL OF JESUS CHRIST ACCORDING TO

ST. MATTHEW

CHAPTER 1

THE ANCESTRY OF JESUS

1 A record of the life of Jesus Christ, the Son of David, the Son of Abraham.

2 Abraham was the father of Isaac; Isaac, the father of Jacob; Jacob, the 3 father of Judas and his brothers; Judas, the father of Phares and Zara, by Thamar; Phares, the father of Esron; Esron, the father of Aram; 4 Aram, the father of Aminadab; Aminadab, the father of Naasson; 5 Naasson, the father of Salmon; Salmon, the father of Booz, by Rahab; 6 Booz, the father of Obed, by Ruth; Obed, the father of Jesse; Jesse, the father of King David; David, the father of Solomon, by the wife of Urias; Solomon, the father of Roboam; Roboam, the father 7 of Abia; Abia, the father of Asa; Asa, the father of Josaphat; Josaphat, 8 the father of Joram; Joram, the father of Ozias; Ozias, the father of 9 Joatham; Joatham, the father of Achaz; Achaz, the father of Ezechias; Ezechias, the father of Manasses; Manasses, the father of Amon; 10 Amon, the father of Josias; Josias, the father of Jechonias and his 11 brothers, at the time of the migration to Babylon.

12 After the migration to Babylon, Jechonias was the father of Salathiel; Salathiel, the father of Zorobabel; Zorobabel, the father 13

1:1. It seems that both SS. Matthew and Luke (3:23–38) give the genealogy of Joseph. The latter traces Joseph's line not by way of physical descent, but by way of juridical ancestry (perhaps as in Lk. 20:28; for which see Deut. 25:5). Christ's Davidic origin, and hence his claim to the throne of David, are legally established through his foster father, and physically through his Virgin Mother who was of David's family (see Lk. 1:32, 69). Note that the word "father" is often equivalent to "ancestor." Mary and Joseph seem to have been closely related. See *A Commentary of the New Testament*, prepared by the Catholic Biblical Association (New York: Sadlier, 1942).

of Abiud; Abiud, the father of Eliachim; Eliachim, the father of
14 Azor; Azor, the father of Sadoc; Sadoc, the father of Achim; Achim,
15 the father of Eliud; Eliud, the father of Eleazar; Eleazar, the father
16 of Matthan; Matthan, the father of Jacob; Jacob, the father of
Joseph, the husband of Mary; and of her was born Jesus, who is
called Christ.

17   In all, therefore, the generations from Abraham to David number
fourteen; again, from David to the migration to Babylon there are
fourteen generations; and once again, fourteen from the migration
to Babylon on to the Christ.

THE CONCEPTION OF JESUS

18   Regarding the conception of Jesus Christ, the circumstances were
as follows: his mother Mary had been espoused to Joseph; but before
they lived together, it was found that she was pregnant by the Holy
19 Spirit. Joseph, her husband, being right-minded and unwilling to
20 expose her, resolved to put her away without public formalities. He
had just made up his mind to this course when an angel of the Lord
appeared to him in a dream and said: "Joseph, son of David, do
not scruple to take Mary, your wife, into your home. Her conception
21 was wrought by the Holy Spirit. She will bear a Son and you are
22 to name him Jesus; for he will save his people from their sins." This
event with all its circumstances was to fulfill the Lord's prediction
made through the prophet, who says:
23   "Behold! The virgin will be pregnant
                          and give birth to a Son,
                    who will be called 'Emmanuel' " —
which means "God with us."

24   After awaking from his sleep, Joseph did as the angel of the
25 Lord had directed him, and took his wife into his home. He had

---

1:17. In order to have fourteen generations in each division, St. Matthew
suppresses some of the links in the genealogy.

1:18. *espoused:* an "espoused wife" was one bound by a solemn betrothal, but
not yet conducted to the home of her husband. The actual marriage ceremony
seems to be indicated in 1:24. It is not certain to what extent the details in the
parable narrated in 25:1 ff. are applicable to this ceremony.

1:23. *the virgin:* could be rendered "a virgin" with no difference in the sense.
See Isa. 7:14.

1:25. St. Matthew is solely concerned with what happened *before* the virginal
birth of Jesus. His words cannot be forced to mean that the marriage was consummated afterward. See notes on 12:46 and on Lk. 2:7.

16

no conjugal relations with her before she gave birth to a Son, whom he named Jesus.

CHAPTER 2

THE MAGI

After Jesus was born at Bethlehem in Judea, in the days of King 1
Herod, a commotion arose in Jerusalem when Magi from the East
arrived and inquired: "Where is the newborn King of the Jews? 2
It was his star we saw in the East, and we came to offer homage
to him."

The news threw King Herod into consternation, shared by all 3
Jerusalem. Assembling the whole body of the high priests and 4
Scribes — the nation's Council — he inquired of them where the
Messias was to be born. "At Bethlehem in Judea," they said to 5
him; "for this is what has been written by the prophet:

> 'And you, Bethlehem, in the land of Juda,   6
> are not the least of Juda's principalities;
> for out of you shall come forth a Ruler,
> who will shepherd my people Israel.' "

Then Herod secretly summoned the Magi and, after carefully 7
ascertaining from them the time during which the star had been
visible, he sent them to Bethlehem with this injunction: "Go and 8
make careful inquiries about the child, and, when you have found
him, report to me. I, too, wish to go and do homage to him."
So they obeyed the king and went their way; and, unexpectedly, 9
the star they had seen in the East preceded them till it came and
stopped over the place where the child was! At sight of the star 10

2:1. *Magi:* the learned class in Persia and Chaldea. The same word has a different meaning in Acts 13:6.

2:2. *his star:* probably a preternatural phenomenon, analogous to "the pillar of fire" (Exod. 13:21) which guided the Israelites through the desert.

offer homage to him: that special form of obeisance shown in the Orient to men of superior rank; it consisted in kneeling and kissing the ground or the feet or garments of the person so honored. When rendered by a believer to God, such homage was an act of "adoration."

2:4. *Scribes:* religious teachers, teachers of the Law, legal experts. They generally belonged to the Pharisaical party. In contrast with the Scribes, who generally repeated what others had taught, Jesus spoke with authority. He was also able to enforce his teaching by the working of miracles.

Herod's appeal to *the nation's Council* was the providential means of informing the Jews officially of the arrival of the Messias.

17

11 they were supremely happy. And so, entering the house and seeing
the child with his mother Mary, they threw themselves down to do
homage to him. Opening also their treasure chests, they presented
12 him with gifts: gold, frankincense, and myrrh. But advised in a
dream not to return to Herod, they departed for their country by
a different route.

THE FLIGHT INTO EGYPT

13   When they had departed, an angel of the Lord appeared, just
in time, in a dream to Joseph, saying: "Rise! Take with you the
child and his mother and flee into Egypt! Remain there till I give
you further notice! Herod is on the point of searching for the child
14 in order to take his life!" So he arose, and taking the child and
his mother with him, withdrew by night into Egypt, where he
15 stayed until the death of Herod. This event was to fulfill the Lord's
prediction made through the prophet, who said:
                    "Out of Egypt have I called my Son."
16   When at last Herod realized that he had been tricked by the
Magi, he flew into a fierce rage and issued orders to massacre all the
male children in Bethlehem and the whole vicinity who were two
years old or under, reckoning by the time he had ascertained from
17 the Magi. It was then that the prediction made through the prophet
Jeremias was fulfilled:
18   "A cry was heard at Rama,
                    there was weeping and sore lament.
                    Rachel wept for her children;
                    she would not be consoled,
                    because they were no more."

THE RETURN TO THE LAND OF ISRAEL

19   In due time after the death of Herod, an angel of the Lord
20 appeared in a dream to Joseph in Egypt and said: "Rise! Take with
you the child and his mother, and set out for the land of Israel.
21 They who were plotting against the life of the child are dead." He
rose and, taking the child and his mother with him, returned to
22 the land of Israel. But when he learned that Archelaus had succeeded

---

2:15. Christ was born some time before 4 B.C., the year of Herod's death.
The beginning of our Christian era does not coincide with our Lord's birth.

18

his father Herod as king of Judea, he was afraid to go there; so, after being advised in a dream, he withdrew to the province of Galilee. Thither he went, making his home in a town called Nazareth; 23 that so might be fulfilled the prediction made through the prophets, that he was to be called a Nazarene.

CHAPTER 3

JOHN THE BAPTIST

In those days John the Baptist arrived to preach in the desert 1 of Judea, and his theme was: "You need a change of heart; the 2 kingdom of heaven is close at hand." This is the man spoken of 3 by Isaias the prophet, who says:

"A herald's voice rings out in the desert:
'Make ready the way of the Lord;
make straight his paths.' "

John wore a distinctive garment of camel's hair and a leathern 4 girdle was round his loins; his food was locusts and wild honey. Soon Jerusalem and the rest of Judea, as well as the entire region 5 on either side of the Jordan, went out to meet him. They confessed 6 their sins and were baptized by him in the Jordan River.

WARNING TO THE PHARISEES AND SADDUCEES

On seeing many of the Pharisees and Sadducees coming to the 7

3:2. *the kingdom of heaven* (Dan. 2:44; 7:13 f.): the expression sometimes means the royal power or dominion of God in the hearts of men, and sometimes signifies the Church, through which this power is ordinarily exercised. The other evangelists prefer the expression "the kingdom of God." In Semitic literature, the word "heaven" is often a reverential reference to "God."

a change of heart (and mind): before the Jewish people were prepared for the kingdom of God (Lk. 1:17), they had to undergo a complete change of heart and mind. Their whole spiritual attitude unfitted them for the teachings of Christ. The "new wine" of the Gospel required "fresh wine skins" (see the note on 9:16). The "old leaven" had to be purged out (1 Cor. 5:7). The Greek term is more inclusive than our words "penance" and "repentance."

3:3. Isa. 40:3.

3:7. *Pharisees and Sadducees:* the two religious parties. The former were sticklers for the Law, and laid stress on the observance of external rites and outward forms of piety, to the neglect of the spirit of the Law (see 23:13 ff.). They were bitterly hostile to Jesus, who often rebuked them for their avarice, ambition, and affectation of piety (see 6:5). The Sadducees were distinguished for birth, wealth, and influential position; they rejected the tradition of the elders, and denied both the immortality of the soul and the resurrection of the body. They were the rationalists and freethinkers among the Jews.

scene of his baptism he said to them: "Brood of vipers! Who advised
8 you to flee before the gathering storm of anger? Well, then, let your
9 conduct show your change of heart! And do not presume to say to
yourselves: 'We have Abraham for our father!' I tell you, God is
10 able to raise up children to Abraham out of these very stones. Besides,
from now on the axe lies ready to strike at the root of the trees;
any tree, therefore, that does not produce sound fruit is cut down
11 and thrown into the fire. I baptize you with water to help you make
a change of heart; but One shall come after me who is mightier than
I and whose sandals I am not worthy to take off his feet. He for
his part will baptize you with the Holy Spirit — or else with fire.
12 His winnowing fan in hand, he will thoroughly cleanse his threshing
floor: the wheat he will store in his barn, and the chaff he will burn
in unquenchable fire."

JESUS IS BAPTIZED BY JOHN

13   At that time Jesus arrived from Galilee to meet John at the
14 Jordan and be baptized by him. John tried to stop him. "It is I who
15 should be baptized by you," he said, "and you come to me?" Jesus
remonstrated. "Let me have my way for the present," he said to
him; "after all, it is only so that we fulfill, as is proper for us, all
just demands." Then he let him have his way.

16   No sooner was Jesus baptized, than he came up out of the water,
and there and then the heavens opened to his view: he saw the
Spirit of God descend in the shape of a dove, and alight on him.
17 And lo! a voice rang out upon the air:
                "This is my Son, the beloved,
                  with whom I am well pleased."

3:11. *I baptize you with water:* the baptism of John did not confer sanctifying grace. See also the note on Lk. 3:16. This is to explain his rendering "or else with fire."

3:15. *remonstrated:* the Greek word, when following a question, means to "answer." When no question has been asked, a statement prefaced by that word either answers a purpose, meets a suggestion (as in Lk. 4:4), registers a protest, corrects an erroneous notion, is appropriate to the occasion (as in Mk. 9:5, 6), or is an answer to a question not expressed but latent in the mind of the person addressed. There are 226 occurrences of this word in the Gospels.

it is only so: note this alternative rendering: "It is proper for us to comply, without more ado, with all just demands."

3:16. The words *to his view* are not found in all manuscripts.

3:17. *upon the air:* the Greek word may, however, mean "from heaven," that is, "from God." See the first note on 3:2.

Chapter 4

JESUS IS TEMPTED BY THE DEVIL

Then Jesus was led on by the Spirit into the desert to be put 1
to the test by the devil. Forty days and forty nights he fasted and 2
after that he was hungry. Now then the tempter approached and 3
said to him: "If you are the Son of God, command these stones to
turn into loaves of bread." But he met the proposal by replying: "It 4
is written, 'Man does not live by bread alone: but by every word
coming from the lips of God.'"

Then the devil took him up into the holy city and set him down 5
upon the gable-peak of the temple. "If you are the Son of God," he 6
said to him, "fling yourself down; for the Scripture says: 'to his
angels he will give charge of you' and 'Upon their hands they
will bear you up that you may not strike your foot against a stone.'"
Jesus answered him: "On the other hand, the Scripture says: 'You 7
shall not tempt the Lord your God!'"

Again, the devil took him up to a very high mountain and let 8
him see all the kingdoms of the world and their splendor. "All 9
these things I will give to you," he said to him, "if you go down on
your knees and do homage to me." Then Jesus said to him: "Begone, 10
Satan! The Scripture says: 'You shall do homage to the Lord your
God, and him alone shall you adore!'" So then the devil left him 11
undisturbed and, presently, angels approached and waited on him.

JESUS WITHDRAWS TO GALILEE

At the news of John's imprisonment he withdrew to Galilee. 12
There, after leaving Nazareth for good, he went to make his home 13
in Capharnaum, which is situated by the sea in the region of
Zabulon and Nephthalim. Thus was to be verified the prediction 14
made through the prophet Isaias, who said:

"Land of Zabulon and land of Nephthalim,   15
     stretching as far as the sea;
     land beyond the Jordan;
     Galilee of the Gentiles!

4:4. Deut. 8:3.
4:6. Ps. 90:11 f.

21

16   The people dwelling in darkness
        have beheld a great Light,
        and over the dwellers
        in the shadowland of death
        has arisen a Light."

17   From that time on, Jesus set himself to preach and proclaim:
"Do penance, for the kingdom of heaven is close at hand."

THE FIRST CALL OF SOME APOSTLES

18   Walking about by the Sea of Galilee one day, he saw two
brothers, Simon, surnamed Peter, and his brother Andrew, who
were flinging a casting net into the sea; for they were fishermen.
19 "Come, follow me," he said to them; "and I will make you fishers
20 of men." At once they abandoned their nets and became his follow-
21 ers. Thence he went on and saw another pair of brothers, James,
the son of Zebedee, and his brother John. They were in a boat with
their father Zebedee, mending their nets, and he called them.
22 Forthwith they abandoned their boat and their father, and followed him.

MIRACULOUS CURES

23   And so Jesus toured the whole of Galilee, instructing the people
in their synagogues and preaching the Good News of the kingdom,
besides healing every disease and every infirmity found among his
24 countrymen. The result was that the report about him spread to
every place in Syria. And all those suffering from various diseases
were brought to him, whether they were racked with pain, or
possessed by demons, or epileptic, or paralyzed. And he cured them.
25 On his wanderings he was joined by numerous groups from Galilee
and the Decapolis, from Jerusalem and the rest of Judea, and from
the other side of the Jordan.

4:23. *the Good News:* see the General Introduction.
4:25. *the Decapolis:* a confederation of ten cities in northeastern Palestine; there
were, however, smaller towns scattered among them. The inhabitants were chiefly
pagan.

22

Chapter 5

CHRIST BEGINS THE SERMON ON THE MOUNT

One day when his eyes fell on the multitude, he went up a   *1*
mountainside, where he sat down, with his disciples close to him.
Opening his lips he gave to his hearers a lengthy instruction, saying: *2*

> "Blessed are the humble souls,   *3*
> for theirs is the kingdom of heaven.
>
> Blessed are the meek and gentle,   *4*
> for they will inherit the land.
>
> Blessed are the sorrowing,   *5*
> for they will be consoled.
>
> Blessed are those who hunger and thirst after holiness,   *6*
> for they will be fully satisfied.
>
> Blessed are the merciful,   *7*
> for they will have mercy shown to them.
>
> Blessed are the singlehearted,   *8*
> for they will see God.

5:1. There is no uniform tradition regarding the place where the Sermon on the Mount was delivered. See Lk. 6:17.

5:3. Since Christ came to establish *the kingdom of heaven*, which is begun on earth and consummated in heaven, and since our true "blessedness" consists in belonging to it both here and hereafter, he states the qualifications of the true members of this Messianic kingdom. In interpreting the rewards, some of the Fathers stress more the earthly character of the kingdom, others its consummation in heaven.

the humble souls: the kind of people whom St. Paul describes in 1 Cor. 1:26–28. The Greek adjective means "of low rank in life, downtrodden, oppressed, mean in the eyes of the world," rather than "poor" or "beggarly." The expression generally rendered "in spirit" (here implied in the noun *souls*) means that persons so situated are blessed if they accept their lot willingly and with due submission to Divine Providence.

5:4. *the meek and gentle:* two aspects of "patience" are required to merit this blessedness: the absence of passion or anger in the face of injury suffered, and the consistent meekness or gentleness of temper which refuses to injure others. The Promised Land was a type of the Messianic kingdom.

5:5. *the sorrowing:* again another aspect of the humble, etc. A true Christian's life is not one of unalloyed joy, but a continual war on the appetites of his lower nature.

5:8. The most notable trait in the character of the Pharisees was hypocrisy, duplicity, lack of singleness of purpose. Even their observance of the Law was intended to win them honor from men; see 6:1; 6:5; Jn. 5:44. The rendering "clean of heart" seems too narrow. The Fathers of the Church are not unanimous in interpreting this beatitude.

9   Blessed are the promoters of peace,
        for they will rank as children of God.
10   Blessed are the victims of persecution for conscience' sake
        for theirs is the kingdom of heaven.
11 Blessed are you when you are reviled, or persecuted, or made a
12 target for nothing but malicious lies — for my sake. Rejoice; yes,
    leap for joy; a rich reward awaits you in heaven. So, too, were
    persecuted the prophets who preceded you.

DUTIES TOWARD OTHERS

13   "You are the salt of the earth. But suppose salt should lose
    its savor, what is there to restore its nature? It is no longer good for
    anything except to be thrown out of doors and trampled upon by
    passers-by!
14   "You are the light of the world. It is impossible for a city to
15 escape notice when built on a mountain top. Nor do people light a
    lamp and then hide it under a bushel-basket. No, it is set on a
16 lampstand that it may give light to all in the house. Just so let
    your light shine before your fellow men, that they may see your good
    example and praise your Father who is in heaven.

CHRIST'S MISSION IS TO FULFILL THE LAW

17   "Do not think it is my mission to annul the Law or the Prophets.
18 It is not my mission to annul, but to fulfill. I assure you emphatically:

5:16. *example:* an effort has been made in this version to find suitable modern equivalents for the Greek word commonly rendered "work." See *The Catholic Biblical Quarterly*, Vol. 6, p. 61 ff.

5:17. *it is my mission:* literally, "I came, *sc.* into the world." A comparison of Mk. 1:38 with the parallel account in Lk. 4:43 shows that the idea of "being sent," *sc.* by the Father, was ever present to our Lord's mind when he spoke of his "coming into the world." The Fourth Gospel lays particular stress on the fact that Christ was "the Father's ambassador."
Christ fulfilled the prophets by fulfilling their predictions. The Mosaic Law was partly ceremonial, partly moral. The former (embracing religious rites, sacrifices, distinction of clean and unclean foods) was a type, "a shadow of the good things to come" (Hebr. 10:1). This law, which had but a temporary purpose, served its usefulness in its proper time, and had its natural fulfillment when the realities replaced the shadows. By bringing the realities, Christ fulfilled this law. He fulfilled the moral law (or brought it to its perfection) by enforcing it more fully and describing its implications in more precise terms. The rabbis had glorified the letter; Christ stressed the spirit of the Law. In such ways Christ "superseded the law" (Rom. 10:4).
5:18. *I assure you emphatically:* the Hebrew word *Amen*, when introducing a saying of special solemnity, means "Yes, it is really so!"

before heaven and earth pass away, not a single letter or one small detail will be expunged from the Law — no, not until all is accomplished. Whoever, therefore, breaks one of these least command- 19 ments and instructs his fellow men to do likewise, will be of lowest rank in the kingdom of heaven. He, on the contrary, who both observes and inculcates them will win high distinction in the kingdom of heaven. Yes, let me tell you: if your religion is not 20 very much better than that of the Scribes and Pharisees, you will not enter the kingdom of heaven.

THE LAW OF CHARITY

"You have heard that it was said to the men of old: 'Do not 21 murder' and 'He who commits murder is answerable to the court.' I, on the contrary, declare to you: anyone who is angry with his 22 brother is answerable to the court; anyone who says to his brother, 'You imbecile,' is answerable to the Supreme Council; anyone who says, 'You fool,' must answer for it in the fiery pit. Suppose, then, 23 you are about to offer your gift at the altar, and there remember that your brother holds something against you: leave your gift there 24 before the altar, and first go and make up your quarrel with your brother; and then come back to offer your gift.

"Show a kindly disposition toward your opponent in good time, 25 while you are on the way to court with him; otherwise, your opponent hands you over to the judge, and the judge to the jailer, and you are thrown into prison. And mark my words: you will not be 26 released from that place until you have paid the last penny.

LUSTFULNESS AND DIVORCE

"You have heard it said: 'Do not commit adultery.' 27 I, on the contrary, declare to you: anyone who glances at a woman 28 with a lustful intention has already committed adultery with her in his heart. If your right eye tempts you to sin, pluck it out and throw it 29

5:21. Exod. 20:13; Deut. 5:17.

5:22. *I . . . declare to you:* throughout this chapter Christ speaks as the Supreme Lawgiver. See the first note on 2:4.

is angry: some manuscripts add "without cause." *the fiery pit:* called Gehenna (Mk. 9:45), a valley southeast of Jerusalem, lit., "valley of lamentation," so called from the cries of little children thrown into the fiery arms of Moloch, the idol-god of the Ammonites.

5:27. Exod. 20:14; Deut. 5:18.

away; it is better for you that one of your members should perish than that, body and all, you should be thrown into the infernal pit.
30 And if your right hand tempts you to sin, cut it off and throw it away; it is better for you that one of your limbs should perish than that you should be thrown, body and all, into the infernal pit.
31 "It has been said: 'To effect a divorce, let a man give his wife a
32 writ of separation.' I, on the contrary, declare to you: anyone who divorces his wife — except on the score of lewdness — makes her a party to adultery; and so, too, he who marries a divorced woman is an adulterer.

DO NOT SWEAR

33 "Again, you have heard it was said of old: 'Do not swear falsely, but you must redeem your promises made under oath to the Lord.'
34 I, on the contrary, declare to you: do not swear at all, whether by
35 heaven, for it is God's throne; or by the earth, for it is his footstool;
36 or by Jerusalem, for it is the city of the Great King; nor should you swear by your own head, for you cannot make a single hair white
37 or black. Let your speech be 'Yes,' when you mean Yes, and 'No,' when you mean No. Whatever is in excess of these expressions is due to the evil in the world.

DO NOT REPAY EVIL BY EVIL

38 "You have heard it said: 'An eye for an eye, and a tooth for a

---

5:31. Deut. 24:1.

5:32. *except on the score* (i.e., setting aside the case) *of lewdness:* since the absolute indissolubility of the marriage tie under the New Law is clearly taught in Mk. 10:11, 12; Lk. 16:18; 1 Cor. 7:10–11, the clause *except*, etc., cannot be taken as a mitigation of it. Its meaning here is disputed. One rabbinical school held that divorce with the consequent right to remarry was justified by adultery; another allowed divorce for almost any cause. Christ here condemns both views. The Church allows a husband to "divorce" (that is, put away) his wife if she has been unfaithful, without, however, granting him the right to marry again; and if in such a case the wife remarries, her husband is not answerable for her adultery.

5:33. Lev. 19:12; Num. 30:3; Deut. 23:21.

5:34. Christ certainly forbids taking an oath on every trivial occasion. His sweeping statement also indicates that in an ideal order there would be no need of taking an oath on any occasion. That his seemingly outright condemnation of swearing admits of exceptions in an imperfect society such as ours, is indicated in verse 37. For Christ's "way of teaching," see the note on Lk. 17:6.

5:36. *swear by your own head:* an imprecatory oath, a calling down destruction on oneself in case of perjury.

tooth.' I, on the contrary, declare to you: do not meet evil with evil. 39
No, if someone strikes you on your right cheek, turn to him the other
as well. And if a man intends by process of law to rob you of your 40
coat, let him have your cloak as well. And if someone forces you to 41
go one mile with him, go two miles with him. Give to anyone who 42
asks you, and if someone would borrow from you, do not turn away.

LOVE OF ENEMIES AND PERSECUTORS

"You have heard it said: 'Love your neighbor, and hate your 43
enemy.' I, on the contrary, declare to you: love your enemies and 44
pray for your persecutors, and thus prove yourselves children of your 45
Father in heaven. He, certainly, lets his sun rise upon bad and good
alike, and makes the rain fall on sinners as well as saints. Really, if 46
you love those that love you, what reward do you deserve? Do not
tax collectors do as much? And if you have a friendly greeting for 47
your brothers only, are you doing anything out of the common? Do
not the heathen do as much? Be perfect, then, as your heavenly 48
Father is perfect.

5:39. The Old Law allowed retaliation; the New inculcates readiness to
suffer even grievous wrong without feelings of resentment or revenge. This is
an illustration of Christ's way of "fulfilling" the Law. The use of the imperative
(turn to him, let him have, go . . . with him, etc.) does not necessarily argue
a strict command. "These precepts are to be observed in readiness of heart;
that is, we must be ready to carry them out according to circumstances, which
sometimes render their literal observance obligatory, at other times — and that
oftener than we are apt to allow — advisable. There are times when such literal
observance would be unadvisable and not to the mind of Divine Wisdom" (St.
Augustine; see Rickaby). In practical life we have to distinguish between duties
and counsels. See the note on Lk. 17:6.
   5:43. You have heard it said: the words love your neighbor are from Lev.
19:18; the others represent the current rabbinical teaching. The Jews were
often bidden to treat enemies harshly, to wage war on them, even to exter-
minate them (Deut. 7:2; 15:3; 20:13–18); but they were never commanded
to hate them. Note that the Jews often restricted the word "neighbor" to men
of their own race, and called Gentiles "enemies." Jesus corrected this notion
in the parable of the Good Samaritan (Lk. 10:36). This is another example
of our Lord's "fulfilling" the Law. For a special sense of the biblical expression
hate, see the note on Lk. 14:26.
   5:48. Applied to God, the Greek word rendered perfect means both that he
lacks no perfection and that he has power to bring others to a state of perfection.
Here the immediate context suggests the first of the two senses; but if this verse
is taken as the conclusion of the whole preceding discussion, the sense is: "Strive
to arrive at the perfection which God possesses, and at which he enables you to
arrive under the New Law." The Fathers generally apply the oft-quoted text
in this fuller sense.

CHAPTER 6

DO NOT TRUMPET ABROAD YOUR GOOD WORKS

1   "Take care not to practice your religion before your fellow men just to catch their eyes; otherwise, you have no reward with your Father in heaven.

2   "For example: when you are about to give alms, do not send a trumpeter ahead of you, as the hypocrites do in the synagogues and streets to win the applause of their fellow men. I tell you plainly,

3   they have their reward already. When you give alms, your left hand

4   should not know what your right is doing. Thus your alms is given in secrecy, and your Father, who sees what is secret, will reward you.

YOUR GUIDES FOR PRAYER

5   "Again, when you pray, do not be like the hypocrites, for they love to pray standing in the synagogues or at street corners to attract the attention of their fellow men. I tell you plainly, they have their

6   reward already. When you pray, retire to your private room and bolt the door, and then pray to your Father in secrecy; and your Father, who sees what is secret, will reward you.

7   "Moreover, when you pray, do not use many and idle words, as the heathen do; for they think that their glibness will win them a

8   hearing. So do not imitate them. Surely, your Father is acquainted

9   with your needs before you ask him. The following, then, must be the pattern of your prayer:

Our Father in heaven!

May you be known and glorified,

10   your kingdom come,

your will be done,

on earth as well as in heaven;

11   give us this day

our daily bread;

6:1. The Greek word (with its Semitic background), here rendered *religion*, sometimes means "almsgiving."

6:11. The Greek may be rendered "give us today the bread we need for the morrow." The Vulgate uses the expression "supersubstantial bread," the meaning of which is not certain. Many Fathers understood *bread* as including the Holy Eucharist.

> forgive us our debts   12
> as we also forgive our debtors;
> and do not expose us to temptation,   13
> but deliver us from evil.

For if you forgive your fellow men their offenses, your heavenly   14
Father will, in turn, forgive you; but if you do not forgive your fellow   15
men their offenses, neither will your Father forgive your offenses.

BE NOT GLOOMY WHEN YOU FAST

"Again, when you fast, do not imitate the gloomy-looking hypo-   16
crites: they go about unkempt and unwashed, so that their fasting
may be noticed by their fellow men. I tell you plainly: they have
their reward already. When you fast, anoint your head and wash   17
your face; thus your fasting will be noticed, not by your fellow men,   18
but by your Father in secrecy; and then your Father, who sees
what is secret, will reward you.

LAY UP TREASURES IN HEAVEN

"Do not lay up treasures for yourselves on earth, where moth   19
devours and rust consumes, and where thieves break in and steal;
but lay up treasures for yourselves in heaven, where neither moth   20
devours nor rust consumes, nor thieves break in and steal. After all,   21
where your treasure is, there, too, your heart is bound to be.

KEEP YOUR INWARD LAMP BURNING

"The eye serves your person as a lamp; so long, then, as your   22
eye is sound, your whole person will have light; but when your eye is   23
defective, your whole person will grope in the dark. Consequently,
if your inward lamp is darkened, how dense will that darkness be!

YOU CANNOT SERVE MONEY AND GOD

"A man cannot be the slave of two masters. He will either hate   24
the one and love the other, or, at least, be attentive to the one and
neglectful of the other. You cannot have money and God for masters.

6:13. Some texts add the beautiful doxology: "For yours is the kingdom and
the power and the glory forever. Amen." As the word *Amen* indicates, this was
a liturgical addition.

6:24. *money*: literally, *Mammon*, a Phoenician word meaning "the god of
riches," much as we speak of "the almighty dollar."

HAVE FAITH AND DO NOT FRET

25 "I tell you therefore: do not fret about what to eat, or what to drink, to sustain your life, or about what to wear on your bodies. Is not life more precious than food, and the body more precious than
26 clothing? Look at the birds of the air: they do not sow, or reap, or store up provisions in barns, and yet your heavenly Father feeds
27 them! Are not you more precious than they? And which of you can
28 by fretting add one minute to his span of life? And as for clothing, why do you fret? Observe the lilies in the field! How they grow! They
29 do not toil or spin; and yet, I tell you, even Solomon in all his glory
30 did not dress like one of these. Now if God so clothes the grass in the field, which is there today and is thrown into the furnace tomorrow, will he not much more readily clothe you? What little faith you have!

31 "Therefore, have done with fretting, and do not constantly be asking; 'What are we going to eat?' or, 'What are we going to
32 drink?' or, 'What are we going to wear?' Why, the heathen make all these things an object of eager search; besides, your heavenly
33 Father knows that you need all these things. No, let your first concern be the kingdom of God and what he requires of you; then
34 you will have all these things thrown in for good measure. In short, have done fretting about the morrow. The morrow, surely, can do its own fretting. One evil a day is burden enough.

6:26. In contrast to fowls that have a definite owner who provides them with a fixed roosting place and their daily food, the expression the birds of the air, so strange to modern ears, denotes birds that "freely roam the air" in quest of food and resting place; yet they are not on that account uncared for, their great "Caretaker," so to say, being the heavenly Father.

6:27. The words may mean "add one cubit to his stature"; but one cubit added to one's size is not "a very small thing" (Lk. 12:26), while one minute added to one's life is inconsiderable. We should prolong our life by avoiding danger and by rational methods of living. Christ forbids, not reasonable provision for, but excessive attention to, future wants. The harassing anxiety here condemned implies lack of trust in Divine Providence and leads to neglect of one's spiritual interests. See the note on Lk. 17:6.

Chapter 7

FORBEAR RASH JUDGMENT

"Do not judge, that so you may not be judged; 1 for the sentence you pass will be passed upon you, and the measure 2 you use in measuring will be used to measure out your share.

"Strange that you see the splinter in your brother's eye and do 3 not notice the log in your own! Or, how can you say to your brother, 4 'Let me take the splinter out of your eye,' when, think of it, there is the log in your own eye! Hypocrite! First take the log out of your 5 own eye, and then you will see clearly enough to take the splinter out of your brother's eye.

"Do not give to dogs what is sacred. And do not throw your 6 pearls before pigs; otherwise, they may trample them underfoot, and then turn round and tear you to pieces.

HAVE CONFIDENCE

"Ask, and you will receive; seek, and you will find; knock, 7 and you will gain admission. In fact, only he who asks receives; 8 only he who seeks finds; only he who knocks will gain admission. Really, will anyone among you give a stone to his son 9 that asks him for bread? or a snake, when he asks for a fish? 10 Well, then, if you, bad as you are, choose to give useful gifts to 11 your children, how much more will your Father in heaven give what is good to those that ask him!

"In short, in all respects do by your fellow men exactly as you 12

7:1. The word *judge* often means "judge unfavorably, condemn." Christ condemns rash judgment, judgment based on "appearances" (Jn. 8:15). We should judge of things as they are in reality (Jn. 7:24), and of persons always on the favorable side. The universal prohibition, to be valid, requires obvious restrictions. See the note on Lk. 17:6.

7:6. We should avoid rash judgment, yet without exposing sacred things (as, for example, Christian doctrine) to the ridicule of persons wholly wanting in appreciation of their true worth. See the note on Mk. 6:5, and compare Christ's silence before Pilate, Jn. 19:9. The early Church kept the Holy Eucharist a secret from all but the baptized.

7:7. Christ here inculcates both the necessity and the efficacy of prayer. Elsewhere we learn that his sweeping statement needs certain modifications; see, for instance, vv. 9–11; also 6:33; James 1:5–7; 4:3; especially 1 Jn. 5:14. See the note on Lk. 17:6.

wish them to do by you. This, surely, is the gist of the Law and the Prophets.

FINAL COUNSELS

13 "Enter by the narrow gate; for wide and spacious is the gateway
14 that leads to destruction; and many there are that enter by it! But oh, how narrow and obstructed is the gateway that leads to life, and few there are that find it!

15 "Beware of false prophets — people that come to you in sheep's
16 clothing, but inwardly are ravenous wolves. By their conduct you can tell them. Are grapes picked from thornbushes? or figs from thistles?
17 In the same way, as every good tree bears healthy fruit, so a sickly
18 tree bears fruit that is bad. As a good tree cannot bear fruit that is
19 bad, so a sickly tree cannot bear healthy fruit. Any tree that does not
20 produce healthy fruit is cut down and thrown into fire. Evidently, then, by their conduct you can tell them.

21 "Not everyone that says to me, 'Lord, Lord,' will enter the kingdom of heaven, but only he that does the will of my Father
22 who is in heaven. Many will say to me on that Day: 'Lord, Lord, did we not prophesy in your name, and in your name drive out demons,
23 and perform many miracles in your name?' But I will tell them plainly: 'I have never had anything to do with you! Leave my presence, you inveterate evildoers!

THE END OF THE SERMON ON THE MOUNT

24 "In short, whoever hears these words of mine and acts accordingly is like a sensible man who built his house upon rock:
25 the rain poured down and the floods came and the winds blew and beat against that house; but it did not collapse. It was founded
26 upon rock. And whoever hears these words of mine and does not act accordingly is like a foolish man who built his house upon sand:
27 and the rain poured and the floods came and the winds blew and beat against that house, and it collapsed. It fact, the collapse of it was complete."

28 When Jesus had finished these discourses, the crowds were lost
29 in admiration of his teaching; he certainly had a way of teaching them as one that has authority, and not as their Scribes and Pharisees.

CHAPTER 8

He then came down the mountainside and great crowds followed *1*
him.

EXAMPLES OF CONFIDENCE

One day a leper approached without warning and, prostrating *2*
himself before him, said: "Sir, if you are willing, you can make
me clean." He extended his hand and touched him, saying: "Yes, *3*
I am willing; be clean." Instantly the man was cleansed of his leprosy.

"Be sure," Jesus then said to him, "that you do not say a word to *4*
anyone. But go and have yourself examined by the priest and make
the offering which Moses enjoined, to serve them as evidence."

When he returned to Capharnaum, a centurion approached *5*
and appealed to him in the following words: "Sir, my slave lies *6*
sick at home; he is paralyzed and suffers frightfully." Jesus said to *7*
him: "Am I to come and cure him?" By way of answer the cen- *8*
turion said: "Sir, I am not fit to have you come under my roof.
No, only utter a word, and my slave will be cured. It is the same *9*
with me: I am only an inferior officer, but have soldiers under me,
and when I say to one, 'March,' he marches; to another, 'Come,'
he comes; and to my slave, 'Do this,' he does it." On hearing this, *10*
Jesus was struck with admiration, and said to the accompanying
crowd: "I tell you frankly, I have never found such lively faith any-

8:4. Jesus wished to avoid unnecessary excitement and ill-timed enthusiasm
among the hotheaded Galileans, who expected a worldly king (see Jn. 6:15). *the
priest:* any local priest had power to certify the cure. Later the leper had to go
to Jerusalem and there to make the prescribed offerings (see Lev 14). The
current rendering "as a testimony unto them" fails to express the different connotations implied in different contexts. Compare 10:18; 24:14; Mk. 1:44; 6:11;
13:9; Lk. 5:14; 9:5; 21:13. Jesus wants the leper to notify the ruling class that
it is his mission not to violate but to observe the Law (see 5:17); moreover,
if they failed to recognize his divine nature, which enabled him to cure a leper
by an act of his will, they were inexcusable.

8:7. This verse is best read as a question, to which verse 8 is the answer.

8:10. *such lively faith:* the centurion, a pagan and evidently a devout proselyte
(Lk. 7:5), had, like the Jews, witnessed several miracles or heard about them
(Jn. 4:50; Lk. 4:33; 4:39–41); but, unlike the Jews, he had formed certain
conclusions regarding Christ's supernatural power. His reverence for Jesus won
him the distinction of having his immortal words enshrined in the liturgy of
the Mass.

in Israel: the mass of the Jewish people. This is one of those universal statements (occasionally occurring in the Gospels; see the note on Lk. 17:6) which

11 where in Israel! I tell you, multitudes will arrive from east and west and, in the company of Abraham, Isaac, and Jacob, will recline
12 at table in the kingdom of heaven, when, at the same time, the born citizens of the realm will be hurled into the outer darkness. And oh, how that region will resound with 'the weeping and gnash-
13 ing of teeth!'" Jesus then said to the centurion: "You may go. In answer to your faith, your wish shall be granted." The slave was cured that same hour.

FURTHER MANIFESTATIONS OF POWER

14   After entering Peter's house, Jesus saw Peter's mother-in-law in
15 bed in a feverish condition. He grasped her hand and the fever
16 left her. She then rose and waited on him. Late in the evening many persons possessed by demons were brought to him. He drove the
17 spirits out with a word and cured all the sick. Thus the event was to fulfill the prediction made through Isaias the prophet, who said:
"Upon himself he took our infirmities,
and our illnesses he bore."

COURAGE, CONFIDENCE, AND RENUNCIATION

18   One day, seeing crowds about him, Jesus gave orders to set sail
19 for the opposite shore. Just then a scribe approached and said to him:
20 "Rabbi, I would like to follow you wherever you go." Jesus said to him: "Foxes have holes, and the birds of the air have places of
21 shelter; but the Son of Man has no place to lay his head." Another, one of his disciples, said to him: "Lord, allow me first to go and
22 bury my father." "Stay in my company," Jesus replied; "leave the dead to bury their own dead."

---

yet admit of exceptions (Christ's mother, John the Baptist, the Apostles, etc.). Not every "all" in the Gospels represents a mathematically exact quantity (see, for instance, Mk. 1:27, 37; etc.). Besides, being a pagan, the centurion had risen to his faith from lower depths than had the Jews, with whom belief in the true God was hereditary. For a similar summary comparative statement, see the note on 18:13.

8:11. In the Scriptures the happiness of heaven is often conceived as a banquet at which God entertains his friends; compare Isa. 25:6; Ps. 35:9; Mt. 22:2; Lk. 14:15; 14:16; Apoc. 19:9. Christians who are converts from paganism are true children of Abraham (Rom. 11:17).

8:20. *the Son of Man:* a Messianic title (Dan. 7:13), applied only by Christ to himself.

8:22. The meaning is: "Let other relatives, who are not my followers, perform this duty." Compare 12:47 ff.; see Lk. 14:26 and the accompanying note. See also the note on Lk. 17:6.

He now entered the boat and his disciples accompanied him. 23
Suddenly, there was a violent upheaval on the sea, so that the boat 24
threatened to be buried under the waves. Meanwhile he was asleep.
The disciples therefore rushed up and woke him with the cry: 25
"Lord! Help! We are going down!" "How timid you are!" he said to 26
them; "what little faith you have!" Then, rising to his full height,
he sternly rebuked the winds and the sea. And there was stillness
everywhere. The people were puzzled. "What is one to make of 27
this man!" they commented; "why, even the winds and the sea
obey him!"

THE TWO DEMONIACS

When he had come to the country of the Gadarenes on the 28
other shore, two demoniacs came out of the tombs to meet him.
They were extremely fierce, so that nobody was able to pass that way.
Yet, unexpectedly, they cried out: "Leave us alone, Son of God! 29
Have you come here to torment us before the appointed time?"
Now, at some distance from them, a numerous herd of pigs was 30
feeding; and so, since the demons had implored him, saying: "If 31
you mean to drive us out, let us go into the herd of pigs," he said 32
to them: "Go!" And out they went, and off into the pigs. And lo!
The whole herd dashed down a steep decline into the sea and
perished in the water! The herdsmen took to flight and entering 33
into the town reported everything, especially what concerned the
demoniacs. The result was striking: the whole town turned out to 34
meet Jesus and, when they saw him, requested him to quit their
coasts.

CHAPTER 9

THE CURE OF THE PARALYTIC

So he entered a boat and, after crossing over, came to his own 1
town. Here a strange thing happened: some men were trying to 2
bring before him a paralytic lying on a mat. When Jesus saw their
faith, he said to the paralytic: "Have courage, my son; your sins
are now forgiven." Immediately some of the Scribes said to them- 3

9:1. *his own town:* Capharnaum, Christ's headquarters during his Galilean
ministry. See Lk. 4:16 and the note on Mt. 13:54.

4 selves: "This man blasphemes!" Jesus read their thoughts. "Why
5 do you," he said, "entertain thoughts that are absurd? Really, which
is easier, to say, 'Your sins are now forgiven,' or to say, 'Rise and
6 walk'? Now I want you to understand that the Son of Man has
power here on earth to forgive sins." He then addressed the para-
7 lytic: "Rise; take up your mat and return home." He rose and went
8 home. As the crowds saw this, a feeling of awe came over them,
and they praised God who had given such power to men.

THE CALL OF MATTHEW

9 As Jesus went on from there, he noticed a man at his counter
in the customhouse — Matthew was his name — and said to him:
"Follow me." At that the man quit his business and became one
of his followers.

CRITICS OF THE SAVIOR

10 One day he was at table in the house, and it so happened that
many tax collectors and sinners were reclining at table with Jesus
11 and his disciples. The Pharisees noticed it. "Your Rabbi," they
said to his disciples, "takes a meal with sinners and tax collectors.
12 How is that?" Jesus heard of it and said: "The sick have need of
13 a physician, not the healthy. Make off, and learn what is meant by
the words: 'Compassion is what I desire, and not sacrifice.' Indeed,
it is my mission to call sinners, not saints."

14 Then the disciples of John came up to him. "We and the
Pharisees," they said, "fast frequently; your disciples do not fast.
15 How is that?" Jesus said to them: "Can wedding guests be in
mourning while the bridegroom is with them? However, a time is
coming when the bridegroom is torn away from them; and then
16 they will fast. No one sews a patch of new cloth on an old cloak;
for it tears off the part of the cloak all round it, and the rip is worse
17 than before. Nor is new wine poured into old wineskins; otherwise,
the skins burst, and thus both the wine is spilled and the skins are

---

9:5. *which is easier:* in reality neither of the two things is easier than the other;
both require divine power. Hence, if Jesus could cure the man, he could also
forgive sins.

9:16. See the second note on 3:2. The spirit of the New Law cannot be
forced into the rigid framework of the Old. It was necessary to form a new
generation, capable of appreciating the teachings of Christ.

ruined. No; new wine is poured into fresh skins, and thus both
are preserved."

A SUCCESSION OF MIRACULOUS EVENTS

He was giving them this explanation when, unexpectedly, an 18
official came up, prostrated himself before him, and said: "My
daughter has just died. Please, come and lay your hand upon her,
and she will return to life." Jesus rose and, accompanied by his 19
disciples, started to follow him when, without warning, a woman, 20
who had been afflicted with hemorrhages for twelve years,
approached from behind and touched the tassel of his cloak. She 21
had been saying to herself: "If I only touch his cloak, I shall get
well." Jesus turned round and caught sight of her. "Have courage, 22
my daughter," he said; "your faith has cured you." The woman was
cured that moment.

Arrived at the home of the official, Jesus saw the flute players 23
and the noisy crowd. "Leave the room," he said; "the girl is not 24
dead; she is asleep." They laughed at him; but no sooner had the 25
crowd been cleared out, than he went into the room and took hold
of the girl's hand; and she awoke to life. The news of this incident 26
spread throughout that whole country.

As Jesus walked on from that place, two blind men followed 27
him, shouting the words: "Take pity on us, Son of David." When 28
he got indoors, the blind men came up to him. "Do you believe,"
Jesus said to them, "that I have power to do this?" "Yes, Lord,"
they replied. He then laid his hands on their eyes and said: "In 29
answer to your faith, your wish shall be granted." Their eyes were 30
opened. But assuming a stern tone, Jesus said to them: "No one is
to know of this! See to it!" They, however, went out and spread 31
his fame over that whole country.

They were just going out when people brought to him a man 32
who was dumb and possessed. The demon was driven out and the 33
dumb man spoke. The crowds were enraptured and declared:
"Never has the like been seen in Israel!" The Pharisees, however, 34
remarked: "He is a tool of the archdemon; that is how he drives
out demons!"

9:22. Jesus required faith in his power as a condition of its exercise. See
verse 28.

35   And so Jesus traveled about from town to town, from village
to village, instructing the people in their synagogues and preaching
the Good News of the kingdom, besides curing every disease and
every infirmity.

36   One day the sight of the masses touched his heart, for they
were bruised and battered down — just like sheep that have no
37   shepherd. It was on this occasion that he said to his disciples: "The
38   harvest is plentiful; but the laborers are few. Therefore, pray the
Owner of the harvest to send out laborers to do his harvesting."

CHAPTER 10

JESUS SUMMONS HIS TWELVE APOSTLES

1   He then called to him his twelve apostles and gave them power
to drive out unclean spirits, as well as power to heal any disease
2   and any infirmity. The names of the twelve apostles are as follows:

   First, Simon, surnamed Peter;
   then Andrew, his brother;
3   James, the son of Zebedee,
   and his brother John;
   Philip and Bartholomew;
   Thomas and the tax collector Matthew;
   James, the son of Alpheus, and Thaddeus;
4   Simon the Cananaean;
   and Judas Iscariot,
   the same that eventually betrayed him.

5   These Twelve Jesus sent on a missionary tour, after giving them
the following instructions:

10:3. *Bartholomew:* most probably the Nathanael mentioned in Jn. 1:45.
Thaddeus: the Apostle Jude.

10:4. *the Cananaean:* also called "the Zealot" (Lk. 6:15). This latter name
is generally interpreted to mean that he belonged to a group of men especially
remarkable for their zeal for the observance of the Law. It is possible, however,
that he and a few others of the Apostles (besides Barabbas and the two bandits
crucified with Jesus) were also members of the League of Freedom which about
that time was assuming political importance and did not shrink from advocating
violent opposition to the Romans. See the note on 27:16.

10:5. The present mission was temporary, a sort of practice tour, and confined
to a limited district. Later the Apostles were commissioned to preach to the
Gentiles. See Mt. 28:19; Mk. 13:10.

ADVICE FOR THEIR MISSIONARY TOUR

"Do not turn aside into Gentile territory, and enter no Samaritan town. Instead, go to the lost sheep of the house of Israel. 6 As you go along, preach on this text: 'The kingdom of heaven 7 is close at hand.' Attend to the sick; raise the dead; make lepers 8 clean; drive out demons. Gratis you have received; gratis you must give. Do not procure pocket money, whether gold or silver or copper; 9 or a traveling bag, or an extra coat, or sandals, or a staff. After all, 10 a laborer is entitled to his support.

BE CONTENT WHERE YOU ARE WELCOMED

"Once you enter a town or village, search out a worthy citizen, 11 and in his home make your headquarters till you leave that locality. On entering the house, salute it saying: 'Peace be to this house,' 12 and in case the household is responsive, your blessing will alight 13 on it; if it is not responsive, your blessing will be no loss to you. But should the people not make you welcome and not listen to your 14 preaching, leave that house or town, and shake the dust off your feet. I tell you the plain truth: on Judgment Day it will go less hard 15 with Sodom and Gomorrha than with that town.

IN PERSECUTION THE DIVINE SPIRIT WILL INSPIRE YOU

"Listen! I am sending you like sheep among a pack of wolves. 16 Be prudent, then, like serpents; yet, for all that, as innocent as doves. Beware of your fellow men: they will try to hand you over 17 to courts of justice and to flog you in their synagogues; you will 18 even be brought before governors and kings for my sake. It will be your chance to testify to Jew and Gentile. But once handed over, 19 do not be uneasy about how or what to speak; for at that moment the words will be put into your mouth. In fact, not you are then 20 the speakers; no, the Spirit of your Father is then the Speaker inspiring you. Brother will give up brother, and father will give 21 up child, to have them put to death. Children will rise against

---

10:9. These directions are meant to inculcate the lesson that material means are relatively unimportant in spreading the kingdom of God. Jesus does not deny that such means are also helpful and may indeed be necessary at times. See the note on Lk. 17:6. Another lesson was that a missionary needs complete trust in Divine Providence. See Lk. 22:35.

10:11. The translation follows the oldest and best manuscripts in omitting the words contained in the Vulgate "saying: Peace be to this house."

22 parents and secure a death warrant against them. You will be the
scorn of all because you profess my name. But he who holds out
to the end will be saved.

23 "When you are persecuted in one city, flee to another; and when
you are persecuted in the other, flee to still another. I positively
assure you: you will not make the round of the towns in Israel
before the Son of Man comes.

DO NOT FEAR PEOPLE WHO CANNOT KILL THE SOUL

24 "No pupil is above his teacher, and no slave above his master.
25 It is enough for a pupil to be treated like his teacher, and for a
slave, like his master. If people called the head of the household
26 'Beelzebul,' how much more so the members of his family! Therefore, do not be afraid of them. After all, nothing is concealed but
must be revealed some day; nothing is hidden but must be made
27 known some day. What I tell you in the dark you have to speak
out in broad daylight; and what you hear in a whisper you have
28 to proclaim from the housetops. And do not fear people that kill
the body, but have no power to kill the soul; rather, fear him who
29 has power to ruin both body and soul in the infernal pit. Do not
two sparrows sell for a penny? And yet, not one of them can drop
30 dead to the ground without the consent of your Father. As for
yourselves, the very hairs on your head have all been numbered.
31 Away, then, with all fear; you are more precious than whole flocks
of sparrows.

32 "In short, everyone who acknowledges me before the world will,
33 in turn, be acknowledged by me before my Father in heaven; but
he who disowns me before the world will himself be disowned by
me before my Father in heaven.

A MAN'S ENEMIES WILL BE HIS OWN FOLK

34 "Do not suppose that it is my mission to shed peace upon the

---

10:23. Either (1) "*before* the Son of Man comes"; in a certain sense, he
"came" in the destruction of Jerusalem (A.D. 70); or (2) "*till* the Son of
Man comes"; the Apostles (and their successors) will not finish converting the
nations until the Day of Judgment. Compare 24:34 and 24:14.

10:25. Beelzebul: a Philistine god, identified in 12:24 with the archdemon.

10:34. These utterances must be viewed in the light of the precept of loving
God above all else and loving one's neighbor only for God's sake. See the note
on Lk. 17:6. the sword: Christ's doctrine is like a two-edged sword that cuts
deep and "separates." See Lk. 2:34 and Hebr. 4:12.

earth; it is not my mission to shed peace but to unsheath the sword. For example, it is my mission to set a man at variance with 35 his father, a daughter with her mother, and a daughter-in-law with her mother-in-law. In fact, a man's enemies will be the members of 36 his own household. He who is fonder of father or mother than of 37 me is not worthy of me; he who is fonder of son or daughter than of me is not worthy of me. Again, he who will not shoulder his 38 cross and follow me is not worthy of me. He who wins a reprieve 39 from death must part with his life at any rate; but he who freely parts with his life for my sake will win it in the end.

HE WHO BEFRIENDS YOU BEFRIENDS ME

"He who befriends you befriends me, and he who befriends me 40 befriends him whose ambassador I am. He who befriends a prophet 41 on the ground that he is a prophet will get the reward of a prophet; and he who befriends a holy man on the ground that he is holy will get the reward of a holy man. And whoever gives only a 42 refreshing drink to one of these little ones, doing so because he is a disciple, will not, I tell you truly, go without his reward."

CHAPTER 11

MISSION OF JOHN THE BAPTIST

When Jesus had at last finished giving rules of conduct to his 1 twelve disciples, he removed thence to teach and preach in the Jewish towns.

Now John was informed in his prison of Christ's mode of 2 acting; so he sent through his disciples the following message to him: "Are you the One who is to come, or are we to await another?" 3 By way of answer Jesus said to them: "Go and bring word to 4 John about what you hear and see: the blind recover sight and 5 the lame walk; lepers are made clean and the deaf hear; dead

---

10:39. A Christian must be ready to lay down his life for Christ. See Mk. 8:35 ff. Note the play on the Greek word which may mean "life" (both physical and eternal) and "soul."

11:3. See the note on Lk. 7:20.

11:5. Christ's deeds (predicted by Isa. 35:5; 61:1) prove that he was the Messias.

men rise again and the humble have the Good News preached to
6 them"; and, "happy is he to whom I am not a stumbling block."
7 When the men were departing, Jesus began to speak to the
crowds concerning John: "What did you go out into the desert
8 to see? A reed waving in the wind? Well, then, what did you go
out to see? A man dressed in fine, soft garments? But notice: those
9 who wear fine, soft clothes are in the palaces of kings! Well, then,
what did you go out to see? A prophet? Yes, I tell you, and more
10 than a prophet! This is the one of whom Scripture says:

> 'Look! I am sending ahead of you
> a messenger who is to prepare
> the road for you to travel.'

THE GREATNESS OF JOHN THE BAPTIST

11 I positively assure you: among all men born of woman no one has
risen to greater heights than John the Baptist. In the kingdom of
12 heaven, it is true, the least is greater than he; and yet, from the
day when John the Baptist appeared down to this day, the kingdom of heaven is to be taken by storm — and only by storm do
13 men lay hold of it! Yes, indeed; while prior to John the Law and
14 the Prophets were the only inspired spokesmen, his own role, if
you are willing to admit it, is that of Elias, who is expected to come.
15 Let everyone heed what he has heard.
16 "But how can I characterize this generation? It reminds me
17 of little children sitting about in the market place and calling out
to their partners:

> 'We played you a tune to make you merry,
> and yet you did not dance;
> we played you a tune to make you sorry,
> and yet you did not strike your breasts!'

11:11. The Baptist, being the direct precursor of the Messias, held the most
exalted position under the old dispensation; yet his position is less in dignity
than that which Christian baptism confers. There is here no question of John's
personal sanctity.

11:12. Since the arrival of the Messias, it was everyone's duty to make a
supreme effort (by storm) to enter the kingdom.

11:14. The prophet Malachias (3:1) had predicted that Elias would come
to prepare the way for the Messias; but his words are here applied to the
Baptist (see Lk. 1:17): as Elias was to prepare Christ's second coming, so the
Baptist did the first.

"To illustrate: John came on a special mission, and he abstains 18
from food and drink; yet people say: 'He is out of his mind!'
The Son of Man came on a special mission, and he takes food and 19
drink; yet people say: 'Look at that glutton; that boon companion
of tax collectors and sinners!' For all that, Wisdom has justified
herself by the mission she assigned to each."

He then proceeded to heap reproaches on the cities in which 20
most of his miracles had been performed, because they had not
repented: "Woe to you Corozain! Woe to you, Bethsaida! Had 21
the wonders done in your midst been done in Tyre and Sidon, they
would long ago have repented in sackcloth and ashes. At all events, 22
it will go less hard on Judgment Day with Tyre and Sidon than
with you. And you, Capharnaum, do you expect to soar as high 23
as heaven? As deep as hell shall you sink! Had the wonders done
in your midst been done in Sodom, it would have survived to this
day. At all events, it will go less hard on Judgment Day with Sodom 24
than with you."

SOVEREIGN POWER IN THE HANDS OF CHRIST

Inspired by the occasion, Jesus said: "I praise you, Father, Lord 25
of heaven and earth, for hiding these things from wise and prudent
men and revealing them to little ones! Yes, Father — for such has 26
been your good pleasure! Sovereign power has been put into my 27

11:18. John's austerity was proper to a stern preacher of penance; Christ's
conformity to ordinary life was more suitable to his joyous message. See
Titus 3:4.

11:25. The current version, "At that time Jesus answered and said," does not
convey the solemnity of the moment which elicited our Lord's beautiful prayer
to the Father. The Greek pronoun is here, as often in the New Testament, not
merely deictic, "that," but rather descriptive, "of such a nature"; besides, since
no question has been asked, it seems odd to say "he answered." For this idiom,
see the note on Mt. 3:15. After heaping reproaches on the worldly and impenitent cities, Jesus turns to the group around him, his followers, the little ones,
who were receptive of his teachings. It was a solemn and inspiring moment, and
this contrast (and back of it the secret and unsearchable way of God's dealings
with mankind) wrung from him a deep-felt prayer of thanks to the Father. To
prepare the reader, the Evangelist (who had heard his trembling voice, and seen
his reverent attitude) prefaces the prayer by some such words as "inspired by the
occasion, he said" or, "on that occasion, at that particular juncture, he felt
moved to say."

The wording of our Lord's prayers recorded in the Gospels will repay careful
study. Compare Mt. 26:39; Jn. 17.

11:27. The knowledge which the Father and the Son have of each other

hands by my Father, and as no one knows the Son except the Father, so no one knows the Father except the Son and anyone to whom the Son decides to reveal him.

28   "O come to me, all you who are weary and overburdened, and I
29 will refresh you. Take my yoke upon you and master my lessons, for I am gentle and humble of heart. Thus you will find refreshment
30 for your souls. My yoke is easy and my burden light."

Chapter 12

JESUS THE MASTER OF THE SABBATH

1   One Sabbath about that time Jesus passed through the wheatfields. His disciples, who were hungry, set about plucking heads of
2   wheat and eating them. The Pharisees noticed it. "See here," they said to him, "your disciples are doing what it is not right to do on
3   the Sabbath!" He replied: "Did you never read what David did one
4   day when he and his companions were hungry? How he went into the house of God and ate the presentation loaves, which neither he nor his companions, nor, in fact, anybody except the priests, had
5   'a right' to do? Or did you not read in the Law that Sabbath after Sabbath the priests in the temple violate the Sabbath without in-
6   curring blame? I tell you something greater than the temple is here!
7   If you understood what is meant by the words, 'Compassion is what I desire, and not sacrifice,' you would not have condemned innocent
8   men. After all, the Son of Man has authority over the Sabbath."
9, 10 Leaving that place, he went to their synagogue. Just then, a man with one arm withered was present. So the question was put to him: "Is it lawful on the Sabbath to heal?" Their object was to
11 bring a charge against him. But he said to them: "Suppose some one of you has just one sheep, and suppose this sheep falls into a hole on the Sabbath, will he not take hold of it and pull it out?

is exclusive, and therefore incommunicable; and, even so far as it can be communicated, only the Son can reveal the Father.

11:29. The Pharisees were harsh and proud, and imposed burdens "heavy and hard to bear" (23:4); Christ is gentle and humble, and his yoke is easy, his burden light. The Pharisees did not stir a finger to lift the burdens; Christ merited for us the grace we need to bear his yoke. The text states both the reason why we should become his disciples, and the lesson which we should learn of him.

Now, how much more precious than a sheep is a human being? 12
It follows, then, that it is 'right' on the Sabbath to do an act of
kindness." Then said he to the man: "Stretch out your arm." He 13
stretched it out. It was restored to health and as good as the other.

THE PREDICTION OF ISAIAS REGARDING JESUS

The Pharisees then walked out and resolved to put him out of 14
the way. Jesus was aware of this and withdrew from that district. 15
Many people accompanied him, and he cured all the sick among
them. He sternly forbade them, however, to turn public attention 16
on him; and thus the prediction made through Isaias the Prophet 17
was to be fulfilled:

"Behold my Servant, whom I have chosen, 18
my Beloved, in whom my soul delights.
My Spirit I will repose on him,
and to the nations will he proclaim
the right order of things.
He will not wrangle or rend the air, 19
nor will his voice be heard
in the thoroughfare.
The reed that is bruised he will not crush, 20
or quench the smoldering wick,
till he has pushed the cause of right
on to victory.
And in his name the nations will put their hope." 21

CHRIST WARNS THE PHARISEES

At that time a demoniac who was blind and dumb was brought 22
to him. He cured the disabled man so that he could both speak
and see. The crowds were all enraptured and remarked: "May not 23
this man, perhaps, be the Son of David?" But when the Pharisees 24
heard this, they said: "This man drives out the demons merely as
a tool of Beelzebul, the archdemon!"

12:18–21. This is one of the gems of this Gospel: a picture of Christ of
great beauty, borrowed from Isaias (42:1–4; 41:9), the evangelist of the Old
Testament. Isaias pictures Christ's union with the Father, his mission to instruct
the nations, his gentleness in dealing with suffering humanity, his final victory;
there is no "hope" for the world except in his name. "Christ — the Savior of
the world" — not expressed in dry scholastic terms, but clothed in rich Oriental
imagery.

45

25 Jesus knew their sentiments. "Any kingdom torn by civil strife,"
he said to them, "is laid in ruins, and no city or household split into
26 factions can last. So, too, if Satan drives out Satan, he is in revolt
27 against himself; but then, how can his kingdom last? And furthermore: if I drive out demons as a tool of Beelzebul, whose tools are
your children when they do the driving out? Therefore, judged by
28 them, you must stand condemned! But if, on the contrary, I drive
out demons by the Spirit of God, then evidently the kingdom of
29 God has by now made its way to you. Or how can anyone enter the
castle of a mighty lord and plunder his possessions unless he first
imprisons this mighty lord? Then only can he plunder his castle.
30 He who is not with me is against me, and he who does not gather
with me scatters.

31 "Therefore I warn you: any sin, were it even blasphemy, may be
forgiven a human being; but the blasphemy against the Spirit cannot
32 be forgiven. And whoever utters a word against the Son of Man may
be forgiven, but he who speaks against the Holy Spirit cannot be
33 forgiven either in this world or in the world to come. Either grant
that the tree is healthy, if you judge its fruit to be healthy; or consider the tree diseased, if you judge its fruit to be diseased; for by its
34 fruit a tree is known. Brood of vipers! How can you say anything
good when you are wicked! After all, a man's speech is but the
35 overflow of his heart. A good man dispenses what is good from his
store of good things, and a wicked man dispenses what is wicked
36 from his store of wicked things. I tell you, moreover, that of every
loose and random word which men speak they must give an account
37 on Judgment Day. Yes, by your word you will be pronounced innocent, and by your word found guilty."

THE SCRIBES DEMAND A PROOF OF CHRIST'S CLAIMS

38 Some of the Scribes and Pharisees were provoked. "Rabbi," they
said to him, "we want to see you give a proof of your claims."
39 He answered their challenge by saying: "A headstrong and adulterous

---

12:31. *cannot be forgiven:* the accusation made by the Pharisees sprang from
an habitually bad disposition, their resistance to the known truth. This is *the
blasphemy against the (Holy) Spirit* and the unpardonable sin.

12:38. *a proof of your claims:* the Jews wanted Jesus to furnish them a *proof*
to show that he had a right to teach and, in general, "to act the way he did"
(Mk. 11:28). In modern parlance, they asked for his credentials.

generation demands a proof of my claims! But a proof will not be given it except the proof which Jonas gave: just as Jonas spent 40 three days and three nights in the belly of the sea monster, so the Son of Man will spend three days and three nights in the heart of the earth.

"Ninevites will rise at the Judgment together with this generation 41 and put it in the wrong, for on the preaching of Jonas they changed their evil ways. And observe, there is something more than Jonas here! A queen of the South will rise at the Judgment together with 42 this generation and put it in the wrong, for she came from the ends of the earth to listen to the wisdom of Solomon. And observe, there is something more than Solomon here!

"When the unclean spirit is driven out of a man, he haunts 43 waterless regions in quest of refreshment, and does not find any. Then he says: 'I will return to the house from which I have been 44 driven out,' and if on his return he finds it vacant, swept, and tidy, he goes off and gets seven other spirits, who are worse than himself, 45 to join him, and they enter and make themselves at home there. In the end that man is worse off than he was in the beginning. The same will happen to this wicked generation."

WHO ARE "BROTHER OR SISTER OR MOTHER" TO CHRIST?

He was still speaking to the crowds when who should be waiting 46 outside but his mother and his brothers, desiring to speak to him. "Please," someone said to him, "your mother and your brothers are 47 waiting outside, wishing to speak to you." But he protested and said 48 to the messenger: "Who is my mother? And who are my brothers?" Then, with a wave of his hand toward his disciples, he said: "Look! 49 Here are my mother and my brothers. Yes, anyone that does the 50 will of my Father in heaven is brother or sister or mother to me."

12:45. *worse off than he was:* the Jews at the time of Christ, who stubbornly refused to acknowledge his Messianic claims, were worse off than the earlier generation that did not hear his message.

12:46. The use of the term *brothers* as such is no proof that Jesus had brothers by blood. In every language this word is capable of a wider and a narrower sense.

12:47. This verse is not found in all manuscripts. Jesus does not repudiate family ties, but indicates that there are ties more honorable and more binding than those of flesh and blood. See 8:22 and the note. Compare Mk. 3:35.

Chapter 13

THE SOWER AND HIS SEED

1 That same day Jesus left the house to linger by the sea,
2 and so great was the concourse of people that he went into a boat
3 and sat down. While the throng stood crowding the shore, he taught
them many lessons in parable style.

4 "Look! The sower goes out to sow. As he sows, some of the seed
falls close to the footpath; and the birds of the air come and eat
5 it up. Other seed falls on stony ground, where it does not have
much soil; and, because it has no soil of any depth, it shoots up at
6 once; but by the time the sun has climbed the heavens, it is
7 scorched and, because it cannot strike root, withers away. Other
seed falls among the thorns, and the thorns come up and choke it.
8 Still other seed falls on the right kind of soil, and this at last
bears fruit, in some cases a hundredfold, in others sixtyfold, in yet
9 others thirtyfold. Let everyone heed what he has heard."

BLUNTED IS THE SENSE OF THIS PEOPLE

10 The disciples then came up and said to him: "Why do you
11 speak to them in parable style?" "Because," was his answer, "you
are privileged to know the mysteries of the kingdom of heaven, but
12 those others are not so privileged; for the man of means will be
given yet more till he abounds in wealth while the man of no
13 means will have taken away from him even what he has. That is
why I speak to them in parable style. For all their seeing they do

---

13:3. *in parable style:* "A parable is an utterance or a story about some actual
or possible event or happening that is taken from the world of nature or from
human life for the purpose of illustrating some spiritual truth or teaching. The
parables of the Gospels are of inestimable beauty and reveal the rich treasure
of knowledge employed by Jesus in his teaching. There are images from the flora
and fauna of Palestine; illustrations drawn from every period of life; from childhood to old age; pictures sketched from various stations in life . . . stories based
upon the various social classes of the people, as rich and poor, master and servant,
employees and employers, debtors and creditors, etc. Although these parables were
primarily intended by Jesus for his immediate audience in Palestine, they are yet
applicable to all times and peoples" (see John E. Steinmueller and Kathryn
Sullivan, *A Companion to the New Testament* [New York: Joseph F. Wagner,
1944], p. 91 ff.).

13:11. The hidden meaning of a parable is revealed to such as make a sincere
effort to know it and profit by it.

not see, and for all their hearing they do not so hear as to understand; and thus the prophecy of Isaias is more and more fulfilled in   14
them. It says:

> 'Your ears will hear,
> yet you will not understand;
> your eyes will look,
> yet you will not see.
> For blunted is the sense of this people: 15
> their ears are hard of hearing,
> and their eyes are shut;
> thus neither their eyes see,
> nor their ears hear,
> nor their minds understand;
> and they are not converted and healed by me.'

But your eyes are blessed, for they see; and your ears are blessed,   16
for they hear. I tell you frankly: many prophets and saints have   17
longed to see what you are looking upon, yet they did not see it,
and to hear what you are listening to, yet they did not hear it!

EXPLANATION OF THE PARABLE OF THE SOWER

"For your part, then, listen to the explanation of the parable of   18
the sower. Whenever anyone hears the message announcing the king-   19
dom and does not really grasp it, on comes the evil one and steals
what has been sown in his mind. Such a one is described by the
words 'sown close to the footpath.' The words 'sown on the stony   20
ground' describe one who, the moment he hears the message,
receives it with joy; but he does not let it take root in himself;   21
on the contrary, he is a timeserver and, when distress or persecution
comes on account of the message, he is at once upset. The words   22
'sown among the thorns' describe one who hears the message, but
the cares of this world and the deceitful attractions of wealth utterly
choke the message, and it turns out barren. The words 'sown in the   23
right kind of soil' describe one who hears and grasps the message;
and he, of course, bears fruit and yields as much as a hundredfold,
or sixtyfold, or thirtyfold."

THE PARABLE OF THE WEEDS AMONG THE WHEAT

Another parable which he proposed to them was this: "The   24

49

kingdom of heaven reminds me of a man who has sown good seed
25 in his field. But, while everybody is asleep, his enemy comes and
26 sows weeds among the wheat, and goes away. Eventually the blades
spring up and put forth heads, but by that time the weeds also
27 crop out. So the help of the landowner approach him and say: 'Sir,
was it not good seed that you sowed in your field? How, then, is it
28 overrun with weeds?' 'That is the work of an enemy!' he replies.
'Well,' say the help to him, 'do you want us to go and gather them
29 up?' 'Not at all,' he answers; 'otherwise, in gathering the weeds, you
30 might pull up the wheat along with them. Let both grow until
the harvest, and, when harvest time has come, I will say to the
reapers: 'Gather up, first of all, the weeds and bind them in
bundles to be burnt; after that, store the wheat in my barn.'"

THE PARABLES OF THE MUSTARD SEED AND YEAST

31   Still another parable proposed by him was this: "The kingdom
of heaven reminds me of a mustard seed which a man carefully
32 plants in his field. This is the tiniest of all seeds; but the full-grown
plant is larger than any garden herb and, in fact, becomes a tree,
so that the birds of the air come and settle in its branches."

33   He told them yet another parable: "The kingdom of heaven
reminds me of a handful of yeast which a housewife mixes with
three measures of flour, to work there till the whole mass has risen."

34   All these lessons Jesus taught the crowds in parable style; indeed, without the use of parables he would not teach them anything.
35 Thus his practice fulfilled the prediction made through the prophet,
who says:

        "I will open my mouth to speak in parables;
        I will utter things that have lain hidden
           since the world's foundation."

CHRIST EXPLAINS THE PARABLE OF THE WEEDS

36   He then left the crowds and went indoors. Here the disciples
interviewed him. "Explain to us," they said, "the parable of the
37 weeds in the field." And this was his answer: "The sower of the
38 good seed is the Son of Man. The field is the world. The good seed
are the born citizens of the realm. The weeds are the brood of the
39 wicked one. The enemy who planted them is the devil. The harvest

time is the end of the world. The reapers are the angels. Just as the *40*
weeds, therefore, are gathered in bundles and burnt, so it will be
at the end of the world: the Son of Man will send his angels, and *41*
they will weed his kingdom of all seducers and evildoers, and hurl *42*
them into the fiery furnace. Oh, how that region will resound with
'the weeping and gnashing of teeth!' Then the saints will shine *43*
like the sun in the kingdom of their Father. Let everyone heed what
he has heard.

THE BURIED TREASURE, THE PEARL, THE DRAGNET

"The kingdom of heaven reminds me of a treasure buried in the *44*
field: as soon as a person discovers it, he hides it again, and off he
goes in his joy and sells all his possessions and buys that field.

"Again, the kingdom of heaven reminds me of a merchant in *45*
quest of beautiful pearls: as soon as he discovers one pearl of great *46*
value, off he goes and promptly sells all his possessions and buys it.

"Again, the kingdom of heaven reminds me of a dragnet thrown *47*
into the sea and taking in fish of every description: when it is filled, *48*
the crew haul it on the beach and settle down to sorting what is
usable into receptacles, and throwing away what is worthless. So it *49*
will be at the end of the world: the angels will go forth and separate
the sinners from among the saints and consign them to the blazing *50*
furnace. Oh, how that region will resound with 'the weeping and
gnashing of teeth!'

"Do you understand all these lessons?" "Yes," they replied. *51*
"Therefore," he continued, "every teacher initiated in the mysteries *52*
of the kingdom of heaven is like the head of a household who produces from his store new things and old."

WHENCE THIS WISDOM?

When Jesus had at last finished these parables he went away *53*
from there. Arrived in his own country, he instructed the people in *54*
their synagogues with such effect that they were puzzled. "This
wisdom!" they said; "where did this man get it?" "And these powers! *55*

13:52. *new things and old*: perhaps, matters concerning the Synagogue and
the Church. More generally: old truths must be adapted and applied to new
needs. With every age new problems arise. Their solution lies in a deeper
understanding (see 5:17) of the "old truths."
13:54. *his own country*: Nazareth. See the note on 9:1.

Is not this man the son of the carpenter?" "And his mother —
is not Mary her name?" "And his brothers — are they not James
56 and Joseph and Simon and Jude?" "And his sisters — are they not
our next-door neighbors? How, then, did this man come by all this?"
57 And so his person was a puzzle to them. But Jesus said to them:
"No prophet is discredited — except in his own country and in his
58 own household." And owing to their unbelief he did not work
many miracles there.

CHAPTER 14

THE BEHEADING OF JOHN THE BAPTIST

1   At that time the tetrarch Herod heard the current talk about
2 Jesus. "This man is John the Baptist," he said to his courtiers; "yes,
it is he, risen from the dead. And that is why the miraculous powers
are active in him!"

3   Just at that time Herod had John arrested, put in chains, and
removed to a dungeon. He did it to humor Herodias, his brother
4 Philip's wife, because John had said to him: "You have no right to
5 live with her." And he would have liked to put him to death, but
6 he feared the people who regarded him as a prophet. However, when
Herod's birthday came round, the daughter of Herodias danced at
7 the party and charmed Herod, so much so that he agreed under oath
8 to give her whatever she might ask. So, prompted by her mother,
she said: "Give me, here and now, on a platter, the head of John
9 the Baptist." At this the king was greatly disturbed; but, out of
regard for the oath and the company at table, he ordered that it
10 should be given to her. He dispatched an executioner and had John
11 beheaded in the dungeon. His head was brought on a platter and
12 presented to the girl, who then brought it to her mother. After
gaining access to his body, his disciples removed and buried it. Then
they came and told Jesus.

MULTIPLICATION OF LOAVES AND FISH

13   On hearing the news, Jesus withdrew from there in a boat to
an unfrequented place for the sake of privacy. But the crowds heard
14 of it and followed him on foot from the towns. When he went

ashore, he saw a multitude of people. His heart went out to them
and he ministered to the sick among them.

Late in the afternoon, the disciples came up to him. "The place," 15
they said, "is unfrequented, and the day is all but gone; dismiss the
crowds so that they can reach the villages and buy themselves something to eat." But Jesus said to them: "They have no need to go 16
away; it is for you to give them something to eat." "We have nothing 17
here," they replied, "except five loaves and two fish." "Bring them 18
here," he said. He then ordered the crowds to recline on the grass, 19
took the five loaves and the two fish into his hands, looked up to
heaven, and, after saying grace, broke the loaves into portions, which
he gave to his disciples. The disciples then passed them out to the
crowds. All ate, and everyone had a plentiful meal. Besides, they 20
gathered what was left over till they had twelve baskets of remnants.
The persons who had eaten numbered about five thousand, not 21
counting women and children.

CHRIST WALKS OVER THE SEA

Immediately he obliged the disciples to re-enter a boat and 22
precede him to the other shore, while he would dismiss the crowds.
After dismissing them, he went up the mountainside alone to pray. 23
Night fell and he was still there alone, while the boat was far out 24
at sea, hit hard by the waves, since the wind was against them.
During the last part of the night, however, he came toward them, 25
walking over the sea. But when they saw him walk upon the sea, they 26
were perplexed. "It is a ghost!" they said, and from fright cried out.
But Jesus at once addressed them. "Take heart," he said; "it is I! 27
Do not be afraid."

Thus reassured, Peter said to him: "Lord, if it is you, tell me to 28
come to you over the water." "Come," he replied. So Peter climbed 29
out of the boat and, starting in the direction of Jesus, walked over
the water; but when he felt the stiff breeze, he took alarm and, 30
since he began to sink, cried out: "Lord, save me!"

Jesus immediately reached out his hand and took hold of him. 31
"How little faith you have!" he said to him; "what made you
doubt?" Then they climbed up into the boat and the wind subsided. 32
The men in the boat prostrated themselves before him and said: 33
"You are indeed the Son of God."

TOUCHING ONLY THE TASSEL OF HIS CLOAK

34 They now went straight across and put ashore at Gennesaret.
35 When the inhabitants of this region recognized him, they sent word round that whole neighborhood, and all the sick were brought to
36 him. He was asked to allow them to touch were it only the tassel of his cloak, and as many as made physical contact were cured.

CHAPTER 15

LIP SERVICE

1 At that time Pharisees and Scribes from Jerusalem interviewed
2 Jesus. "Why," they said, "do your disciples go against the tradition of the elders? For example, they do not wash their hands when
3 about to take a meal." But he had an answer for them. "And why,"
he said, "do you go against God's commandment merely to uphold
4 your tradition? For example, God has declared: 'Honor father and mother,' and, 'Whoever curses father or mother shall be put to
5 death.' Yet you maintain: 'Once a person has said to his father or his mother, Any support you might get from me has already been
6 made a gift to God, he need not honor his father or mother.'
And thereby you render null and void the word of God merely to
7 uphold your tradition. Hypocrites! Rightly has Isaias prophesied about you when he said:
8   'This race honors me with its lips,
          but its heart is far away from me.
9   They worship me in vain,
          for they teach as binding precepts
          mere rulings made by man.'"

BLIND GUIDES OF BLIND FOLK

10 He then called the crowd around him and said to them: "Give

---

14:36. *made physical contact:* the Greek word means much more than a mere casual touch. See Jn. 20:17, and Christ's and Peter's words in Lk. 8:45 ff.

15:2. *the tradition of the elders:* the interpretations of the Mosaic Law, given by former Scribes. The Pharisees regarded them as binding.

15:5. Vows made by a son must not stand in the way of his natural duty to support his parents. The abuse here censured was, no doubt, due to the interpretations of the Scribes. See 23:24.

ear, and use your understanding! Not what goes into the mouth 11
defiles a person, but what comes out of the mouth is the thing that
defiles a person." Then the disciples came up and said to him: 12
"Do you know that the Pharisees, on hearing your remark, were
horrified?" "Any planting," he replied, "not planted by my heavenly 13
Father, must be uprooted. Do not mind them. Blind guides of blind 14
folk they are! And when one blind man guides another, both will
fall into the ditch."

   Peter was puzzled. "Explain to us," he said to him, "this parable." 15
   "So you, too," he replied, "are still without understanding! 16
Do you not comprehend that anything which enters a man's mouth 17
goes into the stomach and is then thrown off as waste? On the other 18
hand, what comes out of the mouth proceeds from the heart, and
this is what defiles a person; for out of the heart proceed evil 19
thoughts — murder, adultery, fornication, theft, false witness, and
blasphemy. These are the things that defile a person. To eat with 20
unwashed hands does not defile anybody!"

CHRIST CURES THE DAUGHTER OF THE CANAANITE WOMAN
   Jesus now left that place and withdrew into the neighborhood 21
of Tyre and Sidon. And behold, out of that district came a Canaanite 22
woman who exclaimed: "Take pity on me, Lord, Son of David!
My daughter is sorely tormented by a demon." But in answer to her 23
request, he did not say a word. Finally his disciples approached and
pleaded with him. "Let her go home contented," they said; "she
cries so after us!" He protested. "My mission," he said, "is exclu- 24
sively to the lost sheep of the house of Israel." At last she herself 25
came and, prostrating herself before him, said: "Lord, help me!"
He demurred. "It is not fair," he said, "to take the children's bread 26
and throw it to the dogs." "You are right, Lord," she replied; "and 27
the dogs eat only of the crumbs that fall from the table of their
masters." Then Jesus acquiesced. "My good woman," he said, 28
"great is your faith! Your wish shall be granted." Her daughter
was cured that very moment.

THE DUMB SPEAK, THE LAME WALK, THE BLIND SEE
   When Jesus had gone away from there he came to the Sea of 29
Galilee. Going up into the mountainside he there sat down, and a 30

multitude of people flocked to him, who brought along with them persons that were lame, blind, dumb, or crippled besides many others. These they put down at his feet, and he healed them.
31 As a result, the crowds were enraptured on seeing the dumb speak, the lame walk, the blind with their sight restored; and they glorified the God of Israel.

ANOTHER MULTIPLICATION OF LOAVES AND FISH

32 Jesus then called his disciples to him and said: "My heart goes out to the multitude. For full three days they have been staying with me and have nothing left to eat. I am unwilling to send them home
33 fasting; they might break down on the way." The disciples then said to him: "Where can we get bread enough to satisfy so large a
34 crowd in a desert!" "How many loaves have you?" Jesus asked
35 them. "Seven," they replied; "besides a few small fish." Then,
36 passing word round for the crowd to recline on the ground, he took the seven loaves and the fish into his hands and, after saying grace, broke them into portions, which he gave to the disciples; and the
37 disciples passed them out to the crowds. All ate, and had a plentiful meal. Besides, they gathered what was left over and filled seven
38 baskets with the remnants. The persons who had eaten numbered
39 four thousand, not counting women and children. After dismissing the crowds, he re-entered the boat and set sail for the district of Magadan.

CHAPTER 16

THE LEAVEN OF THE PHARISEES AND SADDUCEES

1 One day the Pharisees and Sadducees came up and, intending to test him, asked that he show them, in the sky, a proof of his
2 claims. Taking up the challenge, he said to them: "In the evening
3 you say, 'The sky is red; therefore, a fine day tomorrow!' and in the morning you say, 'The sky is red and lowering; therefore, a storm today!' You know how to read the features of the sky: and you
4 cannot read the signs of the times? A headstrong and adulterous generation demands a proof of my claims; but a proof will not be

---

16:1. *in the sky:* implying, of course, that such a "sign" was wrought by "heaven," that is, "by God." See the note on 3:17.

given it except the proof which Jonas gave." And turning his back on them, he walked away.

Now in setting out for the opposite shore, the disciples had 5 forgotten to provide themselves with bread. So, when Jesus remarked 6 to them: "Look out, and beware of the leaven of the Pharisees and Sadducees," they had a discussion among themselves, their thought 7 being, "He said this because we did not provide ourselves with bread." Jesus was aware of this and said: "Why that discussion 8 about your having no bread? What little faith you have! Is the 9 truth not yet dawning on you? And do you not remember the five loaves for the five thousand, and how many basketfuls you gathered up? Or the seven loaves for the four thousand, and how many 10 basketfuls you gathered up? Strange, that you do not understand 11 that it was not bread at all I spoke to you about! But do beware of the leaven of the Pharisees and Sadducees." At last it dawned upon 12 them that he had warned them against the teaching of the Pharisees and Sadducees, and not against the yeast used in baking bread.

CHRIST'S CHURCH TO REST ON PETER, "THE ROCK"

When Jesus had reached the environs of Caesarea Philippi, he 13 put this question to his disciples: "Who do the people say the Son of Man is?" "Some say, John the Baptist," they replied; "others 14 say, Elias; still others, Jeremias, or some other prophet." "But you," 15 he went on to say, "who do you say I am?" Then Simon Peter 16 spoke up: "You are the Messias, the Son of the Living God." Jesus 17 acquiesced and said to him: "Blessed are you, Simon, son of Jona. It was my Father in heaven that revealed this to you, and not flesh and blood. And I, in turn, say to you: You are Peter, and upon this 18

16:18. *upon this rock:* note the play on the words *petra,* "rock," and *Petros,* as it were, "the Rock-man." Christ promises to make Peter the principle of unity and stability of his spiritual building, the Church. He fulfilled his promise when he made Peter the supreme shepherd (Jn. 21:15 ff.). Note the expression "*my*" *Church:* Christ is the invisible Head (Eph. 2:20).

my Church: this is the first of 115 occurrences of this noun in the New Testament. The organized society which Christ established is not called "synagogue" but "Church," because "he did not institute his society as something which was to remain a mere religious unit within the social fabric of the racial Israel, but as the corporate body which was to succeed the Israelitic community as God's kingdom in this world" (Fenton). The Greek term *ecclesia* means an assembly "called out" or convoked by legitimate authority for the purpose of governing the community. Hence the members of this Church are called "the elect" or "the chosen," as in Rom. 1:6. The most common

rock I will build my Church, and the gates of hell shall not prevail
19 against it. I will give you the keys of the kingdom of heaven, and
whatever you bind on earth shall be bound in heaven, and whatever
20 you loose on earth shall be loosed in heaven." But then and there
he enjoined the disciples not to tell anyone that he was the Messias.

CROSS AND CROWN

21   From that time on Jesus began to make plain to his disciples
that it was necessary for him to go to Jerusalem, suffer much at
the hands of the elders, high priests, and Scribes, be put to death,
22 and on the third day rise again. At this Peter drew him aside and
proceeded to lecture him. "May God spare you, Lord," he said:
23 "this must never happen to you!" But he turned on Peter with
the words: "Back to your place; follow me, Satan! You are a
stumbling block to me, for you do not take God's view of things,
but men's."
24   Then Jesus said to his disciples: "If anyone wants to become
my follower, he must renounce himself and shoulder his cross; then
25 he may be a follower of mine. Indeed, he who is bent on saving
his life, must part with it anyway; but he who freely parts with his
26 life for my sake will secure it in the end. Clearly, what will it profit
a man to gain the whole world when his life is forfeited in any case?
27 Or, what price can a man pay down to purchase life forever? Furthermore: the Son of Man is to come hereafter wrapt in his Father's
glory and escorted by his angels; and then he will repay everyone
28 according to his conduct. I tell you truly: some of those present here
will not taste death before they see the Son of Man coming in his
royal state."

---

designation of the Church in the Gospels is "kingdom of God." See the first
note of 3:2. *the gates* (an Oriental metaphor for "the power") *of hell* or "of
death": lit., the gates of Hades: the realm of the dead, or the infernal regions.
These, of course, no mortal can force open. The Church is externally indestruc-
tible and internally indefectible. "To bind" and "to loose" are Oriental metaphors
describing the exercise of supreme authority (executive, legislative, judicial). See
18:17 and 18. The Church can exclude undesirable members (1 Cor. 5:5); she
can "remit" or "retain" sins (Jn. 20:23).

16:23. *Back to your place:* Peter had come out of the group and drawn Jesus
aside for a lecture. Jesus orders him back to his place in the group, whose duty
it was to "follow" him and obey. Note the important omission of the words
"follow me" in Christ's rebuke to Satan in 4:10. Peter is unwittingly playing
the part of Satan: both tried to draw Jesus away from doing the will of God.

16:25. The same truth is taught a little more emphatically in Mk. 8:35 ff.,
where see the note.

CHAPTER 17

CHRIST'S BRILLIANT TRANSFORMATION

Six days later, Jesus took with him Peter, James, and the latter's 1
brother John, and led them up a high hill for the sake of privacy.
Here he changed his appearance before their eyes. His face became 2
radiant like the sun, and his garments turned as white as light.
Presently Moses and Elias were seen by them conversing with him. 3
Then Peter felt moved to say to Jesus: "Lord, it is well that we are 4
here! If you wish, I will put up three tents here — one for you,
one for Moses, and one for Elias."

He was still speaking when, suddenly, a luminous cloud enveloped 5
them and, unexpectedly, a voice rang out in the cloud:
"This is my beloved Son,
with whom I am well pleased.
Listen to him!"
On hearing it, the disciples fell prone upon their faces; so thoroughly 6
frightened were they. But Jesus approached and, laying his hand 7
upon them, said: "Rise and do not be afraid." When they raised 8
their eyes, they saw no one but Jesus only.

JOHN THE BAPTIST REFERRED TO AS "ELIAS"

As they were coming down the hill, Jesus gave them a strict 9
command: "Do not," he said, "tell the vision to anyone till the
Son of Man has risen from the dead." His disciples then asked him: 10
"Why, really, do the Scribes say that Elias is to come first?" "Yes," 11
he replied, "Elias will come and restore everything. But I am telling 12
you, Elias has already come, and people did not appreciate him; on
the contrary, they worked their will on him. And this is just what
the Son of Man is destined to suffer at their hands." Then it dawned 13
on the disciples that he had spoken to them about John the Baptist.

A DEVIL DRIVEN FROM A BOY

When they rejoined the crowd, a man approached and, falling 14
on his knees before him, said: "Sir, take pity on my son. He is 15
subject to fits, and oh, he suffers so badly! Often he throws himself
into the fire and often, too, into water. I brought him to your 16
disciples, but they were unable to cure him." "O unbelieving and 17

perverse generation," Jesus replied. "How long must I be with you!
18 How long must I bear with you! Bring him here to me." Jesus then
spoke sternly to him, and the demon went out of him. The lad
19 was cured that very hour. Thereupon the disciples came up to Jesus
and asked him privately: "Why were we unable to drive him out?"
20 "Because of your little faith," he replied; "I tell you positively, if
you have faith as small as a mustard seed, you may say to this hill,
'Move away from here to there,' and it will move away. Nothing will
21 be impossible to you. As to this particular kind, it cannot be driven
out except by prayer and fasting."

PREDICTION OF THE PASSION AND RESURRECTION

22   They were still wandering about in Galilee when Jesus said to
them: "The Son of Man is to be betrayed into the hands of men:
23 they will put him to death, but on the third day he will rise again."
They were exceedingly distressed.

TEMPLE DUES FOUND IN THE MOUTH OF A FISH

24   When they had entered Capharnaum, the collectors of the temple
dues interviewed Peter and said: "Does not your Rabbi pay the
25 temple dues?" "He certainly does," he replied. But as soon as he
came indoors, and before he had said a word, Jesus asked him:
"What do you think, Simon? On whom do earthly sovereigns levy
custom dues or the poll tax? On their own children or on out-
26 siders?" When he replied, "On outsiders," Jesus said to him: "Then,
27 evidently, the children are exempt! However, we must give them no
offense. Go down to the sea, throw in a hook, and land the first
fish to come up. Then open its mouth, and you will find a stater.
Take that, and give it to them to pay for me and you."

CHAPTER 18

THE WORTH OF A LITTLE CHILD

1   On that occasion the disciples came up to Jesus and said: "Who,
2 really, is the greatest in the kingdom of heaven?" He called a little
3 child to him, and placed him in front of them. "I tell you frankly,"
he said, "if you do not change and become like little children, you

will not enter the kingdom of heaven. Therefore, he who, like this 4
little child, makes little of himself is the greatest in the kingdom of
heaven. And he who befriends one such child out of consideration 5
for me befriends me. On the other hand, he who has been an 6
occasion of sin to one of these little ones that believe in me, it would
be better for him if he had a millstone hung around his neck and
were drowned in the depth of the sea. Oh, cursed is the world 7
because of its temptations to sin! It is unavoidable, to be sure, that
temptations should come; for all that, perdition awaits him through
whom the temptation comes.

"But if your own hand or foot tempts you to sin, cut it off and 8
throw it away; it is better for you to enter life crippled or lame
than to keep both hands or both feet and be consigned to the
everlasting fire. And if your eye tempts you to sin, pluck it out 9
and throw it away; it is better for you to enter life deprived of one
eye than to keep both eyes and be consigned to the fire of the
eternal pit.

"Take care you do not despise any one of these little ones. I tell 10
you, their angels in heaven look continually upon the face of my
Father in heaven; besides, it is the mission of the Son of Man to 11
save what is lost. What do you think? When a man has a hundred 12
sheep and one of them strays, will he not leave the ninety-nine on
the hillside and go in search of the straggler? And when he succeeds 13
in finding it, he is better pleased with it, I assure you, than with the
ninety-nine that have not gone astray! So, too, it is not the will of 14
your Father in heaven that even one of these little ones should
be lost.

HOW TO CORRECT OTHERS

"But when your brother does you wrong, go and, between you 15
and him alone, convict him of his fault. If he listens to you, you
have won your brother over; but should he not listen to you, then 16
take one or two along with you, so that 'every case may be decided

18:13. The recovery of the one lost sheep gives the owner a very special joy
for which the ninety-nine had given no occasion. Compare the reason which
the father of the prodigal son gives for "celebrating" his return; Lk. 15:6.
18:15–20. These verses are a unit, enlarging on the function of the Church
in two respects. The Church has power to sit in judgment and pronounce
sentence when quarrels arise between individual members. This power is vested

17 on the testimony of two or three witnesses.' If he pays no attention
    to them, then notify the Church; and if he pays no attention to the
    Church, then treat him as a heathen and publican.

18 "I tell you with assurance: whatever you bind on earth shall be
    bound in heaven; whatever you loose on earth shall be loosed in
19 heaven. But I tell you with the same assurance: when any two of
    you are in agreement here on earth regarding anything they ask for,
20 their prayer shall be granted by my Father in heaven. Where two or
    three are assembled in my name, there I am in the midst of them."

THE PARABLE OF THE MERCILESS DEBTOR

21   Then Peter came up and said to him: "Lord, how many times may
    my brother wrong me and still claim my pardon? As many as seven
22 times?" "No," Jesus replied; "I do not say, 'as many as seven times,'
23 but 'as many as seventy times seven!' That is why the kingdom of
    heaven reminds me of an earthly king who, once upon a time,
24 desired to settle accounts with his officials. In the course of the
    settlement one who owed him ten thousand talents presented him-
25 self; and since he had no means of paying, the master ordered him
    to be sold with wife, children, and all he had, and payment to
26 be made. Then the official went down on his knees and, prostrating
    himself before him, said: 'Have patience with me, and I will pay
27 you everything.' Touched to the heart, the master of that official
28 canceled his debt and set him free. But no sooner had that official
    gone outside than he met one of his fellow officials who owed him

---

in the Church's officials, as is evident (Mt. 16:18). A notable example of the
use of this judiciary power is given in 1 Cor. 5:5. What is done on earth (by
human officials) is ratified by God, the reason being that the Church is the
"Body of Christ" (Eph. 1:23). Another, and more consoling, result of Christ's
presence in the Church (see verse 20) is God's greater readiness to help when
members of the Church "unite" in prayer.

18:23. *officials*: our word "slave" fails to convey to a modern mind the meaning
of the Greek term. In Oriental monarchies, the king alone was "free"; all
others, including even high officials, were "slaves," that is, subjects in the fullest
sense of the term. Note St. Paul's use of the word to express his utter subjection
to Christ. English has no expression to do justice to all the connotations of
the Greek.

18:24. There were *talents* of gold and of silver, varying in value in different
periods of time and localities. *Ten thousand talents* would approximate twelve
million dollars; one hundred denarii (see note on Mk. 6:37) would be about
seventeen dollars. This is not taking account of the latest depreciations that
may have taken place since this estimate was made.

a hundred denarii; and, grasping him, he was about to choke him, saying: 'Pay what you owe.' Then his fellow official went down on 29 his knees and pleaded with him: 'Have patience with me and I will pay you.' But he would not hear of it; on the contrary, he went and 30 had him thrown into prison until he should pay the amount owed. Naturally, his fellow officials, who saw what had happened, were 31 deeply grieved; and they went to their master to tell him all that had taken place. Then the master summoned him. 'You merciless 32 man,' he said to him; 'I canceled that whole debt of yours because you pleaded with me. Was it not proper for you, too, to take pity 33 on your fellow official just as I had taken pity on you?' And with 34 indignation his master turned him over to the jailors until such time as he should pay the whole debt. In the same way my heavenly 35 Father will treat you if you do not each forgive your brother from your heart."

CHAPTER 19

When Jesus had at last completed these discourses, he took final 1 leave of Galilee and set out for the province of Judea by the Transjordanian route. Large groups of people joined him, and he 2 ministered to the sick that came his way.

THE QUESTION OF DIVORCE

One day Pharisees interviewed him to sound him out. "Is it 3 right," they asked, "to divorce one's wife for any reason whatever?" He answered as follows: "Did you never read that the Creator in 4 the beginning made human beings male and female, and declared: 'For this reason a man must leave father and mother and indissolubly 5 cling to his wife,' and, 'The two are to become one person'? It 6 follows, then, that they are no longer two persons but one. Consequently, what God has yoked together man may not separate."

"Why, then," they went on to say, "did Moses enjoin divorcing 7 one's wife by serving her with a writ of separation?" "Because," he 8 replied, "Moses had an eye to your hardness of heart. That is why he allowed you to divorce your wives. But originally there was no

9   such thing. And I declare to you: whoever divorces his wife, except
    on the score of lewdness, and marries another is an adulterer; and
    he who marries a divorced woman is an adulterer."

10 "If that is the predicament of a married man," the disciples said
11 to him, "then one had better not get married!" "Not all master
    this lesson," he said to them, "but only such as have received a
12 special gift: as there are those barred from marrying by a natural
    defect, and those barred by an act of man, so there are those who
    bar themselves from marrying for the sake of the kingdom of heaven.
    Only a strong soul should try to master this lesson."

CHRIST'S LOVE OF LITTLE CHILDREN

13 Then people brought little children to him, that he might lay
    his hands on them and pray; but the disciples scolded them for
14 doing so. Jesus, however, said: "Let the little children alone, and
    do not stop them from coming to me. The kingdom of heaven
15 belongs to such as these." He then laid his hands on them and
    went his way.

DIFFICULTIES FOR THE RICH

16 Presently someone approached him and said: "Rabbi, is there
17 something good that I can do so as to win eternal life?" He said
    to him: "Why do you consult me about something good you could
    do? There is One who is absolutely good! If you want to enter
18 eternal life, keep the commandments." "Which?" the man asked,
    and Jesus said: "These: 'Do not murder; do not commit adultery;
19 do not steal; do not bear false witness; honor father and mother;
20 and, love your neighbor as yourself.'" "I have observed all these
21 things," the young man replied; "what am I still lacking?" "If you

19:9 ff. Compare 5:32. Not celibacy for its own sake is better than marriage,
but virginity embraced for the love of God and the furtherance of his kingdom.
This teaching was clearly understood and widely practiced from the very beginning
of the Church. Examples of such celibacy at the time of Christ were Jesus,
his Mother, John the Baptist, and the Apostle John. The "lesson" in verse 11
is explained in verse 12.

19:17. See the note on Lk. 18:19.

19:21. All that is needed to enter the kingdom of God is to keep his
commandments; one may, however, by the grace of God (19:11), strive after
a more "perfect" mode of life. The idea of "perfection" as a desirable goal
for a Christian is often expressed in the New Testament; see, for instance,
Eph. 4:13; 1 Cor. 14:20; Mt. 5:48; Phil. 3:15; James 3:1; Col. 1:28. Such

want to be perfect," Jesus said to him, "go and sell all your possessions and give the proceeds to the poor — for which you will have
an investment in heaven; then come back and be my follower."
When the young man heard the answer, he went away with a heavy 22
heart; for he had much property.

Then Jesus said to his disciples: "I tell you frankly: a rich man 23
will find it difficult to enter the kingdom of heaven. I repeat: it is 24
easier for a camel to pass through the eye of a needle than for a
rich man to enter the kingdom of God." On hearing this, the 25
disciples were completely bewildered. "In that case," they said, "who
can be saved?" But Jesus looked straight at them and said: "Where 26
man fails, God still avails." Here Peter took occasion to say to him: 27
"We, you see, have given up everything and become your followers.
What, then, are we to get?" Jesus said to them: "I tell you with 28
assurance: in the final regeneration, when the Son of Man takes
his seat on a throne befitting his glory, you, my followers, will, in
turn, be seated on twelve thrones and have jurisdiction over the
Twelve Tribes of Israel. And so in general: whoever gives up home, 29
or brothers, or sisters, or father, or mother, or children, or lands, for
the sake of my name, will receive a hundred times as much and
inherit eternal life. Many that are first will be last, and many that 30
are last will be first."

CHAPTER 20

THE LANDOWNER AND THE LABORERS

"To illustrate: the kingdom of heaven reminds me of a land- 1
owner who went out at break of day to hire laborers for his vineyard.
After agreeing with the laborers on one denarius a day, he sent them 2
into his vineyard. Again he went out about nine in the morning 3
and saw others loitering about the market place. 'You men, too,' 4

striving is not a command. Effective means to securing perfection are voluntary poverty (indicated in this verse), voluntary continence (see 19:12), and
perfect obedience practiced in the "following" of Christ.

19:24. A camel or an elephant "passing through the eye of a needle" was
a common Oriental metaphor to express a matter of extreme difficulty. Inordinate
attachment to wealth is apt to stifle interest in spiritual things. Compare Lk.
21:34 and Mt. 13:22.

he said to them — 'go into my vineyard, and I will give you what-
5 ever is right.' So they went. Again he went out about noon and
6 three in the afternoon, and acted in the same way. Finally, going
out at five o'clock, he found still others loitering about, and said
7 to them: 'Why have you been loitering here all day?' 'Because,'
they replied, 'no one has hired us.' 'Well, then,' he went on to say,
8 'you too — go into my vineyard.' When evening came, the owner
of the vineyard said to the overseer: 'Call the laborers together and
pay them their wages; begin with the last group and end with the
9 first.' Then the five o'clock group came forward, and everyone
10 received one denarius. Now, when the first group came, they
supposed they would receive more; but they, too, received one
11 denarius each. They accepted it, but grumbled against the land-
12 owner. 'These late arrivals,' they said, 'have done but one hour's
work; yet you put them on the same level with us who have borne
13 the whole day's burden and scorching heat.' 'But, my friend,' he
argued with one of them, 'I am doing you no wrong. Did you not
14 agree with me on one denarius? Take what is yours and make off;
15 but I choose to give this last arrival as much as I gave you. Have
I not a right to do as I please with what is my own? Or, are you
16 jealous because I am generous?' Just so will the last be first, and
the first will be last."

THE CRUCIFIXION AND RESURRECTION AGAIN FORETOLD

17 As Jesus was going up to Jerusalem, he took the twelve disciples
18 aside for the sake of privacy, and on the way said to them: "Listen!
We are going up to Jerusalem, where the Son of Man will be
betrayed to the high priests and Scribes, and they will condemn him
19 to death, and hand him over to the Gentiles to mock and scourge
and crucify; but on the third day he will rise again."

SEATS AT THE RIGHT AND LEFT OF CHRIST

20 At that time the mother of the sons of Zebedee came up to
him with her sons and, prostrating herself, asked a favor of him.
21 "What is your request?" he said to her. She replied: "Arrange for
these two sons of mine to have a seat, one at your right, the other
22 at your left, in your kingdom." Jesus answered by saying: "You
do not realize what you are asking. Can you drink the cup which

I am to drink?" "We can," they replied. "Yes," he said to them, 23
"you will drink my cup; but as for a seat at my right or my left —
that is not in my power to grant except to those for whom it has
been reserved by my Father." When now the ten others heard of 24
this incident, they became indignant at the two brothers. But Jesus 25
called them into his presence and said: "You know that the rulers
of the Gentiles lord it over their subjects, and that their princes
tyrannize over them. That must not be your way! On the contrary, 26
he who would be a prince among you must be your servant, and 27
he who would be a leader among you must be your slave. So, too, 28
the Son of Man did not come into the world to be served, but to
serve and to give his life as a ransom for many."

TWO BLIND MEN RECEIVE SIGHT

They were now journeying on, at some distance from Jericho, 29
and a numerous crowd accompanied him. Suddenly two blind men, 30
who sat by the road, shouted when they heard that Jesus was passing
by: "Lord, Son of David, take pity on us!" The crowd indignantly 31
told them to be quiet; but they shouted all the louder: "Lord, Son
of David, take pity on us." Then Jesus stopped and called for them. 32
"What do you want me to do for you?" he asked. "Lord," they 33
said to him, "we wish our eyes were opened." And pitying them 34
from his heart, Jesus laid his hands on their eyes. Immediately they
received sight, and then followed him.

CHAPTER 21

CHRIST ENTERS JERUSALEM

When they had come into the vicinity of Jerusalem and reached 1
Bethphage on the slope of the Mount of Olives, Jesus then and there
sent two disciples on an errand with these instructions: "Go to the 2
village facing you, and at once you will find tied an ass and a foal
with her. Unhitch them and bring them here. And in case anybody 3
says anything to you, just say that the Lord has need of them and
will send them back without delay." This incident was to fulfill 4
the prediction made through the prophet, who says:

20:30. Only one blind man is mentioned in the parallel account: Mk.
10:46 and Lk. 18:35.

5   "Say to the daughter of Sion:
            Behold your King coming to you —
            gentle and seated upon an ass
            and a foal of the beast of burden."

6   The disciples went and did as Jesus had directed them.
7   They brought the ass and the foal, and, after they had thrown
8   their cloaks on them, Jesus seated himself on these. Most of the
    crowd carpeted the road with their cloaks, while some lopped
9   branches off the trees and strewed the way with them. The crowds
    that marched in front and those that followed in the rear kept
    shouting the words:
            "Hosanna to the Son of David!
            A blessing on him
            who comes in the name of the Lord!
            Hosanna in the heavens above!"

10 Upon his entry into Jerusalem, the whole city was thrown into
11 commotion and asked, "Who is this man?" And the crowds
    responded: "This is the Prophet Jesus of Nazareth in Galilee!"
12   Jesus now entered the temple of God and expelled all the sellers
    and buyers on the temple grounds; he overthrew the counters of
13 the money-changers and the seats of the pigeon dealers, saying
    to them:
            "The Scripture says:
            'My house shall be what its name declares,
            a house of prayer';
14 but you are turning it into 'a den of robbers.' " Blind and lame
    persons came to him on the temple grounds, and he healed them.
15 But when the high priests and the Scribes saw the astonishing
    activity he displayed, and heard the children cry out on the temple
16 grounds: "Hosanna to the Son of David," they indignantly said to
    him: "Do you hear what these are saying?" "Certainly," he replied;
    "did you never read this text:
            'From the lips of infants and of babes
            you have drawn a fitting hymn of praise'?"
17 And, turning his back on them, he left the city for Bethany and
    passed the night there.

21:9. *Hosanna:* originally a cry for help, "Save us"; later, a cry of enthusi-
astic acclamation, because of its use in the ritual of the feast of Tabernacles.

THE BARREN FIG TREE

In the morning he returned to the city. He was hungry and, *18*
seeing a fig tree by the road, went up to it. But he found nothing *19*
on it except leaves. He then said to it: "Hereafter no fruit shall
ever again grow on you!" The fig tree dried up immediately. The *20*
disciples noticed it and expressed astonishment: "How suddenly
the fig tree dried up!" Jesus took advantage of the opportunity and *21*
said: "I tell you positively: if you have faith and do not doubt, you
can do what was done to the fig tree; yes, more than that: you can
say to this mountain, 'Up with you, and down into the sea!' and it
will be done. And in general: you will receive anything you ask in *22*
your prayer, provided you have faith."

THE HIGH PRIESTS AND ELDERS ANSWERED

When he had entered the temple grounds, the high priests and *23*
the elders — the nation's Council — approached him while he was
teaching, and said: "By what authority do you engage in this activity?
That is, who gave you this authority?" Jesus parried their question *24*
by saying: "Let me, too, ask you one question; and, in case you
answer me, then I, for my part, will tell you by what authority I
engage in this activity. John's baptism — where did it come from? *25*
From heaven or from men?" Then they discussed the matter privately. "In case we say, 'From heaven,'" they argued, "he will ask *26*
us, 'Then why did you not believe him?' But if we say, 'From men,'
we have to fear the people, because, one and all, they consider John
a prophet." So their answer to Jesus was: "We do not know." *27*
Then he, in turn, said to them: "Neither will I tell you by what
authority I am acting the way I am."

"What do you think of this? Once upon a time a man had two *28*
sons. He went to the first and said: 'My son, go and spend today
working in my vineyard.' But he refused and said: 'I do not want *29*
to go.' In the end, however, he felt remorse and went anyway.
He then went to the second and told him the same thing. He *30*
acquiesced and said: 'I will, sir.' But he did not go. Which of the *31*
two complied with his father's wishes?" "The first-mentioned," they
replied. Then Jesus said to them: "I tell you frankly: the tax
collectors and the prostitutes have got the start of you in entering
the kingdom of God; for, although John's mission was strictly within *32*

the limits of the law, you did not believe him; but the tax collectors
and the prostitutes did believe him. You saw what happened, but
in the end you did not feel remorse and believe him."

THE PARABLE OF THE UNJUST VINEDRESSERS

33   "Listen to another parable: Once upon a time there was a landowner who planted a vineyard, set up a fence round it, dug a wine
vat in it, and built a tower; he then leased it out to vinedressers
34 and went abroad. When the harvest season drew near, he sent his
35 agents to the vinedressers to receive his share of the vintage. But
the vinedressers seized his agents, beat one of them, killed another,
36 and stoned a third. So he sent another group of agents, more
numerous than the first; but they treated them in the same way.
37 Finally, he sent to them his own son, saying: 'They will respect
38 my son.' But when the vinedressers saw his son, they said among
themselves: 'This is the heir; come, let us kill him and seize upon
39 his inheritance.' So they laid hold of him, drove him out of the
40 vineyard, and killed him. Now, then, when the owner of the
41 vineyard returns, what will he do to those vinedressers?" They said
to him: "He will put those wretches to a wretched death. And
besides, he will lease the vineyard out to other vinedressers, who
will give him his due share of the vintage at its proper season."
42   Jesus continued: "Did you never read this Scripture text:
         'The very stone which the builders rejected
             has become the cornerstone:
                 this is the Lord's own doing,
             and it is a wonderful sight for us'?
43 For this reason I tell you: the kingdom of God will be taken away
from you and turned over to a nation that will produce the fruits
44 expected of it. He who dashes against this stone will be crushed;
and he on whom it falls will be ground to powder."
45   On hearing his parables, the high priests and the Pharisees
46 understood that he had been referring to themselves. They would
have liked to arrest him, but they feared the masses, since these
regarded him as a prophet.

CHAPTER 22

THE PARABLE OF THE WEDDING FEAST

Once again Jesus took occasion to speak to them in parable 1
style. "The kingdom of heaven reminds me of a king who prepared 2
a wedding feast for his son, and sent his servants to bid those come 3
to the festivities who had received invitations. But they refused to
come. So he sent other servants, with these instructions: 'Take this 4
message to those who have been invited: Consider, please, that I
have finished the preparations for my dinner; my beeves and fatted
calves are killed; in short, everything is ready. Come to the wedding
feast.' But they carelessly went their several ways, one to his farm, 5
another to his business; the rest laid hold of the servants, and mal- 6
treated or killed them. Then the king, in a fit of anger, sent his 7
troops to put to death those murderers and lay their city in ashes.
He then said to his servants: 'The wedding feast is ready, but the 8
persons invited to it did not prove worthy. Go, therefore, where 9
the streets issue into the open country, and invite to the wedding
feast as many as you find.' So the servants went out on the open 10
roads and brought together all they found, bad as well as good, so
that the wedding hall was filled with guests. But when the king 11
came in to look at the guests, he noticed there a man who was not
wearing a wedding robe. 'My good sir,' he said to him, 'how did 12
you come in here without a wedding robe?' The man was struck
speechless. Then the king said to the servants: 'Bind him hand and 13
foot, and throw him into the darkness outside.' Oh, how that region
will resound with 'the weeping and the gnashing of teeth!' After all, 14
many are invited, but few chosen."

THREE ATTEMPTS TO ENTRAP JESUS

Then the Pharisees went to hold a consultation as to how to trap 15
him in an argument. So they sent to him their disciples together 16
with the Herodians. "Rabbi," these men said, "we know you are
an honest man and truthfully teach the way of God; you never
worry as to who anyone is, for you do not look to men's rank or

---

22:11. In the application of this parable, the wedding robe is interpreted as
charity or the state of grace, by St. Gregory the Great and many others.
22:16. *Herodians:* the partisans of King Herod.

17 station in life. Tell us, then, what you think. Is it right to pay a poll tax to Caesar or is it not?"

18 Jesus saw through their malice. "Hypocrites!" he said; "what do
19 you mean by sounding me out? Show me the coin with which you
20 pay the poll tax." So they brought him a denarius, and he asked them: "Whose head is this? And whose title is here inscribed?"
21 "Caesar's," they replied. He then said to them: "Therefore render
22 to Caesar what is Caesar's — and to God what is God's." On hearing this, they were nonplused; and turning their backs on him, they made off.

23 That same day Sadducees — the men that deny the resurrection —
24 came to him and laid this case before him: "Rabbi, Moses has declared: 'In case a man dies childless, his brother is to marry the
25 widow and raise children for his brother.' Now once upon a time there were seven brothers living with us. The first got married and
26 died, and, since he had no issue, left his wife to his brother. So did
27 the second and the third and all the rest down to the seventh. Last
28 of all the woman also died. At the resurrection, therefore, which of the seven shall have her to wife? They all, you see, had married her."

29 By way of answer Jesus said to them: "You are wide of the mark, since you understand neither the Scriptures nor the power of God.
30 In the risen life, nobody marries or is given in marriage, but all
31 are like angels in heaven. As to the rising from the dead, did you not read what God expressly declared when he said:

32 'I am the God of Abraham,
and the God of Isaac,
and the God of Jacob'?

33 He is not the God of dead men, but of living!" When the crowds heard this, they were lost in admiration of his teaching.

34 But when the Pharisees learned that he had effectively silenced
35 the Sadducees, they held a meeting; as a result, one of their legal
36 experts proposed this question by way of sounding him out: "Rabbi,
37 which is the great commandment in the Law?" He replied: " 'Love the Lord your God with your whole heart, and with your whole
38 soul, and with your whole mind.' This is the great and first com-
39 mandment. But a second commandment is like it: 'Love your
40 neighbor as yourself.' On these two commandments hinge the whole Law and the Prophets."

THE PHARISEES SILENCED BY JESUS

While the Pharisees were still grouped around him, Jesus put 41
this question to them: "What do you think about the Messias?" 42
he said; "whose Son is he?" "David's," they replied. "What sense, 43
then," he asked them, "does David, prompted by the Spirit, call
him 'Lord,' when he says:

> 'The Lord said to my Lord: 44
> Be seated at my right hand
> until I make your foes
> the footstool for your feet'?

If, then, David calls him 'Lord,' in what sense is he his 'Son'?" 45
No one was able to say a word to answer him; nor did anyone have 46
the face, from that time on, to ask him any more questions.

CHAPTER 23

PERDITION AWAITS THE SCRIBES AND PHARISEES

Then Jesus addressed the crowds and his disciples: 1
"The Scribes and the Pharisees occupy the chair of Moses. 2
Obey, therefore, any precepts or rules they lay down for you; only 3
do not imitate their conduct; for they do not practice what they
preach. They make up bundles of burdens which are heavy and 4
hard to bear, and lay them on the shoulders of their fellow men;
but they will not stir a finger of their own to lift them. Their 5
whole conduct has but one aim — to attract public attention. For

---

22:44. *my Lord:* not a mere temporal ruler, nor in fact any man, but God
himself.

23:2. *occupy the chair of Moses:* act as teachers of the Jewish people. It is
not clear whether Jesus here acknowledges their authority or condemns them as
usurpers. In either case he enjoins or permits obedience to their rulings, with
the evident proviso: "insofar as they correctly explain the Mosaic Law," which
they, no doubt, often did. Elsewhere he condemns their misinterpretations of the
Law (see verses 16 ff.). Verse 3, therefore, must be read in connection with
what follows. However the precise use of the Greek word here rendered "observe"
is not wholly cleared up. For Christ's "way of teaching," see the note on
Lk. 17:6.

23:5. *phylacteries:* two small capsules into which were compressed parchments
containing the words of Deut. 6:3–9. The Pharisees, literally fulfilling Deut.
6:8, fastened them on the forehead and left arm.

example: they widen their phylacteries and lengthen the tassels of
6 their cloaks; they are fond of places of distinction at meals and of
7 front seats in the synagogues; they crave ceremonious greetings in
the public places and love to be styled 'Rabbis' by their fellow men.
8 For your own part, do not have yourselves styled 'Rabbis,' for
One only is your Teacher. Among yourselves you are just brothers.
9 And do not style anyone your 'Father' upon earth, for One only
10 is your Father — he who is in heaven. And do not have yourselves
11 styled 'leaders,' for One only is your Leader — the Christ. He who
12 ranks highest among you must be your servant. He who exalts himself shall be humbled, and he who will humble himself shall be
exalted.

YOU HYPOCRITES

13   "Perdition awaits you, Scribes and Pharisees! Hypocrites! You
14 shut the kingdom of heaven in men's faces; for, besides not going
in yourselves, you block those that try to go in.
15   "Perdition awaits you, Scribes and Pharisees! Hypocrites! You
scour sea and land to make one convert, and when you succeed,
you make of him a devil twice as bad as yourselves.
16   "Perdition awaits you, blind guides! You say, 'If one swears by
the sanctuary, it means nothing; but if one swears by the gold of
17 the sanctuary, he is under obligation.' Foolish and blind men!
What is more important, the gold or the sanctuary which sanctifies
18 the gold? Again, 'if one swears by the altar, it means nothing; but
if one swears by the offering placed upon it, he is under obligation.'
19 How blind you are! What is more important, the offering or the
20 altar which sanctifies the offering? Therefore, he who swears by the
21 altar swears by it and everything upon it. And he who swears by
22 the sanctuary swears by it and by him who dwells in it. And he
who swears by heaven swears by the throne of God and by him who
is seated on it.

23:8. *Rabbis:* that is, teachers. Not the bearing of these titles, but a vain-
glorious parade of them, is forbidden. *just brothers:* to interpret this term to
mean that Christ did not confer on some members of the Church the power
to "rule" (with the consequent duty of others to obey), would be to deny the
monarchical constitution of the Church established elsewhere (Mt. 16:18;
19:20). See the note on Lk. 17:6. Christ warns his disciples against exercising
their power in a domineering spirit. See the note on Jn. 13:15.

"Perdition awaits you, Scribes and Pharisees! Hypocrites! You 23 pay a ten per cent tax on mint and anise and cummin, but disregard the weightier things of the Law — justice, mercy, and fidelity. One ought to attend to the latter without neglecting the former. Blind 24 guides! You strain out the gnat, but swallow the camel whole!

"Perdition awaits you, Scribes and Pharisees; Hypocrites! You 25 clean the outside of cup and dish, but inside they reek with greed and self-indulgence! Blind Pharisee, first clean the inside of the cup 26 so that the outside of it, too, may be clean!

"Perdition awaits you, Scribes and Pharisees! Hypocrites! You 27 resemble whitewashed sepulchers, which outwardly look attractive, but inwardly are full of dead men's bones and all kinds of filth. So you, too — outwardly, in the eyes of your fellow men, you are 28 observers of the Law, but inwardly you reek with insincerity and contempt for the Law.

"Perdition awaits you, Scribes and Pharisees! Hypocrites! You 29 rebuild the sepulchers of the prophets and decorate the tombs of the saints; at the same time you boast: 'Had we lived in the days 30 of our forefathers, we should not have been their partners in shedding the blood of the prophets!' Thus, by your own testimony, you 31 are the lineal descendants of those murderers of the prophets. There- 32 fore, fill up the measure of your forefathers! Serpents! Vipers' brood! 33 How are you to escape being sentenced to the pit of hell! For this 34 reason, mark my words, I am sending to you prophets and wise and learned men. Of these, you will kill and crucify some; others you will flog in your synagogues or pursue from city to city. As a 35 result, all the innocent blood ever shed on earth — beginning with the blood of the innocent Abel to the blood of Zachary, son of Barachias, whom you murdered between the sanctuary and the altar — shall be avenged upon you. Yes, indeed, I tell you, all this 36 bloodshedding must be avenged upon the present generation.

Jerusalem, Jerusalem!   37
Murderess of prophets!

23:35. How were the living Jews punishable for the murders of old? In slaying Christ, the Jews imitated the iniquity of their fathers who shed innocent blood, and thus came under the law by which "temporal" punishment goes down to the third and fourth generation (Exod. 20:5); hence the destruction of Jerusalem, the dispersion of the race, etc. (see verse 37). No one is punishable in the next world except for his own sins; hence the warning given in verse 33.

75

Stoner of the messengers sent to you!
How often have I been willing
to gather your children
as a mother bird gathers her brood
under her wings!
But you refused it!

38 Mark well: you will find your house abandoned — a prey to desola-
39 tion. Yes, I tell you, you will not see me again till you cry out:
'A blessing on him who comes in the name of the Lord!' "

CHAPTER 24

HORRORS OF THE DESOLATION TO COME

1   Jesus now left the temple grounds and, as he went on his way,
his disciples approached to call his attention to the sacred edifice.
2 He read their thoughts. "You admire this mass of buildings, do
you not?" he said to them; "I tell you plainly, not one stone will
3 here be left upon another. All will crumble to pieces." So when
he was seated on the Mount of Olives, the disciples came up and
asked him confidentially: "Tell us, when shall this catastrophe
take place? And what is the sign to herald your coming and the
end of the world?"
4   By way of answer Jesus said to them: "See to it that no one
5 leads you astray. Many will come and, assuming my title, say:
6 'I am the Messias,' and they will lead many astray. You are going
to hear of wars and rumors of wars. See that you are not alarmed.
7 These things must happen, but they are not yet the end. Besides,
nation will rise against nation, and kingdom against kingdom;
8 there will be famines, plagues, and earthquakes here and there: all
9 this is but the prelude to the throes. Then you will be subjected
to afflictions, put to death, and become the scorn of all the nations,
10 because you profess my name. Then, too, multitudes will lose their
11 faith, and betray and hate one another. Many, moreover, will falsely
12 set themselves up as prophets and lead many astray; and because

---

24:2. The temple was destroyed in A.D. 70. Some of the predictions in this
chapter apply to the same event; others more specifically to the end of the
world. The former was a type of the latter.

lawlessness will be rampant, most men's love will grow cold. But he 13
that holds out to the end will be saved. Furthermore: this gospel 14
of the kingdom must be preached throughout the whole world,
so that all nations may have valid evidence. And then will come
the end.

"Now, when you see the horrors of desolation whereof the prophet 15
Daniel speaks, enacted in the holy place — let the reader comprehend! — then those that are in Judea should flee to the mountains; 16
he that is on the housetop must not go down to fetch his things 17
which are in the house; and he that is in the field must not turn 18
back to fetch his cloak. How pitiful the women that are with child 19
or nursing in those days! Pray that your flight may not take place 20
in winter or on the Sabbath; for then there will be sore distress, 21
such as has not existed from the beginning of the world down to
this day, and never will exist again. And had those days not been 22
cut short, not one human being would be saved; but in consideration of the elect those days will be shortened.

BEWARE OF FALSE CHRISTS

"If anyone then says to you, 'Look, here is Christ!' or, 'There 23
he is!' do not believe it. False christs and false prophets will appear 24
and give striking exhibitions of power, so that even the elect, if it
were possible, would be led astray.

"There now; I have forewarned you. Therefore, when you are 25, 26
told, 'Listen, he is in the desert,' do not stir abroad; or, 'Listen,
he is in his hiding place,' do not believe it. As the lightning starts 27
in the east and blazes its way to the west, so it will be with the
advent of the Son of Man. Wherever the corpse is, there the 28
birds of prey assemble.

SIGNS BEFORE THE END OF THE WORLD

"Directly after the distress of those days, the sun will darken, 29
the moon cease to shed her light, and the stars fall from heaven.

24:20. *the Sabbath*: up to the destruction of Jerusalem, the early Christian
community observed the Mosaic Law (Acts 21:20).

24:28. A proverbial saying: "In those days you cannot miss the advent of
the Son of Man any more than birds of prey can miss a dead body."

24:29. The collapse of the universe is described in figurative language.

30 The foundations of the universe will rock. And then the sign of the Son of Man will appear in the sky, and then all the tribes of the earth will lament when they see the Son of Man riding the
31 clouds overhead with great might and majesty. And he will send forth his angels sounding a mighty trumpet, and they will assemble his elect from the four winds, from one edge of the horizon to the other.

32   "From the fig tree learn the lesson it points: as soon as its branch grows tender and puts forth its leaves, you know that summer
33 is near. Apply this to yourselves: as soon as you witness all these
34 events, you know that he is near, yes, at the door! I assure you, this generation will not pass away till all these events have set in.
35 Heaven and earth will fail; my words will never fail.
36   "But regarding that day and hour, no one knows, not even the
37 angels in heaven, nor yet the Son, but only the Father. As it was in the days of Noe, so it will be at the advent of the Son of Man:
38 in the days preceding the flood, people went on eating and drinking, marrying and giving in marriage, till the day when Noe entered
39 the ark; and they suspected nothing till the flood came and swept
40 them all away. So it will be at the advent of the Son of Man. At that moment, if two are in the field, one may be taken up and one
41 abandoned; if two women are grinding with the handmill, one
42 may be taken up and one abandoned. Keep awake, therefore; you do not know on what day your Lord returns.

43   "You understand that, if the owner of a house knew at which of the night watches the thief was coming, he would stay awake
44 and not let his house be broken into. Therefore you, too, must be ready. The Son of Man returns at an hour you do not expect.
45 Suppose a master puts overseers in charge of his household to give its members their rations at the proper time — in that case, which
46 is the faithful and prudent overseer? It is he whom the master on his return finds attending to his duties, and a happy man is he!
47 I assure you, he will put him in charge of his entire estate.
48 But if such an overseer proves good for nothing and says to himself:

24:30. *the sign of the Son of Man:* that is, says St. John Chrysostom, "the Cross, brighter than the sun."

24:34. "One part of the Jewish people saw the destruction of Jerusalem, the other part (of the people) will live until the second coming of Christ" (Arndt, S.J.).

'My master is long in coming,' and then proceed to maltreat his *49*
fellow slaves and feast in the company of drunkards, the master of *50*
that overseer will return on a day he is not expecting him and at a
time not known to him. He will then have him split right down *51*
the middle and assign him a place among the hypocrites. Oh, how
that region will resound with 'the weeping and gnashing of teeth!'

CHAPTER 25

THE WISE AND FOOLISH VIRGINS

"On that day the same will happen in the kingdom of heaven *1*
that once happened to ten bridesmaids who, being provided with
their lamps, had gone out to meet the bridegroom. Now, five of *2*
these were foolish, and five wise: the foolish, though provided with *3*
their lamps, had yet taken no oil with them; the wise, on the *4*
contrary, had besides their lamps taken oil with them in their jars.
But the bridegroom was long in coming, and so they all nodded off *5*
to slumber and, finally, slept. Suddenly, at midnight, a shout is *6*
raised: 'Wake up there! The bridegroom! Come out to meet him!'
At this, all the bridesmaids woke up and began to trim their lamps. *7*
Then the foolish said to the wise: 'Give us some of your oil; our *8*
lamps are going out.' But the wise demurred. 'There might not be *9*
oil enough for both us and for you,' they said; 'better go to the
dealers and buy some for yourselves.' So they went to buy some; *10*
but meanwhile the bridegroom arrived, and those who were ready
entered with him to take part in the festivities. Then the door was
barred. Later the other bridesmaids arrived; but when they pleaded, *11*
'O sir, sir, open the door for us,' back came his answer, 'Upon my *12*
word, I have nothing to do with you.' Keep awake therefore; you *13*
know neither the day nor the hour.

THE PARABLE OF THE TALENTS

"Furthermore: imagine a man who, before going abroad, sent for *14*

25:1. The circumstances described or taken for granted in this parable are
not clear. "The bridegroom in this case is coming to the bride's house, not
bringing his bride with him, but expecting to find her there" (Rickaby). Here,
as elsewhere, the details of the parable must not be pressed too curiously and
minutely. In the application the bridegroom is, of course, Christ, and his bride
the Church (Apoc. 21:9), represented in the parable by the wise virgins.

15 his officials and entrusted to them his money. To one he gave five talents, to another two, and to a third just one — to each the amount
16 proportioned to his individual ability. He then went abroad. At once the recipient of the five talents went to invest them in enterprise
17 and made another five. In like manner, the recipient of the two
18 talents made another two. But the recipient of the one talent went away to dig a hole in the ground and buried his master's money.
19 After a long delay the master of those officials returned and settled
20 accounts with them. So the recipient of the five talents came forward and presented five additional talents. 'Master,' he said, 'you
21 trusted me with five talents; look, I made another five.' 'Well done, my good and faithful servant,' the master said to him; 'you were faithful in managing something small; I will now put you in charge of something great: share to the full your master's happiness.'
22 When the recipient of the two talents came, he said, in turn: 'Master, you trusted me with two talents; look, I made another two.'
23 'Well done, my good and faithful servant,' his master said to him; 'you were faithful in managing something small; I will now put you in charge of something great: share to the full your master's happi-
24 ness.' Finally the recipient of the one talent came before him and said: 'Master, I know you are a hard taskmaster; you reap where you have not sown, and you store away what you have not winnowed.
25 So I shrank from doing anything at all and went to bury your
26 talent in the ground. Here you have your capital back again.' But his master had an answer for him: 'You lazy, good-for-nothing fellow!' he said to him; 'you knew that I reap where I have not sown, and store
27 away what I have not winnowed! Then you ought to have put my money in the bank, and on my return I might at least have recovered
28 my capital plus the interest. Therefore take the talent away from
29 him and give it to the one who has the ten talents. Every man of means will be given yet more till he abounds in wealth, while from the man without means will be taken away even what he has.
30 And as for that unprofitable official, throw him into the darkness outside.' Oh, how that region will resound with 'the weeping and gnashing of teeth!'

MANKIND PARTED INTO TWO GROUPS

31   "When the Son of Man returns in his glory, and escorted by all the angels, he will seat himself on a throne befitting his glory. All the nations will assemble in his presence, and he will part mankind into two groups just as a shepherd parts the sheep from the goats. The sheep he will range at his right, and the goats at his left.

"Then the King will say to those at his right: 'Come, the elect of my Father! Take possession of the kingdom prepared for you at the beginning of the world. For I was hungry, and you gave me to eat; I was thirsty, and you gave me to drink; I was a stranger, and you took me into your homes; I was naked, and you covered me; I was sick, and you visited me; I was in prison, and you came to see me.' Then the saints will be surprised and say to him: 'Lord, when did we see you hungry and feed you? or thirsty and give you to drink? And when did we see you a stranger and take you into our homes? or naked and cover you? When did we see you sick or in prison, and come to visit you?' And in explanation the King will say to them: 'I tell you the plain truth, inasmuch as you did this to one of these least brethren of mine, you did it to me.'

"Next he will say to those at his left: 'Out of my sight, you cursed ones! Off into the everlasting fire prepared for the devil and his ministers! For I was hungry and you did not give me to eat; I was thirsty and you did not give me to drink; I was a stranger and you did not take me into your homes; naked, and you did not cover me; sick and in prison, and you did not visit me.' Then they, in turn, will be surprised and say to him: 'Lord, when did we see you hungry or thirsty or a stranger or naked or sick or in prison, and did not minister to your wants?' Then will he hurl back at them this answer: 'I tell you the plain truth: insofar as you failed to render these services to one of those least ones, you also failed to render them to me.' And so the latter will be consigned to everlasting punishment, while the saints will enter into everlasting life."

CHAPTER 26

THE EMBALMMENT OF CHRIST ANTICIPATED

When Jesus had finished all these discourses, he said to his disciples: "You know that in two days the Passover is kept. On that occasion the Son of Man will be delivered up to be crucified."

81

3   About that time, the high priests and the elders — the nation's
    Council — met in the place of the high priest, whose name was
4   Caiaphas, and decided to arrest Jesus by stealth and have him put
5   to death. "Not, however, during the festival," they said; "or a riot
    might break out among the people."
6   One day, when Jesus was in the home of Simon the leper at
7   Bethany, a woman approached him with an alabaster flask of very
    costly perfume, and emptied it over his head as he reclined at table.
8   The disciples were indignant when they saw it. "What good is this
9   waste!" they commented. "Why, this perfume could have been
10 sold for a good sum and the money given to the poor." Jesus knew
    how they felt about it. "Why do you molest this woman?" he said
    to them. "She has certainly given beautiful expression of her devo-
11 tion to me. After all, you always have the poor with you; but you
12 will not always have me. In truth, by pouring this perfume over my
13 body, she has anticipated my embalmment. I assure you that wher-
    ever, in any part of the world, this gospel is preached, what this
    woman has just done will likewise be proclaimed to perpetuate
    her memory."

PREDICTION OF THE BETRAYAL BY JUDAS

14 Then one of the Twelve — the man named Judas Iscariot —
15 went to meet the high priests. "What are you willing to give me?"
    he asked; "I, for one, am ready to deliver him to you." Then they
16 paid him thirty pieces of silver. And from that time on he looked
    for an opportunity to betray him.
17 On the first day of the feast of the Unleavened Bread, the
    disciples approached Jesus and asked: "Where do you want us to
18 make ready for you to eat the paschal supper?" "Go into the city
    to so-and-so," he replied, "and say to him: 'The Rabbi says: My
    time is close at hand; at your house I intend to celebrate the pass-
19 over with my disciples.'" They did as Jesus had instructed them,
    and prepared the paschal supper.
20 When evening came, he reclined at table with the Twelve.
21 During their meal Jesus said: "Frankly I tell you, one of you will

---

26:15. *thirty pieces of silver:* an allusion to the thirty shekels which a man
had to pay if his ox killed the slave of his neighbor! See Exod. 21:32. Contrast
with this what St. Peter says of the value of the blood of Christ: 1 Pet. 1:19.

betray me." In their great distress, they proceeded to inquire of him, 22
one after another: "It is not I, is it, Lord?" By way of answer he said: 23
"One who dips his hand into the same bowl with me is the one
that will betray me. The Son of Man departs, indeed, as the Scrip- 24
ture says concerning him; but perdition awaits that man who is
instrumental in betraying the Son of Man. It would be better for
that man had he never been born." When Judas, who was about 25
to betray him, took his turn in asking, "It is not I, is it, Rabbi?"
He replied: "Yes, it is you."

THE TRANSUBSTANTIATION

Before supper was over, Jesus took bread into his hands and, 26
after saying grace, broke it into portions, which he gave to the disciples with the words: "Take! Eat! This is my body." He also took 27
a cup and, after saying grace, passed it on to them with the words:
"Drink of it, every one of you; for this is my covenant-blood, which 28
is about to be shed for the sake of many, with a view to forgiveness
of sins. I tell you, I shall never drink again of this product of the 29
vine till that day when I drink new wine with you in the kingdom
of my Father."

PREMONITIONS OF THE PASSION

After chanting the hymn of thanks, they set out for the Mount 30
of Olives. Then Jesus said to them: "You will, all of you, be shaken 31
in your faith in me this night; for the Scripture says: 'I will strike
the shepherd, and the sheep of the flock will be scattered.' But after 32
I am risen from the dead, I will go to Galilee to await you there."
Here Peter spoke up. "Even if all the rest are shaken in their faith 33

26:23. "One" who dips his hand: the Greek article here is generalizing. The
identity of the traitor was not made known to the group, but only to John
and Peter. See Jn. 13:26.

26:25. It seems that Judas left the room before the Apostles received Holy
Communion.

26:26. This is my body: the Catholic Church understands these important
words in their obvious sense. "The Body of Christ is not bread; therefore, to
verify our Lord's words, we must say, this is bread no longer, but the Body of
Christ. Such is the whole account of transubstantiation; to hold it, we need no
medieval metaphysics. Metaphysics, medieval or modern, may discuss it; they
can never explain it, nor disprove it. It is 'the mystery of faith' " (Rickaby).

26:29. new wine: a reference to the heavenly banquet.

34 in you," he said to him, "I shall never be shaken in mine." Jesus replied: "Yes, I have to be plain with you: this night, before a
35 cock crows, you will disown me thrice." "Even if I have to die with you," Peter replied, "I will not disown you!" The other disciples
36 too spoke in a similar way. Accompanied by them, Jesus now came to a place called Gethsemani. "Rest here," he said to the disciples,
37 "while I go over there and pray." Then, taking Peter and the two sons of Zebedee with him, he gave way to sorrow and weariness;
38 and in this mood he said to them: "I am plunged in sorrow — enough to break my heart! Tarry here and keep awake with me."
39 Then, going a short distance forward, he threw himself upon his face to pray. "My Father," he said, "if it is possible, let this cup be spared me! And yet, not as I will, but as you will!"
40 After that he came back to the disciples and found them sleeping. "So you were not able," he said to Peter, "to keep awake one hour
41 with me? Keep awake and pray, that you may not succumb to temp-
42 tation. The spirit is willing, but the flesh is weak." Again he went away and prayed a second time. "My Father," he said, "if this cup cannot be spared me, and I must drink it, may your will be done."
43 Once more then he returned and found them asleep, for their eyes
44 were heavy from drowsiness. So again he left them and went away to pray for the third time, offering the same petition.
45 Finally, he returned to the disciples and said to them: "So you continue to sleep and rest! I warn you, the hour has struck when
46 the Son of Man is betrayed into the hands of sinful men. Rise; let us go; look, my betrayer is close at hand."

THE BETRAYAL AND ARREST OF JESUS

47 He was still speaking when, strange to say, Judas, one of the Twelve, came upon the scene. A numerous throng of men armed with swords and clubs, who had been sent by the high priests and elders, the nation's Council, accompanied him.
48 Now his betrayer had agreed with them upon a signal. "The one
49 I shall kiss," he said, "that is the one. Arrest him." So he went straight up to Jesus and said: "I greet you, Rabbi," and kissed him
50 affectionately. Jesus said to him: "So this is the errand, my friend,

26:50. Another possible rendering would be: "For what purpose, on what errand, have you come?"

on which you have come!" Then they approached and laid hands
on Jesus and arrested him.

Instantly one of the companions of Jesus reached out for his 51
sword, unsheathed it, and, striking at the high priest's servant, cut
off his ear. Then Jesus said to him: "Put your sword back into its 52
place. All those that have recourse to the sword will perish by the
sword. Besides, do you think that I cannot call upon my Father 53
for help, and that he will not instantly put more than twelve legions
at my disposal? But then, how are the Scriptures to be fulfilled which 54
say that events must take this course?"

In that solemn moment, Jesus made this speech to the crowds: 55
"As though to capture a bandit, you have come out, armed with
swords and clubs, to capture me! Day after day I frequented the
temple halls, teaching the people, yet you did not arrest me!
However, all these incidents have but one purpose: to fulfill the 56
writings of the prophets!" Then the disciples, one and all, turned
their backs upon him and took to flight.

THE TRIAL OF JESUS BEFORE CAIAPHAS

The men who had arrested Jesus led him before the high priest 57
Caiaphas, in whose palace the Scribes and the high priests had assembled. Peter, meanwhile, had been following him at a distance, as 58
far as the high priest's palace, where, after going inside, he loitered
among the guards to see how all would end.

Now, the high priests — in fact, the Supreme Council as a body 59
— were looking for false testimony, unfavorable to Jesus, in order
to have him put to death; yet they did not find any although many 60
false witnesses had come forward. Finally, however, two men advanced and declared, respectively: "This man has said, 'I can destroy 61
the sanctuary of God,' and, 'Within three days I can build it up
again.'" Then the high priest rose and said to him: "Have you 62
nothing to say in your own defense? What about the evidence these
men are furnishing against you?" But Jesus remained silent. The 63
high priest then said to him: "I adjure you by the living God to
tell us outright, are you the Messias, the Son of God?" "I am, as 64
you say," replied Jesus; "but I warn you: hereafter you will see the

---

26:53. A Roman legion consisted ordinarily of 6000 men.

Son of Man enthroned at the right hand of the Almighty and returning upon the clouds in the sky."

65   At this, the high priest rent his garments. "He has blasphemed,"
he said; "what further need have we of witnesses? Listen, then!
66 You have just heard his blasphemy; what is your verdict?" And back
67 came the answer: "He is liable to the penalty of death!" Then they
spat in his face and dealt him blows with the fist, while others
68 struck him with the open hand and said: "Prophesy to us, Messias,
who is it that struck you?"

JESUS DISOWNED BY PETER

69   Peter meanwhile was lingering in the courtyard outside, where
a servant girl came up to him and said: "You were in the company
70 of Jesus the Galilean." But he denied it in the presence of all. "I
71 do not understand what you mean," he said. He then went into the
gateway where another girl saw him and said to the bystanders:
72 "This man was in the company of Jesus the Nazarene." But he again
denied it, this time with an oath: "I have nothing to do with the
man."

73   After a little while the bystanders faced Peter and said to him:
74 "You, certainly, are one of them! Your accent betrays you!" And now
he burst out cursing and swearing: "I have nothing to do with the
75 man." And immediately a cock crowed. Then Peter recalled the
prediction of Jesus, who had said: "Before a cock crows, you will
three times disown me." And he went out and wept bitterly.

CHAPTER 27

THE BETRAYER HANGS HIMSELF

1   Early in the morning the high priests and the elders — the
nation's Council — in full assembly reached a decision unfavorable
2 to Jesus, so as to have him condemned to death. They led him
away bound and handed him over to Pontius Pilate, the governor.
3   Judas, his betrayer, now realized that judgment had gone against
him and, stricken with remorse, brought back the thirty pieces of
4 silver to the high priests and elders. "It was wrong for me," he said,
"to betray innocent blood." "What does that matter to us?" they

replied: "that is your worry!" He then threw the silver pieces into 5
the sanctuary and withdrew. And he went away and hanged himself.

The high priests took the silver pieces and said: "It is not right 6
to put them in the temple treasury, because it is the price for a deed
of blood"; and so, after a consultation, they bought with it the 7
potter's field to serve as a burial ground for strangers. For this reason 8
that field was called "Blood Field," a name it bears to this day.
It was then that the prediction made through Jeremias the prophet 9
was fulfilled. He says: "And they took the thirty pieces of silver,
the price which some of the children of Israel had set upon the
Priceless One, and paid them down for the potter's field. Thus the 10
Lord has directed me."

THE TRIAL AND CONDEMNATION OF JESUS

When Jesus was confronted with the governor, and the governor 11
questioned him, saying: "You are the King of the Jews?" Jesus
replied: "I am, as you say." But when charges were being made 12
against him by the high priests and elders, he said nothing in his
own defense. Finally Pilate said to him: "Do you not hear all the 13
evidence they are furnishing against you?" But he did not reply 14
to him in answer to a single charge, so that the governor was
exceedingly surprised.

Now, at the festival it was customary for the governor to release, 15
at the request of the people, some one prisoner of their own choosing; and it happened that they had on hand a notorious prisoner 16
called Barabbas. So, when they were assembled, Pilate said to them: 17
"Which do you want me to release as your choice, Barabbas or Jesus
called the Messias?" He knew, of course, that they had handed him 18
over out of mere spite; besides, while he was still on the bench, his 19
wife sent him a message to this effect: "Do not meddle with that
holy man. I suffered a great deal in a dream last night on his
account." But the high priests and the elders had persuaded the 20
people to demand the release of Barabbas and the death of Jesus.
So, when the governor, in answer to their request, said to them: 21
"Which of the two do you want me to release as your choice?" they
replied: "Barabbas." "Then what am I to do with Jesus, called the 22

27:16. *a notorious prisoner:* some, however, would render: "a captive leader"
of the Liberty League. See the note on 10:4 and Lk. 6:15.

Messias?" Pilate said to them. They all replied: "Have him cruci-
23 fied." He retorted: "Why, what wrong has he done?" But they
vigorously shouted: "Have him crucified."

24   Pilate now realized that he was gaining nothing and that, instead,
a riot was breaking out. So, before the eyes of the people, he washed
his hands in water presented to him, and declared: "I am innocent
25 of the blood of this just man. The responsibility is yours!" By way
of answer, the whole mob shouted: "His blood be upon us and
26 upon our children!" He then released Barabbas to please them, but
turned Jesus over for a scourging, preliminary to crucifixion.

JESUS CROWNED AND MOCKED

27   The soldiers of the governor now took Jesus in charge and
28 gathered round him the entire company in the praetorium. They
29 stripped him and put a scarlet cloak on him; next they put upon
his head a plaited crown of thorns, and placed a reed in his right
hand; then they knelt down before him with the mock salute: "Long
30 live the King of the Jews!" They also spat on him and, taking the
31 reed, struck him on his head. When they had done making sport
of him, they stripped him of the cloak and dressed him in his own
clothes. And so they led him away to be crucified.

CHRIST CRUCIFIED AND INSULTED

32   On their way out, they came upon a Cyrenean, named Simon,
33 whom they commandeered to carry his cross. On arriving at a place
34 called Golgotha, which means "Skull's Mound," they gave him a
drink of wine mixed with gall. He tasted it, but did not care to
35 drink it. When they had crucified him, they divided his clothes
36 among them by drawing lots. Then they sat down there to guard
37 him. Over his head they placed the inscription stating his guilt:
38 "This is Jesus, the King of the Jews." At the same time two rebels
were crucified with him, one at his right, the other at his left.

39   Meanwhile the passers-by kept insulting him, shaking their
40 heads and saying: "You are the one that can pull down the
sanctuary and build it up in three days!" "Help yourself if you are
41 the Son of God, and come down from the cross!" The high priest

---

27:34. *wine mixed with gall:* the morphine of those days. See the notes on
Mk. 15:36 and Jn. 19:29.

joined the Scribes and elders and said in the same taunting manner:
"He helped others! He cannot help himself!" "He is the king of   42
Israel; let him this instant come down from the cross, and we will
believe in him!" "He trusts in God: let God deliver him if he cares   43
for him. Did he not say, 'I am the Son of God'?" The rebels who   44
had been crucified with him insulted him in the same way.

About noon darkness fell upon the whole land and lasted till   45
three o'clock. About three o'clock Jesus cried out with a strong   46
voice: *Eli, Eli, lema sabachthani,* that is, "My God, my God, why
do you abandon me?" But some of the bystanders who heard it   47
said: "This man is calling for Elias." And at once one of them ran   48
off, took a sponge, soaked it in sour wine, put it on a reed, and
offered it to him to drink. The rest said: "Let us see whether   49
Elias is coming to help him!" But Jesus again cried out with a   50
strong voice and gave up his spirit.

HAPPENINGS AFTER THE DEATH OF JESUS

Then strange things happened: the curtain of the sanctuary was   51
torn in two from top to bottom; the earth shook; the rocks split;
the tombs opened and many of the saints whose bodies were asleep   52
in death, rose to life. They came out of the tombs after his resurrec-   53
tion and entered the holy city, where they showed themselves to
many. When the centurion and his men who were keeping guard   54
over Jesus noticed the earthquake and all that happened, they were
overcome by a sense of awe and said: "Assuredly, this man was the
Son of God." Many women, too, were there, looking on from a   55
distance. They had followed Jesus from Galilee, ministering to his
needs. Among them were Mary Magdalen, Mary, the mother of   56
James and Joseph, and the mother of the sons of Zebedee.

Late in the afternoon there came a rich man from Arimathia,   57
by the name of Joseph, who had himself been a disciple of Jesus.
This man interviewed Pilate and petitioned for the body of Jesus.   58

27:46. *why do you abandon me?*: no human mind can fathom the depth of
depression that wrung this cry from Jesus. How was it possible that, while
enjoying the beatific vision, he could consider himself abandoned by the Father?
No ordinary psychology has an answer. All we can say is that the Son of God
was at the same time a son of man. At bottom, we face the same mystery in
his praying the Father to relieve him of the necessity of undergoing the most
painful death when he knew of God's irrevocable decree that he must undergo
it to save the world.

59 Then Pilate ordered it to be given up. Joseph took possession of the
60 body, wrapped it in a clean shroud, and laid it in his tomb as yet
unused, which he had cut in the rock. He then rolled a large
slab of stone against the entrance of the tomb, and went away.
61 Mary of Magdala, however, as well as the other Mary, lingered
behind, seated opposite the grave.
62 On the next day, that is, the day after Preparation Day, the high
63 priests and the Pharisees met at Pilate's headquarters and said to
him: "Sir, we just remember that when this impostor was still alive
64 he said: 'In three days I shall rise again.' Please, therefore, give
orders that the grave is made secure against violation till the third
day; otherwise, his disciples might come and steal him, and then
tell the people 'He is risen from the dead.' And thus the last
65 imposture would be worse than the first." Pilate said to them: "You
have a guard at your disposal. Go and take measures of safety at
66 your own discretion." So they went and secured the grave by sealing
the slab and setting the guard.

CHAPTER 28

AFTER THE SABBATH

1 When the Sabbath was over and the first day of the new week
was dawning on the world, Mary Magdalen and the other Mary
2 set out to visit the grave. All of a sudden there was a mighty earthquake; an angel of the Lord had descended from heaven and,
alighting at the entrance, had rolled away the slab of stone and then
3 seated himself upon it. His appearance was like a flash of lightning
4 and his garment as white as snow. By the terror he inspired, the
guards were struck down and became like dead men.
5 But the angel reassured the women. "You have nothing to fear,"
6 he said; "I know you are looking for Jesus the Crucified. He is not
here. He has risen as he predicted. Come here: inspect the place
7 where he was laid to rest — now go quickly, and take this message
to his disciples: 'He has risen from the dead'; and take note of
this: 'He is going to Galilee to await you there. There is where you
are to see him.' Mind what I told you."
8 They hurriedly left the tomb and, with mingled awe and keen

delight, ran to carry the news to his disciples when who should meet 9
them but Jesus in person! "I greet you!" he said; but they approached
and clasped his feet, prostrated before him. Then Jesus said to them: 10
"Do not be afraid; go and bring word to my brethren that they are
to go to Galilee; and there they will see me."

As they were going on their errand, some of the guards quite 11
unexpectedly turned up in the city and reported to the high priests
what had taken place. The latter at once arranged a meeting with 12
the elders and, after holding a consultation, gave the soldiers a
considerable sum of money with these instructions: "This is what 13
you must give out: 'His disciples came by night and stole his body
while we were asleep.' And in case this is reported at the governor's 14
headquarters, we will satisfy him and see that you have nothing to
worry about." They accepted the bribe and did as they had been 15
directed. Accordingly, this version of the story was circulated in
Jewish communities and is current to this day.

As for the eleven disciples, they betook themselves to the 16
mountain in Galilee to which Jesus had ordered them. When they 17
saw him, they adored him, although at first they had doubts. Jesus 18
then came closer to them and spoke to them the following words:

"Absolute authority in heaven and on earth
has been conferred upon me.
Go, therefore,   19
and initiate all nations in discipleship:
baptize them in the name
    of the Father
    and of the Son
    and of the Holy Spirit,
and teach them to observe   .   20
all the commandments I have given you.
And mark:
I am with you at all times
as long as the world will last."

28:18–20. Here Christ appears in all his splendor. His last thoughts are with
his beloved Church. Under impressive circumstances (Mt. 16:18) he had
promised to found her. Here he equips her with all powers necessary for
carrying on his work in the world. Her mission is universal in space and time.
His continual presence is solemnly assured her. Compare Mk. 16:19–20.

SAINT MARK

The New Testament gives some details about the person and life of St. Mark, while early Christian writers supply additional information regarding his authorship.

The author of this Gospel is "John, who was surnamed Mark" (Acts 12:12). He was the son of a certain Mary, in whose house the Christians of Jerusalem were assembled for worship at the time when St. Peter was miraculously delivered from prison. There is little doubt, moreover, that the upper room of this house was the scene where Jesus held the paschal supper at which he instituted the Holy Eucharist (Mk. 14:15 and Lk. 22:12). Young Mark accompanied St. Barnabas and St. Paul on their missionary tour to Seleucia and Cyprus. After evangelizing the island, the party sailed for Asia Minor, but St. Mark, for one reason or another, returned to Jerusalem. The breach between him and St. Paul was soon healed. Writing from his prison in Rome, the Apostle sent greetings to the Colossians from St. Mark (Col. 4:10). His Epistle to Philemon again conveys a greeting from his "fellow worker" St. Mark (Philemon 24). Shortly before his martyrdom in Rome, St. Paul begs Timothy, who was then at Ephesus, to bring St. Mark with him to Rome, because he could use his services in the interests of the Gospel (2 Tim. 4:11). The last mention of St. Mark comes in St. Peter's first Epistle addressed to the Churches in Asia, in the form of a greeting from his "son" (1 Pet. 5:13). Mark, moreover, was the cousin of St. Barnabas (Col. 4:10), that organizer and mainstay of the nascent Church in Antioch. He was probably of levitical rank and possessed of some means (Acts 4:16, 17).

In recounting the life and teachings of Christ, St. Mark does not generally speak with the authority of an eyewitness. But it has been surmised that the youth mentioned in 14:51 was young Mark, and, if the reading "and still another" (sc. asked the Lord) in 14:19 is genuine, then this, too, may be a veiled reference of the author to himself. At all events, from the circumstances of his family, we may gather that Mark was acquainted with persons well qualified to furnish reliable information. He had numerous contacts with St. Barnabas and St. Paul. But tradition points to another authentic source of knowledge, which puts his narrative in a class all by itself. Papias, the bishop of Hierapolis in Phrygia, states that St. Mark was the "interpreter" of St. Peter while at Rome. According to this writer, the Apostle St. John, when the Christians of Ephesus brought up the subject of the Second Gospel and belittled it for its brevity and scantiness of detail, as compared with the other narratives, frankly admitted that it was incomplete, but found compensation, however, in the fact that it was a faithful reproduction of St. Peter's instructions to the early Christians at Rome. This accounts for St. Mark's style being graphic, direct, dramatic, very popular, and at times uncouth when measured by the canons of art.

The fragment in question runs as follows: "This, too, the old man said: 'When Mark became the interpreter of Peter, he wrote down, though by no means with full detail, as much as he accurately remembered of the words and works of the Lord; for he had neither heard the Lord nor followed him. Subsequently, however, he joined Peter, as I said. Now, Peter did not intend to give a complete exposition of the Lord's ministry, but delivered his instructions to suit the varying needs of the people. It follows, then, that Mark was guilty of no blunder if he wrote, simply to the best of his recollections, an incomplete account. For, of one matter he took forethought, not to omit anything he had heard or to falsify anything in recording it.' "*

The Gospel according to St. Mark is called by the Evangelist himself "a beginning," that is, "a summary," of the Gospel of Jesus Christ, the Son of God. It opens with an account of the appearance of John the Baptist in the desert near the banks of the River Jordan (1:1-8). There follows a brief mention of the baptism of Jesus, and of his temptation in the desert. The rest of the Gospel falls into two sections: the first dealing with our Lord's ministry in Galilee (Chapters 1-10), the other, with our Lord's last days in

---

* See *St. Louis University Studies*, Series A, Vol. 1, No. 1, 1945.

Jerusalem, followed by his resurrection and ascension (Chapters 11–16). By far the greater part of this narrative is taken up with our Lord's deeds, in particular with his miracles, which effectively proved his divine sonship.

Because St. Mark but rarely refers to the Old Testament and explains occasional Semitic expressions and customs, it is assumed that the first readers of the Gospel were converts from paganism. This conclusion tallies with the assumption that he wrote as St. Peter's interpreter at Rome. In 11:21 and 16:7, for instance, he mentions the Apostle by name, while the parallel accounts omit such mention. On the other hand, St. Mark is silent about the promises made to St. Peter in response to the latter's confession of faith (Mt. 16:17–18). His silence has been explained on the assumption that personal privileges promoting the prince of the Apostles to high rank and authority were not likely to be revealed by St. Peter himself in his Roman surroundings. But St. Mark does mention our Lord's sharp rebuke administered to St. Peter (8:33), and narrates in detail the Apostle's denial of his Master. We should, therefore, assume that these humiliating incidents were not withheld by St. Peter from his instructions to the people.

Some of the better manuscripts and earliest versions of this Gospel end with verse 8 of Chapter 16, while others add twelve more verses. The question of the Marcan authorship of this addition, is, therefore, a matter of dispute. Its canonicity or inspiration is guaranteed by the Church, whoever was the author. The last two verses beautifully round out the Gospel with the statement that the Lord Jesus

"After discoursing to them,
was borne aloft to heaven,
and seated himself at the right hand of God.
But they, for their part, went forth
and preached everywhere,
while the Lord assisted them in their work
and confirmed the message
by the proofs of their claims
that followed them."

It may be remarked, in passing, that St. Mark's Gospel opens — almost with the same abruptness as the Prologue of St. John — with the statement namely that Jesus Christ was "the Son of God." Nor is this a merely casual or stereotyped reference to Christ. It may be truly said that the entire Gospel is almost an uninterrupted string of events that prove Christ's divine nature. That, by the way, is the reason why the close of his Gospel, just quoted, looks like a return to the theme of the opening verse.

In the year 63, St. Mark was at Rome, at the end of St. Paul's first captivity. It is probable that he went to Asia soon after (Col. 4:10), and with St. Peter returned to Rome (1 Pet. 5:13). Again he was absent from Rome, until St. Paul, during his second captivity (A.D. 66–67), recalled him to the capital (2 Tim. 4:10), where he probably remained until the death of the Apostle. It is not certain when or where he wrote his Gospel. That it was written before the year 70 is an inference from its prediction of the destruction of Jerusalem. There is a tradition that he was the first bishop of Alexandria, but this notice of Eusebius is difficult to verify. The Church reveres him as a martyr; his feast is kept on April 25. The Basilica of St. Mark in Venice is supposed to contain his relics.

THE HOLY GOSPEL
OF JESUS CHRIST
ACCORDING TO

ST. MARK

CHAPTER 1

JOHN BAPTIZES THE SAVIOR

A summary of the gospel of Jesus Christ, the Son of God. 1
It is written in Isaias the prophet: 2

> "Look! I am sending ahead of you a messenger,
>> who is to prepare your road;
>> a herald's voice rings out in the desert: 3
>> 'Make ready the road of the Lord;
>> make straight his paths.'"

And so it was that John the Baptist appeared in the desert to 4
preach a baptism which signified a change of heart and looked to
forgiveness of sins. The whole of Judea, including all the inhabitants 5
of Jerusalem, went out to meet him. They confessed their sins and
had themselves baptized by him in the Jordan River. John wore a 6
covering of camel's hair and a leathern garment round his loins;
his food was locusts and wild honey. The burden of his preaching 7
was this: "Following me is One mightier than I, and I am not fit
to stoop and untie the strap of his sandals. I baptized you with 8
water; he will baptize you with the Holy Spirit."

One day about that time Jesus came from Nazareth in Galilee 9
and had himself baptized by John in the Jordan. As soon as he 10

1:1. *A summary of the gospel:* see the Introduction, p. 94. *the Son of
God:* these words, omitted in some manuscripts, are strictly pertinent to St.
Mark's purpose of setting forth the divinity of Jesus. Christ's supernatural power
is indicated on almost every page.

1:2. This part of the quotation is from Malachias (3:1).

1:4. *a change of heart* (and mind): see the second note on Mt. 3:2.

1:8. The baptism instituted by Christ not only signifies, but also effects,
interior sanctification.

was coming up out of the water, he saw the heavens opened and
11 the Spirit in the shape of a dove descend upon him. Moreover, a
voice rang out upon the air:

"You are my Son, the beloved;
with you I am well pleased."

12 Without delay the Spirit impelled him to go out into the desert
13 and he remained in the desert forty days, being put to the test by
Satan. He lived among wild beasts, and the angels waited on him.

JESUS CALLS HIS FIRST DISCIPLES

14 After John had been imprisoned, Jesus returned to Galilee to
15 preach God's Good Message. This was his theme:

"The time of waiting is over;
the kingdom of God is close at hand.
Change your evil ways;
believe in the Good Message."

16 Passing by the Sea of Galilee one day, he saw Simon and Simon's
brother Andrew throw casting nets into the sea. They were fisher-
17 men. "Come, follow me," Jesus said to them; "and I will make
18 you fishers of men." At once they abandoned their nets and became
19 his followers. After going on a short distance, he saw James, the
son of Zebedee, and James's brother John. They, too, were in their
20 boat, getting their nets in shape. He at once called them; and they
abandoned their father Zebedee with the hired help in the boat,
and became his followers.

THE DIVINE POWERS OF JESUS

21 They now entered Capharnaum, where on the very next Sabbath
22 he went to the synagogue to teach. The people were lost in
admiration of his teaching. He had a way, certainly, of teaching
them as one possessed of authority, and not as their Scribes.

23 Presently there came into the synagogue a man under control
24 of an unclean spirit, who shouted the words: "Ha! Why do you
meddle with us, Jesus of Nazareth? Have you come to destroy us? I

1:11. *upon the air:* see the note on Mt. 3:17.
1:14. *God's Good Message:* this expression avoids taking the word "Gospel"
in its later technical sense. See the Introduction, p. 5.
1:22. See the notes on Mt. 2:4 and 3:7.

know who you are — God's Holy One!" Jesus sternly rebuked him: 25
"Hold your peace, and come out of him!" The unclean spirit then 26
threw the man into convulsions, uttered a shriek, and went out
of him. A sense of awe came over all, so much so that, in discussing 27
the incident with one another, they said: "What does this mean?"
"A novel way of teaching with authority!" "He even commands
the unclean spirits, and they obey him!" As a result, the report 28
about him spread on and on to every place within and beyond the
boundaries of Galilee.

Immediately now they left the synagogue and entered the house 29
of Simon and Andrew, accompanied by James and John. Simon's 30
mother-in-law lay in bed in a feverish condition, and they at once
appealed to him on her behalf. He approached and, taking her by 31
the hand, raised her to her feet. The fever left her, and she waited
on them. Late in the evening, after the sun had set, all the sick 32
as well as possessed persons were brought to him. Presently the 33
whole town was assembled at the door. He cured many that were 34
suffering from various diseases, and drove out demons in great
numbers; but he would not let the demons go on speaking, because
they knew who he was.

Very early the next morning — it was still dark — he rose, left 35
the house, and went to an out-of-the-way place; and there he
prayed. But Simon and his companions started in pursuit of him, 36
and, when they found him, said to him: "All seek for you." 37
He replied: "Let us go elsewhere and visit the neighboring hamlets. 38
I want to preach there also. That is the purpose of my mission."
So he went through the length and breadth of Galilee to preach 39
in their synagogues and drive out demons.

One day, a leper came to him to implore his help and, kneeling 40
down, said to him: "If you will, you can make me clean." Stirred 41
with pity, Jesus extended his hand to lay it upon him. "Yes," he
said, "I am willing; be clean." At once the leprosy left the man 42
and he was made clean. But strictly Jesus charged him and sent 43
him away immediately. "Be sure," he said to him, "you do not say 44
a word to anyone. But go and have yourself examined by the priest;

1:32. *after the sun had set:* when the Sabbath was over. Carrying the sick
through the streets was considered a violation of the Sabbath. See Jn. 9:1–16.
1:38. *my mission:* see the first note on Mt. 5:17.

moreover, offer the gift for your purification which Moses enjoined.
45 The priests must be informed." The man went out and made a
point of talking freely about the incident; in fact, he published the
news so widely that Jesus could no longer proceed openly into
town, but stayed in unfrequented places at the outskirts. Yet people
came to him from everywhere.

CHAPTER 2

THE POWER TO FORGIVE SINS

1, 2 When he returned to Capharnaum some days later, the
news spread that he was at home. Then a crowd gathered, so
large that even the space about the entrance could hold no more.
3 While he was explaining the message, a group arrived trying to
4 bring a paralytic before him. Four men were carrying him and
since they did not succeed in bringing him into his immediate
presence, owing to the crowd, they removed the roof over the place
where he was, and through an opening let down the mat on which
5 the paralytic was lying. When Jesus saw their faith, he said to
6 the paralytic: "My son, your sins are forgiven you." Now some of
the Scribes were in the audience, and they assumed a critical
7 attitude: "How can the man talk in that way?" "Why, he blas-
8 phemes!" "Who can forgive sins except God alone!" Jesus at once
read their minds and, aware of their inward criticism, said to them:
9 "Why are you in such a critical mood? Which is easier, to say to
the paralytic, 'Your sins are now forgiven,' or to say, 'Rise; take up
10 your mat and walk'? Now I want you to understand that the Son
of Man has power here on earth to forgive sins." He then addressed
11 the paralytic: "I command you: rise; take up your mat, and go
12 home." He rose and, taking up his mat, walked out before the eyes
of all. As a result, all were enraptured and praised God with the
words: "Never did we see the like!"
13 Again he went out to the seashore. From all sides the people

1:45. *made a point of talking:* the rendering "he began" does not exhaust
the connotations of the Greek verb. See *The Gospel of St. Mark*, p. 154 ff.
  Jesus: inserted in the translation to clarify the text, where the Greek
has "he."
2:9. See the note on Mt. 9:5.

flocked to him, and he instructed them. As he went along, he noticed 14
Levi, the son of Alpheus, at his counter in the customhouse, and
said to him: "Follow me." He quit his business and followed him.
One day he was at table in the man's home, and many tax collectors 15
and sinners were reclining at table with Jesus and his disciples, for
the number of his followers was considerable. When now the 16
Scribes of the Pharisaical party noticed that he was taking a meal
with sinners and tax collectors, they said to his disciples: "He takes
a meal with tax collectors and sinners! How is that?" Jesus heard 17
of it and said to them: "The sick have need of a physician, not
the healthy. It is my mission to call sinners, and not saints."

NEW WINE IN FRESH SKINS

One day, when John's disciples and the Pharisees were fasting, 18
he was approached and asked: "The disciples of John and the
disciples of the Pharisees are fasting; your disciples are not fasting.
How is that?" Jesus said to them: "Can wedding guests fast while 19
the bridegroom is with them? As long as they have the bridegroom
with them, they cannot fast. However, a time is coming when the 20
bridegroom is torn away from them, and then they will fast —
yes, on that day! No one sews a patch of new cloth on an old 21
cloak; otherwise, the patch tears off a piece — the new cloth from
the old — and the rip is worse than before. Again, no one pours 22
new wine into old wine skins; otherwise, the wine will burst the
skins, and the wine is lost as well as the skins. No; new wine
belongs in fresh skins."

CHRIST'S AUTHORITY OVER THE SABBATH

The following happened on a Sabbath. Leaving the highway, 23
he passed through the wheatfields and the disciples, as they went
along, set about plucking the heads of wheat. The Pharisees said 24
to him: "See here! Why are they doing on the Sabbath what it is

2:14. *Levi:* the same person as Matthew. See Mt. 9:9.
2:16. *sinners and tax collectors:* since in the eyes of the Pharisees the tax
collectors were, above all others, "*the* sinners" in the Jewish community, the
expression may simply mean "the tax collectors, those sinners," "that dis-
reputable lot of tax collectors." See the note on Mt. 3:7.
2:17. See the note on Mt. 5:17.
2:22. The last words are omitted in some manuscripts.

25 not right to do?" "Did you never read," he replied, "what David did when he felt the pinch of hunger — he and his companions?
26 How he went into the house of God, when Abiathar was high priest, and ate the presentation loaves, which no one has 'a right' to eat except the priests, and shared them with his companions?"
27 He also said to them: "The Sabbath was made for man, not man
28 for the Sabbath. It follows that the Son of Man has authority also over the Sabbath."

CHAPTER 3

MANY PERSONS CURED

1 Once again he went into the synagogue. A man with one arm
2 withered was present. Now Jesus was being narrowly watched, to see whether he would heal him on the Sabbath. The purpose was
3 to bring a charge against him. "Rise, and come forward," he said
4 to the man with the withered arm. He then said to them: "Is it right on the Sabbath to do an act of kindness, or must one inflict evil? to save a life, or must one kill?" But they remained silent.
5 Then, glancing round at them in anger, and deeply grieved at the hardness of their hearts, he said to the man: "Stretch out your arm."
6 He stretched it out, and his arm was fully restored. The Pharisees walked out at once and consulted with the Herodians to plot against his life.
7 Accompanied by his disciples, Jesus withdrew to the seashore. A
8 large multitude from Galilee followed him. In fact, from Judea, (including Jerusalem) and from Idumea, from beyond the Jordan and from the neighborhood of Tyre and Sidon, people came to him — an immense crowd — when they heard of all the things he
9 was doing. So he told his disciples that a boat should be in readiness
10 for him to avoid being crammed in by the crowd; for he had cured many persons, so that all those who had ailments pressed round
11 to make contact with him. The unclean spirits, when they saw him, would throw themselves down before him and shout the words:
12 "You are the Son of God." But he sternly warned them not to draw public attention on him.

3:6. See the note on Mt. 22:16.

102

2nd

Mark 3:7-19

ENARAX

® *antispasmodic/tranquilizer for the treatment of G. I. dysfunctions*

NEW IMPROVED HEPTUNA PLUS

THE GROUP OF TWELVE APOSTLES FORMED

He then went up the hillside, where he summoned into his 13
presence men of his own choosing. They came forward to join him;
and he formed a group of twelve, who were to be his constant com- 14
panions. His intention was to send them on preaching tours equipped 15
with power to heal sicknesses and to drive out demons. And to Simon 16
he gave the name Peter. Included further were James, the son of 17
Zebedee, and John, the brother of James, together surnamed by him
Boanerges, Sons of Thunder; besides, Andrew, Philip, Bartholomew, 18
Matthew, Thomas, James (son of Alpheus), Thaddeus, Simon the
Cananaean, and Judas Iscariot, the same that eventually be- 19
trayed him.

CAN SATAN DRIVE OUT SATAN?

He then went home. And again the crowd flocked together, so 20
that they could not even take a meal. When his own people heard 21
of it, they set out to seize him. "He is out of his mind," they said.
Moreover, the Scribes who had come down from Jerusalem were 22
saying: "He is possessed by Beelzebul," and, "He drives out the
demons as a tool of the archdemon." He therefore called them 23
into his presence and said to them in parable style: "How can
Satan drive out Satan? Suppose a kingdom is torn by civil strife: 24
that kingdom cannot last; and suppose a family is split into factions: 25
that family cannot possibly last. Consequently: if Satan is in revolt 26
and at war with himself, he simply cannot last. No, his end is come.
Now mark: no one can enter the castle of a mighty lord and 27
plunder his possessions unless he first imprisons the mighty lord; then
only can he plunder his castle. I warn you solemnly: anything may 28
be forgiven a human being — his sins, even his blasphemies, any

3:14. *a group of twelve:* some texts add "whom he named Apostles." For
the number "twelve," see Mt. 19:28.

3:17. *Sons of Thunder:* perhaps so called because of their impetuous temper.
See Mk. 9:38 and Lk. 9:54.

3:18. *Thaddeus, etc.:* see the notes on Mt. 10:3 and 10:4.

3:21. *his own people:* his relatives (and friends). No doubt, they wished to
prevent him from doing things calculated to arouse popular excitement or even
violence. The words *He is out of his mind* may, however, mean: "It (the crowd)
is beside itself."

3:23. *in parable style:* see the note on Mt. 13:3.

3:28. *I warn you solemnly:* see the note on Mt. 5:18.

29 blasphemies he utters; but he who blasphemes against the Holy
    Spirit can never obtain forgiveness, but remains forever burdened
30 with sin." He stated this because they had said: "He is possessed
    by an unclean spirit."

CHRIST'S MOTHER, BROTHERS, AND SISTERS

31 Now his mother and his brothers arrived and, waiting outside,
32 sent word to him, bidding him to come out. There was a crowd
    sitting about him; so he was told: "Please, your mother, your
33 brothers, and your sisters are outside, wishing to see you." But he
    protested and said to them: "Who is my mother? And who are
34 my brothers?" Then, looking at the group seated in a circle about
35 him, he said: "Here are my mother and my brothers! Yes, anyone
    that does the will of God is brother or sister or mother to me."

CHAPTER 4

PARABLE OF THE SEED AND SOIL

1   Once again he set himself to teach by the seaside; and so great
    was the concourse of people that he went into a boat and sat down,
    off the shore, while the whole throng was on land, by the water's
2   edge. And he taught them many lessons in parable style. For
3   instance, he said to them in the course of his teaching: "Give ear!
4   Look, the sower goes out to sow. As he sows, it happens that some
    of the seed falls close to the footpath; and the birds come and eat
5   it up. Other seed falls on the stony ground, where it does not have
    deep soil and, because it has no soil of any depth, shoots up at once;
6   but by the time the sun has climbed the heavens, it is scorched
7   and, because it cannot strike root, withers away. Other seed, again,
    falls among the thorns; and the thorns come up and utterly choke it;
8   and it produces no fruit. Still other seed falls on the right kind of
    soil; and this at last produces fruit, because it sprouts and keeps on
9   growing; and it bears fruit thirty-, sixty-, or a hundredfold." He then
    added: "Let everyone heed what he has heard."
10 When he was alone, those around him, including the Twelve,

---

3:31. *his brothers:* see the note on Mt. 12:46.
3:33. *he protested:* see the note on Mt. 3:15.

asked him for an explanation of the parables. He said to them: 11
"You are privileged to know the mystery of the kingdom of God;
but to those outside your group all instruction is given in parable
style so that as a result 12
     'for all their looking they do not see,
       and for all their hearing they do not understand;
       and so they are not converted and forgiven.' "

He then said to them: "If you do not know the meaning of this 13
parable, how, then, will you understand the parables in general? The 14
'sower' is he who sows the message; the words 'close to the footpath' 15
describe those in whom the message is sown; but, as soon as they
hear it, Satan comes and steals the message in them. In like manner, 16
the ones described by the words 'sown in the stony places' are such
as receive the message with joy as soon as they hear it; but they 17
do not let it strike root in them; on the contrary, they are time-
servers and, when distress or persecution comes, are at once upset.
The words 'sown among the thorns' describe another class; they 18
are such as hear the message, but then the cares of this world and 19
the deceitful attractions of wealth and the other allurements to
passion creep in and utterly choke the message; and it turns out
barren. Finally, those described by the words 'sown in the right 20
kind of soil' are those who warmly welcome the message they hear,
and bear fruit thirty-, sixty-, or a hundredfold."

OTHER LESSONS IN PARABLE STYLE

Again he said to them: "Is the lamp brought into the room to 21
be placed under the bushel-basket or under the couch? Is it not
to be put on the lampstand? After all, there is nothing hidden but 22
must be made known some day; nothing concealed but must be
brought to light some day. Let everyone heed what he has heard." 23
Again he said to them: "Look well what it is you hear. The 24

4:13. The first parable is the key to all the others.
4:17. *they . . . are at once upset:* the Greek word, commonly rendered "to
scandalize," occurs thirty times in the New Testament. Its general sense is "to
cause one to sin or take offense" in one way or another, or "to lay a trap for
someone." Significant illustrations of its use are in Mk. 6:3; 9:42; 14:27; Lk.
17:2. See the note on Lk. 7:23.
4:24. The lamp of truth which the disciples received was not intended for
them alone. They were to impart to others the knowledge given to them;
hence "look well, etc."

measure you use in measuring will be used to measure out your
25 share; in fact, more will be given to you. The man of means will
be given yet more, and the man of no means will have taken away
from him what he has."

26   Further he said: "What happens in the kingdom of God is
something similar to what takes place when a man has sown the
27 seed in his field: he sleeps at night and awakes in the morning;
meanwhile the seed is sprouting and shoots the stem into the
28 air — he himself does not know how. By an inward force the earth
29 bears fruit, first blade, then ear, then ripe grain in the ear; and
when the crop permits, he at once applies the sickle, for the time
for harvesting has come."

30   Again he said: "How can we illustrate the kingdom of God? Or
31 by what parable can we set it forth? It is like a mustard seed: when
this is sown in the ground, it is the tiniest of all the seeds in the
32 ground; but once it has been sown, it springs up and becomes larger
than any garden herb, and puts forth spreading branches so that
the birds of the air can nest in its shade."

33   It was by many such parables that he announced to the people
34 the message in a manner suited to their capacity. Without parables
he would not speak to them; privately, however, he interpreted
everything to his immediate disciples.

EVEN WIND AND SEA OBEY HIM

35   At a late hour that same day he said to them: "Let us cross
36 to the other shore." They left the crowd and took him along, just
as he was, in their boat. Other boats were accompanying him.
37 Suddenly a violent storm broke, and the waves were dashing into
38 the boat, so that it was beginning to fill. Meanwhile, he himself
was in the stern, sleeping, with his head on the cushion.

They therefore awoke him with the cry: "Rabbi! We are going
39 down! Is that nothing to you?" Then, rising to his full height, he
sternly said to the wind: "Silence!" and commanded the sea: "Be

---

4:25. Anyone seeking to profit by Christ's words will be richly rewarded in
proportion to the effort he makes. One not interested in the deeper meaning
of a parable will profit nothing by hearing it. In ordinary life, too, "the rich
man with his capital easily adds to his wealth; the poor man just as easily loses
the little he has. He who endeavors earnestly to co-operate with grace shall
every day receive further and more abundant grace; he who by sloth neglects
the grace he has, shall lose even that" (Darby and Smith).

still!" The wind subsided, and there was stillness everywhere. He *40*
also said to them: "Why are you so timid?" and, "How is it you are
still without faith?" For they had been struck with great fear, and *41*
had said to one another, "Who, really, is this man? Why, even
wind and sea obey him!"

CHAPTER 5

AN UNCLEAN SPIRIT CAST OUT

They now came to the country of the Gerasenes on the other *1*
side of the sea. He had just come out of the boat when a man *2*
under the control of an unclean spirit came forth from the tombs
to meet him. This person lived among the tombs, for no one was *3*
any longer able to keep him down even with a chain. In fact, he *4*
had often been bound with handcuffs and chains, but he had
snapped the chains and broken the handcuffs, so that no one was
able to tame him. Night and day, without a break, he remained *5*
among the tombs on the hillside, shrieking and gashing himself
with stones. When he saw Jesus at a distance, he ran and, prostrat- *6*
ing himself before him, shouted at the top of his voice: "Leave me *7*
alone, Jesus, Son of the Most High God. In God's name, do not
torment me," for Jesus was about to say to him: "Unclean spirit, *8*
go out of the man."

He then asked him: "What is your name?" and he replied: *9*
"Legion is my name, for there are many of us." Now he had *10*
earnestly begged him not to put them out of the country; but *11*
since a numerous herd of pigs happened to be feeding there on the
hillside, the spirits ended by asking him: "Allow us to go among *12*
the pigs so that we may go into them." He allowed them, and the *13*
unclean spirits went out of the man and entered into the pigs. And
now the herd dashed down the slope into the sea — some two
thousand head — and were drowned in the sea. The herdsmen took *14*
to flight and carried the news to town and countryside. The inhabitants then came out to see what had taken place. They came to *15*
Jesus, and looked at the possessed man, now seated, clothed, and
in his right mind — the man who no longer had the legion in him.
They were struck with awe. When the eyewitnesses explained to *16*

107

17 them how it had fared with the demoniac, and about the pigs, they
18 earnestly begged him to quit their territory. As he re-entered the
boat, the man previously possessed asked leave to stay with him,
19 but, instead of giving him this, Jesus said to him: "Go home to
your people and relate to them all the Lord has done out of sheer
20 pity for you." He went away and made a point of proclaiming
throughout the Decapolis all that Jesus had done for him. All men
expressed astonishment.

JAIRUS ASKS FOR A CURE

21 When Jesus had crossed in the boat to the other side, a large
crowd once more flocked together to meet him. So he remained
22 close by the sea. Here one of the officials of the synagogue, Jairus
by name, came and, at sight of him, threw himself down at his feet
23 and earnestly pleaded with him. "My little daughter," he said, "is
at the point of death. Please, come and lay your hands upon her.
24 How I wish she would be restored to life!" So he went along with
the man, accompanied by so large a crowd that they were all
but smothering him.

THE WOMAN WITH HEMORRHAGES CURED

25 Now a woman who had endured hemorrhages for twelve years
26 had suffered much under the hands of many physicians, on whom
she had spent all her means; yet instead of improving, she had
27 on the contrary gone from bad to worse. Now hearing the
people talk about Jesus, she came along in the crowd behind and
28 touched his garment. For she kept saying: "If I touch but his
29 garment I shall be well." Instantly the source of her hemorrhage
dried up and she felt the sensation of being permanently cured of
30 her complaint. Instantly, too, Jesus, knowing his healing power
had been active, turned round in the crowd and asked: "Who is it
31 that touched my garments?" But his disciples said to him: "You
see, the crowd is all but smothering you, and you ask, 'Who has
32 touched me?'" He, however, looked round to see her who had
done it.
33 Then the woman, trembling from fright, and conscious of what

5:20. the Decapolis: see the note on Mt. 4:25.
5:30. his healing power had been active: see the note on Lk. 6:19.

had happened to her, came forward and, throwing herself down
before him, told him the whole truth, whereupon he said to her: 34
"Daughter, your faith has cured you. Go home and be at peace. I
want you to be cured, once for all, of your complaint."

THE CURE OF THE DAUGHTER OF JAIRUS

He was still speaking, when messengers from the household of 35
the synagogue official arrived to say: "Your daughter is dead. Why
trouble the Rabbi any further?" But disregarding the words of the 36
messengers, Jesus said to the official: "You have nothing to fear.
Only have faith." He did not allow anyone to accompany him 37
except Peter, James, and John, the brother of James. So, then, 38
they arrived at the home of the official, where Jesus noticed a noisy
crowd of weeping and wailing people. Entering he said to them: 39
"Why this tumult, why this weeping? The child is not dead; she
is asleep." They laughed at him; but he put them all out and, 40
taking with him the child's father and mother and his own companions, entered the room where the child was. He then took the 41
child by the hand and said to her: "*Talitha koum*" — which in our
language means, "Little girl, I command you to awake." The girl, 42
who was twelve years of age, arose immediately and walked about.
At once the people were utterly beside themselves with wonder. But 43
he strictly charged them not to let anyone know of this incident;
besides, he ordered that something to eat should be given the girl.

CHAPTER 6

JESUS LITTLE CREDITED IN HIS OWN COUNTRY

He now left that place and came to his own country, accom- 1
panied by his disciples. When the Sabbath came around, he applied 2
himself to teaching in the synagogue; and most of his hearers were
puzzled. "How came the man by all this?" they said; and, "The
wisdom bestowed on this man — what sort of thing is it?" and, "His
hands — what mighty works they can do!" "Is not this man the 3

5:41. "*Talitha koum*": Aramaic was the dialect of Palestine at the time of
Christ. It was a distinct language similar to Hebrew. St. Mark's Gospel is mainly
addressed to non-Jewish communities. See 14:36.
6:1. Jesus left Capharnaum for Nazareth.

carpenter, the son of Mary, and brother to James and Joseph and Jude and Simon?" and, "Are not his sisters our nextdoor neigh-
4 bors?" So, therefore, his person was a puzzle to them. Then Jesus said to them: "No prophet is discredited, except in his own country
5 and among his own kinsfolk and in his own household." And he could not work any miracle there, except that he cured a few ailing
6 persons by laying his hands on them. Wondering at their unbelief, he went on a teaching journey through the villages round about.

THE MISSION OF THE TWELVE APOSTLES

7 One day he called the Twelve to him and prepared to send them on a mission two by two, and gave them power over the
8 unclean spirits. He also told them not to go and get things for their journey: they were to have a staff only, but no provisions, no
9 traveling bag, no pocket money; they were, however, to wear
10 sandals, and, he added, "Do not put on an extra coat." He further said to them: "In any district, once you enter a house, make it
11 your headquarters till you leave that locality. But should a place not make you welcome and the people not listen to you, leave that place and shake off the dust from under your feet as a warning to
12 them." Accordingly, they set out and exhorted the people to a change
13 of heart; they also drove out many demons and cured many sick persons by anointing them with oil.

JOHN THE BAPTIST PUT TO DEATH

14 One day King Herod, since his name had become well known, heard it said that "John the Baptist is risen from the dead, and
15 that is why the miraculous powers are active in him." But others said: "It is Elias." Still others maintained: "He is a prophet, like
16 one of the old prophets." So, when word came to Herod's ears, he said: "The John whom I have had beheaded is risen from the dead."

6:5. Not because he lacked the power to work miracles, but because the people's lack of faith in his divine mission made them unworthy of these favors. See Mt. 7:6.
6:13. The practice of anointing the sick with oil was widespread in antiquity. Some think that the anointing on this occasion was more than a mere "type" of the Sacrament of Extreme Unction. See James 5:14.
6:14. *heard it said:* some texts read "he, sc. Herod, said."

The facts are these: Herod had John arrested and thrown
into prison to humor Herodias, his brother Philip's wife; for, when
Herod had married her, John kept saying to him: "You have no 18
right to live with your brother's wife." Now Herodias bore him 19
a grudge and would have liked to put him out of the way, but she
was powerless. Herod knew John to be an innocent and holy man, 20
and held him in reverence; in fact, he shielded him, and, on
listening to him, had many qualms of conscience; and yet he liked
to listen to him. But there came a welcome opportunity when 21
Herod, on his birthday, gave a banquet to his high dignitaries, his
army officers, and the leading men in Galilee, and the daughter of 22
this very Herodias came in and, by her dancing, charmed Herod
and his guests. "Ask me," said the king to the girl, "for anything
you wish, and I will give it to you"; he even made an oath to her: 23
"I will give you anything you ask of me, were it even one half of
my kingdom." So she went out and said to her mother: "What 24
shall I demand?" "The head of John the Baptizer," was her reply.
At once she returned with eager haste into the presence of the 25
king, and this is what she demanded: "I want you to give me,
here and now, on a platter, the head of John the Baptist."

The king was extremely annoyed; yet out of regard for the oath 26
and the guests, he dared not disappoint her. So the king at once 27
dispatched an executioner with orders to bring his head. The man 28
went and beheaded John in the dungeon; and he brought his head
on a platter and gave it to the girl. The girl then gave it to her
mother. When his disciples heard of it, they went to remove his 29
corpse and lay it in a tomb.

JESUS FEEDS FIVE THOUSAND

The apostles now rallied round Jesus and made their report to 30
him. They were full of all they had done and all they had taught.
"Come away," he said to them, "for the sake of privacy to a lonely 31
place, and take a little rest." The fact is, a stream of people had
been coming and going, so that they had no leisure even for a meal.
They consequently set out in a boat for a lonely place to secure 32

6:20, 21. Evidently Herod was much impressed by John's rebuke as well as by
his holy life; but the sinful attachment to Herodias stifled his qualms of conscience. See Mk. 4:19.

33 privacy. People, however, had seen them depart, and many more
came to know about it. The result was that groups from all the
towns flocked together and arrived there before them.

34 On landing, he saw a multitude of people, and his heart went out
to them. They were like sheep that have no shepherd, and he
35 diligently set about instructing them. It was already late in the
day when his disciples approached him. "This is a lonely place,"
36 they said, "and it is already late in the day; dismiss the people so
that they can reach the farms and villages round about and buy
37 themselves something to eat." But he met their suggestion by
saying: "It is for you to give them something to eat." "Are we to
go," they replied, "and buy bread for two hundred denarii, and
38 give it to them to eat?" "How many loaves have you?" he asked
them; "go and find out." After making sure, they reported: "Five
39 loaves and two fish." He then told them to have the crowd recline
40 on the green grass in groups resembling table companies. So they
reclined in groups resembling garden plots, of a hundred or fifty
41 persons each. Then, taking the loaves and the two fish into his
his hands, he looked up to heaven and, after saying grace, broke the
loaves into portions, which he gave to his disciples to serve to the
42 people. He also had the two fish distributed among all. All ate, and
43 everyone had a plentiful meal. Moreover, they gathered up remnants
of bread enough to fill twelve baskets, besides what was left over of
44 the fish. The persons who had eaten the loaves numbered five
thousand men.

JESUS WALKS ON THE WATER; HE CALMS THE SEA

45 Without delay he obliged his disciples to re-enter the boat and
go in advance to a place on the other shore opposite Bethsaida,
46 while he himself would dismiss the crowd. After bidding the people
farewell, he withdrew to the mountainside to pray.

47 Night had fallen and the boat was far out at sea, while he was
48 still on land; but when he saw them in distress, trying to make
headway — for the wind was against them — he came toward them
during the last part of the night, walking upon the sea, and he
49 would have passed them by. But seeing him walk upon the sea,

---

6:37. A "denarius" was equivalent to about 17 cents, then an ordinary day's
wages. See Lk. 10:35.

they thought it was a ghost and cried out aloud. They all had seen 50
him and were perplexed. He at once, however, addressed them, and
said to them: "Take courage! It is I! Do not be afraid!"

He then climbed up to join them in the boat. The wind sub- 51
sided; and they were utterly beside themselves. The truth is, they 52
had not yet learned the lesson at the multiplication of the loaves; on
the contrary, their minds were a perfect blank.

MIRACLES AT GENNESARET

After going straight across, they drew to land at Gennesaret and 53
moored there. When Christ had left the boat, some immediately 54
recognized him and ran up and down the countryside. And now 55
people made themselves busy carrying the sick on their mats here
and there, wherever they heard he was. And in any place he visited, 56
whether village, town, or farm, they set down the sick in the streets,
and asked permission for them to touch were it only the tassel of
his cloak; and as many as came in contact with him were cured.

CHAPTER 7

THE PHARISEES REBUKED

One day the Pharisees and a group of Scribes who had come from 1
Jerusalem gathered round him, and noticed that some of his disciples 2
ate their meals with common, that is, with unwashed, hands. Now 3
the Pharisees, like the Jews generally, do not eat unless they wash
their hands up to the wrist, merely to uphold the tradition of the
elders; and when they return from the market, they do not eat 4
unless they first bathe; and there are many other things handed
down to them as binding, such as the washing of cups, jugs, pans,

6:52. The lesson which the disciples should have learned from the multiplication of the loaves was that Jesus had power over nature.

7:3. No altogether satisfactory explanation of the Greek expression here
rendered up to the wrist has yet been advanced. the elders: men of position and
influence in their communities. Many of them served as members of the Sanhedrin, or Supreme Council. See 15:1.

7:4. An alternative rendering would be: "they do not eat things bought in
the market place without thorough cleansing." The object of this ceremony
was to remove any levitical defilement which might cling either to them or to
the food from contact with "unclean" persons or things.

5 and beds. The Pharisees and the Scribes, therefore, asked him: "Why do not your disciples live up to the tradition of the elders,
6 but eat their meals with unwashed hands?" He replied: "Rightly has Isaias prophesied about you, hypocrites, in the Scripture text:

'This race honors me with its lips,
but its heart is far away from me.
7   They worship me in vain;
for they teach as binding precepts
mere rulings made by man.'

8 Setting aside the commandment of God, you cling to the tradition of men. The washing of pots and of cups, and many other things
9 you do like to these." And he went on to say to them: "Well, indeed, do you nullify God's commandments merely to cherish your
10 tradition! For instance, Moses has declared: 'Honor your father and your mother,' and 'Whoever curses a father or a mother shall
11 be put to death.' Yet your teaching is different: Once a person says to his father, or his mother, 'Any support you might get from me
12 is korban' (that is, a gift already made to God), you no longer
13 permit him to do anything for his father or mother; and thus you render null and void the word of God by your tradition — a tradition which you are handing down. And you do many other things similar to these."
14   He then called the crowd around him again, and said to them:
15 "Give ear, all of you, and use your understanding! There is nothing outside a person which, by going into him, can defile him. On the contrary, the things that come out of a person are the things
16 that defile him. Let everyone heed what he has heard."
17   When he had come indoors, away from the crowd, his disciples
18 asked him about that obscure saying. "So you, too," he said to them, "are still without understanding? Do you not comprehend that whatever goes into a person from outside has no power to defile him,
19 since it does not go into his soul, but only into his body, and then
20 passes out as waste?" And thereby he declared all foods clean. He continued: "What comes out of a person is the thing that defiles a
21 person. Yes, it is from within, out of the hearts of men, that evil
22 intentions proceed — fornication, theft, murder, adultery, greed,

7:19. The Mosaic Law distinguishes between clean and unclean foods. See Acts 10:9 ff.

malice, fraud, wantonness, envy, profanity, pride, folly. All these 23
wicked things come from within and defile a person."

CURE OF THE CANAANITE WOMAN'S DAUGHTER

Jesus now left that place and set out for the district of Tyre and 24
Sidon. Here he entered a house and wanted no one to know of it;
but he could not escape notice. The fact is, a woman, whose daughter 25
was possessed by an unclean spirit, at once heard of him, and she
came and threw herself down at his feet. This woman was a Greek- 26
speaking heathen, a Syrophoenician by birth. She implored him to
drive the demon out of her daughter. He said to her: "Let first the 27
children have their fill; it surely is not fair to take the children's
bread and throw it to the dogs." "You are right, Lord," she promptly 28
assented; "and the dogs under the table eat only of the crumbs of
the children's bread." "For that remark," he said to her, "you may 29
go home. The demon is driven out of your daughter." So when she 30
arrived home she found her little daughter lying on the bed and
the demon driven out of her.

HEARING RESTORED

He then left the district of Tyre and went, by way of Sidon, to 31
the Sea of Galilee and into the heart of the Decapolis. Here people 32
brought to him one who was deaf and spoke but imperfectly, and
they begged him to lay his hand upon him. Taking him away 33
from the crowd, to be alone with him, he put his fingers into the
man's ears, and, with his own spittle, touched the man's tongue.
He then looked up to heaven, sighed, and said to him: "*Ephphata*," 34
which means "Open." At once his ears were opened, the impediment 35
in his speech was removed, and he spoke plainly. Jesus then charged 36
the people to tell no one; but the more strictly he charged them,
the more freely, for their part, they published the fact. Indeed, they 37
went beyond all bounds in expressing their delight: "Everything he
has done is wonderful! He gives hearing to the deaf and enables
the dumb to speak."

CHAPTER 8

FOUR THOUSAND FED MIRACULOUSLY

One day about that time, when again a large crowd was present 1

and had nothing to eat, he called the disciples to him and said
2 to them: "My heart goes out to the multitude. For three days already
3 they have been clinging to me and have nothing to eat! If I let them
go home fasting, they may break down on the way. And some of
4 them have come a great distance!" In this predicament his disciples
said to him: "How can anybody manage to give these people bread
5 enough for a plentiful meal in a desert?" "How many loaves have
6 you?" he asked them. "Seven," they replied. He then sent word
round among the crowd to recline on the ground. Next he took the
seven loaves into his hands and, after saying grace, broke them into
portions, which he gave to his disciples to serve. They served them
7 to the crowd. They also had a few small fish; and, after saying grace,
8 he had these also served. The people ate and had a plentiful meal.
Besides, they gathered what was left over and filled seven baskets
9 with the remnants. There were about four thousand men present.
10 After dismissing them, he went at once into the boat, accompanied
by his disciples, and set out for the district of Dalmanutha.

THE PHARISEES REFUSED A SIGN

11   Here the Pharisees came to meet him and set about having an
argument with him. By way of testing him, they demanded of him
12 a proof of his claims, to be shown in the sky. He sighed from the
depths of his soul. "Can it be that this generation," he said,
"demands a proof of my claims! I tell you outright, no such proof
13 will be granted to this generation!" And turning his back on them,
he re-embarked in the boat and set out for the opposite shore.

THE LEAVEN OF THE PHARISEES

14   Now they had forgotten to provide themselves with bread, and
a single loaf was all the bread they had with them in the boat.
15 As it happened, he gave them an instruction in which he said:
"Look out! Beware of the leaven of the Pharisees and of the leaven
16 of Herod." Puzzled at this they remarked to one another: "Oh, it is
17 because we have no bread!" Jesus noticed it and said to them: "Why
are you puzzled over having no bread? Are your minds still a com-
18 plete blank? Have you eyes and do not see? Have you ears and
19 do not hear? And furthermore: do you not remember the time

---

8:11. See the note on Mt. 12:38.

when I broke the five loaves for the five thousand? How many
basketfuls of remnants did you then gather up?" "Twelve," they
replied. "And when I broke the seven loaves for the four thousand,   20
how many basketfuls of remnants did you gather up?" "Seven,"
they replied. And he said to them: "Can you not yet understand?"   21

SIGHT RESTORED

They now arrived at Bethsaida. Here a blind man was brought   22
to him, and Christ was asked to lay his hand upon him. Taking   23
the blind man by the hand he led him out of the village. Then,
after spitting into his eyes and putting his hands on him, he asked
him: "Do you see anything?" Since the man had begun to see,   24
he replied: "I see the people; they look to me like trees that move
about." He then laid his hands on the man's eyes a second time. As   25
a result, he began to see, and was completely cured so that he saw
everything distinctly. He sent him home with the warning: "Go   26
into your house, and if you enter into the town tell nobody."

"YOU ARE THE MESSIAS"

Accompanied by his disciples, Jesus left for the villages of   27
Caesarea Philippi. On the way he put this question to his disciples:
"Who do the people say I am?" Some replied: "John the Baptist";   28
others, "Elias"; still others: "One of the prophets." But he went on   29
questioning them: "But you — who do you say I am?" Here Peter
spoke up and said to him: "You are the Messias." He then strictly   30
charged them not to speak about him to anyone.

He now made it a point to teach them that it was necessary   31
for the Son of Man to suffer much, be rejected by the elders, the
high priests, and the Scribes, be put to death, and after three days
to rise again. And he drove the lesson home in plain words. Then   32
Peter drew him aside and proceeded to lecture him. But he turned   33
round and, in sight of his disciples, lectured Peter: "Back to your
place," he said; "follow me, Satan! You do not take God's view
of things, but men's."

SHOULDERING THE CROSS

He then called to him the crowds as well as his disciples and   34

8:26. Jesus avoided attracting attention since he did not wish to remain in
this district.

said to them: "If anyone wants to be my follower, he must renounce himself and shoulder his cross; then he may be a follower of mine.
35 Why, he who would save his life shall lose it; but he who freely parts with his life for the sake of the gospel will save it in the end.
36 Clearly, what does it profit a man to gain the whole world when
37 his life is forfeited in any case? Or what price can a man pay down
38 to purchase life forever? Furthermore: if one is ashamed of me and my message before this adulterous and sinful generation, of him the Son of Man will, in turn, be ashamed when he returns wrapt in his Father's glory and escorted by his holy angels."

CHAPTER 9

JESUS CONVERSING WITH ELIAS AND MOSES

1   He also said to them: "I tell you truly: some of those present here will not taste death before they see the kingdom of God set
2 up in power." Six days later, Jesus took Peter, James, and John with him and led them up a high hill to be in a group by them-
3 selves. Here he changed his appearance before their eyes: his garments became an exceedingly brilliant white, such as no dyer on
4 earth can produce by bleaching. Moreover, Elias and Moses were
5 seen by them, and they were conversing with Jesus. Then Peter felt moved to say to Jesus: "Rabbi, it is well that we are here. Let us put up three tents — one for you, one for Moses, and one for
6 Elias." Really, he was at a loss for appropriate words: they were so
7 afraid. Then a cloud formed and enveloped them, and a voice rang
8 out in the cloud: "This is my beloved Son. Listen to him!" Suddenly looking round, they saw no one but Jesus alone with themselves.
9   As they were going down the hill, he enjoined them not to tell anyone what they had seen till after the Son of Man had risen from
10 the dead. So they kept the matter to themselves, and discussed with one another what "the rising from the dead" really meant.
11   They also asked him: "Why do the Scribes say that Elias has to
12 come first?" "Yes," he replied, "first Elias comes and restores everything. But then, why does the Scripture say about the Son of Man

9:1. Some of Christ's hearers would live to see the kingdom of God, the Church, firmly established and even widely spread.

that he will suffer much and be treated with contempt? Well, I   13
tell you: Elias has already come, and people worked their will on
him just as the Scripture says concerning him."

JESUS DRIVES OUT A DEAF-AND-DUMB SPIRIT

They started to rejoin the disciples, and noticed that a large   14
crowd surrounded them and that Scribes were arguing with them.
Suddenly, the whole multitude caught sight of him, and, struck   15
with reverence, ran up to salute him. "What are you discussing with   16
them?" he asked the people. "Rabbi," someone out in the crowd   17
answered him, "I brought you my son, who is possessed by a dumb
spirit. Whenever he takes hold of the lad, he dashes him to the   18
ground; and he foams and grinds his teeth and becomes rigid. I
asked your disciples to drive him out, but they were unable to do so."
"O unbelieving generation," he was moved to say to them; "how   19
long must I be with you; how long must I bear with you! Bring
him to me." So they brought him to Jesus. The moment the spirit   20
caught sight of him, he threw the lad into convulsions, and, after
being thrown to the ground, he rolled about, frothing at the mouth.
He then asked his father: "How long is it since he has had this   21
affliction?" "Ever since he was a child," he answered; "and many   22
a time the spirit threw him into fire or into water to kill him. Oh,
if you can do anything, take our trouble to heart and help us."
Jesus said to him: "As to that 'if you can do anything,' one who   23
believes can do everything." The child's father at once cried out: 24
"I do believe! Help me if I do not!" Seeing that a fresh group came   25
running up, Jesus spoke sternly to the unclean spirit and said to
him: "Deaf-and-dumb spirit, I command you: go out of him, and
never again go into him." He screamed and threw him into fierce   26
convulsions, and went out of him. The lad was like a corpse, and
everybody said: "He is dead." But Jesus took him by the hand and   27
helped him to rise. And he rose to his feet.

When he had come indoors, his disciples asked him confidentially: 28
"Why were not we able to drive him out?" "This particular kind,"   29
he replied, "cannot be driven out by anything except prayer and
fasting."

9:29. Some ancient manuscripts omit the words *and fasting.*

119

CHRIST'S DEATH AND RESURRECTION FORETOLD

30   They left that district and, avoiding the highways, passed through
31   Galilee. He wished to remain incognito, because he was engaged
in teaching his disciples. He said to them: "The Son of Man will
be betrayed into the hands of men, and they will put him to
death; but, although put to death, he will rise on the third day."
32   But they could not see the drift of his remark, and yet were too
timid to ask him.

SPIRITUAL GREATNESS

33   They now arrived at Capharnaum. Having come indoors, he asked
34   them: "What were you discussing on the way?" They remained
silent, for on the way they had discussed among themselves which
35   one of their group was the greatest. So he seated himself, called the
Twelve, and said to them: "If anyone would like to be the first,
36   he will have to be the last of all, that is, the servant of all." He
then took hold of a little child, placed it in front of them, and,
37   folding it in his arms, said to them: "Whoever befriends one of
these little children in my name, befriends me, and he who befriends
me befriends not me but him whose ambassador I am."

DO GOOD, AVOID EVIL

38   Here John said to him: "Rabbi, we saw somebody drive out
demons in your name, and we were for stopping him because he
39   is not of our company." "Do not stop him," Jesus said; "after all,
one who works miracles in my name will not the next minute bring
40   himself to speak evil of me; and he who is not against us is for us.
41   In fact, anyone that gives you a cup of water on the ground that you
belong to Christ, will not, I assure you, go without his reward.
42   Furthermore: when one has been an occasion of sin to one of these
little ones who believe in me, he would be better off if he lay at
the bottom of the sea with a great millstone hung round his neck.
43   "Again: if your hand is a temptation to you, cut it off; it is better
for you to go into life maimed than to keep both your hands and go

---

9:43. Sinful occasions must be shunned even at the cost of great personal
sacrifices. The precept "to cut off one's hand, etc.," is not to be interpreted
literally. See the note on Lk. 17:6. For the expression *is a temptation to you,*
see the note on 4:17.

into the unquenchable fire in the infernal pit. And if your foot *44*
tempts you to sin, cut it off; it is better for you to go into life *45*
crippled than keep both your feet and be thrown into the infernal
pit. And if your eye tempts you to sin, put it out; it is better for *46, 47*
you to go into the kingdom of God deprived of one eye than keep
both eyes and be thrown into the infernal pit, where their worm *48*
does not die and the fire does not go out.

"Yes, everyone must be seasoned with fire, just as every sacrifice *49*
must be seasoned with salt. Salt is an excellent thing; but should *50*
salt ever lose its saltness, by what means could you flavor it? Have
salt within you, and be at peace with one another."

CHAPTER 10

MAN AND WIFE ARE ONE PERSON

Leaving that country for good, he set out for the province of *1*
Judea by the Transjordanian route. And again people flocked to him,
and again, as was his wont, he instructed them.

One day the Pharisees approached and, with a view to sounding *2*
him out, laid this case before him: "Is it right for a husband to
divorce his wife?" He answered by asking them: "What ruling *3*
has Moses given you?" They replied: "Moses gave permission to *4*
write a bill of separation and thus effect a divorce." "It was with *5*
an eye to your intractable temper," Jesus said to them, "that Moses
drew up this ruling for you. At the beginning of creation God *6*
made human beings male and female; and for this reason a man *7*
must leave his father and his mother, and the two are to become *8*

9:45. *the infernal pit:* called Gehenna. See the second note on Mt. 5:22.

9:48. This verse is printed in some texts three times, numbered as verses 44, 46, 48. The quotation is from Isa. 66:24.

9:49. *seasoned* (made palatable, savory, agreeable to God) *with fire* (through suffering): see verses 43–47.

9:50. The sense of this saying in this place is not clear. Christ seems to mean: as salt "gone flat" is utterly useless, so followers of his, who afterward abandon him, are fit only to be excluded from his kingdom. In Mt. 5:13 the disciples are called "the salt of the earth" because it is their duty to "season" others by doctrine and example.

10:8. *one person:* the Greek noun so rendered is capable of various senses: flesh, body, human nature, person, etc. The rendering "one flesh" is better suited to other contexts, as, for instance, Eph. 5:31.

9 one person, so that they are no longer two persons but one. Consequently, what God has yoked together man may not separate."

10 After coming indoors, the disciples asked him still further about
11 the matter. "Whoever," he said to them, "divorces his wife and
12 marries another commits adultery in regard to the former; and if a wife divorces her husband and marries another, she commits adultery."

LET THE LITTLE CHILDREN COME TO ME

13 One day people brought little children to him, that he might lay his hands on them, but the disciples scolded them for doing so.
14 Jesus saw this and became indignant. "Let the little children come to me," he said to them, "and do not stop them; to such as these
15 belongs the kingdom of God. I assure you, whoever does not receive the kingdom of God as does a little child, will not enter it."
16 He then folded them in his arms and, laying his hands on them spoke a fervent blessing.

TRUST IN WORLDLY GOODS

17 As he was leaving the house to pursue his journey, someone ran up and, kneeling before him, asked this question: "Good Rabbi,
18 what must I do to inherit eternal life?" "Why do you call me good?" Jesus replied; "Nobody is good except One alone — God!
19 You know the commandments: Do not murder; do not commit adultery; do not steal; do not bear false witness; do not commit
20 fraud; honor your father and mother." "Rabbi," he said to him,
21 "I have guarded against all these things from my youth." Jesus looked at him intently and loved him. Then he said to him: "One thing is still wanting to you: go, sell all you have and give the proceeds to the poor, and you will have an investment in heaven; then come
22 back and be my follower." But he frowned at the words and went away with a heavy heart; for he had much property.

23 Then, looking round, Jesus said to his disciples: "Oh, with what difficulty will those who have the goods of this world enter the
24 kingdom of God!" The disciples were dumfounded at his words. But Jesus took occasion to repeat his statement: "Children, how

10:18. See the note on Lk. 18:19.
10:19. Exod. 20:12–16.

difficult it is for those who put their trust in worldly goods to enter
the kingdom of God! It is easier for a camel to pass through the 25
eye of a needle than for a rich man to enter the kingdom of God!"
They were completely bewildered and said to one another: "In 26
that case, who can be saved?" Jesus looked straight at them and 27
said: "Where man fails, God still avails. God can do all things."
Then Peter made bold to say to him: "We, you see, have given 28
up everything and have become your followers!" Jesus replied: "I 29
tell you with assurance; no one gives up home, or brothers, or sisters,
or mother, or father, or children, or lands, for my sake and for the
sake of the gospel, but receives a hundred times as much — now, in 30
this world, homes and brothers and sisters and mothers and children
and lands, along with persecutions, and, in the world to come,
eternal life! Many that are first will be last, and the last will be first." 31

THE SON OF MAN WILL BE BETRAYED

They were now on their way going up to Jerusalem, and Jesus 32
was walking ahead of them; they were terrified, yet kept following
although they were afraid. Once again he took the Twelve aside
and made a point of telling them what was destined to happen to
him. Namely: "Listen! We are going up to Jerusalem, and the Son 33
of Man will be betrayed to the high priests and the Scribes, and they
will condemn him to death and hand him over to the Gentiles;
and they will mock him and spit on him and scourge him and put 34
him to death; but after three days he will rise again."

TO SERVE AND NOT TO BE SERVED

Then James and John, the sons of Zebedee, approached him. 35
"Rabbi," they said to him, "we would like you to do for us whatever we ask of you." He replied: "What would you like me to do 36
for you?" They said to him: "Give us a seat, one at your right, the 37
other at your left, in your glory." "You do not realize what you 38
are asking," Jesus said to them; "can you drink the cup that I am
to drink, and be baptized with the baptism with which I am to be
baptized?" "We can," they replied. Then Jesus said to them: "Yes, 39
you will drink the cup that I am to drink, and be baptized with the
baptism with which I am to be baptized; but as for a seat at my 40

10:40. Even as Judge, Christ regulates his conduct by the will of the Father.
See Jn. 8:16.

right or my left, that is not in my power to assign except to those for whom it has been reserved."

41 When the other ten heard of this incident, they gave way to
42 indignation at James and John. Jesus called them into his presence and said to them: "You know that the distinguished rulers of the Gentiles lord it over their subjects, and that their princes tyrannize
43 over them. That is not your way! On the contrary, he who would
44 be a prince among you must be your servant, and he who would be a
45 leader among you must be the slave of everyone. Why, even the Son of Man did not come into the world to be served but to serve and to give his life as a ransom for many."

"YOUR FAITH HAS CURED YOU"

46 They were now setting out for Jericho. His disciples and a considerable crowd were with him. While he journeyed on just off Jericho, Bartimaeus, the son of Timaeus, sat by the road. He was
47 a blind beggar. On hearing that it was Jesus of Nazareth, he
48 shouted vigorously: "Son of David, Jesus, take pity on me." The people indignantly told him to be quiet; but he shouted all the
49 louder: "Son of David, take pity on me." Then Jesus stopped and said: "Call him." So they called the blind man. "Take heart," they
50 said to him; "rise; he is calling for you." He flung aside his cloak,
51 sprang to his feet, and came to Jesus. Jesus reassured him and said: "What do you wish me to do for you?" "Rabbi," the blind man said
52 to him, "I wish I could see." "Go home," Jesus said to him; "your faith has cured you." He at once regained his sight, and then followed him on the way.

CHAPTER 11

THE TRIUMPHAL ENTRY OF JESUS

1 When they had come into the vicinity of Jerusalem and reached Bethphage on the slope of the Mount of Olives, he sent two of
2 his disciples on an errand, with these instructions: "Go to the village facing you, and just as you enter it, you will find tied a foal on which no man has ever sat. Unhitch it and bring it here.
3 And in case anybody says to you, 'What do you mean by doing

that?' just say, 'The Lord has need of it, and he will send it back
without delay.'" So they went and found the foal tied to the gate, *4*
in the street outside, and unhitched it. And when some of the *5*
bystanders said to them, "What do you mean by unhitching the
foal?" they told them what Jesus had said to them. Then they let *6*
them have their way. They brought the foal to Jesus and threw their *7*
cloaks over it; and he seated himself on it. Besides, many people *8*
carpeted the road with their cloaks, while others scattered green
things about, which they had cut off in the fields. Those that *9*
marched in front and those that followed in the rear kept shouting:

> "Hosanna!
> A blessing on him
> who comes in the name of the Lord!
> A blessing on our father David's throne   *10*
> which is now to be restored!
> Hosanna in the heavens above!"

And so he made his entry into the temple at Jerusalem. There he *11*
looked keenly at everything; but since it was already late in the
day, he went out to Bethany, accompanied by the Twelve.

The following morning, after they had set out from Bethany, *12*
he was hungry. Seeing in the distance a fig tree in full leaf, he went *13*
to see if he could not, perhaps, find something on it; but when he
came close to it, he found nothing on it except leaves. It was not
the season for figs. He then took occasion to say to it: "May nobody *14*
ever again eat fruit from you!" His disciples were within earshot.

SELLERS AND BUYERS EXPELLED FROM TEMPLE GROUNDS

After arriving in Jerusalem, he entered the temple and proceeded *15*
to expel the sellers and buyers on the temple grounds; he over-
threw the counters of the money-changers and the seats of the
pigeon dealers; nor would he allow anyone to carry any baggage *16*
across the temple grounds. To teach them a lesson he said: "Does *17*
not the Scripture say:

11:10. Ps. 117:26.
11:12. This episode is a parable in action, meant as a warning against
spiritual sterility. The enthusiasm which Jerusalem had just displayed in wel-
coming Christ bore no fruit. After the death of Christ, the Synagogue was like
a dried-up tree. See second note on Mt. 5:17.
11:17. Isa. 56:7; Jer. 7:11.

'My house shall be what its name declares,
a house of prayer for all the nations'?
But you have turned it into 'a den of robbers.'"

18   The high priests and the Scribes heard of it, and they looked
for ways and means of doing away with him. The fact is, they
were afraid of him, since the people were lost in admiration of his
19   teaching. When evening came, he went out of the city.

HAVE FAITH IN GOD. FORGIVE YOUR FELLOW MAN

20   In the early morning they saw, in passing, the fig tree dried up,
21   root and all. Peter had not forgotten. "Look, Rabbi," he said to him;
22   "the fig tree which you cursed is dried up!" Jesus replying said to
23   them: "Have faith in God. I tell you positively: if anyone says to
that mountain, 'Up with you and down into the sea!' and does not
let a doubt rise in his mind, but believes that what he says will
24   come true, it shall be as he desires. For this reason I tell you: plead
for anything you like, and believe that you will surely get it; and
25   it shall be granted to you. And when you compose yourselves for
prayer, forgive anything you may have against a person, so that
26   your Father in heaven may, in turn, forgive your offenses. If you
do not forgive, neither will your Father in heaven forgive your
offenses."

"BY WHAT AUTHORITY?"

27   Again they entered Jerusalem. As he walked about the temple
grounds, the high priests, the Scribes, and the elders, approached
28   him. "By what authority," they said to him, "do you engage in this
activity? In other words, who gave you this authority — the authority
29   to do these things?" But Jesus said to them: "Let me ask you one
question; and I will tell you by what authority I engage in this
30   activity. John's baptism — was it from heaven or from men? Answer
31   me." Then they discussed the matter privately. "In case we say,
'From heaven,'" they argued, "he will ask, 'Then why did you not
32   believe him?' Well, shall we say, 'From men'?" They were afraid
of the people, for one and all they really considered John a prophet.
33   So their answer to Jesus was: "We do not know." Then Jesus said
to them: "Neither will I tell you by what authority I am acting the
way I am."

11:26. Some texts omit this verse.

Chapter 12

THE MAN WHO PLANTED A VINEYARD

He then proceeded to warn them in parable style: "Once upon 1
a time a man planted a vineyard, set up a fence round it, dug a
wine vat, and erected a tower. He then leased it out to vinedressers
and went abroad. In due time he sent an agent to the vinedressers 2
to receive from them a share of the vintage. They seized and beat 3
him, and sent him back with empty hands. So he sent to them 4
another agent; but they struck him on the head and insulted him.
Yet another he sent, and this one they killed; and so they treated 5
many others, beating some and killing others. He still had a beloved 6
son, whom he sent to them last of all, saying: 'They will respect
my son.' But those vinedressers said to one another: 'This is the 7
heir; come, let us kill him, and the inheritance will be ours.'
They laid hold of him, drove him out of the vineyard, and killed 8
him. What, then, will the owner of the vineyard do to them? He 9
will return, and put the vinedressers to death. Yes, and he will give
the vineyard to others! Did you never read this Scripture text: 10
'The very stone which the builders rejected
    has become the cornerstone;
    this is the Lord's own doing, 11
    and it is a wonderful sight to us'?"
They would have liked to arrest him, but they feared the people. 12
They understood, of course, that he had aimed this parable at
themselves. So, turning their back on him, they walked away.

THE PHARISEES AND HERODIANS WOULD TRAP JESUS

They now sent some of the Pharisees and the Herodians to meet 13
him in order to trap him in an argument. These came and said to 14
him: "Rabbi, we know you are an honest man, and who anyone
is never worries you; you do not look to men's rank or station in
life, but truthfully teach the way of God. Is it right to pay a poll
tax to Caesar, or is it not? Shall we pay it, or shall we not?"
But he knew they were playing a part. "What do you mean by 15
sounding me out?" he said to them, "Bring me a denarius. I want

12:10. Ps. 117:22 f.; Isa. 28:16.

16 to look at it." So they brought one. "Whose head is this?" he
then asked them; "and whose title is here inscribed?" "Caesar's,"
17 they replied. Jesus then said to them: "Render to Caesar what is
Caesar's, and to God what is God's." They were nonplused by
his reply.

THE SADDUCEES CONFOUNDED BY JESUS

18   Also Sadducees — the men that deny the resurrection — came to
19 him and laid this case before him: "Rabbi, Moses has made this
ruling for us: 'In case a man's brother dies and leaves a wife but
no child behind, he is to marry his widow and by her raise issue
20 for his brother.' Once upon a time, there were seven brothers.
21 This first took a wife and died without leaving issue. Then the second
took her to wife, and died without leaving issue. And so the third.
22 In a word, the seven left no issue. Last of all the woman also died.
23 At the resurrection, when everybody rises from the dead, which
one's wife will she be? You see, the seven had had her to wife."
24   Jesus said to them: "Does not this show that you are wide of
the mark, since you understand neither the Scriptures nor the power
25 of God? Once people are risen from the dead, they neither marry
26 nor are given in marriage, but are like angels in heaven. And as to
the rising from the dead, did you not read in the Book of Moses,
in the passage about the Bush, that God expressly declared to him:

'I am the God of Abraham,
and the God of Isaac,
and the God of Jacob'?

27 He is not the God of dead men, but of living. You are very wide
of the mark."

THE FIRST AND SECOND COMMANDMENTS

28   Then one of the Scribes came forward. He had listened to their
discussion, and when he perceived that he had answered them to
the point, proposed this question to him: "Which is the very first
29 commandment?" Jesus answered: "The first is this:

'Listen, Israel,
the Lord our God is one Lord;

12:18. *Sadducees:* see the note on Mt. 3:7.
12:26. Exod. 3:6.
12:29. Deut. 6:4 f.

         therefore love the Lord your God   30
         with your whole heart,
         and with your whole soul,
         and with your whole mind,
         and with your whole strength.'
A second commandment is this: 'Love your neighbor as yourself.' 31
Greater than these, there is no other commandment." "Very well, 32
Rabbi," replied the Scribe; "you are right in saying that he is one,
and there is none other but he. Moreover, to love him with one's 33
whole heart, and with one's whole mind, and with one's whole
strength, and to love one's neighbor as oneself, is more precious
than all the burnt offerings and sacrifices." Seeing that he had 34
expressed himself sensibly, Jesus said to him: "You are not far from
the kingdom of God." From that time on, no one had the face to
ask him any more questions.

THE MESSIAS IS NOT THE SON BUT THE LORD OF DAVID

    Again, while teaching in the temple, Jesus took occasion to say: 35
"In what sense do the Scribes say the Messias is the Son of David?
David himself, prompted by the Holy Spirit, said: 36
         'The Lord said to my Lord:
         Be seated at my right hand,
         until I make your foes
         a footstool for your feet.'
David himself calls him 'Lord'; in what sense, then, is he his Son?" 37
Of course, the common people liked to listen to him.

    He also said in the course of his teaching: "Beware of the 38
Scribes, who fancy fine robes for outdoor wear, and ceremonious
greetings in public places, and front seats in the synagogues and 39
places of honor at meals. These men that devour the fortunes 40
of widows and recite long prayers for show will receive a more
than ordinary punishment."

THE GIFT OF THE BEGGAR WOMAN

    Taking a seat opposite the treasury, he observed how the people 41
were putting money into the treasury. Many well-to-do folk were
putting in great amounts. There also came a widow, a beggar woman, 42

12:36. Ps. 109:1.

43 who put in two small coins, that is, one quarter. He then called his disciples to him and said to them: "I tell you the plain truth, this
44 widow, the beggar woman that she is, has put in more than all the others that put money into the treasury: all the others took from their superfluities what they put in; but this woman, in her extreme want, put in all she possessed, yes, all she had to live on."

CHAPTER 13

THE DESTRUCTION OF THE TEMPLE. THE END OF THE WORLD

1 As Jesus left the temple grounds, one of his disciples said to him: "Look, Rabbi, what wonderful slabs of stone! What a wonderful
2 edifice!" Jesus replied: "You admire this mighty edifice? Not one stone will here be left upon another, but all will crumble to pieces."
3 When he was seated on the Mount of Olives, facing the temple,
4 Peter, James, John, and Andrew asked him confidentially: "Tell us, when will this catastrophe take place? And what is the sign to indicate when the whole world is coming to an end?"
5 Jesus then composed himself and said to them: "See to it that
6 no one leads you astray. Many will come and, assuming my title,
7 say: 'I am he!' and many will they lead astray! And when you hear of wars or rumors of wars, do not be alarmed. These things
8 must happen, but the end is not yet. Nation will rise against nation, and kingdom against kingdom. There will be earthquakes here and there; there will be famines. This is but the prelude to the throes.
9 "Look to yourselves. You will be handed over to courts of justice, and flogged in synagogues, and confronted with governors and kings for my sake. It will be your chance to testify to them.
10 Furthermore: all the nations must first have the Gospel preached
11 to them. But, once led away to be handed over, do not be uneasy beforehand as to what you are to say. No, just say what will be put into your mouth at that moment. In fact, the Holy Spirit is
12 then the Speaker, and not you. Brother will give up brother and father will give up child for capital punishment; children will rise
13 up against parents and have them condemned to death. You will be the scorn of all because you profess my name. But he who holds out to the end will be saved.

THE HORRORS OF DESOLATION

"Now, when you see the horrors of desolation enacted where 14
they should not be — let the reader comprehend! — then those who
are in Judea should flee to the hills; he that is on the housetop 15
must not come down and enter the house to fetch something that
is in his house; he that is in the field must not turn back to 16
fetch his cloak. How pitiful the women that are with child 17
or are nursing in those days! Pray that it may not happen in winter; 18
for those days will be a trying time, such as has never existed from 19
the beginning when God created the world down to this day, and
never will exist again. And if the Lord had not shortened the days, 20
not one human being would be saved; but in consideration of his
own elect he has shortened the days. If anyone then says to you: 21
'See, here is the Christ!' 'See, there!' do not believe it; for false 22
christs and false prophets will appear and give striking exhibitions
of power in order to lead the elect astray, if possible. But you — 23
look out! I have foretold you everything.

THE SON OF MAN RIDING THE CLOUDS

"Furthermore: in those days, after that distress, the sun will 24
darken, the moon cease to shed her light, and star after star will 25
fall from heaven; indeed, the foundations of the universe will rock.
Then the Son of Man will be seen riding the clouds with great 26
might and majesty. And then he will send forth the angels and 27
assemble the elect in all four quarters from one edge of the horizon
to the other. From the fig tree learn the lesson it points: the 28
moment its branch grows tender and puts forth its leaves, you
know that summer is near. Apply this to yourselves: as soon as 29
you witness all these events, you can tell that he is near, yes, at
the door! I assure you, this generation will not pass away till all 30
these events have set in. Earth and heaven will fail; my words will 31
never fail.

REMAIN AWAKE!

"But regarding that day or hour no one knows, not even the 32
angels in heaven, nor yet the Son, but only the Father. Look out, 33

13:25. *the foundations of the universe will rock:* seems better suited to the
context than "the heavenly bodies will wander from their course."

34 be wide awake! You do not know when the moment arrives. It is as
when a man goes abroad: on leaving his house, he gives his servants
their authority, assigning to each his special task, but he directs the
35 doorkeeper, in particular, to keep awake. Remain awake, therefore;
for you do not know when the master of the house returns, whether
late in the evening or about midnight, whether at cockcrow or in
36 the small hours of the day. Otherwise, he returns unexpectedly
37 and finds you sleeping. What I say to you, I mean for all. Remain
awake!"

CHAPTER 14

THE WOMAN WITH THE ALABASTER FLASK

1   It was now two days before the Passover or the feast of the
Unleavened Bread. The high priests and the Scribes were looking
for ways and means of arresting him and putting him to death by
2   stealth; "but not during the festival," they said; "or a riot may
break out among the people."

3   One day he was in the home of Simon the leper at Bethany.
While he reclined at table, a woman with an alabaster flask of pure
and very costly nard perfume entered the room. She broke the
4   alabaster flask and emptied it over his head. Now some were
indignantly saying to one another: "What good is the waste of
5   this perfume? Why, this perfume could have been sold for upwards
of three hundred denarii and the money given to the poor!" So
6   they gave way to bitter feelings toward her. But Jesus said: "Let
her have her way. Why do you molest her? She has given beautiful
7   expression of her devotion to me. After all, you always have the
8   poor with you, but you will not always have me. She did what she
could: by anointing my body she embalmed it just in time!
9   I assure you, wherever the gospel is preached, in any part of the
world, what this woman has just done will likewise be proclaimed to
perpetuate her memory."

JUDAS ISCARIOT, THE TRAITOR

10 Then Judas Iscariot, one of the Twelve, went to meet the
11 high priests and arrange for betraying him to them. They were

132

delighted to hear it and agreed to give him money; and he looked
for a convenient opportunity to betray him.

PREPARING THE PASCHAL LAMB

On the first day of the feast of the Unleavened Bread, when   12
it was customary to sacrifice the paschal lamb, his disciples said to
him: "Where do you want us to go and get things ready for you
to eat the paschal supper?" So he sent two of his disciples with   13
these instructions: "Go into the city and you will meet a man
carrying a pitcher of water; follow him, and, where he enters, say   14
to the owner of the house: 'The Rabbi says: Where is my dining
room, where I may eat the paschal supper with my disciples?'
He will then show you a room upstairs, spacious, furnished, and   15
ready for use; and there get things ready for us." The disciples went   16
and came into the city, and when they found things as he had
told them, they prepared the paschal supper.

JESUS FORETELLS THE BETRAYAL

When evening came, he arrived with the Twelve.   17
While they reclined at table and were still eating, Jesus said: "I   18
frankly tell you, one of you will betray me — one who is eating
with me." In their distress, they set about inquiring of him, one   19
by one: "Not I, is it?" and again, "Not I, is it?" He replied: "One   20
of the Twelve, one who dips his hand into the same bowl with me.
The Son of Man departs, indeed, just as the Scripture says about   21
him; but perdition awaits that man who is instrumental in betraying
the Son of Man! It would be better for that man had he never
been born."

THE CONSECRATION

Before supper was over, he took bread into his hands and, after   22
saying grace, broke it into portions, which he gave them with the
words: "Take it! This is my Body." He also took a cup and, after   23
saying grace, passed it on to them and everyone drank of it. He   24
said to them: "This is my covenant-blood, which is about to be
shed for the sake of many. I tell you truly, I shall never again   25

14:18. *they reclined at table:* the ancients did not "sit" at table, but reclined,
leaning on the left elbow, on couches ranged around the table. See. Jn. 13:33
and 21:10.

drink of the product of the vine till that day when I drink new wine in the kingdom of God."

26 After chanting the hymn of thanks, they set out for the Mount
27 of Olives. Then Jesus said to them: "You will, everyone of you, be shaken in your faith; for the Scripture says: 'I will strike the shep-
28 herd, and the sheep will be scattered.' However, when I am risen from the dead, I will go to Galilee to await you there."

PETER FOREWARNED OF HIS DENIAL

29 Then Peter said to him: "Even if all the rest are shaken in
30 their faith, I shall not be shaken in mine!" "Yes," Jesus said to him, "I have to be plain with you: today, this very night, before a cock
31 crows twice, you will disown me three times." But he kept protesting beyond all bounds: "If I have to die with you, I shall not disown you!" All the rest spoke in the same way.

GETHSEMANI

32 They now came to a place called Gethsemani. "Rest here," he
33 said to his disciples, "till I finish praying." Then, taking Peter, James, and John with him, he gave way to terror and weariness,
34 and said to them: "I am plunged in sorrow, enough to break my
35 heart! Stay here and keep awake." He then went a short distance forward, threw himself on the ground, and prayed that, if it were
36 possible, he might be spared the ordeal. He said: "Abba, Father, you can do all things! Spare me this cup! No, not what I will, but what you will!"
37 He then came back and found them sleeping. "Simon," he said to Peter, "are you sleeping? Were you not able to stay awake
38 one hour? Keep awake and pray, all of you, that you may not succumb to temptation. The spirit is willing, but the flesh is weak."
39 Again he went away and prayed, using the same words.
40 On returning, he again found them sleeping. Their eyes had been yielding to drowsiness; and they were at a loss what to say
41 to him. When he returned the third time, he said to them: "So you continue to sleep and rest! It is enough. The hour has struck. Look, the Son of Man is being betrayed into the hands of sinful
42 men! Rise; let us go. Look, my betrayer is close at hand."

14:27. Zach. 13:7.

THE BETRAYAL

There was no delay. He was still speaking when Judas, one of 43
the Twelve, came upon the scene, accompanied by a numerous
throng armed with swords and clubs — emissaries of the high priests,
Scribes, and elders. Now, his betrayer had prearranged with them 44
a signal. "The one I kiss," he had said, "that is he. Arrest him,
and lead him away — carefully." When he arrived, therefore, he 45
went straight up to him and said: "Rabbi!" and kissed him affectionately. Then the men laid their hands on him and arrested him. 46
But someone of the bystanders drew his sword and, striking the 47
high priest's servant, cut off his ear.

Jesus then remonstrated with the crowd: "As though to capture 48
a bandit, you came out armed with swords and clubs to arrest me!
Day after day I was with you, teaching in the temple: yet you did 49
not arrest me! But then, let the Scriptures be fulfilled."

Now all turned their backs on him and took to flight. 50
A lad was following him with a linen sheet on his bare body; 51
but when they tried to arrest him, he let go the sheet and ran away, 52
stripped.

They led Jesus before the high priest, and all the high priests, 53
the elders, and the Scribes assembled. Peter, meanwhile, had been 54
following him at a distance all the way into the palace of the high
priest, where he loitered among the guards, warming himself in the
glow of the fire.

THE CONDEMNATION OF JESUS

Now the high priests — in fact, the Supreme Council as a 55
body — were looking for testimony unfavorable to Jesus in order to
have him put to death; but they did not find any. Many, it is true, 56
had testified falsely against him, but their testimony did not agree.
Finally, some stood up and, falsely testifying against him, declared, 57
respectively: "We ourselves have heard him say: 'I can tear down 58
this sanctuary made by the hands of men,' and, 'Within three
days, I can build up another not made by the hands of men.'"
And thus, again, their testimony did not agree! 59

Then the high priest rose in full view and asked Jesus: "Have 60
you nothing to say in your own defense? What about the evidence
these men are furnishing against you?" But he remained silent, 61

and said nothing in his own defense. Again the high priests asked
62 him: "Are you the Messias, the Son of the Ever Blessed?" "I am,"
replied Jesus; "moreover, you are going to see the Son of Man
enthroned at the right hand of the Almighty and coming wrapt in
the clouds of the sky."

63   The high priest tore his garments and said: "What further need
64 have we of witnesses? You heard the blasphemy! What is your ver-
65 dict?" They all voted him liable to the penalty of death. And now
some made free to spit on him and blindfold him and slap him
in the face and say to him: "Play the prophet!" Even the guards
struck him with the open hand.

PETER DENIES CHRIST

66   While Peter was in the courtyard below, one of the high priest's
67 servant girls came and, catching sight of Peter, who was warming
himself, looked straight at him and said: "You were with Jesus the
68 Nazarene." But he denied it. "I do not in the least understand
what you mean," he said. He then went out into the gateway, and a
69 cock crowed. There the servant girl noticed him and, in turn,
made herself busy saying to the bystanders: "This man is one of
70 them!" But he again denied it. After a little while the bystanders
for their part said to Peter: "You are certainly one of them; why,
71 you are a Galilean!" Then he burst out cursing and swearing: "I
72 have nothing to do with this man you are talking about." And
immediately, now for the second time, a cock crowed. Then Peter
recalled the prediction — how Jesus had said to him: "Before a
cock crows twice, you will disown me three times." And he broke
out into sobs and tears.

CHAPTER 15

CHRIST CONDEMNED TO SCOURGING AND CRUCIFIXION

1   Very early in the morning, the high priests along with the
elders and Scribes — that is, the Supreme Council as a body —
prepared a resolution and, after ordering Jesus bound, led him away
2 to hand him over to Pilate. Pilate questioned him: "You are the
3 King of the Jews?" He answered: "I am, as you say." When the

---

14:69. *servant girl*: a different person from the one mentioned in verse 66.

high priests were urgent in accusing him, Pilate questioned him 4
again: "Have you nothing to say in your own defense? Listen to all
the charges they bring against you!" But Jesus said nothing further 5
in his own defense, so that Pilate was surprised.

Now at the festival he was wont to humor them and release one 6
prisoner — the one they petitioned for; and it so happened that the 7
man called Barabbas was in prison with his fellow rioters who had
committed murder during the riot. So, when the multitude came up 8
and set about petitioning him to comply with their custom, Pilate 9
answered their request by saying: "Do you want me to release as
your choice the King of the Jews?" He understood, of course, that 10
it was from sheer malice that the high priests had handed him
over. But the high priests had stirred up the mob to demand the 11
release of Barabbas as their choice. So, when Pilate again, in answer 12
to their request, said to them: "What, then, do you want me to do
with him whom you call the King of the Jews?" they shouted back: 13
"Crucify him!" But Pilate said to them: "Why, what wrong has 14
he done?" Then they shouted all the more: "Crucify him!" Finally, 15
Pilate, desiring to satisfy the mob, released Barabbas as their choice,
and had Jesus turned over for a scourging preliminary to crucifixion.

THE PURPLE CLOAK AND CROWN OF THORNS

The soldiers then led him away into the interior of the palace, 16
that is, the praetorium, and called together the entire cohort.
They clothed him in a purple cloak, and put on him a plaited 17
crown of thorns. Then they proceeded to salute him: "Long live 18
the King of the Jews!" They also struck his head with a reed, and 19
spat on him, and paid him homage on bended knees. When they 20
had done making sport of him, they stripped him of the scarlet
cloak and dressed him in his own clothes. Then they led him out
to be crucified.

THE CRUCIFIXION AND DEATH OF CHRIST

They compelled a certain Simon of Cyrene, the father of 21
Alexander and Rufus, who was passing by on his return from the
country to carry his cross. They led him to a place called Golgotha, 22
which means "Skull's Mound." Here they offered him drugged 23
wine; but he did not take it. Then they crucified him. His clothes 24

they divided among them by drawing lots for them, to see what each one was to get.

25 It was nine in the morning when they crucified him.
26 There was also the usual inscription stating his guilt: "The King
27 of the Jews." Together with him they crucified two rebels, one at his
28 right, the other at his left. Thus the Scripture was fulfilled which says: "He was classed with lawless men."

29 Meanwhile the passers-by kept insulting him. They shook their heads and said: "Bah! You are the one that can pull down the
30 sanctuary and build it up in three days!" "Save yourself and come
31 down from the cross!" The high priests joined the Scribes and said in the same taunting manner to one another: "He saved others!
32 He cannot save himself!" "Let the Messias, the king of the Jews, come down from the cross this instant: we want to see and believe!" And they who were crucified with him, reviled him.

33 About noon darkness fell upon the whole land and lasted till
34 three o'clock. At three o'clock Jesus cried out with a strong voice: "Eloi, Eloi, lama sabachthani," which means: "My God, my God, why do you abandon me?"

35 Some of the bystanders who heard it, said: "Listen, he is calling
36 for Elias." Then someone ran and soaked a sponge in vinegar and, putting it round a reed, offered him a drink, saying: "Let us see
37 whether Elias is coming to take him down." Jesus uttered a loud cry and expired.

38 Then the curtain of the sanctuary was torn in two from top
39 to bottom. When the centurion, who stood by facing him, saw that he had expired under such circumstances, he said: "This man was really the Son of God."

15:25. *nine in the morning:* this seems to contradict John's statement in 19:14: "the time was about noon." The discrepancy may, perhaps, be explained by assuming that Mark and John followed different ways of counting the hours of the day.

15:28. This verse is not found in all manuscripts. The prophecy of Isaias (53:12) was fulfilled at the trial and at the death of Jesus. He was rated lower than the murderer Barabbas and executed between two bandits.

15:35. *he is calling for Elias:* probably a deliberate misunderstanding of the words of our Lord and therefore a piece of cruel mockery.

15:36. *someone:* probably one of the soldiers. Since it was their task to carry out the official sentence of crucifixion, it is not likely that they allowed a civilian to add to the pains of the victim. See the parallel accounts in Mt. 27:27–31 and Jn. 19:29.

Also women were present, looking on from a distance. Among 40
them were Mary Magdalen, Mary the mother of James the Younger
and of Joseph, and Salome. They had accompanied him and minis- 41
tered to his wants while he was still in Galilee. Besides these, there
were many others who had come up with him to Jerusalem.

JOSEPH OF ARIMATHIA RECEIVES THE BODY OF JESUS

It was now late in the afternoon. And because it was the Day 42
of Preparation, that is, the eve of the Sabbath, Joseph of Arimathia, 43
a councilor in good standing, who was himself waiting for the
kingdom of God, came and made bold to interview Pilate in order
to petition for the body of Jesus. Pilate was surprised that he was 44
already dead. So he sent for the centurion and asked him whether
he was already dead. On learning the facts from the centurion, he 45
made Joseph a gift of the body. Joseph took him down and wrapped 46
him in the linen shroud which he had bought, laid him in a tomb
which had been cut out of the rock, and rolled a slab of stone
against the entrance of the tomb. Mary Magdalen and Mary, the 47
mother of Joseph, carefully noted where he was laid to rest.

CHAPTER 16

HE IS RISEN; HE IS NOT HERE

When the Sabbath had passed, Mary Magdalen, Mary the mother 1
of James, and Salome bought spices in order to go and anoint him.
At a very early hour in the morning on the first day of the week, 2
they set out for the tomb and arrived at sunrise. Now, they had been 3
saying to one another: "Who will roll away for us the slab of stone
at the entrance of the tomb?" when, straining their eyes, they saw 4
that the stone had already been rolled away. It certainly was very
large.

On entering the tomb, they saw a young man seated at the 5
right, dressed in a white robe; and they were frightened. But he said 6
to them: "Do not be frightened. You are looking for Jesus the
Nazarene, the Crucified. He is risen; he is not here. Look, here
is the place where they laid him to rest. Go now, and say to his 7
disciples, in particular to Peter: 'He is going to Galilee to await

you there; there you are going to see him, just as he has told you.' "
8 They hurriedly left the tomb, for they were panic-stricken; and they
did not say a word to anyone; they were so afraid.
9   After he had risen early on the first day of the week, he appeared
first to Mary Magdalen, out of whom he had driven seven demons.
10 She went to bring the news to those who had been in his com-
11 pany and were now sorrowing and lamenting. But when they heard
her say that he was alive and had been seen by her, they did not
12 believe it. Later he appeared in disguise to some on the way to a
13 country place. These men, too, returned to bring the news to the
the others; but even they were not believed.
14   Lastly, he appeared directly to the Eleven as they were reclining
at table, and reproved them for their unbelief and hardness of heart,
because they had not believed those who had seen him risen from
15 the dead. He also said to them:
        "Go into the whole world
         and preach the gospel to all creation.
16   He that believes and is baptized
            will be saved;
            he that does not believe
            will be condemned.
17   And in the way of proofs of their claims,
            the following will accompany those who believe:
            in my name they will drive out demons;
            they will speak in new tongues;
18   they will take up serpents in their hands,
            and if they drink something deadly,
            it will not hurt them;
            they will lay their hands on the sick,
            and these will recover."
19   And so the Lord Jesus, after discoursing to them, was borne
aloft to heaven and took his seat at the right hand of God.
20 But they went forth and preached everywhere, the Lord assisting
them in their work and confirming their message by the proofs
of their claims that followed them.

16:9–20. These verses are not found in all manuscripts. See the Introduction,
p. 95.

SAINT LUKE

Regarding the person of St. Luke we have some scanty, but authentic, information. St. Paul, writing to the Colossians (4:10–11) from his captivity in Rome, mentions several fellow workers who were of Jewish descent, and then separates from this group, besides Epaphras and Demas, "Luke the beloved physician" (4:13–14). We are at a loss to know how the two men became so intimately associated with each other. The Church historian Eusebius writes that St. Luke was of Antioch, the capital of Syria, and from the Acts (11:19 ff.) we learn that St. Peter, St. Paul, and St. Barnabas established there a flourishing community. With these facts for a clue, it has been surmised that St. Paul, of whose mysterious illness we hear in 1 Cor. 1:8; 2 Cor. 12:7; and Gal. 4:13, one day consulted Luke the physician, and that the latter, impressed by the high idealism and overpowering personality of his patient, volunteered to accompany him on his journeys in a professional capacity. Where and when he became a Christian is not known. We find St. Luke in the company of the Apostle on his second missionary journey at Troas, where the latter, accepting a dream as a divine voice, crossed over to Macedonia; "As soon as he had the vision, we were eager to sail for Macedonia" (Acts 16:10). This is the first of the so-called "We-accounts" in the Acts (16:10–17; 20:5–15; 21:1–18; 27:1–28, 16). St. Luke followed St. Paul to Caesarea and Jerusalem, and finally to Rome. There are no certain data regarding his later career. Achaea and Boeotia are sometimes mentioned as his field of labor. According to St. Gregory Nazianzen, he died a martyr for the faith. His feast is kept on October 18.

In narrating the public ministry of Jesus, St. Luke covers in all essentials the accounts given by the other Synoptics. But there are two priceless additions which are St. Luke's peculiar contribution:

141

first, the brief, but classic, introduction (1:1-4); second, the beautiful story of the infancy of Jesus (1:5-2:52). The first great section of the Gospel (4:14-9:50), preceded by a brief preparatory narrative (3:1-4:14), describes the ministry in Galilee. There follows the account of Christ's work on his journey to Jerusalem (9:51-18:30). A third section sketches Christ's activity in Judea and Jerusalem (18:31-21:38). The story of the Passion, the Death, and the Resurrection closes the Gospel (22:1-24:53).

The tradition concerning this Gospel goes back to several old documents, such as the Old Prologue and the Muratorian Fragment, both of which state that St. Luke wrote his Gospel as a disciple and companion of St. Paul. Statements to the same effect are made by St. Irenaeus, Tertullian, and Origen. Eusebius and St. Jerome say that when St. Paul speaks of "my Gospel" (2 Tim. 2:8) he means the Third Gospel. The same is true, according to St. John Chrysostom, of the reference in 2 Cor. 8:18. Be this as it may, there is a strong Pauline note recognizable in St. Luke's account. St. Luke and St. Paul agree in recounting the institution of the Eucharist (Lk. 22:19 ff. and 1 Cor. 11:24 ff.). Both mention the Lord's apparition to St. Peter (Lk. 24:34 and 1 Cor. 15:5). Above all, it is the idea of the universality of the Gospel that impressed both writers. Compare Rom. 1:16 and especially Chapters 9 to 11. Echoes of this idea are numerous in St. Luke. We may mention the hymn of the angels (2:14), the prayer of old Simeon (2:31-32), the Baptist's sermon to the Jews (3:7-8), as contrasted with that to the tax collectors and pagan officials (3:12 ff.). The genealogy of Jesus is traced to Adam and God (3:23 ff.). The words "You will catch men" (5:10) hint that the Gentiles will be called. The Lucan report of the Sermon on the Mount (6:17 ff.) omits details of direct interest only to Jews, in contrast to St. Matthew's account (5 to 7). The heathen centurion is praised for his faith (7:3-9). The Gerasene demoniac is sent home to prepare the ground for the later preaching of the Gospel in his country (8:39). The final rejection of Israel is predicted in the parable of the dried-up fig tree (13:6-9). The kingdom of God shall be open to men from all parts of the world (13:29). The Gospel shall reach all nations (24:27).

The prologue of the Gospel according to St. Luke raises the

question how it was possible for him to gather so much authentic material from the original eyewitnesses. To account for this fact does not seem difficult if we remember that as a companion of St. Paul he was in a position to meet many persons acquainted with the life and teaching of Christ "from the beginning." St. Paul visited Caesarea, Antioch, and especially Jerusalem. At the time of his visit to the Jewish capital, many of the leading men of the early Church were still gathered about the temple, as James, the "brother" of the Lord, and other witnesses of the Resurrection (1 Cor. 15:6–7). It is possible, also, that he obtained reliable data from some of the pious women who had accompanied Jesus from Galilee, and especially from St. John. We may surmise that it was through the last-named channels, the pious women and St. John, "who took Mary into his own home" (Jn. 19:27), that much of the more intimate information revealed in the story of the infancy of Jesus, came into his possession. It has also been thought that the Gospels according to St. Matthew and St. Mark may have been among the "many" accounts available to St. Luke. The latter's place in the Synoptic Problem has given rise to interesting, though as yet inconclusive, speculation.

We are likewise left to more or less probable conjectures in discussing the date as well as the place of composition. In regard to the former, it has been argued that, since the first captivity of St. Paul ended in 63, and the Acts was written after the Gospel (Acts 1:1), the latter was probably composed within the period from 60 to 63. Nor does tradition permit any certain conclusion regarding the place of composition. Among the cities mentioned as the birthplace of this Gospel, Caesarea seems to have the greatest probability in its favor.

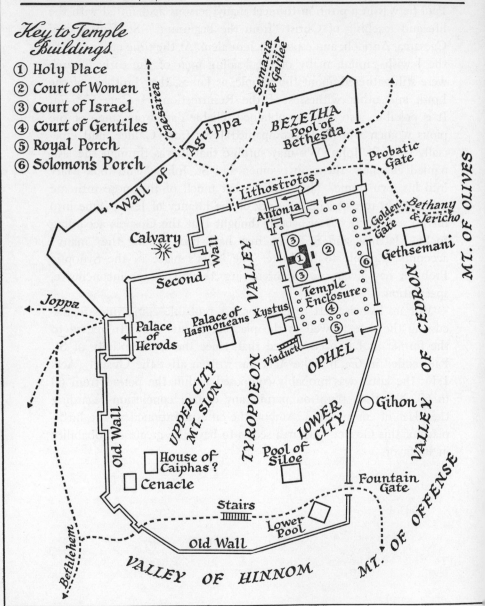

JERUSALEM ~ AT THE TIME OF CHRIST

Key to Temple Buildings
1. Holy Place
2. Court of Women
3. Court of Israel
4. Court of Gentiles
5. Royal Porch
6. Solomon's Porch

Wall of Agrippa

to Caesarea

Samaria & Galilee

BEZETHA
Pool of Bethesda

Probatic Gate

Golden Gate

Bethany & Jericho

Gethsemani

MT. OF OLIVES

Lithostrotos
Antonia

Calvary

Second Wall

Joppa

Palace of Herods

Palace of Hasmoneans

Xystus

Temple Enclosure

Viaduct

OPHEL

Gihon

VALLEY OF CEDRON

UPPER CITY
MT. SION

TYROPOEON VALLEY

LOWER CITY

House of Caiphas?
Cenacle

Pool of Siloe

Old Wall

Fountain Gate

Stairs

Lower Pool

Old Wall

Bethlehem

VALLEY OF HINNOM

MT. OF OFFENSE

THE HOLY GOSPEL
OF JESUS CHRIST
ACCORDING TO

ST. LUKE

CHAPTER 1

PROLOGUE

Many an attempt has been made before now to present the 1
drama of events that have come to a climax among us, so as to 2
accord with the tradition which the original eyewitnesses and ministers of the gospel have handed down to us. And, therefore, 3
Theophilus, I, too, after accurately tracing the whole movement
to its origin, have decided to write a consecutive account for your
excellency. It is my aim that you should appreciate the certainty 4
on which the oral instruction you have already received is grounded.

ZACHARY AND ELIZABETH

In the days of Herod, king of the Jewish land, there lived a 5
priest by the name of Zachary, a member of the weekly class of
Abia. His wife, whose name was Elizabeth, was a descendant of
Aaron. Both were conscientious in serving God, making the Lord's 6
commandments and ordinances their sole rule of life. In this they

---

1:2. St. Luke is careful to state the authorities for his narrative: the living
stream of original eyewitnesses and ministers of the Gospel. Among the many
writers of previous accounts we should, perhaps, include St. Mark. Compare the
"testimony" in Jn. 21:24. For the word *gospel*, see the note on Mk. 1:1.
   1:3. Theophilus was evidently a man of rank. It is not known whether he was
a Christian or a pagan. His previous instruction was either too summary to
satisfy him or else based on misinformation or mere rumors.
   1:1–4. This introduction, classic in spirit and diction, shows the Greek scholar.
The language of the rest of this account is heavily indebted to reports from
Jewish sources.
   1:5. David divided the entire priesthood into twenty-four groups, each of
which served in the temple for one week. Lot was cast to distribute the various
priestly functions among the members of each class.

7 were above reproach. But they had no child, for Elizabeth was
barren; both, moreover, were advanced in years.

THE ANGEL PREDICTS THE BIRTH OF JOHN

8 In the course of his priestly service, while his weekly class was
9 serving its turn in the presence of God, it fell to his lot one day,
according to a custom observed by the priests, to enter the sanctuary
10 of the Lord and burn the incense. The vast throng of worshipers
11 was praying in the outer court during incense time. Suddenly, there
appeared to him an angel of the Lord, standing at the right of the
12 altar of incense. Zachary was startled at the sight, and a feeling of
13 awe came over him. But the angel said to him: "Do not be afraid,
Zachary. Your petition has been granted: your wife Elizabeth shall
14 bear you a son, and you are to name him John. Your heart will
overflow with joy, and multitudes of people will rejoice in his birth.
15 He will be a great man in the eyes of the Lord: wine and liquors
he will not drink; the Holy Spirit will take full possession of him
16 while yet in his mother's womb; he will rally many of the children
17 of Israel round the Lord their God: he will be his forerunner,
endowed with the spirit and might of Elias; he will reconcile
fathers and sons; he will teach the rebellious the wisdom of the
saints. He is to prepare for the Lord a people perfect in every way."

18 "How can I be sure that this is so?" Zachary said to the angel;
19 "I am an old man, and my wife is far advanced in years." In answer
the angel said to him: "I am Gabriel, and my place is in the
presence of God; I have been sent to speak to you and bring you
20 this good news. Now mark: because you did not believe my
message, which must come true in its appointed time, you shall
be silent and unable to speak till the day when these events take
place."

21 Meanwhile the people were waiting for Zachary, and wondering
22 at his delay in the sanctuary. When he came out, he was unable to
speak to them, and they understood that he had seen a vision in

1:10. The altar of incense was in the sanctuary, or holy place, the first of
the two rooms in the temple building. The officiating priest could not be seen
by the people, who prayed in the outer court.

1:15. Gabriel predicted four marks of "greatness" in John's character: continual asceticism, interior holiness, success in securing conversions and in preparing
apt pupils for the Messias (Jn. 1:35 ff.). See the notes on 7:24 ff. and on
Mt. 11:11.

the sanctuary. All he could do was to nod to them; and he remained
speechless.

ELIZABETH CONCEIVES

When finally the term of his liturgical service was over, he 23
departed for his home. Shortly afterwards, his wife Elizabeth con- 24
ceived. For five months she lived in deep retirement, constantly
repeating: "How good the Lord was to me that day! How graciously 25
he effaced the reproach I had incurred in the eyes of the world!"

THE ANGEL GABRIEL APPEARS TO MARY

In the course of the sixth month, the angel Gabriel came with 26
a message from God to a town in Galilee called Nazareth. He was 27
to speak to a virgin espoused to a man named Joseph, a descendant
of David. The name of the virgin was Mary. On coming into her 28
presence, he said: "Rejoice, child of grace! The Lord is your

---

1:25. Among the Jews barrenness was considered a reproach.

1:28. The time-honored rendering "full of grace," supported by the Vulgate
and adopted by the Latin Fathers and the ancient Syriac and Arabic versions,
testifies to the high esteem in which the Church has held Mary from the
beginning. Christians feel that, greeted by a heavenly messenger and asked to
consent to become the Mother of the Savior, she must have been uniquely
pleasing to God and possessed of an exceptionally abundant measure of "grace."
Even so her "fullness" was only relative, as that of other saintly men and women
(e.g., John the Baptist, 1:15; Elizabeth, 1:41; Zachary, 1:67; Stephen, Acts 6:8).
It is also evident that her holiness was based on the (anticipated) merits of
Christ. To honor Mary is to honor our Lord.

But since in the New Testament the word "grace" at times means, not that
inward endowment of the soul which we call "sanctifying grace," but a task,
office, function, position, etc., imposed on men by the grace of God for some
important work in the Church, and since it is not certain in which of the two
senses the word was understood by the angel, it seems advisable in the translation to choose an expression that leaves this question undecided. The Challoner
version "full of grace" has, therefore, been avoided. But whatever translation is
adopted, the word "grace" itself must be retained.

However we interpret the Greek word, it means "a special grace has been
conferred on you" or "you are the recipient of a very special grace." Perhaps,
however, the joyful as well as solemn moment when this announcement was
made to Mary requires something less plain than this. Now we remember that
Christ, in an important statement (Acts 9:15), speaks of St. Paul as "a chosen
instrument of mine"; and so here, too, we may suppose the angel to greet Mary
as "(God's) chosen instrument." Again, the liturgy has no hesitation in addressing
Mary as "spiritual vessel," "vessel of honor," "singular vessel of devotion," which
reminds us of the Challoner version in Acts 9:15: "vessel of election." With
these precedents in mind, we may venture to render the angel's word "singular
vessel of grace." The renderings just suggested express the Greek word perfectly

147

29 helper! You are blessed beyond all women!" But she was profoundly disturbed by the address, and debated within herself what
30 this greeting might mean. So then the angel said to her: "Do not
31 .tremble, Mary! You have found favor in the eyes of God. Behold: you are to be a mother, and to bear a son, and to call him Jesus!
32 He will be great: 'Son of the Most High' will be his title, and the Lord God will give to him the throne of his father David. He will
33 be king over the house of Jacob forever, and to his kingship there will be no end!"
34 Then Mary replied to the angel: "How will this be, since I remain a virgin?"

MARY GIVES HER CONSENT

35 In explanation the angel said to her: "The Holy Spirit will come upon you, and the power of the Most High will overshadow you. For this reason the child to be born will be acclaimed 'Holy'
36 and 'Son of God.' Note, moreover: your relative Elizabeth, in her old age, has also conceived a son and is now in her sixth month —
37 she who was called 'the barren'! Nothing indeed is impossible with
38 God." Then Mary said: "Regard me as the humble servant of the Lord. May all that you have said be fulfilled in me!" With that, the angel left her.

---

and do not seem unsuited to the solemn occasion. Thus, too, we preserve the neutrality of the word "grace." In the Church's mind, at any rate, Mary's inward grace and her exalted position in the economy of salvation go hand in hand. The rendering *child of grace* was here chosen because it seems to express the reverent affection with which the angel must have addressed Mary.

1:32–35. Verses 32 and 33 describe the exalted dignity of the Messias; verse 35 reveals his divine nature. It is impossible to believe that Mary did not then and there understand that her son would be divine.

1:34. The Greek is capable of a fuller meaning than appears in the Vulgate. Mary may have recalled the prophecy of Isaias (see Mt. 1:23) and, enlightened by the Holy Spirit, understood that, however the Jews at the time interpreted it, it was verified in her own person: "A virgin shall be pregnant." If so, it was clear to her that the proposed motherhood would not interfere with her cherished virginity. The Greek lends support to this view, for the negative present indicative often expresses resolve. Hence her exclamation of glad surprise (Lagrange). Her words may, however, be read as a question, inquiring what, under the circumstances, she was expected to do. (See *The American Ecclesiastical Review*, Vol. 114, p. 161 ff.)

1:35. *In explanation:* see the note on Mk. 3:33.

MARY VISITS ELIZABETH

In those days Mary set out in haste to go into the mountainous 39
region to visit a town of Juda. There she entered the home of 40
Zachary and greeted Elizabeth. The moment Elizabeth heard the 41
greeting of Mary, the babe in her womb leaped, and Elizabeth,
inspired by the Holy Spirit, exclaimed in a ringing voice: "Blessed 42
are you beyond all women! And blessed is the fruit of your womb!
How privileged am I to have the mother of my Lord come to 43
visit me! Hear me now: as the sound of your greeting fell upon my 44
ears, the babe in my womb leaped for joy! Happy is she who be- 45
lieved that what was told her on behalf of the Lord would be
fulfilled!"

And Mary said: 46

"My soul extols the Lord;
and my spirit leaps for joy in God my Savior.   47
How graciously he looked upon his lowly maid!   48
Oh, behold, from this hour onward
age after age will call me blessed!
How sublime is what he has done for me —   49
the Mighty One, whose name is 'Holy'!
From age to age he visits those   50
who worship him in reverence.
His arm achieves the mastery: 51
he routs the haughty and proud of heart;
he puts down princes from their thrones,   52
and exalts the lowly;
he fills the hungry with blessings,   53
and sends away the rich with empty hands.
he has taken by the hand his servant Israel,   54
and mercifully kept his faith
— as he had promised our fathers —   55
with Abraham and his posterity
forever and evermore."

Mary was her guest for about three months, and then departed 56
for her home.

1:46. The *Magnificat* is a lyrical outpouring of the first rank. Mary rejoices
in her blessedness and is humbly appreciative of God's signal favor bestowed
on the people and herself.

149

ELIZABETH BEARS A SON: "JOHN IS HIS NAME!"

57   At last the time came for Elizabeth to be delivered, and she
58 gave birth to a son. Word reached her neighbors and kinsfolk that
the Lord had given her a signal proof of his mercy, and they con-
59 gratulated her. The following happened on the eighth day when
they had come together to circumcise the child. They were for
60 calling him Zachary after his father; but his mother protested.
61 "Indeed, no!" she said. "His name will be John!" "But," they said
to her, "there is no one among your relatives who bears that name!"
62 Finally they motioned to his father to indicate what he wished the
63 child to be called. And asking for a writing tablet, he wrote the
64 words: "John is his name!" Everyone was astonished. And there and
then his lips were unsealed and his tongue untied, and he spoke
65 in praise of God. A sense of awe came over all their neighbors, and
throughout the mountainous region of Judea these events were the
66 sole topic of conversation. All those who heard the account were
deeply impressed by it. "Surely," they commented, "this child is
destined to be a great man!" And really, the hand of the Lord was
with him.

PROPHETIC WORDS OF ZACHARY, THE FATHER OF JOHN

67   Zachary, his father, was inspired by the Holy Spirit; and spoke
these prophetic words:
68   "Blessed be the Lord, the God of Israel!
He has visited his people
and brought about its redemption.
69   He has raised for us a stronghold of salvation
in the house of David his servant,
70   and redeemed the promise he had made
through the mouth of his holy prophets of old —
71   to grant salvation from our foes
and from the hand of all that hate us;

1:68. The *Benedictus*, Zachary's hymn of thanks, has a truly priestly ring.
It echoes the ancient prophecies about the coming reign of justice and holiness,
and announces the beginning of their fulfillment.
1:69. *a stronghold* (literally, *a horn*) *of salvation*: the horn was a common
symbol of power and strength.

to deal in mercy with our fathers   72
and be mindful of his holy covenant,
of the oath he had sworn to our father Abraham,   73
that he would enable us —
rescued from the clutches of our foes —   74
to worship him without fear,
in holiness and observance of the Law,   75
in his presence, all our days.
And you, my little one, will be hailed   76
'Prophet of the Most High';
for the Lord's precursor you will be
to prepare his ways;
you are to impart to his people   77
knowledge of salvation
through forgiveness of their sins.
Thanks be to the merciful heart of our God!   78
A dawning Light from on high will visit us
to shine upon those who sit in darkness   79
and in the shadowland of death,
and guide our feet into the path of peace."

The little child grew strong in body and soul, and lingered in   80
the desert till the day of his installation as a messenger to Israel.

CHAPTER 2

THE BIRTH OF THE CHRIST CHILD

Long before that day a decree had been issued by order of   1
Caesar Augustus that a census of the whole world should be taken.
This census was the first to take place while Cyrinus was in charge   2
of Syria.

Accordingly, the people went, each to the city of his ancestor,   3
to be registered; and so Joseph, too, being a member of the house   4
and family of David, went up from the town of Nazareth in Galilee
to David's town in Judea, called Bethlehem, in order to be registered.   5
He was accompanied by his espoused wife Mary, who was with child.
In the course of their stay there, the time came for her delivery;   6

7 and she gave birth to her first-born son. She wrapped him in
swaddling clothes, and laid him in a manger, because there was
no accommodation for them in the lodging.

THE SAVIOR'S BIRTH ANNOUNCED TO SHEPHERDS

8   In the same region shepherds were camping in the open and
9 keeping watch over their flocks by night. Suddenly, an angel of the
Lord stood facing them, and the glory of the Lord shone round
10 about them, so that they were struck with terror. "Do not fear,"
the angel said to them. "Listen: I am bringing you good news of
11 great joy which is in store for the whole nation. A Savior, who is
12 the Lord Messias, was born to you today in David's town! And this
will serve you as a token: you will find an infant wrapped in
13 swaddling clothes and cradled in a manger." All of a sudden, the
angel was joined by a multitude of the heavenly host, praising God
with the strain:
14   "Glory to God in the heavens above,
              and on earth peace to men of good will."
15   When at last the angels had withdrawn from them and returned
to heaven, the shepherds said to one another: "Let us go over to
Bethlehem and find out the truth about this thing the Lord has
16 made known to us." So they set off in haste, and sought out Mary
17 and Joseph and the infant cradled in a manger. And when they saw
them, they made known what had been told them about this little
18 child. All those who heard the account given them by the shepherds
19 expressed surprise, while Mary treasured all these incidents and
20 meditated on them in her heart. At last the shepherds returned,

---

2:7. The text seems to favor the view that, when Mary and Joseph arrived
at Bethlehem, every available room in the "inn" or place of lodging, whether
public or private, was taken. If so, Jesus was born in a stable (indicated by
the presence of a manger), which adjoined the place of lodging. Perhaps, however, Mary and Joseph arrived well ahead of the time of birth and found room,
but, when the hour of her delivery drew near, looked for greater privacy and,
since they did not find it in the inn, retired to one of the numerous grottoes in
some hill nearby.
her first-born Son: among the Jews "every male that opened the womb"
(Exod. 13:2; Num. 8:17) was called "first-born," whether there were other
sons or not. Under the Law, a first-born son had special privileges and special
duties.
2:14. Some manuscripts read "peace, good will among men." men of good
will: men who are the objects of God's good will, God's friends.

glorifying and praising God for everything they had heard and which afterwards was seen to be just as they had been told.

HE WAS NAMED "JESUS" AND PRESENTED TO THE LORD

When seven days had elapsed, it was time for him to be 21 circumcised; and he was named Jesus. It was the name pronounced by the angel before his conception.

When the prescribed days had elapsed, it was time for them 22 to be purified according to the Law of Moses. So they took him up to Jerusalem in order to present him to the Lord; for it was a 23 ruling of the Law of the Lord that "every first-born male child is to be consecrated to the Lord." They were also to sacrifice, accord- 24 ing to the regulation in the Law of the Lord, "a pair of turtle doves or two young pigeons."

THE HYMN OF SIMEON

Just at that time there was a man in Jerusalem by the name of 25 Simeon. He was a devout and conscientious person, longing for the consolation of Israel; and the Holy Spirit was hovering over him. Now it had been revealed to him by the Holy Spirit that he was 26 not to see death before seeing the Lord's Anointed; and so, impelled 27 by the Spirit, he betook himself to the temple. And there, just when the parents had brought in the child Jesus, intending to perform in his behalf the customary rites of the Law, he took him 28 into his arms and spoke this hymn to God:

"Now you may release 29
your bondsman, O Master,
according to your promise,
in peace!
For my eyes have looked upon the salvation 30
which you have prepared 31
for all the nations to behold,
a Light to illumine the Gentiles, 32
a Glory to grace your people Israel."

2:22. *them to be purified*: a somewhat summary expression, combining the purification of the mother with the presentation of the child, or, perhaps, stating that Mary and Joseph discharged the obligation which bound Mary alone.

2:25. *consolation of Israel*: the expression recalls "the redemption of Israel" in verse 38. Compare Jn. 14:16.

33   His father and his mother were wrapt in wonder at what was
34 being said about him. Simeon blessed them, and then said to Mary
his mother:
                  "Alas! This babe is destined
                  to be the downfall no less
                  than the restoration of many in Israel!
                  His very name will provoke contradiction,
35   and your own soul, also,
                  shall be pierced by a sword!
                  And thus the secret thoughts of many a heart
                  shall be laid bare."

THE PROPHETESS ANNA GIVES THANKS TO GOD

36   Also a prophetess named Anna, the daughter of Phanuel, of the
tribe of Aser, was present. This woman was very far advanced in
years. After her girlhood she had lived in wedlock for seven years,
37 and then as a widow for as many as eighty-four years. She never
quit the temple, and worshiped day and night with fasting and
38 prayer. Having come upon the scene that very moment, she
thanked God. She would also speak about him to all who were
waiting for the redemption of Israel.

39   When they had complied with every detail of the Law of the
40 Lord, they returned to their own town Nazareth in Galilee. The
child grew strong in body and soul as his intelligence developed;
and the grace of God rested upon him.

THE CHILD JESUS SEATED AMONG THE RABBIS

41   Year after year his parents went to Jerusalem for the feast of

---

2:34. Jesus was not only "to adorn the people of Israel," but also to occasion
"the downfall of many." Christ is "the parting of the way" (Jn. 9:39).

2:37. for as many as eighty-four years: an alternative rendering would be "up
to her eighty-fourth year."

2:38. about him: the child.

2:40. In Jesus, unimpeded as he was by either natural or acquired defects,
body and soul developed harmoniously. See 2:52. The "grace" of God rested
visibly upon him (as it had on little John: Lk. 1:66). At twelve years of age,
his hearers in the temple were charmed by his "intelligence." Later, the people
of Nazareth were puzzled about his "wisdom." During his childhood, many a
Jewish mother, we may be sure, envied Mary her having a child so healthy, so
pious, so obedient, so intelligent, and so apt at any task assigned him in the
daily routine at Nazareth. St. Luke here records this popular impression. See
also 11:27.

the Passover. And so, too, when he was twelve years old, they went 42
up according to their custom at the time of the feast. After 43
spending there the required number of days, they prepared to return,
but the child Jesus remained behind at Jerusalem, without his
parents knowing about it. Supposing him to be in the caravan, 44
they finished a day's journey, and began to search for him among
their relations and acquaintances. When they did not find him, 45
they retraced their steps to Jerusalem, there to renew their search
for him. It was only on the third day that they discovered him in 46
the temple, seated among the rabbis, now listening to them, now
asking them questions, while all those that heard him were charmed 47
by his intelligence and his answers. They were overjoyed to see him. 48

His mother said to him: "Child, why did you behave toward us
in this way? Oh, our hearts were heavy — your father's and mine —
as we searched for you!"

He said to them: "Why did you search for me? I had to answer 49
my Father's call, and did you not know it?" But they did not grasp 50
the meaning of the reply he made to them. He then went down in 51
their company and came to Nazareth, where he was subject to them.
His mother treasured all these incidents in her memory, and Jesus 52
made steady progress, proportionately to his age, in understanding
and in favor with God and men.

CHAPTER 3

THE SUMMONS TO JOHN THE SON OF ZACHARY

In the fifteenth year of the reign of Emperor Tiberius — when 1
Pontius Pilate was governor of Judea; Herod, tetrarch of Galilee;
Philip, his brother, tetrarch of Iturea and Trachonitis; Lysanias,
tetrarch of Abilene; under the high priests Annas and Caiaphas — 2

2:50. Mary did not yet understand that the time would come when Jesus was
to be completely withdrawn from her parental authority, to devote himself
exclusively to "the business, the affairs, of the Father." The Greek may, however,
mean that he was expected to be "in his Father's house," the temple. His
reply to Mary was enigmatic, inviting her to treasure his words and meditate
on them (see 2:19 and 2:51). A final lesson was imparted to her at the
wedding feast of Cana. (See *The American Ecclesiastical Review*, Vol. 114, p.
81 ff.)

3:1. In A.D. 26.

a summons from God came in the desert to John, the son of Zachary.
3 He appeared in public to preach to the whole region on either side
of the Jordan a baptism which signified a change of heart and looked
4 to forgiveness of sins. For thus it is written in the book of
the sayings of Isaias the prophet:

"A herald's voice rings out in the desert:
    'Make ready the road of the Lord;
    make straight his paths;
5   every hollow must be filled,
    and every mountain and hill brought low;
    what is crooked must be straightened,
    and the rough roads smoothed.
6   And all mankind shall see
        the salvation of God.' "

JOHN'S WORDS TO THE PEOPLE

7   He would, for example, say to the crowds that came out to be
baptized by him: "Brood of vipers! Who advised you to flee before
8 the gathering storm of anger? Well, then, let your conduct be in
keeping with your change of heart. And do not make a point of
saying to yourselves: 'We have Abraham for our father!' I tell
you, God is able to raise children to Abraham out of these stones.
9 Besides, from now on the axe lies ready to strike at the root of the
trees; any tree, therefore, that does not produce sound fruit is cut
down and thrown into fire."
10   When the crowds consulted him, asking: "What, then, are we
11 to do?" he answered them as follows: "He who has two coats
should give one to him that has none; and he who has food should
12 do likewise." Also tax collectors came to be baptized by him.
13 "Rabbi," they said to him, "what are we to do?" "Exact nothing,"
was his answer to them, "in excess of the rate prescribed to you."
14 Also men of the police force consulted with him. "And for our
part," they said, "what are we to do?" He replied: "Browbeat
no one; blackmail no one; and be content with your pay."

3:12. John does not require the tax collectors and other public officials to quit
their jobs, but merely to refrain from sharp practices.

JOHN ANNOUNCES THE MESSIAS

Now the public was in a state of expectation, and everybody 15
was puzzled with regard to John, suspecting he might, perhaps, be
the Messias. So John cleared up all doubts by this statement: "I 16
baptize you with water; but following me is one mightier than I,
and I am not fit to untie the straps of his sandals. He, for his part,
will baptize you with the Holy Spirit, or else with fire. His winnow- 17
ing fan in hand, he will thoroughly clean his threshing floor: the
wheat he will store in his barn, the chaff he will burn in unquenchable fire."

In these and many other ways, then, he would exhort the people, 18
while announcing the Good News. The tetrarch Herod, however, 19
who had been taken to task by him on account of Herodias, his
brother's wife, and, in general, for his whole career of crime,
crowned all by shutting John up in prison. 20

The following happened after the people at large had received 21
baptism and Jesus, too, had been baptized: he was still praying
when the heavens opened and the Holy Spirit descended upon him 22
in bodily shape like a dove; moreover, a voice rang out upon the
air, saying:

"You are my Son, the beloved;
I am well pleased with you."

THE FAMILY TREE OF JESUS IN THE EYES OF THE LAW

Jesus was about thirty years of age when entering on his ministry; 23
he was, in the eyes of the Law, the Son of Joseph, who in turn was
the son of Heli, the son of Matthat, the son of Levi, the son of 24
Melchi, the son of Janne, the son of Joseph, the son of Matthathias, 25
the son of Amos, the son of Naum, the son of Esli, the son of

3:16. *or else with fire:* those who accept the baptism of the Messias will receive
the Holy Spirit; those who reject it will meet with eternal punishment (see verse
17, and Mk. 16:16). The fire may, however, be interpreted as the outpouring
of the Holy Spirit, mentioned in Acts 2:3.

3:23. The current rendering "as was supposed" means, of course, "as was
rightly supposed," the "supposition" being based on the fact that Joseph was
the husband of Mary, which no one doubted; but he was her "husband" only
"in the eyes of the Law." This "legal" fatherhood of Joseph is the first link
in the following genealogy which extends from Jesus to Adam. St. Luke is
writing mainly for Gentile readers, to whom it was of interest to know that
Jesus is the first-born of the whole race, while St. Matthew traces the descent
back to Abraham only. See the note on Mt. 1:1.

26 Nagge, the son of Maath, the son of Matthathias, the son of Semei,
27 the son of Josech, the son of Joda, the son of Joanna, the son of
   Resa, the son of Zorobabel, the son of Salathiel, the son of Nari,
28 the son of Melchi, the son of Addi, the son of Cosam, the son of
29 Elmadam, the son of Her, the son of Jesus, the son of Eliezar, the
30 son of Jorim, the son of Matthat, the son of Levi, the son of Simeon,
   the son of Judas, the son of Joseph, the son of Jona, the son of
31 Eliachim, the son of Melea, the son of Menna, the son of Matthata,
32 the son of Nathan, the son of David, the son of Jesse, the son of
33 Obed, the son of Booz, the son of Salmon, the son of Naasson, the
   son of Aminadab, the son of Aram, the son of Esron, the son of
34 Phares, the son of Judas, the son of Jacob, the son of Isaac, the
35 son of Abraham, the son of Thare, the son of Nachor, the son of
   Sarug, the son of Ragau, the son of Phalec, the son of Heber, the
36 son of Sale, the son of Cainan, the son of Arphaxad, the son of Sem,
37 the son of Noe, the son of Lamech, the son of Mathusale, the son
   of Enoch, the son of Jared, the son of Malaleel, the son of Cainan,
38 the son of Enos, the son of Seth, the son of Adam, who was the
   son of God.

CHAPTER 4

JESUS IS TEMPTED BY THE DEVIL

1   Jesus, full of the Holy Spirit, turned away from the Jordan and
2 was led by the Spirit into the desert to be put to the test by the
   devil for forty days. He did not eat anything in all that time and,
3 when it elapsed, was hungry. The devil said to him: "If you are
4 God's son, command this stone to turn into a loaf of bread." But
   Jesus met his proposal by saying: "The Scripture says: 'Man does
5 not live by bread alone.'" The devil also led him up to an eminence
   to let him see, in a flash, all the kingdoms of the inhabited world,
6 and then said to him: "To you I am ready to give the whole extent
   of this vast empire and its splendor. It has been put at my disposal,
7 and I give it to whom I please. If you, therefore, do homage to me,
8 you shall have all of it." But Jesus countered by saying to him:
   "The Scripture says: 'You shall do homage to the Lord your God,

4:5. *in a flash:* it is not certain how this was done.

and him alone shall you adore.' " Finally, he took him to Jerusalem 9
and after setting him down upon the gable-peak of the temple,
said to him: "If you are God's son, fling yourself down from this
place. The Scripture says: 'To his angels he will give charge of you 10
to keep you safe,' and, 'Upon their hands they will bear you up, 11
that you may not strike your foot against a stone.' " But Jesus 12
retorted: "The Scripture says: 'You shall not tempt the Lord your
God.' " When the devil had exhausted every test, he withdrew from 13
him till a more convenient time.

Invested with the power of the Spirit, Jesus now returned to 14
Galilee, and news concerning him spread far and wide in the region
round about. He instructed the people in their synagogues, and 15
won applause from all.

JESUS COMES TO NAZARETH

One day he came to Nazareth, the home of his childhood. On 16
the Sabbath, he went according to his custom to the synagogue and
stood up to read. A scroll of the prophet Isaias was handed him, 17
and, after unrolling the scroll, he came upon the place where the
following text occurs:

> "The Spirit of the Lord broods over me,   18
> because he has anointed me.
> He has appointed me a messenger
> to bring the Good News to the humble;
> to announce release to captives,
> and recovery of sight to the blind;
> to set the oppressed at liberty;
> to proclaim a year of grace   19
> ordained by the Lord."

He then rolled up the scroll and, after handing it back to the 20
attendant, sat down. The eyes of everyone in the synagogue were
fixed upon him, and he proceeded to speak to them: "Today the 21
Scripture text you have just heard has been fulfilled."

4:13. That more convenient time or favorable opportunity was probably the
time of the Passion.

4:19. a year of grace: an allusion to the Jewish jubilee year, which occurred
every fiftieth year. See Lev. 25:8–10. This year was a type of the whole period
of the Christian dispensation, in which men are freed from the slavery of sin
and the devil.

22   Everyone spoke highly of him and was charmed by the winning
words that fell from his lips; but the remark was also made: "This
23   man is the son of Joseph, is he not?" So he said to them: "Doubtless,
you will quote to me this proverb, 'Physician, cure yourself,' and
say: 'We have heard of all that was done at Capharnaum: do the
same here in your own home town.'"
24   He replied: "I tell you the plain truth: No prophet is acceptable
25   in his own country. It is really so! I tell you, there were many widows
in Israel in the time of Elias when the clouds withheld their rain
for three years and a half, and there was an oppressive famine all
26   over the country; and yet, to none of these was Elias sent, but
27   instead, to a widow at Sarepta in Sidon! Again, there were many
lepers in Israel in the time of the prophet Eliseus; and yet, none
of them was made clean, but instead, Naaman the Syrian!"
28   On hearing this, there was not a man in the synagogue but
29   brimmed over with fury. And they rose in a mass and, driving
him out of the town, led him right up to a steep cliff of the hill
on which their town was built. They meant to hurl him over the
30   precipice. But he passed through the midst of them and quietly
went his way.

JESUS AT CAPHARNAUM; HE DRIVES OUT A DEMON

31   One day, he went down to Capharnaum, a town in Galilee. It
32   was his habit to teach the people on the Sabbath, and they were
lost in admiration of his teaching, because his discourse was delivered
33   with authority. Now, there came into the synagogue a man possessed
by the spirit of an unclean demon, who shouted at the top of his
34   voice: "Ha! Why do you meddle with us, Jesus of Nazareth? Have
you come to destroy us? I know who you are — God's Holy One!"
35   Jesus sternly rebuked him. "Hold your peace," he said, "and
come out of him." The demon then threw the man down in front
36   of all, and went out of him without harming him in the least. A
sense of awe came over all, and, discussing the incident with one
another, they said: "What kind of language is this?" "Why, with
absolute authority he commands the unclean spirits, and they go

---

4:22. What gave offense to the people of Nazareth was not our Lord's
message, but his humble parentage. Jealousy, no doubt, had much to do with
their indignation.

out!" As a result, news concerning him spread to every place in the   37
region round about.

OTHER MIRACULOUS CURES

After leaving the synagogue, he entered Simon's house. Simon's   38
mother-in-law happened to be suffering from an acute attack of
fever, and they appealed to him in her behalf. So he stood over her   39
and sternly rebuked the fever; and it left her. She rose immediately
and waited on them.

When the sun went down, everybody interested in persons   40
suffering from various diseases brought them to him. He laid his
hands on each one of them and cured them. Demons, too, were   41
driven out of many people. They would shriek out the words: "You
are the Son of God!" but he was stern and would not let them go
on speaking. They knew that he was the Messias.

At daybreak he left the house and went to an out-of-the-way   42
place. The crowds searched up and down for him and, after over-
taking him, tried to prevent him from going away from them.
But he said to them: "I must preach the Good News of the king-   43
dom of God to other towns as well. This is the purpose of my
mission." And so he kept preaching in the synagogues of Galilee.   44

CHAPTER 5

THE MIRACULOUS HAUL OF FISH

One day the crowd was surging up against him and listening   1
to the word of God. While he was standing on the beach of Lake
Gennesaret, he saw two boats drawn up on the beach. The fishermen   2
had disembarked and were washing the nets. After entering one   3
of the boats, which was Simon's, he asked him to push out a little
from the shore. He then sat down and taught the crowds from
the boat.

When he had finished speaking, he said to Simon: "Launch out   4
into the deep water, and have your men lower the nets for a haul."
"Master," Simon explained, "we worked all night without catching   5
anything. However, since you tell me to do so, I will have the nets
let down." When they had done this they caught, in a single haul,   6
an extraordinary number of fish; in fact, their nets threatened to

7 break. Then they beckoned their partners in the other boat to come
and lend them a helping hand. They came, and both boats were
filled so that they were on the point of sinking.

THE CALL OF SIMON PETER AND COMPANIONS

8   When Simon Peter saw what had happened, he threw himself
down at the feet of Jesus. "Lord, leave my boat," he said; "I am
9 a sinful creature." A feeling of awe had gripped him, as it had all
his associates, because of the number of fish caught in the haul;
10 so, too, it had seized James and John, the sons of Zebedee, who
were Simon's partners. Jesus then said to Simon: "You have nothing
11 to fear. Hereafter you will be a fisher of men." When they had
brought the boats to shore, they abandoned everything and became
his followers.

THE CURE OF A LEPER

12   One day during his stay in one of the towns, there came without
warning a man covered all over with leprosy. At the sight of Jesus
he threw himself down upon his face and appealed to him in these
13 words: "Lord, if you are willing, you can make me clean." He extended his hand and laid it on him. "Yes," he said, "I am willing;
14 be clean." At once the leprosy left the man. He then ordered the
man not to tell anyone. "But go," he said, "and have yourself examined by the priest; besides, offer the gift for your purification
15 which Moses enjoined, for a testimony to them." But the talk
about him spread all the more, and great crowds flocked together
16 to be instructed and cured of their infirmities. He, however, withdrew to lonely places to pray.

THE CURE OF A PARALYTIC

17   One day about that time he was engaged in teaching. In the
audience there were Pharisees and teachers of the Law, who had
come from every village in Galilee and Judea, including Jerusalem;
18 and the Lord's power was active, enabling him to cure. Here a
strange thing happened: a group of men, carrying upon a mat a
man who was paralyzed, endeavored to bring him in and set him

---

5:17. See the note on Mt. 3:7. *the Lord's power was active:* as everybody
could see. Luke does not mean to imply that this power was "present" on
some occasions and "absent" on others.

down in front of him; but owing to the crowd, they found no way 19
of edging him in; so they went up to the roof and, through a hole
in the tiles, let him down, mat and all, right under the eyes of Jesus.
When he saw their faith, he said: "My good man, your sins are 20
now forgiven." The Scribes and the Pharisees assumed a critical atti- 21
tude. "Who is this man," they said, "who utters blasphemies? Who
has power to forgive sins except God alone?" Aware of their 22
criticism, Jesus reasoned with them as follows: "Why are you in
such a critical mood? Which is easier, to say, 'Your sins are now 23
forgiven,' or to say, 'Rise, and be on your feet again'? But I want you 24
to understand that the Son of Man has power to forgive sins on
earth." He then addressed the paralyzed man: "I command you: rise,
take up your mat, and go home." Immediately the man rose in 25
the presence of all, took up the mat he had been lying on, and
went home glorifying God. All were enraptured and praised God; 26
and, overwhelmed by a sense of awe, exclaimed: "We have seen
extraordinary things today!"

CHRIST'S MISSION TO CONVERT SINNERS, NOT SAINTS

Going out after this incident, he observed a tax collector at 27
his counter in the customhouse, and said to him: "Be one of my
followers." Leaving everything behind, he quit his business and 28
henceforth was one of his followers. One day Levi arranged a great 29
reception in his honor at his home, where a large group of tax
collectors and other people were at table with him. The Pharisees 30
and their Scribes were grumbling. "You eat and drink," they said,
addressing his disciples, "with tax collectors and sinners. How is
that?" By way of answer Jesus said to them: "The sick have need 31
of a physician, not the healthy. It is my mission to call sinners, 32
and not saints, to a change of heart."

But they said to him: "John's disciples fast frequently and recite 33
prayers; so, also, those of the Pharisees; yours eat and drink."
Jesus said to them: "Can you make wedding guests fast while 34
the bridegroom is with them? However, a time is coming when the 35
bridegroom is torn away from them, and then they will fast — yes, in
those days."

5:23. Which is easier: see the note on Mt. 9:5.

PIECE OF A NEW GARMENT NOT PLACED ON AN OLD ONE

36   He also told them a parable: "Nobody cuts a piece out of a new cloak to sew it on an old one; otherwise, not only would he cut up the new, but the piece taken from the new would not match
37   with the old. Again, no one pours new wine into old wine skins; otherwise, the new wine will burst the skins, and the wine will run
38   out and the skins be ruined. No; new wine must be poured into
39   fresh skins. Besides, nobody who has drunk old wine, at once cares for new; 'the old,' he says, 'is good.'"

CHAPTER 6

TWO SABBATH EVENTS

1   The following happened on a Sabbath — the second after the first — when he was passing through the wheatfields and his disciples were plucking the heads of wheat and, after rubbing them with
2   their hands, eating them. "Why," some of the Pharisees remarked,
3   "are you doing what it is not right to do on the Sabbath?" Jesus had an answer for them. "Did you not read," he said to them, "what
4   David did when he was hungry — he and his companions? How he went into the house of God and, helping himself to the presentation loaves, ate them and shared them with his companions — loaves
5   which it is not 'right' for anyone to eat except the priests?" Then he added: "The Son of Man has authority also over the Sabbath."
6   The following occurred on another Sabbath. He went to the synagogue to teach, and a man whose right arm was withered was
7   present. The Scribes and the Pharisees were closely watching him, to see whether he would heal on the Sabbath. They wanted to find
8   grounds for accusing him. He was well aware of their thoughts; so he said to the man with the withered arm: "Rise, and come forward."
9   He rose and came forward. Jesus then said to them: "I ask you: is it 'right' on the Sabbath to do an act of kindness, or must one inflict
10   evil? to save a life, or must one kill?" Then, glancing round at them all, he said to the man: "Stretch out your arm." He did so,

---

6:2. The Sabbath rules laid down by the Pharisees were man-made, and so numerous as to become an unbearable burden (Lk. 11:46). Jesus ignored them and excused the Apostles from following the Pharisaical interpretations, on the simple ground that he had the authority to do so. See the note on 11:52.

and his arm was fully restored. But they brimmed over with fury, *11* and discussed together what they should do with Jesus.

CHRIST CHOOSES HIS TWELVE APOSTLES

One day about that time, he went out to the hillside to pray, *12* and spent the whole night in praying to God. When day broke, he *13* called his disciples into his presence, and chose from among them twelve, whom he called apostles:

Simon, whom he surnamed Peter; *14*
his brother Andrew;
James and John;
Philip and Bartholomew;
Matthew and Thomas; *15*
James, the son of Alpheus;
Simon, called the Zealot;
Jude, the brother of James, *16*
and Judas Iscariot,
who eventually turned traitor.

JESUS BEGINS THE SERMON ON THE MOUNT

He then came down with them and stopped on some level *17* ground. A large group of his disciples was present, besides a great many people from all over the Jewish country, including Jerusalem, and from the seacoast of Tyre and Sidon. They had come to hear *18* him and be cured of their diseases; such, also, as were molested by unclean spirits were healed. And everybody in the crowd endeavored *19* to come in touch with him, for power was going out from him and healing everyone.

TWO GROUPS, THE BLESSED AND THE WRETCHED

It was then that he raised his eyes and fixed them upon his *20* disciples, and spoke as follows:

6:15. *the Zealot:* also called "the Cananaean" (Mt. 10:4; Mk. 3:18). See the note on Mt. 10:4.

6:17. St. Luke's account of the Sermon on the Mount is more condensed than that of St. Matthew. Each evangelist selected from it such details as he judged suited to his (Greek or Jewish) audience.

6:19. *power was going out from him:* a graphic way of saying that "his healing power was active."

"Blessed are you, the humble,
for yours is the kingdom of God.
21   Blessed are you who now go hungry,
for you shall have your fill.
Blessed are you who now weep,
for you shall laugh.

22 Blessed are you when the world hates you, and bars you from its
society, and reviles you, and brands you as criminals — and that for
23 the sake of the Son of Man. Rejoice at such moments; yes, leap
for joy! Mark my words: there is a rich reward for you in heaven.
Besides, that was the way their fathers treated the prophets.

24   On the other hand,
utterly wretched are you, the rich,
for you have your comfort here and now.
25   Utterly wretched are you
who have now your fill of everything,
for you shall go hungry.
Utterly wretched are you
who now are merry,
for you shall mourn and weep.

26 Utterly wretched are you when all the world speaks well of
you; for so, too, the false prophets were treated by their fathers.

LOVE OF THOSE WHOM YOU DISLIKE

27   "But to you who are listening I say: love your enemies; treat
28 kindly those that hate you; bless those that curse you; pray for those
29 that revile you. If someone strikes you on your cheek, present to him
the other as well; if someone takes away your cloak, do not stop
30 him from taking your coat also. Give to anyone that asks you;
31 and if someone robs you of your property, do not claim it. In general,
do by your fellow men exactly as you wish them to do by you.

32   "Again, if you love those that love you, what thanks can you
33 expect? Why, even sinners love those that love them. So, too, if
you are kind to those that are kind to you, what thanks can you
34 expect? Even sinners do as much. And if you lend to those from
whom you expect repayment, what thanks can you expect? Even
sinners lend to sinners on condition that they recover the same
amount.

"On the contrary, love your enemies; do acts of kindness and 35
lend without expecting any return. Then your reward will be abundant, and you will prove yourselves children of the Most High,
who is kind to the ungrateful and the wicked. Be merciful just as 36
your Father is merciful.

"Again, do not judge, and you will not be judged; do not 37
condemn, and you will not be condemned; acquit, and you will be
acquitted. Give, and you will receive; a goodly measure — pressed 38
down, shaken together, running over — will be poured into your lap.
The measure you use in measuring will be used to measure out
your share."

CONCLUDING WORDS OF COUNSEL

He also told them a parable: "Can one blind man lead another? 39
Will not both fall into the ditch? No pupil is above his teacher; 40
when perfectly trained, he is only like his teacher. Strange that you 41
see the splinter in your brother's eye, and do not notice the log in
your own! Or how can you say to your brother: 'Brother, let me 42
take out the splinter in your eye,' when you do not see the log
in your own? Hypocrite, first take the log out of your own eye, and
then you will see distinctly enough to take out the splinter in your
brother's eye. For as no healthy tree bears sickly fruit, so, no sickly 43
tree bears healthy fruit. In fact, each tree is known by its distinctive 44
fruit. Surely, figs are not picked from thornbushes, nor are grapes
harvested from thistles.

"A good man dispenses what is good from the good things 45
stored in his heart, and a wicked man dispenses what is wicked
from his store of wicked things. After all, a man's speech is but
the overflow of his heart.

"Why do you address me 'Lord, Lord,' when you do not do 46
what I say? When anyone comes to me who listens to my teaching 47
and acts accordingly — let me show you whom such a one is like:
he is like a man who carefully builds a house; he digs deep into 48
the ground and lays a foundation upon rock; and, in case a flood
comes, the torrent may beat against that house, but is unable
to shake it off its base, for it has been solidly built. But he who 49
just listens and does not act accordingly is like a man who hastily
builds a house upon the bare ground without a foundation: the

167

torrent beats against that house, and it immediately collapses and is reduced to a mighty heap of ruins."

CHAPTER 7

"UTTER A WORD AND CURE MY SLAVE"

1 After he had completed his instructions in the hearing of the
2 people, he visited Capharnaum. A centurion there had a slave who
   was so ill as to be at the point of death. He thought very highly
3 of him, and so, since he had heard about Jesus, sent a delegation
   of Jewish elders to him, requesting him to come and save the life
4 of his slave. When these men came face to face with Jesus, they
   earnestly pleaded with him. "He is the right man," they said, "for
5 you to grant this favor to. He is, certainly, fond of our nation and
   has built the synagogue for us at his own expense."

6 So Jesus went along with them. But when he was only a short
   distance from the house, the centurion sent to him friends with
   this message for him: "Sir, do not trouble any further; I am not
7 fit to have you come under my roof. That, too, was why I did not
   think I had a right to come to you in person. No, utter a word and
8 cure my slave. It is the same with me: I am an inferior officer,
   and have soldiers under me; and when I say to one, 'March,' he
   marches; to another, 'Come,' he comes; and to my slave, 'Do this,'
9 he does it." On hearing this, Jesus was struck with admiration
   for him and, turning round, said to the accompanying crowd: "I
10 tell you, I have not found such lively faith even in Israel." When
   the messengers returned to the house, they found the slave in
   good health.

A WIDOW'S ONLY SON RESTORED TO LIFE

11 Shortly afterwards he set out for a town called Naim. His dis-
12 ciples and a great crowd accompanied him. Just when he came near
   the gate of the town, a dead man — his mother's only son — was
   being carried out for burial. This woman was a widow, and a con-
13 siderable number of townspeople were with her. The sight of her
   touched the Lord's heart, and he said to her: "Do not weep."
14 He then went up to the coffin and laid his hand on it. The bearers

stopped, and he said: "Young man, I command you, awake!" The   *15*
dead man sat up and began to speak. He then restored him to
his mother. A feeling of awe came over all, and they praised God.   *16*
"A mighty prophet has risen among us!" they commented, and,
"God has visited his people!" This talk about him spread through-   *17*
out the Jewish land and the whole adjacent country.

JOHN: A PROPHET AND MORE THAN A PROPHET

One day, news of all these incidents was brought to John by   *18*
his disciples. So John summoned two of his disciples and sent them   *19*
to the Lord to propose this question: "Are you the one who is to
come, or are we to wait for another?" When the men came into   *20*
his presence, they said: "John the Baptist sends us to you with
this question: 'Are you the one who is to come, or are we to wait
for another?' " At that particular time, he had cured many persons   *21*
of diseases, afflictions, and evil spirits, and made many people
happy by granting them sight. So, taking advantage of the oppor-   *22*
tunity, he said to them: "Go and bring word to John about all
you see and hear: the blind recover sight, the lame walk, lepers are
made clean, the deaf hear, dead men rise again, the humble have
the Good News preached to them"; and, "Happy the man to whom   *23*
I am not a stumbling block!"

When John's messengers had departed, he made a point of   *24*
speaking to the crowds about John: "What did you go out into the
desert to look at? A reed waving in the wind? Well, then, what   *25*
did you go out to see? A man dressed in fine, soft clothes? But

---

7:20. The purpose of John's inquiry is much disputed. We may, perhaps,
suppose that, while for himself he knew that Jesus was "he that was to come,"
yet he wishes him to express himself more clearly on this point for the sake
of his disciples. However, we are doing John no injustice if we suppose that, in
spite of his holiness and the revelations he had received, he was tempted to
doubt. He had proclaimed Christ as the Judge who was "to clean his threshing
floor" (Lk. 3:17); but he could not help seeing that Jesus went about quietly,
preaching and doing good to all sufferers (Acts 10:38). His vision of the Messias
was correct, but incomplete. To remedy the deficiency, Jesus called attention to
what Isaias had foretold of him (Isa. 35:5; 61:1). His word in 7:23 is no
criticism of John, but an encouragement to hold out bravely in his temptation.
See his eulogy of John in verses 24–28. John's appeal to Jesus is proof that
he did not allow his temptation to ripen into an actual doubt.

7:23. *to whom I am not a stumbling block*: in this version the expression
"to be scandalized" has been avoided. See the note on Mk. 4:17. The Greek
word occurs 26 times in the Gospels. (See *The Gospel of St. Mark*, p. 166 ff.)

notice: the people that wear fine clothes and live in luxury are in the
26 royal palaces! Well, then, what did you go out to see? A prophet?
27 Yes, I tell you, and more than a prophet! This is the man of whom
it is written:

> 'Look! I am sending ahead of you
> a messenger who is to prepare
> the road for you to travel.'

28   Yes, I assure you, among the men born of women there is no
greater prophet than John, although in the kingdom of heaven
the least is greater than he.

THE CRITICS OF JOHN THE BAPTIST AND CHRIST

29   "The people at large and the tax collectors acknowledged God's
30 just demands and submitted to John's baptism; the Pharisees and
the teachers of the Law, for their part, frustrated God's intention
31 and did not submit to his baptism. How, then, shall I characterize
32 the men of this generation? Of whom do they remind me? They remind me of little children sitting about the market place and calling
out to their partners:

> 'We played you a tune to make you merry,
> and yet you did not dance;
> we played you a tune to make you sorry,
> and yet you did not strike your breasts.'

33 To illustrate: John the Baptist is here on a special mission, and
he abstains from eating bread and drinking wine; yet you say: 'He
34 is out of his mind.' The Son of Man is here on a special mission,
and he eats and drinks; yet you say: 'Look at that glutton and
35 and drinker; that boon companion of tax collectors and sinners!'
For all that, wisdom has been justified by all that live by her."

SHE HAS SHOWN SO MUCH LOVE

36   One day, one of the Pharisees invited him to a meal with him.
He entered the home of the Pharisee and reclined on a couch;
37 and without warning a woman who was a scandal in the town came

---

7:32. The Pharisees were like petulant children, always doing the opposite of
what they were expected to do.
7:37. a woman: the evidence of the Gospels strongly favors the view that
this unnamed woman, Mary Magdalen, and Mary, the sister of Lazarus, were
three distinct persons.

in. After making sure that he was at table in the home of the
Pharisee, she brought with her an alabaster flask of perfume,
took her stand behind him at his feet, and wept. Yielding to an 38
impulse, she rained her tears on his feet and wiped them with
her hair; she tenderly kissed his feet and anointed them with the
perfume. His host, the Pharisee, noticed this, and said to himself: 39
"This man, if he were a prophet, would know who and what
sort of creature this woman is, that makes so much fuss over him!
Why, she is a scandalous person!"

Jesus read his thoughts and said to him: "Simon, I have something 40
to tell you." "Tell it, Rabbi," he replied. "Once upon a time two 41
men were in the debt of a moneylender. The one owed him five
hundred denarii; the other, fifty. Neither of them was in a position 42
to pay; so he made both of them happy by canceling their debts.
Under these circumstances, which of them will be more generous
in loving him?" "The one, I suppose," answered Simon, "whom he 43
made happy by canceling the greater amount." "Your judgment
is correct," he replied. Then, turning to the woman, he said to 44
Simon: "Do you see this woman? I came into your house, and you
offered me no water for my feet: but this woman rained her tears
upon my feet and wiped them dry with her hair. You gave me no 45
kiss of welcome; but this woman has not left off, from the time I
entered, tenderly kissing my feet. You did not anoint my head 46
with oil: but this woman anointed my feet with perfume. And in 47

7:39. For the Greek word generally rendered "to touch," see the note on
Mt. 14:36. Note Simon's speech, every word of which reflects his typically
Pharisaical attitude. He certainly judged "according to appearances" (Jn. 8:15).

7:44. Washing the feet of a distinguished guest, giving him the kiss of welcome, and anointing his hair with perfume, were customary marks of courtesy.

7:47. Simon condemned the woman as "a scandal in the town" (verse 39).
Jesus undertakes to rebuke him for this rash judgment, which, in typical
Pharisaical fashion (see Jn. 8:15), was based on appearances. He does this by
means of an illustration from ordinary life. A debtor, whose debt has been
canceled, shows his gratitude by "loving" his creditor. In such a case, the
remission of the debt precedes the love, as the cause precedes the effect.
Applying this principle to the conduct of the woman on the present occasion,
Jesus says: "in consideration of this" (that is, the many tokens of love given by
the woman), "I tell you: many sins have been forgiven her. How do I know this?
Because she has loved so much." This interpretation is demanded by the parable,
fits in well with the words that follow, and is compatible with the text, provided we consider it an instance of brachylogy common in Greek literature. In
reading the text we merely insert a pause before the words: "Because she has
loved much." The parable loses much of its force unless we keep in mind the

consideration of this I tell you: her sins, numerous as they are, are
forgiven. You see, she has shown so much love! One, of course,
48 who has but little forgiven him, shows but little love." He then
49 said to her: "Your sins are forgiven." At once his fellow guests gave
way to thoughts like this: "Who is this individual who even forgives
50 sins!" He finally said to the woman: "Your faith has saved you.
Go home and be at peace."

Chapter 8

THE GROUP CLOSE TO JESUS

1   There followed a period of wandering about, during which he
preached in town after town, in village after village, and announced
the Good News of the kingdom of God. He was accompanied by
2 the Twelve, as well as by certain women who had been cured of
evil spirits and infirmities: Mary, surnamed the Magdalene, out of
3 whom seven demons had been driven; Joanna, the wife of Chuza,
Herod's manager, Susanna, and many others. These women were
ministering to the company out of their own means.

PARABLE OF THE SOWER AND HIS SEED

4   One day, when a large crowd and the people from town after
5 town flocked to him, he said in parable style: "The sower goes
out to sow his seed. As he sows, some of the seed falls close to the
footpath, where it is trampled down, or else the birds of the air eat
6 it up. Other seed falls upon the stony ground; and as soon as
7 it sprouts, it withers away because it can get no moisture. Other seed,

---

proper balancing of cause and effect. There is, however, a widespread interpretation which reverses the process: many sins are forgiven her because she loved
much. One may admit that a slight inversion of the order does not at once make
a parable nugatory. The views of the Fathers are divided in explaining this
text. In the second interpretation, the woman's sins were forgiven both because
of her faith (see verse 50) and of her love (verse 47). This tallies with Gal.
5:5–6. "Our hope of justification . . . rests on *faith* . . . the faith that finds
expression in *love*."

The application of the parable to Simon himself is somewhat unexpected,
almost a casual remark thrown in, though a much needed lesson. Note that
the word "little" in this context is probably a delicate euphemism for "nothing";
and so the upshot of the discourse is that the woman is a saint, and Simon
a sinner.

again, falls among the thorns, and the thorns grow up along with it and utterly choke it. Still other seed falls on the right kind of 8 soil; and it sprouts and bears fruit a hundredfold." To enforce the lesson he exclaimed: "Let everyone heed what he has heard."

His disciples then asked him what the meaning of this parable 9 was. "You are privileged," he replied, "to understand the mysteries 10 of the kingdom of God; but to the rest they are presented in parable form, with the result that

'for all their seeing they do not see,
    and for all their hearing they do not understand.'
This is the meaning of the parable: The 'seed' is God's message. 11 Those described by the words 'close to the footpath' are such as 12 listen indeed, but later the devil comes and steals the message from their minds, with the result that they do not believe and are not saved. Those described by the words 'on the stony ground' are 13 persons who, on hearing the Message, receive it with joy; however, they do not let it strike root in them; for a while they have faith, but fall away in a moment of temptation. The words 'fallen among 14 the thorns' describe persons who listen indeed; but as they go through life, they are stifled under cares, riches, and pleasures, and mature no fruit. Those described by the words 'in the right kind 15 of soil' are persons who listen to the message in the right and proper spirit, and therefore hold it fast and patiently bear fruit.

"No one lights a lamp and then covers it up with a bucket or 16 puts it under a couch. No; it is put on the lampstand, so that those who come in see the light. After all, there is nothing hidden but 17 must be made known some day; nothing concealed but must be made known and brought to light some day. Consider therefore 18 with what care you listen; for the man of means will be given yet more, and the man of no means will have taken away from him what he thinks he has."

CHRIST'S MOTHER AND BROTHERS

Once his mother and his brothers came to visit him, but owing 19 to the crowd could not get an interview with him. So this message 20 was brought to him: "Your mother and your brothers are waiting outside, wishing to see you." He protested: "My mother and my 21

8:16. Compare Mk. 4:21, and see the note on Mk. 4:24.

brothers," he said to them, "are those who hear God's word and
live up to it."

WINDS AND WATER OBEY HIM

22   The following occurred one of those days when he and his
disciples had gone into a boat. He said to them: "Let us cross to the
23   opposite shore of the lake." Accordingly they set sail. As they were
sailing along, he fell asleep. Suddenly a gale of wind swooped down
upon the lake; and they were shipping water and facing danger.
24   So they rushed up and woke him with the cry: "Master! Master! We
are going down!" Then, rising to his full height, he sternly rebuked
the wind and the surging waves. They subsided, and all was still.
25   "Where is your faith?" he said to them; for, struck with awe, they
were puzzled, saying to one another: "Who, really, is this man?
Why, he commands both the winds and the water, and they obey
him!"

THE MAN POSSESSED BY DEMONS

26   They now put in at the country of the Gerasenes, which is oppo-
27   site Galilee. When he had gone ashore, a man from town came to
meet him. He was possessed by demons and, for a long time, had
worn no clothes; nor would he live in a house, but stayed among
28   the tombs. At sight of Jesus, he gave a shriek, threw himself down
before him, and shouted at the top of his voice: "Leave me alone,
Jesus, Son of the Most High God. I beg you, do not torment me,"
29   for he was about to order the unclean spirit to go out of the man.
It had for a long time past had a firm grip on the man; and, although
bound with handcuffs and chains and kept under guard, he had
broken the bonds and was driven by the demon into unfrequented
30   haunts. Jesus then asked him: "What is your name?" "Legion,"
he replied; for demons in great numbers had entered into him.
31   Now, they had begged Christ not to order them back into the
32   abyss; but, since a numerous herd of pigs happened to be feeding
there on the hillside, the demons ended by asking him to allow
33   them to enter into these. He gave them permission, and out of

---

8:27. Matthew mentions two demoniacs.
8:33. Christ permitted the destruction of the herd, partly, perhaps, to punish
the people for their worldliness, partly, to show them the destructive power of
the demons, from which he had come to deliver mankind.

the man they went, and entered into the pigs, whereupon the herd
dashed down the slope into the lake and was drowned. When the 34
herdsmen saw what had happened, they took to flight and carried
the news to town and countryside. Then the inhabitants went out 35
to see what had taken place. They came to Jesus, and found the
man from whom the demons had been driven out, clothed, in his
right mind, and seated at the feet of Jesus. They were struck with
awe. When the eyewitnesses told them how the possessed man had 36
been cured, the whole population of Gerasa and vicinity requested 37
him to quit their territory; for they were gripped by an overpowering
fear. So he entered a boat to return. The man, however, out 38
of whom the demons had been driven, asked leave to stay with
him; but he sent him away with the remark: "Go back home, and 39
explain all that God has done for you." So he went away and published all over town what Jesus had done for him.

TWO FURTHER CURES

When Jesus returned, the crowd welcomed him; for they had 40
all been waiting for him. Presently, there came a man whose name 41
was Jairus, an official of the synagogue. Throwing himself down at
the feet of Jesus, he implored him to come to his house; for he had 42
an only daughter, twelve years of age, who was at the point of death.
As he made his way to the place, the crowds all but smothered
him.

Meanwhile, a woman who had had hemorrhages for twelve 43
years, and had spent all her means of sustenance on physicians, but
could not be cured by anyone, approached from behind and touched 44
the tassel of his cloak. Her hemorrhage stopped immediately. "Who 45
has touched me?" Jesus asked. But all denied having done so, and
Peter remarked: "Why, Master, the crowds are pressing round you
and all but crush you!" But Jesus said: "Someone has touched 46
me. I was aware that my healing power had been at work." When 47
the woman realized that she had not escaped notice, she came
tremblingly forward and, throwing herself down before him, told,
in the hearing of all the people, her reason for touching him, and

8:45. See the note on Mt. 14:36.
8:46. Christ's power of healing could not be operative without his knowledge
and will. See the note on 6:19.

48 how she had been instantly cured. He then said to her: "My
   daughter, your faith has cured you. Go home and be at peace."
49   He was still speaking, when a messenger from the household of
   the synagogue official arrived to say: "Your daughter is dead. Do
50 not trouble the Rabbi any further." But Jesus, on hearing the
   message, reassured him: "You have nothing to fear. Only have
51 faith, and she will be safe." Arrived at the home, he did not allow
   anyone to enter with him except Peter, James, and John, besides
52 the child's father and mother. Everyone was weeping and lamenting
53 her. But he said: "Stop crying; she is not dead; she is asleep." They
54 laughed at him, knowing that she was dead. But he took her by the
55 hand and said in a loud voice: "My child, awake." Her spirit
   returned, and she rose immediately. He then ordered that some-
56 thing to eat should be given her. Her parents were beside themselves with wonder; but he enjoined them not to tell anyone what
   had taken place.

CHAPTER 9

CHRIST SENDS FORTH THE TWELVE

1   After calling the twelve apostles together one day, he gave
   them power and authority — authority over all the demons and
2 power to cure diseases. He then sent them out to preach the
3 kingdom of God and heal the sick, after giving them the following
   instructions: "Do not go and get anything for your journey, whether
   staff or bag or provisions or money; and do not have an extra coat.
4 Once you enter a household, make your headquarters there till you
5 leave that locality. And if any people do not make you welcome,
   quit that town and shake the dust off your feet as a warning to
6 them." So they set off and traveled about, preaching the Good
   News in village after village, and everywhere curing the sick.
7   On hearing of all that was going on, the tetrarch Herod was
8 puzzled because it was said by some that John had risen from the
   dead; by others, that Elias had reappeared; by still others, that one
9 of the old prophets had come back to life. Herod, however, declared:
   "As to John — I have myself had him beheaded; but who is this
   man about whom I hear such reports?" As a result, he was anxious
   to see him.

• The apostles finally returned and told him in detail what success 10
they had had. He then took them with him and, for the sake of
privacy, withdrew in the direction of a town called Bethsaida. The 11
crowds came to know about it and followed him. He received them
kindly, spoke to them about the kingdom of God, and cured those
in need of attention.

MULTIPLICATION OF LOAVES AND FISH

The day was now well on its way to decline. So the Twelve 12
approached and said to him: "Dismiss the crowd so that they can
reach the villages and farms round about, and find lodging and
provisions. Here we are in a lonely place." But he replied: "It is 13
for you to give them something to eat." "We do not have more
than five loaves and two fish," they said, "unless we go ourselves
and buy eatables for this whole crowd." There were, in fact, about 14
five thousand men present. He then said to his disciples: "Have
them recline in groups of about fifty persons each." They did so, 15
and had them all recline. Then he took the five loaves and the two 16
fish into his hands, and, looking up to heaven, said grace over them,
and broke them into portions which he gave to the disciples to
serve to the crowd. All ate, and everyone had a plentiful meal.
Besides, what was left over from their meal was gathered up, in 17
all twelve basketfuls of remnants.

WHO DO YOU SAY I AM?

On one occasion he was praying all by himself. Only the 18
disciples were with him. He then put this question to them: "Who
do the people say I am?" "John the Baptist," they answered; "but 19
others say, Elias; still others, one of the old prophets has come back
to life." "But you," he said to them, "who do you say I am?" Then 20
Peter spoke up and said: "The Anointed of God." He sternly 21
enjoined them, however, not to tell this to anyone, adding: "The 22
Son of Man has yet to suffer much, be rejected by the elders, high
priests, and Scribes, put to death, and on the third day rise again."

TO BE CHRIST'S FOLLOWER

The following he addressed to all: "If anyone wants to be my 23
follower, he must renounce himself and shoulder his cross day by

24 day; then he may be a follower of mine. He who is bent on saving his life must part with it anyway; but he who freely parts with his
25 life for my sake will save it in the end. Really, what does it profit a man to gain the whole world once he has paid the price and
26 thrown his own self away? For, if one is ashamed of me and my message, of him the Son of Man will be ashamed when he returns
27 wrapt in his own glory and that of his Father and the holy angels. I tell you truly, some of those present here will not taste death before they see the kingdom of God."

CHRIST WITH MOSES AND ELIAS

28 About eight days after this discourse, he took Peter, James, and
29 John, with him and went up the hill to pray. In the course of his prayer, the expression of his countenance changed and his clothes
30 turned a brilliant white. And presently two men, Moses and Elias,
31 were conversing with him; they were seen with a halo of glory and spoke of his departure from the world, which was to round out his career at Jerusalem.
32 Peter and his companions, in the meantime, were struggling with drowsiness; but, on being thoroughly awakened, they saw the
33 halo surrounding him and the two men by his side. When these were about to withdraw from him, Peter said to Jesus: "Master, it is well that we are here! Let us put up three tents, one for you, one for Moses, and one for Elias." He did not realize what he
34 was saying. And as he spoke this, a cloud formed and enveloped them. And as they entered into the cloud, a feeling of awe came
35 over them; moreover, a voice rang out from the cloud, which said: "This is my Son, the Chosen One; listen to him."
36 When the voice had died away, it was found that Jesus was alone. They kept silence regarding this incident and, for some time afterwards, told no one what they had seen.

CURE OF THE CONVULSED BOY

37 It happened the following day, when they had come down the
38 hill, that a great crowd of people came to meet him. And behold,

9:24. See the note on Mt. 16:25. "The words are made to fit only the highest act of Christian obedience, obedience unto death, but they are meant to apply, with due proportion, to every act of fidelity or infidelity to God" (Darby and Smith).
9:27. See the note on Mk. 9:1.

a man among the crowd cried out: "Rabbi, I beg you to look at
my son; he is the only one I have; and without warning a spirit   39
seizes him; he suddenly shrieks, and the spirit convulses him till he
foams at the mouth, and throws him on the ground. It is only with
difficulty, and after nearly crushing him, that he leaves him. I asked   40
your disciples to drive him out, but they could not do it." "O   41
unbelieving and perverse generation," Jesus was moved to say; "how
long must I be with you! How long must I bear with you! Bring
your son here." Before he had come into his presence, the demon   42
dashed him to the ground and violently convulsed him. But Jesus
spoke sternly to the unclean spirit, cured the lad, and restored him
to his father. Everybody was delighted with the manifestation of   43
God's Majesty.

STILL OTHER DEEDS AND SAYINGS

But while all expressed admiration for all he did, he said to his
disciples: "Let what I now say to you sink deep into your ears: the   44
Son of Man is destined to be betrayed into the hands of men."
They could not see the drift of his remark; it was a mystery to them,   45
and they failed to grasp it. Besides, they were too timid to ask him
what he meant.

One day the thought occurred to them as to which one of their   46
group was the greatest. Knowing what was uppermost in their minds,   47
Jesus took hold of a little child and placed it close beside him.
"Whoever," he then said to them, "befriends this little child for   48
the sake of my name, befriends me; and he who befriends me
befriends him whose ambassador I am. You see, then, he who is
the least among you all is the greatest."

Here John broke in with the remark: "Master, we saw somebody   49
drive out demons in your name, and we were for stopping him
because he is not of our company." But Jesus said to him: "Do   50
not interfere; after all, he who is not against us is for us."

The day of his assumption was now drawing nearer and nearer.   51
So he set out, openly and resolutely, on his pilgrimage to Jerusalem,
and dispatched messengers ahead of him. They went and entered   52
a Samaritan village to provide accommodations for him. But the   53
people offered him no hospitality because it was evident that he

9:51. *his assumption:* sc., into heaven.

54 was bound for Jerusalem. When the disciples James and John saw this, they said: "Lord, do you want us to order fire to drop from
55 the sky and consume them?" But Jesus turned upon them with a
56 stern rebuke; and they journeyed on to another village.

57   As they journeyed along, someone said to him: "I would like to
58 follow you wherever you go." Jesus said to him: "Foxes have holes, and the birds of the air have places of shelter; but the Son of Man
59 has no place to lay his head." To another he said: "Stay in my company," and on the man's replying: "Lord, allow me first to go
60 and bury my father," he said to him: "Let the dead bury their own dead. You go and spread the news of the kingdom of God."
61 Still another said: "I would like to follow you, Lord: but first allow
62 me to say farewell to my folks at home." But Jesus replied: "No one who puts his hand to the plow and then looks back is fit for the kingdom of God."

CHAPTER 10

CHRIST'S INSTRUCTION TO HIS MISSIONARIES

1   After these incidents, the Lord appointed another group, seventy-two in all, and sent them out two by two to go ahead of him to
2   every town and place which he intended to visit personally. He said to them: "The harvest is plentiful, but the laborers are few. Pray the Owner of the harvest, therefore, to send out laborers to do his
3   harvesting. Go now; but mind: I am sending you out like lambs
4   among a pack of wolves. Do not burden yourselves with purse, or
5   bag, or sandals. And greet no one by the way. Whatever house you enter, the first thing you say must be: 'A blessing on this
6   household.' If there is a soul in it responsive to a blessing, your
7   blessing will alight on him; if not, it will be no loss to you. Make

---

9:55. Some ancient manuscripts add: "saying you do not know what sort of spirit animates you; for the Son of Man did not come to destroy men's lives, but to save them."

9:60. Compare Mt. 8:22 and accompanying note.

10:4. Not greetings as such were forbidden, but greetings by the way. Jesus insisted on wholehearted devotion to the work in hand. Here, as elsewhere (see the note on 17:6), Christ's specific injunctions to his disciples on any given occasion are not meant to be obligatory for all time and under all circumstances.

your headquarters in just that house, and eat and drink whatever
they have to offer. After all, the laborer is entitled to his wages. Do
not be constantly shifting from house to house. Whatever town   8
you enter, if the people make you welcome, eat what is set before
you; take care of the sick in the place; and speak to the inhabitants   9
on this theme: 'The kingdom of God has finally come to you.'
But if, in any town you enter, the people do not make you welcome,   10
go out into the streets and say: 'Even the dust of your town that   11
sticks to our feet we are wiping off for you to keep. Nonetheless,
be sure of one thing: The kingdom of God has finally come.' I tell   12
you, on that Day it will go less hard with Sodom than with that town.

"Down with you, Corozain! Down with you, Bethsaida! If   13
the wonders done in your midst had been done in Tyre and Sidon,
they would long ago have repented in sackcloth and ashes. At all   14
events, at the judgment it will go less hard with Tyre and Sidon
than with you. And you, Capharnaum, do you expect to soar as   15
high as heaven? As deep as hell shall you sink! He who listens to   16
you listens to me, and he who despises you despises me; but whoever despises me despises him whose ambassador I am."

RETURN OF THE MISSIONARIES

The seventy-two returned in high spirits. "Lord," they said,   17
"even the demons are subject to us because we use your name!"
"Yes," he said to them, "I was watching Satan fall like lightning   18
that flashes from heaven. But mind: it is I that have given you the   19
power to tread upon serpents and scorpions, and break the dominion
of the enemy everywhere; nothing at all can injure you. Just the   20
same, do not rejoice in the fact that the spirits are subject to you,
but rejoice in the fact that your names are engraved in heaven."

Inspired by the occasion, he exulted in the Holy Spirit and said: 21
"I praise you, Father, Lord of heaven and earth, for hiding these
things from wise and prudent men and revealing them to little
ones. Yes, Father, for such has been your good pleasure! All things   22
have been put into my hands by my Father, and no one knows

10:12. *that Day:* Judgment Day.
10:18. *I was watching Satan fall:* these words do not refer to Satan's fall from
heaven. The expression *from heaven* qualifies the word *lightning.* Through the
ministry of the disciples, Satan's power was rapidly and irretrievably lost.
10:21. *Inspired by the occasion:* see the note on Mt. 11:25.

who the Son is except the Father, or who the Father is except the Son and anyone to whom the Son decides to reveal him."
23 Then, turning to his disciples, he said privately: "Happy the eyes
24 that see what you are seeing. Indeed, I tell you, many prophets and kings would have liked to see what you are looking upon, but did not see it, and to hear what you are listening to, but did not hear it."

WHAT IS REQUIRED FOR SALVATION?

25 Presently a legal expert came forward to sound him out. "Rabbi,"
26 he said, "what must I do to obtain a place in eternal life?" "Well," he replied, "what does the Law say about it? What do you read
27 in it?" He answered: " 'Love the Lord your God with your whole heart, and with your whole soul, and with your whole strength, and with your whole mind'; and besides, 'Love your neighbor as
28 yourself.' " "Your answer is correct," he said to him; "act accordingly,
29 and you will have life." But, being anxious to justify his question, the man said to Jesus, "And whom, pray, must I consider a neighbor?"
30 Jesus complied with his request and said: "Once upon a time, a man who was on his way from Jerusalem down to Jericho fell in with bandits; they stripped and beat him, and then went their way,
31 leaving him half dead. By some chance a priest was going down the same road; but when he saw the man, he made a detour.
32 In like manner a levite came near the spot and he, too, made a
33 detour at sight of him. Finally a traveling Samaritan came near him,
34 and he, on seeing the man, was stirred to pity. He went up to him and bound up his wounds, pouring wine and oil into them. He then mounted him on his own beast of burden and brought him to an
35 inn, where he took care of him. Moreover, on the morrow he produced two denarii to pay the innkeeper, and left these instructions: 'Take good care of him; and in case you spend anything over and
36 above this sum, I will repay you on my way back.' Now which of these three men seems to you to have taken a neighborly interest
37 in the man who had fallen in with bandits?" "The one," he replied, "who pitied him in that practical way." "Very well, then," Jesus said to him, "model your conduct on his."

10:32. Levites (much like our deacons) assisted the priests at their services in the temple.

MARY HAS CHOSEN THE GOOD PART

As they pursued their journey, he came to a certain village 38
where a woman called Martha offered him the hospitality of her
house. This woman had a sister called Mary; and she seated herself 39
at the Lord's feet to listen to his instruction. Martha, meanwhile, 40
was all in a flutter, trying to provide ample cheer for the guests.
So she confronted him and said: "Lord, is it no concern to you that
my sister leaves me all alone to prepare the meal? Tell her, therefore, to lend me a helping hand." By way of answer Jesus said to 41
her: "Martha, Martha, you are fretting and greatly disturbing yourself about many things. There is need of one thing only: Mary has 42
chosen the good part, which must not be taken away from her."

CHAPTER 11

OUR LORD'S PRAYER

Once he was somewhere engaged in praying. When he had 1
finished, one of his disciples said to him: "Lord, teach us how to
pray, just as John taught his disciples."

He said to them: "When you pray, say as follows: 2
  'Father, may you be be known and glorified;
  may your kingdom be established;
  give us day after day our daily bread; 3
  and forgive us our sins, 4
  for we also forgive everyone indebted to us;
  and do not expose us to temptation.' "

10:42. *the good part:* the Vulgate reads: "has chosen the best part." The
lesson imparted seems to be: "Do not spend much time over the meal; after
all, there is need of one thing only; and this one thing is 'the good part' that
Mary has chosen: to receive my teachings and counsels." The expression *"the
good part"* seems to imply "the only good part." The part Martha had chosen
was not good; in her love for the Master, mingled, perhaps, with a little house-
wifely pride, she yielded to "worry and anxiety" (condemned by Jesus on
another occasion: see Lk. 12:25, 26). Many Fathers see in Martha and Mary
the types of the active and the contemplative life; but it is doubtful whether
Jesus meant to stress this point here. Both these kinds of life are "good,"
each in its own way, whereas here Martha's part was not good under the circumstances. Mary was interested, first of all, "in the kingdom of God" (Mt. 6:33).

FURTHER INSTRUCTIONS ON PRAYER

5   "Suppose," he also said to them, "some one of you has a friend and goes to him at midnight and says to him: 'Friend, lend me
6 three loaves of bread; a friend of mine has just turned in from the road to visit me and I do not have a thing to set before him':
7 shall then the man inside remonstrate and say: 'Do not pester me; at this late hour the door is barred; my little ones are in bed with
8 me; I cannot get up and accommodate you'? I tell you, he may not get up and accommodate him just because he is his friend, but he will certainly get up for shame's sake and give him all he asks for.

9   "That is why I say to you: ask, and you will receive; seek, and
10 you will find; knock, and you will gain admission. In fact, only he who asks receives; only he who seeks finds; only he who knocks will gain admission.

11   "Again, suppose some one of you, fathers, is asked by his son for a loaf of bread: will he hand him a stone? Or, when he asks
12 for a fish, will he hand him a serpent instead of a fish? Or, when
13 he asks for an egg, will he hand him a scorpion? Now, then, if you, bad as you are, are disposed to give your children useful gifts, how much more readily will the Father in heaven give the Holy Spirit to those that ask him!"

CHRIST DRIVES OUT A DEMON. OUR LORD'S REPLY

14   Once he was driving out a demon, and this particular demon was dumb. The demon was driven out, the dumb man spoke, and
15 the crowds were enraptured. But some among the people remarked: "He is a tool of Beelzebul, and that is how he drives out demons!"
16 Another group, intending to test him, demanded of him a proof of
17 his claims, to be shown in the sky. He knew their inmost thoughts.

11:8. *for shame's sake*: a homely illustration to show God's readiness to answer our prayers. In a Palestinian farming community it would be a "shame" (a disregard of "decency" and a violation of the most ordinary laws of hospitality) not to help a neighbor under the circumstances supposed in the parable; therefore the man inside could not be expected to say what, in the current translations, he is made to say (Fridrichsen). On the contrary, to avoid "the imputation of being shameless" he will accommodate his friend. For another homely illustration of the power of prayer, see Lk. 18:1–8 (though there the effectiveness of persistent prayer is emphasized).

"Any kingdom torn by civil strife," he said to them, "is laid in ruins; and house tumbles upon house. So, too, if Satan is in revolt *18* against himself, how can his kingdom last, since you say that I drive out demons as a tool of Beelzebul! And furthermore: if I *19* drive out demons as a tool of Beelzebul, whose tools are your pupils when they do the driving out? Therefore, judged by them, you must stand condemned. But, if, on the contrary, I drive out *20* demons by the finger of God, then, evidently the kingdom of God has by this time made its way to you! As long as a mighty lord in *21* full armor guards his premises, he is in peaceful possession of his property; but should one mightier than he attack and overcome *22* him, he will strip him of his armor, on which he had relied, and distribute the spoils taken from him. He who is not with me is *23* against me, and he who does not gather with me scatters.

"When the unclean spirit is driven out of a man, he haunts *24* waterless regions in quest of refreshment, and, when he does not find any, says: 'I will return to the house from which I have been driven out.' Then, if on his return he finds it swept and tidy, *25* he goes and gets seven other spirits, who are worse than himself, to *26* join him, and they enter and make themselves at home there. Such a man is worse off in the end than he was at the beginning."

As he was giving these explanations, a woman in the crowd *27* cried out aloud: "Blessed the womb that has borne you; blessed the breasts that have suckled you!" "Blessed, rather," he replied, "are *28* those that hear the word of God and observe it!"

OUR LORD'S WARNING

As the crowds were flocking closer together, he delivered a warn- *29* ing: "This generation is a headstrong generation. It demands a proof of my claims, but a proof will not be given to it except the proof that Jonas gave. In the same way that Jonas proved his claims *30* before the Ninevites, will the Son of Man prove his before this generation. A queen of the South will rise at the judgment together *31*

11:19. Jewish exorcists often relied on charms and incantations. Christ expelled the demons "by the finger (the power) of God." Any observer could see this; hence the warning in verse 20 ff.

11:28. Faith and obedience, or readiness to do the will of God, are greater blessings than merely physical relationship. The words are, of course, no slur on Mary, whose faith and obedience are brought out in the account of the Anunciation and in Lk. 1:45.

with the men of this generation and put them in the wrong; for, from the ends of the earth she came to listen to the wisdom of Solomon. And observe: there is something more than Solomon here! 32 Ninevites will rise at the judgment together with this generation and put it in the wrong; for, on the preaching of Jonas they changed their evil ways. And observe: there is something more than Jonas here!

33 "No one lights a lamp and then puts it in a cellar or under a bushel-basket. No; it is put on the lampstand, so that all who come 34 in can see the light. Your eye serves your person as a lamp; as long as your eye is sound, your whole person has light; but, when your 35 eye is defective, your whole person gropes in the dark. Consider, therefore, whether your inward lamp is not, perhaps, darkened; in 36 other words, whether your entire person has light. Only when no part of your person is dark, will your entire person have light, as when a brightly burning lamp enlightens you."

"PERDITION AWAITS YOU PHARISEES!"

37 He had just finished speaking when a Pharisee invited him to 38 lunch at his home. He entered and reclined on a couch. But the Pharisee noticed with surprise that he did not bathe before the 39 lunch. "So this is your way, Pharisees!" the Lord said to him; "the outside — cup and dish — you clean, but the inside — yourselves — 40 reeks with greed and depravity! How foolish you are! Did not he who 41 made the outside make the inside also? In any case, give what you can afford by way of alms, and in that way, do you not see, you make everything clean!

42 "As it is, perdition awaits you, Pharisees! You pay a ten per cent income tax on mint and rue and every garden herb, but disregard justice and the love of God. One ought to attend to the latter 43 without neglecting the former. Perdition awaits you, Pharisees! You set great store by front seats in the synagogues and ceremonious 44 greetings in public places. Perdition awaits you, for you are like those obliterated graves which one walks over without being aware of it!"

11:41. *give what you can afford*: an alternative rendering would be "give what is at hand, or on the table, in the cups and dishes" or "give in alms what remains over from the meal." The sense is practically the same.

Here one of the legal experts protested. "Rabbi," he said to 45
him, "in saying that, you insult us as well." "The same perdition 46
awaits you, the legal experts," he replied, "you burden your fellow
men with burdens hard to bear, but do not stir a finger of your own
to lay hold of the burdens. Perdition awaits you; for you build 47
the tombs of the prophets — you whose fathers murdered them!
Evidently, you witness to this fact and sympathize with the conduct 48
of your fathers: they killed them, and you build their tombs!
And that is why God's wisdom has declared: 'I will send to them 49
the prophets and apostles; some of these they will kill or persecute.'
The result will be that the blood of all the prophets, shed since 50
the foundation of the world, shall be avenged upon the present
generation. Yes, I tell you that, from the blood of Abel down to 51
the blood of Zachary, who perished between the altar and the
sanctuary, it must be avenged upon the present generation!

"Perdition awaits you, legal experts, for you have taken away 52
the key that opens the door of knowledge. You yourselves did not
go in, and when others wanted to go in, you blocked their way."

When he had left the house, the Scribes and the Pharisees were 53
deeply resentful and made a point of getting him to express himself
offhand on a variety of things. They lay in wait to catch some 54
unguarded expression from his lips.

CHAPTER 12

A DISCOURSE DIRECTED PARTICULARLY TO THE DISCIPLES

It was under such circumstances, when the thousands of people 1
were pressing near him so as to trample on one another, that he
addressed a discourse, first of all, to the disciples: "Beware of the
leaven of the Pharisees, that is, hypocrisy. Nothing is hidden but 2
must be revealed some day, and nothing concealed but must be made
known some day. That is why whatever you say in the dark shall be 3
divulged in broad daylight, and whatever you whisper within doors
shall be proclaimed from the housetops. But I tell you, my friends: 4
do not fear those who kill the body and, that done, have no power

---

11:52. *you have taken away the key:* by obscuring the real meaning of the Law
through your false interpretations and burdensome traditions.

5 to inflict anything worse. I will show you whom you ought to fear: fear him who, after killing a man, has power to consign him to the pit of hell. Yes, I tell you, he is the one to be afraid of.

6 "Do not five sparrows sell for two pennies? And yet, in the providence of God, not one of them is a poor, forgotten creature!

7 No, even the hairs on your head are all numbered. Have no fear;

8 you are more precious than whole flocks of sparrows. I assure you, everyone who acknowledges me before the world will himself be

9 acknowledged by the Son of Man before the angels of God; but he who disowns me before the world will be disowned before the angels

10 of God. And furthermore: anyone who utters a word against the Son of Man may be forgiven, but he who blasphemes the Holy Spirit

11 cannot be forgiven. When you are led into the synagogues or before magistrates and their tribunals, do not be uneasy as to how or

12 what to plead in self-defense or what to say; for at that moment the Holy Spirit will teach you what to say."

PARABLE OF THE RICH MAN, ADDRESSED TO THE PEOPLE

13 Someone out in the crowd said to him: "Rabbi, tell my brother

14 to divide the inheritance with me." "Why, man," he replied, "who

15 has appointed me judge or arbiter over you two?" He then addressed the people: "Look out, and guard against greed in any form. When a man abounds in riches, his life is not assured just because he is well-to-do."

16 He then spoke to them in parable style: "Once upon a time," he said, "there was a rich man whose land yielded an abundant

17 crop. So he soliloquized as follows: 'What shall I do since I have

18 no place to store my crops?' Finally he said: 'This is what I will do: I will pull down my barns and build larger ones; and there I

19 will store my wheat and all my goods; and then I will say to myself: My good fellow, you have many possessions laid up to last for many

20 a year; take life easy now: eat, drink, and enjoy yourself.' But God said to him: 'You fool! This very night your soul will be demanded from you: who is then going to get what you have provided?'

21 It is the same with anyone who hoards to indulge himself and does not think of God in amassing wealth."

ADDRESS TO HIS DISCIPLES

22 He then said to his disciples: "For this reason I say to you: do

188

not fret about what to eat to sustain your life, or what to wear on
your body. Life, surely, is more precious than food, and the body   23
more precious than clothing. Observe the ravens! They neither sow   24
nor reap, nor have they storeroom or barn. God feeds them just the
same. How much more precious you are than birds! Besides, which   25
of you can by fretting add even a minute to his span of life?
Well, then: if you cannot do even so small a thing, why should   26
you fret about all the rest?

"Observe the lilies! How they grow! They do not toil or spin;   27
yet, I tell you, even Solomon in all his splendor did not dress like
one of these. Now, if God so clothes the grass, which is in the field   28
today and thrown into the furnace tomorrow, how much more
readily will he clothe you! What little faith you have! You, there-   29
fore, must not be anxious about your food and drink, or live in
constant suspense. Why, the heathens, all the world over, make all   30
these things an object of eager search; but you have a Father who
knows that you need these things. Instead, make his kingdom your   31
concern; then you will have those other things thrown in for good
measure.

"Do not live in fear, my little flock! Your Father, certainly, has   32
been pleased to give you his kingdom. Sell all your possessions and   33
give alms; make yourselves purses that do not wear out — an unfailing treasure in heaven, where no thief has access and no moth devours. After all, where your treasure is, there, too, your heart is   34
bound to be.

"Keep your loins girt and your lamps burning. Yes, be like   35, 36
men who are on the lookout for their master, uncertain when he
starts for home from the wedding feast. Thus, the moment he arrives, they will at once open the door for him. Well for those slaves   37
whom the master on his return finds awake. I assure you, he will
gird himself and bid them recline at table and personally wait on
them! And whether he returns before midnight or after, well for   38
those slaves if he finds them so engaged! Of one thing you are sure: 39
if the owner of a house knew at what hour the thief was coming,
he would stay awake and not let his house be broken into. So you,   40
too: be in constant readiness; the Son of Man returns at an hour
you do not expect."

OUR LORD REPLIES TO PETER

41   Here Peter interposed: "Lord, do you mean your parable for us
42 or for everybody else as well?" The Lord replied: "Suppose a
master puts a manager in charge of his household to distribute the
rations of food at the proper time — in that case, who is the faithful,
43 prudent manager? It is the slave whom the master on his return
44 finds attending to his duties; and a happy man is he! I tell you
45 truly, he will put him in charge of his entire estate. But if the
manager says to himself: 'My master is long in coming,' and then
proceeds to maltreat the men and women slaves, and to eat and to
46 drink till he is drunk, the master of that overseer will return on a
day he is not expecting him and at an hour not known to him, and
shall separate him, and assign him a place among the unbelievers.
47   "If such an overseer knows his master's intentions, yet fails to
make preparations or act according to his intentions, he will be
48 severely punished. Of course, if he does not know them, yet does
things that deserve punishment, he will be but slightly punished.
Anyone that has received much will be required to return much;
and he that has a large capital entrusted to him will be required to
pay back interest as well.

49   "To throw a firebrand upon the earth — that is my mission! And
50 oh, how I wish it were already in a blaze! But then, I have yet to
undergo a baptism, and oh, in what an agony I am till it is
accomplished!

51   "Do you suppose that I came to shed peace upon the earth?
No, I tell you; quite the contrary! I came to sow dissension.
52 For example, from now on there will not be five persons in one
family without a quarrel; two will be on one side, and three on the
53 other; father will quarrel with son, and son with father; mother
with daughter, and daughter with mother; mother-in-law with daughter-in-law, and daughter-in-law with mother-in-law."

12:49. Verse 51 suggests that the firebrand is here a symbol of the strife and
dissensions which the teachings of Christ must necessarily occasion. The reference
may, however, be to the fire to be kindled in the souls of his disciples (see Lk.
24:32 and Acts 2:3). This was to take place after the death of Christ; hence
the reference to his "baptism" (see Mk. 10:38).

12:51. This statement is not contradicted by Jn. 14:27; each statement, though
universal in form, is limited in sense. See the note on 17:6.

WORDS ADDRESSED TO THE CROWDS

He also addressed the crowds: "When you see a cloud rise in the 54
west, you immediately say: 'A shower is coming'; and so it turns
out. And when you notice that the wind is blowing from the south, 55
you say: 'There will be scorching heat'; and it turns out that way.
Hypocrites! You know how to read the features of earth and sky: 56
how is it you do not read the signs of the times? And why do you not 57
look into your own conscience to decide what is the right thing
to do? For example: while you are on the way to a magistrate side 58
by side with your creditor, make an effort to get rid of him on the
way; otherwise, he drags you before the judge, and the judge hands
you over to the sheriff, and the sheriff puts you in jail! I tell you, 59
you will not be released from that place till you have paid the
last penny."

CHAPTER 13

WARNING TO MEND EVIL WAYS

About that very time some persons arrived to bring him word 1
about the Galileans whose blood Pilate had mingled with their
sacrifices. Taking advantage of the opportunity, he said to them: 2
"Do you suppose that these Galileans were worse sinners than
their countrymen, just because they suffered this fate? No, indeed, 3
I assure you; in fact, if you do not mend your evil ways, you will,
everyone of you, likewise perish. Or, take those eighteen persons 4
whom the Tower at the Pool of Siloam crushed to death by its fall
— do you suppose they were worse offenders than the rest of the
inhabitants of Jerusalem? No indeed, I assure you; in fact, if you 5
do not mend your evil ways, you will, everyone of you, likewise
perish."

He then told them the following parable: "Once upon a time, 6
a man had a fig tree planted in his vineyard. One day he came to
look for fruit on it, and did not find any. So he said to the vine- 7
dresser: 'It is now three years since I have been coming to look for

---

13:6. The fig tree planted in the vineyard is, no doubt, a figure of Jerusalem,
placed, as it was, in the midst of the Holy Land. Both vineyard (Isa. 5:2) and
fig tree (Jer. 24) were recognized types of the Chosen People.

fruit on this fig tree, and have not found any! Cut it down! Why,
8 really, should it impoverish the soil?' But the man pleaded with him.
'Sir,' he said, 'let it stand one year more. In the meantime, I will
9 dig up the ground about it and put in manure. If after that it
bears fruit, well and good; if not, you may have it cut down.'"
10   One Sabbath, he was teaching in one of their synagogues.
11 Just then a woman who, for eighteen years, had been suffering from
an infirmity caused by a spirit was present. She was actually bent
12 double and completely unable to raise her head. When Jesus saw her,
he called her to come forward. "My good woman," he said to her,
13 "you are now rid of your infirmity." He laid his hands upon her, and
she immediately straightened up and gave glory to God.

CHRIST HEALS ON THE SABBATH

14   But the head official of the synagogue, enraged because Jesus
had healed on the Sabbath, took occasion to lecture the crowd:
"Six days there are wherein you may work; on those days, therefore,
15 come and get yourselves cured, and not on the Sabbath!" But the
Lord taught him a lesson. "Hypocrites!" he said; "Does not everyone
of you unhitch his ox or his ass from the stall and drive them away to
16 water on the Sabbath? But here is a woman, a daughter of Abraham,
whom Satan bound, think of it, eighteen years ago, and it was not
17 all right to free her from this impediment on the Sabbath?" As he
said this, all his critics blushed with shame, while the people at
large expressed their joy at all the glorious things he was doing.

SIMILES OF THE KINGDOM OF GOD

18   He resumed therefore: "Of what does the kingdom of God
19 remind me? Or how shall I characterize it? It reminds me of a
mustard seed which a man carefully plants in his garden: eventually
it grows to be a stately tree, and the birds of the air nest in its
20 branches." Again he said: "How shall I characterize the kingdom
21 of God? It reminds me of a handful of yeast which a housewife
hides away in three measures of flour, to work there till the whole
mass has risen."

ENTER BY THE NARROW DOOR

22   And so he kept traveling about, teaching in town after town,

in village after village, while steadily pursuing his pilgrimage to Jerusalem. One day someone said to him "Lord, will the elect be 23 few in number?" "Strain every nerve," he replied, "to enter by the 24 narrow door; for many, I assure you, will be anxious to go in, but will not succeed once the head of the house has risen to shut the 25 door. Then you, standing outside, will be busy knocking at the door. 'Lord,' you will plead, 'open the door for us.' But his answer to you will be: 'I do not know what sort of people you are.' You will then 26 enter into an argument: 'Why, we ate and drank under your eyes, and you taught in our streets.' But he will retort: 'I am telling you, 27 I do not know what sort of people you are. Get out of my sight, the whole pack of you evildoers.' Oh, how that place will resound with 28 'the weeping and gnashing of teeth!' when you see Abraham, Isaac, and Jacob, with all the prophets, inside the kingdom of God, but yourselves turned out! Yes, guests will keep arriving from east and 29 west and north and south, and recline at table in the kingdom of God. Mark well: there are last ones that will be first, and first 30 ones that will be last."

JERUSALEM, MURDERESS OF PROPHETS

Just at that time some Pharisees approached to say to him: 31 "Quit this vicinity and keep going on your way. Herod has a mind to kill you." "Go," he said to them, "and say to that fox: 'Note 32 that I am driving out demons and performing cures today and tomorrow; it is on the third day that I reach my goal.' For all 33 that, I must keep going on my way today, tomorrow, and the following day. It surely will not do for a prophet to come to grief outside Jerusalem!

Jerusalem, Jerusalem!   34
Murderess of prophets!
Stoner of the messengers sent to you!

13:24. *many . . . will not succeed*: not, of course, because the door is too narrow, but because they come too late.

13:32. *I reach my goal*: the rendering is designedly vague to allow for the connotations of the Greek verb which was a technical term in the current mystery cults. It means not only "My end is coming," but "I enter into a higher state of life, I crown my career, I am perfected, I reach my full growth, I fill the measure of my achievement." The Greek word no doubt includes a reference to his death and his consequent glorification. Compare Hebr. 2:10; 5:9; 7:28; 11:40.

How often have I been willing
to gather your children
as a mother bird gathers her brood
under her wings!
But you refused it!

35 Mark well: you will find your house abandoned. And I tell you, you will not see me until the day comes when you cry out: 'A blessing on him who comes in the name of the Lord.'"

CHAPTER 14

HEALING ON THE SABBATH

1   The following occurred when he had entered the home of one of the leading men of the Pharisaical party to take a meal on the
2   Sabbath. The company was narrowly watching him. Suddenly a
3   man who had the dropsy stood in front of him, and Jesus took occasion to say to the legal experts, who were Pharisees: "Is it right
4   on the Sabbath to heal, or is it not?" But they held their peace. So
5   he laid his hand on the man, healed him, and sent him away. He then addressed the company: "Suppose your son or your ox falls into a well, will you not at once pull him up even though it is a
6   Sabbath?" Of course, they could raise no objection against that.

HE WHO HUMBLES HIMSELF WILL BE EXALTED

7   He then told the guests a parable, noticing how they were choosing the best places at table for themselves. He said to them:
8   "When you have been invited by someone to a wedding feast, do not recline on the first couch; or, possibly, someone more dis-
9   tinguished than you has been invited by him; and in that case your common host will come and say to you: 'Make room for this man.' And then you will have to be content, to your confusion, to occupy
10   the lowest place. No; when you are invited, go to the lowest place and recline, so that, when your host enters, he can say to you: 'My friend, come up higher.' Then you will win distinction from
11   all your fellow guests. Whoever exalts himself will be humbled; he who humbles himself will be exalted."

COMPENSATION AT THE RESURRECTION

He also had a word for his host: "Whenever you give a lunch 12
or supper, do not invite your friends or brothers or relatives or
well-to-do neighbors. Otherwise, they might, perhaps, invite you in
turn, and that would then be your compensation. No; when you 13
give an entertainment, invite persons that are poor, crippled, lame,
or blind; and you will be happy, because they have no means of 14
compensating you; for compensation will be made to you at the
resurrection of the saints."

INVITATIONS SPURNED. THE CONSEQUENCE

On hearing this, one of the fellow guests said to him: "O what 15
bliss it must be for anyone to feast in the kingdom of God!"

He replied: "Once upon a time, a man planned giving a great 16
supper and sent out many invitations. About the time set for the 17
supper he sent his servant to give notice to those invited: 'Come;
everything is now ready.' Then all alike proceeded to beg off. The 18
first said to him: 'I have bought a farm, and I must of necessity go
and inspect it. I beg you, consider me excused.' Another said: 'I 19
have bought five teams of oxen; and I am just going to try them
out. I beg you, consider me excused.' Still another said: 'I just got 20
married, and for that reason I cannot come.' When the servant re- 21
turned, he reported these excuses to his master. The head of the house
flew into a rage. 'Go out quickly,' he said to his servant, 'into the
streets and lanes of the city, and bring in here the poor and crippled
and blind and lame.' Again the servant reported: 'Master, your 22
order has been carried out, and there is still room for more.' The 23
master then said to the servant: 'Go out on the highways and among
the hedges, and compel people to come in. My house must be filled
to capacity.' I tell you, therefore, not one of those originally invited 24
will taste my supper."

RENOUNCE ALL TO FOLLOW CHRIST

One day when great crowds were journeying along with him, he 25
turned round and said to them: "If anyone comes to follow me and 26

14:26. A Christian must not love his relatives more than his divine Master.
There is here no question of real "hatred." Compare the wording in Mt. 10:37,
and see the note on Mt. 5:43.

Note from the Douay Bible: "The law of Christ does not allow us to *hate*

does not hate his father and mother, his wife and children, his brothers and sisters, and even his life, he cannot be my disciple.
27 He who comes to follow me but will not shoulder his cross, cannot
28 be my disciple. Really, which of you, intending to build a tower, will not first sit down and calculate the cost, to see whether he has
29 the wherewithal to finish it? Otherwise, if after laying a foundation he has not money enough to complete the work, the curious crowd
30 will indulge in mockery at his expense. 'Here is a fellow,' they will say, 'who began building without having means enough to finish!'
31 Or, again, where is there a king that intends to mobilize his troops against a rival king, but does not first sit down and hold a council to see whether he with his ten thousand men is a match for the
32 other who mobilizes twenty thousand to attack him? And if he is not, he sends an embassy to inquire about terms of peace while the
33 other is still far off. On the same principle, none of you can be my disciple unless he first renounces all his possessions.
34 "So, too, salt is an excellent thing. But suppose salt should ever
35 go flat, by what means could its nature be restored? It would be fit for neither soil nor dunghill. People would throw it away. Let everyone heed what he has heard."

CHAPTER 15

TAX COLLECTORS AND SINNERS LISTEN TO JESUS

1 The tax collectors as a class and the sinners were in the habit
2 of being near him and listening to him. At this, however, the Pharisees and the Scribes were grumbling. "This man," they would
3 say, "attracts sinners and feasts with them." So one day Jesus
4 addressed to them the following parable: "Suppose one of you has a hundred sheep: will he not, if he loses one of them, leave the ninety-nine in the desert and go in search of the one that is lost
5 until he finds it? And when he has found it, he joyfully puts it on
6 his shoulders, and, on coming home, calls his friends and neighbors

---

even our enemies, much less our parents; but the meaning of the text is, that we must be in that disposition of soul, as to be willing to renounce, and part with everything, how near or dear soever it may be to us, that would keep us from following Christ."

196

together and says to them: 'Congratulate me, for I have found my
sheep that was lost.' I tell you, there is joy in heaven over one 7
repentant sinner — more, in fact, than over ninety-nine saints that
have no need of repentance.

"Or suppose a woman has ten drachmas and loses one: does she 8
not light a lamp and sweep the house and search carefully till she
finds it? And when she has found it, she calls her friends and 9
neighbors together and says: 'Congratulate me, for I have found the
drachma which I had lost.' For the same reason, I tell you, there 10
is joy among the angels of God over one repentant sinner.

PARABLE OF THE TWO SONS

"Once upon a time," he said, "a man had two sons. 11
One day the younger of them said to his father: 'Father, give me 12
the part of the property that falls to my share.' So he divided his
property between them. Not many days later, the younger son cashed 13
everything and went off to a far-off country, where he squandered
his money by licentious living. When he had spent everything, a 14
terrible famine swept over that country and he faced starvation.
So he went to throw himself on the mercy of a citizen of that 15
region, who sent him to his farm to tend pigs. And oh, how heartily 16
he would have feasted on the carob pods on which the pigs were
feeding! But no one would give them to him. At last he came to 17
his senses. 'How many of my father's hired men,' he said, 'have food
enough and to spare, while I am here perishing with hunger! I will 18
quit this place and go to meet my father. Father, I will say to him,
I have sinned against heaven, and you know that I am no longer fit 19
to be considered your son. Treat me as one of your hired help.' So he 20
quit the place and went to meet his father.

"He was still a good way off when his father caught sight of him
and, stirred to pity, ran and threw his arms round his neck and kissed
him affectionately.

"The son then said to him: 'Father, I have sinned against heaven 21
and before you, and you know that I am no longer fit to be considered your son.' But the father said to his slaves: 'Quick; bring 22
out the finest robe and put it on him; then put a ring on his hand
and sandals on his feet; also fetch the fatted calf and kill it; let us 23
feast and celebrate. This son of mine was dead and has come back 24

197

to life again, was lost and has been found again.' And so they gave themselves up to celebrating.

25 "Meanwhile the elder son was in the field. When he returned and came near the house, he heard strains of music and dancing,
26 and, calling one of the farmhands aside, inquired what all this meant.
27 'Why,' the lad said to him, 'your brother has come back; so your father had the fatted calf killed because he received him back safe
28 and sound.' Thereupon he grew angry and refused to go in. So
29 his father came out and pleaded with him. But he protested and said to the father: 'Look at all these years that I have been toiling like a slave for you! I never disobeyed any of your orders, and yet you never gave me a kid, that I might celebrate with my friends!
30 But here comes that son of yours who wasted his property in the company of lewd women, and right away you kill the fatted calf to
31 humor him!' He replied: 'My son, you have always been with me,
32 and all that is mine is yours; but as to this feasting and celebrating — it simply has to be done, because that brother of yours was dead and has come to life again, was lost and has been found again!' "

CHAPTER 16

THE UNSCRUPULOUS MANAGER

1 He also said to the disciples: "Once upon a time, there was a rich man who had a manager, and complaints were made to him about this man that he was letting his estate go to rack and ruin.
2 So he summoned him and said: 'What is this I hear about you?
3 Submit your balance sheet! You can be manager no longer!' The manager then reasoned as follows: 'My master is taking the management away from me. What shall I do? To dig I am not strong
4 enough; to beg I am ashamed. Ah, I know what to do, so that, when I am ousted from the management, people will welcome me
5 in their homes!' And calling his master's debtors to appear before him, one by one, he said to the first: 'How much do you owe my
6 master?' 'One hundred barrels of oil,' he replied. 'Take your note';

16:1. The parable of the unscrupulous manager illustrates the ways of men of the world — masters, managers, debtors — among themselves. The lesson is pointed out in the second half of verse 8 and the following.

he said to him: 'quick, sit down and write fifty.' 'And you,' he said 7
to another, 'how much do you owe?' 'Fourteen hundred bushels of
wheat,' he replied. 'Take your note,' he said to him, 'and write
eleven hundred.' And the master commended the unscrupulous 8
manager for his shrewd way of acting.

USE MONEY CONSCIENTIOUSLY

"The fact is, in dealing with their own kind, the children of the
world are shrewder than the children of the light. And so I say to 9
you: money is a worthless thing; but use it to make friends for
yourselves, so that, when it gives out, they may receive you in the
everlasting homes. He who is conscientious in small things is 10
conscientious in big things also; he who is unscrupulous in small
things is unscrupulous in big things also. Therefore, if you do not 11
prove conscientious in handling so worthless a thing as money, who
will trust you with a genuine good? And if you do not prove 12
conscientious in handling what is not your own, who will trust you
with what is your own?

"A servant cannot be the slave of two masters; for either he will 13
hate the one and love the other, or, at least, be attentive to the one

---

16:8 *the children of the world*: a Hebraism for men dominated by the principles of the world. "The disciples of Christ, although their light is so much
clearer, are so much less prudent in making provision for the life to come than
worldlings are in making provision for their future in this life" (Darby and
Smith).

16:9. Money as such is *worthless* because it has no necessary connection with
eternal life; but, used from a religious motive, it may become a means of securing
salvation. See the note on 11:41. The rendering "the mammon of iniquity" (see
the note on Mt. 6:24) is erroneous. Christ is not here speaking of money unjustly
acquired (Lagrange). To the Greeks anything "not up to the mark, no longer
fit for use or service" was "unjust, iniquitous, not right."

16:10. *small things*: money, worldly goods; *big things*: virtue, divine grace, etc.
Undue attachment to worldly goods is a hindrance to spiritual life and, often
enough, to eternal salvation. See Mt. 13:22.

16:11. *who will trust you with a genuine good?*: God will not give you the
grace needed for salvation.

16:12. The language in this verse is colored by current philosophical termi-
nology. Money (and, in general, material goods) is "not our own," literally,
"foreign, extraneous, not under our control, not making us better when we
possess it." Divine grace, on the other hand (and, in general, the blessings of
Christianity), is "our own"; for, although it comes from God, it is meant as a
help to eternal salvation. *who will trust you*: see the note on 16:11. Compare
12:20.

199

and neglectful of the other. You cannot have God and money for masters."

14 The Pharisees, who were fond of money, were within earshot
15 when he said all this, and sneered at him. So he said to them: "You are the type of men that make the world believe they are saints; but God knows your hearts. Rest assured: what is exalted in men's eyes is an abomination in the sight of God.

TO ENTER HEAVEN DO VIOLENCE TO SELF

16 "The Law and the Prophets prevailed till John's time; since then, the Good News of the kingdom of God is being preached, and one
17 has to do violence to himself to enter it. Nevertheless, it is easier for heaven and earth to go out of existence than for one detail of
18 the Law to go out of force. Anyone who divorces his wife and marries another is an adulterer, and he who marries a woman divorced from her husband is an adulterer.

THE RICH MAN AND THE BEGGAR LAZARUS

19 "Once upon a time there was a rich man who dressed in purple
20 and fine linen, and feasted sumptuously day after day. Close by the portal of his mansion there lay a beggar named Lazarus — a
21 mass of sores! And oh, how he would have liked to satisfy his hunger with the mere refuse from the rich man's table! Not only that: even the prowling dogs would come and lick his sores.
22 Eventually the beggar died and was carried by the angels into Abraham's bosom. The rich man also died and was buried in hell.
23 Finding himself in extreme torment in hades, he raised his eyes
24 and saw at a distance Abraham with Lazarus in his lap. So he called out: 'Father Abraham, take pity on me and send Lazarus to dip the tip of his finger in water and cool off my tongue; I am in
25 agony in this flame.' 'But remember, my son,' replied Abraham, 'that you received all you cared for during your lifetime, while Lazarus, for his part, was in misery. At present, he is here in bliss while you are in
26 agony. And in addition to all this, a deep chasm is once for all fixed between us and you, so that no one who might wish to cross from here to you can do so, nor can any that are there come over

---

16:16. See Mt. 11:12.
16:17. Although the new era (the kingdom of God) has arrived, *nevertheless* the Mosaic Law in its pristine purity continues. See Mt. 5:17.

to us.' He then said: 'I beg you therefore, Father, to let him go 27
to my father's house; for I have five brothers; let him give them 28
solemn warning; otherwise, they, too, will come to this place of
extreme torment.' But Abraham replied: 'They have Moses and the 29
prophets; let them listen to these.' 'No, father Abraham,' he replied, 30
'but in case somebody comes to them from the dead, they will mend
their evil ways.' But he said to him: 'If they do not listen to Moses 31
and the prophets, neither will they take advice in case a dead man
rises again.' "

Chapter 17

BE THE OCCASION OF SIN TO NO ONE

He said to his disciples: "It is impossible that temptations to 1
sin should not come; but O the wretchedness of him through whom
they come! It would be better for him if he lay at the bottom of 2
the sea with a heavy millstone hung round his neck, instead of being
an occasion of sin to even one of these little ones.

OTHER SPIRITUAL ADVICE

"Be considerate of one another. In case your brother sins, reprove 3
him; and in case he is sorry, forgive him. And should he sin against 4
you seven times a day, and seven times return to tell you, 'I am
sorry,' forgive him."

One day the disciples said to the Lord: "Give us more faith." 5
The Lord replied: "If you have faith as small as a mustard seed, you 6

17:6. Christ's method of teaching is apt to puzzle the modern mind. We
are accustomed, in studying the commandments, to have them explained with
due regard to varying circumstances (see the note on Mt. 5:39). This is not
our Lord's way in the Gospels. He, as a rule, emphasizes one aspect of the
matter under discussion to the seeming exclusion of all others; but no such
exclusion is intended. So here: undoubting faith is put down absolutely as though
it were by itself sufficient for an infallible answer to one's prayer. This is the
one condition pointed out here, because the disciples (see Mt. 17:14-21) were
"unable" to cure the lunatic because of their "little faith." That other conditions
are required to make prayer successful is not only obvious, but also taught expressly
elsewhere; for example, the thing prayed for must be "a good gift" (Lk. 11:13),
something that is helpful to us and promotes the glory of God. So again, the
words "do not swear at all" (Mt. 5:34) do not forbid taking an oath under
certain circumstances. The prohibition in Mt. 10:9 is not meant to be a binding
rule for missionaries of all times. The statement in Mt. 10:34 needs to be supplemented by that in Jn. 14:27. In short: the meaning of Christ's words on any

might say to this mulberry tree, 'Up with you, root and all, and plant yourself in the sea!' and it would obey you.

7   "Suppose some one of you has a slave who is plowing or tending sheep, and then comes in from the field. Will he say to
8   him: 'Come here at once and recline at table'? Will he not, rather, say to him: 'Get my dinner ready; and gird yourself to wait on me while I eat and drink; after that, you can eat and drink'?
9   Does he feel obliged to the slave for carrying out his orders?
10   Apply this to yourselves: when you have carried out all the orders given you, just say: 'We are good-for-nothing slaves; we have merely done our duty.' "

TEN LEPERS CLEANSED. ONE ALONE GRATEFUL

11   The following occurred on his pilgrimage to Jerusalem, as he
12   passed along the borders of Samaria and Galilee. He was about to enter a village when ten lepers came his way. They stopped at some
13   distance, and with raised voices cried out: "Rabbi Jesus, take pity
14   on us." Noticing them, he said: "Go, and get yourselves examined by the priests." And this is what happened: while still on their way,
15   they were made clean. Now one of them, seeing that he was cured,
16   turned back, loudly praising God; he threw himself on his face at
17   Jesus' feet and thanked him. And this was a Samaritan! "Were not
18   the ten made clean?" Jesus asked; "Where are the other nine? Oh to find that not one has returned to give glory to God except this
19   foreigner!" He then said to him: "You may rise and go home. Your faith has cured you."

THE KINGDOM OF GOD

20   Being asked one day by the Pharisees when the kingdom of God was coming, he gave them this answer: "The kingdom of God
21   is not coming with visible pomp that can be watched for; nor will people have to say: 'See there!' or 'See here!' Why, open your eyes;

occasion is not necessarily clear from an isolated text, but must be gathered from the whole of his teaching. Common sense, the context, and such other limitations as circumstances may suggest must be duly weighed before we can be sure of knowing the mind of Christ. The Gospels are not a catechism that teaches Christian doctrine in set form, but a string of occasional (and often fragmentary) utterances that need explanation.

the kingdom of God is already in your midst." "But a time is 22
coming," he said to his disciples, "when you will long to see were
it only one day of the Son of Man, and you will not see it. You will 23
then be told, 'See there!' or 'See here!' Stay where you are, and do
not run in pursuit. For just as the lightning flares up at one end of 24
the firmament and blazes its path to the other, so it will be with the
Son of Man on his day. First, however, he has yet to suffer much, 25
and meet with rejection at the hands of this generation.

WHEN THE SON OF MAN REVEALS HIMSELF

"And what happened in the time of Noe will happen again in 26
the days when the Son of Man appears: people went on eating and 27
drinking, marrying and giving in marriage, up to the day when Noe
entered the Ark; then the flood burst and destroyed every living soul.
The same happened in the time of Lot: people went on eating 28
and drinking, buying and selling, planting and building; but the day 29
Lot left Sodom, fire and brimstone rained from the sky and destroyed
every living soul. The very same will happen when the Son of Man 30
reveals himself. On that day, if one is on the roof and his belongings 31
are in the house, he must not go down to fetch them; and so, too,
he who is in the field must not turn back. Remember Lot's wife! 32
He who seeks ways and means of saving his life must part with it 33
anyway; but he who freely parts with his life will preserve it.
On that night, I tell you, two may be lying on one bed: one will be 34
taken along, and the other abandoned; two women may be grinding 35
together: one will be taken along, and the other abandoned." 36, 37
And when they inquired, "Where, Lord?" he replied: "Where the
dead body is, there, too, the birds of prey will assemble."

Chapter 18

PERSEVERANCE IN PRAYER

He also told them a parable to show that they must persevere 1

17:22. Sorely tried by persecutions, the disciples will long for Christ's glorious
return. But God has his own time for helping his distressed children in the
world. See 21:19. That God is not indifferent to our cries is clearly taught
in 18:1-7.
17:32. See Gen. 19:26.
18:1-8. A homely illustration, as in 11:8.

2 in prayer and not lose heart. "Once upon a time," he said, "there
   was a judge in a town somewhere who did not fear God and had no
3 regard for man. In the same town, there lived a widow who used
   to come to him and say: 'See that justice is done me! Rid me of
4 my persecutor!' For a time he refused; but later he said to himself:
5 'I do not fear God and have no regard for man; but, at any rate,
   since this widow is pestering me, I will see that justice is done her.
6 I am afraid she may finally come and beat me black and blue.' " The
7 Lord then added: "Listen to what the unjust judge says! And God
   will not see full justice done to his elect who cry to him day and
8 night? Will he really delay acting in their behalf? I tell you, he
   will see that justice is done them with all speed! But, oh, when the
   Son of Man returns, will he find the necessary faith on earth?"

PRIDE VERSUS HUMILITY

9 He also addressed the following parable to some of those who
   confidently believed that they were observers of the Law and, at
10 the same time, despised everybody else: "Once upon a time, two
   men went up to the temple to pray, the one a Pharisee, the other a
11 tax collector. The Pharisee stood conspicuously apart and soliloquized
   this prayer: 'O God, I thank you that I am not like the rest of men
   — robbers, rogues, adulterers — or like that tax collector over there.
12 I fast twice a week; I pay a tax of ten per cent on every item of
13 my income.' The tax collector, on the contrary, kept in the background and would not so much as raise his eyes to heaven, but
   struck his breast and said: 'O God, have mercy on me the sinner.'
14 I assure you, this man went down to his home acquitted of all guilt;
   not so the other. Everyone who exalts himself shall be humbled,
   and he who humbles himself shall be exalted."

LET THE LITTLE CHILDREN COME TO ME

15 One day people brought to him even their infants, that he might
   lay his hands upon them; but the disciples, who saw this, scolded
16 them for doing so. Jesus called for the infants and said: "Let the

18:8. In heaven the elect will see, in retrospect, that after all Christ did
come "with all speed." See Apoc. 22:7. In God's view of things, even a lifetime
of suffering is but "a momentary affliction" (2 Cor. 4:17). There was a widespread belief among the early Christians that the end of the world was near
at hand. St. Paul corrected this impression in 2 Thess. 2:1 ff.

little children come to me, and do not stop them. The kingdom
of God belongs to such as these. Yes, I assure you: he who does 17
not accept the kingdom of God as a little child does will never
enter it."

SACRIFICE FOR THE SAKE OF GOD'S KINGDOM

One of the leading men put this question to him: "Good Rabbi, 18
what must I do to inherit eternal life?" "Why do you call me good?" 19
Jesus said to him; "nobody is good except One — God! You know 20
the commandments: do not commit adultery; do not murder; do
not steal; do not bear false witness; honor your father and mother."
"All these commandments," he said to him, "I have observed from 21
my youth." When Jesus heard this, he said to him: "One thing is 22
still wanting to you: sell all you have and distribute the proceeds
among the poor, and you will have an investment in heaven; then
come back and be my follower." On hearing that, he became ex- 23
tremely sad, for he was exceedingly rich. Jesus then looked at him 24
and said: "Oh, with what difficulty will those who have the goods of
this world enter the kingdom of God! Yes, it is easier for a camel 25
to pass through the eye of a needle than for a rich man to enter
the kingdom of God!" Here the hearers said: "In that case, who can 26
be saved?" He replied: "Where man fails God still avails!" 27
Then Peter remarked: "We, you see, have given up our possessions 28
and become your followers." "I tell you with assurance," he said 29
to them, "no one gives up home, or parents, or brothers, or wife, or
children, for the sake of the kingdom of God, but receives many 30
times as much in this world and eternal life in the world to come."

Taking the Twelve aside, he said to them: "Listen! We are going 31
up to Jerusalem, and every detail written by the prophets about the
Son of Man must be fulfilled. Namely: he will be betrayed to the 32
Gentiles, and mocked, and outraged, and spat upon, and scourged 33
and put to death, and on the third day rise again." They, however, 34

18:19. To make sense in this context, the question, *why do you call me
good?* must be supplemented by the question in Mt. 19:17: "Why do you
consult me about something good" Jesus means to say: since you call me good,
and want to know what is really good, keep the commandments, because they
are the expression of him who alone is good! He does not wish to deny that
he, too, is God and therefore good.
18:20. Exod. 20:12–16.

understood nothing of this. His speech was a mystery to them, and they could not make out what he meant.

THE BLIND BEGGAR REGAINS HIS SIGHT

35 The following happened as he was coming into the vicinity of
36 Jericho. A blind beggar sat by the road. Hearing a crowd pass by,
37 he inquired what it all meant, and when the people informed him
38 that Jesus of Nazareth was passing by, he shouted the words: "Jesus,
39 Son of David, take pity on me." Those who marched in the van
sternly bade him be quiet; but he shouted all the more vigorously:
40 "Son of David, take pity on me." Jesus stopped and ordered him to
41 be fetched. When he had come near, he asked him: "What do you
42 wish me to do for you?" "Lord," he replied, "I wish to see." "Have
43 your sight," Jesus said to him; "your faith has cured you." And immediately he saw, and then followed him, glorifying God. So, too,
all the people who had witnessed the scene gave praise to God.

CHAPTER 19

ZACCHEUS WELCOMES JESUS

1 He now entered Jericho. As he made his way through the town,
2 there was a stir: a man named Zaccheus, a high official among the
3 tax collectors and rich as well, was curious to find out who Jesus
was, but owing to the press of people had no chance to do so, for
4 he was small of stature. In order, therefore, to get a glimpse of
Jesus, he ran ahead and climbed up into a sycamore tree, because
5 he was expected to pass that way. When Jesus came to the spot,
he looked up. "Zaccheus," he said to him, "come down quickly;
6 today I must be your guest." And, coming down quickly, he wel-
7 comed him joyfully. But a murmur ran through the crowd of
spectators. "He has turned in," they commented, "to accept the
8 hospitality of a sinner!" Then Zaccheus drew himself up and
addressed the Lord: "Upon my word, Lord, I will give to the poor
one half of my possessions and, if I have obtained anything from
9 anybody by extortion, I will refund four times as much." Then, in
his presence, Jesus said: "Today salvation has visited this household,

---

18:35. *coming into the vicinity of Jericho*: this does not conflict with the parallel accounts in Mt. 20:29 or Mk. 10:46. The rendering "leaving Jericho" in Mt. and Mk. is erroneous.

because he, too, is a son of Abraham. After all, it is the mission of 10
the Son of Man to seek and save what is lost."

BE LOYAL WHILE I AM AWAY

His words were still ringing in their ears when he followed up 11
with a parable, for he was in the neighborhood of Jerusalem and
they expected the kingdom of God to make its appearance at any
moment. He said, then: "Once upon a time, a man of noble birth 12
set out for a distant country in order to obtain the title of king and
then return. So, after summoning ten of his officials, he distributed 13
among them ten minas, with this injunction: 'Do business while I
am away.' His fellow citizens, however, hated him, and sent a 14
delegation after him with this message: 'We do not want this man
to be our king.' As things went, he obtained the title of king. When 15
he returned, he ordered these officials to be summoned before him
to find out what each had gotten out of his business transactions.
The first to present himself said: 'My lord, your mina has earned an 16
additional ten.' 'Capital!' he said, 'You are a first-rate official. You 17
have been faithful in managing a very small amount; therefore you
shall have the governorship over ten cities.' Then the second 18
came and reported: 'Your mina, my lord, has made five more.' To 19
this one he said, in turn: 'You shall be placed over five cities.'
When the third, who was of a different type, came in, he made 20
this speech: 'Well, sir, here is your mina. I have kept it laid aside
in a napkin. I was afraid of you, because you are a merciless task- 21
master; you pick up what you have not laid down, and you reap
what you have not sown.' 'Out of your own mouth,' he replied, 22
'will I pass sentence on you, good-for-nothing fellow. So you knew
that I was a merciless taskmaster, picking up what I have not laid
down, and reaping what I have not sown? Then why did you not 23
put my money in the bank, and on my return I might at least have
claimed it back plus the interest?' He then said to the bystanders: 24
'Take the mina away from him, and give it to the one who has the
ten minas.' 'But, lord,' they interposed, 'he has ten minas already.' 25

19:12. Foreign princes subject to the Roman Empire had to obtain their title
from the emperor.

19:13. See the note on Mt. 18:23. A *mina* was the sixtieth part of a talent
(see the note on Mt. 18:24), equivalent to about 30 dollars at an earlier date
than the present writing.

26 'I tell you, every man of means will be given yet more, while the
    man without means will have taken from him even what he has.
27 But as to those enemies of mine who do not want me to be their
    king, bring them in here and dispatch them before my eyes.'"

ON THE WAY TO JERUSALEM

28   After saying this, Jesus went right on, taking the lead on the
29 way up to Jerusalem. When he arrived at the outskirts of Bethphage
    and Bethany, on the slope of the so-called Mount of Olives, he
30 sent two of his disciples on an errand, with this instruction: "Go into
    the village directly in front of you and, as you enter, you will find
    hitched a foal on which no man has ever sat. Unhitch it and bring
31 it here. And in case anybody asks you, 'Why do you unhitch it?'
32 just say: 'Because the Lord has need of it.'" The messengers went
33 and found everything as he had told them. As they were un-
    hitching the foal, its owners said to them, "Why do you unhitch
34 the foal?" and they replied: "Because the Lord has need of it."
35 They brought the foal to Jesus, and, after throwing their cloaks on
    it, seated Jesus upon it.
36   As he proceeded, the people carpeted the road with their cloaks.
37 Finally, they came to the spot where the Mount of Olives slopes
    down, and now the whole throng of the disciples became enthusiastic
    and burst into praising God for all the deeds of power they had
38 witnessed, and exclaimed:

            "A blessing on the King
            who comes in the name of the Lord!
            Peace in heaven
            and glory in the heights above!"

39 Then some of the Pharisees in the crowd said to him: "Rabbi,
40 reprove your disciples!" But his answer was: "I tell you, if these are
    dumb, the stones will cry out."

CHRIST SOBS OVER THE CITY

41   When at last he came near enough to have a view of the city, he
    sobbed out his grief over it, saying:
42   "O if you, too, did know,
                at least on this your day,

19:38. From the Psalm 117.

208

what makes for peace!
But alas, it is hidden from your eyes!
Days are coming upon you   43
when your enemies
will throw a rampart round you,
and encircle you,
and press hard upon you on every side;
and they will dash to the ground   44
both you and your children within,
nor will they leave stone upon stone
within your walls;
because you did not recognize
the time of your visitation."

After entering the temple grounds, he proceeded to drive out   45
the sellers. "The Scripture says," he said to them,   46
" 'My house shall be a house of prayer;
        but you have turned it into a den of robbers.' "

He spent day after day in the temple. Meanwhile, the high   47
priests and the Scribes, as well as the leaders of the people, were
scheming to destroy him; but they could not discover just what to 48
do, for the mass of the people hung upon his words.

Chapter 20

BY WHAT AUTHORITY?

The following happened one day about that time when he   1
instructed the people in the temple and preached the Good News.
The high priests and the Scribes, accompanied by the elders, confronted him, and put this question to him: "Tell us outright by   2
what authority you engage in this activity; in other words, who is
he that gave you this authority?" But he parried their question by 3
saying to them: "Let me, in turn, ask you a question, and tell me
outright: the baptism of John — was it from heaven or from men?" 4
Then they privately took counsel together: "In case we say, 'From 5
heaven,' " they argued, "he will say, 'Then why did you not believe
him?' But if we say, 'From men,' the people to a man will stone us, 6
for they are convinced that John was a prophet." So their answer 7

209

8   to Jesus was: "We do not know where it came from." Then Jesus
said to them: "Neither will I tell you by what authority I am
acting the way I am.'"

THE PARABLE OF THE HUSBANDMEN

9   He then proceeded to warn them in parable style as follows:
"Once upon a time, a man planted a vineyard and leased it out
to vinedressers. He then went abroad for a long period of time.
10 In due season he sent an agent to the vinedressers, demanding
that they should give him a share of the vintage. But the vine-
11 dressers beat him and sent him back empty-handed. But he followed
up with sending another agent; and this one, again, they beat and
12 insulted and sent back empty-handed. He persisted, however, and
sent a third agent; and this one, too, they wounded and forced off
13 the premises. Finally, the owner of the vineyard said: 'I am at a
loss what to do. Ah, I will send my beloved son! Perhaps they will
14 respect him.' But when the vinedressers saw him, they consulted
with one another. 'This is the heir,' they said; 'let us kill him, so
15 that the inheritance may be ours.' So they forced him out of the
vineyard and killed him. Under these circumstances, what will the
16 owner of the vineyard do to them? He will come and put those
vinedressers to death. Yes, and he will give the vineyard to others."
17 On hearing this, they said: "God forbid!" But he looked straight
at them and said: "What, then, is the meaning of this Scripture text:
'The stone which the builders rejected
has become the cornerstone'?
18 Whoever dashes against that stone will be crushed; and he on whom
19 it falls, will be ground to powder." The Scribes and the high priests
were eager to lay their hands on him there and then; but they feared
the people. They understood, of course, that he had aimed this
parable at themselves.

SEEKING TO ENSNARE JESUS

20 So they watched their opportunity and sent spies to act
the part of honest men and take him in his speech, in

20:9. The *vineyard* is the Chosen People of Israel; the *vinedressers* are the
rulers of the people; the *agents* are the prophets.
20:16. *to others*: the Gentiles.
20:17. Ps. 117:22; Isa. 28:16.

order to hand him over to the civil power, that is, the
tribunal of the governor. They put this question to him: 21
"Rabbi, we know that in all your teaching you speak straightforwardly, and who a person is never worries you; on the
contrary, you teach the way of God truthfully. Is it right for us 22
to pay the poll tax to Caesar, or is it not?" Jesus saw through 23
their cunning. "Show me a denarius," he said to them; "Whose 24
head is this? And whose title is here inscribed?" "Caesar's," they
replied. "Therefore," he said to them, "render to Caesar what is 25
Caesar's, and to God what is God's." And so they were unable to 26
take him in his speech in the hearing of the people. They admired
his answer, and said nothing more.

THE JUST IN HEAVEN SHARE IN THE NATURE OF GOD

Then some of the Sadducees interviewed him — the men that 27
deny the resurrection — and proposed a case to him. "Rabbi," they 28
said, "Moses has made this ruling for us: 'If a man's brother dies and
is childless, his brother is to marry the widow and raise issue for him.'
Now, once upon a time there were seven brothers. The first took 29
a wife and died childless; the second then took her to wife; 30
and so did the third; and in like manner all the seven died without 31
leaving issue. Last of all the woman also died. What, then, about 32
the woman at the resurrection? Of which of them does she become 33
the wife? All the seven, you see, had her to wife." Jesus said 34
to them: "It is only while living in this world that people marry and
are given in marriage; but once happily admitted to the world 35
beyond and to the resurrection from the dead, they neither marry
nor are given in marriage; nor, indeed, are they any longer subject 36
to death, because they are like angels; and, once they share in the
resurrection, they share in the nature of God. But as to the rising 37
from the dead, even Moses has hinted at it in the passage about
the Bush, where he speaks of 'the Lord, the God of Abraham,'
and 'the God of Isaac,' and 'the God of Jacob.' But he is not the 38
God of dead men, but of living; indeed, all are living to him." Then 39
some of the Scribes expressed their assent and said: "Well said,

---

20:23. *a denarius:* see the note on Mk. 6:37.
20:27. *the Sadducees:* see the note on Mt. 3:7.
20:37. Exod. 3:6, 15 f.

40 Rabbi!" The fact is, nobody after this dared ask him any more questions.

41 But he said to them: "In what sense do people say the Messias
42 is the Son of David? David himself, you know, says in the Book of Psalms:

> 'The Lord said to my Lord:
> Be seated at my right hand
43 > until I make your foes
> a footstool for your feet.'

44 David, therefore, calls him 'Lord.' In what sense, then, is he his son?"

BEWARE OF THE SCRIBES

45 In the hearing of all the people he said to the disciples:
46 "Beware of the Scribes, who fancy fine robes for outdoor wear, and crave ceremonious greetings in public places, and front seats in the
47 synagogues, and places of honor at meals. These men that devour the fortunes of widows and recite long prayers for show will receive a more than ordinary punishment."

CHAPTER 21

THE BEGGAR WOMAN'S GIFT

1 Looking up, he saw the people putting their offerings into the
2 treasury. They were well-to-do folk. He also noticed a poor widow
3 putting in two small coins. "I tell you the plain truth," he said, "this widow, the beggar woman that she is, has put in more than
4 all the others; for all the others took from their superfluities what they put in as offerings to God; but this woman, in her extreme want, put in all that she had to live on."

5 When some remarked that the temple with its wonderful slabs
6 of stone and votive offerings was a thing of beauty he said: "You regard this structure with admiration; yet days are coming when not one stone will be left upon another. All will crumble to pieces."
7 They then asked him this question: "When, then, Rabbi, will this catastrophe take place? And what is the sign to indicate that this

is about to happen?" He replied: "See to it that you are not led 8
astray. Many will come and, assuming my title, say: 'I am he,' and,
'The moment is at hand.' Do not run after them. When you hear of 9
wars and revolutions, do not be alarmed. These things must happen,
but the end is not imminent."

FUTURE PERSECUTIONS

He then gave them this explanation: "Nation will rise against 10
nation, and kingdom against kingdom; there will be severe earth- 11
quakes and, here and there, famine and pestilence; there will be
frightening occurrences and striking portents in the sky. But before 12
all these things happen, men will lay their hands on you and
persecute you; they will deliver you up to synagogues and pris-
ons, and bring you before kings and governors because you
profess my name. That will be your chance to testify. 13
Make up your minds, therefore, not to premeditate speeches of 14
self-defense. I will give you ability to speak and wisdom, and your 15
adversaries will not be able to resist the one or contradict the other.
You will be betrayed even by parents and brothers, by relatives and 16
friends; and they will have some of you put to death. You will be 17
the scorn of all because you profess my name. Yet not a hair on your 18
head will perish. Your patient endurance will be your salvation. 19

THE DESTRUCTION OF JERUSALEM. THE COMING OF CHRIST

"And when you see a ring of armies round Jerusalem, then you 20
may be sure that her devastation is close at hand. Then those who 21
are in Judea should flee to the hills; those within her walls should
leave; and those in the country should not re-enter her. It will be 22
a time of vengeance, and every detail of the Scriptures must be
fulfilled. How pitiful the women that will be with child or nursing 23
in those days! There will, surely, be sore distress throughout the
land, and the vials of wrath will be poured out upon this people.
Men will fall by the edge of the sword, or be carried off captive 24
among the nations of the world. Jerusalem will be under the heel
of the Gentiles until such time as the Gentiles have run their
allotted course.

21:10. See the note on Mt. 24:2.
21:15. The special assistance here promised the defenders of the faith is well
illustrated in Acts 7.

25   "There will be striking phenomena in sun and moon and stars;
on the earth throes will grip the nations, perplexed by the roar of
26   sea and surge; men will faint away from fright and expectation of
what is yet to befall the world; for the foundations of the universe
27   will rock. At last they will see the Son of Man riding upon a cloud
28   with great might and majesty. When these phenomena are well under
way, raise your heads and look up, for then your redemption is
close at hand."

29   He also told them a parable: "Look at the fig tree, or any of the
30   trees: the moment they begin to shoot, you need but open your
31   eyes to know that summer is near. Apply this to yourselves: as soon
as you see these events in progress, you know that the kingdom of
32   God is at hand. Yes, I assure you, this generation will not pass away
33   before all these events have set in. Heaven and earth will fail; my
words will never fail.

34   "Keep watch over yourselves; otherwise the spirit in you is
smothered by heavy eating, drinking, or worldly cares; and that day
35   will unexpectedly spring upon you like a trap; indeed, it will burst
in upon all no matter where on the face of the earth they dwell.
36   Be vigilant at all times, praying that you may succeed in escaping
all these things that are bound to come, and that you may stand
your ground when confronted with the Son of Man."

37   The daytime he spent teaching in the temple, but passed the
38   nights in the open on the so-called Mount of Olives. Early in the
morning the people flocked to him in masses in order to hear him in
the temple.

CHAPTER 22

JUDAS CLOSES HIS BARGAIN

1   The feast of the Unleavened Bread, the so-called Passover, was
2   now drawing near, and the high priests and Scribes looked for ways
and means of doing away with him. They were afraid of the people.
3   Meanwhile Satan had taken full possession of Judas, surnamed
4   Iscariot, who was numbered among the Twelve. So he went to confer

22:3. This does not mean that Judas became a demoniac, but that he freely
yielded to the suggestions of Satan. See the note on Jn. 13:27.

with the high priests and temple officers as to how he might betray
him. They were delighted and agreed to pay him a sum of money. 5
He closed the bargain, and from then on looked for a convenient 6
opportunity to betray him to them in the absence of a crowd.

PETER AND JOHN PREPARE THE PASCHAL SUPPER

At last the day of the Unleavened Bread arrived, and the paschal 7
lamb had to be sacrificed. So Jesus sent Peter and John on an 8
errand, with this instruction: "Go to prepare the paschal supper for
us to eat." "Where," they asked him, "do you want us to make 9
preparations?" "Listen," he replied; "on entering the city, you will 10
meet a man carrying a pitcher of water; follow him into the house
he enters, and say to the proprietor of the house: 'The Rabbi asks, 11
Where is the dining room in which I can eat the paschal supper with
my disciples?' He will show you a room upstairs which is spacious 12
and well furnished. There get things ready." They went and found 13
everything as he had told them, and prepared the paschal supper.

THE PASCHAL SUPPER. THE BETRAYER IS PRESENT

When the hour had come, he took his place on a couch, and so 14
did the apostles. "It has been my heart's desire," he said to them, 15
"to eat this paschal supper with you before I suffer. I tell you, I shall 16
not eat it again till it is fulfilled in the kingdom of God." And after 17
receiving a cup and saying grace, he said: "Take this, and divide it
among you. I tell you, I shall not again drink of the produce of the 18
vine till the kingdom of God is set up."

He also took bread into his hands and, after saying grace, broke 19
it into portions, which he gave to them with these words: "This is
my body, which is about to be given for your sake. Do this as my

22:6. *in the absence* (from the city) of a crowd, or, "so as to avoid a popular
riot." Since the hotheaded Galileans would crowd the city during the feast,
Jesus was to be arrested either before or after the festivities.

22:17. "It was part of the ceremonial of the paschal supper to pass round
three, sometimes four, cups of wine mingled with water. It is to these ceremonial
chalices that the present verse refers, and not to the Blessed Eucharist" (Darby
and Smith).

22:19. *Do this as my memorial*: these words and verse 20 are omitted in some
manuscripts. The syntax of this sentence is not beyond cavil. The pronoun *this*
may refer to the whole action (including words and gestures) just described,
or only to *my body*. But the sense is the same in either interpretation, provided
the Greek verb rendered *do* is given a sacrificial sense (well known to Greek

20 memorial." He did the same with the cup when supper was over,
and said: "This cup is the new covenant sealed by my blood, which
21 is about to be shed for your sake. And yet, think of it, at this table,
22 within reach of me, there is the hand of my betrayer! The Son of
Man departs, indeed, according to the fixed decree; but perdition
23 awaits that man who is instrumental in betraying him!" At once
they set about inquiring which one of their group, then, might be the
likely perpetrator of this deed.

WHO SHOULD BE DEEMED THE GREATEST?

24   They also had a discussion among them as to which one in their
25 group should be considered the greatest. He said to them: "The
kings of the Gentiles lord it over them, and their princes have them-
26 selves styled benefactors. That must not be your way! No, the greatest
in your group must be like the youngest, and the leader like the
27 servant. For example, which is the more distinguished, the diner
at table or the waiter in attendance? The diner at table, of course;
28 and yet, I am in your midst like a waiter in attendance! You have,
29 however, stood by me in my trials; and therefore, as my Father has
willed that I should inherit royal power, so I, in turn, will to you
30 the rights of royalty, namely, to eat and drink at my table in my
kingdom and be seated on thrones with jurisdiction over the Twelve
Tribes of Israel.

PETER'S TRIPLE DENIAL FORETOLD

31   "Simon, Simon, mark my words: Satan has demanded the sur-
32 render of you all in order to sift you like wheat; but I have prayed
for you personally, that your faith might not fail. Later on, therefore, when you have recovered, it is for you to strengthen your
33 brethren." "At your side, Lord," he said to him, "I am ready to go
34 to prison and to death." "I tell you, Peter," he replied, "the cock will

---

writers): "offer this (my body) by way of sacrifice." The Catholic Church holds
that by these words Christ appointed his Apostles to be the priests of the New
Testament; see the Council of Trent, sess. 22, ch. 1.

22:32. Satan wants to sift you all, but I prayed for you, Peter, personally or
in particular. This recalls the promise made to Peter in Mt. 16:18. "Your
faith": in the supernatural character of Jesus (5:20; 7:9; 8:25; 16:16, etc.).
Peter "disowned" Jesus three times, but never denied that he was the Messias.
when you have recovered: when you have come back to me, when you have been
converted (for this sense of the Greek word, compare Mt. 13:15; Acts 9:35;
11:21; 28:27; etc.).

not crow today before you three times deny having anything to do with me."

He also said to them: "When I sent you on a mission tour without 35 purse or bag or sandals, did you lack anything?" "No," they replied. 36 "It is different now," he said to them; "he that has a purse must take it with him; so, too, he that has a bag; and he that has not either of these must sell his cloak to buy a sword. Yes, I tell you, this 37 Scripture text must be fulfilled in me: 'And he was classed with the lawless.' Indeed, my career is at an end." "Look, Lord," they said: 38 "here are two swords." "It is enough," he replied.

"FATHER . . . YOUR WILL NOT MINE BE DONE!"

He now went out and made his way, according to his custom, 39 to the Mount of Olives. The disciples accompanied him. Arrived 40 at the place, he said to them: "Pray, that you may not succumb to temptation." He then tore himself away from them and, with- 41 drawing about a stone's throw, knelt down and prayed to this effect: 42 "Father, if it pleases you, spare me this cup! However, may your will, not mine, be done!" An angel from heaven appeared to him, and 43 strengthened him. Now his struggle became intense, and he prayed 44 the more earnestly, so that his sweat became like clots of blood that fell to the ground. At last he rose from his prayer and returned to 45 the disciples to find them sleeping for sorrow. "How can you be 46 sleeping?" he said to them; "Rouse yourselves and pray, that you may not succumb to temptation."

JUDAS BETRAYS JESUS WITH A KISS

He was still speaking when, presently, there came upon the scene 47 a throng, with the man named Judas, one of the Twelve, leading the way! He approached Jesus to greet him with a kiss. "Judas," 48 Jesus said to him, "with a kiss you betray the Son of Man?"

22:36. The Apostles are here advised to take precautions for their personal safety. See Mt. 10:23.

22:44. Our word "agony" is correctly used in this verse if it does not mean "the pangs of death; the last struggle of life; the death struggle; extreme bodily pain." Jesus did not die from physical exhaustion; his life did not flicker out like a dying flame. See the note on Jn. 19:28. The Greek word here means the utmost will power which Jesus put forth to overcome his natural horror of death; his struggle to accept the will of the Father in spite of the excruciating pain awaiting him. This effort (struggle, exertion) reached its climax after the angel had strengthened him.

49 Then those about him, who saw what was coming, said: "Lord,
50 shall we strike with the sword?" And one of them actually struck the
51 servant of the high priest and cut off his right ear. Jesus interposed.
"Stop!" he said; "This is enough!" He then touched the man's ear
and healed him.

52 Jesus now addressed the high priests, or temple officers, and
elders, who had come to arrest him: "As though to capture a bandit
53 you came out armed with swords and clubs! Day after day I was
in your midst in the temple, yet you did not move a finger to arrest
me! But then, this is your chance and the triumph of darkness!"

PETER'S TRIPLE DENIAL OF JESUS

54 Under a strong escort they marched him off and took him to
the palace of the high priest. Peter, meanwhile, followed at a distance.
55 When the men had lit an open fire in the courtyard and seated
56 themselves round it, Peter was sitting among them. As he sat with
his face to the fire, a slave girl caught sight of him and, looking
57 straight at him, said: "This man was with him." But he denied it.
58 "Woman," he said, "I have nothing to do with him." After a little
while, another person saw him and said: "You are one of them."
59 "No, sir," Peter said, "I am not." After the lapse of about one hour,
another stoutly affirmed: "This man was certainly with him. Why,
60 he is a Galilean." "Sir," Peter rejoined, "I do not know what you
are talking about." And immediately, while he was speaking, a cock
61 crowed. Then the Lord turned round and looked full upon Peter,
and Peter remembered the Lord's prediction — how he had said to
him: "Today, before a cock crows, you will disown me three times."
62 And he went out and wept bitterly.

63 The men who had him in custody now mocked and cuffed him;
64 they also blindfolded and challenged him: "Act the prophet, please!
65 Who is it that struck you?" And there were many other blasphemies
they uttered against him.

CHRIST DECLARES HIMSELF TO BE THE SON OF GOD

66 As soon as day broke, the senate of the people, composed of high
priests and Scribes, met and hurried him off to their Supreme

---

22:62. *he . . . wept bitterly*: the first step toward that "recovery" predicted by
Jesus. See the note on 22:32.

Council. "If you are the Messias," they said, "then tell us so."
He replied: "If I do tell you so, you will not believe me; 67
and if I, in turn, ask you a question, you will not answer me. 68
However, from this time forward the Son of Man will be enthroned 69
at the right hand of Almighty God." They all broke in: "Therefore, 70
you are the Son of God!" "I am, as you say," he replied. Then 71
they said: "What further need have we of witnesses! Why, we have
heard it from his lips!"

CHAPTER 23

CHRIST BEFORE PILATE

Their meeting now broke up and, in a body, they took him to 1
Pilate. Here they brought a series of charges against him. "We 2
caught this man," they said, "inciting our nation to revolt: he opposes
the paying of taxes to Caesar and passes himself off as the Messias —
King." Pilate asked him: "Are you the King of the Jews?" To 3
which he replied: "I am, as you say." Then, turning to the high 4
priests and the crowds, Pilate declared: "I can detect no guilt in
this man." But they grew ever more insistent. "He stirs up the 5
nation," they said, "by his teaching throughout the whole Jewish
country. He began in Galilee and ended here."

PILATE REFERS THE CASE TO HEROD, WHO RETURNS HIM

When Pilate heard that, he asked whether the man was a 6
Galilean and, after learning that he belonged to Herod's jurisdiction, 7
referred his case to Herod, who was himself at Jerusalem in those
days. Herod was exceedingly well pleased to see Jesus. He had for 8
a long time been anxious to see him, because he had been receiving
news of him; and now he indulged the hope of witnessing some
striking exhibition at his hands. He plied him with a string of 9
questions, but he would not give him any answer. Meanwhile the 10
high priests and the Scribes stood by, vehemently accusing him.
Finally Herod, joined by his military, treated him with contempt 11
and mockery, and, after having a gorgeous robe put on him, referred
him back to Pilate. Herod and Pilate became mutual friends again 12
that very day; up to then they had been at enmity.

13 Pilate now called together the high priests, the leading men,
14 and the people at large. "You brought this man before my tribunal,"
he said to them, "on the ground that he incited the nation to revolt.
Now see the result: in your presence I personally conducted the
hearing, but detected no guilt in him regarding the charges you
15 preferred against him. Nor did Herod either, for he referred his
case back to us. This, then, is the upshot: he has done nothing to
16 deserve the penalty of death. Accordingly, I will discipline him, and
then set him free."

THE PEOPLE PREFER THE MURDERER BARABBAS TO CHRIST

17 Now he was under an obligation at the festival to release at the
18 people's request one prisoner. So they shouted in chorus: "Put this
19 man out of the way. We want you to release Barabbas" — a man, by
the way, thrown into prison for a riot which had occurred in the
20 city, and for murder. Pilate addressed them a second time, still
21 desirous of setting Jesus free. But they kept shouting back: "Crucify,
22 crucify him." Yet a third time he spoke to them: "Why, what crime
has this man committed? I found nothing in him to deserve capital
punishment. Accordingly, I shall have him scourged and then set
23 free." But they were insistent and vehemently clamored for his
24 crucifixion. Their shouts prevailed more and more. Finally Pilate
25 ruled that their demand should be satisfied. So he released the man
confined to prison for riot and murder — the one they had clamored
for — but surrendered Jesus to their will.

CHRIST'S WORDS TO THE WOMEN WHO BEWAIL HIM

26 When they led him forth, they requisitioned on the way one
Simon of Cyrene, who was just returning from the country, and
27 put the cross on him to carry it behind Jesus. A great multitude
of the people accompanied him, notably women who bewailed and
28 lamented him. Turning to them, Jesus said: "Daughters of Jerusalem,
29 do not weep for me; weep for yourselves and your children; for,
mark my words, a time is coming when people will say, 'How
blessed the barren are! How blessed the wombs that have never
30 borne children, and the breasts that have never nursed!' Then they
will actually cry out to the mountains, 'Fall upon us!' and to the

hills, 'Bury us!' Yes, if this is done to the green wood, what must be   *31*
the fate of the dry!"

CRUCIFIED BETWEEN TWO CRIMINALS

Besides him two criminals were led out to be executed.   *32*
When they reached the place called the Skull, they crucified him   *33*
there, as well as the criminals, one at his right, the other at his
left. But Jesus said: "Father, forgive them; they do not know what   *34*
they are doing." His clothes they divided among them by drawing lots.

Meanwhile the people stood by, witnessing the scene, and   *35*
sneering remarks were made even by the magistrates, such as: "He
saved others; let him save himself if he is the Anointed of God,
the Chosen One"; the soldiers, too, made sport of him by coming   *36*
up and offering him vinegar with the remark: "If you are the King   *37*
of the Jews, then save yourself." There was also an inscription over   *38*
his head in Greek, Latin, and Hebrew characters: "This is the
King of the Jews."

ONE OF THE CRIMINALS DEFENDS CHRIST

One of the criminals who had been hanged insulted him, saying: *39*
"Are not you the Messias? Save yourself and us." But the other   *40*
protested and sternly rebuked him: "Do you not even fear God,
though you have been condemned to the same punishment? Besides,   *41*
we suffer justly and are getting what we have deserved for our
crimes; but this man has done no wrong." He then went on: *42*
"Jesus, remember me when you return in your royal glory." "Indeed,"   *43*
he replied, "I assure you, this very day you will be with me in
paradise."

THE VEIL IN THE SANCTUARY TORN THROUGH THE MIDDLE

It was now about noon, and darkness fell upon the whole land.   *44*

23:31. *green wood:* the *green wood* is a symbol of the innocent Christ; the
dry, of the guilty nation. There is, perhaps, an allusion to the dried-up fig tree.
23:33. The *Skull* is known to us from the Latin word "Calvary."
23:34. *do not know:* the soldiers did not realize what they were doing, nor did
the Jews in general fully comprehend the enormity of their crime. See Acts
3:17; 13:27; 1 Cor. 2:8.
23:43. *paradise:* the place of rest where the souls of the just were awaiting
their entrance into heaven with Christ on Ascension day. It is often called the
Limbo of the Fathers.

45 It lasted till about three in the afternoon, the sun having ceased to shine. The veil of the sanctuary was torn right through the middle.
46 At last Jesus gave a loud cry. "Father," he said, "into your hands
47 I commit my spirit." With that, he expired. When the centurion saw what had happened, he praised God. "Truly," he exclaimed,
48 "this man was innocent." Crowds had gathered to witness this spectacle, and when they saw what had taken place, they all struck
49 their breasts and returned home. All his acquaintances and especially the women who had accompanied him from Galilee stood by at some distance, watching what was going on.

THE BURIAL OF JESUS

50   And unexpectedly there came a man by the name of Joseph, a member of the Supreme Council, a good and fair-minded person,
51 who had not concurred with the rest in either their verdict or their proceedings. He was from Arimathia, a Jewish town, and
52 looked forward to the kingdom of God. This man interviewed
53 Pilate and petitioned for the body of Jesus. He took it down from the cross and, after wrapping it in a linen shroud, laid him in a tomb cut out of the rock, in which no one had ever been laid to rest.
54   It was the Day of Preparation, and already the lights of the
55 Sabbath were gleaming. The women who had accompanied him from Galilee followed close behind, and took note of the tomb and how
56 his body was laid to rest. Then they returned to provide spices and perfume. The Sabbath they spent quietly, obedient to the Law.

CHAPTER 24

"HE HAS RISEN"

1   On the first day of the week, however, when night was in its last stage, they set out for the tomb, carrying the spices they
2 had provided. They found the stone rolled away from the tomb;
3 on entering, however, they did not find the body of the Lord
4 Jesus. They were at a loss what to make of this, when, to their surprise, they were confronted by two men in dazzling clothes.
5 Seized with fright, they bowed their faces to the ground, but the men said to them: "Why do you look among the dead for him who

is alive? He is not here. No, he has risen. Recall what he told you 6
when he was still in Galilee, namely, that the Son of Man must 7
be betrayed into the hands of sinful men, and be crucified, and on
the third day rise again."

Then they recalled his words, and they returned from the 8
tomb to report all these incidents to the Eleven and all the rest. 9
These women were Mary Magdalen, Joanna, and Mary, the mother 10
of James. The others who were with them gave the same report to
the apostles. But to them these accounts seemed like foolish talk, 11
and they would not believe them. Peter, however, started off for 12
the tomb at a run; but, when he stooped to look in, all he saw was
the linen cloths; and he went home puzzling over what had
taken place.

A NEW SURPRISE

There was a new surprise, that same day, when two of their 13
company were on the way to a village named Emmaus, sixty stadia
from Jerusalem. Their whole conversation was about these recent 14
events; and, while they were conversing and putting this and that 15
together, who should draw near and join them on their journey
but — Jesus! Their eyes, however, were prevented from recognizing 16
him. "What is it," he said to them, "you are so earnestly discussing 17
on your walk?" They stopped, and sadness clouded their faces.
Then one of them, Cleopas, by name, spoke up. 18

"Are you," he said to him, "the only visitor to Jerusalem that
does not know what happened there these days?"

"Well, what?" he replied. 19

"Why," they said to him, "all about Jesus of Nazareth, who
proved himself a prophet mighty in deed and word in the eyes of
God and the mass of the people, and how the high priests and our 20
authorities delivered him up for capital punishment and finally
had him crucified, although for our part we had hoped he might be 21
the man destined to redeem Israel. But, in addition to all, this is
the third day since these events took place! And furthermore: some 22
women of our company, too, have upset us: they went to the tomb
at dawn, and, when they did not find his body, came back saying 23

24:12. This verse is omitted in some manuscripts.
24:13. *sixty stadia:* about seven miles; some manuscripts read 160 stadia.

they had actually seen a vision of angels who declared that he was
24 alive! Then some of our company set out for the tomb and found
the report of the women to be correct; but they did not see him
in person!"

25 "O how dull you are!" he then said to them; "How slow to understand when it comes to believing anything the prophets have said!
26 Was it not necessary that the Messias should undergo these sufferings
27 and thus enter into his glory?" And now, beginning with Moses and
going right through the prophets, he interpreted to them whatever is
said about himself anywhere in the Scriptures.

28 Meanwhile, they had come near the village for which they were
bound, and when he gave the impression of intending to go on,
29 they used gentle force to dissuade him. "Please, be our guest,"
they said; "the day is fast declining, and it is close to evening." So he
30 went in to be their guest. And this is what happened when he
had reclined at table in their company: he took the bread into his
hands and, after saying grace, broke it into portions, which he gave
31 to them. At last their eyes were opened, and they recognized him;
but he vanished from their sight.

32 "Were not our inmost hearts on fire," they said to each other,
"as he spoke to us by the way, explaining to us the Scriptures?"
33 And setting out that very hour, they retraced their steps to Jerusalem.
34 Here they found assembled the Eleven and their companions, who
35 said: "Actually, the Lord is risen! He appeared to Simon!" Then
they, in turn, related what had taken place on the journey, and
how they had recognized him in the breaking of the bread.

CHRIST APPEARS IN PERSON

36 They were still rehearsing their experiences when he himself
37 appeared to them and said: "Peace be to you!" But they were in a
38 perfect panic, fancying they were seeing a ghost. "Why are you
disturbed?" he said to them; "And why do you let doubts come
39 into your minds? Look at my hands and my feet. Surely, it is my
very self! Feel me, and convince yourselves; no ghost has flesh and
40 bones such as you see I have!" With that, he showed them his
hands and his feet.

24:27. We may render the Greek either as in the text above, or: "taking
his text from Moses and all the prophets, he interpreted to them what is
contained about him in the Scriptures."

But they still refused to believe — it was too good to be true! — *41*
and continued in their perplexity. So he said to them: "Have you
something here to eat?" Then they offered him a piece of broiled *42*
fish, which he accepted and ate before their eyes. *43*

He said to them: "These events are the fulfillment of what I *44*
predicted to you when I was still with you, namely, that anything
ever written concerning me, whether in the Law of Moses, or in the
prophets, or in the Psalms, must needs be fulfilled." He then gave *45*
them the key to the understanding of the Scriptures. "This," he said *46*
to them, "is the gist of the Scriptures: the Messias must suffer and
on the third day rise from the dead. Furthermore: in his name the *47*
need of a change of heart and forgiveness of sins must be preached
to all the nations; the preaching must begin in Jerusalem, and you *48*
are the witnesses of all this. And note: I am going to send down *49*
upon you him whom the Father has promised; but you must tarry
in the city until you are invested with power from on high."

One day he led them forth to the spot where the road turns *50*
off toward Bethany, and there, with uplifted hands, gave them his
blessing. And in the act of blessing them, he finally parted company *51*
with them, mounting higher and higher heavenward. For their part, *52*
they adored him and, in a transport of joy, retraced their steps to
Jerusalem. They were regular in their visits to the temple, praising *53*
and blessing God.

24:50. *where the road turns off toward Bethany:* on the Mount of Olives.
Luke's summary account of the Ascension may be supplemented by his narrative
in Acts 1:1; 1:11.

SAINT JOHN

The name of the fourth evangelist is John, that is, "he to whom Yahweh is gracious," or "he whom Yahweh has graciously given." He was the son of Zebedee, a Galilean fisherman, probably of Bethsaida (1:44; Mt. 4:18 ff.), and of Salome, one of the pious women who accompanied Jesus from Galilee and ministered to his needs. On a memorable occasion (Mk. 3:17), he and his brother James the Elder (or Greater) were called *Boanerges*, that is "peals of thunder." He was among the first disciples whom the Baptist won for Jesus (1:37 ff.). His final call to discipleship is narrated in Mt. 4:21 f. and Mk. 1:19 f.

In the course of time St. John formed a strong attachment for his divine Master, which was reciprocated and manifested on several occasions. Together with St. Peter and St. James, he was singled out to be present at the home of Jairus, when this man's daughter was raised to life (Mk. 5:37 and Lk. 8:51), at the transfiguration (Mt. 17:1; Mk. 9:1; Lk. 9:28), and at the scene in Gethsemani (Mt. 26:37; Mk. 14:33). He was "the disciple whom Jesus loved," and it was surely no mere accident that at the Last Supper he was privileged to "lie resting in the bosom of Jesus" (13:23). On that occasion Jesus whispered into his ear the name of the traitor. He alone of all the disciples followed Jesus to Calvary, where the dying Savior entrusted his mother to his care. "He took her into his home" (19:26) and was henceforth her protector and her "son," most probably until her death at Jerusalem or, possibly, at Ephesus. His strong love for Jesus clung to him through life. "The man who is not loyal to Christ's teaching," he says in 2 Jn. 9, "loses hold of God."

After the Ascension we find St. John in Jerusalem, where he and St. Peter cured a man "lame from birth" (Acts 3:1 ff.). When the Apostles heard that Samaria had received the word of God, they sent St. Peter and St. John to visit them (Acts 8:14). He attended the Apostolic Council at Jerusalem in 49 or 50. Tradition says that he left Jerusalem and made his home in Ephesus. Under Domitian he was taken to Rome and thrown into a caldron of seething oil, but escaped uninjured. Banished to the island of Patmos, he wrote the Apocalypse. The date of his death is not certain. It must have occurred somewhere between 98 and 117, during the reign of Trajan, in Ephesus.

The Gospel opens with a lofty vision of the pre-existent Christ, which strikes the keynote of the twenty-one chapters: Jesus Christ is coequal with the Father; he is the Messias; he is the Author of all supernatural light and life (1:1–18). Then follow the testimony of the Baptist and the call of the first disciples (1:19–51). The first great section of the narrative deals with the public ministry of Jesus, describing his five journeys to Jerusalem (2:1–4:54; 5:1–6:71; 7:1–10:21; 10:22–12:50). Each of the journeys is lit up by some outstanding event, as the wedding feast at Cana, the visit of Nicodemus, the conversation with the Samaritan woman, the cure of the cripple at the pool of Bethesda, the miraculous feeding of the multitude, the promise of the institution of the Eucharist, the conflict with the Jewish authorities. At the end of the last visit to the capital, the high priests definitely resolve to put Jesus to death.

The second section of the Gospel deals with the Passion, the Death, and the Resurrection (13:1–21:25). Here we find Jesus pictured in intimate converse with his beloved disciples. Then follow the scenes in Gethsemani and on Golgotha (18:1–19:42). A series of apparitions closes the Gospel: to Mary Magdalen, to the unbelieving Thomas, and to several Apostles by the sea of Tiberias.

This bare framework of the Gospel is filled with details not touched upon by the Synoptists. In fact, after reading the Synoptic accounts, we find ourselves almost in a different world on turning to St. John's narrative. It is at once evident that his object in writing was different from theirs. Clement of Alexandria relates that the disciples approached St. John one day and asked him to give them a "spiritual" Gospel instead of a "material" or "bodily" one. They meant to say that, while the other evangelists had devoted their attention mainly to the external facts in the life of Jesus, there was need of a Gospel that would describe his inner life, or, as we should say, lay bare the secrets of the Sacred Heart of Jesus. St. John alone mentions the opening of his side by the lance of the Roman soldier. It is for this reason, too, that St. John allows so much room to our Lord's private conversations with individuals, to his almost endless discussions with the Jewish authorities, and most of all, to his heart-to-heart talks with his most intimate friends, the disciples. The crown of all these self-revelations is the sacerdotal prayer in Chapter 17, which shows his love for the Father, for the Church, and for us.

St. John, though one of the two "peals of thunder," was yet a deeply meditative soul. Aided by an extraordinary memory, he loved to ponder over every word from the lips of the Master. If the development of the theme in some of the longer discourses is at times a little slow, it is because he desired to omit none of the precious jewels. Chapters 13 to 17 are like a quietly moving stream; there are not a few windings in its course, but eventually it reaches the ocean, and our final impression is that of unfathomable depths. So, after all, St. John did give us a "spiritual Gospel." The reader who goes in quest of "precious pearls" will find most of them in the Fourth Gospel.

It must not be forgotten that St. John also wrote with an eye to the needs of the growing Church in her struggle with the rampant heresies of the day. Mention may be made of the Nicolaites, the Ebionites, the Gnostics, and the Docetists, or the forerunners of these heresies. Living to a ripe old age, he was able to watch the progress of the young Church for more than half a century after her Founder's death. He knew what was most needed to strengthen the faithful in their loyalty to Jesus. He tells us that, while there are many other proofs of his claims which Jesus gave in the presence of his disciples, "this much, at any rate, has been recorded that you may grow in your belief that Jesus is the Messias, the Son of God, and that, through your belief, you may have life in his name" (21:31).

The date of composition is not certain. It is generally admitted that the Gospel was written toward the end of the first century. At times, doubt has been thrown on St. John's authorship. But the singular view of Eusebius, the Church historian, who lived in the fourth century, that "the Presbyter John," mentioned in a fragment of Papias, bishop of Hierapolis, was not John, the son of Zebedee, cannot shake the unanimous tradition of the first two centuries that the author of the Gospel was none other than John, the son of Zebedee.[1] The last two verses were probably added by men of his immediate surroundings. They testify that St. John was "the witness of the facts" and "the recorder of the facts" here described. The story of the adulterous woman in 8:1–11 is not found in all manuscripts. Its canonicity or inspired character is guaranteed by the Church.

[1] See J. A. Kleist, "The Fragments of Papias," in *Ancient Christian Writers*, 6 (Westminster, Md.: The Newman Press, 1948), pp. 105–124, 204–210.

THE HOLY GOSPEL
OF JESUS CHRIST
ACCORDING TO

ST. JOHN

CHAPTER 1

PROLOGUE

When time began, the Word was there,   *1*
    and the Word was face to face with God,
    and the Word was God.
This Word, when time began,   *2*
    was face to face with God.
All things came into being through him,   *3*
    and without him there came to be
    not one thing that has come to be.
In him was life,   *4*
    and the life was the light of men.

1:1–18. These eighteen verses, called the Prologue, are the majestic portal through which we accompany John into the Holy of Holies, the eternal home of the pre-existent Christ. They are also the gates through which we must accompany him into his recital of Christ's earthly activities. The leading ideas of the Prologue are the leitmotif of his Gospel. John, "the disciple whom Jesus loved," also had an open eye for the human traits in our Lord's character. See, for instance, 1 Jn. 1:1–3.

1:1. *When time began:* compare Gen. 1:1: "The Word": the Intelligence, the Wisdom, of God, conceived as a person. Col. 1:15–17 reads like a commentary on this verse.

was there: was already in existence. Compare 8:58. *face to face:* the Greek preposition here denotes neither extraneousness nor inferiority; it implies distinctness of person, coupled with intimate communion. Compare 1:18: "in the Father's bosom." The Son's equality with the Father is one of the keynotes of this Gospel; see, especially, Chapters 13–17.

1:3. *All things:* note John's elaborate way of saying that *all* things owe their existence to the Word. Some ancient philosophers and Christian heretics believed in beings between God and man, that were not created by God. *through him:* the preposition implies neither instrumentality in the ordinary sense nor inferiority. Compare Col. 1:16–17; 1 Cor. 8:6; Hebr. 1:2.

1:4. *life:* essential, substantial life, and the source of life in the world. *light:* essential, substantial light, and the source of spiritual, supernatural light in men. Compare 8:12 and 14:6. *of men:* all men, of course.

231

5   The light shines in the darkness,
and the darkness did not lay hold of it.

6   There came upon the scene a man,
a messenger from God,
whose name was John.

7   This man came to give testimony —
to testify in behalf of the light —
that all might believe through him.

8   He was not himself the light;
he only was to testify in behalf of the light.

9   Meanwhile the true light,
which illumines every man,
was making its entrance into the world.

10   He was in the world,
and the world came to be through him,
and the world did not acknowledge him.

11   He came into his home,
and his own people did not welcome him.

12   But to as many as welcomed him
he gave the right to become children of God —
those who believe in his name;

13   who were born not of blood,
or of carnal desire,
or of man's will;
no, they were born of God.

14   And the Word became man

1:5. *the darkness:* the world buried in spiritual ignorance; *did not lay hold of it:* did not master it (Knox); the world neither overcame and quenched this light, nor absorbed and assimilated it.

1:6 ff. Note John's precise statement of the role of the Baptist. The forerunner made so deep an impression on his contemporaries that many attributed to him an importance that did not belong to him. See 1:19–33. Compare Mt. 11:7–15.

1:9. The Vulgate reads: "That was the true light which enlightens every man that comes into the world."

1:11. *into his home:* more generally, "into his property," that is, the Jewish nation (Exod. 19:5; Deut. 4:20; 7:6; 26:18; etc.); *his own people:* the Jews. In a wider sense all the world is God's home.

1:12. *children of God:* this spiritual rebirth, accomplished by baptism, was a puzzle to Nicodemus (3:5).

1:14. *the Word became man:* see verse 1, "the Word was God" — Christ

and lived among us;
and we have looked upon his glory —
such a glory as befits
the Father's only-begotten Son —
full of grace and truth!

John testifies in his behalf,   15
and the cry still rings in our ears:
"This is the one of whom I said:
'The one expected to follow me
takes precedence over me,
because he was in existence before me.'"

And of his fullness   16
we have all received a share —
yes, grace succeeding grace;

for the Law was granted through Moses,   17
but grace and truth have come
through Jesus Christ.

On God no man ever laid his eyes;   18
the only-begotten Son,
who rests in the Father's bosom,
has himself been the interpreter.

"I AM A HERALD'S VOICE"

The testimony which John gave when the Jews of Jerusalem sent   19
priests and levites to him is as follows. They were to ask him: "Who 20
are you?" He acknowledged the truth without reserve and frankly
declared: "I am not the Messias." "What, then?" they asked him; 21
"Are you Elias?" He answered: "I am not!" "Are you the Prophet?"

---

is very God and very man. "Many deceivers have appeared in the world, who
will not acknowledge that Jesus Christ has come in human flesh" (2 Jn. 7).
See the note on 6:61.

his glory: the glory of his divinity, manifested in his teachings and miracles,
and reflected in his human traits and demeanor. Also as man, Christ was "full
of grace and truth." There is an affectionate recollection of the sacred humanity
in 1 Jn. 1:1–4.

1:15. *testifies*: his testimony is valid for all time.

1:18. Some texts read "God, the only-begotten."

1:19. *the Jews of Jerusalem*: the highest Jewish authority, and the declared
enemies of Jesus throughout the Gospel.

1:21. *Elias*: John was "Elias" in an entirely different sense: see Lk. 1:17 and
Mt. 17:10. "The Prophet": promised to Moses (Deut. 18:15–19). See Acts
3:22 and 7:37.

22   "No!" he replied. Finally they said to him: "Who are you? We have
to give an answer to those who sent us. What do you say about
23   yourself?" He said: "I am a herald's voice which rings out upon
the desert:

'Make straight the road of the Lord,'

as the Prophet Isaias has said."

24   Also   delegates   of   the   Pharisaical   sect   were   present,
25   and they put this question to him: "Why, then, do you baptize, if
26   you are not the Messias, or Elias, or the Prophet?" John gave them
this explanation: "I baptize with water; there is already one in your
27   midst whom you do not know — the one who is to follow me,
28   the strap of whose sandal I am not fit to untie." These incidents
occurred in Bethany beyond the Jordan, where John was baptizing.

"THERE IS THE LAMB OF GOD"

29   The following day he saw Jesus coming toward him. "Look," he
said, "there is the lamb of God, who takes away the sin of the world.
30   This is he of whom I said: 'There is a man to follow me who takes
31   precedence over me because he existed before me.' I, too, had not
known him; but he had to be made known to Israel, and it is for
this purpose that I came to baptize with water."

32   Now, John testified as follows: "I have seen the Spirit coming
down in the shape of a dove from heaven; and he rested upon him.
33   I, too, had not known him, but he who sent me to baptize with
water also said to me: 'If you see the Spirit come down upon
someone and rest upon him, that is the one who baptizes with the
34   Holy Spirit.' Therefore, as an eyewitness I declare: This is the Son
of God."

ANDREW AND SIMON PETER FOLLOW JESUS

35   The next day John was again at his station, and so were two of

---

1:25. *Why, then, do you baptize?*: later Jesus reminded the Jews of this episode and asked a pointed question: Mk. 11:30.

1:26. *with water*: with water only, not with the Holy Spirit. See 1:33. John's
baptism was not a sacrament.

1:29. The image of *the lamb of God* was probably suggested to John by "the
lamb" foretold by Isaias (53:7). In the temple a lamb was offered morning and
evening for the sins of the people.

his disciples. Fixing his eyes on Jesus, who was walking by, he said: 36
"Look! There is the Lamb of God." After hearing what he said, the 37
two disciples followed Jesus. Jesus turned round and, seeing them 38
follow, said to them: "What is your wish?" They replied: "Rabbi"
— which in our language means "teacher" — "where are you staying?"
"Come, and you will see," he said to them. So they went and saw 39
where he was staying. They were his guests that day. It was about
four in the afternoon.

Now Andrew, the brother of Simon Peter, was one of the two 40
men who heard what John said and followed Jesus. The first whom 41
he met was his own brother Simon. "We have found," he said to
him, "the Messias!" which in our language means "Christ." He 42
then introduced him to Jesus, and Jesus, looking intently at him,
said: "You are Simon, the son of John. Your name shall be 'Cephas' "
which in our language means "Peter."

PHILIP AND NATHANAEL, THE NEXT TO JOIN JESUS

The following day he decided to leave for Galilee, and so he came 43
upon Philip. Jesus said to him: "Be one of my followers." Philip, 44
by the way, was from Bethsaida, the home town of Andrew and
Peter. Philip then met Nathanael and said to him: "The One 45
about whom Moses has written in the Law, and the Prophets, too,
we have found him! — Jesus of Nazareth, the son of Joseph!"
Nathanael replied: "Can any good come out of Nazareth?" "Well," 46
Philip said to him, "come and see!"

When Jesus caught sight of Nathanael as he was coming toward 47
him, he said to the bystanders: "Look! Here is a true Israelite! A
good and honest soul!" "How do you know me?" Nathanael asked 48
him. To which Jesus made this answer: "Before Philip called you,
when you were still under the fig tree, I saw you." "Rabbi," 49
Nathanael burst out, "you are the Son of God! You are the King
of Israel!" "Because I told you that I saw you under the fig tree," 50
replied Jesus, "is that why you believe? You will see greater things

1:42. For the name *Peter*, "the Rock-man," see Mt. 16:18. The word
Christos is sometimes best rendered: "the Anointed" (Lk. 2:26; 23:35), sometimes "the Messias" (Mt. 16:16), sometimes "Christ," our Lord's proper name
(Mt. 1:17).
1:46. *Nathanael:* most probably identical with the Apostle Bartholomew.

51 than that!" He then continued, still speaking to him: "Yes, so it really
is! I tell you all, you will see heaven opened and the angels of
God going up and coming down upon the Son of Man."

CHAPTER 2

THE WEDDING AT CANA. WATER TURNED INTO WINE

1   Two days later a wedding took place at Cana in Galilee, at which
2   the mother of Jesus was present. Jesus and his disciples were also
3   invited to the festivities. When the wine had run short, the mother
4   of Jesus said to him: "They have no wine." Jesus replied: "Leave
5   that to me, mother! My time has not yet come!" His mother then
said to the waiters: "No matter what he tells you, be sure you do it!"
6   Now there were six water jars of stone standing there, to meet
the needs of the Jewish rite of purification, each holding about
7   twenty gallons. "Fill the jars with water," Jesus said to the waiters.
8   And they filled them up to the brim. "Now draw off some," he said
to them, "and bring it to the steward in charge." So they brought it
9   to him. After tasting the water now turned into wine, the steward
did not know how to account for it; of course, the waiters who had
drawn off the water knew very well. So the steward called the
10 bridegroom and said to him: "Everybody serves his good wine first,
and only when the guests have had their fill of it does he put out

---

1:51. *heaven opened:* opened, and remaining open during the life of Christ.
The expression recalls the vision of Jacob (Gen. 28:12). There was constant
communication between the Father and the Son; and of its results (the miracles)
the disciples were to be witnesses.

It is somewhat disputed in what sense Jesus called himself here and elsewhere
in the Gospels "the Son of Man." See Lagrange's note on Mk. 2:10 and compare Dan. 7:13–14.

2:4. *Leave that to me:* the Greek idiom thus rendered deprecates undue interference. Its tone depends on the context: "leave me alone; mind your own
business; why do you meddle with me?" Mary's request interfered with the *time*
which the Father had set for the first miracle (see verse 11). But our Lord's
refusal was in fact assent. Mary inferred this from the accent in his voice and
the look in his eye; hence her directions to the waiters. *mother:* in modern
American daily life a son is not expected to address his mother as "woman."
Other instances of the use of the same Greek word are 4:21; 8:10; 19:26;
20:13; Lk. 22:57; 13:12.

2:6. *purification:* the Jews always washed their hands before a meal, often
during it, and always after it. One reason for this practice was that they ate
with their fingers; another is indicated in Mk. 7:4.

the poorer sort. But you have kept back the good wine till now!"
This is the first proof of his claims that Jesus gave, and he gave it *11*
at Cana in Galilee. He revealed his glory, and his disciples believed
in him.

After this, he went down to Capharnaum with his mother, his *12*
brothers, and his disciples. They did not stay many days.

THE DEALERS DRIVEN OUT OF THE TEMPLE

The Passover of the Jews was now near, and Jesus went up to *13*
Jerusalem. There, on the temple premises, he came upon the dealers *14*
in oxen, sheep, and pigeons, as well as upon the money-changers
at their counters. So he made a whip of small cords and drove all *15*
the men out of the temple; so, too, the sheep and the oxen; the
coin of the money-changers he scattered about by overturning the
tables. He said to the pigeon dealers: "Get these things out of the *16*
way! Do not turn my Father's house into a market place!" His *17*
disciples remembered that the Scripture says: "The zeal for your
house will consume me." The Jews remonstrated. "What proof do *18*
you give us," they said to him, "to show your right to do these
things?" "If you destroy this sanctuary," Jesus answered them, "I *19*
will build it up again in three days." The Jews then said to him: *20*
"Six and forty years this sanctuary was in building; and you will
build it up again in three days?" He, however, was speaking of *21*
the sanctuary of his body. After he had risen from the dead, there- *22*
fore, his disciples remembered that he had said this; and they
believed both the Scripture and the statement Jesus had made.

While he was at Jerusalem during the feast of the Passover, *23*
many believed in his name after seeing the proofs of his claims
that he was giving. But Jesus did not confide in them. He knew *24*

2:11. The Greek word generally rendered "sign" denotes an action by which
Jesus proved his divine nature; hence "miracle." Christ's miracles were the
credentials which attested his authority. See Mk. 11:28.
2:12. *his brothers:* perhaps the sons of Mary's sister; see 19:25. Their names
are given in Mt. 13:55.
2:13. *The Passover:* the great Jewish festival kept in memory of the time when
the Jews, preparing to depart from Egypt, sprinkled their doorposts with the
blood of a lamb, that the destroying angel might "pass over" their dwellings.
Exod. 12:13.
2:17. See Ps. 68:10, and compare Mt. 26:61; Mk. 14:58. consume: devour,
ruin.

25 them all, nor did he need anyone's testimony regarding any man.
He was able to read men's character.

CHAPTER 3

YOU MUST ALL BE BORN ANEW

1 A member of the Pharisaical party, Nicodemus by name, a
2 leader in the Jewish community, came to him one night, and said
to him: "Rabbi, we know that you have a mission from God to
teach. Surely, no one can give such striking proofs of his claims as
3 you are giving, unless God is with him." Jesus seized the opportunity
and said to him: "I must be frank with you: if one is not born
4 anew, he cannot see the kingdom of God." "But how," replied
Nicodemus, "can a man be born in his old age? Can he really enter
5 his mother's womb a second time and have another birth?" Jesus
answered: "I am telling you the plain truth: unless a man is born
of water and the Spirit, he cannot enter the kingdom of God!
6 What is born of the flesh is flesh, and what is born of the Spirit
7 is spirit. Do not be perplexed because I said to you: you must all
8 of you be born anew. The breeze blows at will, and you can hear
its sound; but you do not know where it comes from or whither
it goes. Something like this takes place in everyone born of the

---

3:2. *one night*: perhaps, "by night." Nicodemus may have feared his col-
leagues, the majority of whom were hostile to Jesus; besides, the night afforded
more leisure for undisturbed conversation.

3:3. *seized the opportunity* afforded by the good will of this man, Jesus frankly
declared: "in order to see" (and enjoy the blessings of) "the kingdom of God,
you must be born anew." The idea of being "born anew" (now so familiar
to us; compare 1 Pet. 1:3, 23; Tit. 3:5: "the bath of regeneration and renewal
by the Holy Spirit) was new to Nicodemus. The word rendered "anew" may also
mean "from above," that is, from God. Compare Jn. 1:13.

3:5. Jesus very patiently explains that this new birth must be brought about by
water and the (Holy) Spirit. A spiritual effect demands a spiritual cause. The
mention of *water* is ultimately a reference to the sacrament of Baptism; but for
the moment it was enough for Nicodemus to be reminded of the words of the
Baptist: "I baptize you with water, but the One who is following me will
baptize in the Holy Spirit" (Mt. 3:11).

3:8. Nicodemus still puzzles over this mysterious rebirth. To tide him over
his difficulty, Jesus shows that it would be unreasonable to deny the fact, just
because we cannot understand the nature, of this regeneration. We hear and
feel the wind that plays about us, and from these effects we are sure of its
existence, though of its origin or nature we can give no account. Something

Spirit." Nicodemus demurred. "How," he said to him, "are such 9
things possible?" "You are the teacher of Israel," Jesus answered 10
him, "and do not understand things like this! I tell you the plain 11
truth: we speak what we know, and testify to what we have seen;
but you all refuse to accept our testimony! If I have told you of 12
earthly things and you refuse to believe, how will you believe if I
should tell you of heavenly things! Of course, no one has ever 13
ascended into heaven; but mind — there is one who has come down
from heaven, the Son of Man, whose home was in heaven!

BELIEF IN THE ONLY-BEGOTTEN SON OF GOD

"And just as Moses lifted up the serpent in the desert, so the 14
Son of Man must needs be lifted up, that everyone who believes in 15
him may have eternal life." So marked, indeed, has been God's love 16
for the world that he gave his only-begotten Son: everyone who
believes in him is not to perish, but to have eternal life. The fact is, 17
God did not send the Son into the world to condemn the world.
Not at all; the world is to be saved through him. He who believes 18
in him is not liable to condemnation, whereas he who refuses to
believe is already condemned, simply because he has refused to
believe in the name of the only-begotten Son of God. And this is 19
how the sentence of condemnation is passed: the light has come
into the world, but men loved the darkness more than the light,
because their lives were bad. Only an evildoer hates the light and 20

---

like this takes place when a man is born anew. Rebirth is a fact, though we
do not understand the process by which it is brought about. Nicodemus admitted
that Jesus "had a mission from God to teach," and should therefore have accepted
the fact of this spiritual rebirth without any further argument regarding its
nature. The rest of the conversation with Nicodemus culminates in showing
the need of implicit faith in Jesus as a condition of entering the kingdom of God.

3:11. Two leading ideas inculcated in this conversation are (1) the need of
a spiritual birth, in the sense hinted at by the Baptist (Mt. 3:11) and specified
in Jn. 1:13; (2) faith in Jesus, who speaks with authority. This tallies with
what Jesus said to the Apostles on Ascension Day: "He who believes and is
baptized will be saved" (Mk. 16:16).

we: probably, Christ and the Baptist.

3:13. Jesus is a competent witness of these "heavenly things," because he is
the Son of Man, that has come down from heaven. "He is the interpreter" (1:18).

whose home was in heaven: omitted in some manuscripts. See 1:18.

3:16–21. These words (as well as verses 31–36) are, most probably, John's
own reflections. It is likely that even verse 13 was not spoken by Jesus. lifted
up: a reference to the lifting up of the serpent by Moses for the cure of the
Israelites (Num. 21:8) and to the crucifixion of Jesus (Jn. 8:28).

refuses to face the light, for fear his practices may be exposed;
21 but one who lives up to the truth faces the light, so that everybody
can see that his life is lived in union with God.

THE PEOPLE CAME AND WERE BAPTIZED

22   After this, Jesus and his disciples went into the country of
23 Judea, and there he stayed with them and baptized. John, however,
continued to baptize in Ainon near Salim, because there was much
24 water there, and people came and were baptized. As yet, John had
not been put in prison.

25   One day the disciples of John and a certain Jew were arguing
26 about purification. So they interviewed John. "Rabbi," they said to
him, "the man who visited you on the other side of the Jordan and
in whose favor you testified — why, he is himself baptizing and all
27 the world is flocking to him!" John set them right. "No man,"
he said, "can take anything. One has to be content with what has
28 been assigned him by heaven. You yourselves give me credit for
having said: 'I am not the Messias; no, my whole mission consists
29 in being his forerunner.' He who has the bride is the bridegroom.
The bridegroom's friend, who stands at attention and lends a ready
ear to him, is overjoyed when he but catches the bridegroom's voice.
30 Such is my joy, and it is now complete. Of him there must be
more and more; there must be less and less of me."

GOD'S AMBASSADOR PROCLAIMS GOD'S MESSAGE

31   He who comes from above is above all; he who is sprung from
the earth is earthly through and through, and his speech savors of
32 the earth. He who comes from heaven is above all: what he has
seen and heard — that is the sum of his testimony; yet no one accepts
33 his testimony! Everyone who accepts his testimony thereby puts
34 his seal upon the truthfulness of God; for he who is God's ambassador proclaims God's message; besides, he communicates the
Spirit in no stinted measure.

35   The Father loves the Son and has put all things at his disposal.
36 He who believes in the Son possesses eternal life; he who refuses to

3:25–30. The Baptist's last testimony, the swan song of the forerunner, takes
rank with the finest passages in our Gospels. Verse 30 shows his complete
absorption in the task divinely assigned to him. The verses that follow record
the evangelist's own reflections.

believe in the Son will not see life. No, the anger of God lies upon him!

CHAPTER 4

JESUS AND THE SAMARITAN WOMAN

Now word had come to the Pharisees that Jesus was gaining and 1 baptizing more disciples than John. Jesus was aware of this, and 2 therefore — though, really, it was not Jesus that did the baptizing, but his disciples — he quit Judea and went back again to Gal- 3 ilee. Since it was arranged that he should pass through Samaria, 4 he came to a Samaritan town called Sychar near the place which 5 Jacob had given to his son Joseph. Jacob's well was there; and so, 6 since he was fatigued from journeying on foot, he simply sat down by the well. It was about noon.

Now there came a Samaritan woman to draw water. "Let me 7 have a drink," Jesus said to her. His disciples had gone off to town 8 to buy provisions. "How can you, a Jew," the Samaritan woman 9 said to him, "ask me, a Samaritan woman, for a drink?" The fact is, Jews have no dealings with Samaritans. Jesus answered her: "If 10 you understood God's gift and knew who he is that said to you, 'Let me have a drink,' you would have asked him, and he would have given you living water." "Sir," the woman replied, "you have no 11 means of drawing water, and the well is deep. Where, then, do you get the living water? Are you greater than our father Jacob, who 12 gave us the well out of which he and his children and his flocks used to drink?" "Anyone," replied Jesus, "who drinks of this water 13 will thirst again; but he who drinks of the water which I will give him will never thirst. No, the water which I will give him will 14 become in him a fountain of water welling up into eternal life." "Sir," replied the woman, "let me have the water you speak of. I do 15 not want to keep on getting thirsty and making this trip to draw water."

"Go," he then said to her, "call your husband and come back 16 here." "I have no husband," the woman frankly admitted. "You 17 were right," Jesus said to her, "when you said you had no husband.

4:10. *living water:* spring water; here a metaphor for truth and grace (1:17). Compare 4:13-14; 7:37.

18 You had five husbands, and the man with whom you are now living
is not your husband. What you said is perfectly true."

19 "I see, sir," the woman said to him, "you are a prophet!
20 Our fathers worshiped on this mountain, and your people say that
21 Jerusalem is the place for worshiping." "Take my word for it,
madam," Jesus replied, "a time is coming when you will worship
22 the Father neither on this mountain nor in Jerusalem. You worship
what you do not know; we worship what we do know. Salvation
23 comes from the Jews. And yet a time is coming, in fact, it is now
here, when true worshipers will worship the Father in spirit and
24 in truth. Such are the worshipers the Father demands. God is
25 Spirit, and his worshipers must worship in spirit and in truth." "I
know very well," the woman said, "that the Messias" — the Christ,
as he is called — "is to come and, when he comes, will tell us
26 everything." Jesus then said to her: "I am he — I who now speak
to you."

27 At this point the disciples returned and were surprised to find
him conversing with a woman; but no one asked: "What do you
28 want?" or, "Why did you talk to her?" The woman then left her
29 pitcher behind and went into town. "Come and see a man," she
said to the inhabitants, "who told me everything I ever did! Can
30 he, perhaps, be the Messias?" And some actually stirred out of town
and came to meet him.

CHRIST'S FOOD: TO DO GOD'S WILL

31 Meanwhile his disciples were pleading with him: "Rabbi, eat,
32 please." Jesus replied: "I have a food to eat of which you are
33 ignorant." Then the disciples said among themselves: "Did some-
34 one, perhaps, bring him something to eat?" Jesus said to them: "To
do the will of him whose ambassador I am, and to complete the

4:20. *this mountain*: Mount Garizim, the Samaritan place of worship.
4:23. We worship God *in truth* (in reality; really; as we should) if our worship is *in spirit*, that is, spiritual. Limitations of time, place, and nationality,
though necessary, do not touch the essence of religion. Both Garizim and
Jerusalem were to be superseded by the universal Church, whose worship is
essentially spiritual, although for its practice it, too, makes use of places, times,
and other contingencies. Both the Samaritans and the Jews erred in thinking
that God's worship was essentially local.
4:27. Scribes and Pharisees were not allowed to converse with a woman
in public.
4:34. *whose ambassador I am*: a favorite expression with John; for its first

work he has assigned — that is my food! Would you not say, 'Four 35
months yet — then is the time for harvesting'? Now mark what I
tell you: raise your eyes and look at the fields! Already they are
white and ripe for the harvest! The reaper is getting wages and 36
gathering fruit for eternal life, so that planter and reaper may
rejoice together; for in this case the saying, 'One does the planting, 37
and another the reaping,' is to the point. I am sending you to reap 38
a field in which you have not toiled; others have done the toiling,
and to the fruits of their toil you have fallen heirs."

Many of the inhabitants of that Samaritan town believed in 39
him because the woman testified that he had told her everything
she had done. So when the Samaritans met him, they pressed him 40
to stay with them; and he did stay there two days. As a result, many 41
more believed in him thanks to his preaching; and then they would 42
say to the woman: "Now we no longer believe on account of your
story. We have heard for ourselves and are convinced that this is
indeed the Savior of the world."

After the two days, he left that country for Galilee. Jesus himself 43, 44
had declared that a prophet is not respected in his own country;
but when he returned to Galilee, the Galileans gave him a hearty 45
welcome, after seeing all he did at the feast in Jerusalem; for they,
too, had gone to the feast.

JESUS CURES THE SON OF A ROYAL OFFICIAL

So he came again to Cana in Galilee, where he had changed 46
the water into wine. Now the son of a certain royal official was ill
at Capharnaum. When this person learned that Jesus had come 47
from Judea into Galilee, he went to meet him and begged him to
come down and heal his son, who was at the point of death. "If 48

intimation in the Gospels, see Mt. 5:17. It is interesting to search the Gospels
for significant references to Christ: Word, light, life, the Father's ambassador,
grain of wheat (12:24), vine, shepherd, and others.

4:35. *Four months yet:* this conversation probably took place in December or
January. Jesus stresses the fact (*Now mark,* etc.) that on this occasion no such
space of time has elapsed between the sowing and the reaping: but a few
moments ago the Father (planter) sowed the good seed in the heart of this
woman (as in the hearts of other Samaritans), and *already* Christ (the reaper)
is gathering in the fruit! Jesus here very humbly attributes the planting to the
Father (in accordance with the statement in 6:44). Verse 38 shows that he
wants his Apostles to do the same in their later missionary work.

4:48. *you:* the use of the plural ("you and the rest of your people") seems
intended to soften the reproach somewhat.

you do not see striking exhibitions of power," Jesus said to him, "you
49 will not believe." "Come down, sir," the royal official urged, "before
50 my child dies." Jesus then said to him: "Go; your son is safe and
sound." The man had faith in the word Jesus had spoken to him,
51 and went his way. He was still on his way down when his slaves
52 met him and said: "Your son is safe and sound." He then inquired
of them at what hour he had shown improvement. "Yesterday," they
53 replied, "at one in the afternoon the fever left him." The father
knew, therefore, that it was the very hour in which Jesus said to him,
"Your son is safe and sound." As a result, he and his entire family
54 became believers. This is the second time that Jesus gave a proof
of his claims after returning from Judea to Galilee.

CHAPTER 5

CHRIST CURES AN INVALID OF THIRTY-EIGHT YEARS

1   Some time later there was a feast of the Jews, and Jesus went up
2 to Jerusalem. There is a pool near the Sheepgate in Jerusalem which
3 in Aramaic is called Bethesda. It has five porticoes. In these a number of bedridden invalids — blind, crippled, decrepit people — were
4 always awaiting the motion of the water; for an angel of the Lord
would descend into the pool from time to time and stir the water;
and the first invalid then to go in after the stirring of the water would
get well, no matter with what disease he was afflicted.

5   There was a man there who had been an invalid for thirty-eight
6 years. When Jesus caught sight of him lying on his mat, and learned
of his long-standing affliction, he said to him: "Would you like to
7 get well?" "Why, sir," replied the invalid, "I have nobody to put
me into the pool the moment the water is stirred up, and by the
8 time I get there, someone else has gone down ahead of me." Jesus
9 then said to him: "Stand up; take your mat and walk." Immediately
the man got well, took up his mat, and walked.

JEWISH OBJECTION TO CURING ON THE SABBATH

10   That day was a Sabbath. So the Jews said to the man who had
been cured: "Today is a Sabbath. You are not allowed to carry the

---

5:4. This verse is omitted in some manuscripts.

mat." "But," he replied, "he who made me well also told me: 'Take   *11*
up your mat and walk.'" Then they asked him: "Who is the man   *12*
who told you to take up your mat and walk?" But the cured man   *13*
did not know who he was; for, since there was a crowd of people in
the place, Jesus had left unnoticed. Later Jesus met him in the   *14*
temple and said to him: "Listen; you are now well and strong. Do
not sin any more, or something worse may happen to you." The man   *15*
went away and told the Jews that it was Jesus that had made him
well again.

For this reason the Jews persecuted Jesus, namely, that he did   *16*
things like this on the Sabbath. But Jesus answered their charge.   *17*
"My Father," he said, "has been working to this hour; and so I, too,
am working." The result was that the Jews were all the more eager   *18*
to kill him, not only because he broke the Sabbath, but also because
he spoke of God as his own Father, thereby claiming equality
with God.

"THE FATHER DEARLY LOVES THE SON"

Jesus, therefore, resumed the argument and said to them. "I tell   *19*
you the plain truth: the Son can do nothing on his own initiative;
he can only do what he sees the Father do. Yes, what he is doing —
that, and nothing else, the Son does likewise. The Father dearly   *20*
loves the Son, and lets him see everything he himself is doing; in
fact, he will let him see even greater exercises of power than the
ones you witnessed, so that you will be astonished. For example,   *21*
just as the Father raises the dead and gives them life, so, too, does
the Son give life to anyone he chooses. Nor, again, does the Father   *22*
judge anyone; no, the right to judge he has turned over wholly to
the Son. All men are to honor the Son just as they honor the Father.   *23*
He who does not honor the Son does not honor the Father, whose
ambassador he is.

"Yes, I tell you frankly: he who heeds my message and believes   *24*
him whose ambassador I am, is in possession of eternal life, and is
not liable to judgment. On the contrary, he has once for all passed
out of the realm of death into that of life. It is the truth when I   *25*

5:17. After the six days of the creation, God "rested"; but his "work" for
man's salvation went on, and still goes on, without interruption.
5:19. The Son carries out the will of the Father in every detail. His will
and the will of the Father are one and the same. See the third note on 1:1.

tell you that a time is coming, in fact, it is already here, when the
dead will hear the voice of the Son of God, and those who heed it
26 will have life. Just as the Father is the source of life, so, too, has
27 he given the Son the power to be a source of life; and he has
28 authorized him to pass judgment, because he is a son of man. Do not
be surprised at this, for a time is coming when all the dead and
buried will hear his summons, and out of the grave they will come —
29 those who have lived good lives will rise to live, those whose lives
30 have been ill-spent will be condemned. I have no power of my own
to do anything: I pass judgment only as I am told to do, and
therefore my judgment is just; after all, I am not seeking to do my
will, but the will of him whose ambassador I am.

31 "Suppose I testify in my own behalf; well, my testimony is not
32 true. There is another who does the testifying in my behalf, and I
33 know that the testimony he bears in my favor is true. You sent a
delegation to John, and he has, once for all, testified to the truth;
34 but for myself, I refuse to accept the testimony issuing from man.
35 I merely mention this that you may be saved. That man was the
burning and shining light; but all you cared for was to bask in his
light for a while.

CHRIST, THE FATHER'S AMBASSADOR

36 "But the testimony which I have is weightier than that of John:
the work which the Father has appointed me to complete, the very
work in which I am engaged, bears me witness that I am the Father's
37 ambassador. Besides, the Father, whose ambassador I am, has himself
borne witness to me. You have neither heard his voice nor seen his
38 face. Nor do you make his word your rule of life, because you do
39 not believe the very one who is his ambassador. You have the
Scriptures at your finger ends, since you think you have in them
a source of eternal life; and, in fact, they are my standing witnesses;

5:27. "because he is a son of man (a human being)": see Hebr. 4:15.
5:31. my testimony is not true: a provisional statement, made for the sake of
argument. In 8:14 Jesus takes occasion to show why his testimony is true.
5:32. another: the Father, or, more probably, the Baptist. See verse 36.
5:37. God the Father had manifested himself (Hebr. 1:1) to the Chosen
People, but on the whole it remained "deaf to his voice and blind to the vision
of him" (Knox). The Word manifested himself to the Jews of his own time
(Hebr. 1:2), but "a veil hung over their hearts" (2 Cor. 3:15). They did not
read Scripture with open minds and hearts (Jn. 3:19, 20). See 5:39.

but you do not care to come to me in order to have life. Not that 40, 41
I court honor from men; no, but I know you through and through; 42
you do not have the love of God in your hearts. Here I am — 43
come in the name of my Father, and you do not welcome me! Let
someone else come in his own name, and you will welcome him!

"How is it possible for you to believe — you who court honor 44
from one another, and, at the same time, are not concerned about
the honor which the only God bestows! Do not think that I shall 45
accuse you before the Father. Moses, on whom you have pinned
your hopes — there is your accuser! Yes, if you believed Moses, you 46
would believe me; for he has written concerning me. But if you do 47
not believe his writings, no wonder you will not believe my words."

CHAPTER 6

MIRACULOUS MULTIPLICATION OF LOAVES AND FISH

Some time later Jesus went across the Sea of Galilee, that is, 1
the Lake of Tiberias. A great crowd followed him, because they were 2
witnesses of the miracles which he used to perform on the sick.
After going up the mountainside, Jesus seated himself there, sur- 3
rounded by his disciples. The Passover, the feast of the Jews, was 4
near at hand.

Lifting up his eyes and noticing that a multitude of people were 5
coming to meet him, Jesus said to Philip: "Where shall we buy bread
enough for these people to have a meal?" He said this by way of 6
testing him, for he knew his own mind as to what he intended to
do. "Bread for two hundred denarii," Philip answered him, "is not 7
enough for each of them to get even a little." Then one of his 8
disciples, Andrew, the brother of Simon Peter, said to him: "There 9
is a lad here who has five barley loaves and two fish; but what
is that for so many!" "Make the people recline on the ground," 10

5:43. *someone else:* about a hundred years later a certain Bar Kochba set
himself up as the Messias and secured a large following. Perhaps the antichrist
is meant; but the general statement may include the past as well. See 10:8.

6:2. *witnesses of the miracles:* see the note on 2:11. The multitude was
prompted more by curiosity and excitement than by a genuine desire to understand Christ's miracles as his credentials. Compare 6:26.

6:7. *two hundred denarii:* about 35 dollars.

Jesus said. There was much grass in the place. So they reclined, the men numbering about five thousand.

11   Jesus then took the loaves into his hands and, after saying grace, had the loaves as well as pieces of the fish distributed among the people reclining about the ground. Everyone got as much as he
12   wanted. When all had had their fill, he said to his disciples: "Gather
13   up the pieces that are left over; nothing must be wasted." They gathered them up, therefore, after they had finished their meal, and filled twelve baskets with the remnants of the five barley loaves.

JESUS WALKS UPON THE SEA

14   When the people realized what miracle he had performed, they said: "This is really the Prophet who is to come into the world!"
15   Jesus, accordingly, knowing that they intended to come and carry him off to make him King, withdrew, all by himself, still deeper
16   into the mountainous region. When evening came, his disciples
17   went down to the seashore and, embarking in a boat, steered for Capharnaum on the other side of the sea. Darkness had already
18   fallen, and Jesus had not yet come to join them; besides, the sea
19   was rising since a strong breeze kept blowing. When they had rowed about twenty-five or thirty furlongs, they suddenly saw Jesus walking
20   upon the sea and coming near the boat. They were terrified. But he
21   said to them: "It is I. Do not be afraid." Then they were only too glad to take him into the boat; and at once the boat was at the land for which they had been heading.
22   The next morning the crowd was still lingering on the other side of the sea. They had noticed the day before that there was only one boat at the place, and that Jesus did not go into that boat
23   with his disciples. The disciples had left by themselves. But meanwhile other boats had arrived from Tiberias and put in near the spot where the people had eaten the bread blessed by Jesus.

THE FOOD THAT AFFORDS ETERNAL LIFE

24   When the people saw that neither Jesus nor his disciples were there, they entered the boats and went to Capharnaum, looking for
25   Jesus. When they found him on the other shore of the sea, they
26   said to him: "Rabbi, when did you come here?" "I tell you the

---

6:19. About three or four miles.

plain truth," Jesus answered them, "you are looking for me, not because you saw manifestations of power, but because you partook of the loaves and made a hearty meal of them. Do not be concerned 27 about the food that is bound to perish, but about the food that affords eternal life — the food which the Son of Man will give you; for on him God the Father has set his seal of approval."

"Well," they replied, "what must we do to be concerned about 28 what God requires?" Jesus answered them: "This is what God 29 requires: believe in his ambassador." "What proofs of your claims, 30 then," they rejoined, "do you give so that we may see it and believe you? What can you do? Our fathers ate the manna in the desert, 31 as the Scripture says: 'He gave them bread from heaven to eat.'"

"I tell you the plain truth," replied Jesus, "Moses did not give 32 you the bread from heaven; not at all: my Father gives you the real bread from heaven; for only the bread that comes down from heaven 33 for the purpose of giving life to the world is God's bread." "Well, 34 sir," they said to him, "then let us always have the bread you speak of."

CHRIST IS THE BREAD OF LIFE

"I am the bread of Life," replied Jesus; "he who comes to me 35 will never hunger, and he who believes in me will never thirst. The pity is, as I said, you have seen me, and yet refuse to believe. 36 Only one whom the Father entrusts to me will come to me; and 37 when anyone comes to me, I will certainly not reject him; for I have 38 come down from heaven not to do my own will, but the will of him whose ambassador I am. Now, this is the will of him whose 39 ambassador I am: I must not lose anything of what the Father has entrusted to me, but raise everything from the dead on the last day. Yes, it is my Father's will that everyone who looks at the Son and 40 believes in him shall have eternal life and be raised by me on the last day."

The Jews were grumbling at him for saying: "I am the bread 41 that came down from heaven." "Is not this man Jesus, the son of 42 Joseph?" they remarked; and, "Do we not know his father and

6:28. *to be concerned about:* sometimes rendered, "to work the works of God." See the note on 9:3.
6:31. The crowd is willing to believe in Jesus (as the Messias) if he were able to perform a miracle to match that performed by Moses. Exod. 16:12.

mother? How can he now say that he has come down from heaven?"

43   Jesus answered their challenge by saying to them: "Do not
44   grumble among yourselves. Nobody is able to come to me unless the
Father, whose ambassador I am, draws him, that I may raise him
45   from the dead on the last day. It says in the Book of Prophets:
'And all will be learners in God's own school.' Only he who has
46   heard the Father's voice and learned the lesson comes to me. Not
that anyone has actually seen the Father; only one has seen the
47   Father — he who is here with authority from God. I tell you the
plain truth: he who believes is in possession of eternal life.

48, 49   "I am the bread of life. Your fathers ate the manna in the desert,
50   and they died. The bread which I speak of, which comes down from
51   heaven, is such that no one who eats of it will ever die. I am the
living bread that has come down from heaven. If one eats of this
bread, he will live forever; and, furthermore, the bread which I shall
give is my flesh given for the life of the world."

"THE BREAD THAT HAS COME DOWN FROM HEAVEN"

52   The Jews then had a violent discussion among themselves. "How,"
they argued, "can this man give us his flesh to eat?"

53   Resuming, therefore, Jesus said to them: "What I tell you is
the plain truth: unless you eat the flesh of the Son of Man and
54   drink his blood, you have no life in you. He who eats my flesh
and drinks my blood is in possession of eternal life; and I will
55   raise him from the dead on the last day; for my flesh is real food,
56   and my blood is real drink. He who eats my flesh and drinks my
57   blood is united with me, and I am united with him. As the living
Father has appointed me his ambassador, and I live because of the

---

6:45. See Isa. 54:13.

6:48–59. Jesus distinguishes between "coming to him" (through faith in him)
and "eating his flesh and drinking his blood." The latter expression would
not be an intelligible metaphor for the former. Besides, Jesus compares the
giving of his flesh to the giving of the manna, and at the same time contrasts
the two; evidently, in both instances there is question of real food. Finally,
he prepared the multitude for the Eucharist by the miraculous feeding.

6:53 ff. Christ's promise to give his real flesh and real blood as food for the
nourishment of our souls was fulfilled by the institution of the Blessed
Eucharist (Mt. 26:26 ff.; Mk. 14:22 ff.; Lk. 22:19 f.; 1 Cor. 11:23–25). John
supplements the accounts of the Synoptics by narrating the promise and stressing
the need of faith as an indispensable condition of the acceptance of this
mysterium fidei.

Father, so, too, he who eats me will have life because of me. This 58
is the bread that has come down from heaven. It is not what your
fathers ate; they ate and died. He who eats this bread will live
forever."

This discourse he delivered in an instruction at a synagogue service 59
in Capharnaum. The result was that many of his disciples among 60
the hearers said: "Such language is hard to bear; who can listen
to it!" But Jesus, inwardly aware that his disciples were grumbling 61
on this account, said to them: "Does this make you waver in your
faith? Suppose, then, you see the Son of Man ascend to where he 62
was before? The spirit is the life-giving thing; the flesh as such is 63
worthless. The words I have spoken to you are spirit and, therefore,
life. The trouble is, there are some among you that have no faith." 64

Jesus knew, of course, from the outset, who those were that had
no faith, and, in particular, which of them was to betray him.
So he continued: "This is what I meant when I said to you: 'No 65
one can come to me unless he has received the gift from the Father.'"

Thereupon many of his disciples went back to their old life and 66
would no longer associate with him. Jesus then said to the Twelve: 67
"Are you, too, minded to go away?" Simon Peter spoke up. "Lord," 68
he said to him, "to whom shall we go? You have a message of
eternal life; we firmly believe and are fully convinced that you are 69
the Holy One of God!" Jesus interposed. "I personally chose you, 70
the Twelve, did I not? And yet, one of you is a devil!" He meant 71
Judas, the son of Simon Iscariot; for he was eventually to betray
him, and he was one of the Twelve.

CHAPTER 7

JESUS TARRIES IN GALILEE

For some time afterwards Jesus kept moving about in Galilee. 1
Since the Jews were anxious to kill him, he did not wish to tour

---

6:61. were grumbling: this grumbling may be said to have been the germ
of the later heresy called "Docetism," which denied the reality of Christ's human
nature, and consequently undermined all Christian faith.

6:62. If Christ could ascend into heaven, he could also make his body and
blood fit to serve as food for the soul. In either case the body is stripped, by
the power of God, of its raw, material qualities.

2 Judea. But when the Jewish feast of Tabernacles was near,
3 his brothers said to him: "Quit this part of the country and go
4 to Judea. Your disciples, too, should see what you are doing. Nobody,
surely, acts in secret and, at the same time, wants to be in the public
eye. Since you are having such success, let your light shine before
5 the world." Even his brothers, by the way, did not believe in him.
6 "My time," replied Jesus, "is not yet at hand; but your oppor-
7 tunity is always ready to hand. The world cannot hate you. It does
8 hate me, because I expose its wickedness. You may go to the feast;
I am not going up to this feast; my time has not quite come as yet."
9 After saying this, he himself tarried in Galilee.
10 However, when his brothers had gone up to the feast, then he,
11 too, went up, not so as to attract attention, but incognito. The Jews,
therefore, made search for him at the feast. "Where is this man?"
12 they asked. There was also much whispering among the crowds.
Some said: "He is a good man." Others said: "Not at all; he leads
13 the masses astray." No one, however, expressed his opinion of him
openly, because of their fear of the Jews.

JESUS TEACHES IN THE TEMPLE

14 By the time the feast was half over, Jesus went up to the temple
15 to teach. The Jews were puzzled. "How is it," they said "that this
16 man is able to read? He has had no regular schooling!" In explanation, therefore, Jesus said to them: "My teaching is not my own
17 invention. It is his whose ambassador I am. Anyone in earnest about
doing his will can form a judgment of my teaching, to decide
whether it originates with God, or whether I speak my own mind.
18 He who speaks his own mind is looking for his personal glory; but
he who looks for the glory of him whose ambassador he is, is truthful
19 and not given to deception. Did not Moses give you the Law? And

---

7:2. The feast of Tabernacles was the annual harvest festival, which also
commemorated the forty years of wandering in the desert. During it, the Jewish
families lived in booths made from the boughs of trees.

7:8. *I am not going up:* here, it seems, the Greek verb for *going up* is taken
in the more restricted and technical sense of joining a caravan of pilgrims who
went up to Jerusalem for the festivities. A few days later Jesus "did go up"
privately, incognito (verse 10).

7:19. The mention of Moses seems abrupt. This verse is best taken as an
a pari argument: "You are not doing the will of the Father, *and therefore* do not
recognize me as his ambassador" (verse 17); "*just so,* you are not living up

yet, not one of you lives up to the Law! Why are you so anxious   20
to kill me?" "You are not in your right mind," the crowd replied;
"who is anxious to kill you?" Jesus explained. "One deed I have   21
done," he said to them, "and you are all surprised at this. Moses gave   22
you the rite of circumcision" — not that it originates with Moses, but
with the fathers — "and you practice circumcision on the Sabbath.
If a man may be circumcised on a Sabbath to prevent the Law of   23
Moses from being broken, why are you enraged at me for restoring
a whole man to health on a Sabbath? Do not judge according to   24
appearances, but form your judgments on just grounds."

Then some of the inhabitants of Jerusalem said: "Is not this   25
the man they are anxious to kill? And here he is, speaking right out   26
in the open, and they say nothing to him. Maybe, the authorities
have really discovered that this man is the Messias. On the other   27
hand, we know this man's parentage; but when the Messias comes,
nobody will know his parentage!" Jesus, therefore, while teaching   28
in the temple, cried out: "You know me, and you know my parentage! And yet, I am not here by my own authority. No, in reality
I am but the ambassador of him whom you do not know. I know   29
him, for he is the very one from whom I have come with a mission."
Upon this, they would have liked to arrest him, but no one laid   30
his hand on him. His hour had not yet come. But among the people   31
many believed in him. "When the Messias comes," they said, "can
he give more proofs of his claims than this man has done?"

PHARISEES GIVE ORDERS FOR THE ARREST OF JESUS

These whispered comments of the crowd came to the ears of   32
the Pharisees; so the high priests and the Pharisees sent policemen
with orders to arrest him. Jesus said, therefore: "Only a little while   33
longer shall I be with you, and then I go home to him whose
ambassador I am. You will miss me, and you will not find me, and   34
where I am you cannot come." The Jews then said among them-   35
selves: "Where does this man intend to go, since he says that we

---

to the Law of Moses, and therefore do not recognize me as the one of whom
Moses has testified; on the contrary, you wish to kill me."

7:21. *One deed:* see 5:2 ff. In many manuscripts, the words "on this account"
are printed as the beginning of verse 22.

7:27. The Messias was expected to appear suddenly, without anyone knowing
his hiding place. See Mt. 24:23.

shall not find him? Does he, perhaps, intend to visit the Jews
36 dispersed among the Greeks and to teach the Greeks? What did
he mean when he said, 'You will miss me, and you will not find
me,' and, 'Where I am you cannot come.'"

DISSENSIONS AMONG THE PEOPLE REGARDING JESUS

37 On the last and solemn day of the feast, Jesus stood erect and
cried out: "If anyone thirsts, let him come to me and drink.
38 He who believes in me will, as the Scripture has said, himself
become a fountain out of which streams of living water are flowing
39 forth." He meant by this the Spirit whom those who believed
in him were destined to receive. As yet there was no outpouring
40 of the Spirit, because Jesus was not yet glorified. Then some of the
crowd who had heard these words, said: "This is really the Prophet!"
41 Others said: "This is the Messias!" But some remarked: "Surely, the
42 Messias is not coming from Galilee, is he? Has not the Scripture
said that the Messias is to come of the line of David, and from
43 the village of Bethlehem, where David lived?" So there was a
44 dissension among the people on his account. Some of them, too,
would have liked to arrest him, but no one laid his hands on him.

45 The police finally returned to the high priests and Pharisees,
46 who asked them: "Why did you not bring him?" "Never," the
47 policemen explained, "has man spoken as this man speaks!" The
48 Pharisees replied: "Have you, too, perhaps, been led astray? Has
anyone of the authorities or of the Pharisees ever believed in him?
49 Oh, this rabble which does not know the Law is a damnable pack!"
50 But Nicodemus, the man who had previously interviewed him and
51 was one of their group, said to them: "Does our Law condemn a
man without first hearing what he has to say and inquiring what he
52 is doing?" By way of answer, they said to him: "Are you, too,
perhaps from Galilee? Search the Scriptures and see for yourself
that prophets are not raised in Galilee!"
53 Then all went home.

7:37. Christ's exhortation was suggested by the ceremony of pouring water at
the base of the altar during the festivities. See the note on 4:10.

7:38. Those who believe in Jesus will not only have their own thirst quenched
(verse 37), but also be able to impart the gifts of the Holy Spirit to others
(verse 39). *as the Scripture has said:* perhaps Isa. 58:11.

CHAPTER 8

"GO AND SIN NO MORE"

Jesus, however, went to the Mount of Olives. In the morning 1, 2
he again appeared in the temple, where the people flocked to him in
crowds; and he sat down to teach them. Here the Scribes and the 3
Pharisees brought a woman caught in adultery and, placing her in
view of all, said to him: "Rabbi, this woman has been caught in 4
the act of committing adultery. Now in the Law, Moses has com- 5
manded us to stone women of this kind. What, then, do you say?"
They said this to set a trap for him, to have matter for accusing 6
him. But Jesus stooped down and with his finger drew figures on
the ground. They persisted, however, in questioning him; so he 7
raised his head and said to them: "If there is one among you free
from sin, let him be the first to throw a stone at her." Then, 8
stooping again, he continued drawing figures on the ground; but, on 9
hearing this, they stole away, one by one, beginning with the older
men, till he was left alone with the woman still standing in full
view. Jesus then raised his head and said to her: "Madam, where 10
are they? Has no one condemned you?" "No one, sir," she replied. 11
Then Jesus said to her: "Neither do I condemn you. Go, and
from now on sin no more."

"I AM THE LIGHT OF THE WORLD"

Once more Jesus addressed them. He said: "I am the light of 12
the world. He who follows me will not walk in the dark, but have
the light of life." "You testify in your own case," the Pharisees 13
said to him; "your testimony is not valid." Jesus answered the charge. 14
"Suppose," he replied, "I do testify in my own case: my testimony
is valid even then, for I know where I came from and where I am
going; but you do not know where I came from or where I am
going. You judge according to outward appearances: I judge no 15

8:1. The story of the adulterous woman is not found in some of the best
manuscripts.

8:6. *continued drawing figures on the ground:* perhaps, to show his complete
indifference to what the Jews were saying.

8:14. *my testimony is valid:* as God and essential truth, Jesus needs no further
testimony. See 5:34.

16 one. And even if I judge, my judgment conforms to rule, for I am
not alone. No, there are two: I and the Father, whose ambassador
17 I am. Even in your own Law it is laid down that the testimony of
18 two men is valid. I am the witness in my own case, and the Father,
19 whose ambassador I am, witnesses in my behalf." Then they said
to him: "Where is your Father?" Jesus replied: "You know neither
me nor my Father. If you knew me, you would also know my
20 Father." He spoke these words in the treasury while teaching in
the temple; and no one arrested him, for his hour had not yet come.

"HE WHOSE AMBASSADOR I AM IS WITH ME"

21 Again he said to them: "I am going away. You will miss me,
and you will die in your sin. Where I am going you cannot come."
22 At this, the Jews said: "Does he perhaps mean to commit suicide,
23 since he says, Where I am going you cannot come?" He replied:
"You come from below; I come from above. You are part and
24 parcel of this world; I am not of this world. That is why I told
you that you will die in your sins. If you do not believe that I am
he, you must die in your sins."

25 Then they replied: "Who are you, anyway?" Jesus said to them:
26 "Oh, that I should speak to you at all! There is much that I might
say about you and condemn in you. I forbear; he whose ambassador
I am speaks the truth, and I proclaim to the world only what I
have heard from him."

27 They did not understand that he was speaking to them of the
28 Father. Jesus resumed: "When you have lifted up the Son of Man,
then at last you will understand that I am he, and that I act in no
wise at my own discretion, but speak only as the Father has taught
29 me. He whose ambassador I am is with me. He has not left me
30 alone, because at all times I do what is pleasing to him." As he
delivered this discourse, many believed in him.

8:24. *I am he:* the one for whom the Jews were waiting; the Messias.

8:25. The Vulgate reads: "I am the beginning, I who speak to you."

8:27. He had just said, "he whose ambassador I am," but did not add,
"my Father," as he had done in 8:18. Perhaps, too, his audience had somewhat shifted from verse 18.

8:28. *lifted up:* his crucifixion was followed by his Resurrection and his ascent
into heaven. These events were sufficient proofs of his divinity. Compare 3:14.

"YOU ARE ANXIOUS TO KILL ME"

Jesus then said to the Jews that had just begun to believe in 31
him: "If you make my teaching your rule of life, you are truly my
disciples; then you will know the truth, and the truth will make you 32
freemen." They remonstrated. "Descendants of Abraham we are," 33
they said to him, "and we have never been any man's slaves! What
do you mean by saying, You will become freemen?" "I must be 34
frank with you," Jesus explained; "I tell you, everyone who commits
sin is the slave of sin. Now a slave does not stay in the household 35
forever; a son does stay forever. Consequently, if the son should make 36
you freemen, you will be freemen in reality.

"I know that you are descendants of Abraham; but the pity is, 37
you are anxious to kill me, because my teaching finds no room in
your hearts. What I have seen in the bosom of the Father — that 38
is the burden of my teaching; and, of course, you, too, are doing
what your father has suggested to you." But they protested and said 39
to him: "Our father is Abraham!" "If your are children of Abraham,"
Jesus retorted, "you ought to do what Abraham did. As it is, you 40
want to kill me — a man that has told you the truth; and this truth
I have heard from God. Abraham did not act like that! You are 41
following in the footsteps of your father." "We are not born out
of wedlock," they rejoined; "we have one Father — God!"

"THE FATHER WHOSE SONS YOU ARE IS THE DEVIL"

Jesus then said to them: "If God were your Father, you would 42
love me, for it is from God that I am come and am now here. I
certainly have not come by my own choice. No, he appointed me
his ambassador. Why will you not understand my language? Because 43
you cannot bring yourselves to give ear to my message. The father 44
whose sons you are is the devil, and you are bent on carrying out
the wishes of your father. He proved himself a murderer at the very
beginning, and did not loyally stand by the truth; in fact, there is

8:33. *They remonstrated:* the Jews in general, rather than those who had
just begun to believe.
8:37. *finds no room in your hearts:* because your malice (the attempt to kill
him) makes you incapable of understanding what I teach. Compare 3:19, 20.
8:44. *the very beginning:* not the moment of his creation, but the time when
he entered into the history of mankind (Gen. 3:1 ff.). The sentence may be

no spark of truth in him. Whenever he gives utterance to the lie in
his soul, then he is in his native element; for he is a liar and the
45 father of lies. I, on the contrary, speak the truth, and therefore you
46 do not believe me. Which of you can prove me guilty of sin? If I
47 speak the truth, why, then, do you not believe me? He who is sprung
from God gives ear to God's message. You do not give ear, because
you are not sprung from God."

"I AM HERE — AND I WAS BEFORE ABRAHAM!"

48 By way of answer the Jews said to him: "Are we not right in
49 saying that you are a Samaritan and possessed by the devil?" "I am
not possessed by the devil," Jesus protested; "on the contrary, I
50 honor my Father, and you dishonor me. Not that I am looking for
my own glory: there is one who makes a point of looking after it
51 and of judging. I tell you the plain truth: if anyone treasures my
52 teaching, he will not see death in all eternity." "Now we are
convinced," the Jews replied, "that you are possessed. Abraham died,
and so did the prophets: yet you say: 'If anyone treasures my teach-
53 ing, he will not taste death in all eternity!' Are you, perhaps, greater
than our father Abraham? He died, and the prophets died! What
54 do you make of yourself?" "If I glorify myself," replied Jesus, "my
glory is worthless. It is my Father that glorifies me. You call him
55 your God; yet you do not know him, whereas I do. Were I to say
that I do not know him, I should be a liar like yourselves. The
56 truth is, I know him, and I treasure his message. Abraham, your
father, exulted in the thought of seeing my day. He did see it, and
57 was glad." Then the Jews said to him: "You are not yet fifty years
58 old, and you have seen Abraham?" "I tell you the plain truth,"

rendered either as in the text, or: "he has been (i.e., was and still is) a murderer
from the very beginning."

8:47. not sprung from God: see 1:18. This verse is supplemented by verse
43: "and because you do not give ear to my message, you do not understand
my language." give ear means, of course, "heed."

8:48. a Samaritan: an enemy of the Jewish people.

8:56. Abraham exulted (Gen. 15) in the thought of being a progenitor of
the Messias, and ardently longed to see the fulfillment of the promise made
to him. He did see it (my day): he saw the time of Christ's life on earth, not
actually, but in faith and prophetic vision, because in the birth of Isaac he saw
the first step toward the fulfillment of that promise.

8:58. Christ here states (1) that he "was" already "in existence" before
Abraham "came into being"; and (2) that, since then he has always been, and
"still is," in existence. The two statements, fused into one grammatical expres-

replied Jesus; "I am here — and I was before Abraham!" At this they 59
took up stones to throw at him; but Jesus was lost to sight and made
his way out of the temple.

CHAPTER 9

CURE OF THE MAN BLIND FROM BIRTH

One day he saw, in passing, a man blind from birth. So his 1, 2
disciples asked him: "Rabbi, who has sinned, this man or his parents,
to account for his being born blind?" "Neither this man has sinned," 3
replied Jesus, "nor his parents. No. God simply wants to make use of
him to reveal his ways. Our duty is, while it is day, to conform to 4
the ways of him whose ambassador I am. Night is coming on, when
no man can do anything. As long as I am in the world, I am the 5
light of the world." With these words spoken, he spat on the ground, 6
and by means of the spittle made a lump of clay, and then spread the
clay over his eyes, and said to him: "Go, and wash in the pool of 7
Siloam" — a word which in our language means "Ambassador." So
he went, and washed, and came back able to see.

Now the neighbors and the people who had seen him before — 8
for he was a beggar — said: "Is not this the fellow who used to sit
and beg in such and such a place?" Some said: "This is the man."
Others said: "Not at all; he only looks like him." He himself 9
declared: "I am the man." They asked him therefore: "How, then, 10
were your eyes opened?" "The man called Jesus," he replied, "made 11
a lump of clay and spread it over my eyes and said to me. 'Go to
Siloam and wash.' So I went and washed, and got my sight." When 12
they asked him: "Where is this man?" he replied: "I do not know."

THE ONCE BLIND MAN BEFORE THE PHARISEES

The man who had been blind was then taken before the Pharisees. 13
Now it happened that the day on which Jesus had formed the lump 14

---

sion, stress the idea of continuity from before Abraham's time down to the
present moment, and intimate his eternity. The statement in Exod. 3:14 is
different: "I am he whose essence it is to be."

9:2. It was a current belief that all physical ailments were punishments for
sin. This is true if by "sin" we mean original sin. The case in 5:14 is different.

9:3. *to reveal his ways*: the rendering "work" for the Greek *ergon* is replaced
in this translation by a more expressive term. Compare 6:28. See the *Catholic
Biblical Quarterly*, January, 1944, p. 61 ff.

15 of clay and opened his eyes was a Sabbath. So the Pharisees, for their part, asked him how he had obtained sight. He replied: "He put a lump of clay on my eyes, and I washed, and now I see."

16 Then some of the Pharisees said: "That man has no authority from God; he does not observe the Sabbath." Others argued: "How can a sinner give such proofs of power!" As a result, there was dis-

17 agreement among them. So they asked the blind man again: "What do you say about him, because he opened your eyes?" He answered: "He is a prophet."

18 The Jews, therefore, did not believe that he had been blind and then obtained sight, until they summoned the parents of the man

19 himself who had regained his sight, and put this question to them: "Is this your son? And do you say he was born blind? How, then, is

20 he at present able to see?" His parents gave this explanation: "We

21 know that this is our son, and that he was born blind; but how he is now able to see we do not know, nor do we know who opened his eyes. Ask him himself; he is old enough; he will give his own

22 account." His parents said this because they were afraid of the Jews; for the Jews had already agreed among themselves that, if anyone should acknowledge Christ as the Messias, he should be put out of

23 the synagogue. That was why his parents said: "He is old enough; ask him himself."

24 So they summoned a second time the man who had been blind, and said to him: "Give glory to God! We know that this man is a

25 sinner." "Whether or not he is a sinner I do not know," he replied;

26 "one thing I do know: I was blind and now I see." Then they asked

27 him: "What did he do to you? How did he open your eyes?" "I told you already," he replied, "and you did not listen. Why do you want to hear it again? Do you, too, perhaps, want to become his disciples?"

28 Then they heaped abuse on him. "You are a disciple of that man,"

29 they said; "we are disciples of Moses. We know that Moses is God's spokesman, but whose mouthpiece this man is we do not know."

30 "Why," the man retorted, "the strange thing is that you do not know whose mouthpiece he is when, as a matter of fact, he has

31 opened my eyes! We know that God does not listen to sinners; but when one is God-fearing and does his will, he does listen to him.

32 Since the world began, it is unheard of that anyone opened the eyes

33 of one born blind! If this man had no mission from God, he

could do nothing!" By way of answer they said to him: "You were 34
wholly born in sin, and you mean to teach us?" And they
expelled him.

Jesus was informed that they had expelled him. When he met 35
the man, he said: "Do you believe in the Son of God?" "Well, who 36
is he, sir?" the man answered; "I want to believe in him." "You are 37
now looking in his face," replied Jesus; "yes, it is he who is now
speaking to you!" "I do believe, sir," he said; and he fell on his knees 38
before him. Jesus continued: "To be the parting of the way — that 39
is my mission to the world: henceforth the sightless are to have sight,
and those who see are to become blind." Some of the Pharisees, who 40
happened to be near, heard this and said to him: "Maybe we, too,
are blind, are we?" "If you were blind," replied Jesus, "you would 41
have no sin; as it is, you claim to have sight. Your sin remains."

CHAPTER 10

THE TRUE SHEPHERD

"I tell you the plain truth: he who does not enter the sheepfold 1
by the door, but climbs into it some other way, is a thief and a
robber. But he who enters by the door is the shepherd of the sheep. 2
He is the one for whom the keeper opens the door; and the sheep 3
hear his voice. He calls his own sheep individually, and leads them
out. After taking out all that are his own, he marches in front of 4
them; and the sheep follow him because they know his voice. But 5
they will never follow a stranger; on the contrary, they run away
from him, because they do not know the voice of strangers."
This was the parable which Jesus told them; but they did not grasp 6
the meaning of what he said to them.

Jesus resumed, therefore. "I must be very plain with you," he 7
said to them; "I am the door for the sheep; any and all that came 8
before me are thieves and robbers. But the sheep did not listen to

---

9:35. Some manuscripts read "the Son of Man." The man already believed
(verse 17) that Jesus was a prophet; when asked whether he believed in the
Son of God, he naturally wished to learn who that person was. His readiness
to believe in him was well prepared by all that Jesus had done for him.

9:39. "the parting of the way": see Lk. 2:34. "Those who see": who think
themselves wise and prudent. Compare Mt. 11:25.

10:8. thieves and robbers: a reference either to the Scribes and Pharisees,
who had often abused their spiritual leadership (Mt. 23), or, more probably,

9 them. I am the door; if one goes in through me, all will be well
10 with him; he will go in and out, and find pasture. The thief does not
come except to steal and slaughter and destroy. I have come that
they may have life and have it in abundance.

CHRIST THE GOOD SHEPHERD

11 "I am the good shepherd. A good shepherd lays down his life to
12 save his sheep. If a hired man, who is not a shepherd and has no
sheep of his own, sees the wolf coming, he abandons the sheep and
13 runs away; and the wolf carries them off or scatters them. After
14 all, he is only a hired man and has no interest in the sheep. I am
15 the good shepherd; and I know mine and mine know me, as the
Father knows me and I know the Father; and I lay down my life to
16 save the sheep. Still other sheep I claim as my own, which are not
of this fold. I must lead them also to pasture, and they will listen to
17 my voice, and there will be one flock, one shepherd. The Father loves
me because I lay down my life, and he wills that I should take it
18 back again. No one can rob me of it. No, I lay it down of my own
will. I have power to lay it down, and power to take it back again.
Such is the charge I have received from my Father."

19 Again there was disagreement among the Jews because of what
20 he had just said. Many of them remarked: "He is possessed by a
21 demon and out of his mind. Why do you listen to him?" Others
said: "This is not the language of one possessed by a demon! Can
a demon open blind men's eyes?"

"THE FATHER AND I ARE ONE"

22 Then came the feast of the Dedication at Jerusalem. It was

to certain revolutionaries who had come with Messianic pretensions, but were
not followed by the people as a whole. See 5:43.

10:16. *other sheep:* the Gentiles. *one flock, one shepherd:* the Vulgate and,
consequently, the Douay-Challoner version ("one *fold:* one shepherd") gave
rise to heated discussions in Reformation times. Christ came to redeem both
the Chosen People and the Gentiles; he was, therefore, the shepherd of both
groups or folds, the one made up of the children of Abraham, the other, of
outsiders. But once Jew and Gentile have come into the Church, "the inter-
vening wall of the enclosure is broken down" (Eph. 2:14), and then there is
only one Church (Mt. 16:18) and "one fold." Some consideration like this
may have led the author of the Vulgate to use the word "fold" where the
Greek has flock.

10:22. This feast commemorated the restoration of the temple by Judas
Machabee.

winter; and Jesus was walking about in the porch of Solomon inside 23
the temple premises. So the Jews surrounded him and said to him: 24
"How long will you keep us in suspense? If you are the Messias, tell
us outright." Jesus answered their challenge: "I told you, but you 25
refuse to believe. The things I am doing in the name of my Father
testify in my behalf. The pity is, you refuse to believe, because you 26
do not belong to my sheep. My sheep listen to my voice. I know 27
them, and they follow me; and I give them eternal life; they will not 28
be lost in eternity, for no one can snatch them out of my hand.
The Father, who has entrusted them to me, is all-powerful; and no 29
one can snatch anything out of my Father's hand. The Father and 30
I are one."

Once again the Jews brought stones, ready to stone him to death. 31
Jesus remonstrated with them: "Many a kindly deed have I performed, 32
under your eyes, with power from my Father, for which particular
deed do you mean to stone me?" "Not for a kindly deed," the Jews 33
retorted, "do we mean to stone you, but for blasphemy and because
you, a man, make yourself God." Jesus replied: "Is it not written in 34
your Law, 'I said, you are gods'? If it called 'gods' those to whom the 35
word of God was addressed — and the Scripture cannot be annulled
— will you then say, 'You are a blasphemer,' to him whom the 36
Father has consecrated to his service and made his ambassador to
the world, just because I said, 'I am the Son of God'? If I do not 37
act as my Father does, then do not believe me; but if I do, then 38
believe on the strength of my actions even if you do not believe
my words. Thus the truth will dawn on you, and you will understand that the Father is in me and that I am in the Father." Again 39
they were eager to arrest him; but he eluded their grasp.

He then went again to the place across the Jordan where John 40
had begun his career as a baptizer; and there he tarried. A great 41
many people came to meet him. "John, to be sure," they remarked,
"did not work a single miracle; yet whatever John said about this 42
man has proved true." The result was that many believed in him
there and then.

10:34. In Ps. 81 (82):6, rulers are called "gods," because they represent God.

CHAPTER 11

THE ILLNESS OF LAZARUS

1   Now a man named Lazarus was ill. He was of Bethania, the
2   village where Mary and her sister Martha were living. Mary is the
    person who anointed the Lord with perfume and wiped his feet with
3   her hair. It was her brother Lazarus that was ill. So the sisters sent
4   this message to him: "Please, Lord, your dear friend is ill." "This
    illness," Jesus said on receiving the news, "will not result in death.
    No, it is to promote the glory of God. Through it the Son of God
    is to be glorified."
5, 6 Now Jesus loved Martha and her sister and Lazarus. So, when he
    learned that he was ill, he tarried, it is true, for two days in the
7   place where he was; but after that space of time he said to the
8   disciples: "Let us go back into Judea." "Rabbi," the disciples said
    to him, "only recently the Jews wanted to stone you to death, and
9   you mean to go back there again?" Jesus answered: "Are there
    not twelve hours to the day? As long as a man walks in the day, he
10 does not stumble, because he sees the light of this world. But when
    a man walks in the night, he stumbles, because he has no light to
    guide him."
11 After saying this, he paused, and then continued: "Lazarus, our
    friend, has fallen asleep. Well, then, I will go and wake him from
12 his sleep." "Lord," the disciples said to him, "if he has fallen asleep,
13 he will be all right." But Jesus had spoken of his death, whereas they
14 imagined he had referred to the restfulness of sleep. Jesus now told
15 them plainly: "Lazarus is dead. For your sake I am glad I was not
16 there, so that you may believe. Come now; let us go to him." Here
    Thomas, called the Twin, said to his fellow disciples: "Let us go
    along and die with him."

"YOUR BROTHER WILL RISE AGAIN"

17 When Jesus arrived, he found that Lazarus had already been
18 four days in the tomb. Bethany was near Jerusalem, about two miles
19 away; and many Jews had called on Martha and Mary to express their

11:9. The time allotted to me by my Father has not yet run out; not until
then will my enemies prevail against me.

264

sympathy with them in the loss of their brother. As soon as Martha   20
heard that Jesus was coming, she went to meet him, while Mary
remained at home. Martha said to Jesus: "Lord, if you had been   21
here, my brother would not have died. And even now I know that   22
whatever you ask of God, God will grant you." Jesus replied: "Your   23
brother will rise again." "I know," Martha said to him, "he will   24
rise again at the resurrection on the last day." "I am the resurrection   25
and the life," Jesus said to her; "he who believes in me will live even
if he dies; and no one that lives and believes in me shall be dead   26
forever. Do you believe this?" "Yes, Lord," she replied; "I firmly   27
believe that you are the Messias, the Son of God, who was to come
into the world."

With this, she returned and called her sister Mary privately.   28
"The Master is here and asks for you," she said. As soon as Mary   29
heard this, she rose quickly and went to meet him. Jesus had not   30
yet entered the village, but was still at the spot where Martha had
gone to meet him. Then the Jews who were with her in the   31
house to offer their sympathy, on seeing Mary rise hurriedly and
go out, followed her, supposing she was going to the tomb, there
to give vent to her tears. When Mary came where Jesus was, she   32
threw herself down at his feet as soon as she saw him, and said
to him: "Lord, if you had been here, my brother would not have
died." She was weeping; and weeping, too, were the Jews who accom-   33
panied her. The sight of them stirred Jesus deeply and shook his
inmost soul. "Where have you laid him to rest?" Jesus asked.   34
"Come, and see, Lord," they replied. Jesus burst into tears;   35
and the Jews remarked: "Look, how dearly he loved him!"   36
But some of them said: "He opened the eyes of the blind man; was   37
he not able to prevent this man's death?"

"LAZARUS COME FORTH!"

Then Jesus, his inmost soul shaken again, made his way to the   38
tomb. It was a cave, and a slab of stone lay against the entrance.
"Remove the slab of stone," Jesus said. "Lord," Martha, the dead   39
man's sister, said to him, "his body smells by this time; he has been
dead four days." "Did I not tell you," replied Jesus, "that, if you   40
have faith, you will see the glory of God?" So they removed the slab   41

11:26. He will die indeed, but with the right to eternal life.

of stone. Then Jesus lifted up his eyes and said: "Father, I thank
42 you for giving ear to me. For myself, I knew that you always hear
me; but I said it for the sake of the people surrounding me, that
they might believe that I am your ambassador."

43 Having said this, he cried out in a strong voice: "Lazarus, come
44 forth!" And he who had been dead came forth, wrapped hand and
foot with bandages, and his face muffled with a scarf. Jesus said to
them: "Unwrap him and let him go."

45 Now many of the Jews — those who had called on Mary and
46 witnessed what he did — believed in him; some of them, however,
went to see the Pharisees and told them what Jesus had done.
47 Thereupon the high priests and the Pharisees convened a meeting
of the Supreme Council. "This man," they urged, "is giving many
48 proofs of power! What, then, are we to do? If we let him go without
interference, all the world will believe in him; and then the Romans
will come and put an end to our rank and race alike."

RESOLUTION PASSED TO PUT JESUS TO DEATH

49 One of them, however, Caiaphas, who was high priest in that
50 year, said to them: "You are not men of vision! Can even you not
understand that it is to our advantage that one man should die for
51 the people so that the whole nation may be saved from ruin?" In
saying this, he was wiser than he knew; the truth is, being high priest
in that year, he revealed God's design that Jesus was to die for the
52 whole nation; and not only was he to save the whole nation, but
53 to unite in one body all the scattered children of God. On that
day, accordingly, they passed a resolution to put him to death.

54 As a result, Jesus would no longer move freely among the Jews,
but left the place and, retiring to a town called Ephraim in the
55 region skirting the desert, tarried there with his disciples. The Passover of the Jews was now at hand, and multitudes went up from the
country to Jerusalem in order to purify themselves before the
56 Passover. Of course, they were looking for Jesus and, as they stood
about in groups on the temple grounds, would say to one another:
"What do you think? You think he will not come to the feast?"
57 By that time, the high priests and the Pharisees had given orders

---

11:52. See Jer. 29:14 and 10:16.

that, if anyone knew of his whereabouts, he should make it known so that they might arrest him.

CHAPTER 12

JESUS DEFENDS MARY

Six days before the Passover, Jesus came to Bethania, where 1 Lazarus, whom Jesus had raised from the dead, was living. Here 2 a dinner was given in his honor, at which Martha acted as hostess, while Lazarus was one of the guests reclining at table with him. On this occasion Mary took a pound of perfume made of very 3 costly spikenard, anointed the feet of Jesus, and wiped his feet with her hair. The whole house was filled with the fragrance of the perfume. But Judas Iscariot, one of his disciples, who intended to 4 betray him, said: "Why was not this perfume sold for three hundred 5 denarii and the money given to the poor?" He said this, however, 6 not because he was interested in the poor, but because he was a thief and used to pilfer what was put into the purse, which he carried. Jesus then said: "Let her have her way. It will turn out that 7 she has reserved this perfume for the day of my embalmment. Besides, the poor you always have with you, but you do not always 8 have me."

Now it became widely known among the common people of 9 the Jews that he was there; so they came, not exclusively for Jesus' sake, but also to get a glimpse of Lazarus, whom he had raised from the dead. The high priests, thereupon, resolved to kill Lazarus as 10 well, because many of the Jews went there and then believed 11 in Jesus.

THE SAVIOR'S GLORIOUS ENTRY INTO JERUSALEM

The next day, the common people who had come to celebrate 12 the feast, on hearing that Jesus was coming to Jerusalem, provided 13

12:2 In the house of Simon the Leper. Mt. 26:6.
12:5. See the note on 6:7.
12:7. After the crucifixion in the late afternoon there was no time for the customary Jewish embalmment. It will then turn out that by her action, the significance of which she did not at first understand, Mary had anticipated the embalmment, because Jesus very graciously accepted it as such.

themselves with branches from the palm trees nearby, and went out to meet him, shouting:

> "Hosanna! A blessing on him
> who is coming in the name of the Lord,
> who is also Israel's King!"

14 When Jesus had procured an ass's foal, he seated himself on it, in accordance with the Scripture text:

15 > "Have no fear, O daughter of Sion!
> Look! Your King is coming
> seated on an ass's foal."

16 His disciples did not at first understand the meaning of all this; but, after Jesus was glorified, they remembered that this text had reference to him, and that what they did for him on this occasion
17 was its fulfillment. Of course, the crowd that had been with him when he called Lazarus out of the tomb and raised him from the
18 dead, spoke favorably of this event; and this was the reason why the crowd now went out to meet him, namely, that they had heard
19 of his having given this particular proof of his claims. The Pharisees then said among themselves: "You see that you are profiting nothing! Look, the whole world is running after him!"

20 Among the pilgrims going up to Jerusalem to worship at the
21 feast were some Greeks. These people interviewed Philip, who was from Bethsaida in Galilee, and made this request of him: "Sir, we
22 would like to see Jesus." Philip then went and spoke to Andrew,
23 and Andrew and Philip, in turn, went and spoke to Jesus. Jesus was moved to say: "Come at last is the hour for the Son of Man to be
24 glorified! I tell you the plain truth: unless the grain of wheat falls
25 into the earth and dies, it remains just one grain; but once it has died, it bears abundant fruit. He who holds his life dear destroys it; he who sets no store by his life in this world will preserve it for
26 eternal life. Whoever would be in my personal service must follow me; and then, wherever I am, there, too, my servant will be. Whoever is in my personal service will be honored by the Father.

12:13. *Hosanna:* literally, "save, I pray"; "be propitious."

12:20. *some Greeks:* proselytes, who had come to Jerusalem to worship the true God.

12:24. *the grain of wheat:* an allusion to himself (see the note on 4:34), who had to die before abundant fruit for eternal life could be reaped. See Lk. 24:26.

JESUS APPROACHES HIS GREAT ORDEAL

"Now is my soul shaken in its inmost depths; and what shall 27
I say? 'Father, save me from this ordeal'? No, no; for this very
purpose I am facing this ordeal. Father, glorify your name." Then 28
a voice rang out from heaven: "I have glorified it, and I will continue to glorify it." At this, the crowd which stood by within hearing 29
distance said: "It has thundered." Others said: "An angel has spoken
to him." Jesus explained: "Not for my sake," he said, "has this 30
voice rung out, but for yours. Now is the sentence of condemnation 31
being passed upon this world; now is the prince of this world being
evicted; and I, once I have been lifted up from the earth, will draw 32
all men to myself."

This he said to signify what kind of death he was to die. 33
The crowd, therefore, argued with him: "We have been taught by 34
the Law that the Messias is to remain forever. How, then, can you
say that the Son of Man must be lifted up? Who is this Son of
Man?" "A little while longer," Jesus replied, "will the light be 35
among you. Walk while you have the light, or darkness will overtake
you. He who walks in the dark does not see where he is going. As 36
long as you have the light, believe in the light so that you may
become shining lights." After delivering this discourse, Jesus went
away and hid himself from them.

WHY SO MANY REFUSED TO BELIEVE

But although he had given such strong proofs of his claims 37
under their very eyes, they refused to believe in him. Thus the 38
saying of Isaias the prophet was to be fulfilled:

"Who, O Lord, believed the message preached to us!

To whom was the power of the Lord made known!"

The reason why they could not believe was that, as again Isaias says, 39

12:27. The thought of his own death is a painful ordeal to Jesus; his soul
is deeply stirred, and he momentarily considers (as he will again in the garden
of Gethsemani) the possibility of saving the world without undergoing death.
for this very purpose: namely, of suffering death, he submits to the present ordeal.

12:38. The unbelief of the Jews was foretold by Isaias. After stating (52:15)
that the Gentiles would acknowledge and honor the Messias, he pictures the
Jews (53:1) as lamenting, in retrospect, their own former rejection of the
message of salvation.

12:39. The persistent refusal of grace results in spiritual callousness, which,
morally speaking, is incurable. See Mt. 12:31.

40   "He has blinded their eyes,
                       and hardened their hearts,
                       that their eyes might not see
                       and their hearts not understand,
                       and they might not be converted
                       and healed by me."
41 Isaias said this because it was he whose glory he envisioned and of
42 whom he spoke. Just the same, even among the leading classes a
good many individuals believed in him; only, on account of the
Pharisees, they would make no open profession of it, for fear they
43 might be put out of the synagogue. After all, they cared more for
the approval of men than for the approval of God.

THE WARNING OF JESUS

44   But Jesus cried out these words: "He who believes in me believes
45 not in me but in him whose ambassador I am, and he who looks at
46 me looks at him whose ambassador I am. I have come into the world
as a light, so that no one who believes in me might remain in
47 darkness. If anyone hears my teachings and does not observe them,
it is not I that condemns him. It is not my mission to condemn
48 the world; but, on the contrary, to save the world. He that rejects
me and does not accept my teachings will find his judge. The doctrine I have taught — that is what will condemn him on the last
49 day. I do not teach on my own authority. Quite the contrary; the
Father, whose ambassador I am, has laid on me a commandment
50 as to what I am to say and what I am to teach. And I know that
his commandment means eternal life. Therefore, whatever I teach,
I teach exactly as the Father has instructed me."

CHAPTER 13

JESUS WASHES THE FEET OF HIS DISCIPLES

1   The feast of the Passover was now approaching, and Jesus knew
that his time for passing from this world to his Father had arrived.

13:1. This solemn verse reads like a prologue to John's story of the Passion,
Death, and Resurrection of Jesus. To the evangelist, the whole drama presents
itself as an all-embracing act of love. Jesus had always loved his own; but the

He had always loved his own who were in the world; and now he gave them a last proof of his love.

Supper was still in progress, and the devil had by now firmly 2 fixed in the heart of Judas Iscariot, Simon's son, the purpose of betraying him. He, however, being conscious that the Father had 3 put sovereign power into his hands, and that he had come as a messenger from God and was now going home to the Father, rose 4 from supper, laid aside his outer clothing, and provided himself with a towel, which he girt round his waist. He next poured water 5 into the basin, and proceeded to wash the feet of the disciples and wipe them with the towel which he had girt round him. So he 6 came to Simon Peter, who said to him: "Lord, do you mean to wash my feet?" "What I intend to do," Jesus explained to him, "you 7 do not understand right now, but you will understand by and by." "You are not going to wash my feet in all eternity!" Peter said 8 to him. To which Jesus replied: "If I do not wash you, I have nothing more to do with you!" "Lord," Simon Peter said to him, 9 "then wash not only my feet, but my hands and my head as well!" Jesus said to him: "After a bath, all one needs is to have his feet 10 washed; then he is perfectly clean. And you are clean, though not all of you." He knew, of course, his betrayer; that is why he said: 11 "You are not all of you clean."

"WHAT I HAVE DONE TO YOU, YOU TOO SHOULD DO"

After he had washed their feet and resumed his outer clothing, 12 he again took his place on the couch. "Do you appreciate," he said to them, "what I have just done to you? You call me 'Rabbi,' 13 and 'Lord'; and you are right. That is what I am. Well, then if I 14 have washed your feet — I, the Lord and Rabbi — you, too, ought to wash one another's feet; for I have set you an example, so that what 15

---

time had arrived for a *last proof* of his love. This proof was the last in the order of time, and the last or supreme in the order of excellence. See 15:13. Chapters 13 to 17 show Jesus in familiar intercourse with his beloved disciples. No other evangelist was capable of baring the secrets of the Sacred Heart as fully and warmly as was John. It is impossible to restrict this verse as merely introductory to the washing of the feet. The specific purpose of this ceremony is given in verses 12–15.

13:15. In the exercise of their exalted position in the Church, the Apostles must preserve due humility and not be overbearing. To teach this lesson, Jesus goes through the ceremony of washing their feet, a service, by the way, which a

16 I have done to you, you, too, should do. "Most certainly, a slave does not take precedence over his master, or an envoy over his
17 sender! If you bear this lesson in mind, happy are you in case you
18 put it in practice. I am not referring to all of you; I know very well whom I have chosen; but then, the Scripture has to be fulfilled:
19 'He who eats my bread has lifted up his heel against me.' I tell you this here and now before it happens, so that when it does
20 happen you may believe that I am he. I am telling you the plain truth: he who welcomes anyone of my ambassadors welcomes me, and he who welcomes me welcomes him whose ambassador I am."

"ONE OF YOU WILL BETRAY ME"

21 When Jesus had said this, he was shaken in his inmost soul, and with great emphasis declared: "I tell you truly, one in your
22 group will betray me!" The disciples then looked at one another,
23 at a loss to know whom he meant. Now one of the disciples of
24 Jesus lay resting in his bosom — the one whom Jesus loved. To him, therefore, Simon Peter nodded, whispering: "Ask who it is
25 he means." Then he, freely drawing close to Jesus' breast, said to him: "Who is it, Lord?"
26 Jesus answered: "It is he to whom I will give the morsel after dipping it in the bowl."

So he dipped the morsel, and with his own hand reached it to
27 Judas, Simon Iscariot's son. And directly after the morsel Satan took full possession of him. Then Jesus said to him: "Do quickly what
28 you mean to do." Of those at table, however, not one understood
29 the meaning of the remark he made to him. In fact, some of them supposed that, since Judas kept the purse, Jesus meant to say: "Buy what we need for the feast," or that he was to give an alms
30 to the poor. After taking the morsel, then, he went out immediately. It was night.

---

host was accustomed to render his guests (Lk. 7:44). That Peter needed a special lesson in this respect is not surprising (Mt. 16:18; Jn. 21:15 ff.). Some of the Fathers see in the "bath" (see verse 10) a reference to baptism, and in the "washing of the feet" a reference to postbaptismal absolution.
    13:23. The ancients reclined at table, leaning on the left elbow.
    13:27. From the service of Christ, Judas passed into the slavery of Satan. See Lk. 22:3.

"LOVE ONE ANOTHER AS I LOVE YOU"

When he had left, Jesus said: "At last the Son of Man is 31
glorified, and in him God is glorified! Since God is glorified in him, 32
God, in turn, will glorify him in himself; and without delay will
he glorify him. Dear children, only a little while longer am I with 33
you. You will miss me and, as I told the Jews, so I tell you at present:
where I am going you cannot come. A new commandment I give 34
you: love one another; as I love you, so I want you, too, to love
one another. By this token all the world must know that you are 35
my disciples — by cherishing love for one another."

Here Simon Peter said to him: "Lord, where are you going?" 36
Jesus explained: "Where I am going you cannot at present follow
me. But you will follow me later." "And why, Lord," replied Peter, 37
"cannot I follow you right now? I will lay down my life for you!"
Jesus answered: "You will lay down your life for me? I must be 38
frank with you: before cockcrow you will disown me three times."

CHAPTER 14

"HE WHO SEES ME SEES THE FATHER"

"Do not let your heart be troubled! You have faith in God. I 1
have faith in me also. In my Father's house are many rooms. I 2
should have told you if it were not so. The fact is, I am now about
to go for the very purpose of preparing a place for you. And when 3
I am gone and have prepared a place for you, I will come back and
take you home with me. I want you to be where I shall be. The way 4
to where I am going you know, of course." "Lord," Thomas then 5
said to him, "we do not know where you are going; how do we
know the way?"

13:33. you cannot come: you are destined to carry on my work after my death.
13:34. The commandment is old, but its motivation is new: Christians love
one another because they are members of the Mystical Body. Rom. 12:5. See
Theological Studies, 3 (1942), p. 260 ff.
14:2. I should have told you: a much-disputed passage. When Jesus "called"
his disciples (Mk. 1:20), he thereby invited them to be his "followers" (Mt.
4:19). This call to "fellowship with Christ" (1 Cor. 1:9) was obviously intended for life and "eternity" (Jn. 12:26), and therefore implied that there
was "room" for them in heaven by the side of Christ (12:26). Had this not been
so, he would, in fairness, have told them.

273

6   Jesus replied: "I am the way, and the truth, and the life. No
7   one comes to the Father except through me. Since you know me,
    you will also know my Father. In fact, you know him now, and are
8   looking him in the face." Here Philip broke in: "Lord, let us see
9   the Father, and we shall be satisfied!" "Philip," Jesus then said to
    him, "so long a time have I been in your midst, and you do not
    know me? He who sees me sees the Father. How, then, can you
10 say: 'Let us see the Father'? Do you not believe that I am in the
    Father and the Father is in me? Take the words I speak to you:
    they are not my own invention, are they? And as for the things I do,
    the Father who dwells in me, is personally responsible for them.
11 Believe me, all of you, when I say that I am in the Father and the
    Father is in me; but if not, at least believe on the strength of what
    I am doing.
12   "I tell you the truth: he who believes in me will himself do the
    things I am doing; in fact, he will do even greater things than I do,
13 now that I am going home to the Father; and should you ask for
    anything in my name, I will do it, that the Father may be glorified
14 in the Son. If you ask me for anything in my name, I will do it.
15   "If you love me, you will treasure my commandments.

"HE WILL GRANT YOU ANOTHER ADVOCATE"

16 And I will ask the Father, and he will grant you another Advocate
17 to be with you for all time to come, the Spirit of Truth! The world

---

14:6. *the way, and the truth, and the life*: this is one of those important self-
revelations in which this Gospel abounds. Note the definite article with each
noun. Compare the elegant variation of the same idea in 8:12. *The truth*: both
the noun and the corresponding adjective are more frequently used by John than
by any other sacred writer. Christ, both as God and as Man, is *the truth*,
both subjectively (essential truthfulness) and objectively (the great reality).

14:7. The Greek text is not certain. Jesus leads his Apostles to a deeper
understanding of his equality with the Father.

14:12. *even greater things*: Jesus confined his ministry to Palestine, and even
there had comparatively little outward success. His disciples are to preach the
Gospel everywhere and with much greater visible results. The liturgy applies to
their activity Ps. 18 (19):6:

> "To all the earth their sound goes forth;
> their message, to the world's extremity."

14:16. *Advocate*: a "Paraclete" is one called in to act as legal assistant or
counsel to his client; then, generally, a helper, consoler, counselor, *another
Advocate*: implying that Christ, too, was during his lifetime an Advocate for his
disciples; and stating that after his departure from the world the Holy Spirit
would take his place.

is incapable of receiving him, because it neither sees him nor knows him. You will know him, because he will make his permanent stay with you and in you. I will not leave you orphans; I am coming 18 back to you. Yet a little while, and the world sees me no longer; 19 but you will see me, because I live, and you, too, shall live. On that 20 day you will come to understand that I am in the Father, and you are in me, and I in you. He who accepts my commandments and 21 treasures them — he is the one that loves me. And he that loves me will, in turn, be loved by my Father; and I will love him, and will manifest myself to him."

Then Judas, not the Iscariot, said to him: "And what is the 22 reason, Lord, why you intend to manifest yourself to us and not to the world?" By way of answer Jesus said to him: "Anyone who 23 loves me will treasure my message, and my Father will love him, and we shall visit him and make our home with him. He who 24 does not treasure my message does not love me; and, mind you, the message you have heard is not mine but the Father's, whose ambassador I am!

"I have told you all this while I am still lingering in your midst; 25 but the Advocate, the Holy Spirit, whom the Father will send in 26 my name, will teach you everything, and refresh your memory of everything I have told you. Peace is my legacy to you: my own 27 peace is my gift to you. My giving to you is not like the world's way of giving.

"Do not let your heart be troubled! Do not let your heart despair! You heard me say to you: 'I am going home and I am coming 28 back to you.' If you loved me, you would rejoice that I am going to the Father, because the Father is greater than I. I have told 29 you this now before it takes place, so that, when it does take place, you may revive your faith. I am not going to converse with you 30 much longer, for already the prince of this world is on his way. Not that he can claim anything in me as his own; no, but 31

14:27. Christ here wishes nothing less than that his peace, his own majestic serenity of soul, the untroubled harmony of his own will with that of the Father, should be ours!

14:28. As man, Jesus is subordinate to the Father.

14:31. It is not certain where the following discourse was delivered. Such words could not be spoken on the way through the city. They were spoken either in the upper room (where the group lingered after rising) or else in the temple. See the next note.

then, the world must come to know that I love the Father and am acting strictly according to the Father's instructions. Rise; we must be going on our way.

Chapter 15

"I AM THE VINE, YOU ARE THE BRANCHES"

1 "I am the real vine, and my Father is the vinedresser.
2 He prunes away any branch of mine that bears no fruit, and cleans any branch that does bear fruit, that it may bear yet more abundant
3 fruit. By now you are clean, thanks to the lessons I have given you.
4 Remain united with me, and I will remain united with you. A branch can bear no fruit of itself, that is, when it is not united with the vine; no more can you, if you do not remain united with me.
5 I am the vine, you are the branches. One bears abundant fruit only when he and I are mutually united; severed from me, you can
6 do nothing. If one does not remain united with me, he is simply thrown away like a branch, and dries up. Such branches are gathered
7 and thrown into the fire to be burned. As long as you remain united with me, and my teachings remain your rule of life, you may ask for
8 anything you wish, and you shall have it. This is what glorifies my Father — your bearing abundant fruit and thus proving yourselves my disciples.

"BE SURE TO HOLD MY LOVE"

9 "Just as the Father loves me, so I love you. Be sure to hold
10 my love. If you treasure my commandments, you will hold my love, just as I treasure my Father's commandments and thus secure his
11 love. I have told you this, that my joy may be yours, and your joy may be perfect.

"LOVE ONE ANOTHER AS I LOVE YOU"

12 "This is my commandment: love one another as I love you.

15:1. *I am the real vine:* compare 6:32: "the real bread from heaven." Jesus saw, we may perhaps suppose, on the high gate leading to the holy of holies, the great Golden Vine with its branches, symbolizing Israel and the Synagogue. "Not that is the real vine," we seem to hear him say; "no, I am the real vine." As the vital force of the vine permeates and vivifies every branch united with it, so Christ is the vital principle that unites his true followers into the Mystical Body, the Church. Eph. 1:23.

No one can give a greater proof of his love than by laying down his 13
life for his friends. You are my friends, provided you do what I 14
command you. No longer do I call you servants for a servant is 15
not in his master's confidence. But I have called you friends, because
I have made known to you all that I have heard from my Father.
Not that you chose me; no, I have chosen you, and the task I 16
imposed upon you is to go forward steadfastly in bearing fruit; and
your fruit is to be lasting. Thus the Father will grant you any
petition you may present to him in my name. This is all I command 17
you: love one another.

"THEY HAVE HATED ME WITHOUT CAUSE"

"If the world hates you, bear in mind that it has hated me first. 18
If you were children of the world, the world would cherish its own 19
flesh and blood. But you are not children of the world; on the
contrary, I have singled you out from the world, and therefore the
world hates you. Remember what I told you: a slave is not better 20
off than his master. If they persecuted me, they will persecute you
also; if they took my teaching to heart, they will take to heart
yours also. Not only that: it is because you profess my name that 21
they will treat you in all these ways; for they do not know him whose
ambassador I am. Had I not come with a message to them, they 22
would have no sin: as it is, they have no excuse for their sin.
He who hates me hates my Father also. Had I not done in their 23, 24
midst what no one else has ever done, they would have no sin;
as it is, they have seen and hated both me and my Father. How 25
pitiful that this saying in their Law must needs be fulfilled 'They
have hated me without cause!'

"When the Advocate whom I am going to send you with a 26
mission from the Father — the Spirit of truth, who proceeds from
the Father — has come, he will witness in my behalf. And you, too, 27
will witness, because you have been with me from the beginning."

15:24. *they have seen . . . me and my Father:* in seeing him, they saw the
Father, because of his equality with the Father. See 14:9. The context in
5:37 is different.

CHAPTER 16

THINGS THAT THE FUTURE HOLDS IN STORE

1 "I have told you this, that you may not waver in your faith.
2 You will be put out of the synagogue. Not only that: a time is
coming when anyone who kills you will think he is offering to God
3 an act of supreme worship. And they will do this because they
4 know neither the Father nor me. But enough! I have told you
this, so that, when the time comes for it to happen, you may recall
that I told you so. I did not tell you all this at the outset, because
I was still with you.

5 "But now I am going home to him whose ambassador I am. Yet
6 none of you asks me: 'Where are you going?' Well, because I told
7 you this, sorrow fills your hearts! But I tell you the truth: it is to
your advantage that I depart. Unless I depart, the Advocate will not
8 come to you; whereas, if I depart, I will send him to you. And
when he comes, he will prove the world wrong about guilt, about
9 innocence, and about condemnation; about guilt: they do not be-
10 lieve in me; about innocence: I am going home to the Father and
11 you will see me no longer; about condemnation: the prince of this
world stands condemned.

12 "There is still much I might say to you; but you are not strong
13 enough to bear it at present. But when he, the Spirit of truth,
has come, he will conduct you through the whole range of truth.
What he will tell does not originate with him; no, he will tell only
14 what he is told. Besides, he will announce to you the future. He is

---

16:8. *prove the world* (primarily, the impenitent Jews) *wrong*: the two an-
tagonists in this gigantic struggle are Jesus and the impenitent Jews. For the
moment, the latter seem to triumph; but the Holy Spirit, through the preaching
of the Apostles, will reverse the world's verdict.

16:9. The Jews are the guilty party: their sin is unbelief; Jesus is the innocent party: his death leads to his glorification in heaven (which will involve a
temporary absence from his disciples); the sentence of condemnation will
fall on the prime instigator of the crimes of the Jews, the prince of this world.

16:13. *conduct you*: as it were, take you by the hand and show you the
way *through the whole range of truth*: that is, the truth already made known to
the disciples by the teaching of Jesus, or yet to be made known to them by
the Holy Spirit. After the death of the Apostles, the deposit of faith is incapable of further enrichment, though there will be further clarification through
the unerring teaching of the Holy Spirit.

to glorify me, for he will draw upon what is mine and announce it
to you. Whatever the Father possesses is mine; that is why I said 15
that he will draw on what is mine and announce it to you.

"YOUR SORROW WILL BE TURNED INTO JOY"

"A little while and you see me no longer, and again a little 16
while, and you will see me." Then some of his disciples remarked to 17
one another: "What does he mean by saying to us: 'A little while
and you do not see me, and again a little while, and you will see me,'
and, 'Because I am going home to the Father'?" They asked, there- 18
fore: "What does he mean by the words 'a little while'? We do
not understand what he means." Jesus understood that they wished 19
to ask him; so he said to them: "Is this what you are discussing
among yourselves, my saying: 'A little while, and you do not see me;
and again a little while, and you will see me'? I must be perfectly 20
frank with you: you will weep and lament, while the world rejoices.
You will be plunged in sorrow, but your sorrow will be turned into
joy. When a woman is about to give birth, she is in sorrow because 21
her hour has come; but when she has brought forth her child, she
no longer remembers her pangs for sheer joy that a human being
has been born into the world. So you, too: at present you are in 22
sorrow; but I shall see you again, and then your hearts will rejoice,
and no one will take your joy away from you. That will be the 23
time when you ask me no more questions. It is the real truth when
I tell you that, if you make any request of the Father, he will
grant it to you in my name. Up to the present you made no 24
requests in my name. Make them, and they will be granted. Thus
nothing will be wanting to your joy.

"HAVE COURAGE; I HAVE OVERCOME THE WORLD"

"Thus far I have spoken to you in figures. A time is coming 25
when I no longer speak to you in figures, but tell you about the
Father in plain language. That will be the time when you make 26
requests in my name; and I do not tell you that I shall then petition
the Father in your behalf. Of his own accord the Father loves you 27
dearly, because you are settled in your love for me and in your
conviction that I come from the Father. I come from the Father 28

16:16. *you will see me*: after the Resurrection.

and have come into the world. And now I am leaving the world and
29 going home to the Father." "There now," his disciples said, "you
30 are speaking plainly and avoid all figures of speech. Now we know
that you know everything and need not wait till someone asks
you. And that is why we believe that you come from God."
31, 32 "You now believe?" Jesus interposed; "mark well: a time is coming,
in fact, it is at hand, when you will scatter, each going back to his
home, and leave me all alone! Not that I am really alone, for the
33 Father is with me. I have forewarned you of this event, that you
may find peace of soul in union with me. In the world, afflictions
are in store for you. But have courage; I have overcome the world."

CHAPTER 17

CHRIST PRAYS FOR HIMSELF

1   When Jesus had delivered this discourse, he raised his eyes to
heaven and said:
      "Father, the hour is come!
        Glorify your Son,
        that your Son may glorify you.
2   You have given him authority over all mankind,
        that he might give eternal life
        to all you have entrusted to him.
3   And this is the sum of eternal life —
        their knowing you, the only true God,
        and your ambassador Jesus Christ.

4   "I have glorified you on earth
        by completing the work you gave me to do.
5   And now, for your part, Father,
        glorify me in your bosom
        with the glory I possessed in your bosom
        before the world existed.

17:1. In this high-priestly or pontifical prayer, Jesus touchingly gives an
account of his stewardship: he chose his Apostles, initiated them in discipleship, trained them for their future work, shielded them from dangers. He then
begs the Father to glorify him, to preserve the Church from the influence of
the world, and to unite all believers in one society where love reigns supreme.

CHRIST PRAYS FOR HIS DISCIPLES

"I have made your name known to the men 6
whom you singled out from the world
and entrusted to me.
Yours they were,
and to me you have entrusted them;
and they cherish your message.
Now they know 7
that whatever you have given me
really comes from you;
for the message you have delivered to me 8
I have delivered to them;
and they have accepted it.
They really understand
that I come from you,
and they believe that I am your ambassador.

"I am offering a prayer for them; 9
not for the world do I pray,
but for those whom you have entrusted to me;
for yours they are.
All that is mine is yours, 10
and yours is mine;
and they are my crowning glory.

"I am not long for this world; 11
but they remain in the world;
while I am about to return to you.
Holy Father!
Keep them loyal to your name
which you have given me.
May they be one as we are one!
As long as I was with them, 12

17:11. *loyal to your name*: that is, to God. God's *name* is his nature, power, and especially his holiness (Lk. 1:49). See the note on 17:26.
17:12. According to Catholic theology, eternal damnation is the result not of predestination, but of one's own choice; hence "a son of perdition" is one who deliberately chooses his own doom.

I kept them loyal to your name.
I shielded and sheltered the men
whom you have entrusted to me;
and none of them is lost
except the one who chooses his own doom.
And thus the Scripture was to be fulfilled!

13   But now I return to you,
and I say this before I leave the world
that they may taste my joy
made perfect within their souls.

14   "I have delivered to them your message;
and the world hates them,
because the world finds nothing kin in them,
just as the world finds nothing kin in me.

15   "I do not pray you
to take them out of the world,
but only to preserve them from its evil influence.

16   The world finds nothing kin in them,
just as the world finds nothing kin in me.

17   Consecrate them to the service of the truth.
Your message is truth.

18   "As you have made me your ambassador to the world,
so I am making them my ambassadors to the world;

19   and for their sake I consecrate myself,
that they, in turn, may in reality be consecrated.

CHRIST PRAYS FOR ALL BELIEVERS

20   "However, I do not pray for them alone;
I also pray for those
who through their preaching will believe in me.

21   All are to be one;
just as you, Father, are in me and I am in you,
so they, too, are to be one in us.
The world must come to believe
that I am your ambassador.

282

"The glory you have bestowed on me   22
I have bestowed on them,
that they may be one as we are one,
— I in them and you in me.   23
Thus their oneness will be perfected.
The world must come to acknowledge
that I am your ambassador,
and that you love them as you love me.

"O Father!   24
I will that those whom you have entrusted to me
shall be at my side where I am:
I want them to behold my glory,
the glory you bestowed on me
because you loved me
before the world was founded.

"Just Father!   25
The world does not know you,
but I know you,
and thus these men have come to know
that I am your ambassador.
I have made known to them your name,   26
and will continue to make it known.
May the love with which you love me
dwell in them
as I dwell in them myself."

17:26. your name: your nature and here especially your will. Jesus will continue and deepen this revelation through the Holy Spirit. And what is to be
the fruit of Christ's work on earth? Verse 11: "May they be one as we are one."
Verse 21: "As you, Father, are in me and I in you, so they, too, are to be one
in us." Verse 23: "Thus their oneness will be perfected." This "oneness" of
the Christian soul with God is a deep reality, the nature of which is defined
in the fervent aspiration which closes this prayer: the vital principle that binds
us all together — the Father, the Son, and ourselves — is love. St. Augustine
remarks on this passage that the Father loves the "whole" Son, that is, him
as the head, and us as the body. Here we have a clear statement of the doctrine
of the Mystical Body of Christ; here the great charter of Christian mysticism.
The writings of the Apostolic Fathers show how thoroughly this truth was
grasped by the early Christians and applied to everyday life. See 15:1 and
13:34.

Chapter 18

THE BAND SENT TO SEIZE JESUS

1 Here Jesus ended and, with his disciples, went out to a place beyond the torrent of Cedron, where there was a garden. This he 2 entered, accompanied by his disciples. But Judas, his betrayer, was also acquainted with the place — for Jesus had often resorted there 3 with his disciples — and so, accompanied by the band of soldiers and servants sent by the high priests and the Pharisees, he went 4 there with lanterns, torches, and weapons. Jesus, who knew well what was awaiting him, came forward and said to them: "Who is 5 it you are looking for?" "Jesus of Nazareth," was their reply. Jesus said to them: "I am he!" Judas, his betrayer, had taken his stand 6 with them. The moment he said to them, "I am he," they fell back and dropped to the ground.

7 He then asked them a second time: "Who is it you are looking 8 for?" "Jesus of Nazareth," was their reply. Jesus went on to say: "I told you that I am he. Therefore, since you are looking for me, let 9 these men go unmolested." This incident was to fulfill the statement he had made, namely: "Of those you have entrusted to me, I have 10 not lost a single one." Then Simon Peter, who carried a sword, unsheathed it and, striking the high priest's servant, cut off his right ear. The name of the servant was Malchus.

11 "Put the sword back into the sheath," Jesus said to Peter; "shall I not drink the cup which the Father has presented to me?"

12 The company of soldiers, led by the chief officer, and the attend- 13 ants of the Jews now arrested Jesus and fettered him. They led him first to Annas, for he was the father-in-law of Caiaphas, who was 14 the high priest of that year. Caiaphas was the man who had counseled the Jews that it was to their advantage that one man should die to save the nation.

PETER'S FIRST DENIAL OF JESUS

15 Simon Peter and another disciple had been following Jesus; but, while the latter disciple, an acquaintance of the high priest, had gone

---

18:13. Annas had been high priest from A.D. 7–11, but continued to wield great influence until his death.

along with Jesus into the palace of the high priest, Peter remained 16
outside at the door. So the other disciple, the acquaintance of the
high priest, went out and, after speaking to the portress, brought
Peter in. Then the girl who was the portress said to Peter; "Are you, 17
perhaps, one of the disciples of that man?" "I am not," he replied.
Meanwhile the officers and the guards, who had made a coal fire, 18
because it was cold, were loitering about and warming themselves.
Peter also wanted to warm himself, and so he mingled with the group.

JESUS STRUCK BY A GUARD

The high priest now questioned Jesus about his disciples and 19
about his teaching. "I have spoken openly," replied Jesus, "where 20
all the world could listen. I have always taught at synagogue meetings
and in the temple, where all the Jews are wont to meet. I have said
nothing in secret. Why do you question me? Question those who 21
heard what I said. You see, they know what I said." No sooner 22
had Jesus said this than one of the guards who stood by, gave him
a blow in the face and said: "Is this the way you answer the high
priest?" Jesus protested. "If I was wrong in speaking this way," he 23
said to him, "then prove me wrong; but if I was right, then why do
you strike me?" The upshot was that Annas sent him fettered to 24
Caiaphas the high priest.

PETER'S SECOND AND THIRD DENIAL OF JESUS

Simon Peter was still lingering about, warming himself. "Are 25
you, perhaps, one of his disciples?" he was asked. He denied it and
said: "I am not." Then one of the servants of the high priest, a 26
relative of the one whose ear Peter had cut off, said: "Did I not
see you in the garden with him?" Again Peter denied it; and im- 27
mediately a cock crowed.

They next led Jesus from Caiaphas to the praetorium. It was 28
early morning. They themselves did not enter the praetorium to
avoid being defiled, since they wanted to eat the paschal supper.
Pilate therefore came out to face them. "What charge," he said, "do 29
you bring against that man?" By way of answer they replied: "If this 30
man were not a criminal, we should not have handed him over to

---

18:21. The Jewish Law did not require a defendant to testify to his own
disadvantage.

31 you." "Then take him in charge yourselves," Pilate said to them, "and try him by your law." "We have no power," the Jews rejoined,
32 "to put anyone to death." This incident was to fulfill the statement Jesus had made when indicating the kind of death he was to die.

THE TRIAL OF JESUS BEFORE PILATE

33   Pilate then went back into the praetorium and summoned Jesus.
34 "Are you the King of the Jews?" he asked him. Jesus answered: "Do you ask this question from personal observation, or have others
35 spoken to you about me?" "Am I a Jew?" replied Pilate; "Your own nation and the high priests have handed you over to me. What
36 have you done?" "My kingdom," Jesus explained, "is not a worldly one. If mine were a worldly kingdom, my subjects would exert themselves to prevent my being surrendered to the Jews. As it is, my
37 kingdom is not of an earthly character." "Then you are a king after all!" Pilate said to him. "You are right," replied Jesus; "I am a king. For this purpose I was born, and for this purpose I came into the world — to give testimony to the truth. Only he who is open to the
38 truth gives ear to my voice." "What is truth?" Pilate said to him, and with that went outside again to face the Jews. He said to them:
39 "I find no guilt in him. It is a custom among you that I release someone at your request at the Passover. Do you want me, therefore,
40 to release as your choice the King of the Jews?" Back came their shout: "No; not this man, but Barabbas." Barabbas was a robber.

18:31. This power was taken from the Sanhedrin in A.D. 6, when Judea became a Roman province.

18:34. Asked whether he was the King of the Jews, Jesus could answer yes and no, according to what Pilate meant by the ambiguous question. He was not a political king, not a menace to the Roman State; his kingship was spiritual. To bring out this important distinction, Jesus asked Pilate whether his question was prompted by *personal observation* in his capacity as Roman official, or was suggested by the Jews. Disregarding the first alternative, Pilate implied that as governor he had no complaints against Jesus. As to the second alternative, he was not a Jew and was not interested in Jewish religious quarrels. Then Jesus explained that his kingship was of a spiritual nature. The result of this conversation satisfied Pilate: "I find no guilt in this man." See the note on 18:38.

18:36. *not a worldly one:* Jesus was King "by right of birth, from the great day of eternity when mysteriously, like the dew before the light of dawn, he was begotten by the Father" (Ps. 109; Foster).

18:38. *What is truth?:* as though he meant to say: "what does religious truth mean to me?" Pilate, the man of the world, treated Jesus as a visionary that could do no harm to the Roman government. At this turn of the trial, the high priests shifted ground: Jesus "was" a political criminal. Lk. 23:5.

CHAPTER 19

PILATE ATTEMPTS TO APPEASE THE JEWS

Then Pilate took Jesus in charge and had him scourged. 1
The soldiers also plaited a crown of thorns and put it on his head; 2
besides, they threw a purple cloak round him and, marching up, 3
saluted him: "Long live the King of the Jews!" They also slapped
him in the face. Pilate went outside once more and said to the 4
crowd: "Now look! I am bringing him out to you, and you must
understand that I find no guilt in him!" Jesus, therefore, came out, 5
wearing the crown of thorns and the purple cloak. "Here is the
man!" Pilate said to them. But when the high priests and their 6
underlings saw him, they burst out shouting: "To the cross! To the
cross!" "Then take him in charge yourselves and crucify him,"
Pilate said to them; "I certainly find no guilt in him." "We have a 7
Law," countered the Jews, "and according to the Law he must die,
for he has declared himself the Son of God."

PILATE SURRENDERS JESUS FOR CRUCIFIXION

The result was that, when Pilate heard this kind of language, he 8
was still more alarmed. He re-entered the praetorium and said to 9
Jesus: "What is your origin?" But Jesus gave him no answer. "You 10
will not speak to me?" Pilate said to him; "Do you not know that I
have power to set you free and power to crucify you?" "You have no 11
power whatever to harm me," replied Jesus, "unless it is granted to
you from above. That is why he who surrendered me to you is
guilty of a graver offense." As a result, Pilate was anxious to release 12
him; but the Jews kept shouting: "If you release this man, you are
not a friend of Caesar. Anyone who declares himself a king renounces
allegiance to Caesar."

Pilate accordingly, on hearing such language, had Jesus led out, 13
and seated himself on the judge's bench at a place called Lithostrotus,

---

19:11. *he who surrendered me*: Judas or Caiphas. As Caesar's representative,
Pilate had no authority over Jesus; just the same, he carried out God's decree
that Jesus should die to save the world. To that extent, he had power
from above.

14 or in Hebrew Gabbatha. It was the Day of Preparation for the Passover. The time was about noon. He then said to the Jews: "Look,
15 there is your king!" Then they shouted: "Away with him! Away with him! Crucify him!" "Your king am I to crucify?" Pilate replied.
16 The high priests answered: "We have no king but Caesar!" Then at last he handed him over to them for crucifixion. And so they took Jesus in charge.

"JESUS THE NAZARENE, KING OF THE JEWS"

17 Carrying his own cross, he went out to the place called Skull's
18 Mound, which is the rendering of the Hebrew, Golgotha. Here they crucified him, and two others at the same time, one on one
19 side, one on the other, while Jesus was in the center. Pilate also had a notice inscribed and posted on the cross. The inscription ran
20 as follows: "Jesus the Nazarene, King of the Jews." Many of the Jews read this notice, since the place where Jesus was crucified was near the city. It was drawn up in Hebrew, Latin, and Greek.
21 The high priests of the Jews, therefore, said to Pilate: "Do not let your inscription be, King of the Jews, but: He said, I am
22 the king of the Jews." Pilate replied: "My inscription stands!"

THE SOLDIERS DISTRIBUTE HIS CLOTHES AMONG THEMSELVES

23 When the soldiers had crucified Jesus, they took his clothes and made four parts of them, one for each soldier, besides the coat. This coat was seamless, woven from top to bottom in a single piece.
24 So they said to one another: "Do not let us tear it. Rather, let us draw lots for it, to see to whom it shall belong." Thus the Scripture text was to be fulfilled:

> "They distributed my clothes among them,
> and for my garment they cast lots."

This is what the soldiers did.

JESUS COMMITS HIS MOTHER TO JOHN

25 There stood beside the cross of Jesus his mother, his mother's
26 sister, Mary, the wife of Cleophas, and Mary Magdalen. Seeing his

19:14. *about the sixth hour:* this seems to conflict with Mk. (15:25) where it is stated that Jesus was crucified "at the third hour." Evidently, John and Mark followed two different ways of counting the hours of the day.

19:25. John means, it seems, four persons, and not three.

mother and the disciple whom he loved standing by, Jesus said to
his mother: "Mother, this is your son." He then said to the disciple: 27
"This is your mother." That same hour the disciple took her into
his home.

After this, knowing that all the details would presently be com- 28
pleted so as to fulfill the Scripture, Jesus said: "I am thirsty."
A jar containing vinegar was standing there; so a sponge soaked in 29
the vinegar was put on a stalk of hyssop and reached up to his lips.
As soon as Jesus had taken the vinegar, he said: "It is now com- 30
pleted." And he bowed his head and surrendered his spirit.

JESUS' SIDE PIERCED WITH A LANCE

Since it was Preparation Day, the Jews did not wish the corpses 31
to remain on the crosses during the Sabbath, for that Sabbath was
a holy day; so they requested Pilate to order that the men's legs
should be broken and the bodies removed. Accordingly, the soldiers 32
came and broke the legs both of the one and of the other that were
crucified with him. When they came to Jesus, they saw that he was 33
already dead. So they did not break his legs, but one of the soldiers 34
pierced his side with a lance, and immediately there came out blood
and water. This statement is the testimony of an eyewitness. His 35
testimony is true, and he knows that he is speaking the truth, so
that you, too, may believe. In fact, these incidents took place that 36
the Scripture might be fulfilled: "Not a bone of his shall be broken."

19:28. *all the details*: that is, of the work of redemption. *I am thirsty*: there
is no such text in the Old Testament. Ps. 21:16 and 68:22 say that in Christ's
thirst his enemies would, in cruel mockery, give him vinegar and gall to drink.
This "vinegar" was not, it seems, a refreshing soldier potion, the soldiers' sour
wine (*posca*), hence a humane tonic, but a drink intended to add to the pains
of the victim. This was a general practice of Roman soldiers during crucifixion.
Jesus, then, cried out, "I thirst," not to fulfill any Scripture text, but to reveal
the excruciating pains he was suffering. This gave the soldiers an occasion to
add a further pain. The Greek word generally rendered "to fulfill" does not
have this meaning anywhere in the New Testament; it always means "to
complete." See next note.

19:30. *It is now completed*: the work of the redemption is now accomplished.
Jesus died as it were triumphantly, as one that has gained a victory, not from
physical exhaustion, but because he willed to die (10:18, "I lay down my life
of my own free will"). All the Synoptics state that he "cried out with a
strong voice"; and John testifies that he *surrendered his spirit*. Jesus died with
his mind unclouded by grief or pain, and with his will ready to make the
supreme sacrifice. He refused to take "wine and myrrh," which would have
clouded his consciousness.

37 And still another Scripture text says: "They will look upon him whom they have pierced."

THE BURIAL OF JESUS

38 After this, Joseph of Arimathia, a disciple of Jesus, though but a secret one because of his fear of the Jews, petitioned Pilate for permission to remove the body of Jesus, which Pilate granted. So he

39 came and removed his body. Also Nicodemus, the man who had at first visited Jesus by night, appeared on the scene, bringing with him

40 a mixture of myrrh and aloe, of about one hundred pounds. They took the body of Jesus and wrapped it in a shroud along with the

41 spices, in accordance with the Jewish custom of embalming. There was a garden at the place where Jesus was crucified, and in the garden there was a fresh tomb, in which no one had as yet been laid to rest.

42 Here, then, because it was the Preparation Day of the Jews and the tomb was close by, they laid Jesus to rest.

CHAPTER 20

THE RESURRECTION

1 On the first day of the week — it was an early hour and still dark — Mary Magdalen came to the tomb and noticed that the slab

2 of stone had been dislodged from the entrance of the tomb. So she ran and came to Simon Peter and to the other disciple, whom Jesus loved, and said to them: "They have taken the Lord out of the tomb!

3 We do not know where they have laid him!" Thereupon Peter and the other disciple left the house and set out for the tomb.

4 The two started running together; but the other disciple ran faster

5 than Peter and was the first to reach the tomb. He stooped to look in and saw the linen cloths lying there; but he did not enter.

6 In due time Simon Peter, who had been following him, arrived and went into the tomb. He looked at the cloths lying there,

7 and at the scarf, which had been round his head, not lying with

8 the cloths, but folded up in a separate place. Then the other disciple, who was the first to reach the tomb, also went inside, and

9 because of what he saw, believed. They had not as yet understood

the Scripture text which says that he must rise from the dead. The 10
disciples then left for home.

MARY MAGDALEN MEETS THE RISEN SAVIOR

Mary, meanwhile, had been lingering outside the tomb, weeping. 11
As she was giving vent to her tears, she stooped to look into the
tomb, and saw two angels dressed in white, seated where the body 12
of Jesus had lain, one at the head, the other at the feet. "Good 13
woman," they said to her, "why are you weeping?" "Because," she
replied, "they have taken away my Lord, and I do not know where
they laid him!" With this, she turned round to look behind and 14
saw Jesus standing by, but did not know that it was Jesus. "My 15
good woman," Jesus said to her, "why are you weeping? Who is it
you are looking for?" Taking him for the gardener, she replied: "Sir,
if you carried him away, tell me where you laid him. I want to
remove him." Then Jesus said to her: "Mary!" Turning round, she 16
said to him in Hebrew: "*Rabbouni!*" which means "My Master."
"Do not hold me any longer," Jesus then said to her; "I have not 17
yet ascended to the Father; go therefore to my brethren and say to
them: 'By and by I will ascend to my Father and your Father, to
my God and your God.'" Mary Magdalen went to carry the message 18
to the disciples. "I have seen the Lord!" she said, and that he had
told her so and so.

JESUS CONFERS THE POWER OF REMITTING SINS

Late in the evening that same day — the first day of the week — 19
although the doors of the place where the disciples had gathered
were bolted for fear of the Jews, Jesus came and stood before them,
and said: "Peace be to you!" With that, he let them see his hands 20
and his side. The disciples were delighted to see the Lord. Then 21
Jesus said to them again: "Peace be to you! As the Father has made
me his ambassador, so I am making you my ambassadors." With 22

20:17. *Do not hold me any longer:* after recognizing her Master, Mary was
no doubt allowed to "hold" Jesus, that is, to clasp his feet (see Mt. 28:9);
but in her intense love for Jesus she seemed disposed to prolong the happy
moment. For this there was no time now. The happiness of heaven must not
be anticipated.

20:22. This bestowal of the Holy Spirit was formal, solemn, and official.
It has been remarked that the consoling power of forgiving sin was appropriately
conferred on Easter Day.

23 this, he breathed on them and said: "Receive the Holy Spirit. Whenever you remit anyone's sins, they are remitted; when you retain
anyone's sins, they are retained."

24 Thomas, one of the Twelve, called the Twin, was not with the
25 group when Jesus came. So the other disciples said to him: "We
have seen the Lord!" But he replied: "Unless I see in his hands the
print of the nails, and put my finger into the place where the nails
were, and lay my hand into his side, I am not going to believe!"

INCREDULOUS THOMAS IS CONVINCED

26 Eight days later, his disciples were again in the room, and Thomas
was with them. Jesus came, though the doors were bolted, and,
27 standing before them, said: "Peace be to you!" He then addressed
Thomas: "Let me have your finger; put it here, and look at my
hands. Now let me have your hand, and lay it into my side. And
28 do not be incredulous, but believe!" Then Thomas burst out into
29 the words: "My Lord and my God!" "Because you have seen me,"
Jesus said to him, "is that why you believe? Blessed are those who
have not seen me and yet believe!"

30 To sum up: Jesus gave many other proofs of his claims in the
31 presence of his disciples, which are not on record in this book. This
much, however, has been recorded that you may persevere in
your belief that Jesus is the Messias, the Son of God, and that,
through your belief, you may have life in his name.

CHAPTER 21

THE THIRD APPEARANCE OF CHRIST TO HIS DISCIPLES

1 On a later occasion Jesus showed himself again to the disciples,
this time by the Lake of Tiberias. He did so under the following
2 circumstances: Simon Peter, Thomas called the Twin, Nathanael of
Cana in Galilee, the sons of Zebedee, and two others of his disciples,
3 happened to be together. Simon Peter said to them: "I am going
fishing." "We will go along with you," they replied. So they set out
and got into the boat, and during that entire night they caught
4 nothing. But just as day was breaking, Jesus stood on the beach.
5 The disciples did not know, however, that it was Jesus. "Well, lads,"

Jesus said to them, "you have no fish there, have you?" "No," they replied. "Throw your net to the right of the boat," he said to them, and you will find something." So they threw it in, and now they were not strong enough to haul it up into the boat because of the great number of fish in it. Then the disciple whom Jesus loved said to Peter: "It is the Lord!" No sooner did Simon Peter learn that it was the Lord than he girt his upper garment about his shirt — for that was all he was wearing — and plunged into the lake. Meanwhile the other disciples came on in the boat — for they were not far from the shore, only about two hundred yards — dragging along the net full of fish.

When they had come ashore, they noticed a charcoal fire on the ground, with fish and bread lying on the fire. Jesus said to them: "Bring some of the fish you caught just now." So Simon Peter climbed into the boat and hauled the net upon the beach. It was full of fish, one hundred and fifty-three in all, and in spite of the great number the net did not break. "Come, now," Jesus said to them, "and have breakfast." Not one of his disciples could find it in his heart to ask him, "Who are you?" They knew it was the Lord. Then Jesus approached, took the bread in his hands, and gave them of it. He did the same with the fish. This was now the third time that Jesus showed himself to the disciples after he had risen from the dead.

CHRIST CONFERS ON PETER IMPORTANT RESPONSIBILITIES

After they had breakfasted, Jesus said to Simon Peter: "Simon, son of John, do you love me more than these others do?" "Yes, my Lord," he replied; "you know that I really love you." "Then," Jesus said to him, "feed my lambs." He asked him a second time:

21:14. the third time: there is some difficulty in arranging the different appearances in chronological order.

21:15. The variations in noun (lambs, sheep) and verb (feed, shepherd) serve no other purpose than that of signifying the whole of the flock entrusted to Peter. The threefold repetition of the same question and the same answer in identical words is intended to impress Peter and the rest of the Apostles with the solemnity of the moment. The promise made to Peter (also made in surroundings and circumstances not easily forgotten; Mt. 16:18) was a response to his profession of faith; here the fulfillment of that promise comes in response to his profession of love. Faith in Jesus and consummate love for him (compare 15:13 with 21:19) must characterize the supreme shepherd of Christ's flock.

"Simon, son of John, do you love me?" "Yes, Lord," he replied, "you know that I really love you." "Then," he said to him, "be a
17 shepherd to my sheep." For the third time he put the question to him: "Simon, son of John, do you really love me?" It grieved Peter that he had asked him the third time: "Do you really love me?" and he replied: "Lord, you know everything; you know that I really
18 love you!" "Then," Jesus said to him, "feed my sheep. I tell you the plain truth: when you were young, you used to put on your own girdle and go where you wished; but when you grow old, you will stretch out your arms for someone else to gird you and carry you
19 where you have no wish to go." He said this to signify the kind of death by which he was to glorify God. And having said this, he said to him: "Follow me."
20 Turning round, Peter saw the disciple whom Jesus loved following them, the same who at the supper had been resting against his bosom and had asked: "Lord, who is it that is going to betray you?"
21 So, at sight of him, Peter said to Jesus: "And what about him,
22 Lord?" Jesus replied: "If I should want him to stay till I return, what difference does this make to you? Your duty is to follow me."
23 Accordingly, the report became current among the brethren that that disciple was not going to die. But Jesus had not said to him that he was not to die, but simply: "If I should want him to stay till I return, what difference does this make to you?"
24 This is the disciple who is both the witness of these facts and the recorder of these facts; and we know that his testimony is true.
25 There are, however, many other things that Jesus did — so many that, should they all be recorded in full detail, the world is not likely to hold all the volumes that would have to be compiled.

21:17. Peter was grieved at being asked the same question three times, because, no doubt, Jesus seemed to him to doubt his sincerity. It may also be that the triple question recalled his triple denial.

21:18. Peter was imprisoned and martyred thirty years before this Gospel was written. The words *someone else to gird you*, etc., are a hint of his crucifixion.

21:19. Follow me: in the full sense of the word. The disciples were warned at the outset (Mt. 10:38) that the "following" of Christ involved acceptance of martyrdom.

21:24–25. These words were added by the disciples of John or other trustworthy witnesses, known to the first readers.

PART TWO

Acts of the Apostles
Epistles and Apocalypse

TRANSLATED BY JOSEPH L. LILLY, C.M.

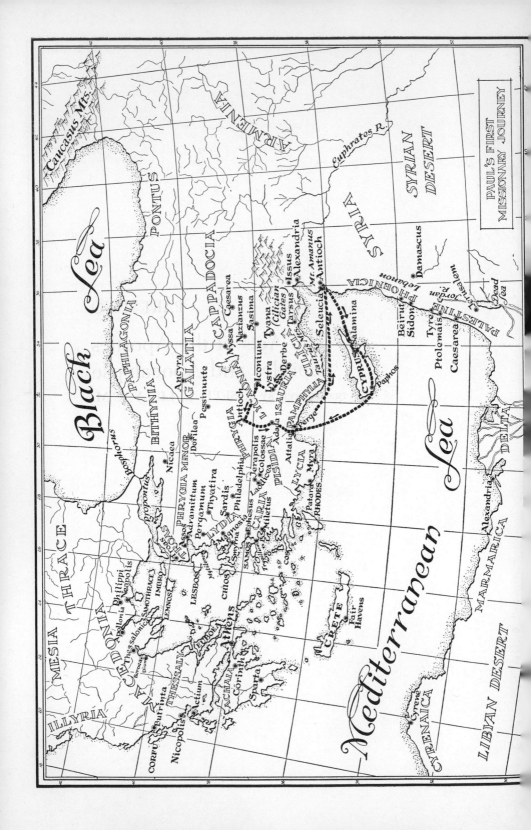

PAUL'S FIRST
MISSIONARY JOURNEY

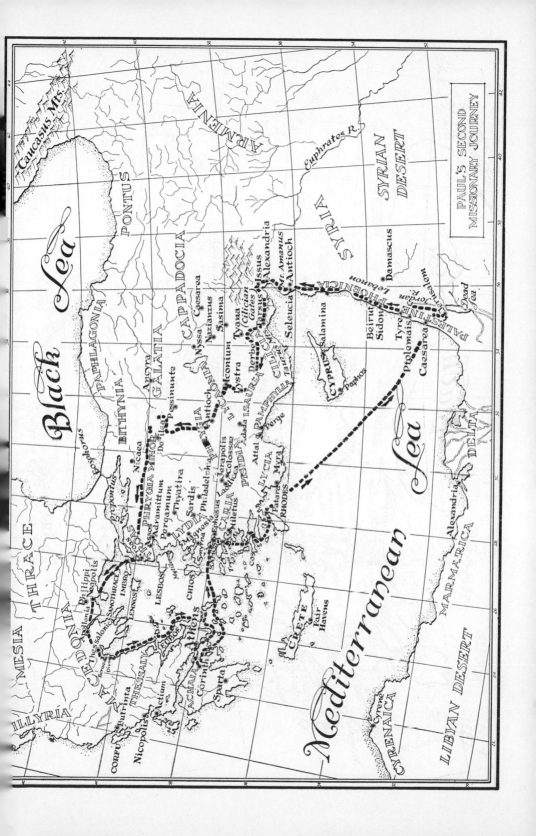

PAUL'S SECOND
MISSIONARY JOURNEY

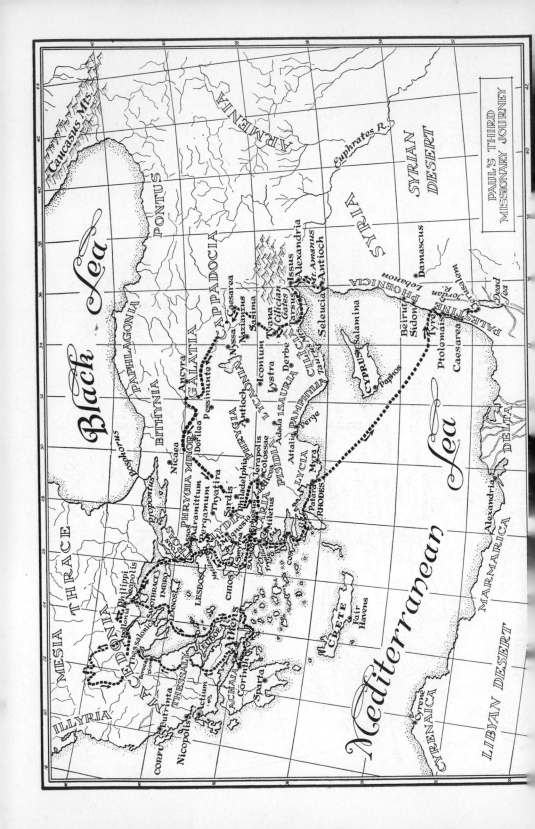

PAUL'S THIRD
MISSIONARY JOURNEY

INTRODUCTION TO THE "ACTS"

This section is in reality a continuation of the Third Gospel. It is the second part of what originally was a single undertaking. In its first section the author, St. Luke, traveling companion and co-worker of St. Paul, gave us the account of Jesus' work; in the second he now tells us how this work of Jesus was continued by his duly commissioned representatives.

The contents can be briefly summarized in the words of our Lord: "You shall be my witnesses in Jerusalem and in all Judea and Samaria, and even to the very ends of the earth." After describing the coming of the Holy Spirit on the Apostles, St. Luke tells us how the Church spread in Judea and Samaria, and thence on to the Gentile world. The story covered is from the Ascension of our Lord to St. Paul's release from prison in Rome, about the year A.D. 62.

The author's purpose is to show that Christianity, according to Roman law, should not merely be granted toleration, but is a religion revealed by God. Through this, its divine Founder, Jesus Christ, continues his work for the instruction and sanctification of mankind. On this Church, in the person of its hierarchical leaders, he poured out the Holy Spirit, who duly abides in it to direct and safeguard it in its divinely appointed mission. In fact, almost every important utterance and undertaking of the Church's leaders is ascribed by St. Luke to the Holy Spirit, dwelling in and operating through the Apostles. Not unfittingly is the Acts often styled "the Gospel of the Holy Spirit." In the words of St. Paul: "The Good News (i.e., Christianity) . . . is the power of God for the salvation of everyone that believes" (Rom. 1:16).

The importance of Acts as an historical record can scarcely be exaggerated. It is the only contemporary document we have of the beginning and development of the Christian Church. Yet the record is fragmentary; it gives us mere glimpses, in broad outlines, of what took place at the inauguration of the Christian Church, first among the Jews and then in various parts of the Gentile world.

Doctrinally the Acts is of the highest importance. It contains every article of the Apostle's Creed, except the virginal birth, and presents the Church from the outset as an authoritarian institution, with the supreme authority vested in St. Peter. The means of salvation are repentance and baptism, and the rite which differentiates Christianity from other forms of worship is the Lord's Supper, referred to in the Acts as the "breaking of bread."

DIVISION OF THE ACTS OF THE APOSTLES

Introduction, 1:1–26.
The Church in Palestine and Syria, 2:1 to 12:25.
    The Church grows in Jerusalem, 2:1 to 8:3.
    The Church grows in Judea and Samaria, 8:4 to 9:43.
    The Church spreads to the Gentiles, 10:1 to 11:30.
    The persecution by Herod Agrippa, 12:1–25.
The Church in Asia Minor and Europe. The missionary journeys of
    St. Paul, 13:1 to 28:31.
    The first missionary journey of Paul, 13:1 to 15:35.
    The second missionary journey of Paul, 15:36 to 18:22.
    The third missionary journey of Paul, 18:23 to 21:16.
    The imprisonment of Paul in Palestine, 21:7 to 26:32.
    The imprisonment of Paul in Rome, 27:1 to 28:31.

ACTS OF THE APOSTLES

INTRODUCTION

CHAPTER 1

THE ASCENSION OF CHRIST

In my former book, Theophilus, I spoke of all that Jesus did 1
and taught from the beginning until the day on which he was taken 2
up, after giving instructions through the Holy Spirit to the apostles
whom he had chosen. To them he also showed himself alive after 3
his passion, giving many conclusive proofs, appearing to them
throughout forty days and discussing matters pertaining to the
kingdom of God. Thus, for example, while eating with them, he 4
charged them not to depart from Jerusalem, but to await what the
Father had promised. "This you have heard from me," he said,
"that while John baptized with water, you shall be baptized with 5
the Holy Spirit not many days hence."

So, when they had come together they asked him, "Lord, will 6
you at this time restore the kingdom to Israel?"

1:1. As the comparison here is merely between the Gospel according to St.
Luke and the Acts, the Greek "first" is translated *former.*

1:3. *proofs:* the appearances of our Lord, together with his words and actions. All this served to establish the reality of his Resurrection. During these
forty days he instructed the Apostles and prepared them for their work of
developing and guiding the Church.

1:4. *eating:* in some manuscripts and translations, "being assembled together."
had promised: the Holy Spirit.

1:5. *you shall be baptized:* not the sacrament of Baptism, which the Apostles
had already, at least equivalently, received, but the fuller outpouring of the
Holy Spirit at Pentecost.

1:6. *So, when they had come:* or, "As they accompanied him," i.e., to the
place of the Ascension.

restore: they are thinking of the external power and splendor of the ancient
political kingdom, according to some Catholic writers. But it is quite likely

7   "It is not for you," he answered them, "to know the times or the
8   dates which the Father has fixed by his own authority; but you
    shall receive power when the Holy Spirit comes upon you, and
    you shall be my witnesses in Jerusalem and in all Judea and Samaria
    and even to the very ends of the earth."
9   After he had said this, he was lifted up before their eyes, and
10 a cloud took him out of their sight. While they were gazing up to
    the sky as he went, at that moment two men stood beside them in
11 white garments and said, "Men of Galilee, why do you stand looking
    up to the sky? This Jesus who has been taken up from you will
    come in the same way as you have seen him going into the sky."
12 Then they returned to Jerusalem from the mount called Olivet,
13 which is near Jerusalem, two thirds of a mile distant. When they
    had entered the city, they went to the upper room where they had
    lodgings — Peter and John and James and Andrew, Philip and
    Thomas, Bartholomew and Matthew, James, the son of Alpheus,
14 and Simon the Zealot, and Jude, the brother of James. All these
    with one mind continued steadfastly in prayer with some women
    and Mary, the mother of Jesus, and with his brothers.

MATTHIAS REPLACES JUDAS

15 During these days Peter arose among the brothers (the number
    of persons was in all about one hundred and twenty), and addressed
16 them: "Brothers, it was necessary that the passage of Scripture in
    which the Holy Spirit by the mouth of David spoke prophetically of
17 Judas be realized, inasmuch as he was numbered among us and was
18 allotted his share in this ministry. Yet he served as guide to those
    who arrested Jesus. (With the price of his iniquity he bought a field,
    and falling face downward burst asunder at the waist, so that all

---

that the Apostles at this time had a more spiritual view of the kingdom, though
their view was still imperfect. "It seems to me that they did not yet have
any clear notion of the kingdom, for the Holy Spirit had not yet instructed
them" (St. Chrysostom).

1:12. *two thirds of a mile:* literally, "a Sabbath day's journey," the distance
one was permitted by Jewish jurisprudence to travel on the Sabbath.

1:15. There is no need, as McNabb remarks, to elect a chairman to preside
over the election of a successor to Judas; St. Peter had already been appointed
the authoritative head of the Church and so takes the lead in this election
as in all subsequent events described in the early chapters of Acts.

1:18. *bought:* the priests really bought the field with Judas' money (Mt.
27:7), and thus in a loose sense Judas can be said to have bought it. The

302

his bowels gushed out. This became known to all the residents of 19
Jerusalem, and hence the field came to be called in their language
Akeldama, that is, the Field of Blood.) Now since it is written in 20
the book of Psalms,

> 'Let his home become desolate
>> and let there be none to dwell in it,'

and,

> 'Let another take over his office,'

therefore, of these men who have been in our company all the 21
time that the Lord moved about among us, from John's baptism 22
until the day that he was taken up from us — of these one must
become with us a witness of his resurrection."

They nominated two: Joseph called Barsabbas, who was sur- 23
named Justus, and Matthias. "Lord," they prayed, "you know the 24
hearts of all, show which one of these two you have chosen to take 25
the place in this apostolic ministry, from which Judas fell away to
go to his own place."

Then they drew lots for them, and the lot fell on Matthias; so 26
he was numbered with the eleven apostles.

THE CHURCH GROWS IN JERUSALEM

CHAPTER 2

THE COMING OF THE HOLY SPIRIT

When the day of Pentecost had come, they were all together in 1
one place. Suddenly there came a sound in the sky, as of a violent 2
wind blowing, and it filled the whole house where they were staying.
And there appeared to them tongues like fire which distributed 3
themselves and settled on each one of them. They were all filled 4
with the Holy Spirit and began to speak in foreign tongues, as the
Holy Spirit prompted them to give utterance.

Now there were staying at Jerusalem devout men of every nation 5

---

words in 18 and 19 are most probably parenthetic, inserted into St. Peter's
speech by St. Luke. It is not probable that the field would have acquired this
name so soon after the event.

2:1. The feast of Pentecost was celebrated on the last day of the period of
fifty days after the Passover.

6 under heaven. When this sound was heard, a crowd of them gathered and were bewildered, because each one heard his own
7 language spoken by the apostles. Everybody was amazed and marveled, saying, "Look, are not all those who are speaking Gali-
8 leans? How then does each of us hear his own native language?
9 Parthians and Medes, and Elamites, and inhabitants of Mesopo-
10 tamia, Judea and Cappadocia, Pontus and Asia, Phrygia and Pamphylia, Egypt and the districts of Libya and Cyrene, and visitors
11 from Rome, Jews and Proselytes, Cretans and Arabians — we hear them declaring in our own languages the wonderful works of God."
12 They were all amazed and perplexed, saying to one another,
13 "What does this mean?" Others said in mockery, "They are full of sweet wine."

PETER'S EXPLANATION OF THE MIRACLE

14 But Peter, presenting himself with the Eleven, raised his voice and addressed them: "Men of Judea and all you who reside in
15 Jerusalem, let me inform you of this, and give ear to my words. These men are not drunk, as you suppose, since it is only nine o'clock in
16 the morning. But this is what was foretold by the prophet Joel:
17   'It shall happen in the last days, says God,
        that I will pour forth my Spirit on all mankind;
    And your sons and daughters shall prophesy,
        and your young men shall see visions,
        and your old men shall dream dreams.
18   And on my slaves too and my handmaids
        in those days will I pour forth my Spirit,
        and they shall prophesy.
19   I will also show wonders in the heavens above
        and signs on the earth below,
        blood and fire and a cloud of smoke.
20   The sun shall be turned into darkness
        and the moon into blood,
    Before the day of the Lord comes,
        the great and manifest day.

2:15. *nine o'clock:* literally, "the third hour." The rabbis prescribed that ten o'clock was the earliest hour for legitimate eating and drinking. The morning prayer was offered in the temple at nine, and only after that prayer were eating and drinking permitted.

And it shall happen
that whoever calls on the name of the Lord
shall be saved.' 21

PETER APPEALS TO THE PEOPLE

"Men of Israel, hear these words. Jesus of Nazareth was a man 22
accredited to you by God through miracles and wonders and signs,
which God did through him in your midst, as you yourselves know.
When he was delivered up by the settled purpose and foreknowledge 23
of God, you crucified and slew him by the hands of wicked men.
But God has raised him up, having put an end to the pangs of 24
death, because it was not possible that death should hold him. For 25
David says of him:

'I saw the Lord before me always,
because he is at my right hand lest I be shaken.

This is why my heart has made merry 26
and my tongue has rejoiced.

Even my flesh will rest in hope,
because you will not abandon my soul to death 27
and you will not let your Holy One see decay.

You have made known to me the path that leads to life; 28
You will fill me with joy in your presence.'

"Brothers, we are permitted to speak with firm assurance to you 29
of the patriarch David who died and was buried. His tomb is with
us to this day. Therefore, since he was a prophet and knew that 30
God had sworn to him with an oath that of his offspring one was to
sit on his throne, he spoke with foreknowledge of the resurrection 31
of the Christ, who was not abandoned to the grave, and whose flesh
did not see decay. God has raised up this Jesus, and of that fact 32
we are all witnesses. Therefore, exalted by the power of God, and 33
receiving from the Father the promised Holy Spirit, he has poured

---

2:23. crucified: literally, "fastening" or "nailing" (to a cross).
2:25. Ps. 15:8.
2:33. exalted: at the Ascension, when the sacred humanity of Jesus received
its full glorification in heaven.
promised: as man, Christ, now in heavenly glory, receives the fulfillment
of the promise concerning the sending of the Holy Spirit. Christ sends the
Holy Spirit and this effusion of the Holy Spirit brought about what was heard
and seen.

34 forth that which you see and hear. David did not ascend into heaven, but he says:

> 'The Lord said to my Lord,
> Sit at my right hand,

35   until I make your enemies
> a footstool for your feet.'

36 "Therefore, let all Israel know most assuredly that God has proved him both Lord and Christ — this very Jesus whom you have crucified."

THE RESULT OF HIS APPEAL

37 On hearing this they were pierced to the heart and said to Peter and the rest of the apostles, "Brothers, what shall we do?"

38 "Have a change of heart and mind," Peter told them, "and be baptized everyone of you in the name of Jesus Christ for the remission of your sins: then you will receive the gift of the Holy

39 Spirit. The promise is meant for you and for your children and for all who are afar off, for all whom the Lord our God may call to himself."

40 With many other words he bore witness and exhorted them, saying, "Save yourselves from this perverse generation."

41 Those who accepted his word were baptized, and there were added that day (to the Church) about three thousand persons.

FERVOR AND GROWTH OF THE EARLY CHURCH

42 They gave steadfast attention to the teaching of the apostles
43 and to union, to the breaking of bread and to the prayers. A sense of awe came on everyone, as many wonders and signs were done by

---

2:34. Ps. 109:1.

2:36. *proved:* literally, "made." by the Resurrection and Ascension Jesus enters into the perfect glory belonging to him and is proved to be the Son of God and the Messias (Christ).

2:38. *in the name,* etc.: this does not designate the words the Apostles used in baptizing but the authority by which they baptized. This is the accepted opinion in Catholic circles, as Jacquier points out. The words used in administering the sacrament are given in Mt. 28:19.

2:39. *afar off:* the Gentiles, the Church universal.

2:42. *breaking of bread:* the Holy Eucharist. *prayers:* certain prayers said in common, which the Apostles had already taught the believers. A form of public worship was developing.

the apostles. All the believers were united, and held all things in 44
common. They would sell their possessions and goods and distribute 45
them to everyone as need required. Daily with one accord they 46
attended the temple, and, breaking bread at their homes, took their
food with gladness and simplicity of heart, praising God and having 47
the good will of all the people. Day by day the Lord added to
their company such as were to be saved.

CHAPTER 3

CURE OF A LAME BEGGAR

As Peter and John were going up to the temple at three o'clock 1
in the afternoon, the hour of prayer, a certain man who had been 2
lame from his mother's womb was carried by. He was placed daily
at that temple gate called Beautiful to ask alms of those going into
the temple. When he saw Peter and John about to enter the temple, 3
he asked for an alms. Peter and John gazed intently at him. "Look 4
at us," Peter said. The lame man fixed his gaze on them, expecting 5
to receive something from them. But Peter said, "Silver and gold 6
I have none; but what I have, that I give you. In the name of Jesus
of Nazareth, walk!"

Taking him by the right hand Peter raised him up, and im- 7
mediately his feet and ankles became strong. Leaping up, he stood 8
erect and began to walk, and went with Peter and John into the
temple, walking, leaping, and praising God. All the people observed 9
him walking and praising God. When they recognized him as the 10
man who used to sit begging at the Beautiful Gate of the temple,
they were filled with wonder and amazement at what had happened
to him.

2:44. *in common:* all were ready to help the needy, and, as occasion required
and the generosity of the faithful prompted, they even sold their possessions
to aid the poor. This spirit of fraternal charity was voluntary and thus widely
differed from modern Communism.

2:46. *the temple:* there was to be no sudden break with the past, but already
the disciples had their own sacrifice, the Eucharist, *at their homes* where they
also took their evening meal beforehand, as did our Lord at the institution
of the Eucharist. So Belser and Knabenbauer.

3:2. *Beautiful:* probably the gate from the Court of the Gentiles to the
Court of the Women.

11   Now as he clung to Peter and John, all the people ran in
amazement to them in the portico called Solomon's.

PETER'S SERMON TO THE AMAZED CROWD

12   When Peter saw this, he began to speak to the people: "Men
of Israel, why do you marvel at this man, or why do you stare at us,
as though by any power or holiness of our own we had enabled him
13   to walk? The God of Abraham, of Isaac, and of Jacob, the God of
our fathers, has glorified his servant, Jesus, whom you indeed delivered up and disowned in the presence of Pilate, when he had
14   decided to release him. You, however, disowned the Holy and Just
15   One, and asked that a murderer be released to you; but you killed
the author of life, whom God has raised up from the dead. Of this
16   fact we are witnesses. And his name, that is when this man had
faith in it, has made him strong whom you behold and recognize.
Moreover it is the faith that comes through Jesus that has given
him this perfect health in the presence of all of you.

17   Now brothers, I know that you acted in ignorance, as did also
18   your rulers. But in this way God fulfilled what he had announced
19   through all the prophets: that his Christ should suffer. Have a
change of heart, therefore; be converted, that your sins may be
20   blotted out, in order that so the times of refreshment may come from
the presence of the Lord, and that he may send him who has been
21   destined beforehand for you as the Christ, Jesus. Heaven must
receive him until the times of the restoration of all things, of which
22   God has spoken through his holy prophets of old. As Moses said:
'The Lord our God will raise up to you
    a prophet from among your brothers,
    as he did me.
To him you must hearken
    in whatever he will speak to you.

3:11. *Solomon's:* the colonnade running along the eastern side of the temple.
3:13. *servant:* an allusion to the "suffering servant" of Isa. 53, the Messias.
3:16. Faith in Christ is the true explanation of the miracle. We have here,
as Knabenbauer remarks, a striking indication of the efficacy of faith, as Christ
had promised (Mt. 17:19).
3:20. *times of refreshment:* the same as "the times of restoration" mentioned
in the following verse, i.e., the second coming of our Lord at the end of time,
according to Jacquier.
3:22. *as he did me:* Both Christ and Moses were mediators between God
and man. On the superiority of Christ to Moses see Hebr. 3:1–6; Deut. 18:15–18.

And it shall be that 23
whoever refuses to hearken to that prophet,
shall surely be destroyed from among the people.'
Now all the prophets from Samuel onward, as many as have 24
spoken, have also announced these days. You are the heirs of the 25
prophets and of the covenant that God made with your fathers,
when he said to Abraham,
'In your offspring shall
all the families of the earth be blessed.'
To you first, God, having raised up his servant, has sent him to 26
bless you, by turning everyone of you away from his own wickedness."

CHAPTER 4

PETER AND JOHN ARRESTED AND FREED

Now while they were speaking to the people, the priests and 1
the chief of the temple police and the Sadducees came upon them,
annoyed because they were teaching the people and proclaiming in 2
the case of Jesus the resurrection from the dead. They arrested 3
Peter and John and placed them in custody till the next day, as it
was already evening. But many of those who had heard the message 4
believed, and the number of the men grew to about five thousand.

It happened on the morrow that their rulers, elders and Scribes 5
were gathered together in Jerusalem with Annas, the high priest, 6
Caiaphas, John, Alexander, and whoever were of priestly family.
Placing the apostles in their presence, they began to inquire, "By 7
what authority or in what name have you done this?"

Then Peter, filled with the Holy Spirit, said to them: "Rulers 8
of the people and elders, if we are on trial today for a benefit con- 9

3:25. Gen. 12:3.
4:1. chief: a priest, next in dignity to the high priest, who had general charge
of the temple. Most of the priests were Sadducees, and one of their tenets was
the denial of the resurrection of the dead.
4:6. Annas: though deposed by the Romans in favor of his son-in-law,
Caiaphas, Annas was still head of the high-priestly family and was probably
looked on by the Jews as the true high priest since, according to the Law, the
office was held for life.
of priestly family: i.e., belonging to those families from which the high priest
was chosen.

10 ferred on a cripple, as to how this man has been cured, be it known
to all of you and to all the people of Israel that in the name of
Jesus Christ of Nazareth, whom you crucified, whom God has
raised from the dead — even through him does this man stand here
11 before you in perfect health. This is

'The stone that was rejected by you, the builders,
which has become the cornerstone.'

12 Nor is there salvation in any other, since there is no other name
under heaven appointed among men as the necessary means of
our salvation."
13   Now seeing the firm assurance of Peter and John, and finding
that they were uneducated and ordinary men, they began to marvel,
14 and then they recognized them as having been with Jesus. But
seeing the man who had been cured standing with them, they
15 could say nothing in reply. So they ordered Peter and John to
withdraw from the council chamber; then they conferred together,
16 saying, "What shall we do to these men, since the fact that a
notable miracle has been done by them is manifest to all the
17 inhabitants of Jerusalem, and we cannot deny it? But lest it spread
further among the people, let us forbid them under threat of
18 punishment to speak further to any man in Jesus' name." Then
summoning the apostles they charged them to make no utterance
and to teach nothing at all in the name of Jesus.
19   But Peter and John answered them and said, "Whether it is
right in the sight of God to listen to you rather than to God,
20 decide for yourselves. We cannot refrain from speaking of what we
21 have seen and heard." The authorities, after further threatening
them, let them go, not finding any way of punishing them, because
of the people, who were all glorifying God because of what had
22 happened. Actually the man for whom the miraculous cure had been
effected was more than forty years old.

THANKSGIVING FOR GOD'S INTERVENTION
23   After their dismissal Peter and John came to their companions

4:11. Ps. 117:22.
4:13. uneducated and ordinary: not trained in the rabbinical traditions, and
having no authority to teach. The Apostles were not necessarily illiterate. St.
Chrysostom says: "One may be uneducated yet not ordinary, and ordinary yet
not uneducated."

and reported all that the chief priests and elders had said to them. When the faithful heard it, they lifted up their voice with one 24 accord to God and said, "Sovereign Master, it is you who did make heaven and earth and the sea and all that is in them, who did say 25 by the Holy Spirit through the mouth of our father, David, your servant:

'Why did the Gentiles rage
and the peoples plan vain things?
The kings of the earth stood by, 26
and the rulers assembled together
against the Lord and against his Christ.'

Truly there assembled together in this city against your holy 27 servant Jesus, whom you have anointed, Herod and Pontius Pilate with the Gentiles and the tribes of Israel, to do what your might 28 and your plan had beforehand decreed to be done. And now Lord, 29 consider their threats, and grant to your servants courage to speak your message with complete and firm assurance, while you exercise 30 your power to effect cures, signs and wonders to be wrought by the name of your holy servant Jesus."

When they had prayed, the place where they were gathered 31 trembled, and they were all filled with the Holy Spirit, and they continued to speak the message of God with firm assurance.

EARLY CHRISTIANS HELP ONE ANOTHER

Now the congregation of believers were of one heart and one 32 soul. Not one of them claimed as his own anything he possessed. They held all things in common. With great power the apostles 33 continued to give testimony to the resurrection of Jesus, the Lord, and without exception to enjoy great popularity. No one among 34 the faithful was in want. Those who owned land or houses would sell them and bring the price of what they sold and lay it 35 at the feet of the apostles, who distributed to each according to his

4:25. Ps. 2:1.
4:33. in common: as in 2:44. While they still held private property, all the faithful were ready to use it for those in want, and the more fervent went to the extent of selling their possessions in whole or in part and turning the proceeds over to a fund for the poor. This latter practice was not obligatory or universal, even in Jerusalem, as is clear from the special mention of Barnabas in verse 36, and from 5:4 in the case of Ananias. enjoy great popularity: literally, "great grace was on them," which could mean God's grace.

36 need. Thus Joseph, whom the apostles had surnamed Barnabas,
which means Son of Consolation, a levite and a native of Cyprus,
37 sold the field that he owned, and brought the price and laid it at
the feet of the apostles.

CHAPTER 5

ANANIAS AND SAPHIRA LIE TO PETER

1 But a man named Ananias, with Saphira his wife, sold a piece
2 of land, and with the connivance of his wife, kept back part of the
price, and bringing a part only, laid it at the feet of the apostles.
3 "Ananias," said Peter, "why has Satan filled your heart, that you
should lie to the Holy Spirit and keep back part of the price of the
4 land? While it remained unsold, did it not remain yours; and after
it was sold, was not the money at your disposal? Why have you
conceived this plan in your heart? You have not lied to men but
5 to God." Ananias, hearing these words, fell down and died. Great
6 fear came on all who heard it. The young men swung into action,
wrapped him up, carried him out, and buried him.

7 About three hours later his wife came in, unaware of what had
8 happened. "Tell me," said Peter to her, "did you sell the land for
9 so much?" "Yes," she said, "for so much." Peter said to her, "Why
have you agreed to put the Spirit of the Lord to the test? Listen,
the feet of those who buried your husband are at the door, and
10 they will carry you out." Instantly she fell dead at his feet. The
young men, coming in, found her dead; and carrying her out, they
11 buried her beside her husband. Great fear came on the whole
congregation and on all who heard of this.

MIRACLES CONFIRM THE CHURCH'S AUTHORITY

12 The apostles worked many signs and wonders among the people.
13 With one accord they all met in Solomon's portico. And although
the common people made much of them, no one of the rest dared
14 join them. More and more came to believe in the Lord and were
15 added to their number — a great crowd of men and women. The

---

5:13. *the rest*: probably "the people" in verse 12 stands for the *common
people* and *the rest* designates the aristocrats, the leaders.

people used to carry the sick into the streets and lay them on beds
and pallets so that, when Peter passed, his shadow at least might
fall on someone of them. Throngs came also from the towns near   16
Jerusalem, bringing the sick and those troubled with unclean spirits,
and they were all cured.

THE APOSTLES ARE PUT IN JAIL

The high priest, however, and all that sided with him (that   17
is, the party of the Sadducees) took action, as they were filled with
jealousy. They seized the apostles and put them in the public   18
prison. But during the night an angel of the Lord opened the prison   19
doors and let them out with the words, "Go, stand in the temple   20
and declare to the people the full message of this life." On hearing   21
this the apostles went to the temple about daybreak and began to
teach. Meanwhile the chief priest and his party came and called
together the Sanhedrin and all the elders of the Israelites. They
sent to the prison to have the apostles brought out. But when the   22
officers came and failed to find them in prison, they returned and
reported, "We found the prison securely locked and the guards   23
standing before the doors; but on opening them we found no one
inside." When the officers of the temple and the chief priests heard   24
this report, they were much perplexed about it as to how this thing
could have happened. Someone, however, came and reported to   25
them, "Why, the men you put in prison are standing in the temple
and teaching the people." Then the officer went off with his men   26
and brought them, but without violence because they feared that
they might be stoned by the people.

Having brought the apostles, they placed them in the Sanhedrin.   27
The high priest questioned them, "We strictly charged you not to   28
teach in this name, and here you have filled Jerusalem with your
teaching. You are determined to make us responsible for this
man's death."

Peter and the apostles answered, "One must obey God rather   29
than men. The God of our fathers raised Jesus, whom you put to   30
death, hanging him on a gibbet. God exalted him by his might   31
to be leader and Savior, to grant a change of heart and mind and

---

5:20. *this life:* i.e., salvation, the life of grace on earth and of glory in
heaven.
5:28. *make us responsible:* literally, "bring this man's blood on us."

32 forgiveness of sins to Israel. And we are witnesses of these events, and so is the Holy Spirit, whom God has given to all who obey him."

GAMALIEL SAVES THEIR LIVES

33 On hearing this they were torn with rage and planned to kill
34 them. A certain Pharisee in the Sanhedrin, however, Gamaliel by name, a teacher of the Law, respected by all the people arose. He
35 requested the men to be put outside for a little while. He then said to them. "Men of Israel, take care what you are about to do to
36 these men. You know that some time ago Theudas revolted, claiming to be somebody, and a number of men, about four hundred, joined him; but he was slain, and all his followers were dispersed and
37 brought to nought. After him Judas the Galilean rose in revolt during the days of the census and drew followers after him. He too
38 perished, and all his followers were dispersed. So now I say to you, keep away from these men; let them alone, for if this plan or
39 movement comes from man, it will be overthrown, but if it comes from God you will not be able to overthrow these men. Otherwise, perhaps, you may find yourselves fighting even against God."
40 They agreed with him, and after they had the apostles scourged they summoned them and charged them not to speak in the name
41 of Jesus, and let them go. So then they departed from the presence of the Sanhedrin, rejoicing that they had been counted worthy to
42 suffer disgrace for the name of Jesus. Nor did they for a single day cease teaching and preaching the good news about Jesus, the Christ, in the temple and from house to house.

CHAPTER 6

SEVEN DEACONS ARE CHOSEN

1 In those days, as the number of disciples was increasing, the Greek-speaking Jews began to murmur against those that spoke Hebrew to the effect that their widows were being neglected in the
2 daily distribution of alms. So the Twelve summoned the congrega-

---

6:1. Greek-speaking: literally, "Hellenists." those that spoke, etc.: literally, "Hebrews." The version here given is based on St. Chrysostom's explanation. Less probably the terms may designate conservative Jews, and those who were inclined to a more liberal attitude toward foreign culture.

tion of the disciples and said, "It is not desirable that we should forsake the preaching of the word of God to serve tables. Therefore, 3 brothers, select from among you seven men of good reputation, full of the Spirit and of wisdom, that we may put them in charge of this work. But we will devote ourselves to prayer and to the work 4 of preaching. The plan met with the approval of the whole congrega- 5 tion, and they chose Stephen, a man full of faith and of the Holy Spirit, and Philip, Prochorus, Nicanor, Timon, Parmenas, and Nicholas, a proselyte of Antioch. These they presented to the 6 apostles who prayed and laid their hands on them.

God's word continued to spread, and the number of disciples 7 increased greatly in Jerusalem. A large number of priests also accepted the faith.

STEPHEN IS ARRESTED

Now Stephen, full of grace and power, was working great wonders 8 and signs among the people. But some members from the synagogue 9 which is called that of the Freedmen, and of the Cyrenians and of the Alexandrians and of those from Cilicia and the province of Asia, began to dispute with Stephen. Yet they were not able to cope 10 with the wisdom and the Spirit by whom he spoke. Then they 11 instigated men to say, "We have heard him speaking blasphemous words against Moses and against God."

Thus they stirred up the people, the elders, and the Scribes, and 12 rushing on him, they seized him and brought him to the Sanhedrin. They also produced lying witnesses who said, "This man never 13 ceases speaking words against the Holy Place and the Law. Why, we 14 have heard him declare that this Jesus of Nazareth will destroy this place and will change the customs which Moses handed down to us." Then all who sat in the Sanhedrin gazed on him. They saw his face 15 as though it were the face of an angel.

6:8. grace: more probably God's grace, but possibly popular favor or pleasing eloquence. power: i.e., of miracles, but possibly forceful arguments and convincing eloquence.

6:9. It is uncertain how many synagogues are here indicated. Opinions vary from one to five synagogues.

CHAPTER 7

1   The high priest asked, "Are these charges true?"

STEPHEN ARGUES FROM JEWISH HISTORY

2   Stephen said in reply: "Brothers and fathers, hear. The God of glory appeared to our father Abraham when he was in Mesopotamia,
3   before he settled in Haran, and said to him, 'Go forth from your country and from your kindred, and come into the land that I will
4   show you.' Then he went forth from the land of the Chaldeans and settled in Haran. From there, after the death of his father, God
5   removed him into this land where you now dwell. But he gave him no property in it, not even a foot of land, although he promised 'to give its possession to him and to his offspring after him,' when as yet
6   he had no son. God spoke thus:

'His offspring shall sojourn in a foreign land.
There they shall be enslaved and mistreated for
four hundred years.
7   And on the nation to which they shall have been in bondage
I will pass sentence,'
said God,
'And afterwards they shall go forth
and shall worship me in this place.'

8   He also gave Abraham a covenant sealed by circumcision, and so Abraham became the father of Isaac and circumcised him on the eighth day; and Isaac became the father of Jacob, and Jacob became father of the twelve patriarchs.

9   "Out of jealousy the patriarchs sold Joseph into Egypt, but God
10   was with him, and rescued him from all his trials, and gave him favor and wisdom in the sight of Pharao king of Egypt, who made
11   him governor over all Egypt and over all his household. Now there came a famine throughout Egypt and Canaan, and no little suffer-
12   ing, since our fathers found no food. But when Jacob heard that
13   there was grain in Egypt, he sent our fathers there a first time, and

7:3. Gen. 12:1.
7:6. Gen. 15:3.
7:10. Gen. 41:37.

316

the second time Joseph was recognized by his brothers, and his
family became known to Pharao. Joseph then sent an invitation to   *14*
his father Jacob and all his kindred, seventy-five persons in all. So   *15*
Jacob went down to Egypt, where he and our fathers died and were   *16*
taken to Sichem and laid in the tomb which Abraham had bought
for a sum of silver from the sons of Hemor in Sichem.

THE TIME OF MOSES

"Now when the time for the fulfillment of the promise God had   *17*
made to Abraham drew near, the people had increased and multiplied
in Egypt till another king arose in Egypt who knew nothing of   *18*
Joseph. He exploited our race and oppressed our fathers by forcing   *19*
them to expose their newborn children so that they might not live.
At this time Moses was born. He was beautiful in God's sight. He   *20*
was nourished for three months in his father's house, but when he   *21*
was exposed, Pharao's daughter adopted him and brought him up
as her own son. Moses was instructed in all the wisdom of the   *22*
Egyptians, and was effective in word and deed. When he was forty   *23*
years old, it occurred to him to visit his brothers, the children of
Israel. When he saw one of them being mistreated, he defended   *24*
and avenged him by striking down the Egyptian. Now he thought   *25*
that his brothers understood that through him God was giving them
deliverance, but they did not understand. The next day he came   *26*
across two of them fighting. He tried to restore them to peace with
the words, 'Men, you are brothers; why do you hurt each other?' But   *27*
the man who was wronging his neighbor thrust him aside with the
remark, 'Who has appointed you ruler and judge over us? Do you   *28*
mean to kill me as you did the Egyptian yesterday?' At this word   *29*
Moses fled, and lived for a time in the land of Madian, where he
begot two sons.

"When forty years had passed, an angel appeared to him in the   *30*
desert of Mount Sinai in a bush that was one flame of fire. When   *31*
Moses beheld this he marveled at the sight; and as he drew near
to look, there came the voice of the Lord, 'I am the God of your   *32*
fathers, the God of Abraham, of Isaac, and of Jacob.' Moses trembled

---

7:17. Exod. 1:7.
7:20. Exod. 2:2.
7:24. Exod. 2:12.
7:30. Exod. 3:2 ff.

33 and dared not look. Then the Lord said to him, 'Remove the sandals from your feet, for the place where you are standing is holy ground.
34 I have seen the oppression of my people in Egypt; I have heard their groaning, and I have come to deliver them. And now, come; I will give you a mission to Egypt.'
35 "This Moses whom they disowned, saying, 'Who has made you ruler and judge?' God sent to be ruler and redeemer with the help
36 of the angel who appeared to him in the bush. This is he who led them out, working wonders and signs in the land of Egypt and at the
37 Red Sea and in the desert for forty years. This is the Moses who said to the children of Israel, 'God will raise up a prophet for you
38 from among your brothers, as he did me.' This is he who was in the assembly in the wilderness with the angel who spoke to him on Mount Sinai and with our fathers. This is he who received life-
39 giving oracles to pass on to you. Our fathers, however, were unwilling to obey him, thrust him aside, and in their hearts turned back to
40 Egypt, saying to Aaron, 'Make us gods to go before us. As for this Moses who brought us out of the land of Egypt, we do not know
41 what has become of him.' So they made an image of a calf in those days and offered sacrifice to the idol, while they rejoiced in
42 the product of their own hands. But God turned away and abandoned them to the worship of the host of heaven, even as it is written in the book of the Prophets:

'Did you offer sacrificial victims to me
     for forty years in the desert, O house of Israel?
43   Why, you took up with the tabernacle of Moloch
     and the star of the god Rephan,
    images that you made to worship.
Therefore I will remove your abode beyond Babylon.'

AFTER THE TIME OF MOSES
44 "Our fathers had in the desert the tent of testimony, as God arranged when he told Moses to make it according to the model he
45 had seen. This tent our fathers inherited, and brought it with them when under Josue they took possession of the territory of the

7:37. Deut. 18:15.
7:40. Exod. 32:1.
7:42. Amos 5:25.
7:44. The preceding part refers to the charge of having spoken against Moses,

Gentiles whom God had driven out before our fathers. This tent
remained down to the time of David. who found favor with God   46
and asked permission to construct a dwelling place for the God of
Jacob. But it was Solomon who built a house for God. Yet not in   47, 48
houses made by hands does the Most High dwell, even as the
prophet says,

       'The heaven is my throne,   49
         and the earth a stool for my feet.
    What kind of a house will you build me, says the Lord,
       or what shall be the place where I may dwell?
    Did not my hand make this entire universe?'   50

"Stiff-necked, ill-disposed to understand or hear, always you oppose   51
the Holy Spirit; as your fathers did, so do you also. Was there a   52
single prophet that your fathers did not persecute? They killed
even those who foretold the coming of the Just One, of whom you
have now become the betrayers and murderers, you who received   53
the Law delivered by angels, yet did not keep it."

THE MARTYRDOM OF STEPHEN

As they listened to this indictment, their hearts were torn with   54
rage, and they gnashed their teeth at Stephen. But, filled with the   55
Holy Spirit, he looked up to heaven and saw the glory of God,
and Jesus standing at the right hand of God. "At this very moment,"   56
he said, "I see the skies opened and the Son of Man standing at the
right hand of God." But they shouted aloud, stopped their ears, and   57
to a man rushed on him. They drove him out of the city and began   58
to stone him. The witnesses laid their garments at the feet of a
young man named Saul. While they were stoning Stephen, he called   59
for aid, "Lord Jesus, receive my spirit." Then falling on his knees,   60
he cried with a loud voice, "Lord, do not charge this sin against
them." With these words he passed away. Saul approved of his   1
being put to death.

Stephen now takes up the charge of having spoken against the temple.
  7:49. Isa. 66:1.
  7:51. ill-disposed, etc.: literally, "uncircumcised of heart and ear."
  7:53. delivered by angels: the phrase in the Greek is obscure and in addition
to the translation given above the text has been rendered: "by means of angelic
ordinances," "as ordinances of angels," etc.
  7:60. passed away: literally, "fell asleep." The Clementine Vulgate adds: "in
the Lord."

Chapter 8

PERSECUTION OF THE CHURCH

There broke out on that day a great persecution against the
Church in Jerusalem, and all except the apostles were scattered
2 abroad throughout the land of Judea and Samaria. Devout men
3 took care of Stephen's burial, and mourned him deeply. But Saul
was ravaging the Church. Entering house after house he dragged out
men and women and committed them to prison.

The Church Grows in Judea and Samaria

THE CHURCH IN SAMARIA

4   Now those who had been scattered abroad went from place to
5 place spreading the Good News of the word. Philip went down to
the city of Samaria and brought the Good News about the Christ to
6 its people. The crowds when they heard, and saw the miracles that
7 Philip worked, gave heed with general accord to what he said, as
unclean spirits, shouting with a loud voice, departed from large numbers of possessed persons, and many paralyzed and lame people were
8 cured. So there was great joy in the city.
9   Now a man named Simon had previously been practicing sorcery
in that city and astounding the people of Samaria, claiming to be
10 a great person, and everybody, prominent or obscure, listened to
him, saying, "This man is the instrument of God's mighty power."
11 They gave heed to him because for a long time he had bewitched
12 them with his sorceries. But when they believed Philip as he proclaimed the Good News of God's kingdom and the name of Jesus
13 Christ, they were baptized, men and women alike. Even Simon
himself believed, and after his baptism attached himself to Philip,
and was amazed at the sight of the signs and exceedingly great
miracles being effected.

8:5. *Philip:* one of the seven deacons named in 6:5.
8:7. *unclean spirits,* etc. Both in the Latin and the Greek the possessed
persons are the subject of the verb. Literally: "for many of those having unclean
spirits, crying with a loud voice, went out," etc.
8:10. *instrument of God's mighty power:* literally, "the power of God which
is called great."

Now when the apostles in Jerusalem heard that Samaria had 14
accepted the word of God, they sent Peter and John to them. On 15
their arrival they prayed for the Samaritans, that they might receive
the Holy Spirit. As yet he had not come on any of them, because 16
they had only been baptized in the name of the Lord Jesus. Then 17
Peter and John laid their hands on them, and they received the Holy
Spirit. When Simon saw that the Holy Spirit was imparted through 18
the laying on of the apostles' hands, he offered them money, saying, 19
"Give me also this power, so that anyone on whom I lay my hands
may receive the Holy Spirit."

But Peter said to him, "May your money go to destruction with 20
you, because you thought that the gift of God could be purchased
with money. You have no part or lot in this matter, for your heart 21
is not right with God. Repent, therefore, of this wickedness of yours 22
and pray to God that perhaps the intent of your heart may be forgiven you, for I see that you have fallen into the depths of 23
viciousness and are held by bonds of wickedness." Simon answered, 24
"Do you pray for me to the Lord, that nothing of what you have
said may happen to me."

So, after they had given testimony and preached the word of the 25
Lord, on their way back to Jerusalem they brought the Good News
to many Samaritan villages.

AN ETHIOPIAN CONVERT

Now an angel of the Lord spoke to Philip, "Get busy and 26
journey south by the road that runs through the desert from
Jerusalem to Gaza." So he got busy and departed. Now just at that 27
time an Ethiopian, a member of the court of Queen Candace of
Ethiopia, holding high office as her treasurer, had come to Jerusalem
to worship, and was returning seated in his carriage reading the 28
prophet Isaias. The Spirit said to Philip, "Go and stay near this 29

8:15. *Holy Spirit*: the Samaritans had received the Holy Spirit in Baptism,
but not in that fullness of his gifts which is imparted in Confirmation. Philip,
being only a deacon, could not administer this sacrament.

8:23. *depths of viciousness*, etc.: literally, "in the gall of bitterness and the
bond of iniquity."

8:26. *desert*: i.e., an uncultivated or uninhabited region. It is possible to con-
strue the word with Gaza: "by the road that runs from Jerusalem to Gaza
the deserted."

8:27. This description leaves us in doubt as to whether the Ethiopian was
Jew or Gentile.

30 carriage." Philip ran up, and overheard the Ethiopian reading the prophet Isaias. He inquired, "Do you really understand what you are
31 reading?" He replied, "Why, how can I, unless someone interprets
32 it for me?" He begged Philip to get in and sit with him. Now the passage of Scripture which he was reading was this:

"He was led like a sheep to slaughter;
and as a lamb dumb before its shearer
he opens not his mouth.
33 In his humiliation fair judgment was denied him.
Who shall describe his contemporaries,
that removed him from the land of the living?"

34 The official spoke to Philip, "I pray you, of whom is the prophet saying this? Of himself or of someone else?"
35 Then Philip began to speak, and starting from this scriptural
36 passage, preached the Good News about Jesus to him. As they journeyed along the road, they came to some water. "Look," said the official, "here is water. What is there to prevent my being
38 baptized?" He ordered the carriage stopped, and both Philip and the official went down into the water, where Philip baptized him.
39 Now when they came up out of the water, a wind sent by the Lord carried Philip away, and the official did not see him, such was
40 his joy as he continued his journey. Then Philip was found in Azotus, and in passing he preached the Good News to all the cities till he came to Caesarea.

Chapter 9

THE CONVERSION OF SAUL

1 But Saul, still breathing threats of death against the disciples
2 of the Lord, went to the high priest, and asked him for letters to the synagogues at Damascus, so that, if he found any men or women belonging to the Way, he might bring them in bonds to Jerusalem.

8:32. Isa. 53:7.
8:36. Some manuscripts of the Latin and Greek here add: "Philip said, 'If you believe with all your heart you may.' And he answered: 'I believe Jesus Christ to be the Son of God.'"
8:40. *was found:* or "found himself."
9:2. *the Way:* i.e., Christianity and the Christian way of life.

During his journey, it happened, as he was approaching Damascus, 3
that suddenly a light from the sky flashed round about him, and 4
falling to the ground, he heard a voice saying to him, "Saul, Saul,
why do you persecute me?" "Who are you, Lord?" he asked. Jesus 5
replied, "I am Jesus whom you are persecuting. Arise and go into 6
the city, and you will be told what you must do." Meanwhile his 7
traveling companions remained speechless. They heard the voice
but saw no one. Then Saul arose from the ground, and although 8
his eyes were open, he could see nothing. So leading him by the
hand, they brought him into Damascus. For three whole days he 9
could not see, neither did he eat or drink.

Now there was in Damascus a disciple named Ananias, to whom 10
the Lord said in a vision, "Ananias!" "Here I am, Lord," he answered.
The Lord said to him, "Arise and go to the street called Straight 11
and ask at the house of Judas for a man of Tarsus named Saul,
who at this very moment is praying." (Saul saw a man named 12
Ananias enter and lay his hands on him that he might recover his
sight.) Ananias, however, objected, "Lord, I have heard from many 13
a person about this man, how much evil he has done to your saints
at Jerusalem. Even here he has authority from the high priest to 14
arrest all who invoke your name." "Go," the Lord commanded him, 15
"for this man is my chosen instrument, to carry my name among
nations and their kings and among the children of Israel as well.
I myself will show him how much he must suffer for my name." 16

So Ananias departed and entered the house. As he laid his hands 17
on Saul he said, "Brother Saul, the Lord has sent me — Jesus, who
appeared to you on your journey — that you may recover your sight
and be filled with the Holy Spirit." Immediately there fell from 18
Saul's eyes something like scales, he recovered his sight, arose, and
was baptized. Then after taking some food, he regained his strength. 19

THE NEW CONVERT'S ZEAL
Now for some days he lived with the disciples at Damascus.

9:12. This parenthesis describes a vision which Saul had while our Lord
was speaking to Ananias.

9:13. *saints:* an ordinary designation of the early Christians, so called because they were separated (the basic meaning of sanctity) from the world and
united to Christ. They are sanctified by the presence in them of the Holy
Spirit, while preserving themselves in the state of grace.

20 Without delay he began to preach Jesus as the Son of God in the
21 synagogues. All who heard him were amazed and remarked, "Is not this he who used to make havoc in Jerusalem of those who call on this name, and who had come here for the purpose of taking them in bonds to the chief priest?"
22 Saul, however, grew all the more confident and confounded the Jews who were living in Damascus, proving that Jesus is the Christ.
23, 24 As time passed on, the Jews plotted to kill Saul, but their plot became known to him. They were even guarding the gates day and
25 night in order to kill him, but his disciples took him by night and let him down over the wall, lowering him in a basket.
26 On his arrival at Jerusalem he tried to join the disciples, but they were all afraid of him, not believing that he was a disciple.
27 Barnabas, however, befriended him and brought him to the apostles, and told them how Saul on his journey had seen the Lord, that the Lord had spoken to him, and how in Damascus Saul had
28 spoken courageously in the name of Jesus. So Saul moved freely among them in Jerusalem, speaking courageously in the name of the
29 Lord. He also spoke and argued with the Greek-speaking Jews, who,
30 however, sought to kill him. When the brethren heard of this attempt, they brought him down to Caesarea and sent him on to Tarsus.

PETER VISITS THE CONGREGATIONS

31 Throughout all Judea, Galilee, and Samaria, meanwhile, the Church was in peace, and it developed spiritually and lived in awe of the Lord. At the same time it increased in numbers through the exhortation inspired by the Holy Spirit.
32 It happened that Peter, while visiting all these places, came
33 to the saints living in Lydda. He found there a man named Aeneas,
34 a paralytic who had been bedridden for eight years. "Aeneas," Peter said to him, "Jesus Christ now heals you; get up and make your
35 own bed." He arose at once, and all who lived at Lydda and in Sharon saw him, and were converted to the Lord.
36 At Joppa there was a disciple, Tabitha (which is translated

---

9:31. *exhortation:* or "consolation," "encouragement." The basic meaning is that the making of new converts is due to the work of the Holy Spirit. He either inspired the preaching of the missionaries or encouraged them to carry on in spite of opposition.

Dorcas). Her life was filled with good deeds and acts of charity which
she was constantly doing. It happened at this time that she fell ill   37
and died. After washing her they laid her out in an upper room. As   38
Lydda was near Joppa, the disciples, hearing that Peter was there,
sent two men to him with the request, "Come over to us without
delay." So Peter arose and went with them, and on his arrival they   39
took him to the upper room. All the widows came to meet him,
and with tears showed him the tunics and cloaks which Dorcas used
to make while she was still with them. Peter, sending them all   40
out, knelt down and prayed. Then turning to the body, he said,
"Tabitha, arise." She opened her eyes and, seeing Peter, sat up. Then   41
Peter gave her his hand and helped her rise. Calling the saints and
widows, he presented her alive. This became known all over Joppa,   42
and many believed in the Lord. It happened that he continued to   43
stay for some time at Joppa with a certain Simon, who was a tanner.

THE CHURCH SPREADS TO THE GENTILES

CHAPTER 10

CORNELIUS, THE FIRST GENTILE CONVERT

Now there was in Caesarea a man named Cornelius, a centurion   1
of the cohort called Italian. He was devout and God-fearing, as   2
was all his household. He gave alms generously to the people and
prayed to God continually. About three o'clock in the afternoon   3
he perceived distinctly in a vision an angel of God enter his house
and say to him, "Cornelius!" Gazing at the angel in awe he said: 4
"What is it, Lord?" "Your prayers," replied the angel, "and your
alms have gone up and been remembered in the sight of God. And   5
now send men to Joppa and fetch Simon, surnamed Peter: he is   6
lodging with Simon a tanner, whose house is by the seaside." When   7
the angel who had spoken to him had departed, Cornelius called
two of his household servants and a God-fearing soldier from among

---

9:36. Dorcas, her Greek name, means gazelle.

10:2. God-fearing: a term frequent in the Acts, used of Gentile converts
to Judaism, who accepted faith in the one true God but without being circumcised or submitting to the full burden of the Mosaic Law.

10:4. gone up . . . God: gone up to please God like the smoke of the sacrifice
which was called a "memorial." Lev. 2:9.

8 his personal attendants, and after telling them the whole story sent them to Joppa.

9 Now the next day, while they were still on their journey and were just drawing near to the city, Peter went up to the roof about

10 noon to pray. He became very hungry and wanted something to

11 eat. While food was being prepared, he fell into an ecstasy, and saw the sky opened and a receptacle descending like a great sheet, let

12 down by the four corners to the earth. In it were all the four-footed beasts and creeping things of the earth and the birds of

13 the air. A voice came to him, "Rise, Peter, kill and eat."

14 "Far be it from me Lord," said Peter, "for never did I eat anything

15 common or unclean." A second time a voice came to him, "What

16 God has cleansed, do not call common." Now this happened three times, when forthwith the receptacle was taken up into the sky.

17 Now while Peter was still perplexed as to what the vision he had seen might mean, just then the men sent by Cornelius stood

18 at the door, inquiring for Simon's house, and calling out to ask

19 whether Simon, surnamed Peter, was staying there. While Peter was pondering over the vision, the Spirit said to him, "At this moment

20 three men are looking for you. Rise, therefore, go down and depart

21 with them without hesitation, for I have sent them." So Peter went down to the men and said, "Here I am, the man you are asking for.

22 What is the reason for your coming?" "Cornelius," they answered him, "a centurion, a just and God-fearing man, who enjoys a good reputation with the whole nation of the Jews, has been directed by a holy angel to fetch you to his house and to hear a message from

23 you." So he invited them in and entertained them.

PETER VISITS AND INSTRUCTS CORNELIUS

The next day he set out and went with them, accompanied by

24 some of the brothers from Joppa. The following day he reached Caesarea. Now Cornelius was waiting for them with a number of

25 his relatives and intimate friends whom he had invited. As Peter

26 entered, Cornelius met him and fell at his feet in reverence. But

27 Peter raised him up, saying, "Get up, I myself also am a man." As he talked with Cornelius, he went in and found many assembled,

---

10:15. The distinction made by the Mosaic Law between clean and unclean food is no longer to hold.

and said to them, "You know it is not permissible for a Jew to 28
associate with a foreigner or to visit him, but God has shown me
that I should not call any man common or unclean. Therefore I 29
came without hesitation when I was summoned. I ask, therefore,
why you have sent for me?"

"Three days ago at this very hour," replied Cornelius, "I was 30
praying in my house at three o'clock in the afternoon, and suddenly a man stood before me in shining garments who said,
'Cornelius, your prayer has been heard and your alms have been 31
remembered in the sight of God. Send therefore to Joppa and sum- 32
mon Simon, surnamed Peter. He is lodging in the house of Simon,
a tanner, by the sea.' Accordingly at once I sent for you, and you 33
have very kindly come. Now, therefore, we are all present before
God to hear whatever the Lord has commanded you."

Peter began to address them: "Now I really understand that 34
God shows no partiality, but in every nation the man that fears 35
him and does what is right is acceptable to him. He sent his word 36
to the children of Israel, proclaiming the Good News of peace
through Jesus Christ, who is Lord of all. You know what took 37
place throughout Judea. Jesus of Nazareth began in Galilee after
the baptism preached by John. You know how God anointed 38
him with the Holy Spirit and with power, and he went about doing
good and healing all who were in the power of the devil because
God was with him. We are witnesses of all that he did in the 39
country of the Jews and in Jerusalem. Yet they killed him, hanging
him on a cross. But God raised him up on the third day and caused 40
him to be plainly seen, not by all the people, but by witnesses 41
designated beforehand by God, that is, by us, who ate and drank
with him after he had risen from the dead. Jesus also charged us 42
to preach to the people and to bear witness that it is he who has
been appointed by God to be judge of the living and the dead. To 43
him all the prophets bear witness that through his name all who
believe in him may receive forgiveness of sins."

BAPTISM OF CORNELIUS

While Peter was still speaking these words, the Holy Spirit 44
came on all who were listening to his message. The Jewish faithful, 45
Peter's companions, were amazed, because the gift of the Holy

327

46 Spirit had also been poured forth on the Gentiles, for they heard
47 them speaking in tongues and magnifying God. Then Peter made
the decision: "Can anyone refuse the baptism of water to these
people, seeing that they have received the Holy Spirit just as we
48 did?" So he ordered them to be baptized in the name of Jesus
Christ. Then they besought him to stay on there for a few days.

Chapter 11

PETER EXPLAINS AT JERUSALEM

1   Now the apostles and brothers all over Jerusalem heard that
2 the Gentiles too had received God's word. When Peter went up
to Jerusalem, the advocates of circumcision found fault with him,
3 saying, "You have visited and even eaten with uncircumcised men!"
4   Then Peter began to explain the matter to them from beginning
5 to end, saying: "I was praying in the city of Joppa and while in
ecstasy I had a vision — a receptacle coming down something like
a great sheet, let down from the sky by its four corners. It came
6 right down to me. Gazing on it I observed and saw the four-footed
creatures of the earth, and the wild beasts and the creeping things,
7 and the birds of the air. I also heard a voice saying to me, 'Rise,
8 Peter, kill and eat.' 'By no means, Lord,' I said, 'for nothing common
9 or unclean has ever entered my mouth.' The voice spoke a second
10 time, 'What God has cleansed, do not call common.' This happened
11 three times, and then it was all drawn up again into the sky. And
just at that moment, three men came to the house where we were
12 staying, sent from Caesarea to me, and the Spirit bade me to accompany them without hesitation. These six brothers also went with me
13 and we entered the man's house. He told us how he had seen the
angel in his house present himself and say to him, 'Send to Joppa
14 and fetch Simon, surnamed Peter. He will speak to you words
15 by which you shall be saved, you and all your household.' When I
began to speak, the Holy Spirit descended upon them, just as he
16 did upon us at the beginning. Then I remembered the Lord's
word, how he had said, 'John indeed baptized with water, but you
17 shall be baptized with the Holy Spirit.' Therefore, if God gave

10:46. *in tongues:* as on Pentecost. See Chapter 2.

to them the same gift as he gave to us who believed in the Lord Jesus Christ, who was I that I could interfere with God?"

On hearing this they acquiesced, and glorified God, saying, 18 "Therefore to the Gentiles too God has given a change of heart and mind leading to life."

MANY CONVERTS AT ANTIOCH

Now those that had been dispersed by the persecution which 19 had broken out in connection with Stephen, went all the way to Phoenicia, Cyprus, and Antioch, speaking the message to nobody but Jews. Some of those dispersed, however, were Cyprians and Cyre- 20 neans, who on reaching Antioch began to speak to the Greeks also, preaching the Lord Jesus. The Lord blessed their efforts and a great 21 number believed and turned to the Lord. News about them came to 22 the ears of the congregation at Jerusalem, and they sent Barnabas to Antioch. When he came and saw the effects of God's grace, he 23 rejoiced and exhorted them all to remain with steadfast heart attached to the Lord, for he was a good man filled with the Holy 24 Spirit and faith. A great multitude was won over to the Lord. Then 25 he went over to Tarsus to look for Saul, and on finding him, brought 26 him to Antioch, where for a whole year they took part in the meetings of the congregation and taught a great multitude. It was in Antioch that the disciples were first called "Christians."

THE FAMINE RELIEF VISIT OF PAUL

In those days some prophets from Jerusalem came down to 27 Antioch, and one of them, named Agabus, arose and revealed through 28 the Spirit that there would be a great famine all over the world. The famine occurred during the reign of Claudius. So the disciples, 29 each according to his means, determined to send relief to the brothers dwelling in Judea. And this they did, sending it through 30 the medium of Barnabas and Saul to the presbyters.

11:28. *Claudius:* Roman emperor from A.D. 41 to 54.

11:30. *presbyters:* literally, "elders." This is the term from which our "priest" is derived. But here and in the rest of the Acts and in many of the Epistles it designates the priests who held office as rulers of the early Church. The term "priest" was probably designedly avoided by the early Christians because the term was used both by Jews and pagans. The translation *presbyters* serves to distinguish these priests from the Jewish "elders."

The Persecution by Herod Agrippa

Chapter 12

PETER IMPRISONED

1 About that time King Herod set hands on certain members of
2 the Church to do them violence. He dispatched the brother of
3 John by the sword, and seeing that it pleased the Jews, he went on
4 to arrest Peter during the days of the Unleavened Bread. After
arresting him, he cast him into prison, committing him to the
custody of four guards of soldiers, four in each guard, intending to
bring him up for trial in the presence of the people after the
5 Passover. So while they were holding Peter in prison, fervent prayer
was being offered to God for him by the Church.

AN ANGEL FREES PETER

6 The very night before Herod was going to bring him up for
trial, Peter was sleeping between two soldiers and fastened by two
7 chains, while outside the door sentries guarded the prison. Suddenly an angel of the Lord stood before him, and a light shone in
the room. He struck Peter on the side and woke him, saying "Get
8 up quickly." The chains dropped from his hands. "Gird yourself,"
the angel said to him, "and put on your sandals." When he had
done so, the angel said to him, "Wrap your cloak about you and
follow me."
9 So he followed the angel out without knowing that what was
being done by the angel was real, since he thought he was having a
10 vision. They passed through the first and second guard and came
to the iron gate that leads to the city. It opened to them of itself.
They went out and passed on through one street; then immediately
11 the angel left him. Then Peter came to himself and said, "Now I
know that the Lord has sent his angel and rescued me from the
power of Herod and from all that the Jewish people were expecting."
12 When he realized his situation, he went to the house of Mary,
the mother of John surnamed Mark, where many had gathered and

---

12:3. *days of the Unleavened Bread:* the seven days following the paschal
supper.

330

were praying. When he knocked at the outer door, a maid named 13
Rhoda came to answer it. As soon as she recognized Peter's voice, 14
for joy she did not open the door but ran in and announced that
Peter was standing at the gate. "You are out of your mind," they 15
said to her. But when she insisted that it was so, they said, "It is
his angel." Meanwhile Peter continued knocking, and when they 16
opened and saw him, they were besides themselves with joy. He 17
motioned with his hand for quiet and related how the Lord had
brought him out of prison. "Report this," he said, "to James and to
the brothers." Then he departed and went to another place.

When morning came, there was no little stir among the soldiers 18
as to what had become of Peter. When Herod had search made 19
for him and could not find him, he examined the guards and
ordered them to be put to death. Then he went down from Judea
to Caesarea and stayed there.

HEROD IS PUNISHED

He was very angry with the Tyrians and Sidonians. So they came 20
in a body to him, and, having won over Blastus, the king's chamber-
lain, they asked for peace, because their country depended on his
kingdom for its food supply. So a day was fixed and on it Herod, 21
arrayed in kingly apparel, sat in the judgment seat and began to
address them. The people shouted, "It is the voice of a god, not 22
of a man." But immediately an angel of the Lord struck him down, 23
because he had not given the honor to God. And he was eaten up
by worms and died. But the preaching of God's word continued 24
to grow and spread.

Now when Barnabas and Saul had fulfilled their mission, they 25
returned from Jerusalem, taking with them John, who was surnamed Mark.

12:15. angel: the Jews at this time believed that each man had a guardian
angel, who could assume the appearance and voice of his charge.

12:17. James: called "the brother of the Lord," i.e., one of Jesus' near
relatives, called also "James the Less," to distinguish him from James the Great,
brother of John the Evangelist. another place: undoubtedly outside the jurisdiction of Herod. Origen and St. Jerome ascribe the establishment of the congregation at Antioch to St. Peter. Possibly it was at this time that Peter went to
Antioch. According to Eusebius, however, St. Peter went to Rome about
this time.

THE FIRST MISSIONARY JOURNEY OF PAUL

CHAPTER 13

DEPARTURE CEREMONY

1 In the congregation at Antioch there were God's inspired spokesmen and teachers: Barnabas, and Simeon who was called Niger, and
Lucius of Cyrene, and Manahen who had been brought up with
2 Herod the tetrarch, and Saul. As they were celebrating the liturgical
worship of the Lord and fasting, the Holy Spirit said, "Set apart
immediately for me Saul and Barnabas for the work to which I
3 have called them." Then after fasting and praying they imposed
hands on them, and sent them on their way.

THE MISSION IN CYPRUS

4 So, sent forth by the Holy Spirit, they went down to Seleucia
5 and from there sailed to Cyprus. On their arrival at Salamina they
proclaimed the word of God in the synagogues of the Jews. John
6 too was their assistant. They passed through the whole island
all the way to Paphos, where they came across a Jewish magician and
7 false prophet, named Bar-Jesus, who was an attendant to the proconsul Sergius Paulus, a man of discernment. Sergius sent for
8 Barnabas and Saul, and asked to hear the word of God. But Elymas
the magician (for so his name is translated) opposed them, trying
9 to turn the proconsul away from the faith. But Saul (also called
10 Paul), filled with the Holy Spirit, looked him in the eye and said,
"You thoroughgoing scoundrel and deceiver, son of the devil, enemy
of all that is holy, will you never stop trying to make crooked the

13:1. *Herod*: Herod Antipas, who beheaded John the Baptist and mocked
our Lord during his Passion. Lk. 23:6 ff.
13:3. *imposed hands on them*: according to Knabenbauer, this was episcopal
consecration, but Jacquier is of the opinion that there is here merely a blessing
for the missionary journey they were beginning.
13:5. *John*: i.e., St. Mark.
13:6. *Bar-Jesus*: a patronymic, *Bar* meaning "son of" as in Barnabas. *Jesus*:
another form of "Josue." His proper name was Elymas, meaning "magician."
13:9. *Saul*: a Jewish name. The Roman name Paul may have been given
him much earlier. Its use is more appropriate among the Gentiles, especially as
Saulos in Greek means "loose," "wanton of gait," "straddling," "wanton."

straight ways of the Lord? And now perceive the hand of the Lord   11
on you; you shall be blind, not seeing the light of day for a time."
Instantly there fell on him a mist of darkness, and he groped about
for someone to lead him by the hand. Then the proconsul, seeing   12
what had happened, and deeply impressed by the Lord's teaching,
accepted the faith.

THEY ARRIVE AT ANTIOCH IN PISIDIA

Putting to sea from Paphos, Paul and his companions came to   13
Perge in Pamphylia, where John deserted them and returned to
Jerusalem. They, however, passing through Perge, reached the   14
Pisidian Antioch, and entering the synagogue on the Sabbath,
took seats. After the reading of the Law and the Prophets, the   15
rulers of the synagogue sent them the message, "Brothers, if you
have any word of exhortation, speak to the people."

PAUL'S SERMON

Then Paul rose, and motioning with his hand for silence said,   16
"Israelites and you who fear God, hearken. The God of this people   17
of Israel chose our fathers and made our people great when they
were sojourners in the land of Egypt. With great might he led
them forth from there, and for a period of forty years he bore with   18
their ways in the desert. After destroying seven nations in the land   19
of Canaan, he divided their territory among the Israelites by lot.
This period covers about four hundred years. After that he provided   20
them with judges, until the time of Samuel the prophet. Then they   21
demanded a king, and for forty years God gave them Saul, the
son of Cis, a man of the tribe of Benjamin. Removing him, God   22
raised up David to be their king, and to him he bore witness in

13:12. accepted the faith: literally, "believed." He became a Christian most
probably. It is not likely that St. Luke would have used the word of mere
intellectual assent not followed by Baptism. At times St. Luke speaks of those
who "believe" with no mention of Baptism, where the believers are certainly
baptized.

13:18. Another variant reading, quite well supported, means "he fed them."

13:20. This period covers: these words are inserted in the translation to give
an acceptable sense to a very troublesome phrase. The period would be either
from the promise made to Abraham or the birth of Isaac to the death of Josue,
or from the entrance of the Israelites into Egypt to the death of Josue.

13:22. 1 Kings 16:13; Ps. 88:21.

the words, 'I have found David, the son of Jesse, a man after my own heart, who will do all that I desire.'

23   "From his offspring God according to promise brought to Israel
24 a Savior, Jesus. Before his coming John had preached to all the people of Israel a baptism as a sign of a change of heart and mind.
25 At the close of his career John said, 'I am not what you think I am. But take heed! One is coming after me, and I am not worthy to
26 untie the shoes of his feet.' Brothers, children of the race of Abraham, and all among you who fear God, to us the message of this
27 salvation has been sent. Really the citizens of Jerusalem and their leaders fulfilled the words of the prophets which are read every
28 Sabbath by condemning Jesus in their ignorance. Though they found no grounds for the death penalty, they asked Pilate to have
29 him put to death. When they had carried out all that had been written concerning him, he was taken down from the cross and
30, 31 laid in a tomb. But God raised him from the dead, and he was seen during many days by those who had come up with him from Galilee to Jerusalem. So they became witnesses of him to the people.
32   "We now bring you the Good News that God has fulfilled the
33 promises made to our forefathers for us, their children, by raising Jesus, as also it is written in the second Psalm,

'You are my son; this day have I begotten you.'

34 And to show that he has raised him up from the dead, never again to return to decay, he has thus said,

'I will give fulfillment of the holy
and unfailing promises made to David.'

35 For this reason in another Psalm he says,

'You will not let your Holy One see decay.'

36 "Now after he had served God's purposes for the benefit of his own generation, David fell asleep and was gathered to his fathers, and did
37 see decay. But he whom God raised to life did not see decay.
38 Be it known to you, therefore, brothers, that it is by him that
39 forgiveness of sins is proclaimed to you, and through this one everybody who believes is acquitted of all the sins of which you could
40 not be acquitted by the Law of Moses. Beware, therefore, that what

---

13:25. Mt. 3:11; Mk. 1:7; Jn. 1:20.
13:33. Ps. 2:1.
13:34. Isa. 55:3.
13:35. Ps. 15:10.

is said in the prophets may not prove true of you,

<blockquote>
'See, you despisers, then wonder and perish,   41
because I do a deed in your days,
A deed which you will not believe,
if anyone relates it to you.' "
</blockquote>

Now as they were going out, the people begged to have all this   42
repeated to them on the following Sabbath. After the assembly had   43
been dismissed, many of the Jews and worshiping converts went
away with Paul and Barnabas, who talked with them and urged
them to hold fast to the grace of God. The next Sabbath almost   44
the whole city gathered to hear the word of the Lord. On seeing   45
the crowds, the Jews were filled with jealousy and contradicted what
Paul had said, and abused him. Then Paul and Barnabas discarding   46
all restraint, said, "It was necessary that the word of God be spoken
to you first, but since you reject it and judge yourselves unworthy
of eternal life, realize that we now turn to the Gentiles. Exactly so   47
the Lord has commanded us,

<blockquote>
'I have set you to be a light to the Gentiles
to be a means of salvation to the very ends
of the earth.' "
</blockquote>

THE REACTION OF THE JEWS

On hearing this the Gentiles were delighted, and glorified the   48
word of the Lord, while all those who were disposed for eternal
life accepted the faith. The word of the Lord spread through the   49
whole country. But the Jews incited the worshiping women of   50
rank and the chief men of the city, they stirred up a persecution
against Paul and Barnabas, and drove them from the district. So   51
they shook the dust from their feet in protest against the Jews and
went to Iconium. But the disciples continued to be filled with joy   52
and the Holy Spirit.

CHAPTER 14

THEIR STAY AT ICONIUM

Now the same things happened at Iconium. They went into   1
the synagogue of the Jews and so spoke that a great throng of

---

13:41. Hab. 1:5.
13:47. Isa. 49:6.

2 Jews and of Greeks accepted the faith. But the disbelieving Jews
stirred up and poisoned the minds of the Gentiles against the
3 brothers. Nevertheless Paul and Barnabas stayed a long time there,
acting with firm assurance in the Lord, who gave testimony to the
message announcing his grace by granting signs and wonders to
4 be done by their hands. The people of the city were divided, some
5 siding with the Jews and some with the apostles. But when there
was a hostile movement on the part of both the Gentiles and the
Jews with their rulers to assault and stone Paul and Barnabas,
6 realizing their situation, they escaped to the Lycaonian cities,
7 Lystra and Derbe, and to the whole country round about, where
they went on spreading the Good News.

THE HAPPENINGS AT LYSTRA

8   In Lystra there sat a man who did not have the use of his feet.
9 As he had been lame from his very birth, he had never walked. This
man listened to Paul as he spoke. Paul, gazing at him and seeing
10 that he had faith to be cured, said with a loud voice, "Stand upright
on your feet!" And he sprang up and began to walk.
11   Then the crowds, seeing what Paul had done, lifted up their
voice, saying in the Lycaonian tongue, "The gods have come down
12 to us in the likeness of men." So they called Barnabas, Jupiter and
13 Paul, Mercury, because he was the chief speaker. The priest of the
Jupiter which is at the entrance to the city brought oxen and
garlands to the gateways, and, with the people, would have offered
14 sacrifice. But on hearing this the apostles Barnabas and Paul
15 rushed into the crowd, tearing their clothes and shouting, "Men,
why are you doing this? We too are mortal, of the same nature as
you are. We bring to you the Good News that you should turn
from these vain gods to the living God who made heaven and earth
16 and the sea and all things that are in them. In the generations that
17 are passed he let all the nations follow their own ways and yet he
did not leave himself without testimony, bestowing blessings, giving
rains from heaven and fruitful seasons, filling your hearts with food
18 and gladness." Yet even with these words they hardly restrained
the crowds from offering sacrifice to them.

14:13. *of the Jupiter:* i.e., of the temple of Jupiter. "The god was said to be
where his temple is" (Zorrell). *to the gateways:* of the temple or the city.

But some Jews arrived from Antioch and Iconium, and after 19
winning over the crowds, they stoned Paul and dragged him outside
the city, thinking that he was dead. But when the disciples gathered 20
round him, he got up and re-entered the city.

DERBE AND THE RETURN JOURNEY

The next day he set out with Barnabas for Derbe. After preaching 21
the Good News to that city and making many disciples, they returned
to Lystra and Iconium and Antioch, reassuring the disciples, and 22
exhorting them to continue in their faith, and reminding them that
through many tribulations we must enter the kingdom of God.
When, with imposition of hands, they had appointed presbyters 23
for them in each congregation after prayer and fasting, they commended them to the Lord in whom they had believed. Crossing 24
Pisidia they came to Pamphylia, and after speaking the word of the 25
Lord in Perge they went down to Attalia, and from there they sailed 26
back to Antioch, where they had been entrusted to the grace of
God for the work which they had now accomplished. On their 27
arrival they called the congregation together and reported all that
God had done with them, and how he had opened to the Gentiles
access to the faith. There they stayed no little time with the disciples. 28

CHAPTER 15

MEETING AT JERUSALEM

Some people came down from Judea and began to teach the 1
brothers: "Unless you are circumcised in accordance with the Law
of Moses, you cannot be saved." When no little dispute and con- 2
troversy arose, with Paul and Barnabas opposing them, it was decided
that Paul and Barnabas and some other representatives should go
up to the apostles and presbyters at Jerusalem to consult about this
question. So they were sped on their way by the congregation, and 3
as they passed through Phoenicia and Samaria, they related the
conversion of the Gentiles. By this news they caused great rejoicing
among all the brothers. On arriving at Jerusalem they were wel- 4

15:2. *some other representatives*: perhaps of the other side of the controversy,
as is attested by some manuscripts which read: "some of the other side."

comed by the congregation and the apostles and the presbyters, to whom they proclaimed all that God had done, working with them.

5 But some of the Pharisee sect who had accepted the faith stood up and said, "These converts must be circumcised and also be told to observe the Law of Moses."

6 So the apostles and presbyters had a meeting to look into this
7 matter. After a long debate Peter stood up and addressed the meeting, "Brothers, you know that some time ago God saw fit in your midst to have the Gentiles hear the word of God from my lips
8 and believe. God, who knows the heart, bore witness in their favor
9 by giving them the Holy Spirit just as he did to us. He made no distinction between them and us, but cleansed their hearts by faith.
10 Why then do you try now to test God by putting on the disciples' neck a yoke which neither our fathers nor we have been able to bear?
11 On the contrary we believe that we are saved through the grace of our Lord Jesus, just as they are."

12 Then the whole meeting became silent, and listened while Barnabas and Paul told of the great signs and wonders God had done among the Gentiles through them.

13 After they had finished speaking James expressed his opinion as
14 follows, "Brothers, listen to me. Symeon has told how God for the first time visited the Gentiles to take from among them a people
15 consecrated to his name. And with this the words of the prophets agree, as it is written:

16   'After these things I will return
           And will rebuild the tabernacle of David
              which has fallen down,
            and the ruins thereof I will rebuild,
            and I will set it up again,
17   That the rest of mankind may seek after the Lord,
           even all the nations on whom my name
            is invoked,

15:10. *which neither . . . to bear:* St. Peter has in mind the Law as interpreted by the rabbis who had added countless restrictions, though in itself the Law imposed burdens which were hard to bear. St. Chrysostom points out how this doctrine is in perfect accord with that of St. Paul in the Epistle to the Romans.

15:14. Here and in 2 Pet. 1:1, the Hebrew name Symeon is used instead of the Greek form "Simon."

15:16. Amos 9:11.

says the Lord, who does these things.'

'To the Lord was his own work known   18
    from the beginning of the world.'

Therefore in my opinion we ought not to disquiet those who from   19
among the Gentiles are turning to God, but to send them written   20
instructions to abstain from anything that has been contaminated
by idols and from immorality and from anything strangled and from
blood. For Moses ever since generations long past has had his   21
preachers in every city in the synagogues, where he is read aloud
every Sabbath.

THE LETTER SENT TO ANTIOCH

Then the apostles and the presbyters with the whole assembly   22
decided to select representatives and send them to Antioch with
Paul and Barnabas. These representatives were Judas, surnamed
Barsabbas, and Silas, leading men among the brothers. They were   23
bearers of the following letter:

"The brothers who are apostles and presbyters send greetings to
the brothers of Gentile origin in Antioch and Syria and Cilicia. As   24
we have heard that some of our number have gone out without any
instructions from us, and have disturbed you with their teaching,
unsettling your minds, we have, after reaching a unanimous decision,   25
determined to select representatives and send them to you with our
beloved Barnabas and Paul — men who have exposed their lives   26
for the name of our Lord Jesus Christ. We, therefore, send Judas   27
and Silas, who themselves by word of mouth will give you the same
message. It is that the Holy Spirit and we have decided to lay no   28
further burden on you but this indispensable one, that you abstain   29
from things sacrificed to idols and from blood and from what is
strangled and from immorality. Keep yourselves from these things,
and you will do well. Farewell."

15:18. Isa. 45:21.

15:20. Idolatry and immorality were so widespread among the pagans that
a special warning was felt to be necessary for the new converts from among
the Gentiles. Some interpreters here understand *immorality* of marriages within
degrees of consanguinity forbidden by Lev. 18:6 ff.

15:21. The Jews of the Dispersion, well instructed in the Mosaic Law, would
find it hard to associate with those converts who did not observe the Mosaic
prescriptions on those points at least. This decree was largely disciplinary,
temporary, and local in application.

30   So the delegates went down to Antioch and, gathering the com-
31 munity together, they delivered the letter. When the faithful had
read it, they were delighted with the encouragement it gave them.
32 As Judas and Silas were God's inspired spokesmen, they exhorted
33 the brothers in a long address and strengthened them. After spending
some time there, the brothers bade them good-by with a greeting for
35 those who had sent them. Paul and Barnabas, however, stayed on at
Antioch, teaching and along with many others preaching the word
of the Lord.

THE SECOND MISSIONARY JOURNEY OF PAUL

PAUL CHOOSES A NEW PARTNER

36   After some days Paul said to Barnabas, "Let us return and visit
the brothers in all the cities where we have proclaimed the word
37 of the Lord, to see how they are doing." Barnabas wanted to take
38 with them John, who was surnamed Mark. Paul, however, judged it
proper that Mark, inasmuch as he had deserted them in Pamphylia
instead of going on with them to their work, should not again be
39 taken along. Then a sharp contention sprang up so that they separated from each other. Barnabas took Mark and sailed for Cyprus.
40 Paul chose Silas and set out commended by the brothers to the
41 grace of the Lord. He traveled through Syria and Cilicia where he
strengthened the congregations.

CHAPTER 16

PAUL TAKES TIMOTHY WITH HIM

1   He also came to Derbe and Lystra where there was a disciple
named Timothy, son of a believing Jewess and a Greek father.
2 Timothy was highly thought of by the brothers in Lystra and
3 Iconium. Paul desired to take this man with him, and so he himself
circumcised him because of the Jews who were in those parts, as they

---

15:33. Verse 34 is omitted by most of the Greek manuscripts and by the
best codices of the Vulgate. It reads: "Silas, however, decided to stay there,
and so Judas departed alone for Jerusalem."
15:41. Some few Greek manuscripts here add: "And commanded them to
keep the precepts of the apostles and presbyters."

all knew that his father was a Greek. As they passed through the 4
cities, they delivered to the brothers for their observance the decisions
arrived at by the apostles and presbyters in Jerusalem. So the con- 5
gregations grew stronger and stronger in the faith and daily increased
in numbers.

THE HOLY SPIRIT GUIDES PAUL TO MACEDONIA

They passed through Phrygia and the Galatian country, because 6
they had been forbidden by the Holy Spirit to speak the word in the
province of Asia. When they came to the frontier of Mysia, they 7
tried to enter Bithynia, but the Spirit of Jesus did not permit them.
So passing along the frontier of Mysia, they went down to Troas. 8
There Paul had a vision one night: a Macedonian was standing, 9
appealing to him in the words, "Come over into Macedonia and
help us." As soon as he had the vision, we forthwith made efforts 10
to set out for Macedonia, concluding that God had called us to
bring the Good News to its people.

THE EVENTS AT PHILIPPI

So sailing from Troas, we ran a straight course to Samothrace and 11
the next day to Neapolis, and from there to Philippi, a leading city 12
of the district of Macedonia, a Roman colony. We stayed some
days in this city, and on the Sabbath we went outside the gate to 13
the bank of the river where we thought there was a place of prayer.
Sitting down we spoke to the women who had gathered there. A 14
certain woman named Lydia, a dealer in purple from the city of
Thyatira, who worshiped God, was listening. The Lord opened her
heart to give close attention to what Paul was saying. When she and 15
her household had been baptized, she urged us, saying, "Since you
have judged me to be a believer in the Lord, come to my home
and stay there." And she insisted on our coming.

Now it happened as we were going to the place of prayer that we 16
came on a girl who had a divining spirit and brought her masters

---

16:10. we: St. Luke, author of Acts, is now accompanying St. Paul.

16:12. a leading city: probably certain cities were given the title "first"
or "leading" in the sense of "important." The exact meaning of the expression
is doubtful.

colony: a group of citizens regularly organized and sent to occupy a city
or part of a city in virtue of a special law or imperial decree. The city thus
occupied was designated as a colony (Jacquier).

17 much profit from fortunetelling. She followed Paul and ourselves
and kept crying out, "These men are servants of the most high God
18 and they proclaim to you a way of salvation." This she did for
many days, until Paul, very much annoyed, turned to the spirit
and said, "I order you in the name of Jesus Christ to depart from
her." And it went out at that very moment.

PAUL AND SILAS ARE ARRESTED

19   On seeing that their hope of profit was gone, her masters seized
Paul and Silas and dragged them into the market place to the
20 authorities. They brought them to the praetors with the words,
"These men are making a great disturbance in our city. They are
21 Jews and are advocates of practices which it is against the law for
22 us to adopt or observe, because we are Romans." The people too
joined in the attack against Paul and Silas, and the praetors had them
23 stripped and ordered them to be beaten with rods. After inflicting
many strokes on them, they cast them into prison, charging the
24 jailer to guard them carefully. On receiving such orders, he cast
them into the inner prison and secured their feet in the stocks.
25   At midnight Paul and Silas were praying and singing the praises
26 of God, while the prisoners were listening to them. Suddenly there
was such a great earthquake that the foundations of the prison were
shaken. At once all the doors flew open, and everyone's chains were
27 unfastened. The jailer, roused from sleep and seeing that the prison
doors were open, drew his sword and was about to kill himself,
28 because he thought that the prisoners had escaped. But Paul
shouted in a loud voice, "Do yourself no harm; we are all here."
29 Then calling for a light, the jailer rushed in and trembling all over
30 fell before Paul and Silas in reverence. Then he brought them out
31 and exclaimed, "Gentlemen, what must I do to be saved?" "Believe
in the Lord Jesus," they replied, "and you and your household shall
32 be saved." Paul and Silas spoke the word of the Lord to him and to
33 all that were in his household. Then at that very hour of the night
the jailer took personal charge of them and washed their wounds.
34 Then and there he and his family were baptized. Taking Paul and
Silas upstairs, he put food before them, and rejoiced with all his
household over his faith in God.

PAUL AND SILAS ARE RELEASED

At daybreak the praetors sent their lictors with the instructions, 35
"Let these men go." The jailer reported these words to Paul, "The 36
praetors have sent word that you are to be released. So come out
right away and go your way in peace." But Paul said to them, 37
"Although we are Roman citizens, publicly they have beaten us and
cast us into prison, and that without trial. Secretly now they are
going to get rid of us. Not at all, but let them come themselves,
and lead us out." The lictors reported these words to the praetors, 38
who on hearing that Paul and Silas were Roman citizens were
alarmed, and came to appeal to them. Leading them out, they begged 39
them to leave the city. On leaving the prison they went to Lydia's 40
home and after seeing and consoling the brothers, they departed.

Chapter 17

THE UPROAR AT THESSALONICA

After passing through Amphipolis and Apollonia, they came to 1
Thessalonica, where there was a synagogue of the Jews. As was his 2
custom, Paul went into their meeting and for three Sabbaths reasoned
with them from the Scriptures, explaining them and showing that 3
the Christ had to suffer and rise from the dead, and that this is
the Christ, "the Jesus whom I proclaim to you." Some of them 4
were won over and were allotted to Paul and Silas, along with a
large number of the worshiping Greeks and not a few women of
rank. But the Jews, moved with jealousy, enlisted the aid of some 5
base loafers, and forming a mob, set the city in an uproar. They
attacked Jason's home and sought to bring Paul and Silas out to
the people. When they failed to find them, they dragged Jason 6
and some brothers before the magistrates of the city, shouting,
"These men who are setting the world in an uproar have come here
too, and Jason has given them hospitality; yet they are all acting 7
contrary to the decrees of Caesar by saying that there is another
king, Jesus." When they heard this the people and the magistrates 8
of the city were aroused, but they accepted bail from Jason and the 9
rest, and let them go.

THEIR STAY AT BERAEA INTERRUPTED

10   The brothers at once sent Paul and Silas away by night to Beraea, and on their arrival they went to the synagogue of the Jews.
11 As these were of a nobler character than those of Thessalonica, they received the word with great eagerness, studying the Scriptures
12 daily to see whether these things were so. Many of them became believers, and so did no small number of prominent Greeks, women
13 and men. But when the Jews in Thessalonica found out that in Beraea too the word of God had been preached by Paul, they came
14 there to stir up and excite the crowds. Then at once the brothers sent forth Paul on his way to the sea, while Silas and Timothy
15 remained there. Those who escorted Paul took him as far as Athens, and returned with instructions from him to Silas and Timothy to rejoin him as soon as possible.

PAUL PREACHES IN ATHENS

16   Now while Paul was waiting for them at Athens, his soul was exasperated on seeing how the city was wholly given to idolatry.
17 He had discussions in the synagogue with the Jews and those that worshiped God, and in the market place every day with those who
18 happened to be there. Some of the Epicurean and Stoic philosophers debated with him. "What is this babbler trying to say," said some, while others said, "He seems to be a herald of strange gods," because he proclaimed to them the Good News about Jesus and the
19 resurrection. They took him and brought him to the Areopagus, saying, "May we know just what is this new doctrine you are
20 teaching? You certainly bring some strange ideas to our ears. We
21 wish, therefore, to know what these ideas mean." (The Athenians in general and the visitors there from abroad used to spend all their leisure telling or listening to the latest news.)

17:18. *babbler:* perhaps a slang expression current in Athens when St. Paul was there, and overheard by St. Luke. The term could mean "beggar," "ignoramus," "plagiarist." It certainly denotes contempt and insolence, as St. Chrysostom remarks.

resurrection: in Greek: *Anastasis,* a feminine noun which St. Paul's audience seems to have mistaken for the name of a goddess.

17:19. *Areopagus:* the hill of Mars, where the council called the "Areopagus" held its meetings.

17:21. *news:* most probably in the realm of philosophical speculation.

Then Paul stood up in the midst of the Areopagus, and said, 22
"Men of Athens, I see that in every respect you are remarkably
religious. For as I was going about and observing objects of your 23
worship, I found an altar with this inscription: 'To the unknown
God.' What, therefore, you worship unknowingly, I make known
to you. God, who made the world and all that is in it, since he is 24
Lord of heaven and earth, does not dwell in temples built by hands,
neither is he served by human hands as though he were in need of 25
anything, since it is he who gave to all men life and breath and
all things. From one man he has created the whole human race 26
and made them live everywhere on the face of the earth, determining
their seasons and the boundaries of their lands, that they should 27
seek God and perhaps find him as they grope after him, though he
is not far from anyone of us. For in him we live and move and 28
have our being, as indeed some of your own poets have said,

'For we are also his offspring.'

If therefore we are the offspring of God, we ought not to imagine 29
that the Divinity is like to gold or silver or stone, to an image graven
by human art and thought. The time of this ignorance, God, it is 30
true, viewed with indulgence, but now he calls on all men everywhere to have a change of mind and heart, inasmuch as he has 31
fixed a day on which he will judge the world with justice through
a Man whom he has appointed. He has given proof of this to all
by raising him from the dead."

Now when they heard of a resurrection of the dead, some began 32
to sneer, while others said, "We shall hear you again on this matter."
So Paul departed from their midst. Some men, however, joined him 33, 34
and became believers, among whom were Dionysius the Areopagite
and a woman named Damaris, and others with them.

17:23. unknown God: any god whom the Greeks might otherwise have neglected. St. Paul takes the expression and applies it to the true God whom in
fact the Athenians did not know. Tertullian and St. Jerome testify to the
existence of such an altar at Athens.

17:24. does not dwell: i.e., "is not confined to."

17:28. The citation may be from Aratus. Cleanthus and Epimenides have
similar words.

CHAPTER 18

PAUL COMES TO CORINTH

1, 2　　After this Paul left Athens and came to Corinth. There he found a Jew named Aquila, a native of Pontus, who had recently come from Italy with Priscilla, his wife, because Claudius had ordered all Jews
3　to leave Rome. Paul visited them, and as he was of the same trade, he stayed with them and went to work for they were tentmakers
4　by trade. He would preach in the synagogue every Sabbath, and
5　try to convince the Jews and Greeks. But when Silas and Timothy arrived from Macedonia, Paul was wholly occupied with preaching,
6　emphatically assuring the Jews that Jesus is the Christ. But as they contradicted and abused him, he shook the dust from his clothes and said to them, "The loss of your souls is your own responsibility; I am not to blame. From now on I will go to the Gentiles."
7　　Leaving there he went to the home of a man named Titius Justus, which adjoined the synagogue. He was a worshiper of God.
8　Crispus, the president of the synagogue, believed in the Lord and so did all his household. Many of the Corinthians also, on hearing
9　Paul, believed and were baptized. One night the Lord said to Paul
10　in a vision, "Do not fear, but speak. Do not be silent, because I am with you and no one shall lay a hand on you to harm you, for I
11　have many people in this city." So he settled there for a year and six months, teaching the word of God among them.
12　　During Gallio's term as proconsul of Achaia the Jews made a
13　concerted attack on Paul and took him before the court. "This fellow," they said, "contrary to the Law is persuading men to worship
14　God." Just as Paul was about to open his mouth, Gallio said to the Jews, "If there were some question of misdemeanor or serious
15　crime, O Jews, I should with reason bear with you. But if these are questions about words or names or your Law, look to it yourselves.
16　I have no desire to decide such matters. With that he drove them
17　from the court. Then all the Greeks seized Sosthenes, the president of the synagogue, and beat him in front of the court, but Gallio paid no attention to these disorders.

346

RETURN JOURNEY TO ANTIOCH

Paul, after staying there a long time, took leave of the brothers 18
and sailed for Syria with Priscilla and Aquila. At Cenchrae Paul had
his head shaved because of a vow he had made. They arrived at 19
Ephesus and there they left him. He himself entered the synagogue
and had a discussion with the Jews. But when they begged him 20
to stay some time longer, he did not consent, but bade them farewell, 21
saying, "I will come back to you, God willing." He put to sea from
Ephesus, and landing at Caesarea, he went up to pay his respects 22
to the congregation and then went down to Antioch.

THE THIRD MISSIONARY JOURNEY OF PAUL

APOLLOS AT EPHESUS

After spending some time there he departed, and traveled through 23
the Galatian country and Phrygia in turn, strengthening all the
disciples.

Now a Jew named Apollos, a native of Alexandria, came to 24
Ephesus. He was an eloquent man and well versed in the Scriptures.
He had been instructed in the way of the Lord, and being fervent 25
in spirit, used to speak and teach accurately whatever had to do
with Jesus, though he knew only John's baptism. This man, there- 26
fore, set himself to speak with firm assurance in the synagogue, and,
on hearing him, Priscilla and Aquila took him home and expounded
the Way of God to him more precisely. As he wanted to cross over 27
to Achaia, the brothers encouraged him and wrote to the disciples
to welcome him. On his arrival there he was of great service by his
gift to those who had believed, for he vigorously refuted the Jews 28
in public and showed them from the Scriptures that Jesus is the
Christ.

CHAPTER 19

PAUL ARRIVES AT EPHESUS

Now it was while Apollos was in Corinth that Paul, after passing 1
through the upper districts, came to Ephesus and found certain

18:18. The vow here referred to may have been the Nazarite vow in an
attenuated form. See Num. 6:2–5.
18:22. *went up:* most probably to Jerusalem.

347

2 disciples. "Did you," he asked them, "receive the Holy Spirit when you became believers?" They replied, "We have not even heard
3 that there is a Holy Spirit." "What kind of baptism then did you
4 receive?" asked Paul. They replied, "John's." "John baptized the people," Paul answered, "with a baptism of repentance, telling them to believe in him who was to come after him, that is, in Jesus."
5 On hearing this they were baptized in the name of the Lord Jesus,
6 and when Paul laid his hands on them, the Holy Spirit came on
7 them, and they began to speak in tongues and to prophesy. These men numbered about twelve in all.

8 For three months Paul went to the synagogue and spoke with firm assurance, holding discussion and trying to persuade the people
9 about the kingdom of God. But when some became obstinate and, speaking evil of the Way in the presence of the gathering, refused to believe, he abandoned them and withdrew his disciples from them
10 to hold daily discussions in the school of one Tyrannus. This went on for two years, so that all who lived in the province of Asia, both
11 Jews and Greeks, heard the word of the Lord. Meanwhile God
12 worked more than the usual miracles by the hand of Paul, so that even handkerchiefs and aprons were carried from his body to the sick, and the diseases left them and evil spirits departed.

THE JEWISH EXORCISTS PUNISHED

13 Some itinerant Jews, exorcists, also attempted to invoke the name of the Lord Jesus over those who were possessed by evil spirits, using the words, "I adjure you by the Jesus whom Paul preaches."
14 Sceva, a Jewish high priest, had seven sons who were doing this.
15 "Jesus I know," the evil spirit answered, "and Paul I am acquainted
16 with, but who are you?" And the man in whom the evil spirit dwelt sprang at them and overpowered them both with such violence that they fled from the house tattered and bruised.
17 This event became known to all the Jews and Greeks living in Ephesus, so that fear fell on them all, and the name of the Lord
18 Jesus came to be held in high honor. Many too of those who believed

---

19:14. *Jewish high priest:* must mean here "of high-priestly family."
19:16. them both: perhaps only two of the seven sons were actively engaged on this occasion. It is not unlikely, however, that the word here translated *both* may have meant "all" or "all together" in the usage of St. Luke's time. So Zorrell.

came and openly confessed their practices. Many who had practiced 19
magical arts collected their books and burned them publicly. The cost
of these books was estimated and was found to be fifty thousand
pieces of silver. Thus mightily did the word of the Lord spread 20
and prevail.

After these events Paul made up his mind to pass through Mace- 21
donia and Achaia en route to Jerusalem, saying, "After I have been
there, I must also visit Rome." So he sent two of his assistants, 22
Timothy and Erastus, to Macedonia, while he himself stayed on for
some time in the province of Asia.

THE RIOT AT EPHESUS

Just at this time there arose no small commotion because of the 23
Way. A silversmith named Demetrius, by making silver shrines of 24
Diana, brought no small gain to the craftsmen. These he assembled 25
together with workmen of like occupation, and said, "Men, you
know that our prosperity comes from this trade, and you see and 26
hear that not only at Ephesus, but almost over the whole province
of Asia, this man Paul has persuaded and turned away numbers of
people with the statement, 'Gods made by human hands are not
gods at all.' Not only is there danger that this business of ours 27
will be discredited, but also that the temple of the great Diana
will be regarded as worthless, and even she whom all Asia and the
wide world worship will be shorn of her majestic rank." On hearing 28
this they were filled with wrath and shouted, "Great is Diana of
the Ephesians."

So confusion spread all over the city, and the people rushed 29
by a common impulse into the theater, dragging along the Macedonians, Gaius and Aristarchus, Paul's traveling companions. Then 30
Paul was minded to enter the crowd, but his disciples would not
let him. Some of the Asiarchs, who were his friends, sent a plea 31
to him not to venture into the theater. Meanwhile some were shout- 32
ing one thing and some another, for the assembly was in confusion
as most of them did not know why they had gathered together.

19:19. *their books:* those containing magical formulas.
19:29. *theater:* the large open-air assembly place.
19:31. *Asiarchs:* officers in charge of the religious feasts and of certain other
matters in the province of Asia.

33 Then some brought out of the crowd Alexander, whom the Jews
had been pushing forward. Alexander, motioning with his hand for
34 silence, wanted to give an explanation to the people. But as soon
as they recognized that he was a Jew, they all with one voice shouted
for almost two hours, "Great is Diana of the Ephesians."
35 When the town clerk quieted the crowd, he said, "Ephesians,
what man does not know that the city of Ephesus is warden of
the great Diana's temple and of her statue which fell from heaven.
36 Since, therefore, this is undeniable, you ought to be calm and do
37 nothing rash. For you have brought these men here who are neither
38 guilty of sacrilege nor blasphemers of our goddess. Therefore, if
Demetrius and the craftsmen with him have a complaint against
anyone, court days are held and there are proconsuls. Let them take
39 action against one another. If you require anything further, it shall
40 be settled in the lawful assembly. Why, we are even in danger
of being accused of riot over today's uproar, since there is no reason
we can give for it." With this he dismissed the assembly.

CHAPTER 20

PAUL FORCED TO LEAVE EPHESUS

1 When the riot had subsided, Paul sent for the disciples and
encouraged them. Then he took leave of them and started for
2 Macedonia. After traveling through those districts and giving them
3 much encouragement, he came to Greece. When he had spent
three months there and was about to sail for Syria, a plot was laid
against him by the Jews. So he resolved to return through Macedonia.
4 He had as companions Sopater of Beraea, the son of Pyrrhus,
Aristarchus and Secundus of the Thessalonians, Gaius of Derbe and
Timothy, and Tychicus and Trophimus of the province of Asia.
5 These having gone on in advance waited for us at Troas,
6 while we sailed from Philippi after the days of the Unleavened
Bread, and five days later joined them at Troas, where we stayed
seven days.

19:35. town clerk: the chief local official. which fell: it was supposed that
the statue of Diana had fallen from heaven.

FROM TROAS TO MILETUS

On the first day of the week, when we had met for the breaking 7
of bread, Paul addressed them. Since he was to leave the next
morning, he prolonged his address until midnight. There were many 8
lamps in the upper room where we were assembled. A youth named 9
Eutychus sitting at a window was overcome with drowsiness and,
as Paul addressed them at great length, the lad went fast asleep
and fell down from the third story to the ground and was picked
up dead. Paul went down and laid himself on him, and embracing 10
him said, "Do not be alarmed; life is still in him." Then he went 11
up and broke bread and ate, and having spoken to them a good
while, he finally departed. They took the lad away alive and were 12
not a little comforted.

We went ahead by ship and sailed for Assos, intending to take 13
Paul on board there. That was the arrangement he had made, as
he intended to travel that far by land. So when he met us at Assos, 14
we took him on board and came to Mitylene. Sailing from there we 15
arrived on the following day off Chios; the next day we made
Samos and the day after we reached Miletus. Paul had decided to 16
sail past Ephesus, lest he spend much time in the province of Asia,
for he was hurrying on so that he might, if he possibly could, reach
Jerusalem by the day of Pentecost.

PAUL'S FAREWELL TO THE EPHESIAN PRESBYTERS

From Miletus, however, he sent to Ephesus for the presbyters 17
of the congregation, and when they had come to him, he said to 18
them, "You know in what manner I have lived with you the whole
time since the first day that I set foot in the province of Asia,
serving the Lord with all humility and with tears and in trials that 19
befell me because of the plots of the Jews; how I have kept back 20
nothing that was for your good, but have declared it to you and
taught you in public and from house to house, urging Jews and 21
Greeks to turn to God with a change of heart and to believe in
our Lord Jesus Christ. And now I am going to Jerusalem under 22
spiritual compulsion, not knowing what will happen to me there,

---

20:7. *the first day of the week:* Sunday had replaced the Sabbath (Saturday)
as the principal day of worship. "It was," as St. Chrysostom remarks, "the
Lord's Day." *breaking of bread:* the Holy Eucharist, celebrated in the evening.

23   except that in every city the Holy Spirit assures me that imprison-
24   ment and persecution are awaiting me. But I count my life as nothing
     nor do I hold it as precious to myself, if only I accomplish my course
     and the ministry that I have received from the Lord Jesus, to bear
     witness to the Good News about God's grace.

25   "And now, I know that none of you among whom I went about
26   preaching the kingdom will ever see my face again. Therefore I call
     you to witness this day that I have nothing with which to reproach
27   myself in regard to your salvation, for I have not shrunk from declar-
28   ing to you the whole design of God. Take heed to yourselves and
     to the whole flock in which the Holy Spirit has placed you as
     bishops to rule the Church of God, which he has purchased with
29   his own blood. I know that after my departure fierce wolves will
30   get in among you, and will not spare the flock. Even from among
     your own selves men will rise speaking perverse things to draw away
31   the disciples after them. Watch, therefore, and remember that for
     three years night and day I did not cease to admonish each one of
     you with tears.

32   "For the present I commend you to the Lord and to his gracious
     message. He has the power to build you up and give you your
33   inheritance among all who have been sanctified. I have coveted no
34   man's silver or gold or apparel. You yourselves know that these hands
     of mine have provided for my needs and those of my companions.
35   In all things I have shown you that by so toiling you ought to help
     the weak, mindful of the word of the Lord Jesus that he himself
     spoke, 'It is more blessed to give than to receive.'"

36   After he had said this, he knelt down and prayed with all of
37   them. They all wept much, embraced Paul and kissed him.
38   They were grieved most of all at his saying that they would see his
     face no more. Then they escorted him to the ship.

20:25. It seems probable from 1 Tim. 1:3 and 2 Tim. 4:20 that St. Paul did
visit Ephesus again. But when he spoke these words in view of the attempts
on his life and his projected journey to Italy and to Spain, he had no human
expectation of again returning to Ephesus.

20:35. The statement here ascribed to Jesus is in none of the canonical
Gospels. Paul may have had it from oral tradition or from a document now lost.

CHAPTER 21

FROM MILETUS TO TYRE

When we had parted from them and set sail, we made a straight 1
course and arrived at Cos, and the next day at Rhodes, and from
there reached Patara. Here we found a ship crossing over to 2
Phoenicia, which we boarded and set sail. After sighting Cyprus 3
and leaving it on the left, we sailed for Syria and landed at Tyre,
as the ship was to unload her cargo there. Having searched out the 4
disciples, we stayed there seven days. Through the Spirit's direction
they told Paul not to go to Jerusalem. But when our time was up 5
we went our way, and all of them with their wives and children
escorted us until we had arrived outside the city. Then we knelt
down on the shore and prayed. After having said farewell to one 6
another, we boarded the ship, and they went home.

FROM TYRE TO JERUSALEM

After completing the voyage from Tyre, we landed at Ptolemais 7
where we greeted the brothers and spent a day with them. The next 8
day we departed and came to Caesarea, where we went to the house
of Philip the evangelist, one of the seven, and stayed with him.
He had four virgin daughters who were gifted with inspired speech. 9
While we were staying on there for some days, a certain inspired 10
spokesman named Agabus came down from Jerusalem. Approaching 11
us and taking Paul's girdle, he bound his own feet and hands with
the words, "Thus says the Holy Spirit, 'The man whose girdle this
is the Jews will bind like this at Jerusalem, and they will deliver
him over to the power of the Gentiles.'" On hearing this, we our- 12
selves and the people there begged Paul not to go to Jerusalem.
But Paul remonstrated with the words, "What do you mean by 13
weeping and breaking my heart? Why, I am ready not only to be
bound but even to die at Jerusalem for the name of the Lord
Jesus." When we could not dissuade him, we acquiesced and said, 14
"The Lord's will be done." After this we made our preparations 15

21:4. *told:* they learned through the Spirit that trials awaited Paul but it
was their own affection which prompted them to beg him not to go to
Jerusalem.

16 and went our way to Jerusalem. Some of the disciples from Caesarea
    went with us, bringing with them Mnason, a Cypriot, an early
    disciple, whose guests we were to be.

The Imprisonment of Paul in Palestine

JERUSALEM

17 On our arrival at Jerusalem the brothers gave us a hearty welcome.
18 The next day Paul went with us to James, and all the presbyters
19 gathered. After greeting them, Paul related in detail what God had
    done among the Gentiles through his ministry.

20   The presbyters praised God when they heard Paul's report and
    said to him, "You see, brother, how many thousands of believers
    there are among the Jews, all of them zealous upholders of the
21 Law. Now, they have heard about you that you teach the Jews who
    live among the Gentiles to depart from Moses, advising them that
    they should not circumcise their children or observe the customs.
22 What then is to be done? They will surely hear that you have
23 arrived. So do what we tell you. We have four men who are bound
24 by vow. Take them and purify yourself along with them, and pay
    their expenses that they may shave their heads. Then everybody
    will know that what they have heard about you is false, but that
25 you too in your actions observe the Law. But as for the Gentile
    believers, we ourselves have written our decision that they abstain
    from what has been sacrificed to idols and from blood and from
    what is strangled and from immorality."
26   Then Paul joined the men, and the next day after being
    purified along with them he entered the temple and announced
    the completion of the days of purification, when the sacrifice was
    to be offered for each of them.

THE RIOT IN THE TEMPLE

27   When the seven days were almost over, the Jews from the
    province of Asia, seeing him in the temple, stirred up all the people
28 and seized him, shouting, "Men of Israel, help! This is the man

---

21:18. *James:* the same as in 12:17 and 15:13.
21:24. Num. 6:18.
21:28. Only Jews were permitted to enter certain parts of the temple area.

who teaches everybody everywhere what is counter to the people
and the Law and this place, and in addition to all that he has even
brought Greeks into the temple, thus desecrating this holy place."
They had seen Trophimus, the Ephesian, in the city with Paul 29
and had supposed that Paul had taken him into the temple. The 30
whole city was thrown into confusion. The people ran together,
and, seizing Paul, proceeded to drag him out of the temple. Immediately the doors were shut.

PAUL'S ARREST

They were trying to kill him when word was brought to the 31
tribune of the cohort that all Jerusalem was in an uproar. He 32
immediately took soldiers and centurions and ran up to the mob.
When they saw the tribune and the soldiers, they stopped beating
Paul. Then the tribune came up, had Paul arrested, and gave orders 33
for him to be bound with two chains. When he inquired who Paul
was and what he had been doing, some of the crowd shouted one 34
thing, some another, and as the tribune could not learn anything
certain on account of the uproar, he ordered Paul to be taken into
the barracks. Because of the violence of the mob, it happened that 35
by the time they reached the steps Paul was actually being carried
by the soldiers, while the mob of people followed, shouting, 36
"Kill him!"

As Paul was about to be taken into the barracks, he said to the 37
tribune, "May I have a word with you?" He answered, "Do you
speak Greek? Are you not the Egyptian who recently stirred up 38
that sedition and led four thousand assassins out to the desert?"
"I am a Jew from Tarsus in Cilicia," replied Paul, "a citizen of no 39
mean city. I beg you, give me leave to speak to the people."

PAUL TALKS TO THE PEOPLE

The tribune gave him leave, and Paul, standing on the steps, 40
motioned with his hand to the people, and when they had become
fairly quiet, he addressed them in Hebrew:

CHAPTER 22

"Brothers and fathers, listen to what I have to say to you in 1
my defense."

2   When they heard him speaking Hebrew, they became still more
3 quiet. He continued:

    "I am a Jew, born at Tarsus in Cilicia, brought up here in this
city, instructed at the feet of Gamaliel according to the strict
acceptation of the Law of our Fathers. I was zealous for God just
4 as all of you are today. I persecuted this Way even to the death,
5 binding and committing to prison both men and women, as the
high priest and all the assembly of the elders can bear me witness.
In fact I received letters from them to the brothers, and I was on
my way to Damascus to bring back in chains to Jerusalem for
punishment those who were there.

THE STORY OF HIS CONVERSION

6   "It happened that, as I was on my way near Damascus, suddenly
about noon there shone round about me a great light in the sky,
7 and I fell to the ground and heard a voice saying to me, " 'Saul,
8 Saul, why do you persecute me?' 'Who are you, Lord?' I answered.
He said to me, 'I am Jesus of Nazareth whom you are persecuting.'
9 My companions saw the light but they did not understand him
10 that spoke to me. 'What shall I do, Lord?' I asked. The Lord said
to me, 'Get up and go into Damascus, and there you shall be told
11 of all that you are destined to do.' As I could not see for the
dazzling light, my companions had to lead me by the hand, and
so I reached Damascus.

12   "Now a certain Ananias, an observer of the Law, respected by
13 all the Jews living there, came to me, and standing beside me said
to me, 'Brother Saul, regain your sight.' And instantly I regained
14 my sight and looked at him. 'The God of our fathers,' he said,
'has appointed you beforehand to learn his will and to see the Just
15 One and to hear the statement from his mouth that you are to be
16 his witness before all men of what you have seen and heard. And
now why delay? Get up and have yourself baptized and your sins
washed away, after you have invoked the Lord's name.'

17   "It happened that when I had returned to Jerusalem and was
18 praying in the temple I was in an ecstasy and saw Jesus as he said
to me, 'Get out of Jerusalem quickly; the people here are not going
19 to receive your testimony concerning me.' But I remonstrated,

---

22:4. Way: the Christian manner of life.

'Lord, they themselves know that I used to imprison and beat in synagogue after synagogue those who believed in you, and when the 20 blood of Stephen, your witness, was shed, I was standing by and approved. I took charge of the garments of those who killed him.' 'Go,' he said to me, 'as it is my will to send you to the Gentiles 21 far away.'"

PAUL INVOKES HIS ROMAN CITIZENSHIP

Now till he said this they listened to him, but then they raised 22 their voice and shouted, "Away from the earth with a man like that, because it is not right that he should live." As they were shouting 23 and throwing off their garments and casting dust into the air, the 24 tribune ordered Paul to be taken to the barracks and to be examined under the scourge to find out why the people shouted so against him.

When they had stretched him out for the scourges, Paul said 25 to the centurion who was standing by, "Is it legal for you to scourge a Roman, and that without trial?" When the centurion heard this, 26 he went to the tribune and reported, "What are you about to do? This man is a Roman citizen!" Then the tribune came and said to 27 Paul, "Tell me, are you a Roman?" "Yes," replied Paul. The tribune 28 answered, "I obtained this citizenship at a great price." "I," said Paul, "am more than that — a citizen by birth." At once, therefore, 29 those who were about to torture him drew back from him. Even the tribune was alarmed to find that Paul was a Roman citizen and because he had bound him.

PAUL ADDRESSES THE SANHEDRIN

The next day as he wished to find out the real reason why 30 Paul was accused by the Jews, the tribune removed the prisoner's chains and ordered the priests and all the Sanhedrin to assemble. He brought Paul and placed him before them.

CHAPTER 23

Then Paul, looking steadily at the Sanhedrin, said, "Brothers, 1 I have conducted myself before God with a perfectly good con-

2 science up to this day." The high priest Ananias ordered those who
3 were standing by Paul to strike him on the mouth. Then Paul
said to him, "God will certainly strike you, you whitewashed wall!
Do you sit there to try me according to the Law, and in violation
4 of the Law order me to be struck?" The bystanders said, "Do you
5 insult God's high priest?" "I did not know, brothers," replied
Paul, "that he was the high priest, for it is written, 'You shall speak
no evil of a ruler of your people.' "

6 Then Paul, aware that some of them were Sadducees and others
Pharisees cried out in the Sanhedrin, "Brothers, I am a Pharisee,
a son of Pharisees. It is about the hope of the resurrection of the
7 dead that I am on trial." When he said that, there arose a dispute
between the Pharisees and the Sadducees, so that the crowd was
8 divided. For the Sadducees say that there is no resurrection and
that there are no angels or spirits, whereas the Pharisees believe in
9 both. So there was a great uproar, and some of the Scribes of the
party of the Pharisees got up and contended fiercely, "We find no
evil in this man. What if a spirit has really spoken to him, or an
10 angel?" As the dispute was becoming violent, the tribune, fearing
lest Paul should be torn to pieces by them, ordered the troops to
come and take him by force from among them and bring him into
11 the barracks. On the following night the Lord stood by Paul and
said, "Be steadfast, for just as you have borne witness to me in
Jerusalem, so also must you bear witness in Rome."

A PLOT AGAINST PAUL

12 When day broke the Jews assembled and bound themselves under
a curse, swearing that they would neither eat nor drink until they
13 had killed Paul. There were more than forty that had made this
14 pact. They went to the chief priests and elders and said, "We have
bound ourselves under a great curse to taste nothing until we have
15 killed Paul. Now, therefore, do you, with the Sanhedrin, suggest
to the tribune that he bring Paul to you as though you mean to
look into his case more carefully, but we are ready to kill him before
he gets here."

23:2. Ananias: high priest from A.D. 47 to 59.
23:3. whitewashed wall: with a thin coating of white to hide its ugliness, or
perhaps in the sense of the "whited sepulchers" of Mt. 23:27.
23:5. Exod. 22:28.

The son of Paul's sister heard of the ambush, came and entered 16
the barracks to tell Paul. Paul called one of the centurions to him 17
and said, "Take this young man to the tribune, for he has something to report to him." So the centurion took him to the tribune 18
and said, "The prisoner Paul called me and asked me to bring this
young man to you, for he has something to say to you." So the 19
tribune took him by the hand, and withdrawing, asked him privately,
"What is it you have to tell me?" "The Jews," he replied, "have 20
agreed to ask you to bring Paul to the Sanhedrin tomorrow, on
the plea that they intend to have a more thorough investigation made
into his case. But do not believe them, for more than forty of them 21
are lying in wait for him, having bound themselves under a curse
not to eat or drink, until they have killed him. At this moment they
are ready, waiting your consent."

PAUL TAKEN TO CAESAREA

The tribune then let the young man go, charging him not to 22
divulge to anyone that "you have given me this information." Then 23
he called two centurions and said to them, "By nine o'clock tonight
get ready two hundred soldiers, seventy cavalry, and two hundred
spearmen to go as far as Caesarea, and provide horses to mount 24
Paul and conduct him safely to Felix the governor."

He wrote a letter in these terms: "Claudius Lysias to His Excel- 25, 26
lency, Felix the governor, greeting. Whereas this man had been 27
seized by the Jews and was on the point of being killed by them, I
came on them with the troops and rescued him, having learned that
he was a Roman citizen. Since I wanted to know what charge they 28
had preferred against him, I took him down into their Sanhedrin.
I found him accused about questions of their Law, but of no charge 29
deserving death or imprisonment. When I was told that there was 30
an ambush against him, I immediately sent him to you, directing
his accusers to state the case before you. Farewell."

So the soldiers in accordance with their instructions took Paul 31
and conducted him by night to Antipatris. The next day they re- 32
turned to the barracks, leaving the cavalry to continue on with him.

23:24. The Vulgate in some manuscripts here adds: "For he was afraid that
the Jews might seize him by force and kill him, and he himself should afterwards be slandered as though he intended to receive money." These words form
verse 25 in the Clementine Vulgate.

33 When they reached Caesarea, they delivered the letter to the
34 governor and handed Paul over to him. On reading the letter he
asked from what province Paul came, and on learning that he was
35 from Cilicia, he said, "I will hear you when your accusers have come."
He ordered Paul to be kept in Herod's palace.

CHAPTER 24

PAUL TRIED BEFORE THE ROMAN GOVERNOR

1 Now five days later the high priest Ananias came with some of
the elders and one Tertullus, an attorney. They presented their case
2 against Paul before the governor. When Paul had been summoned,
Tertullus began to accuse him:

"Whereas we live in secure peace, thanks to you, and whereas
reforms for the good of the nation are in progress, due to your
3 foresight, we always and everywhere receive them, most excellent
4 Felix, with all thankfulness. But not to detain you too long, I
5 entreat you to be kind enough to grant us a brief hearing. We have
found this man a troublemaker and a promoter of seditions among
all the Jews throughout the whole world and a ringleader of the
6 Nazarene sect. He even tried to desecrate the temple, but we caught
8 him. By examining him yourself you will be able to discover all these
9 charges we lodge against him." The Jews also supported Tertullus
declaring that the charges were true.

10 Then when the governor nodded to him to speak, Paul answered,
"As I know that for many years you have been a judge for this
11 nation, I undertake my defense with good courage. You can take
as certain that it is not more than twelve days since I went to
12 Jerusalem to worship, and neither in the temple did they find me
disputing with anyone or creating a disturbance among the people,
13 nor in the synagogues, nor about the city. Neither can they prove
14 to you the charges that they now make against me. This I do admit
to you, that according to the Way, which they call a sect, so I
worship the God of my fathers, believing whatever is written in the

---

24:6. Between verses 6 and 8 the Vulgate and some few Greek manuscripts
add: "And wished to judge him according to our Law. But Lysias, the tribune,
came upon us and with great violence took him away out of our hands,
ordering his accusers to come to you." These words form verse 7 in the Vulgate.

Law and the Prophets, having the hope in God which these men   15
also look for, that there is to be a resurrection of the holy and the
unholy. For this reason too I strive always to have a clear conscience   16
before God and men.

"After several years I came to bring alms and offerings to my   17
nation. While I was engaged in these matters, they found me in   18
the temple, ceremonially pure, with no crowd or disturbance whatever. But there were some Jews from the province of Asia, who   19
ought to have been here before your tribunal and to have presented
their charges, if they had any, against me; or else let these men here   20
say what they found wrong in me when I stood before the Sanhedrin,
unless it be for the one thing I shouted out as I stood among them,   21
'It is about the resurrection of the dead that I am being judged by
you this day.'"

THE TRIAL ADJOURNED

Felix, however, having fairly precise information about the Way,   22
adjourned the trial, saying, "When Lysias the tribune comes down,
I will decide your case." He instructed the centurion to keep Paul   23
in custody, yet to allow him some liberty, and not to prevent any
of his friends from assisting him.

Some days later Felix came with his wife Drusilla, a Jewess, and   24
sent for Paul and heard what he had to say about the faith in
Jesus Christ. As he talked of holiness and chastity and the judg-   25
ment to come, Felix became alarmed and said, "For the present go
your way. When I have an opportunity, I will send for you." At   26
the same time he was hoping that Paul would give him money, and
for this reason he would send for him often and talk with him.
After two years had elapsed, Felix was succeeded by Porcius Festus.   27
As Felix wanted to ingratiate himself with the Jews, he left Paul
in prison.

CHAPTER 25

PAUL BEFORE FESTUS

Festus accordingly entered his province, and three days later   1
he went up from Caesarea to Jerusalem. There the chief priests   2

24:17. offerings: or "sacrifices," such as the Nazarite vow required.

and Jewish leaders presented their charges against Paul, and begged
3 Festus, as a special favor for themselves to the prejudice of Paul, that he would have him brought to Jerusalem. Meanwhile they were
4 laying an ambush to kill him on the way. But Festus answered that Paul was being kept in custody at Caesarea, and that he himself
5 would be going there shortly. "Let, there, your influential men go down with me," he said, "and if there is anything wrong with the man, let them present charges against him."
6 After staying among them not more than eight or ten days he went down to Caesarea, and the next day he took his seat on the
7 tribunal and ordered Paul brought in. When he appeared, the Jews who had come down from Jerusalem surrounded him and brought many serious charges against him, which they were unable to prove.
8 Paul said in his own defense, "Neither against the Law of the Jews nor against the temple nor against Caesar have I committed any
9 offense." Festus, anxious to do the Jews a favor, spoke to Paul and said, "Are you willing to go to Jerusalem, and be tried there on these charges?"
10 "I am standing at the tribunal of Caesar," replied Paul; "there I ought to be tried. To the Jews I have done no wrong, as you yourself
11 very well know. If I have done any wrong and committed a crime deserving of death, I do not ask to be excused from the death penalty. But if there is no ground to these charges against me, no one can give me up to them; I appeal to Caesar."
12 Then Festus, after conferring with the council, answered, "You have appealed to Caesar; to Caesar you shall go."

PAUL BEFORE AGRIPPA

13 After an interval of some days King Agrippa and Bernice came to
14 Caesarea to pay their respects to Festus. As they were to stay there several days, Festus laid Paul's case before the king, saying, "There
15 is a man left prisoner by Felix, and when I was at Jerusalem the chief priests and elders of the Jews presented their case against him
16 and asked for his conviction. My answer was that Romans are not accustomed to give any man up before the accused has met the accusers face to face and has been given a chance to defend himself

25:13. Agrippa: Herod Agrippa II, son of the Herod mentioned in Chapter 12.

against the charge. Therefore, when they had assembled here, I lost 17
no time, and on the following day took my seat on the tribunal
and ordered the man to be brought in. When his accusers gathered 18
about him, they did not charge him with any of the crimes such as
I had expected. They merely had some difference of opinion about 19
their own religion, and about a certain deceased Jesus, who, Paul
insisted, was alive. Being at a loss as to how to investigate such 20
matters, I asked him if he would be willing to go to Jerusalem and
be tried on these charges there. But when Paul entered an appeal 21
to have his case reserved for the decision of Augustus, I ordered
him kept in custody till I could send him to Caesar." "I too," said 22
Agrippa, "would like to hear the man." "Tomorrow," replied Festus,
"you shall hear him."

So the next day Agrippa and Bernice came with great pomp 23
and entered the audience hall with the tribunes and principal men
of the city. When by order of Festus Paul was brought in, Festus 24
said, "King Agrippa and all men here present with us, you see this
man about whom the whole crowd of the Jews pleaded with me at
Jerusalem and here, crying out that he ought not to live any longer.
But I, for my part, found that he had done nothing deserving of 25
death. Since, however, he himself made the appeal, I decided to
send him to Augustus. Still I have nothing definite to write to my 26
lord about him. So I have brought him before you, and especially
before you, King Agrippa, that after an examination of him has been
made I may have something to put in writing. Really it seems 27
unreasonable to me to send a prisoner without stating the charges
against him."

Chapter 26

Then Agrippa said to Paul, "You are permitted to speak for 1
yourself." Then Paul stretched forth his hand and began his defense.
"I consider myself fortunate, King Agrippa, that I am to defend 2
myself today before you against all the accusations of the Jews,
especially as you are well acquainted with all the Jewish customs and 3
controversies. I beg you, therefore, to listen to me with patience.

25:21. Augustus: a title used for the emperors from the time of Augustus
himself.

PAUL PLEADS HIS CASE

4   "My life from my youth, the early part of which was spent
5   among my own nation and at Jerusalem, all the Jews know. In fact
they have long been acquainted with me, if only they are willing
to give evidence, that according to the strictest sect of our religion,
6   I spent my life as a Pharisee. And now because of the hope in the
7   promise made by God to our fathers I stand here on trial. This
promise our twelve tribes hope to attain as they serve God earnestly
day and night. It is about this hope, O king, that I am accused by
8   the Jews. Why is it deemed incredible that God should raise
the dead?

9   "Now I myself thought it my duty to struggle intensely against
10 the name of Jesus of Nazareth. And this I did in Jerusalem. Many
of the saints I shut up in prison, having received authority from
the chief priests to do so, and when the death sentence was proposed
11 I cast my vote against them. Oftentimes in one synagogue after
another I punished them and tried to force them to curse Jesus. In
my extreme rage against them I even pursued them to foreign cities.

12 "But while I was journeying on this business to Damascus with
13 authority and mandate from the chief priests, at midday, O king, I
saw on the way shining about me and my traveling companions
14 a light from the sky, brighter than sunshine. We all fell to the
ground, and I heard a voice speaking to me in Hebrew, 'Saul, Saul,
why do you persecute me? It is hard for you to kick against the
15 goad.' 'Who are you, Lord?' I inquired. 'I am Jesus,' the Lord
16 replied, 'whom you are persecuting. But rise and stand on your
feet, for I have appeared to you for this purpose, to appoint you
to be a minister and a witness to what you have seen, and to
17 the visions you shall have of me. I will deliver you from the
people and from the nations, to whom I am now sending you,
18 to open their eyes that they may turn from darkness to light and
from the dominion of Satan to God, that they may receive the
forgiveness of sins and an inheritance among those sanctified by
faith in me.'

26:14. *It is hard*, etc.: a proverb. Oxen were urged on by goads, and kicking
only made the goading more painful. The grace of God was prodding Paul
in a similar way. St. Chrysostom interprets the proverb as descriptive of the
futility of struggling against an invincible, superior force as is the Church.

"Therefore, King Agrippa, I was not disobedient to the heavenly 19
vision, but set about declaring, first to the people of Damascus and 20
Jerusalem and then all over Judea and to the Gentiles, that they
should have a change of heart and mind and turn to God, performing deeds befitting this change. This is why the Jews seized me in the 21
temple and tried to kill me. But aided to this day by the help of 22
God, I stand here to testify to both high and low, saying nothing
beyond what the prophets and Moses said would happen: that the 23
Christ was to suffer, that he, the first to rise from the dead, was to
proclaim light to the people and to the Gentiles."

PAUL DECLARED INNOCENT

While he was saying this in his defense, Festus said in a loud 24
voice, "Paul, you are mad; your great learning is driving you insane."
"I am not insane, Festus, your Excellency," replied Paul, "but I 25
speak words of sober truth. Why, the king knows about these things 26
and to him also I speak with firm assurance. I am quite sure that
none of these things escaped him, since none of them has transpired
in a corner. Do you believe the prophets, King Agrippa? I know 27
that you do." Agrippa answered Paul, "With a little effort you are 28
confident of making a Christian out of me!" Paul answered, "I would 29
to God that, with little or great effort, not only you but also all who
hear me today might become such as I am, except for these chains."

Then the king and the governor and Bernice, with their retinue, 30
arose, and after withdrawing they kept talking the matter over, 31
saying, "This man is engaged in no activity that deserves death or
imprisonment." Agrippa remarked to Festus, "This man might have 32
been set at liberty, if he had not appealed to Caesar."

26:28. With a little effort: This could mean: "in a little time." For the
rest of Agrippa's statement, probably spoken ironically, there are variant read-
ings and various interpretations. These result in: "In a little time you persuade
me to become a Christian"; "With little ado, you are persuaded that you will
make a Christian of me"; "You almost persuade me to become a Christian."

The Imprisonment of Paul in Rome

Chapter 27

DEPARTURE FOR ROME

1   When it was decided that we should sail for Italy, they entrusted Paul with some other prisoners to a centurion named Julius of the
2 Augustan cohort. We boarded a ship of Adrumytium which was bound for the ports of the province of Asia, and set sail. Aristarchus, a Macedonian from Thessalonica, was one of our party.
3   The next day we put in at Sidon. Julius treated Paul kindly,
4 allowing him to go to his friends and to be cared for. Putting to sea from there, we passed under the lee of Cyprus, as the winds
5 were against us, and sailing across the sea that lies off Cilicia and
6 Pamphylia, we reached Myra in Lycia. There the centurion found a ship of Alexandria bound for Italy and put us on board.
7   For many days we made slow progress and had difficulty in arriving off Cnidus. Then, as the wind here kept us from going on,
8 we sailed under the lee of Crete off Salmone, and coasting along it we came with difficulty to a place called Fair Havens near the town of Lasea.
9   As much time had been spent and navigation was now unsafe,
10 for the Fast was already over, Paul repeatedly warned them, saying, "Men, I see that this voyage is threatening to bring disaster and heavy loss, not only to the cargo and the ship but to our lives also."
11 But the centurion gave heed rather to the pilot and the captain
12 than to Paul's statements, and as the harbor was unsuitable for wintering, the majority favored sailing from there in order, if possible, to reach and winter at Phoenix, a harbor in Crete facing
13 southwest and northwest. So when a light south wind sprang up, thinking that they had practically secured their purpose, they weighed anchor and ran close along the coast of Crete.

A STORM THREATENS THEIR SAFETY

14   But not long afterwards a violent wind, called Euraquilo, burst

---

27:9. *the Fast:* of the Day of Atonement, about September 15. After this time navigation was considered dangerous.
27:14. *Euraquilo:* a northeast wind.

against the coast, and when the ship was caught and could not face 15
the wind, we gave way and were driven along. Running under the 16
lee of a small island called Clauda, we with difficulty managed there
to secure the ship's boat. After hoisting it on board, they used 17
stays to undergird the ship, and, as they were afraid of being driven
on the Syrtes quicksands, they lowered the anchor and so were
driven along. While we were being driven about by the violence 18
of the storm, they threw overboard the next day some of the cargo,
and on the third day, with their own hands, they threw the ship's 19
gear overboard. Since neither sun nor stars were visible for many 20
days, and no small storm was raging, all hope of our being saved
was finally abandoned.

Then after they had eaten nothing for a long time, Paul stood 21
up in their midst and said: "Men, you really should have listened
to me and not have sailed from Crete. Thus you would have spared
yourselves this disaster and loss. But even now I beg you to be of 22
good cheer, for there will be no loss of life among you, but only
of the ship. For last night an angel of the God I belong to and 23
worship stood by me, saying, 'Do not be afraid, Paul; you must 24
appear before Caesar, and note well, God has granted you the lives
of all who are sailing with you.' So, men, be of good cheer; for I have 25
faith in God that it will be as it has been told me. But we are to be 26
stranded on a certain island."

THEY ABANDON THE SHIP

It was the fourteenth night, and we were drifting in the Adriatic 27
sea, when about midnight the sailors began to suspect that they were
approaching land. On taking soundings they found twenty fathoms, 28
and a little further on they found fifteen. Then fearing that we 29
might go on the rocks, they dropped anchors from the stern and
longed for daylight. But as the sailors were trying to escape from 30
the ship and had lowered the ship's boat into the sea, pretending
that they were going to cast anchors from the bow, Paul said to 31
the centurion and the soldiers, "Unless these men remain on the

---

27:16. ship's boat: known as a dinghy. It was used for landing, also for
tacking, and was sometimes kept on deck and sometimes towed after the ship.
    27:17. anchor: alternative translations are "mainsail" and "gear."
    27:19. gear: the same word as translated above "anchor." The word is of
doubtful meaning, and seems to refer generically to the ship's apparatus.

32 ship, you cannot be saved." Then the soldiers cut away the ropes of
the ship's boat and let it fall off.

33   When it began to grow light, Paul begged them all to take food,
saying, "This is the fourteenth day that you have been constantly on
34 the watch, fasting, without taking anything. So I beg you to take some
food, because it is necessary for your safety. Besides, not a hair from
35 the head of a single one of you shall perish." With these words
he took bread and gave thanks to God in the presence of them all
36 and broke it and proceeded to eat. Then all became cheerful and
37 themselves took food. We were in all two hundred and seventy-
38 six persons on board. After eating their fill, they lightened the ship
by throwing the wheat into the sea.

39   When day broke they could not recognize the land, but they
noticed a bay with a beach. They proposed to run the ship ashore
40 there, if they could. So they slipped the anchors and left them to
the sea, at the same time unleashing the fastenings of the rudders,
and hoisting the foresail to the wind, they made for the beach.
41 But they struck here a place open to the two seas, and ran the
ship aground. The prow stuck fast and remained immovable, but
the stern began to break up under the violence of the sea.

42   The soldiers' counsel now was to kill the prisoners, lest any
43 of them might swim ashore and escape, but the centurion, anxious
to save Paul, put a stop to their plan. He ordered those who could
44 swim to jump overboard first and make for land, while the rest
were to make the trip, some on planks and others on various things
from the ship. So it was brought about that all came safely to land.

CHAPTER 28

THE LANDING AT MALTA

1   After our escape we learned that the island was called Malta.
2 The natives showed us extraordinary kindness. They kindled a fire
because of the rain that had set in and the cold, and gave us a
3 hearty welcome. After Paul had gathered a bundle of faggots and

---

27:41. *open to the two seas*: perhaps a projection of land exposed to the
waves on both sides. The storm may have covered it with waves and rendered
it invisible.

laid them on the fire, a viper came out of them because of the heat
and fastened on his hand. When the natives saw the tiny reptile *4*
hanging from his hand, they said to one another, "Surely this man is
a murderer, for though he escaped the sea, Justice does not let him
live." But he shook off the little reptile into the fire and suffered *5*
no harm. They were expecting him to swell up or suddenly drop *6*
dead, but after waiting a long time and seeing nothing amiss happening to him, they changed their minds and said he was a god.

In the vicinity were estates belonging to the chief officer of the *7*
island, named Publius, who received us hospitably and entertained
us for three days. It so happened that Publius' father was laid up *8*
with a fever and dysentery. Paul paid him a visit and after praying
and laying his hands on him healed him. After this the rest of the *9*
sick on the island came and were cured. The people showed us many *10*
marks of honor, and when we sailed, they provided us with such
things as were needed.

FROM MALTA TO ROME

After three months we set sail in an Alexandrian ship which *11*
had wintered at the island. It had "Twins" for its figurehead.
On arriving at Syracuse, we stayed there three days. Then, following *12, 13*
the coast, we reached Rhegium, and one day later a south wind blew,
and on the second day we arrived at Puteoli, where we found *14*
brothers who begged us to stay seven days with them. So then we
came to Rome. The brothers there, having received news of us, *15*
came as far as the Forum of Appius and the Three Taverns. On
seeing them Paul gave thanks to God and took courage. Upon our *16*
arrival at Rome, Paul was given permission to live by himself with a
soldier to guard him.

Three days later he called together the leading Jews and when *17*
they assembled he said to them, "Brothers, although I have done
nothing against the people or against the customs of our fathers,
I nevertheless was handed over to the Romans as a prisoner from
Jerusalem. After examination of my case they were ready to release *18*
me, since I was innocent of any crime that deserved death; but, as *19*

28:4. *Justice:* or "Vengeance." As pursuing criminals this was a familiar goddess
among the Greeks and Romans. The natives here so speak of it.

28:11. *Twins:* on its prow the ship carried the images of Castor and Pollux,
patrons of sailors.

the Jews objected, I was forced to appeal to Caesar — not that I had
20 any charge to bring against my nation. This, then, is why I asked
to see you and speak with you. Actually it is because of the hope
of Israel that I am wearing this chain."
21 "We ourselves," they said to him, "have received no letters about
you from Judea, and none of the brothers on arrival has reported or
22 spoken any evil of you. But we think it right to hear from you what
your views are, because as regards this sect we know that everywhere
it is spoken against."
23   So they fixed a day, and a great many came to Paul at his lodging.
To them he explained the kingdom of God, eagerly giving his
testimony, and trying from morning to night to convince them from
24 the Law of Moses and from the Prophets concerning Jesus. Some
25 believed what was said, and some disbelieved. As they could not
agree among themselves, they were on the point of departing when
Paul added this one word:
    "Well did the Holy Spirit speak through Isaias the prophet to
26 your fathers these words:
    'Go to this people and say:
    With all your hearing you will not understand;
        with all your seeing you will not perceive.
27   For the mind of this people has grown callous,
        and with their ears they have become dull of hearing.
    Their eyes they have closed,
    Lest perhaps they see with their eyes,
        and hear with their ears, and understand with their heart,
    And be converted, and I heal them.'
28 Be it known, therefore, to you that this message of salvation from
God has been sent to the Gentiles; they certainly will listen to it."
30   For two full years Paul remained in his own hired lodging, and
31 welcomed all who came to him, preaching the kingdom of God and
teaching about the Lord Jesus Christ with all assurance and without
hindrance.

28:26. Isa. 6:9.
28:28. Verse 29, found in some Latin manuscripts, reads: "When he had
said this, the Jews departed, having much argument among themselves." It is
not found in the Greek manuscripts.

THE LIFE AND EPISTLES OF ST. PAUL

We do not know with certainty when St. Paul was born, but we can deduce with a fair degree of accuracy and certainty from allusions in the Acts and Epistles that he must have seen the light of day about the time our Lord was born in Bethlehem. Paul's birthplace was Tarsus in Cilicia. His parents were Hebrews, who would have seen to it that from earliest childhood their son received a good religious education.

He grew up in an environment of pagan worship and culture. Here he learned a great deal about pagan depravity. He also learned the Greek language, which was to serve him in good stead in his missionary activities.

He probably received no formal schooling from pagan instructors. His parents were strict Jews, and would have considered it a great neglect of duty to have sent their son to pagan schools. Whatever the future Apostle learned of paganism he learned from observation.

His father, or perhaps some more remote progenitor, acquired in some way the privilege of Roman citizenship. In consequence Paul was born to this privilege, a distinction of which he was proud and which he used to advantage on several occasions during his missionary activities: his Roman citizenship saved him more than one flogging and other penalties from which Roman citizens were exempt.

Since he was born in a foreign country, he probably had from infancy two names, Saul, a Hebrew name, and Paul, a Latin name. Among his own compatriots he was known by his Jewish name, while among the pagans he used his Latin name.

His parents sent him as a youth to Jerusalem, where he was educated in the rabbinical schools and became a member of the Pharisees. As such he was bitterly opposed to the new movement, which later came to be known as Christianity, and persecuted it fiercely. He assisted at the execution of the first martyr, Stephen. Shortly afterward he was miraculously converted to Christianity.

There is no need to tell the rest of the life and activities of the great Apostle, since all that we know of him is found in the Acts and the various Pauline Epistles. Beginning with the ninth chapter of the Acts, we have the first of three accounts of Paul's conversion; and nearly all the remaining chapters of the Acts are devoted to a summary account of the Apostle's missionary activities. Brief though the accounts are, they will in connection with the Pauline Epistles give the reader a deep impression of the greatness of St. Paul. He was a man of deep-seated faith, of tireless zeal for souls, in spite of an illness which through the greater part of his life, and at times painfully, afflicted him. He feared no danger and never hesitated to expose his life when the interests of the Church and of souls called for heroism. He was a clever man, as his calm self-possession and resourcefulness showed on many occasions when he was in difficulties and faced with the threat of death. He had a tender love for his converts, as also for his compatriots, the Jews. Their failure, as a whole, to accept the Christian message was a lifelong source of sorrow to him.

After about thirty years of untiring labor, long and arduous travels, persecutions, calumnies, and imprisonments, he finally died the death of a martyr. Such is the constant tradition, and there is no reason to doubt it. His martyrdom took place at Rome. Scholars are divided as to the year of his death: one school favors the year 64 in the early days of the Neronian persecution; others favor the year 67.

In the midst of an intensely active life, St. Paul also engaged in some literary activity. The results of this activity have not all come down to us; some of his writings are lost. But we have thirteen Epistles in our New Testament which are from the pen of the great Apostle, and a fourteenth, Hebrews, which, according to tradition, contains his ideas and was at least remotely inspired by him.

As to his style, St. Paul professes to hold in considerable contempt the art of the rhetoricians, and it is quite evident that he did not consciously strive after literary perfection. Yet there are passages in his Epistles where he reaches the heights of sublimity and eloquence, such as the thirteenth chapter of 1 Corinthians, the concluding verses of the eighth and the eleventh chapters of Romans. All students of Paul agree that his little letter to Philemon is a literary gem. In other passages he is lyrical, as in the latter part of 1 Corinthians 15.

But on the other hand, the Apostle is often careless of the rules of good writing. He dictated his Epistles to a scribe or secretary, and often his thoughts run faster than his words. Thus he sometimes neglects to complete a sentence; at other times he introduces one relative clause after another which complicate and obscure the thought, or he throws in long parentheses. This carelessness of style is one of the causes of the difficulty of understanding the Apostle's writings.

Another cause is that his letters teem with allusions to circumstances, persons, and situations of which we know nothing, save what we can gather from the vague references to them in the Epistles themselves. The letters of Paul, someone has said, are like a telephone conversation: we hear only one of the two persons engaged in the exchange of words.

A third cause of the difficulty in understanding the Apostle is that he at times gives a brief statement of doctrine which he had already set forth at length to his converts in sermons, instructions, and conversations. There is no intention on the part of the Apostle to present a systematic or a complete statement of Christian doctrine. His letters are occasional, i.e., they were called forth by some problem of discipline or doctrine, and their object is to explain further and clarify what had already been expounded fully by word of mouth.

Yet, in spite of the difficulty of understanding St. Paul, there are many passages which easily yield a satisfactory and a sublime meaning. His Epistles are a mine of information on the beliefs and practices of the early Church. They give us precious data on Grace, the Sacraments, the Redemption, the Incarnation, the future life, and all the basic dogmas of the Christian faith.

In conclusion, a few practical suggestions are offered which, it is hoped, will help them obtain a more meaningful appreciation of the Epistles of St. Paul.

1. Read the Epistles in the order of time in which they were written. It is: 1 and 2 Thessalonians, Galatians, 1 and 2 Corin-

thians, Romans, Ephesians, Philippians, Colossians, Philemon, Hebrews, 1 Timothy, Titus, 2 Timothy.

2. Read them in connection with the Acts: Before reading 1 and 2 Thessalonians, read Acts 17:1–12. Before Galatians, read Acts 15:1–35. Before Philippians, read Acts 16:9–40; before Ephesians, Acts 19:1–40. Before 1 Corinthians read Acts 17:16–18. There are no passages in the Acts directly bearing on the other Epistles.

3. Read a good special introduction to the Epistle and a commentary. The special introduction will explain the circumstances which called forth the Epistle, and the commentary will explain obscure passages. *A Commentary on the New Testament*, prepared by the Catholic Biblical Association of America, is recommended.

THE EPISTLE TO THE ROMANS

INTRODUCTION

St. Paul's Epistle to the Romans is given the position of honor at the head of all the New Testament Epistles because of the doctrinal importance of its contents and also because of the outstanding position that the Roman congregation of Christians early assumed in the Church. It was written at Corinth during the winter of A.D. 57–58, at the close of St. Paul's third missionary journey, prior to his voyage to Jerusalem, where at the instigation of his adversaries he was to be arrested and held prisoner for several years, first at Caesarea in Palestine and then in Rome itself. This date for the composition of the Epistle is arrived at by comparison of the circumstances and persons to which it alludes with those at Corinth during St. Paul's sojourn there at the close of his third missionary journey.

St. Paul during this period of his missionary activity had rather thoroughly covered the territory in the Near East, and was looking for new fields to evangelize in the West. He purposed accordingly after visiting Jerusalem, where he went to bring a collection which he had promoted for the poor Christians at Jerusalem, to journey to Spain, stopping en route at Rome (Rom. 15:18–24). In this letter he wished to inform the Romans of his intended visit and to set before them the fruits of his meditations on the great religious questions of the day: sanctification by faith in Jesus Christ and the relation of this new system of salvation to the Mosaic religion. He proves that, while the Mosaic practices are powerless to sanctify and save, they were the forerunner and historical preparation for the new system. Christianity is the full flowering and historical development of Judaism. Although St. Paul had previously dealt briefly with this question in the Epistle to the Galatians, he had not thus far had the opportunity of fully developing it in writing his doctrine on this point. Years of thought and prayer with the aid of the Holy Spirit had matured his views on this subject. And now wishing to introduce himself to the Roman Christians, he seized the opportunity of setting forth a lengthy statement and proof of his doctrine, not only for the Romans but also for the various Christian communities throughout the world.

In addition to establishing his thesis, St. Paul also discusses the reasons on the part of God and on the part of the Jews why they as a whole failed to come into the blessings of the Messianic reign. He then lays down some practical norms of conduct which the profession of the Christian faith entails, and concludes with a long series of personal greetings.

THE DIVISION OF THE EPISTLE TO THE ROMANS

Introduction, 1:1–17.
Doctrinal part. The Gospel is the power of God for the salvation of all who believe, 1:18 to 11:36.
    Humanity without Christ, 1:18 to 3:20.
    Justification through faith in Jesus Christ, 3:21 to 4:25.
    The superabundance of justification, 5:1–21.
    Justification and the Christian life, 6:1 to 8:39.
    The problem of the rejection of Israel, 9:1 to 11:36.
Moral part. The duties of Christians, 12:1 to 15:13.
Conclusion, 15:14 to 16:27.

THE EPISTLE OF

ST. PAUL THE APOSTLE

TO THE ROMANS

INTRODUCTION

CHAPTER 1

GREETINGS

Paul, servant of Jesus Christ to all God's beloved, saints by voca-   1, 7
tion, at Rome, grace be to you and peace from God our Father and
from the Lord Jesus Christ.

We have been called to the apostolate and set apart to proclaim
the Good News now made known by God, as he had promised it   2
of old through his prophets in Holy Writ. This Good News concerns   3
his Son, who in regard to his human nature was born of the line
of David, but who in regard to his all-holy divine nature was con-   4
stituted the mighty Son of God by his resurrection from the dead,
Jesus Christ our Lord. Through him we have received grace and   5

1:1. *servant*: literally, "slave." The term, frequent in the Pauline Epistles to
designate Paul's relation to God, is expressive of the absolute submission of the
Apostle to God.

1:1–7. The latter part of this greeting comes at the end of the paragraph in
the original, and is separated from the first part by a long parenthesis, made
up of a series of relative clauses. The change in the order and the breaking
up of the lengthy sentence was motivated by the desire to secure greater
clearness.

1:4. *his all-holy divine nature*: literally, "according to the spirit of holiness."
constituted: Jesus Christ was from all eternity the real Son of God in regard to
his divine nature. When he became man, the glory of this nature was hidden
away from men in the human nature which he had taken unto himself. "He
emptied himself" of that divine glory (Phil. 2:7). But at his Resurrection, and
because of it, the process of his glorification in his human nature was begun
and culminated in his Ascension into heaven, where at the right hand of God
the Father he was constituted the mighty Son of God, or Son of God in
power and splendor in that very human nature in which during his sojourn on
earth he had appeared to men weak and lowly. An alternative meaning given
by some to *constituted* is "manifested."

377

the apostolic office, whose purpose is to bring men of all nations
6 to honor his name by the submission of faith. Among these nations
you, who have been called to belong to Jesus Christ, are included.

PAUL AND THE ROMANS

8   First I give thanks to my God through Jesus Christ for all of
9 you, because your faith is proclaimed all over the world. Indeed
God, whom I serve in all sincerity by proclaiming the Good News
about his Son, is my witness how unceasingly I make mention of
10 you, always imploring at my prayers that somehow by God's will
11 I may at last come to you after a safe journey. I really long to see
you that I may impart some spiritual gift to you to strengthen you,
12 or rather, that among you I may be comforted together with you
by that faith which is common to us both, yours and mine.
13   Brothers, I would not have you unaware that I have often proposed to come to visit you, that I may gather some fruit among
you also as well as among the rest of the Gentiles, but I have been
14 prevented until now. To Greeks and to foreigners, to learned and
15 unlearned, I owe a debt, so that for my part I am eager to preach the
Good News to you also who are at Rome.

MAIN THESIS

16   I certainly am not ashamed of the Good News, for it is the
power of God to bring about salvation for everyone that has faith,
17 for Jew first and then Greek. For in it God's way of sanctifying by
an ever increasing faith is revealed. As it is written,
"The holy man lives by faith."

HUMANITY WITHOUT CHRIST

PAGAN DEPRAVITY AND ITS PUNISHMENT

18   The wrath of God is being revealed from heaven against all

---

1:7. Hab. 2:4. *sanctifying:* literally, "of justifying." We have abandoned the
technical theological terms, "justify" and "justice," because in modern usage they
mean something quite different from the theological sense theologians give them.
by an ever increasing faith: literally, "from faith unto faith," i.e., the imperfect
faith of the neophyte gradually increases and disposes the believer for the reception of God's grace, and thus is manifested the holiness which God imparts
to the believer. The faith of the baptized convert is capable of being deepened
and strengthened also.

ungodliness and wickedness of those men who in wickedness stifle the truth of God. Here is the reason: what may be known about 19 God is manifest to them, because God has manifested it to them. Since the creation of the world his invisible attributes are clearly 20 seen — especially his everlasting power and divinity, which are understood through the things that are made. And so they are without excuse, because although they knew God, they did not glorify him 21 as God or give thanks, but their reasonings became absurd, and their senseless minds were darkened. While professing to be wise, they 22 became fools, and they exchanged the glory of the incorruptible 23 God for an image made like corruptible man and to birds and four-footed beasts and creeping things.

Therefore God has given them up, in the lustful desires of their 24 heart, to uncleanness, so that they dishonor their own bodies — they 25 who exchanged the truth of God for a lie and worshiped and served the creature rather than the Creator who is blessed forever, amen.

For this cause God has given them up to shameful lusts; for 26 their women have exchanged natural intercourse for what is against nature, and in the same way men too, having given up natural 27 intercourse with women, have burned in their lusts toward one another, men with men practicing that well-known shamelessness and receiving in their own persons the fitting punishment of their perversity. And as they resolved against having a good knowledge 28 of God, God has given them up to a seared conscience so that they do what is morally disgraceful. They are steeped in dishonesty, 29 wickedness, greed, ill-will; they are overflowing with envy, murderous intent, strife, deceit, rancor; they secretly spread false reports; they openly calumniate, they hate God, they are insulting. They 30 are proud, vain, boastful, ingenious in evil, disobedient to parents. They lack conscience, constancy, affection, piety. Although they are 31, 32 aware of the decree of God that those who do such things are worthy of death, they not only do them, but applaud others who do them.

1:24. *God has given them up:* as St. Thomas Aquinas says, not by impelling them to evil, but by deserting them. He justly withdrew his grace from them in punishment of their idolatry, and being thus abandoned by God, men followed the bent of fallen nature, and fell into the degradation of unnatural vice.

Chapter 2

IMPARTIAL JUDGMENT FOR ALL MEN

1 And so you are inexcusable, O man, whoever you are who judge.
2 Your judgment passed on another is your own condemnation. For
you, who sit in judgment, yourself commit the same sins. We know
that the condemnation of God is in accord with the truth and is
3 leveled against those who are guilty of such sins. Do you think, O
man, who judge those who do such things and do the same yourself,
4 that you will escape the condemnation of God? Or do you despise
the wealth of his goodness, patience, and long-suffering? Do you not
know that the goodness of God is meant to lead you to repentance?
5 But according to your obstinacy and unrepentant heart, you treasure
up to yourself wrath on the day of wrath, when the just judging
6 of God, who will render everyone according to his deeds, will be
7 revealed. Life eternal he will give to those who by persevering in
8 good deeds seek glory, honor, and immortality; but wrath and indignation will he visit on those that are contumacious, that is to
say, who refuse to submit to the truth, but assent to iniquity.
9 Tribulation and anguish shall be the lot of every man who is bent
10 on evil-doing: of the Jew first and then of the Greek; but glory,
honor, and peace will be the lot of every man intent on doing good:
11 of the Jew first and then of the Greek, since with God there is no
favoritism.

STANDARD OF JUDGMENT, REVEALED OR NATURAL LAW

12 Whoever have sinned, not having the Law, will perish without
respect to the Law, and whoever were bound by the Law and have
13 sinned, will be judged by the Law. Really it is not they who hear
the Law that are holy in the sight of God, but it is they who follow
14 the Law that will be sanctified. When the Gentiles who have
no law follow the dictates of reason, and do what the Law prescribes,
15 these, though they have no law, are a law to themselves. They
show that the requirements of the Law are written in their hearts.

2:9. *of the Jew first:* because of his greater responsibility, since he was
enlightened by Divine Revelation, the Jew will have a certain priority on the
Day of Judgment in punishment. The same holds true in regard to rewards,
because he is a member of the chosen race he will have a priority.
2:15. *written in their hearts:* The dictates of human reason and common sense

Their conscience bears the same testimony, as also their thoughts, which alternately accuse or defend them. This will be evident on *16* the day when God will judge the secrets of men by Jesus Christ according to what I preach.

THE RESPONSIBILITY OF THE JEWS

Now you are called "Jew," and you rely on the Law. You glory *17* in God, you know his will; you approve the higher ideals, since you *18* are informed by the Law. You are confident that you are a guide to *19* the blind, a light to those who are in darkness, an instructor of the *20* unwise, a teacher of children, since you have in the Law the pattern of knowledge and of truth. You, therefore, who teach others, do *21* you not teach yourself? You who preach against stealing, do you steal? You who say that men should not commit adultery, do you *22* commit adultery? You who abominate idols, do you plunder temples? You who glory in the Law, do you dishonor God by transgressing *23* the Law? "The name of God," as it is written, "is maligned because *24* of you among the Gentiles."

TRUE CIRCUMCISION

Circumcision is certainly useful if you keep the Law, but if you *25* are a transgressor of the Law, your circumcision is the same as no circumcision. If, then, the uncircumcised person keeps the precepts *26* of the Law, will not his uncircumcision be counted as circumcision? And he who is physically uncircumcised, provided he fulfills the Law, *27* will condemn you who have a written Law and circumcision, and yet transgress the Law. For he is not really a Jew who is so out- *28* wardly, nor is that man circumcised who is so outwardly, in the flesh. But he is a Jew who is so inwardly, and real circumcision *29* is a matter of the heart — something based on the spirit, not just

---

make known to us, independently of Revelation, certain basic principles of conduct. This is what is known as the natural law, which coincides roughly with the Decalogue.

2:24. Isa. 52:5. The misfortunes which the Jews during the time of Isaias brought on themselves by their sins reflected dishonor on God in the eyes of the pagans, who attributed the misfortunes of a people to weakness on the part of the object of their worship.

2:29. Circumcision of the heart means the uprooting of vices and evil tendencies from the heart. The name "Jew" is derived from a Hebrew root meaning "praise." St. Paul is playing on the word.

on the letter of the Law. The praise of such a man comes not
from men but from God.

CHAPTER 3

GOD UNCONDITIONALLY FAITHFUL TO HIS PROMISES

1 What advantage, then, remains to the Jew, or what is the use
2 of circumcision? Much, in every respect. First, the Jews had the
3 oracles of God entrusted to them. What then? If some of them have
not been faithful, will their unfaithfulness nullify the faithfulness
4 of God? That must never be! God must prove true, even if all men
are fickle, as it is written,

"That you may be vindicated as just in your deeds,
And may win your case when you are judged."

5 But if our wickedness shows forth the justice of God, what shall
we say? Is God unjust when he inflicts punishment? (I am speaking
6 according to human standards.) That must never be! Otherwise, how
7 is God to judge the world? But if by means of my fickleness the
fidelity of God to his promises has been more abundantly proved to
8 his glory, why am I still judged as a sinner? And why should we not
do evil that good may come of it, as some calumniously accuse us of
teaching. The condemnation of such is well deserved.

HUMAN SINFULNESS IS UNIVERSAL

9 What then? Are we better off than the Gentiles? Not entirely.
For we have just charged that Jews and Greeks are all under the
10 domination of sin, as it is written,

"There is not one just man;
11   there is none who understands.
There is none that seeks after God.
12   All have gone astray together;
        they have wasted their lives.
There is none who does good,
        no, not even one.

3:4. *all men are fickle:* in comparison with God, who is truth itself, men are
essentially unreliable and, intentionally or unintentionally, often utter untruths
and make insincere promises. Ps. 50:6.

3:11–18. A tissue of Scripture texts from Ps. 13:1–3; 52:2–4; 5:11; 139:4;
9:7; Isa. 59:7; Prov. 1:16; Ps. 35:2.

Their throat is an open sepulcher;   *13*
    with their tongues they have dealt deceitfully.
The venom of asps is behind their lips;
    their mouth is full of bitter curses.   *14*
Their feet run swiftly to the shedding of blood;   *15*
    destruction and misery are in their paths.   *16*
The highway that leads to peace they have not known.   *17*
There is no fear of God in their view of things."   *18*

Now we know that whatever the Law says, is directed to those *19*
who come under the Law, in order that every mouth may be
reduced to silence and the whole world be made accountable to
God. Obviously by the prescriptions of the Law no human being *20*
shall be made holy in God's sight, because through law comes merely
the clearer recognition of sin.

JUSTIFICATION THROUGH FAITH IN JESUS CHRIST

JUSTIFICATION COMES THROUGH FAITH IN JESUS CHRIST

But now, however, the sanctification brought about by God *21*
independently of the Law, yet attested by the Law and the Prophets,
has been made manifest: it is the sanctification brought about by *22*
God through faith in Jesus Christ. It comes to all believers, as
there is no discrimination. All have sinned and lack the approval *23*
of God. They are sanctified freely by his grace through the redemp- *24*
tion which is in Christ Jesus. God has publicly exhibited him as a *25*
sacrifice which is expiatory through the shedding of his blood and

---

3:20. *by the prescriptions of the Law:* it does not follow from this statement that good actions are not necessary for salvation. The sanctification of
which St. Paul here speaks is the infusion of sanctifying grace, which alone
renders a person supernaturally pleasing to God. This grace cannot be merited
either by the performance of legal prescriptions or any other act of unregenerate
man.

3:22. The sanctification brought about by God through faith is not a mere
declaration of holiness with no corresponding interior renovation. It consists
in grace which he imparts to the soul to make it really, intrinsically pleasing
and holy in his sight. The necessary condition for obtaining the infusion of
this divine gift in the case of adults, whom alone St. Paul has in mind here,
is faith — not a bare speculative faith but a practical faith which through the
love of God leads to the observance of the commandments and the practice
of virtue. *approval:* others understand of the goodness of God manifested in
man when he is in the state of grace. Perhaps there is reference to the glorious
adornment of grace which Adam and his posterity lost by original sin.

available to all believers. God's purpose was to vindicate his holiness, since, during the period of tolerance, he had passed over former
26 sins without punishing them. A further purpose was to make known his holiness at the present time in sanctifying him who has faith in Jesus.

NO REASON FOR SELF-COMPLACENCY

27 Where, then, is any reason for boasting? It is excluded. By what kind of law? That of legal prescriptions? No, but by the law of faith.
28 For we hold that a man is sanctified by faith independently of
29 the deeds prescribed by the Law. Is God the God of the Jews only, and not of the Gentiles too? Assuredly he is also the God of the
30 Gentiles. Why, there is but one God who will sanctify the circumcised in consequence of their faith and the uncircumcised by their
31 faith. Do we, therefore, by this faith abolish the Law? By no means! Rather we uphold the Law.

CHAPTER 4

ABRAHAM WAS JUSTIFIED BY FAITH

1 What, then, shall we say that Abraham, our father according
2 to flesh, acquired? If Abraham was sanctified in consequence of his deeds, he has reason to boast. But it is not so in the sight
3 of God. What does the Scripture say? "Abraham believed God
4 and it was credited to him as holiness." Now to him who works,
5 the pay is not credited as a favor but as something due. But to him who does not work, but believes in him who imparts holiness to the
6 impious, his faith is credited to him as holiness. Thus David

---

4:3. Gen. 15:6.

4:5. credited: when God, who is infinite truth, credits something to a man, it is the same as saying that he imparts it really to the man, for there is no make-believe with God. Abraham was sanctified long before the incident Paul here refers to, but this particular act of faith, resulting in an increase of holiness for Abraham, is particularly apt for St. Paul's argument.

4:6. We should distinguish between sanctification and salvation. Sanctification, i.e., the infusion of sanctifying grace, cannot be merited by us; it is an entirely free gift on God's part. But salvation, or perseverance to the end of life in this state of grace, depends largely on right living, and accordingly St. Paul repeatedly insists on the necessity of avoiding evil and doing good.

declared the blessedness of the man to whom God credits holiness
without deeds:

"Blessed are they whose breaches of the Law are forgiven   7
    and whose sins are blotted from sight;
Blessed is the man to whom the Lord will   8
    not credit sin."

FAITH AND CIRCUMCISION

Does this declaration of blessedness hold good, then, only for 9
the circumcised, or for the uncircumcised also? We say that to
Abraham faith was credited as holiness. How, then, was it credited? 10
After he was circumcised or before? Not after he was circumcised,
but while he was still uncircumcised. He received circumcision as 11
the seal of the holiness which comes from faith. He had this
holiness before he was circumcised, that he might be the father of
all who believe, even though uncircumcised, and thus have their
faith credited to them as holiness. He will also be the father of the 12
circumcised, provided they are not merely circumcised but direct
their steps in the path of that faith which was our father Abraham's
before he was circumcised.

THE PROMISE, FAITH AND THE LAW

Not through any law but through the holiness that comes from 13
faith was the promise made to Abraham and to his posterity that he
should be the heir of the world. Now if they are heirs in virtue of 14
the Law, faith becomes meaningless, the promise is reduced to
nought. The Law produces wrath; for where there is no law, there 15
is no transgression. Therefore the promise was the outcome of faith, 16
in order that it might be a favor and might be secure for all the
offspring, not only for those who are adherents of the Law, but
also for those who share the faith of Abraham, who is the father
of us all, as it is written,   17
"I have appointed you the father of many nations." He is our

4:11. Gen. 17:10 f.
4:15. *the Law produces wrath:* a law simply indicates the line of conduct to
be followed. It does not impart the strength of will to fulfill its precepts. Of
itself, then, it becomes an occasion of wrath in that if its precepts are violated,
the lawgiver is provoked to anger and inflicts punishment on the transgressor.
4:17. Gen. 17:5.

father in the sight of God, whom he believed, who gives life to
the dead and calls things that are not as though they are.

18   Abraham, hoping against hope, believed, so that he became the
father of many nations, according to what was said,

"So shall your offspring be."

19   He did not let his faith weaken as he considered his own body with
its already withered vitality, as he was almost a hundred years old,
20   and the withered vitality of Sara's womb. In the light of God's
promise, he did not waver in unbelief, but was strengthened in
21   faith. Thus he gave glory to God, by his strong conviction that
22   whatever God has promised he is able to carry out. Therefore his
faith was credited to him as holiness.

23   Not for his sake alone was it written that "It was credited to
24   him," but for our sake also, to whom it will be credited if we believe
25   in him who raised Jesus our Lord from the dead, who was delivered
up for our sins, and rose again for our sanctification.

THE SUPERABUNDANCE OF JUSTIFICATION

CHAPTER 5

CHRIST'S DEATH GUARANTEES PEACE AND SALVATION

1   Having, therefore, been sanctified by faith, let us have peace
2   with God through our Lord Jesus Christ, through whom also we
have found entrance into this state of grace in which we now abide,
3   and exult in the hope of participating in God's glory. Not only
this, but we exult in tribulations also, aware that tribulation produces
4   endurance, and endurance proven virtue, and proven virtue hope.
5   And this hope does not disappoint, because God's love is poured
forth in our hearts by the Holy Spirit who has been given us.
6   While we were still helpless, Christ at the appointed time died for
7   us wicked people. Why, it is only with difficulty that a person will
die to save a good man. Yes, it is only for a worthy person that a
8   man may, perhaps, have the courage to face death. But God proves
his love for us, because, when we were still sinners, Christ died for us.
9   Much more now that we are sanctified by his blood shall we be

4:18. Gen. 15:5.

saved through him from God's avenging justice. Surely, if when we   *10*
were enemies we were reconciled to God by the death of his Son,
much more, once we are reconciled, shall we be saved by his life.
And more than this, we exult also in God through our Lord Jesus   *11*
Christ, through whom we have now received this reconciliation.

THE SIN OF ADAM AND THE GRACE OF CHRIST

Therefore, as through one man sin entered into the world and   *12*
through sin death, and thus death has spread to all men because all
have sinned — true it is that until the Law sin was in the world,   *13*
but sin is not imputed when there is no law. Yet death held sway   *14*
from Adam until Moses even over those who had not sinned after
the manner of the transgression of Adam, a type of him who was
to come.

But the gift is not at all like the offense. For if by the offense   *15*
of the one the many died, much more has the grace of God, and
the gift which consists in the grace of the one man, Jesus Christ,
overflowed unto the many. Nor is the gift as it was in the case   *16*
of the one man's sin, for the judgment unto condemnation followed
the one man's offense, but grace resulting in sanctification follows
many offenses. For if by reason of the one man's offense death   *17*
reigned through the one man, much more will they who receive
the abundance of the grace and of the gift of holiness reign in life
through the one Jesus Christ. Therefore as from the offense of   *18*
the one man the result was condemnation to all men, so from the
one's fulfillment of a mandate the result is the sanctification which
gives life to all men. In other words, just as by the disobedience of   *19*
the one man the many were constituted sinners, so also by the
obedience of the one the many will be constituted holy.

5:12. *through one man:* i.e., Adam, the moral and physical head of the
human race. The sin of which St. Paul speaks is known as original sin. *all have
sinned:* general statements like this are to be understood with their obvious
exceptions, and those that can be established from other sources of revealed
truth. The two exceptions to the general statement about the universal preva-
lence of sin are our Lord and his mother Mary.

5:13. *sin is not imputed when there is no law:* there was sin against the
law of nature during the period between Adam and Moses, but the sins committed before the Law of Moses were not imputed as a cause of death since
no law prescribed this penalty. Yet all, even infants, underwent the penalty of
death. It must be, then, because all mankind shared in some way in the sin
of Adam, the penalty for which was death.

THE ROLE OF THE LAW

20   The Law intervened that the offense might become greater. But
the greater the offense became, so much the more has grace in-
21   creased. So, just as sin has resulted in the reign of death, so also
grace, which confers holiness leading to eternal life, holds sway
through Jesus Christ our Lord.

JUSTIFICATION AND THE CHRISTIAN LIFE

CHAPTER 6

UNITED TO CHRIST WE ARE DEAD TO SIN

1   What then shall we say? Shall we continue in sin that grace may
2   increase? By no means! For how shall we, who are dead to sin,
3   still live in it? Do you not know that all of us who have been
baptized into union with Christ Jesus have been baptized into union
4   with his death? Yes, we were buried in death with him by means
of Baptism, in order that, just as Christ was raised from the dead
by the glorious power of the Father, so we also may conduct our-
5   selves by a new principle of life. Now since we have grown to be
one with him through a death like his, we shall also be one with
6   him by a resurrection like his. We know that our old self has
been crucified with him, in order that the body enslaved to sin
may be reduced to impotence, and we may no longer be slaves
7, 8   to sin; for he who is dead is once for all quit of sin. But if we have
died with Christ, we believe that we shall also live with him,
9   since we know that Christ, having risen from the dead, will die
10   no more; death shall no longer have dominion over him. The
death that he died was a death to sin once for all, but the life that
11   he lives is a life for God. Thus you too must consider yourselves
dead to sin, but alive to God in Christ Jesus.

6:3 f. St. Paul alludes to the manner in which Baptism was ordinarily conferred in the primitive Church, by immersion. The descent into the water is
suggestive of the descent of the body into the grave, and the ascent is suggestive
of a resurrection to a new life. St. Paul obviously sees more than a mere symbol
in the rite of Baptism; through it we are incorporated into Christ's Mystical
Body and live a new life.

6:6. enslaved to sin: some with St. Chrysostom take this expression to indicate
sin in general, and others understand it of the body inasmuch as it is enslaved
to concupiscence and is an instrument of sin.

Do not then let sin reign in your mortal body so as to obey its 12
lusts. And do not go on offering your members to sin as instruments 13
of iniquity, but once for all dedicate yourselves to God as men
that have come to life from the dead, and your members as instruments of holiness for God; for sin shall not have dominion over 14
you, since you are not subjects of the Law but of grace.

SLAVERY TO SIN GIVES PLACE TO SLAVERY TO HOLINESS

What then? Are we to sin because we are not subjects of the 15
Law but of grace? By no means! Do you not know that when you 16
offer yourselves as slaves to obey anyone, of that one you are the
slaves, whether of sin which leads to death or of obedience which
leads to holiness? But thanks be to God that you who were the 17
slaves of sin have now wholeheartedly obeyed the kind of teaching
you were taught, and after being set free from sin, you have become 18
the slaves of holiness. I am making use of these human analogies out 19
of regard for your weak human nature; for as you offered your members to be slaves of uncleanness and iniquity, culminating in utter
wickedness, so now offer your members to be slaves of right living,
culminating in holiness. When you were the slaves of sin, you 20
rendered no service to holiness. But what advantage had you then 21
from those things of which you are now ashamed? They finally end
in death. But now, set free from sin and become slaves of God, you 22
have your reward in sanctification, which finally leads to life
everlasting. For the wages that sin gives is death, but the gift that 23
God bestows is life everlasting in Christ Jesus our Lord.

CHAPTER 7

CHRISTIANS SET FREE FROM THE LAW

Do you not know, brothers — I am speaking to those who know 1
law — that the Law has dominion over a man as long as he lives?
For example, the married woman is bound by the Law while her 2
husband is alive, but if her husband dies, she is free from the law
binding her to her husband. Consequently, while her husband is 3
alive, she will be called an adulteress if she unites herself to another
man; but if her husband dies, she is set free from the law, so that

4 she is not an adulteress if she unites herself to another man. Therefore, my brothers, you in turn, through the body of Christ, have died to the Law, to unite yourselves to another, to him who has risen from the dead, in order that we may bring forth fruit for God.
5 While we were ruled by our lower nature, sinful passions, aroused by the Law, were at work in our members so that they brought forth
6 fruit for death. But now we have been set free from the Law, having died to that by which we were held down, so that we may render service which is new and according to the spirit, not old and according to the letter.

THE LAW THE OCCASION, SIN THE CAUSE OF DEATH

7   What shall we say, then? Is the Law sin? By no means! Yet I had not known sin save through the Law. For I had not known
8 lust unless the Law had said, "You shall not lust." But sin, having seized a base of operations in the commandment, produced in me by its means all manner of lust, for without law sin lies dormant.
9   Once too I was without law, but when the commandment came,
10 sin was stirred to life, and I died. Thus the commandment that was
11 to lead to life, was discovered in my case to lead to death. Sin, having seized a base of operations in the commandment, deceived me, and
12 thereby killed me. So the Law, surely, is holy and the commandment holy and just and good.
13   Did then that which is good become death to me? By no means! But sin, that it might be manifest as sin, produced death for me through what is good, in order that sin by reason of its abuse of
14 the commandment might become immeasurably sinful. We know

7:4. St. Paul lays down the general principle that death severs the marriage bond. The Christian has died mystically by reason of his union through Baptism with Christ. But since the death was only mystical, the Christian still lives and can enter a new union with Christ and produce spiritual fruit. St. Thomas Aquinas says: "It is evident that through the death by which we die with Christ, the obligation of the old Law ceases."

7:5. *ruled by our lower nature:* deprived of the grace of God, which comes from union with Christ through Baptism. *sinful passions:* i.e., evil inclinations which incite to sin. These evil inclinations were *aroused by the Law.* Prohibition whets desire.

7:7. *I had not known sin:* St. John Chrysostom says that St. Paul here means that a thorough and complete knowledge of sin comes only through law.

7:8. *without law sin lies dormant:* i.e., sin was comparatively weak. The restraint which prohibitive laws put on liberty stirred it up to rebellion, and thus in law found a powerful ally.

well that the Law is spiritual but I am carnal, sold into slavery
to sin. Why, I do not understand what I do, for what I wish, I   15
do not; what I hate, I do. But if I do what I do not wish, I admit   16
that the Law is good. But then it is no longer I who do it, but the   17
sin that dwells in me. Well do I know that in me, that is, in my   18
lower nature, no good dwells, because to wish is within my power,
but I do not find the strength to accomplish what is good. Yes, I   19
do not do the good that I wish, but the evil that I do not wish, that
I do. Now if I do what I do not wish, it is no longer I who do it,   20
but the sin that dwells within me. Therefore, when I wish to do   21
good, I discover this to be the rule, that evil is ready to hand.
I am delighted with God's Law according to the inner man,   22
but I see another norm in my bodily members, warring against the   23
law which my mind approves and making me prisoner to the norm
in my members which allures me to sin.

RESCUE THROUGH THE GRACE OF GOD

Unhappy man that I am! Who will rescue me from this body   24
doomed to death? Thanks be to God! Through Jesus Christ our   25
Lord (rescue is effected). So then, I by myself with my mind serve
the Law of God, but with my lower nature the law which allures
me to sin.

CHAPTER 8

LIVING ACCORDING TO SPIRITUAL IDEALS

So, there is now no longer any condemnation against those who   1
are in Christ Jesus. The norm of action of the spiritually minded   2
which directs my life in Christ Jesus has delivered me from the
inclination that entices me to sin and leads to death. What was   3
impossible to the Law, in that it was helpless because of corrupt
nature, God has effected. By sending his Son in a nature like that of
sinful man and as an offering for sin, he has condemned sin by the

---

7:15 ff. Here St. Paul vividly depicts the inner struggle which goes on in all
human beings between the lower, sensual nature and the higher aspirations of
the soul. He concludes by saying that the higher aspirations gain the victory
only through the grace of God merited by Jesus Christ for mankind.

8:3. *by the incarnation:* the incarnation of itself, since it was destined to

4 incarnation, in order that the requirements of the Law might be fulfilled in us who live no longer according to our lower but according to our higher nature.

5 Now they who live under the control of their lower instincts set their minds on the carnal, but they who live under the control

6 of spiritual ideals set their minds on the spiritual. Sensual-mindedness leads to death, but spiritual-mindedness leads to life and peace.

7 Why? Because sensual-mindedness is hostile to God; it is not sub-

8 ject to the Law of God, nor can it be. The sensual-minded cannot please God.

9 You, however, are not sensual but spiritual, if the Spirit of God really dwells in you, whereas no one who is deprived of the Spirit

10 of Christ belongs to Christ. But if Christ is in you, the body, it is true, is destined to death because of sin, but the spirit has life

11 because of its holiness. And if the Spirit of him who raised Jesus from the dead dwells in you, then he who raised Christ Jesus from the dead will also bring to life your mortal bodies because of his Spirit who dwells in you.

12 Therefore, brothers, you are under no obligation to your animal

13 instincts to live according to those instincts. If you live according to your lower instincts you will die; but if by the spirit you put to death the deeds prompted by your animal instincts, you will live.

CHILDREN OF GOD

14 Whoever are led by the Spirit of God, they are the sons of God.

15 Now you have not received a spirit of bondage so that you are again in fear, but you have received a spirit of adoption as sons,

16 in virtue of which we cry, "Abba! Father!" The Spirit himself joins his testimony to that of our spirit that we are children of

17 God. But if we are children, we are heirs also: heirs indeed of

---

vanquish sin, and since it entailed the presence of the Son of God in a sinless flesh and personally united to it, was the proof that God had condemned sin. The literal meaning is "in the flesh," which some interpret as "our flesh."

8:16. The testimony of the Spirit does not give us absolute assurance of our eternal salvation, and such is not the idea St. Paul intended to convey, for elsewhere he counsels us to "work out our salvation in fear and trembling" (Phil. 2:12); and he warns us, "Whoever believes he is standing firm, should beware lest he fall" (1 Cor. 10:12).

God and joint heirs with Christ, provided, however, we suffer with him that we may also be glorified with him.

Why, I count the sufferings of the present time as not worthy 18 to be compared with the glory to come that will be revealed shining upon us. All creation awaits with eager longing the manifestation 19 of the sons of God. For creation was made subject to vanity not 20 by its own choice but by the will of him who made it subject, yet with the hope that creation itself would be delivered from its 21 slavery to corruption, to enjoy the freedom that comes with the glory of the children of God. For we know that all creation groans 22 and travails in pain until now.

And not only that, but we ourselves who have the Holy Spirit 23 as first fruits — we ourselves groan within ourselves, waiting for the adoption as sons, the redemption of our body. As yet, our salvation 24 is only a matter of hope. Now there is no hope when the object which had been hoped for is seen. How can a man hope really for what he sees? But if we hope for what we do not see, we wait 25 for it with patience.

In the same way the Spirit also helps our weakness. For we 26 do not know what we should pray for as we ought, but the Spirit himself pleads for us with unutterable sighs. And he who searches 27 the hearts knows what the Spirit desires and that he in accord with God's designs pleads for the saints.

GOD'S GREAT LOVE FOR US

Now we know that God causes all things to work together for 28 the good of those, who love him, who according to his purpose are called because those whom he has foreknown he has also predestined 29 to be conformed to the image of his Son, so that this Son should be the first-born among many brothers. Those whom he has pre- 30 destined, he has called; and those whom he has called, he has sanctified, and those whom he has sanctified, he has glorified.

8:18–23. St. Paul in this passage, in a mystical, poetical conception, thinks of the whole world as groaning in subjection to vanity, that is, to corruption, change, and death, as a result of man's fall, and yearning to share in the glorification of the sons of God at the end of time. St. Peter tells us that there "will be a new heaven and a new earth" (2 Pet. 3:13). St. John in vision "saw a new heaven and a new earth" (Apoc. 21:1).

8:30. St. Paul here speaks by anticipation and with certainty. But the cer-

31   What then shall we conclude after that? If God is for us, who
32   is against us? He who has not spared even his own Son but has
delivered him for us all, how can he fail to grant us all other blessings
33   with him? Who shall make accusation against the elect of God?
34   It is God who sanctifies! Who shall condemn? It is Christ Jesus
who died, yes, and who rose again, who is at the right hand of
God, who also intercedes for us!

35   Who shall separate us from Christ's love for us? Shall tribulation,
or distress, or persecution, or hunger, or nakedness, or danger, or
36   the sword? Even as it is written,

"For your sake we are put to death all the day long,
we are regarded as sheep for the slaughter."

37   But in all those things we are more than victorious through him who
38   has loved us. I am sure that neither death, nor life, nor angels, nor
principalities, nor things present, nor things to come, nor powers,
39   nor height, nor depth, nor any other creature can separate us from
God's love for us, which is in Christ Jesus our Lord.

THE PROBLEM OF THE REJECTION OF ISRAEL
CHAPTER 9

PAUL'S SORROW FOR THE JEWS

1   I speak the truth in Christ, I do not lie, my conscience bears
2   me witness in the Holy Spirit, that I have great sadness and con-
─3   tinuous sorrow in my heart. For I could wish to be cut off myself
from Christ for the sake of my brothers, my kinsmen according to
4   the flesh. They are Israelites. Theirs is the adoption as sons, theirs
the glory, the covenants, the legislation, the worship, and the

---

tainty is only on the part of God, who will perform this as the last in a series
of acts leading man to his eternal destiny, provided man does not fall from
grace before the end of his life.
    8:33. Isa. 50:8 f.
    8:36. Isa. 43:22.
    9:3. cut off . . . from Christ: i.e., to be eternally separated from Christ. So
great was St. Paul's longing for the salvation of his own kinsmen that he would
make any possible sacrifice to that end, even to being separated from Christ, if
it were permissible to entertain such a desire. That these words are merely an
emphatic way of declaring his great devotion to his people and that they are
not to be taken literally is evident from what St. Paul has said above (8:38).

promises. The patriarchs are theirs, and from them has been derived 5
the human nature of Christ, who exalted above all beings, is God
blessed forever. Amen.

GOD'S FREE CHOICE

It is not that the word of God has failed. They are not all 6
Israelites who are sprung from Israel; nor, because they are the 7
descendants of Abraham, are they all his children; but

"Through Isaac shall your posterity bear your name."
That is to say, not they are sons of God who are the children by 8
natural descent, but it is the children designated by the promise
who are reckoned as descendants. Here are the terms of the promise: 9
"About this time I will come and Sara shall have a son." And not 10
only she, but Rebecca too conceived by one man, Isaac our father.
Why, before the children had been born, or had done aught of 11
good or evil, in order that God's selective purpose might stand,
depending not on deeds, but on him who calls, it was said to her, 12
"The elder shall serve the younger." So it is written, "Jacob I have 13
loved, but Esau I have hated."

What then shall we say? Is there injustice in God? By no means! 14
Does he not say to Moses, "I shall have mercy on whom I have 15
mercy, and I will show pity to whom I show pity"? So then, there 16
is no question of him who wills or of him who runs, but of God
showing mercy. For example the Scripture says to the Pharao, "For 17
this very purpose I have raised you up, that I may show my power,
and that my name may be proclaimed in all the earth." Therefore 18
he has mercy on whom he pleases, and he hardens whom he pleases.

9:7. Gen. 2:22.
9:9. Gen. 18:10.
9:10–12. Gen. 25:23 ff.
9:13. Mal. 1–2. The hatred toward Esau here ascribed to God should be understood in the light of a familiar Hebrew idiom, according to which "to love less" is equivalent "to hate."
9:15. Exod. 33:19.
9:16. *of him who wills:* the primary and ultimate factor in man's destiny is the activity of God's grace, which of course does not exclude man's co-operation.
9:17. Exod. 9:16. *For this very purpose:* it is not to be understood that God's primary and express purpose in creating Pharao was to make a sinner out of him. But God raised him up to rule the Egyptian people, and, foreseeing that Pharao would abuse grace and fall into sin, God decreed to use Pharao according to his demerits for the further manifestation of his own divine attributes and for the realization of the designs of his all-wise providence.
9:18. *he hardens:* i.e., by withdrawing divine grace in punishment of sin.

19   Then you will ask me: "Why does God still find fault? Does
20 anyone resist his will?" Of course not, O man, but who are you
to answer back to God? Does the object molded say to him who
21 molded it. "Why have you made me thus?" Or is not the potter
master of the clay, free to make from the same material one vessel
22 for honorable, another for dishonorable use? If God who intends to
show his wrath and make his power known, endured long and
patiently those who deserved his wrath and were ripe for destruc-
23 tion, what can be said against that? He intends thus to show the
wealth of his glory on those who are objects of his mercy, whom
24 beforehand he has prepared for that glory. We whom he has called,
Jews and Gentiles alike, are the objects of that mercy.
25   So also he says in Osee:
"A people not mine I will call my people,
and her who was not beloved, beloved,
26   And it shall be in the place where it was said to them:
you are not my people;
there they shall be called sons of the living God."
27 Isaias cries out concerning Israel:
"Though the number of the children of Israel
be as the sands of the sea,
the remnant shall be saved.
28   Surely the Lord will accomplish his word
fully and with dispatch on earth."
29 And as Isaias foretold:
"Unless the Lord of Hosts had left us some descendants,
we should have become as Sodom
and should have been like Gemorrah."

ISRAEL'S RESPONSIBILITY

30   What then are we to say? That the Gentiles who were not

9:21. St. John Chrysostom says: "St. Paul here so speaks not by way of
denying free will but to show to what extent we are to submit to God. For
we should be no more ready to demand reasons from God than the clay
vessel."
9:25. Osee 2:23 f.
9:26. Osee 1:10.
9:27. Isa. 10:22 f.
9:29. Isa. 1:9.

pursuing holiness have secured holiness, the holiness that comes of
faith, while Israel, though pursuing a law leading to holiness, have   31
not attained to holiness. Why? Because they sought it not from   32
faith but from deeds. They stumbled at the stumbling stone,
as it is written,   33

"See, I lay in Sion a stumbling stone and rock to trip over;
But no one who believes in him shall be disappointed."

CHAPTER 10

Brothers, my heart's desire and my prayer are directed to God   1
in their behalf for their salvation. I bear them witness that they   2
have zeal for God, though a zeal that is unenlightened. Ignorant   3
of the sanctification provided by God and seeking to establish their
own, they have not submitted to the sanctification provided by God.
Christ has put an end to the Law and has opened the way to   4
sanctification for everyone who believes.

Moses writes that the man who realizes that holy living which   5
is required by the Law shall find life by it. But the sanctification   6
that comes of faith says, "Do not say in your heart: Who shall
ascend into heaven?" (that is, to bring Christ down); or, "Who   7
shall descend into the abyss?" (that is, to bring Christ up from the
dead). But what does the Scripture say? "The message is near you,   8
on your lips and in your heart" (that is, the message of faith, which

---

9:33. Isa. 28:16.

10:3. *sanctification provided by God:* literally, "justice," which God imparts
to the soul through Christ and the Church. The Jews rejected this and sought
to acquire holiness rather through the observance of the works prescribed by
the Mosaic Law.

10:4. *put an end to the Law:* literally, "is the end," which some understand
as "purpose."

10:5. Lev. 18:5.

10:6-9. Deut. 30:12-14. The words were first spoken of the accessibility of
the Mosaic Law. St. Paul applies them to the revealed message of Jesus Christ.

10:6-13. St. Paul here seeks to establish the ease with which this holiness
of the Christian dispensation may be acquired, in contrast to the system which
prevailed under the Mosaic dispensation. According to this latter, one had to
observe the Law — not an easy thing as St. Paul has shown in Chapter 7. In
the Christian dispensation there is no need of attempting the impossible, like
ascending into heaven to bring Christ down, or descending into the abyss to
bring Christ up from the dead. Christ has already come and has risen from
the dead.

9   we preach). For if you confess with your lips that Jesus is the Lord, and believe in your heart that God raised him from the dead,
10 you shall be saved. Because with the heart a man believes and attains holiness, and with the lips profession of faith is made and salvation secured.
11 "No one who believes in him," says the Scripture, "shall be
12 disappointed." There is no distinction between Jew and Greek. There is the same Lord of all, generous toward all who call upon
13 him, since "whoever calls on the name of the Lord shall be saved."
14 How, then, are people to call upon him in whom they have not attained faith? And how can they attain faith in him whom they
15 have not heard? And how are they to hear if no one preaches? And how are men to preach unless they be sent? As it is written,

> "How welcome is the coming of those who
> proclaim the Good News."

16 But not all have submitted to the Good News. So Isaias says,

> "Lord, who has believed our preaching?"

17 Faith, then, depends on hearing, and hearing on Christ's teaching.
18 But I ask: Have they heard. Yes, assuredly,

> "Their voice has gone forth into all the earth
> and their words unto the ends of the world."

19 But I say: Has not Israel understood? First of all, Moses says,

> "I will provoke you to jealousy of those who
> are not a nation:
> I will stir you to anger against a senseless nation."

20 Then Isaias dares to say,

> "I was found by those who did not seek me;
> I revealed myself to those who made no inquiry
> about me."

10:15. Isa. 52:7.
10:16. Isa. 53:1. preaching: In Isaias the word which literally means "hearing" can be understood either of the prophetic message from God heard by the prophet, or of its deliverance by the prophet to the people and their hearing it.
10:17. Christ's teaching: literally, "word," which some understand of the revealed message or teaching of Christ, others of the commission given by Christ to the Apostles.
10:18. Ps. 18:5.
10:19. Deut. 32:31.
10:20–21. Isa. 65:1 f.

But to Israel he says,   21
    "All the day I stretched out my hands
    to a people unbelieving and contradicting."

Chapter 11

ISRAEL'S REJECTION NOT TOTAL

  I ask then: Has God cast off his people? By no means! Why, I 1
myself am an Israelite, of the posterity of Abraham, of the tribe of
Benjamin. God has not cast off his people whom he foreknew. 2
Or do you not know what the Scripture says in the account of
Elias, how he lodges complaint with God against Israel?
    "Lord, they have slain your prophets,   3
        they have razed your altars,
        and I alone am left,
        And they seek my life."
But what does the divine answer say to him?   4
    "I have left myself seven thousand men,
        who have not bent their knees to Baal."
Even so at the present time there is a remnant left, selected by 5
grace. And if by grace, then not in virtue of deeds; otherwise grace 6
would no longer be grace.
  What then? What Israel is seeking after, that it has not obtained; 7
but the chosen ones have obtained it, and the rest have been blinded,
as it is written,   8
    "God has given them a spirit of stupor
        until this present day,
        Eyes that they may not see,
        and ears that they may not hear."

  11:3. 1 Kings 19:10. Just as in the time of Elias there was a small remnant
who persevered in their fidelity to God, so likewise when St. Paul wrote this
epistle, although the Jewish nation as a whole had refused to believe, there were
not a few converts to Christianity. St. Paul insists, however, that their call
to the faith was due to the free choice of God, and not to the merit of
their deeds.
  11:4. 1 Kings 19:18.
  11:8. Isa. 29:10. God permitted this blindness in punishment of their sins.

9 And David says,
            "Let their table become a snare and a trap
                and a stumbling block and a retribution unto them.
10   Let their eyes be darkened that they may not see,
                and let them bow their backs forever."

ISRAEL'S REJECTION NOT FINAL

11   I ask then: Have they so stumbled as to fall utterly? By no means!
    But by their false step salvation has come to the Gentiles, that they
12 may emulate them. Now if their false step is directed to the enrich-
    ment of the world, and their defection to the enrichment of the
    Gentiles, how much more their full number!
13   Now I say to you Gentiles: As long surely as I am an Apostle
14 of the Gentiles, I shall do honor to my ministry, in the hope that
    I may provoke to emulation those who are my own flesh and may
15 save some of them. If the rejection of them leads to the reconcilia-
    tion of the world, what will taking them back lead to but life
    from the dead?
16   Now if the first handful of the dough is holy, so too is the batch
17 of dough; and if the root is holy, so too are the branches. But if
    some of the branches have been broken off, and if you, a wild olive,
    are grafted in their place, and have become a partaker of the root
18 and richness of the olive tree, do not boast against the branches.
    But if you do boast notwithstanding, remember that it is not you
19 who support the root, but the root you. You will say, then, "Branches
20 were broken off, that I might be grafted in." True, but they were
    broken off because of unbelief, whereas you because of faith hold your
21 position. Be fearful, not conceited, because if God has not spared the
22 natural branches, perhaps he may not spare you either. See, then, the
    goodness and the severity of God: his severity toward those who have
    fallen, but the goodness of God toward you if you abide in his
    goodness; otherwise you also will be cut off.
23   But they too, if they do not continue in unbelief, will be grafted
24 in; certainly God is able to graft them back. Why, if you have
    been cut off from the wild olive tree which is natural to you, and,
    contrary to nature, have been grafted into the cultivated olive tree,

_____
11:9. Ps. 68:23 f.

how much more shall these, the natural branches, be grafted into their own olive tree!

ISRAEL'S CONVERSION FORETOLD

I would not, brothers, have you ignorant of this mystery, lest 25 you should have a conceited opinion of yourselves, that a partial blindness only has befallen Israel, until the full number of the Gentiles should enter, and thus all Israel shall be saved, as it 26 is written,

"There will come out of Sion the deliverer,
he will turn away impiety from Jacob;
And this is my covenant with them, 27
When I shall take away their sins."

For your sake they are enemies in view of the spread of the gospel, 28 but for their fathers' sake they are most dear in virtue of the divine choice. For God does not revoke his gifts and his call. 29

GOD'S INFINITE MERCY

Just as once you did not believe God, and now have obtained 30 mercy, because of their unbelief; even so they too have not believed 31 on the occasion of the mercy shown you, that they too may obtain mercy. For God has imprisoned all mankind in unbelief, that he 32 may have mercy on them all.

Oh, the depth of the riches and of the wisdom and of the knowl- 33 edge of God! How incomprehensible are his judgments and how unsearchable his ways! For 34

"Who has known the mind of the Lord,
or who has been his counselor?
Or who has first given to him 35
and in turn had a recompense due him?"

For from him and through him and unto him are all things. To 36 him be glory forever, Amen.

11:26. Isa. 59:20 f.
11:27. Isa. 27:9.
11:29. God does not revoke: Jews, therefore, always remain the race of God's predilection, and will eventually be converted to the faith and saved.

THE DUTIES OF CHRISTIANS

CHAPTER 12

SELF-IMMOLATION

1   I exhort you, therefore, brothers in view of the mercies of God,
to offer your bodies as a sacrifice, living, holy, pleasing to God —
2   such is the worship reason requires of you. And do not conform to
this world's way of life, but be transformed by the renewal of your
mind, that you may investigate the will of God — all that is good,
all that is acceptable to him, all that is perfect.

HUMBLE ACCEPTANCE OF ONE'S PLACE IN THE CHURCH

3   By the commission that has been given me, I say to each one
among you: Let no one esteem himself more than he ought, but let
him esteem himself in moderation according to the degree of faith
4   which God has apportioned to each one. For just as in one body
we have many organs, yet not all the organs have the same function,
5   so we, the aggregate, are one body in Christ, but individually to one
6   another we stand in the relation of part to part. We have gifts
differing according to the grace that has been given us. If the gift
is that of God's inspired spokesmen, let it be used under the control
7   of faith; if it is ministry, let one minister, or if one is a teacher, let
8   him teach; if one's gift is exhortation, let him exhort; let him who
shares his goods, do so in simplicity; let him who presides, do so
with diligence; let him who shows mercy, do so with cheerfulness.

12:1. *as a sacrifice:* we should daily put to death or mortify the lusts of
the flesh and wholly dedicate our bodies to the divine service in accord with
the requirements of the Christian law of right living. *worship reason requires:*
literally, "spiritual service" or "reasonable service."
12:3. Each must take as the rule of his esteem of self, and as his role in
the Church the measure of faith, that is, probably, the special gifts God has
given him.
12:6. *God's inspired spokesman:* literally, "prophecy" — a supernatural gift
in virtue of which the recipient is given insight into the hidden truths beyond
the power of human reason to discern. The term also designates a special gift of
eloquence in preaching and expounding the mysteries of faith. This gift is
to be exercised *under the control of faith* — literally, "according to the analogy
of faith," i.e., as St. Thomas says, "not in vain, but that the faith may be
confirmed by it; not against the faith."

THE PRACTICE OF BROTHERLY LOVE

Let love be without pretense. Hate what is evil; cling to what 9
is good. Love one another with fraternal charity, anticipating one 10
another with honor. Do not be slothful in zeal; be fervent in spirit; 11
it is the Lord you serve. Rejoice in hope. Be patient in tribulation, 12
persevering in prayer. Relieve the needs of the saints, exercise hos- 13
pitality with eagerness. Bless those who persecute you; bless and do 14
not curse. Rejoice with those who rejoice; weep with those who weep. 15
Agree in thought with another, aspiring not to high things, but 16
agreeing in thought with lowly people. Be not wise in your own
eyes. To no man render evil for evil, but take thought for decent 17
conduct in the sight of all men. If it be possible, as far as lies in 18
your power, be at peace with all men. Do not avenge yourselves, 19
beloved, but give place to the wrath of God, for it is written,

"Vengeance is mine; I will repay, says the Lord."
But 20
"If your enemy is hungry, give him food;
If he is thirsty, give him drink;
For by so doing you will heap coals of fire
on his head."
Be not conquered by evil, but conquer evil by good. 21

CHAPTER 13

OBEDIENCE TO CIVIL AUTHORITY

Let everyone submit himself to the ruling authorities, for there 1
exists no authority not ordained by God. And that which exists has
been constituted by God. Therefore he who opposes such authority 2
resists the ordinance of God, and they that resist bring condemnation
on themselves. Rulers are not a source of fear in regard to good 3
actions, but only in regard to evil ones. You wish, then, not to fear
the authority? Do what is good and you will have praise from him.
For he is God's minister for your benefit. But if you do evil, fear, for 4

12:19. Deut. 32:35.
12:20. Prov. 25:21 f. To heap coals of fire on one's head probably means
to make that person burn with shame and remorse; to overwhelm him with
kindness.

not without reason does he wear the sword. He is God's minister,
5 an avenger to inflict punishment on evildoers. Accordingly we must
needs submit, not only out of fear of punishment, but also for
6 conscience' sake. This is why you pay tribute, for they are public
7 ministers of God, devoting their energies to this very thing. Render
to all men their due: tribute to whom tribute is due; taxes to whom
taxes are due; respect to whom respect is due; honor to whom
honor is due.

LOVE IS PERFECTION

8 Let there be no unpaid debt except the debt of mutual love,
9 because he who loves his neighbor has fulfilled the Law. For the
commandments:
> "You shall not commit adultery;
> You shall not kill;
> You shall not steal;
> You shall not covet";

and if there is any other commandment, all are summed up in this
saying,
> "You shall love your neighbor as yourself."

‒ 10 Love does no evil to a neighbor. Love, therefore, is the complete
fulfillment of the Law.

BREVITY OF TIME CALLS FOR EARNESTNESS

11 And this do with due regard for the time, for it is now the hour
for you to rise from sleep, because now our salvation is nearer than
12 when we came to believe. This night is far advanced; the day is at
‒ hand. Let us, therefore, lay aside the deeds prompted by darkness,
13 and put on the armor of light. Let us conduct ourselves becomingly
as in the day, not in revelry and drunkenness, not in debauchery and
14 wantonness, not in strife and jealousy. But put on the Lord Jesus
Christ, and take no thought for your lower nature to satisfy its lusts.

CHAPTER 14

MUTUAL FORBEARANCE

1 Welcome among yourselves the person who has a weak con-

13:9. Exod. 20:13–17.
14:1. *weak conscience*: those whose faith is not sufficiently enlightened to

science, but avoid disputes about opinions. One person's conscience 2
says that he may eat anything, but he who has a weak conscience
eats only vegetables. He that eats should not despise him that eats 3
not, and he that eats not should not condemn him that eats, since
God has welcomed this latter one into his household. Who are you 4
to condemn another's household servant? It is his master's concern
whether he stands or falls; and he will stand, for God can keep him
standing. Another prefers this day to that; still another puts all 5
days on the same level. Let everyone have his own complete mental
conviction. He who has a mind to observe the day, does so for the 6
Lord's sake; and he who eats does so for the Lord's sake, since he
gives thanks to the Lord. So too he who does not eat, abstains for
the Lord's sake, and gives thanks to God. None of us lives for 7
himself, and none dies for himself. If we live, we live for the Lord, 8
and if we die, we die for the Lord. Whether we live or whether
we die, we are the Lord's. To this end Christ died and lived, that 9
he might be Lord both of the dead and of the living. But you, 10
why do you condemn your brother? Or why do you despise your
brother? We shall all stand before the judgment seat of God.
So it is written, 11

> "As I live, says the Lord,
>> to me every knee shall bend,
>> and every tongue shall give praise
>> to God."

LOVE AND HARMONY

Therefore everyone will render account of himself to God. 12
Let us then no longer judge one another, but rather resolve not to 13
put an occasion of sin or a stumbling block in your brother's way.
I know and I am fully convinced in the Lord Jesus that nothing is 14
of itself unclean; but to him who regards something as unclean, it
is unclean. If then your brother is upset because of what you eat, 15

---

make the practical application of its principles to the affairs of daily life,
particularly in the case under discussion relative to certain foods, whether it
was licit or not to eat them. The strong in faith are those who have a more
enlightened faith and make better application of it to daily moral problems.
St. Paul in this chapter exhorts the strong to bear with and refrain from giving
bad example to the weak, and the weak to refrain from condemning the strong.
Judgment is to be left to the Lord, before whose tribunal all men must appear.
14:11. Isa. 45:23.

no longer do you act according to the demands of love. Do not
16 with what you eat destroy him for whom Christ died. Let not then
17 your privilege be reviled. For the kingdom of God does not consist
in food and drink, but in holiness and peace and joy in the Holy
18 Spirit. He who in this way serves Christ pleases God and is approved
19 by men. Let us, then, pursue the things that make for peace and
20 mutual edification. Do not for the sake of food destroy God's work!
All food is certainly clean, but food is evil for the man who eats it
21 while giving in to bad example. It is good not to eat meat and not
to drink wine, nor to do anything by which your brother is offended
22 or induced to sin or weakened. You have a conscientious conviction:
Keep it to yourself before God. Blessed is he who does not condemn
23 himself by his own decision. But he who eats when he is in doubt,
condemns himself because his act does not come from conscientious
conviction; for every act that does not proceed from conscientious
conviction is sinful.

CHAPTER 15

SELF-DENIAL AND PATIENCE

1 We, the strong, ought to bear the infirmities of the weak, and not
2 please ourselves. Let everyone of us please his neighbor, doing him
3 good by edifying him, since Christ did not please himself, but as
it is written,

> "The reproaches of those who reproach you
> have fallen upon me."

4 For whatever has been written beforehand, has been written for our
instruction, that through the patient endurance and consolation
5 afforded by the Scriptures we may have hope. May then the God
who imparts patience and comfort grant you this unity of sentiments
6 among yourselves according to Jesus Christ, that, one in spirit, you
may in a harmonious chorus glorify the God and Father of our
Lord Jesus Christ.

14:16. *privilege:* literally, "your good," which according to St. Chrysostom
means the treasure of doctrine which Christianity offers. Outsiders, seeing the
Christians arguing about trifles, will be led to despise Christianity. Others
understand this privilege of Christian liberty, based on solid principles of faith.
15:3. Ps. 68:10.

INDULGENT MERCY

Therefore, welcome one another cordially, even as Christ has 7
cordially welcomed you to himself for the glory of God. I declare 8
as a matter of fact that Christ Jesus has been a minister of the
circumcised to show God's fidelity in realizing the promises made to
our fathers, while the Gentiles glorify God because of his mercy, as 9
it is written,

> "There shall I praise you among the Gentiles
> And shall sing to your name."

And again the Scripture says, 10

> "Rejoice, you Gentiles, with his people."

And again, 11

> "Praise the Lord, all you Gentiles;
> and sing his praises, all you peoples."

And again Isaias says, 12

> "There shall be the root of Jesse,
> and he who arises to rule the Gentiles . . .
> in him the Gentiles shall hope."

May God, the source of hope, fill you with all joy and peace based 13
on faith, that you may abound in hope by the power of the
Holy Spirit.

CONCLUSION

APOSTLE OF THE GENTILES

I myself, my brothers, am convinced in your regard that you 14
too are full of goodness, replete with all knowledge, so that you are
able to admonish one another. Yet I have written to you rather 15
boldly here and there, brothers — as it were to refresh your memory
— because of the commission given me by God, to be a public 16
minister of Christ Jesus to the Gentiles, performing priestly functions by means of God's gospel, that the oblation of the Gentiles

---

15:9. Ps. 17:50.
15:10. Deut. 32:43.
15:11. Ps. 116:1.
15:12. Isa. 11:10.
15:16. *performing priestly functions:* St. Paul here uses the metaphorical
language of sacrifice. The Apostle's priestly functions result in the oblation of

17 may become acceptable, being sanctified by the Holy Spirit. I have, therefore, this boast in Christ Jesus as regards the work of God.
18 I do not make bold to mention anything but what Christ has wrought through me to bring about the conversion of the Gentiles,
19 by word and deed, with mighty signs and wonders, by the power of the Holy Spirit, so that from Jerusalem, and that in all directions, as far as Illyricum, I have fully preached the gospel of Christ.
20 But I have made it a point of honor not to preach the gospel where Christ has already been proclaimed, lest I build on another
21 man's foundation. But as it is written,

"They who have not been told of him shall see,
and they who have not heard shall understand."

PAUL'S PLANS

22 This is why I have been hindered these many times from coming
23 to you. But now, having no further field of action in these parts,
24 and having had for many years a great desire to visit you, when I set out for Spain I hope to see you as I pass through and to be sped on my way by you, after I have to some extent satisfied my
25 desire for your company. At the moment, however, I am setting out
26 for Jerusalem to bring help to the saints. For Macedonia and Achaia have thought it well to contribute to the needs of the poor among
27 the saints of Jerusalem. Such has been the good pleasure of the former, who have thus made the latter their debtors. For if the Gentiles have shared in the Jew's spiritual blessings, they should
28 also aid their Jewish brothers with material blessings. So, when I have completed this task, and have turned the proceeds over to
29 them, I will set out by way of your city for Spain. I know that when I come to you, I shall come with the fullness of Christ's blessing.

REQUEST FOR PRAYERS

30 I beseech you, brothers, through our Lord Jesus Christ, and through the love of the Spirit, that you join your efforts with mine
31 in prayers to God for me, that I may be delivered from the un-

the Gentiles as a sacrifice to God, and the means by which this oblation is made worthy of God is the Gospel teaching and its effects. The Gentiles become acceptable to God as an offering because they have been made holy by the Holy Spirit who dwells in the faithful.
15:21. Isa. 52:15.

believers in Judea, and that the proffered help may be acceptable to
the saints at Jerusalem; that I may come to you in joy, by the will   32
of God, and may enjoy a vacation with you. May the God of peace   33
be with you all. Amen.

CHAPTER 16

PERSONAL GREETINGS

I recommend to you Phoebe, our sister, who is a deaconess of   1
the congregation at Cenchrae, that you may welcome her in the   2
Lord, as becomes saints, and that you may assist her in whatever
business she may have need of you. She too has assisted many,
including myself.

Greet Prisca and Aquila, my helpers in Christ Jesus, who for   3, 4
my life have risked their own. To them not only I but all the
congregations of the Gentiles give thanks. Greet also the congrega-   5
tion that meets in her house. Greet my beloved Epaenetus, who
is the first fruits of Asia for Christ. Greet Mary who has labored   6
much for you. Greet Andronicus and Junias, my kinsmen and   7
fellow prisoners, who are distinguished among the apostles, who
also were in Christ before me. Greet Ampliatus, beloved to me   8
in the Lord. Greet Urbanus, our helper in Christ, and my beloved   9
Stachys. Greet Apelles, approved of Christ. Greet the members   10, 11
of Aristobulus' household. Greet Herodion, my kinsman. Greet
the members of Narcissus' household, who are in the Lord.
Greet Tryphaena and Tryphosa who labor in the Lord. Greet the   12
beloved Persis who has labored much in the Lord. Greet Rufus, the   13
elect in the Lord. Greet Asyncritus, Phlegon, Hermas, Patrobas,   14
Hermes, and the brothers who are with them. Greet Philologus   15
and Julia, Nereus and his sister, and Olympias and all the saints
who are with them. Greet one another with a holy kiss. All the   16
congregations of Christ greet you.

WARNING TO TROUBLEMAKERS

I exhort you, brothers, to watch those who cause dissensions and   17
scandals contrary to the doctrine you have learned; avoid them.
Such do not serve Christ our Lord but their own appetites, and   18

by smooth words and flattery deceive the hearts of the simple.
19 Surely your submission to the faith has been published everywhere;
I rejoice over you. Yet I would have you wise as to what is good,
20 and guileless as to what is evil. The God of peace will speedily
crush Satan under your feet. The grace of our Lord Jesus Christ
be with you.

GREETINGS FROM CORINTH

21   Timothy, my fellow laborer, greets you, and Lucius, and Jason,
22 and Sosipater, my kinsmen. I, Tertius, who transcribed this letter
23 greet you in the Lord. Gaius, my host and the host of the whole
24 congregation, greets you. Erastus, the city treasurer, and Quartus,
our brother, greet you.

DOXOLOGY

25   Glory be to God who is able to strengthen you in accordance
with the Good News I preach, which heralds Jesus, the Messias. This
preaching reveals the mystery which has been kept hidden through
26 eternal ages, but which is now made known by the prophetical
writings and proclaimed, by the command of the eternal God, to
the Gentiles, so as to bring about their submission to the faith.
27 Yes, to God, who alone is wise, be glory through Jesus Christ
for ever and ever. Amen.

16:24. Part of this verse is omitted as it appears in only a few Greek codices
and is missing from the best codices of the Vulgate. It reads: "May the grace
of our Lord Jesus Christ be with you all, Amen."

THE FIRST EPISTLE
TO THE CORINTHIANS

Corinth was a Roman colony built upon the remains of an old Greek city. When St. Paul visited it, the city was materially prosperous and morally corrupt.

On his second missionary journey, Paul preached about two years in Corinth, first to the Jews in the synagogue and then to the Gentiles in the house of Titus Justus (Acts 18:1–18). After his disappointment in the use of a philosophical approach to Christianity at Athens (Acts 17:15 ff.), Paul used at Corinth a simpler approach. He preached nothing but Jesus Christ, and especially his crucifixion (1 Cor. 2:2). According to the divine promise (Acts 18:9 f.), he made many converts, but suffered much from the hostility of the Jews. He left for Ephesus some time after Gallio became proconsul of Achaia, i.e., about A.D. 52.

It is quite probable that St. Paul wrote an Epistle to the Corinthians prior to the two which our New Testament contains (1 Cor. 5:9). The Epistle known as the First of St. Paul to the Corinthians was occasioned by the visit to Ephesus of members of the Corinthian congregation (1 Cor. 1:11; 16:12, 17). St. Paul, who had meanwhile returned to Antioch and undertaken his third missionary journey, learned from these messengers of certain disorders in the congregation at Corinth. Questions were also proposed by the neophytes to their spiritual father for solution. To correct these disorders and to answer these questions, St. Paul wrote this masterly Epistle.

From 1 Cor. 16:5–8 it is clear that the letter was written at Ephesus some time before Pentecost, probably in the beginning of the year A.D. 57.

411

THE FIRST EPISTLE OF

ST. PAUL THE APOSTLE

TO THE CORINTHIANS

CHAPTER 1

GREETINGS

Paul, called by the will of God to be an apostle of Jesus Christ, *1* and Sosthenes our brother, to the congregation of God at Corinth, *2* to you who have been sanctified in Christ Jesus and called to be saints in the same way as all who, in whatever place it may be, call upon the name of our Lord Jesus Christ, their Lord as well as ours. Grace be to you and peace from God our Father and the Lord *3* Jesus Christ.

I give thanks to my God always on your behalf for God's grace *4* which was given you in Christ Jesus, because in every respect you *5* have been enriched in him with every form of eloquence and knowledge. In proportion as the testimony borne to Christ has been *6* well established among you, you lack no gift. Meanwhile you await *7* the appearance of our Lord Jesus Christ. He will keep you steadfast *8* to the end, unimpeachable on the Day of our Lord Jesus Christ. God *9* is faithful; it was he who called you into fellowship with his Son, Jesus Christ our Lord.

PARTY SPIRIT

FACTIONS IN THE CHURCH

But I beseech you, brothers, by the name of our Lord Jesus *10*

1:1. *Sosthenes:* possibly the same person mentioned in Acts 18:17.

1:2. *in the same way:* St. Paul reminds the Corinthians who had a tendency to split into factions, of the unity of all Christians the world over.

1:10. The reference is to cliques, not to heresies or schisms.

413

Christ, that you all agree in what you say, and that there be no
factions among you, but that you be perfectly united in the same
11 understanding and disposition of soul. For I have been informed,
concerning you, my brothers, by members of Chloe's household,
12 that there is wrangling among you. I mean namely that each group
among you has its slogan: "I am a follower of Paul," or "I am a
13 follower of Apollos," or "I of Cephas," or "I of Christ." Is Christ
at war with himself? Was Paul crucified for you? Or were you
14 baptized in the name of Paul? I thank God that I baptized none
15 of you but Crispus and Gaius, lest anyone should say that you were
16 baptized in my name. I baptized the household of Stephanus also.
Beyond that I am not aware of having baptized anyone else.

WISDOM OF GOD AND WISDOM OF THE WORLD

17   Christ certainly did not send me to baptize, but to preach the
Good News, not with the orator's devices, lest the cross of Christ
18 should be robbed of its force. Whereas the message that the cross
proclaims is nonsense to those who are on the road to destruction,
to us who are on the road to salvation, it is the power of God.
19 It is written,
    "I will destroy the wisdom of the wise,
        and the cleverness of the clever I will thwart."
20 Where is the "wise" man? Where is the scholar? Where is the
philosopher of this world? Has not God turned to nonsense the
21 "wisdom" of this world? Since the world with all its "wisdom"
did not attain to the knowledge of God from his wisdom (reflected
in creation), it pleased God by the "absurdity" we preach, to save
22 those who believe. The Jews demand miracles and the Greeks look
23 for "wisdom," but we, for our part, preach a crucified Christ — to

---

1:12. *Apollos:* friend and co-worker of St. Paul, an eloquent speaker. *Cephas:*
the Aramaic name ("Rock") of St. Peter. He and others here mentioned,
as St. Chrysostom says, were not leaders of factions; their names are merely
used as examples.

1:17. *to baptize:* this was not the principal work of St. Paul. He usually
left it to his assistants to administer the rite.

1:19. Isa. 29:14.

1:21. God's wisdom is reflected in the created universe. So Tertullian and
St. Thomas. God's wisdom, according to others, is his providence which so disposes things as to permit men to fail to recognize him through the reflection
of his attributes in creation.

414

the Jews certainly a stumbling block and to the Gentiles an absurdity,
but to those who are called, to the Jews and Greeks alike, Christ, 24
the power of God and the wisdom of God. Why, there is more 25
wisdom in the "absurdity" of God than in all the "wisdom" of
men and more might in the "weakness" of God than in all the
might of men.

Just consider, brothers, your own call; not many of you were 26
wise, not many influential, not many noble by worldly standards.
But God chose what the world holds foolish, to put to shame 27
the wise, and what the world holds weak God chose to put to shame
the mighty, and what the world holds ignoble and despicable, 28
and what counts for nought God chose, to bring to nought the
things that count, lest any weak mortal should pride himself in 29
God's sight. From him comes your union in Christ Jesus, who 30
has become for us God-given wisdom and holiness and sanctification
and redemption; so that, just as it is written, "Let him that takes 31
pride, take pride in the Lord."

CHAPTER 2

I, too, brothers, when I came to you did not come with pre- 1
tentious speech or "wisdom," to announce to you the testimony
God has given. I had decided to make known to you nothing but 2
Jesus Christ, and especially his crucifixion. And it was in weakness 3
and fear and much trepidation that I presented myself to you.
My speech and my preaching did not consist of the persuasive 4
words of "wisdom," but of the convincing display of the Spirit's
power. My motive was that your faith should rest not on human 5
"wisdom" but on divine power.

1:25. *"Absurdity"* and *"weakness"* are the pagan's way of regarding Christianity, which has accomplished more for humanity than all the combined systems of human philosophy and efforts at amelioration.

1:31. Jer. 9:23–24.

2:1. *testimony:* some authorities read "mystery." *God:* some authorities read "Christ."

2:5. *divine power:* as shown in the many conversions and the visible gifts, such as tongues, bestowed on the converts.

TRUE WISDOM

6 We do, however, speak wisdom among those that are mature,
yet not the wisdom of this world, or of the rulers of this world
7 who are on the wane. The wisdom we speak is of God, mysterious,
hidden, which God foreordained to our glory before the world's
8 beginning, a wisdom which none of this world's rulers knew,
because if they had known it, they would never have crucified
9 the Lord to whom belongs all glory. It is the wisdom which, in
the words of Scripture, proposes

> "What no eye has ever seen,
> what no ear has ever heard,
> what no human heart has ever thought of,
> namely, the great blessings God holds ready
> for those who love him."

10 But to us God has revealed them through his Spirit, who fathoms
11 all things, even the depths of God. Who among men knows the
inner thoughts of a man save the man's spirit within him? Even
so, the thoughts of God no one knows but the Spirit of God.
12 Now we have received not the spirit of the world, but the spirit
imparted by God. Thus we are enabled to recognize the gifts
13 bestowed on us by God. These are just the things we express in
words taught by the Spirit, not in words taught by human wisdom,
when we make a synthesis of spiritual truths for the spiritually
14 minded. But the nonspiritual man does not accept what the Spirit
of God imparts; it is stupidity to him and he cannot understand,
15 because it demands a spiritual scrutiny. The spiritual man, on the
other hand, can scrutinize all things, while in turn he is subject
16 to no merely human scrutiny. "Who has known the mind of the

---

2:6. *rulers of this world:* the intellectual and political leaders of governments (St. Chrysostom), or the evil spirits who influenced them (St. Thomas).

2:9. Isa. 64:4; Jer. 3:6.

2:13. *make a synthesis:* other proposed translations: "compare spiritual gifts to spiritual" or "explain spiritual truths to spiritual men."

2:15. St. Paul does not wish to imply that the spiritual man is above all criticism. His meaning is that in the realm of revealed truth he is not subject to criticism by those who do not accept revealed truth. St. Chrysostom: "He that sees can see everything, even what concerns the blind man, but no blind man can see what concerns the man with vision."

2:16. Isa. 40:13; Wisd. 9:13.

Lord so as to be able to instruct him?" But we have the mind of Christ.

CHAPTER 3

CORINTHIANS SPIRITUALLY IMMATURE

And I, brothers, could not speak to you as to spiritual men, 1 but only as worldlings, as babes in Christ. I fed you milk, not 2 solid food, since you were not yet strong enough for it. And still you are not strong enough for it, because you are still worldly. Surely as long as there are still jealousy and wrangling among you, 3 are you not worldly and behaving in keeping with human standards?

RESPONSIBILITY AND REWARD OF GOD'S MINISTERS

Certainly, whenever one says, "I am a follower of Paul," and 4 another "I of Apollos," are you not merely human? Why, what is 5 Apollos? What is Paul? They are ministers who serve in the way the Lord assigns to each; through their ministry you have embraced the faith. It was I who planted the seed; it is Apollos who waters 6 it, but it is God who makes it grow. So then, both he who plants 7 and he who waters count for nothing; God who makes the seed grow is what matters. Now he who plants and he who waters the 8 seed work in harmony, yet each will receive his own salary befitting his efforts. We are God's co-workers; you are God's field, God's 9 building.

According to the commission God has given me I have, like a 10 skilled master builder, laid the foundation; others look after the superstructure. But each individual should be careful how he erects that superstructure. Of course no other foundation can anyone 11 lay than the one already laid, and that is Jesus Christ. Whoever 12

3:8. *work in harmony*, literally, "are one," and so, to make them leaders of opposing factions is absurd. Cornely and Catholic interpreters generally see in this verse a basis for the Catholic doctrine of merit.

3:12. *Gold, silver*, etc.: they figuratively represent the various degrees of excellence or lack thereof in the work done by various Christian teachers for the upbuilding of the Church, such as the quality of the new converts, the doctrines and the moral code taught them, and the thoroughness of the instruction. St. Thomas sees in these inferior materials curious or poorly established doctrines, venial sins, and vain concern over temporalities.

builds on this foundation may use gold, silver, precious stone, wood,
13 hay, or straw, but each individual's work will be made manifest.
The day will make it known because fire will lay it bare, and will
14 test the quality of each individual's work. If the work anyone has
15 put into the superstructure stands firm, he will be rewarded, but
if anyone's work is burned up, he will suffer a loss, yet he himself
will be saved, though only by passing, so to speak, through fire.
16 Do you not know that you are God's temple, and that God's
17 Spirit dwells in you? If anyone destroys God's temple, God will
destroy him, for God's temple, which you yourselves are, is holy.

PRIDE NOT TO BE TAKEN IN MEN

18 No one must fool himself: if anyone deems himself wise by
19 worldly standards, he must become stupid to be really wise. Why?
Because this world's wisdom is stupidity in God's estimate. So
the Scripture says,
          "He catches the wise by their cunning."
20 And again,
          "The Lord knows how futile are the reasonings of the wise."
21 So then, no one should boast of men. All things belong to you,
22 whether it is Paul, or Apollos, or Cephas, or the world, or life, or
23 death; or the present, or the future. All things belong to you, and
you to Christ and Christ to God.

CHAPTER 4

THE LORD IS JUDGE

1 Consequently a man should form his estimate of us in as much

---

3:13. *day:* the general judgment. *fire:* a figure designating God's judgment.
According to St. Thomas, the day also means the day of the particular judgment
at death and of visitations of punishment during life.
3:15. *suffer a loss:* i.e., of reward for having propagated the kingdom of God,
the Church, in an imperfect manner, yet if the preacher's conscience is otherwise clear he will be saved. The teaching of this verse implies the doctrine of
the Church on purgatory. If the minor offenses of preachers are punished on
the last day with a punishment less than damnation, similarly other minor
offenses will be punished on the last day with a punishment less than damnation,
before the offender is fit for entrance into heaven.
3:19. Job 5:13.
3:20. Ps. 93:11.

as we are subordinates of Christ and stewards of God's mysteries.
In this case what in the final analysis is required of stewards is that   2
they prove to be trustworthy. As for me, it is the merest trifle to   3
be called to account by you or by any other human day of reckoning.
I do not even judge my own self. True, my conscience makes no   4
charge against me, yet I am not by that fact acquitted. My Judge
is the Lord. Accordingly, pass no judgment before the appointed   5
time, before the Lord comes. His it is to bring to light the secrets
now hidden in darkness, and to disclose the intentions of men's
hearts. At that time the praise due to each individual will come
from God.

CORINTHIANS IRONICALLY REBUKED

These things, brothers, I have applied to myself and Apollos, to   6
serve you as an illustration: from it you are to learn not to run
counter to the Scriptures, and glory in one man to the disparage-
ment of another. Why, who ascribes pre-eminence to you? What   7
have you that you have not received? And if you have received it,
why do you boast as if you had not received it?

Already your every yearning is fully satisfied! Already you have   8
grown rich! Independently of us, you have become kings! Would
that you were kings, so that we might be kings with you! As it is,   9
it seems to me that God has put us apostles on exhibition in the
last place, like men doomed to death, since we have been made a
spectacle to the world, both angelic and human. We are fools   10
for Christ, but you are wise in Christ! We are weak, but you are
strong! You are renowned, but we are without repute! To this very   11
hour we are victims of hunger and thirst; we are poorly clad and
knocked around; we are vagabonds and we wear ourselves out with   12
manual labor. When men call us ugly names, we speak well of
them. When they persecute us, we bear it patiently. When they   13
insult us, we speak gently. We have practically become at present
the world's scum, the scapegoat of society.

4:6. *These things*: i.e., all that the Apostle has been saying from 3:5. What
he says apparently fits others better than it does himself and Apollos, but for
the sake of tact he does not mention their names. *run counter to the Scriptures*:
the more common interpretation of the words. St. John Chrysostom thinks of
a maxim enunciated by our Lord; others see a proverbial expression current at
Corinth with reference to contracts.

14   I write these things not to embarrass you, but to refresh your
15   memory, as my beloved children. Although you may have ten
thousand guides in Christ, you have but one father, myself, who
16   by preaching the Good News to you begot you in Christ. I beg you,
17   then, to follow my example. For this very reason I have sent to you
Timothy, my beloved and faithful son in the Lord. He will recall
to you my teachings and my methods. They are exactly the same
everywhere, in every congregation.
18   Some are arrogant, on the pretense that I am not coming to
19   you. But come I shall, and that very soon, if the Lord wills, and I
shall learn not the talk but the power of these arrogant people.
20   The kingdom of God, you know, does not advance by talk, but
21   by power. What is your choice? Shall I come to you provided with a
rod, or with love, with a spirit of gentleness?

A FLAGRANT CASE OF INCEST

CHAPTER 5

LAXITY IN HANDLING THE CASE

1   There is a widespread report of immorality in your midst and
of such immorality as would not be found among the Gentiles.
2   I refer to a man living with his father's wife. What is worse, you
are arrogant! Should you not rather deplore it with a view of
expelling from your midst the one who has committed that crime?
3   As for me, though absent in body, I am present in spirit, and
have already, as if present, reached the decision against the per-
4   petrator of such a monstrous disorder: You and my spirit, gathered
in the name of our Lord Jesus Christ in general assembly, decree
5   by the authority of our Lord Jesus Christ, to deliver this man to
Satan for the destruction of his corrupt tendencies that his spirit
may attain salvation on the day of the Lord Jesus.

5:5. *to deliver this man to Satan:* i.e., to excommunicate. *for the destruction of his corrupt tendencies:* just how this was to be effected is not clear. Perhaps the man will be surfeited and disgusted with sin and thus be led to abandon it, or his body will be afflicted with a deadly disease and the fear of death will bring him to repentance. So SS. Chrysostom and Thomas.

You have no good reason to boast. Are you not aware that a 6
little yeast leavens all the dough? Clean out the old yeast, that you 7
may be fresh dough (as, of course, you really are). As a matter of
fact, Christ, our paschal victim, has been sacrificed. We should, 8
therefore, celebrate the feast, not with the old yeast, the yeast of
malice and wickedness, but with the unleavened bread of sincerity
and integrity.

PUNISHMENT OF SUCH SINS

I wrote in my letter not to mingle with fornicators. I did not at 9, 10
all mean this world's fornicators, or covetous people or thieves or
idolaters. In that case you would have to withdraw from the world.
Now what my letter really meant was that if anyone who is 11
nominally a Christian is a fornicator, or is covetous, or an idolater,
or indulges in abusive speech, or is a drunkard or a thief, you are not
to mingle with him. Indeed, what business is it of mine to pass 12
judgment on outsiders? Is it not those within the fold that you
judge? God is the judge of outsiders. 13

Expel the wicked men from your midst.

Lawsuits Before Pagan Courts

Chapter 6

Does anyone of you dare, when you have a grievance against 1
another, to bring the case to the courts of the wicked rather than
before the saints? Are you not aware that the saints are to judge 2
the world? And if you are to judge the world, are you unfit to serve
in the most insignificant courts? Are you not aware that we are 3
to judge the angels? How much more, affairs of this life! If, then, 4

5:6–8. Fermentation was considered as a kind of corruption. Therefore, leaven was removed from Jewish houses for the observance of the Passover. The comparison was probably suggested to St. Paul by the nearness of Easter, which for Christians replaced the Jewish Passover.

6:2. Our Lord has been appointed by his Father to be the judge of the world of intelligent creatures human and angelic (Jn. 5:27), and in virtue of the faithful's union with him in his Mystical Body, they will have a share in the judicial power of Christ, their head.

6:4. This advice is given in irony.

you have courts for affairs of this life, appoint those who are the
5 least esteemed in the congregation as judges! I say this to shame
you. Can it be that there is no one among you who is expert and
6 competent to settle a case between brothers? On the contrary, does
brother have to go to law against brother, and that before unbelievers?
7   To begin with, it is, even in any circumstances, a defect in you
to have lawsuits among yourselves. Why do you not prefer to suffer
8 wrong, to be defrauded? But you yourselves inflict wrong and fraud,
9 and that on your brothers. Can it be that you are unaware that the
unjust will not inherit the kingdom of God? Make no mistake; no
10 fornicator, no idolater, no adulterer, no pervert, no homosexualist,
no thief, no slave of avarice, no drunkard, no addict of abusive
11 language, no miser, will inherit the kingdom of God. That is precisely what some of you were. But you have been washed clean;
you have been sanctified; you have been made holy in the name
of our Lord Jesus Christ and in the Spirit of our God.

THE BASIS OF CHRISTIAN CHASTITY

12   All things are permissible to me, but not all things are helpful.
All things are permissible, but I will never yield myself to the control
13 of anybody or anything whatever. Food is for the stomach and the
stomach is for food, yet God will put an end to the use of both
the one and the other. The body is not for immorality but for
14 the Lord, and the Lord is for the body. Just as God raised the Lord,
so he will raise us by his power.
15   Are you not aware that your bodies are members of Christ's
body? Shall I then take the members of Christ and make them the
16 members of a prostitute? Never! Are you not aware that he who
unites himself to a prostitute becomes one body with her? So says
17 the Scripture, "The two shall become one flesh." But he who unites

---

6:7. St. Paul, as Cornely points out, does not absolutely forbid litigation,
but its necessity among Christians is an indication of imperfection.
    6:12. permissible: St. Paul, according to Allo, may have made such a state-
ment relative to the prohibitions of the Mosaic Law which had been abrogated, or
it may be that the statement was made by poorly instructed Christians who
erroneously took the freedom which Christianity granted to imply removal of
all moral restraint.
    6:13. the Lord is for the body: in that he is the model, the source of its
supernatural life and resurrection in glory. We may have here, as St. Cyril
thought, an allusion to the Blessed Eucharist.
    6:16. Gen. 2:24.

himself to the Lord, forms one spirit with him. Shun immorality. 18
Every other sin a man may commit is outside the body, but the
fornicator sins against his own body. Are you not aware that your 19
body is the temple of the Holy Spirit? Him you have received from
God! You are not your own masters. You have been bought, and 20
at a price! So then, glorify God in your body.

MARRIAGE AND CELIBACY

CHAPTER 7

LAWFULNESS AND DUTIES OF MARRIAGE

Now concerning the matters about which you wrote me: It is 1
well for a man to have no intimate relations with woman. Yet to 2
avoid the danger of fornication every man should have a wife of
his own, and every woman should have a husband of her own. The 3
husband must give his wife her due, and so too the wife her husband.
The wife has no right over her own body; that right belongs to 4
her husband. So, the husband has no right over his own body;
that right belongs to his wife. Of this right do not deprive each 5
other except perhaps temporarily by mutual consent, that you may
be free for prayer; then resume your common life, lest in case of
lack of self-control Satan tempt you. This I say, however, by way 6
of concession, not by way of command. I certainly wish that you 7
were all in the same state as I, but each one has his own gift from
God, one to live in one way, another in another.

ADVICE TO MARRIED AND SINGLE

To the unmarried and widows I say: It is well for them to con- 8
tinue in the state in which I am. But in case they lack self-control, 9
they should marry, because it is better to marry than to be on fire
with passion. But to the married, not I, but the Lord commands 10
that a wife is not to leave her husband, and if she does leave, she 11
is to remain unmarried or be reconciled to her husband. And a
husband must not divorce his wife.

6:18. *outside the body:* St. Paul is speaking relatively. This sin needs no
means apart from the body, one's own and that of the accomplice, for its
commission.

THE PAULINE PRIVILEGE

12   To the rest it is I, not the Lord, who gives the precept: If any
brother has an unbelieving wife, and she consents to live with him,
13   he must not divorce her. And if any woman has an unbelieving
husband and he consents to live with her, she must not divorce him.
14   Why? Because the unbelieving husband is consecrated by the
believing wife, and the unbelieving wife is consecrated by the
believing husband. If it were not so, your children would be defiled,
15   but, as it is, they are holy. But if the unbeliever is minded to depart,
let him go. A brother or sister is under no obligation in such cases.
16   God has called us to live in peace. As a matter of fact, how do
you, the wife, know that you will save your husband? Or how do
you, the husband, know that you will save your wife?

CONTENTMENT WITH ONE'S CONDITION

17   Apart from the above-mentioned exception, I always promulgate
this rule in all the congregations: Everyone is to continue in the
condition to which the Lord has assigned him, in which he was at
18   the moment of God's call. If a man was called after circumcision,
he is not to disguise it. If he was called before circumcision, he is
19   not to be circumcised. Being circumcised means nothing; not being
circumcised means nothing. It is the keeping of God's command-
20   ments that counts. Everyone should remain in the circumstances
21   in which he was at the time of his call. Were you called when a
slave? Do not let that bother you. Even if you could win your
22   freedom, rather make the most of your slavery. Why, he who has

---

7:12. *I, not the Lord:* our Lord gave no explicit teaching on this point,
but he empowered the Church with authority to make laws which would be
ratified in heaven. Cf. Mt. 18:18.

7:14. *consecrated:* the nonbelieving party, since he consents to live with
the believing party and thereby accepts Christian principles insofar as their
mutual relations are concerned, becomes to that extent consecrated and is placed
in circumstances favorable for conversion. *defiled:* literally, "unclean." St. Paul
seems to be using Jewish technical legal language. His meaning is that children
born of the union he is discussing, even though not as yet baptized, are accepted into the Christian community by the mere fact that they are born of
one Christian parent. Thus, this attitude to such children indicates that the
union from which they were born is a legitimate union.

7:21. Others translate: "Yet if you can acquire your freedom, make use of
the opportunity."

been called in the Lord, while he was a slave, is a freedman of the
Lord, just as he who has been called while he was a freedman, is
a slave of Christ. You have been bought with a price! Do not 23
enslave yourselves to men. Brothers, each of you should remain 24
before God in the state you were in when called.

As regards virgins, I have no precept of the Lord, yet, as a 25
man who, by the mercy received from the Lord, is worthy of trust,
I think that it is excellent, in view of the present distress, yes, that 26
it is excellent for a person to remain in this state of virginity.
Are you bound by marriage to a wife? Do not seek to be free from 27
her. Are you free of marriage ties? Do not seek them. Yet, if you 28
marry, you commit no sin, and if a virgin marries, she commits no
sin. But the married will have their human trials, and I would like
to spare you that.

THE PASSING WORLD

This I declare, brothers, that the allotted time has become very 29
short. From now on those who have wives should live as though they
had none, and those who weep should be as though they were 30
not weeping, and those who rejoice should be as though they were
not rejoicing, and those who buy as though they had nothing,
and those who make use of this world should live in such a way 31
as not to become engrossed in that use, because the stage setting of
this world is passing away.

MARRIAGE AND VIRGINITY

I would have you free from concern. He who is unmarried is 32
concerned about the interests of the Lord, how he may please the
Lord. But he who is married is concerned about worldly interests, 33
how he may please his wife. Thus his interests are divided. The 34
unmarried woman or the virgin is concerned with the Lord's interests, is intent on being holy both in body and in mind. But the
married woman is concerned with worldly things, how she may

7:26. *present distress*: the trials and worries of life, and possibly the coming
persecution of Christians, which St. Paul may have foreseen.
7:31. St. Paul urges the Christians not to become too attached to the
world and its pursuits. Using the language of the theater, he characterizes the
world as merely the very passing stage where for a brief moment we play our
part. This life and the part we play in it are in comparison to the next life as
unreal and as passing as a theatrical performance.

35 please her husband. I say this for your benefit, not to hold you in check, but that you may conduct yourselves properly and attend assiduously to the Lord without distractions.

THE UNMARRIED DAUGHTER

36 If, however, a father thinks he is acting unbecomingly toward his virgin daughter in case she is past the bloom of youth, and his duty requires it to be so, he may do as he pleases. There is no sin
37 committed. Let her (and her suitor) get married. But the father who continues in a fixed resolve and is under no compulsion, but is free to do as he pleases, and who has made up his mind to keep
38 his daughter unmarried, does well. Thus, he who gives his virgin daughter in marriage does well, yet he who does not give her does better.

WIDOWS

39 A wife is bound as long as her husband is alive. But if her husband dies, she is free. She may marry the man of her choice,
40 provided he is in the Lord. But she is to be congratulated more, in my judgment, if she remains as she is. And I think that I also am inspired by God.

FOOD OFFERED TO IDOLS

CHAPTER 8

GENERAL PRINCIPLES

1 Concerning food offered in idol worship: we know well that all have knowledge. Mere knowledge makes one arrogant, but love
2 builds up character. If anyone thinks he has full knowledge on any
3 subject, he has not yet learned how to know. But if anyone has
4 love for God, he is known approvingly by God. As for eating food offered to idols, we know well that an idol stands for no reality in
5 the world, and that none is God save one. Even though there are pretended gods whether in the sky or on the earth — and truly

---

7:36. Marriage in ancient times was always determined for a girl by her father or guardian.
7:39. in the Lord: i.e., a Christian, a fellow member of the Mystical Body.
8:5. sky: the heavenly luminaries worshiped as gods by some pagans.

there are numerous gods and numerous lords — yet for us there 6
is but one God, the Father, from whom all things have their being,
and who is our last end; and there is but one Lord, Jesus Christ,
through whom all things have their being, especially ourselves.

PRACTICAL APPLICATION

But not everyone has this knowledge. Some by force of a habit 7
still enduring, in regard to idols, look on food while they eat as
really sacrificed to idols, and their conscience, because it is weak,
is defiled. Yet it is not food that will place us near God. We lose 8
nothing if we do not eat, and we gain nothing if we do eat. But 9
take care lest this right of yours should become a stumbling block
to weaklings. Suppose, for example, someone sees you, a man of 10
knowledge, reclining at table in an idol's temple. Might not his
conscience, since it is weak, be encouraged to eat food offered in
idol worship? By your knowledge he is destroyed, this brother for 11
whose sake Christ died! When you so sin against your brothers, and 12
wound their weak conscience, it is against Christ that you sin.
Therefore, never will I eat meat, if food leads to my brother's sinning, 13
lest I should be the cause of my brother's sin.

PAUL GIVES UP HIS RIGHTS

CHAPTER 9

THE GOSPEL MINISTER'S RIGHT TO SUPPORT

Am I not free? Am I not an apostle? Have I not seen Jesus our 1
Lord? Did not my labor make you what you are? Although for 2
others I may not be an apostle, for you I certainly am. Why, you,
who are in the Lord, are the seal affixed to my apostolate. Here is 3
my defense against those who would criticize me: Do we not have 4

8:7. Some converts from paganism had not yet got rid of their habitual attitude
toward idols and still regarded the eating of food which had been offered to
idols as a participation in idol worship. This type of convert, says St. Thomas,
lack knowledge; they think the idol is some kind of god.

8:10. *a man of knowledge:* has an enlightened and correct conscience, but
there are times when acting with the freedom it grants would lead the weak
and poorly instructed to act contrary to their erroneous conscience and sin.

9:3. This refers to what follows, an answer to those who criticized St. Paul's

5 the right to food and drink? Do we not have the right to take
with us in our travels a woman who is a Christian, as do the rest
6 of the apostles and the Lord's brothers and Cephas? Or is it
myself and Barnabas alone who have no right of exemption from
manual labor?
7   What soldier ever serves at his own expense? Who plants a vineyard without eating its fruit? Or who shepherds a flock without
8 drinking some of its milk? Do I say these things on human authority,
9 or does not the Law itself say the same thing? Why, it is written
in the Law of Moses, "You shall not muzzle the ox when it threshes
10 the grain." Is God's concern for the oxen? Or does he say this
especially for our benefit? It is written, of course, for our benefit,
because the plowman should plow with hope and the thresher should
11 thresh with hope of a share in the crop. If we have sown spiritual
12 seed, is it too much if we reap a material harvest? If others have a
share in this right you grant, do we not have a greater claim on it?
But we have made no use of this right, lest we should cause the
least hindrance to the gospel of Christ.
13   Do you not know that those who minister in the temple eat
food that comes from the temple; that those who serve as assistants
14 at the altar have their share of the altar offerings? In the same way
the Lord directed that those who preach the gospel should have
their living from the gospel.

PAUL RENOUNCES THESE RIGHTS

15   But I have availed myself of none of these rights. And I am not
writing this to achieve that purpose for myself. I would rather die
16 than have that. No one is going to nullify my boast. Even though
I preach the gospel, in that fact I have no grounds to boast. I am

---

attitude toward idol offerings. Instead of acting on an enlightened conscience
regardless of the effect of such action on others, those well-instructed Christians
would do better to follow Paul's example. He gave up some of his rights to
avoid placing any obstacle whatever to the spread of Christianity.
   9:5. *a woman who is a Christian:* literally, "a woman" or "wife-sister." The
term "sister" certainly means a sister in the faith, not by blood. As to the
word translated *woman,* many authorities are for translating it "wife." But as
for the preponderance of patristic opinion (Clement of Alexandria, Ambrosiaster,
Jerome, Augustine, and others), the context and the majority of modern Catholic
exegetes seem to favor the translation given above.
   9:9. Deut. 25:4.
   9:12. *right you grant:* or "right you have."

under necessity to do so. Woe betide me if I do not go on preaching the gospel! If I do so willingly, I have a reward, but if unwillingly, I act merely as one entrusted with a commission. What then is my reward? That in preaching I present the gospel free of charge, and thus do not avail myself to the full of the right the gospel grants me.

PAUL'S MOTIVE

Independent though I am of all men, I make myself everybody's slave to win the more converts. For example, I make myself a Jew to the Jews to win over the Jews; to those subject to the Law, a man subject to the Law (though not myself subject to the Law), to win over those subject to the Law; to those not having the Law, a man not having the Law (though I am not without a law, since I am subject to the law of Christ), to win over those that have not the Law. I become like a weak man for the weak to win over the weak. I become all things to all men, by all means to win over some of them. Whatever I do, I do for the sake of the gospel that I may have a share in its blessings.

THE REWARD IS WORTH IT

Do you not know that whenever men run a race in a stadium, all run but only one wins the prize? So run that you will surely win. Every contestant submits to all sorts of privations, and that to win a perishable crown, but we an imperishable one. Therefore I run with a fixed goal in mind; I box not as one beating the air, but I buffet my body and make it my slave, lest, perhaps, after preaching to others, I myself should be eliminated.

THE DANGER OF PRESUMPTION

CHAPTER 10

Brothers, I would not have you remain in ignorance of the following facts. Our fathers all marched under the cloud and all

---

9:17. St. Paul alludes to his life before his conversion. He fiercely persecuted the Church, whereas the other Apostles, friends of Christ from the beginning, eagerly accepted the office of preaching. Paul, so to speak, was forced to preach Christianity after the miracle near Damascus.
10:1–13. These verses contain allusions to the events that transpired in the

2 passed through the sea; they were all united to Moses by being
3 baptized in the cloud and in the sea; they all ate the same spiritual
4 food and all drank the same spiritual drink; they drank in fact
   from the spiritual rock that accompanied them, and that rock was
5 Christ. Yet with the majority of them God was not well pleased,
   since they were strewn prostrate over the desert.

6   These things became examples to teach us not to covet wicked
7 things as they did; not to become idolaters as some of them. So
   the Scriptures testify, "The people sat down to eat and drink and
8 rose up to amuse themselves." We are not to commit fornication
   as some of them committed fornication, and in a single day twenty-
9 three thousand fell dead. We are not to try the Lord's forbearance
10 as some of them did, and were destroyed by serpents. We are not
   to murmur as some of them did and were destroyed by the Destroyer.
11 All these things happened to them to serve as examples, and they
   were written down to challenge the consideration of us on whom
   the final epoch of world history has come.

12   Therefore, whoever believes he is standing firm, should beware
13 lest he fall. No temptation has assailed you except what is common
  ⌄to men. God is faithful and will not let you be tempted beyond
   your strength. On the contrary he will, along with the temptation,
   supply you a way of escape, so that you will be able to hold your own.

THE EUCHARIST OPPOSED TO PAGAN BANQUETS

14   This is why, my dearly beloved, you should flee from idol wor-

---

exodus from Egypt and the wanderings of the Israelites in the desert, as recorded
in Exod. 13–14; Num. 14:21 and 26.

10:2. *united to Moses:* the Israelites were baptized into union with Moses,
i.e., they accepted his leadership which delivered them from the bondage of
Egypt and made them members of God's Chosen People. So Christians are
united to Christ by Baptism and become members of the new Israel, the Israel
of God. So Allo, Cornely, and Catholic commentators generally.

10:3. *spiritual food:* so called because it was supplied by the spiritual rock,
which was Christ in his pre-existence. The rock is an apt image for Christ as
the absolutely solid and unchangeable basis of hope, as it is an apt and oft-
recurring image for God in the Old Testament. It is said to be spiritual because
hidden and invisible, thus stating the pre-existence of Christ and applying
to him the metaphor which the Old Testament applies repeatedly to God as
an indirect assertion of Jesus Christ's divinity. So Sales and others.

10:7. *amuse themselves:* in various diversions including dancing before the
golden calf.

10:10. *the Destroyer:* the angel whom God sent to punish the people with a
virulent pestilence.

ship. I address you as sensible people: judge for yourselves what I 15
say. Does not the chalice of blessings which we bless bring us into 16
union with Christ through his blood, and does not the bread which
we break bring us into union with Christ through his body?
Because the bread is one, we, the many who all partake of that one 17
bread, form one body.

Consider the real Israelite nation. Do not those that eat the 18
victims unite themselves with the altar? What do I say? That food 19
offered to idols amounts to anything, or that the idol stands for any
reality? No, but what the Gentiles sacrifice, they sacrifice to demons, 20
who are not God. I would not have you enter into union with
demons.

You cannot drink the chalice of the Lord and the chalice of 21
demons. You cannot partake of the table of the Lord and the
table of demons. Are we going to provoke the Lord to jealousy? 22
Are we stronger than he?

All things are permissible, but not all things are helpful. All 23
things are permissible, but not all things build up character.
Everyone should seek his neighbor's advantage rather than his own. 24

Eat whatever is sold in the market without asking any questions 25
for conscience' sake. The reason is, "The earth and everything on 26
it belong to the Lord." If anyone of the unbelievers invites you 27
to a meal, and you wish to go, eat whatever is set before you without
asking any question for conscience' sake. But if someone should say, 28
to you, "This food is a sacred victim," do not eat of it for the sake
of him who pointed it out to you and for conscience' sake. I mean 29
not your own but the other person's conscience. Why, in fact,
should my use of liberty be condemned because of another person's
conscience? If I partake of food with thanksgiving, why should I 30
provoke criticism because of that for which I give thanks?

Whether, then, you eat or drink, or do anything else, do every- 31
thing for God's glory. Never be a stumbling block to Jews or Greeks 32

10:16. *the chalice of blessings which we bless*: this has been variously understood. St. John Chrysostom explains the first phrase of the numerous blessings
the chalice contains and imparts to communicants. The latter phrase may be
simply understood of the words of consecration.
10:18. *real Israelite nation*: as contrasted with the spiritual Israel, the
Christian Church.

33 or to God's congregation, just as I try to conciliate all men by seeking not my own advantage but that of the many in order to save them.

Chapter 11

1 Become imitators of me as I am of Christ.

Women's Headdress

2 I praise you because you bear in mind all that I taught you and cling to the traditions precisely as I passed them on to you.

3 I want you to know, however, that Christ is the head of every man, man is the head of woman, and God is the head of Christ.

4 Every man that prays, or speaks under inspiration, with his head

5 veiled brings shame on his head. Every woman that prays, or speaks under inspiration, with her head unveiled brings shame on her head.

6 It really amounts to the same thing as shaving her head. If a woman does not veil herself, then she should shave her head. But if it is a mark of infamy for a woman to shave her head or cut her hair

7 short, she should wear a veil. A man, indeed, has no duty to veil his head, because he is the image and glory of God, but woman

8 is the glory of man. Why? Because man did not spring from woman,

9 but woman from man. The man, in fact, was created not for the

10 woman's sake, but the woman for the man's sake. This is why the women should have a symbol of authority on their head, out of respect for the angels.

11 Yet woman is not independent of man and man is not inde-

12 pendent of woman in the Lord. Just as the first woman was drawn from the first man, so man is born of woman. And all things take their origin from God.

11:4. *on his head:* this can be referred to Christ or to the man's head or to both. Since man is the mirror which immediately reflects Christ, to veil his head would interfere with his function as a reflection of Christ and also detract from man's own dignity.

11:10. *symbol of authority:* according to St. John Chrysostom, the authority of the husband over the wife, but more probably, according to many modern commentators, of the woman's authority or control over herself. In oriental countries the veil on the woman's head was a sign of her dignity as wife or as a respectable woman. She commanded respect in virtue of that veil and could safely go where she pleased without fear of molestation. *angels:* according to St. Cyril of Alexandria, St. Chrysostom, St. Augustine, and others, the heavenly spirits who assist at and watch over the decorum of divine worship.

Judge for yourselves: is it proper for a woman to pray unveiled 13
to God? Does not nature itself teach you that for a man to wear his 14
hair long is an ignominy for him, and that for a woman to wear 15
her hair long is a glory for her, because her hair was given to her
as a covering? But if anyone wants to pick flaws in my argument, 16
neither we nor the congregations of God have any such custom.

The Holy Eucharist

In laying down the following regulations, I cannot commend you, 17
because you hold your gatherings to your harm instead of to your
benefit. First, for example, I hear that when you meet in your 18
gatherings there are cliques among you. To a certain extent I
believe it, since there must be factions among you so that those 19
of proven worth may be easily recognized. So when you meet in the 20
same place there is no eating of the Lord's supper. In fact each one 21
hastens to eat his own supper beforehand with the result that one
man goes hungry and another drinks to excess. Do you have no 22
homes of your own where you can eat and drink? Or do you despise
those assembled to worship God, and bring shame on the poor?
What am I to say to you? Am I to commend you? On this point,
I do not commend you.

The fact is that I have received as coming from the Lord, and 23
have passed on to you, how the Lord Jesus on the night of his
betrayal took bread in his hands and after he had given thanks 24
broke it and said, "This is my body which is given up for you; do
this in remembrance of me." In the same way, after he had finished 25
supper, he took the chalice in his hands and said, "This chalice is
the new covenant sealed with my blood. Do this, as often as you

---

11:13–16. The Apostle makes two points: first, there is a disciplinary tradition in the Church, which the Christians must accept; and second, the disciplinary laws of the Church are in keeping with the laws of nature.
11:22. assembled to worship: literally, "the Church of God."
11:23. as coming from the Lord: i.e., through the Apostles or possibly by direct revelation.
11:24–30. This section teaches that: (1) the Eucharist is really the body and blood of Christ (24 f.); (2) the Apostles and their successors were empowered to perpetuate the act (24–26); (3) the Mass is a sacrifice (25; cf. note); (4) the Mass is one with the sacrifice of the cross (26); (5) the Eucharist must be received worthily.
11:25. the new covenant: sacrificial blood sealed the old covenant (cf. Exod.

26 drink it, in remembrance of me." In reality, every time you eat
   this bread and drink the chalice of the Lord, you proclaim the
27 Lord's death until he comes. Consequently, whoever eats this bread
   or drinks the chalice of the Lord unworthily will be held responsible
28 for a sin against the body and blood of the Lord. A person should
   examine his conscience and after so doing he may eat of the bread
29 and drink of the chalice, because he that eats and drinks without
   recognizing the body, eats and drinks to his own condemnation.
30 For this reason many among you are sick and weak while not a
31 few have died. If we habitually meted out strict judgment on our-
32 selves, we would not receive that condemnation. Yet it is meted
   out by the Lord for our correction, that we may not be condemned
33 with worldlings. So, my brothers, when you assemble for the Lord's
34 supper, wait for one another. If anyone is hungry, he should eat at
   home, lest you turn your assemblies into condemnation proceedings.
   The other matters I shall set in order on my arrival.

UNITY AND VARIETY OF SPIRITUAL GIFTS

CHAPTER 12

PRINCIPLE ON WHICH GIFTS ARE DISTRIBUTED

1   Now concerning spiritual gifts, brothers, I would not have you
2 ignorant. You know that when you were pagans, you were led
3 astray to speechless idols, as the impulse seized you. This is why
   I would have you know that no one that speaks under the influence
   of God's Spirit ever says, "Jesus be cursed," and no one can say
   "Jesus is Lord," except under the influence of the Holy Spirit.
4   There is a distribution of gifts, but the same Spirit distributes
5 them. There is a distribution of ministrations, but it is the same
6 Lord to whom we minister. There is a distribution of activities,
7 but it is the same God who activates them all in everyone. The

---

24:8). This is the sacrificial blood which makes effective the new order established by God through Christ.

11:30. The unusually large number of deaths and cases of illness were regarded by St. Paul as punishment sent by God on the Corinthians for their
laxity in regard to the Lord's Supper.

12:5. ministrations: any kind of service from the loftiest to the most humble
rendered to the Lord or to his Church.

12:7. manifestation of the Spirit: outward signs of the presence and activity
of the Holy Spirit, such as speaking in tongues and working miracles.

manifestation of the Spirit is given to each individual for the common good. For example, to one is imparted the ability to speak with 8 wisdom, to another with knowledge under the guidance of the same Spirit, to another by the same Spirit is imparted wonder-working 9 confidence, to another gifts of healing by the one Spirit, to another 10 the performance of miracles, to another fervent preaching, to another the discernment of spirits, to another the ability to speak in various languages, to another the ability to interpret them. But it is one 11 and the same Spirit who is active in all these gifts, which he distributes just as he wishes.

THE CHURCH IS LIKE A HUMAN BODY

For example, just as the body is a unit, although it has many 12 members, and all the members of the body, many though they are, form but one body, so too is the Christ. In fact, by a single Spirit 13 all of us, whether Jews or Greeks, slaves or free men, were introduced into the one body through baptism, and were all given to drink of a single Spirit. The body, I repeat, is not formed of one but of many 14 members. Suppose the foot should say, "Because I am not a hand, I 15 am no part of the body," is it for all that no part of the body? And suppose the ear should say, "Because I am not an eye, I am 16 no part of the body," is it for all that no part of the body? If the 17 whole body were eye, where would the hearing be? If the whole body were hearing, where would the sense of smell be? But, as it is, 18 God has put the members, every last one of them, in the body, as he wished. Now if they were all one member, where would the 19 body be? But, as it is, there are certainly many members, but a 20 unified body. The eye cannot say to the hand, "I have no need of 21 you," nor the head to the feet, "I have no need of you." On the 22 contrary, much rather are those members of the body necessary, which seem the weakest. Those members which we deem the less 23 honorable, we clothe with more abundant honor. Yes, our unpresentable parts are decently clad, whereas the presentable parts 24 have no need of that. But the fact is that God has fitted the body

---

12:10. *fervent preaching*: literally, "prophecy," not the prediction of future events but a special insight into revealed truth and an inspired eloquence in presenting it to others.

12:13. *drink*: perhaps a reference to the effects of Baptism, or to the Eucharist, or to Confirmation, in which the gifts and graces of the Holy Spirit are imparted.

25 together by giving more abundant honor where it was lacking, to avoid any rift in the body and to secure the same common concern
26 of the members one for another. In case one member is in pain, all the members share it. In case one member is honored, all the members share its satisfaction.
27, 28 You are Christ's body and individually its members. And God has established in his Church some in the first rank, namely apostles, others in the second rank, namely fervent preachers, and still others in the third rank, namely teachers. After that come wonder-workers, then those with the gifts of healing, then assistants, administrators, and those that speak a variety of languages.
29 Are all of us apostles? Are all of us inspired preachers? Are all of
30 us teachers? Are all of us wonder-workers? Do all of us have the gifts of healing? Do all of us speak in languages? Do all of us act as interpreters?
31 Be eager always to have the gift that is more precious than all the others. I am now going to point out to you the way by far the most excellent.

LOVE

CHAPTER 13

ITS NECESSITY AND MORAL BEAUTY

1 If I should speak the languages of men and of angels, but have no love, I am no more than a noisy gong and a clanging cymbal.
2 And if I should have the gift of inspired utterance, and have the key to all secrets, and master the whole range of knowledge, and if I should have absolute faith so as to be able to move mountains,
3 but have no love, I am nothing. And if I should distribute all I have bit by bit, and should yield my body to the flames, but have no love, it profits me nothing.
4 Love is long-suffering; love is kind, and is not envious; love does
5 not brag; it is not conceited; it is not ill-mannered; it is not self-
6 seeking; it is not irritable, it takes no note of injury; it is not glad

---

12:31. way: the way by which what is better than the gifts under consideration can be attained.

when injustice triumphs; it is glad when the truth prevails. Always 7
it is ready to make allowances; always to trust; always to hope; always
to be patient.

ITS EXCELLENCE AND PERMANENCE

Love will never end. If there are inspired utterances, they will 8
become useless. If there are languages, they will be discarded. If
there is knowledge, it will become useless. For our knowledge is 9
incomplete, and our utterances inspired by God are incomplete,
but when that which is perfect has come, what is incomplete will 10
be useless. When I was a little child, I spoke as a little child, I 11
thought as a little child. Now that I am grown to manhood, I have
discarded as useless my childish ways. We see now by means of 12
a mirror in a vague way, but then we shall see face to face. Now my
knowledge is incomplete, but then I shall have complete knowledge,
even as God has complete knowledge of me. So, there abide faith, 13
hope, and love, but the greatest of them is love.

THE GIFTS OF TONGUES AND PROPHECY

CHAPTER 14

SUPERIORITY OF INSPIRED SPEECH

Be in constant pursuit of love. You may desire spiritual gifts 1
but especially that of being God's inspired spokesmen. He who 2
speaks in a foreign language, speaks not to men but to God; no
one understands him, as he is holding mysterious converse with his
own mind. But he who speaks under divine inspiration addresses 3
men for their edification, exhortation, and encouragement. He who 4

13:12. The mirror which in this life reflects God is the visible universe.
In St. Paul's day the only mirrors were pieces of polished metal which did not
give clear reflections as do modern mirrors.

14:1. *inspired:* literally, here and often in this chapter the reference is to
"prophecy." It does not designate, in this chapter, predictions of future events,
but rather a fervent, persuasive eloquence that stirred the minds and wills and
affections to salutary action. This gift, if genuine, was of divine origin, and
might at times entail revealed knowledge. It was to be submitted to the scrutiny
of others who possessed it to determine whether it was genuine. The norm of
judgment was the "analogy of the faith."

speaks in a foreign language, edifies himself, but he who acts
5 as God's inspired spokesman edifies the congregation. I would
be willing to have you all speak in foreign languages, but I would
much rather have you act as God's inspired spokesmen, as he who
discharges this function renders a greater service than he who speaks
in foreign languages, unless someone interprets them for the edification of the congregation.

THE GIFT OF TONGUES NEEDS INTERPRETATION

6   Now, brothers, suppose I visit you and speak in foreign languages,
what benefit will I be to you, unless I impart revealed doctrine to
you as God's inspired spokesmen, or knowledge by instruction?
7 If inanimate instruments which, however, emit a sound, such as a
flute or a harp, have no difference in the notes, how will the melody
8 played on flute or harp be recognized? And suppose the bugle gives
9 a doubtful call, who will get ready for battle? It is exactly the same
in your case. Suppose you give forth unintelligible sounds in a
foreign language, how can anybody know what you are saying? You
10 will be speaking gibberish. There exist in the world as many different
kinds of languages as one could wish, and none is meaningless.
11 But if I do not know the meaning of the language, I am counted
a foreigner to the speaker, and the speaker a foreigner to me.
12 So you too, since you are eager to have spiritual manifestations,
let it be for the edification of the congregation that you seek to
abound in them.
13   For this reason he that speaks in a foreign language ought to
14 pray for the ability to give an interpretation. For example, if I pray
in a foreign language, my affections pray, but my mind gets no
15 fruit from it. What then is to be done? I shall pray with my
affections, and also with my mind shall I pray. I shall sing psalms
with my affections, and also with my mind shall I sing psalms.
16 Else, if you give thanks with your affections, how can he who holds
the position of the uninitiated say the Amen to your thanksgiving,
17 since he does not understand what you say? You certainly give
18 thanks well, but the other person is not edified. I thank God, more
19 than any of you I speak in foreign languages. But in the congregation

14:14. my affections: literally, "my spirit." Here the term excludes the intelligence and seems to designate the purely emotional part of man's make-up.

I would rather speak five words with my mind, so as to instruct others, than ten thousand words in a foreign language.

PURPOSE OF THESE GIFTS

Brothers, do not become children in judgment. Play the part of little children in malice but of grownups in judgment. In the Law it is written,

> "Through men with foreign tongues and lips
> I will speak to this people,
> And even so they will not listen to me,"
> says the Lord.

Consequently foreign languages serve as a sign not to believers but to unbelievers, while an utterance inspired of God is not meant for unbelievers but for believers. Suppose, then, that the entire congregation is gathered in the same place, that all are speaking in foreign languages, and that some of the uninitiated or unbelievers should enter, will they not say that you are insane? But suppose that all act as God's inspired spokesmen, and that an unbeliever or uninitiated person should enter, he is convinced by all the speakers, he is provoked to self-examination; the secrets of his heart are revealed to him, and so he will prostrate himself, worship God, and declare that God is really in your midst.

PRACTICAL RULES FOR ORDER

What then is to be said, brothers? When you assemble each of you has ready a hymn, an instruction, a revelation, a message in a foreign language, or an interpretation. Let all that is done make for edification. If there is speaking in a foreign language, let it be done by two or at most three, and in turn, and have an interpreter. If there is no one to interpret, let the man with the gift of foreign languages keep silent in the congregation. He may speak to himself or to God. Two or three of God's inspired spokesmen should speak,

20
21
22
23
24
25
26
27
28
29

14:21. Deut. 28:49; Isa. 28:11 f. St. Paul cites freely from Isaias. The people of Jerusalem in the time of the prophet failed to hearken to the clear warnings of God, who then threatened to send the Assyrians to invade and take over the city and issue orders in a foreign language. The invasion and foreign language were a sign to the unbelieving Jews. So the gift of tongues was a sign to the Corinthians who did not have a sufficiently strong faith to aspire to less spectacular but more precious gifts.

30 and the rest should weigh what is said. But if something is revealed
31 to another who is seated, the speaker must stop. One by one you
can each deliver an inspired message, and thus all can receive instruc-
32 tion and encouragement. The spiritual gifts of God's inspired
spokesmen must be subject to the control of other inspired spokes-
33 men of God. God is the author not of disorder but of tranquillity.
34 As in all the congregations of the saints, women are to keep
silent at the services. They have been given no commission to
35 speak, but they should keep their place, as the Law directs. If
they wish to inform themselves, they may ask their husbands at
home, since it is not proper for a woman to speak at a service.
36 What! Was it from you that the word of God went forth, or
has it come to you alone?
37 If anyone rates himself as an inspired spokesman of God or as
spiritually gifted, let him recognize that what I am writing to you
38 is the Lord's command. If he fails to recognize this, he will not be
39 recognized. So, then, my brothers, desire earnestly the gift of being
God's inspired spokesman, and do not hinder the gift of speaking
40 in foreign languages. Only see that all things are done properly
and in good order.

THE RESURRECTION

CHAPTER 15

CHRIST'S RESURRECTION IS A FACT

1 I recall to your minds, brothers, the Good News which I preached
to you, which also you received, and in which you continue steadfast,
2 through which, too, you are working out your salvation, if you continue to cling firmly to it, as I preached it to you — unless your faith
has all been for nothing.
3 In fact, I passed on to you as of first importance the message
which I in turn had received, that Christ died, in accordance with

---

14:36. St. Paul here senses opposition to what he has just said, and shows
signs of irritation. He ironically asks if the Corinthians have originated the faith
and alone accepted it, so that they could legislate for it and regulate its exercise
according to their own fancy. The Corinthians' congregation is part of a widespread movement and must submit to its regulations.

the Scriptures, for our sins, and that he was buried, and that he 4
rose again the third day, according to the Scriptures, and that he 5
appeared to Cephas, and after that to the Twelve. Then he was 6
seen by more than five hundred of the brothers at one time, the
majority of whom are still with us, although some of them have
fallen asleep in death. Then he was seen by James, then by all 7
the apostles. Last and least of all, as one born out of due time, 8
he was seen by me. I am the least significant of the Apostles, not 9
worthy to be called an apostle, because I persecuted the Church of
God. By God's grace I am what I am, and the grace which entered 10
me was not fruitless. On the contrary I have worn myself out in
toil more than any of them. No, not I but the grace of God working
with me. Whether, then, it is I or they, we preach as stated above, 11
and that is the belief you accepted.

FAITH IS VAIN IF THERE IS NO RESURRECTION

If what is preached about Christ is that he was raised from the 12
dead, how is it that some of you say there is no resurrection from
the dead? If there is no resurrection from the dead, Christ was 13
not raised. If Christ was not raised, then there is nothing to our 14
preaching, there is nothing to your faith. Further, it is discovered 15
that we are guilty of misrepresenting God, because we testified that
God raised Christ when he did not raise him, if it is true that the
dead are not raised. If the dead are not raised, Christ has not been 16
raised. But if Christ has not been raised, your faith is groundless; 17
you are still in your sins! It follows also that those who have fallen 18
asleep in death in Christ are lost! If in view merely of this present 19
life we have nothing but hope in Christ, we are more to be pitied
than all other men.

15:5. *Twelve:* the Vulgate and some Greek manuscripts read "Eleven."
Though there were only eleven Apostles at the time, the expression "Twelve"
continued to be used as a technical term for the group of originally twelve
of our Lord's Apostles.

15:8. *Last and least:* though grammatically this refers to time, it also refers
in the mind of St. Paul to his position of unworthiness as he goes on to state.
born out of due time: literally, "abortive." The expression indicates how sudden
and unexpected was the Apostle's conversion.

15:19. *merely:* this word could also be construed with "in this life," and
the meaning would be that there was hope of advantage only in this life, none
for the future life. As the version above construes it, the meaning is that the
faithful have hope but it is nothing else; it is illusory.

CHRIST'S RESURRECTION THE MODEL OF OURS

20   But Christ has been truly raised from the dead. He is the first
21   fruits of those that have fallen asleep in death, because since man is
the cause of death, so man is the cause of the resurrection from the
22   dead. Just as in Adam all men die, so too in Christ all men are
23   made alive. But each in his own division: Christ the first fruits; then
24   Christ's own, when he comes. Then the end, when he will hand the
kingdom over to his God and Father once he has reduced to nothing
25   every other principality and every other authority and power. He
must indeed exercise royal authority, "until he has put all his enemies
26   under his feet." The last enemy to be destroyed will be death,
27   because "he put all things under his feet." But when it is said,
"he put all things under his feet," it is evident that he who subjected
28   them is to be excepted. Once everything has been brought into
subjection to him, then the Son himself, in order that God may be
everything to everyone, will be brought into subjection to the
Father who subjected everything to him, in order that God may
be everything to everyone and everything.

ARGUMENTS FOR OUR RESURRECTION

29   If this is not so, what will they accomplish who have themselves
baptized for the dead? If there is absolutely no resurrection of the
30   dead, why do they have themselves baptized for them? Why do
31   we at every moment expose ourselves to danger? I swear, brothers,
by the very pride I take in you in Christ Jesus our Lord, that day
32   after day I face death. If from human motives I fought wild beasts
at Ephesus, what use was it to me? If the dead are not raised, let
us eat and drink since tomorrow we shall die.

15:28. The submission of Christ to the Father, according to St. Hilary, St.
Jerome, and others of the Fathers, is to be understood of Christ as Redeemer.
He will offer the redeemed to the Father as the trophy of his victory, the result
of the mission which the Father gave him to accomplish. In thus submitting to
the Father, Christ will lose none of his prerogatives, since he is God. Then
God will be everything in and to all the elect, the sole object of their contemplation and love, and in God all other creatures will be loved.

15:29. The baptism for the dead seems to have been a sort of sacramental,
a practice different from Baptism, the sacrament. It was possibly a sprinkling
with water accompanied with prayers for the deceased. It is to be noted that
St. Paul does not condemn the practice, and that thus understood it evidences
a belief in purgatory and in the efficacy of prayers and good works offered for
the souls in purgatory.

Do not fool yourselves. "Bad company corrupts good morals." 33
Return, as is proper, to your senses, and do not go on sinning. Some 34
of you actually cling to your ignorance. I so speak to move you
to shame.

But someone will ask, "How can the dead be raised? With what 35
kind of body will they come back?" Senseless man! What you sow 36
is not brought to life unless it dies. And when you sow, you do not 37
sow the body that is to be, but a bare grain, perhaps of wheat or
something else. But God gives it a body such as he wills, and to 38
each kind of seed the body proper to it. All flesh is not the same, 39
but men have one kind of flesh, beasts another, birds another, and
fish still another kind. And there are heavenly bodies and earthly 40
bodies, but the splendor of the heavenly bodies differs from that of
the earthly bodies. The sun has its own degree of splendor, the 41
moon its own, and the stars their own. Yes, star differs from star
in splendor.

It is the same with the resurrection of the dead. 42
What is sown is perishable;
What is raised is imperishable.
What is sown is sordid; 43
What is raised is glorious.
What is sown is weak;
What is raised is mighty.
The body sown is natural; 44
The body raised is glorified.
As surely as there is a natural body,
So surely is there a glorified body.

So the Scriptures say: 45
"The first Adam became a soul having life;
The last Adam became a spirit imparting life."

15:44. *natural . . . glorified:* literally, "psychic . . . pneumatic (spiritual),"
i.e., a body animated with a purely natural soul and subject to the weaknesses
and limitations with which we in this life are so familiar. The pneumatic (spiritual) body is the same body essentially, animated with the same soul as during
life, but now it is controlled by the highest part of the soul, the pneuma (spirit)
which has been transformed and elevated by the indwelling of the Holy
Spirit and is thus enabled to exercise perfect control over the body. The body is
perfectly submitted to the spirit as the spirit is perfectly submitted to the
Holy Spirit.
15:45. Gen. 2:7.

46 Yet the first body was not glorified,
But first came the natural body, then the glorified.
47 The first man was made from the earth's dust;
The second man is from heaven.
48 As was the man of dust,
So are they who are of the dust.
And as is the Heavenly One,
So are those who are heavenly.
49 And just as we have borne the likeness of the man of dust,
So shall we bear the likeness of the Heavenly One.

FINAL VICTORY OVER DEATH

50 But I affirm this, brothers, that flesh and blood cannot inherit
the kingdom of God, any more than what is perishable can inherit
51 what is imperishable. Here I tell you a mystery.
We shall not all fall asleep in death,
But we shall all be changed.
52 In a moment, in the twinkling of an eye,
At the last trumpet call,
When the trumpet sounds,
Then the dead will be raised imperishable,
And we shall be changed,
53 Because this perishable nature of ours is destined to be
clothed in imperishable glory,
And this mortal nature of ours must be clothed
in immortality.
54 When this perishable nature is clothed in imperishable glory,
And this mortal nature is clothed in immortality,
Then will be realized the words of Scripture,
"Death is swallowed up in victory!
55 O Death, where is your victory?
O Death, where is your sting?"
56 Death's sting comes from sin;
Sin's force comes from the Law.
57 But thanks be to God, who gives us the victory
Through our Lord Jesus Christ.

15:50. *flesh and blood*: here designate the natural body before its glorification.
15:51. The Vulgate reads: " We shall all rise but we shall not all be changed."
The Greek text we have translated is certainly the correct reading.

So my beloved brothers, be steadfast, immovable. Devote your- 58
selves fully at all times to the Lord's work, realizing that your toil
in the Lord can never be in vain!

CONCLUSION

CHAPTER 16

THE COLLECTION TO BE TAKEN UP

As to the collection for the saints, follow the arrangements I 1
have made for the congregations in Galatia. On the first day of every 2
week, each of you should set aside in a fund what he has succeeded
in saving, so that the collection will not have to be taken up at the
time of my arrival. As soon as I arrive, I shall send with letters of 3
credit those whom you approve, to bring your gift to Jerusalem.
And if it is important enough for me to go, they will make the 4
journey with me.

PAUL'S PLANS

I shall visit you as soon as I have passed through Macedonia. 5
My intention is merely to pass through Macedonia, but with you, 6
probably, I shall remain for some time, or even spend the winter, so
that wherever I go you may see me off. I do not wish to see you 7
now merely in passing. I hope to spend some time with you, if the
Lord permits. But I shall prolong my stay at Ephesus until Pente- 8
cost. I have evidently a great opportunity there for effective work, 9
although many are my adversaries.

If Timothy comes, see that his visit to you is without anxiety; he 10
is doing the Lord's work, just as I am. Therefore no one is to look 11
upon him as a nobody. See him off in peace, that he may come
to me, for I am expecting him with the brothers.

16:1. The collection for the poor of Jerusalem was requested by the other
Apostles (Gal. 2:10). Cf. Rom. 15:26; Acts 24:17; 2 Cor. 8–9.

16:4. *important enough:* i.e., if the sum is large enough. Paul did eventually
go to Jerusalem with the bearers of the collection (Rom. 15:25; Acts 24:17).

16:6. Paul did spend the winter at Corinth (Acts 20:1–3).

12   As to the brother Apollos, I have strongly urged him and the brothers to visit you, but he was quite unwilling to do so now. He will come when he has the time.

DIRECTIONS AND GREETINGS

13   Be watchful; be steadfast in your faith; act like men; be strong.
14   Let everything you do be regulated by love.

15   I make this plea: Brothers, you know well that the household of Stephanus are the first fruits of Achaia and that they have devoted
16   themselves to the service of the saints. Follow the leadership of men like these, and of everyone who co-operates and toils with them.
17   I am happy over the presence here of Stephanus, Fortunatus, and
18   Achaicus, because they make up for your absence. They have really brought calm to my spirit and yours. Recognize the worth of such men.

19   The congregations of Asia greet you. Aquila and Priscilla with the congregation that assembles at their home, greet you heartily.
20   All the brothers greet you. Greet one another with a holy kiss.
21, 22   I, Paul, greet you in my own handwriting. If anyone loves not the Lord, let him be accursed. The Lord comes.

23, 24   The grace of our Lord Jesus be with you. My love is with you all in Christ Jesus.

16:12. It is clear from this verse that there was no rivalry between Paul and Apollos.

16:22. *The Lord comes*: the Greek is *Maranatha*, an Aramaic expression. The word may also be divided in such a way as to yield: "Our Lord, come!"

THE SECOND EPISTLE TO THE CORINTHIANS

St. Paul followed up his first Epistle to the Corinthians by sending Timothy to them as his personal representative, and then Titus. This latter met St. Paul in Macedonia and reported favorably, for the most part, on the situation at Corinth. The Corinthians had promised to mend their ways, but meanwhile bitter enemies of the Apostle had attacked his authority and criticized him for supporting himself by his own manual labor instead of accepting aid from the Corinthians. They found fault with him for promoting a collection for the poor of Jerusalem. These funds, St. Paul's enemies said, he intended to use for himself. They accused him of ambition, inconstancy, lack of skill in oratory, and of being extremely bold in his letters during his absence, but weak and vacillating when present at Corinth.

In the second Epistle the Apostle undertakes to answer these calumnies in vigorous and forceful language. He is in turn affectionate and indignant, pleading and threatening, ironical and indulgent. There is no more intensely personal letter than 2 Corinthians, in which the Apostle changes his moods so rapidly and gives expression to such a wide variety of emotions.

Apart from answering the charges leveled against him and defending his authority, the Apostle in this letter makes a fervid plea for alms to be sent to the poor at Jerusalem. In this plea the Apostle shows a shrewd understanding of human nature and the various motives which sway men, while at the same time he appeals to some deeply spiritual motives based on his theology of the Incarnation.

The Epistle, written from Macedonia about A.D. 57, is by no means a formal treatise, such as Romans, but rather a familiar letter, penned or rather dictated under the stress of strong emotion, with abrupt transitions and changes of mood from deep tenderness such as is found in Philippians to vigorous reprimand such as characterizes Galatians.

Many commentators think that between 1 and 2 Corinthians there were one and possibly several letters addressed to the Corinthians which have been lost. Other critics, however, think that in 2 Corinthians there is a fusion of several letters, including those which other critics suppose lost.

THE DIVISION OF THE SECOND EPISTLE TO THE CORINTHIANS

Introduction, 1:1–14.
Personal defense, 1:15 to 7:16.
  The Apostle's delay, 1:15 to 2:17.
  The Apostle defends his assurance, 3:1 to 5:10.
  The Apostle defends his sincerity, 5:11 to 7:1.
  The Apostle defends his previous letter, 7:2–16.
The collection for the poor, 8:1 to 9:15.
The Apostle defends his commission, 10:1 to 13:10.
Conclusion, 13:11–13.

THE SECOND EPISTLE OF

ST. PAUL THE APOSTLE

TO THE CORINTHIANS

INTRODUCTION

CHAPTER 1

GREETINGS

Paul, by God's will an apostle of Christ Jesus, and Timothy our 1
brother, to God's congregation at Corinth, as well as to all the saints
throughout Achaia: grace and peace from God our Father and from 2
the Lord Jesus Christ.

THANKS BE TO GOD FOR HIS MERCY

Blessed be the God and Father of our Lord Jesus Christ, the 3
merciful Father who is the source of unalloyed comfort, and con- 4
tinues to comfort us in our every affliction, that we may in turn
be enabled to comfort those who are in any kind of affliction by
imparting to them the comfort we receive from God. As the suffer- 5
ings which we have to endure for Christ's sake are superabundant,
so is the comfort we receive through Christ superabundant. If we 6
are afflicted, it is to comfort and save you. If we are comforted, it is
to bring you comfort. It does its work when you endure the selfsame
sufferings as we. And our hope in your regard is unshaken, since 7
we know well that as you share in our sufferings, so do you also in
our comfort.

We do not want you to be ignorant, brothers, of the affliction 8
which befell us in Asia. We were crushed beyond measure, beyond
our strength, so that we were not sure of even continuing to live.
Why, we had within ourselves the sentence of death. The purpose 9

1:9. *sentence of death:* probably a severe illness St. Paul thought might be
fatal. So Allo.

of that sentence was to bring us to rely not on ourselves but on
10 God who raises the dead. He it is who delivered us from such
deadly peril and is now delivering us. And in him I have put my
11 hope that he will deliver me again, through the help of your prayers.
Thus, thanks will be given by many on our behalf for the gift bestowed on us at the request of many.

PAUL'S SINCERITY

12   Our boast is this, the testimony of our conscience that we have
conducted ourselves in the world at large and particularly in our
relations with you in simplicity and God-given sincerity, not relying
13 on human cleverness but on God's grace. We really write nothing
but what you can read and recognize fully, and I hope that you
14 will recognize it fully (as you have partly recognized us), that we
are one you can be proud of, as we shall be proud of you on the
day of our Lord Jesus Christ.

THE APOSTLE'S DELAY

PAUL NOT FICKLE

15   With this assurance I intended, in order that you may enjoy a
16 second favor, to visit you first and pass through your city on my
way to Macedonia, and to return to you from Macedonia and have
17 you send me off to Judea. Now in this my intention did I show
inconstancy? Or do I make plans, guided by human prudence, in
18 such a way that with me it is now Yes and now No? God is the
trustworthy witness that our message to you is not both Yes and No.
19 The Son of that God, Jesus Christ, who was preached among you
through our instrumentality, mine, Silvanus', and Timothy's, did
not prove to be Yes and No, but in him was realized the Yes.
20 In fact, whatever God promised finds its Yes in him, and for that
21 reason we say the Amen through him to God's glory. It is God who
has established us firmly along with you in communion with Christ,

---

1:10. *is now delivering*: another well-attested reading has: "will deliver."
1:12. Many manuscripts read "holiness" instead of *simplicity*.
1:15. *second favor*: "second joy" in many manuscripts. This visit would be
a token of Paul's esteem for the Corinthians, and thus a favor or a joy to them.
1:21. *anointed*, etc.: these expressions probably refer to Baptism and Confirmation (Tertullian and many Fathers), or possibly to Paul's investiture as
an Apostle (Sickenberger and others).

and has anointed us, and stamped us with his seal, and given us 22
the Spirit as a pledge in our hearts.

PAUL SPARES AND PARDONS
Now I call God to witness against my soul that it was to spare 23
you that I did not come any more to Corinth. Not that we lord 24
it over your faith, but rather we work with you for your happiness.
You do not falter in matters of faith.

CHAPTER 2

But I made up my mind that it was better for me not to come to 1
you again in sorrow. If, in fact, I make you sorrowful, who is there 2
to gladden me save him on whom I have inflicted sorrow? And I 3
wrote as I did that when I come I may not be given sorrow by
those who ought to give me joy. I am convinced in regard to all of
you that my joy is joy to all of you. In much affliction and heartfelt 4
anxiety and with many tears I wrote to you, not to bring you sorrow
but knowledge of the overflowing love I have for you.

If anyone has inflicted sorrow, he did not inflict it on me, but, 5
to a certain extent — not to say too much — on all of you. For such 6
a one this punishment meted out by the many is enough. So now, 7
take the opposite course, and rather forgive and comfort him or he
may be overwhelmed by too much sorrow. For this reason I exhort 8
you to take an official stand of love toward him. With this very 9
object I wrote you to find out by test whether you are in all
points obedient. If you pardon anyone my offense, I too pardon 10
him. Indeed, whatever I have pardoned, if I have pardoned anything, I have done in the person of Christ for your sakes, in order 11
that Satan may not get the upper hand; we are not ignorant of
his schemes.

THE FRAGRANCE OF CHRIST
When I came to Troas to preach the gospel of Christ, although 12

2:4. *I wrote*: probably a reference to a letter now lost.
2:8. *an official stand*: the local authorities are to issue orders putting an end
to all harsh treatment of the offender and directing instead that he be treated
kindly and charitably.

13 in the Lord I had a great opportunity, I had no relief of mind because I did not find my brother Titus there. And so, bidding them farewell, I went on to Macedonia.

14 Thanks be to God, who always leads us in triumphal procession in Christ, and spreads abroad his knowledge like a perfume every-
15 where through our instrumentality. We are the fragrance of Christ for God, alike as regards those who are on the way to salvation and
16 those who are on the way to perdition: to the one group a fragrance which because of their spiritual torpor leads to death, to the other a fragrance which because of their spiritual vitality leads
17 to life. Who is competent to perform such a task? We, at least, are not as many others, dishonest, secondhand dealers in God's word, but as men of sincerity, under God's eye, in union with Christ we deliver the message from God.

The Apostle Defends His Assurance

Chapter 3

LETTER OF RECOMMENDATION

1 Are we beginning to commend ourselves? Or do you suppose we need, as some do, letters of recommendation to you or from
2 you? You are our letter written on our hearts, which is known and
3 read by all men; you are evidently a letter from Christ, drawn up by us, written not with ink but with the Spirit of the living God, not on tablets of stone but on tablets of the human heart.

MINISTERS NOT OF THE LETTER BUT OF THE SPIRIT

4 Such is the assurance we have through Christ with regard to
5 God. Not that we are competent of ourselves to take credit for anything as originating from us. Really our competency is from
6 God. He it is who has made us competent ministers of a new

2:17. *secondhand dealers:* the word is always used of those who traffic in a dishonest manner. It often denotes adulteration or falsification of the goods sold, such as diluting wine with water. "They mix their own ideas with divine truth," says St. Chrysostom.

3:6. *spirit:* the true spirit or deeper meaning of the old Law is unfolded and clarified in the new and better Christian dispensation.

covenant, not of a written code which kills, but of a spirit which gives life.

If the dispensation that brought death, existing in writing and 7 engraved on stones, was inaugurated in such splendor that the children of Israel could not fix their gaze on Moses' face because of the splendor of that face — a splendor that was but passing — shall not the dispensation of the spirit be still more resplendent? 8 Yes, if there was splendor in the dispensation that brought disaster, 9 much more is the dispensation that bestows holiness rich in splendor. Why, that which had splendor is not at all resplendent in this 10 case, since the greater splendor surpasses it. Yes, if the transient was 11 resplendent, how much more so is the permanent.

SUPERIORITY OF THE NEW OVER THE OLD COVENANT

Having, therefore, such hope, we show great boldness. We do 12, 13 not act as did Moses, who used to put a veil over his face that the Israelites might not get a glimpse of the eventual fate of their transitory law. But their minds became dulled; for to this day, when 14 the Old Testament is read to them, the selfsame veil remains. It is not made known to them that the Old Covenant is abrogated by Christ. Yes, down to this very day, when Moses is read, the 15 veil covers their hearts; but as soon as they turn in repentance to 16 the Lord, the veil shall be taken away. Now the Lord is the spirit, 17 and where this spirit of the Lord is, there is freedom. But all of us, 18 reflecting as in a mirror the Lord's glory, are being transformed into his very image from one degree of splendor to another, such as comes from the Lord who is the spirit.

CHAPTER 4

For this reason, since we have this ministry in accordance with 1

3:7. *the dispensation that brought death:* the Mosaic dispensation commanded but of itself did not offer the strength necessary to execute its commands. Thus it was an occasion of sin and death.

3:13. St. Paul here gives a symbolic interpretation of Exod. 34. The rays from Moses' face were but passing and symbolized the transitory character of the Old Law. So Allo and others.

3:17. *the Lord is the spirit:* Jesus Christ is the deeper meaning underlying the letter of the Old Testament. So Prat and others. *freedom:* i.e., from the letter of the Law and from sin.

2 the mercy shown us, we do not lose heart. On the contrary we renounce those dissimulations caused by false shame, we avoid crafty conduct, we do not tamper with the word of God, but by openly proclaiming the truth we commend ourselves to every human
3 conscience with the eyes of God upon us. And if our preaching is still veiled, it is only in the case of those who are bringing about
4 their own destruction. In their case the god of this world has blinded the infidels' thoughts, lest they fix their eyes on the enlightenment afforded by the gospel which proclaims to them the
5 splendor of Christ, who is God's image. For we herald not ourselves, but Christ Jesus as Lord, and ourselves merely as your
6 servants for the sake of Jesus. The God who said, "Let light shine from the midst of darkness," has shone in our hearts, to give enlightenment through the knowledge of God's glory, glowing in the face of Christ.

WEAK IN THEMSELVES, APOSTLES ARE MIGHTY IN GOD

7   Yet we carry this treasure in earthen vessels, to show that its
8 superabundant power comes from God and not from us. On all sides we are hard pressed, but by no means trapped. We have every
9 way blocked, yet we have a way of escape. We are pursued, yet by no means overtaken. We are thrown down, but by no means
10 destroyed. We carry about with us in our bodies at all times Jesus' condemnation to death, so that in these same bodies of ours the
11 living power of Jesus may become evident. Yes, for the sake of Jesus every moment of our lives we are condemned to death, so that the living power of Jesus may become evident in our weak selves
12 so liable to death. Thus death is at work in us, and life in you.
13 But since we have the same spirit of faith as shown in the Scripture passage, "I believe, and so I spoke," we also believe, and that is
14 why we also speak. We are convinced that he who raised Jesus will raise us also with Jesus, and will place us near him with you.
15 All things come to pass for your sake, so that the grace so profusely granted may lead, for God's glory, to profuse thanksgiving
16 as the result of multiplied conversions. This is why we do not lose

---

4:7. *this treasure:* i.e., the message of the Gospel was entrusted to frail mortals for transmission to mankind.
4:13. Ps. 115:10.

heart. On the contrary, although the physical part of our being is
wasting away, yet its spiritual element within is being renewed day
after day. For our present light affliction is producing for us an 17
eternal weight of glory that is beyond all measure, while we direct 18
our gaze not at what is seen but at what is unseen. What we see is
temporary, but what we do not see endures forever.

CHAPTER 5

In fact we are certain that when our earthly dwelling, which 1
is but a tent, is destroyed, we have an edifice made by God, a
dwelling not made with hands, everlasting in the heavens. And in 2
truth we pine in this present dwelling, yearning to have put over it
that dwelling of ours which is from heaven, if indeed we shall be 3
found clothed and not naked. For we who are in this tent sigh 4
under our burden, because we do not wish to be unclothed, but
rather clothed over, that what is mortal may be swallowed up by
life. Now he who fashioned us for this very purpose is God, who 5
has given us the Spirit as a pledge.

We are, then, always full of courage; we know full well that 6
while we are in the body we are exiled from the Lord, since we 7
guide ourselves by faith, not by what is seen. We even have the 8
courage to prefer to be exiled from the body and to be at home
with the Lord. And this is why we strive, whether in the body or 9
outside it, to be pleasing to him. We must all be laid open to 10
inspection before the tribunal of Christ, each to receive his due in
keeping with the good or evil he has done while he was in the body.

THE APOSTLE DEFENDS HIS SINCERITY

PAUL'S LABOR FOR SOULS

Knowing, therefore, what the fear of the Lord means, we try to 11
win men by persuasion. To God our character is perfectly clear;
and I hope that in your inner selves it is also.

5:2. *dwelling of ours which is from heaven*: i.e., the glorified body.
5:3. *if indeed, etc.*: if at the time of the general resurrection, Paul would
still be among the living and not have been divested of the body.
5:11. *fear of the Lord*: which arises from the consideration of the judgment of

12   It is not that we are commending ourselves again to you; we are merely giving you an occasion to boast about us, that you may have an answer for those who glory in outward appearances and
13 not in inward realities. If we were transported with zeal, it was
14 for God; if we restrain ourselves, it is for your sake. Love for Christ impels us. We have come to the conclusion that since one
15 died for all, therefore all died, and that Christ died for all, in order that they who are alive may live no longer for themselves, but for him who died for them and rose again.

16   So, from now on we value no one by what he is externally. Even though we once valued Christ by what he was externally,
17 we now value him by this standard no longer. If, then, any man is in Christ, he is a new creation; the old state of things has gone;
18 wonderful to tell, it has been made over, absolutely new! All this comes from the action of God, who has reconciled us to himself through Christ, and has entrusted us with this ministry of recon-
19 ciliation. We know that God was truly reconciling the world to himself in Christ, not reckoning against men their sins, and entrusting to us the message of reconciliation.

20   We are, therefore, Christ's ambassadors; we know that God makes appeal through us. We beg you, for the sake of Christ, to
21 be reconciled to God. For our sakes God made him who knew no sin the bearer of sin, so that in him we might become the bearers of God's holiness.

CHAPTER 6

1   Yes, as co-workers, we also exhort you that it be not in vain that you have received the grace of God.

---

which Paul has just spoken. In view of this judgment, St. Paul seeks to persuade men of the genuineness of his prerogatives and the sincerity of his motives. He was not prompted by any desire of self-glorification. So St. Chrysostom.

5:16. *by what he is externally:* i.e., lineage, social position, racial privilege, etc. St. Paul may have once rated Jesus according to such standards. From this statement it cannot be deduced that St. Paul had ever seen our Lord prior to the vision near Damascus.

5:21. Jesus, who never committed the slightest sin himself, was treated by God as the greatest of sinners. The sins of all mankind, without impairing in the least his personal holiness, were loaded upon him, and, as the emissary

He says,   2
> "In an acceptable time I have heard you,
> and on the day of salvation I have helped you."

Right now is the acceptable time! Right now is the day of salvation! We give no offense in anything lest our ministry be discredited. 3
On the contrary we reflect credit on ourselves in all circumstances,   4
as befits God's ministers — in great endurance, in afflictions, in
hardships, in straits; in scourgings, in imprisonments, in riots, in   5
fatigues, in sleepless nights, in fastings; in integrity, in knowledge, 6
in long-suffering, in kindness, in the gifts of the Holy Spirit, in
unaffected love; in the preaching of the truth, in the power that   7
comes from God; with the offensive and defensive armor supplied
by holiness; in honor and dishonor, in evil report and good report;   8
as deceivers and yet truthful, as unknown yet well known, as ever   9
at death's door, yet, wonder of wonders, we continue to live; as
chastised but not killed, as sorrowful yet always rejoicing, as beggars 10
yet enriching many, as having nothing yet possessing everything.

PLEA FOR AMENDMENT

We are frank with you, Corinthians. We open wide our heart   11
to you. In us there is no lack of room for you, but in your heart   12
there is no room for us. Now to make a return in kind — I speak   13
as to my children — open wide your hearts to us.

Do not enter into mismated association with unbelievers. What   14
has holiness in common with iniquity? Or what fellowship has
light with darkness? What agreement is there between Christ and   15
Beliar? Or what part has the believer with the unbeliever? And what   16

---

goat, our Lord was sacrificed in expiation of them. The result was that we, who
avail ourselves of his merits, become partakers of the justice or holiness which
God imparts to all who have faith in the Redeemer. So Estius and others.
6:2. Isa. 49:8.

6:14. *mismated association:* literally, "be unequally yoked." The term is used
by the Greek translators of the Old Testament in reference to the prohibition of
yoking or teaming together beasts of different kinds such as an ox and an ass.
While the reference is not primarily to mixed marriages, yet the principle here
enunciated includes and is applicable to them. So Allo.

6:15. *Beliar:* etymologically seems to mean "lord of the forest," but perhaps
the correct reading here should be "Belial," which means "lord of wickedness
(or) nothingness," a name applied to Satan.

6:16. Lev. 26:12; Isa. 52:11; Jer. 51:45; Exod. 20:34 and 41 seem to be
fused here.

harmony has the temple of God with idols? That temple of the
living God you are. So says God,

> "I will dwell and move among them,
>   I will be their God and they shall be my people."

17 For this reason,

> "Come out from their midst, withdraw, says the Lord,
>   and touch not what is unclean;
> And I will welcome you,

18 >   and will be your Father
>   and you shall be my sons and daughters,
>   says the Lord Almighty."

CHAPTER 7

PAUL'S LOVE FOR CORINTHIANS

1   Such being the promises we have, beloved, let us cleanse ourselves
from all bodily and spiritual defilement, putting the finishing touches
on the work of our sanctification out of reverence for God.

THE APOSTLE DEFENDS HIS PREVIOUS LETTER

2   Be bighearted enough to understand us. No one has been
3 treated unjustly by us; no one has been exploited by us. I am not
saying this to condemn you, since I have already said that you are
4 in our heart, united with me in death and in life. Great is my
confidence in you, great my boasting about you. I am filled with
comfort. I overflow with joy in spite of all our troubles.
5   In fact from the time of our arrival in Macedonia, our body
has had no rest; we had troubles on every side, conflicts without
6 and anxieties within. But God who comforts the humble, com-
7 forted us by the arrival of Titus. And not only by his arrival, but
also by the comfort which he himself experienced in you. He told
us of your longing, of your sorrow, of your loyalty to me, so that
I rejoiced yet more.

6:17. 2 Kings 7:14; Isa. 43:6; Jer. 31:9; 32:38; Osee 1:10; Amos 4:13; Soph.
3:20 seem to be alluded to in this free citation.

THEIR REPENTANCE

Yes, although I brought you sorrow by my letter, I do not regret 8
it. And even if I did regret it (for that letter, I see, did for a time
make you sorrowful), now I am glad, not because it brought you 9
sorrow, but because your sorrow led you to repentance. That is, you
had sorrow that was inspired by God, so that you suffered no injury
from what we wrote. Now the sorrow that is inspired by God pro- 10
duces salutary and unalterable change of mind and heart, while
the sorrow based on worldly motives produces death. Consider, as 11
a matter of fact, what earnestness this sorrow inspired by God produced in you; yes, what self-vindication, what indignation, what fear,
what yearning, what zeal, what readiness to avenge! In every point
you freed yourselves from guilt in the affair.

If, then, I wrote to you, it was not for the sake of the one who 12
inflicted the wrong, nor for the sake of the one who was its victim,
but to make clear to you the eager devotion you have for us in the
sight of God. This is why we have been comforted. But besides 13
our own comfort, we more especially rejoiced at the joy of Titus,
because his mind is set at rest by all of you, and because, since I 14
had boasted somewhat to him about you, I was not put to shame,
but just as we had spoken all things in truth to you, so also has
our boasting to Titus been found to be true. And his affection for 15
you is all the more abundant, as he recalls how obedient you all
were and how you received him with fear and trembling. I rejoice 16
that in every respect I can have confidence in you.

The Collection for the Poor

Chapter 8

EXHORTATION TO BE GENEROUS

Now, brothers, we make known to you the grace that God has 1
bestowed on the congregations of Macedonia — namely that in a 2

7:8. The reference, it is generally thought, is to a letter written by St. Paul
to the Corinthians and now lost.

7:12. We do not know who inflicted this wrong, but its victim was most
probably St. Paul himself.

severe ordeal of affliction their overflowing joy shines out, and their
— very deep poverty has resulted in a wealth of simple generosity.
3 According to their means, as I can bear them witness, rather beyond
4 their means, of their own accord, they insistently begged of us the
5 favor of sharing in this charitable service on behalf of the saints. And
   beyond anything we had hoped for, it was themselves that they gave,
6 first to the Lord, and then by God's will to us. This led us to
   request Titus that as he had begun this work of charity among you,
   he should bring it to completion.

7   Now, as you excel in every way, in faith, in eloquence, in knowledge, in every kind of zeal, and in the love we have stirred up in
8 you, so too you should excel in this work of charity. I am not
   speaking by way of command, but to test the genuineness of your
9 love by means of your eagerness to help others. You know, in fact,
   the graciousness of our Lord Jesus Christ. Although he was rich,
   he became poor for your sakes that by his poverty you might
   become rich.

10   And in this matter I am giving advice. It is in line with your
   desires, since a year ago you not only began the project, but began
11 it of your own accord. So now complete the project, so that your
   eagerness in willing it may be equaled by your desire to carry it
   through according to your ability.

12   If, in fact, the good will is there, it is welcome according to what
13 it has to give, not according to what it does not have. I mean the
   relief given to others should not be a hardship to you, but there
14 should be equality; that is to say, your surplus should supply their
   lack, and their surplus should, in turn, supply what you lack, thus
15 establishing an equality. So it is written,

                "He who had much had nothing over,
                    and he who had little had no less."

RECOMMENDATION OF DELEGATES

16   Now thanks be to God, who inspires Titus' heart with the
17 same zeal for you. In fact he not only accepted our request, but

---

8:4. *saints:* the poor Christians at Jerusalem.
8:8. *eagerness to help others:* or "others' eagerness to help." St. Paul in this
latter interpretation would propose for imitation the generosity of the Macedonians.
8:15. These words refer to the manna and are found in Exod. 16:18.

since he is more than eager, he has gone to you of his own choice. And we have sent along with him the brother whose service in 18 spreading the gospel is praised in all the congregations. What is 19 more, he was also appointed by the congregations, to the glory of God and the satisfaction of my own desire, to be my traveling companion in this gracious work which is being directed by me. We 20 are on guard, lest anyone should slander us in the matter of our administration of this generous amount. We take forethought for 21 what is honorable, not only in the eyes of God, but also in the estimation of men. And we have sent with them our brother also, 22 whom we have in many things and on many occasions, proven to to be zealous. He is now more zealous than ever because of the great confidence he has in you. As regards Titus, he is my 23 associate and fellow worker in your service. As regards our brothers, they are the messengers of the congregations, and reflect honor on Christ. Give publicly, therefore, for all the congregations to see, 24 the demonstration of your love and of my right to boast of you.

Chapter 9

It is as a matter of fact superfluous for me to write to you with 1 reference to this charitable service to the saints. I know your eager- 2 ness. I boast of it in your regard to the Macedonians, saying that Achaia has been ready since last year. And your zeal has stimulated the majority of them. Still, I have sent the brothers, so that our 3 boasting concerning you should not be given the lie in this regard, and that, as I was saying, you may be ready. Otherwise, if any 4 Macedonians come with me and find you unprepared, we — to say nothing of yourselves — would be put to shame for having been too sure. I have, therefore, thought it necessary to request the 5 brothers to go to you in advance, and to organize in advance this generosity which was announced in advance, so that it may be ready as a generous offering and not as a grudging gift.

8:18. *the brother whose service,* etc.: it is not known who this was. Some commentators have seen a reference to St. Luke and to his written Gospel. But such a view is a misunderstanding of the word *gospel* in this passage.
8:22. We do not know who this third member of the party was.

BLESSINGS OF GENEROSITY

6   Mark this: he who sows sparingly will also reap a scant harvest,
and he who sows generously will also reap a bountiful harvest.
7 Let each one give as he has determined in his heart, not grudgingly
8 or from compulsion, for "God loves a cheerful giver." And God is
powerful enough to give you an abundance of every blessing, so
that always having ample means, you may have an abundance for
9 every good work, as it is written,

> "He has scattered abroad, he has given to the poor;
> his goodness remains forever."

10   Now he who bountifully provides the sower with seed and gives
you bread to eat, will supply and multiply your resources and will
11 increase the fruits of your holiness. You will enrich yourselves in
everything, acquiring a perfect generosity. That will lead us to give
12 thanks to God. The administration of this sacred service not only
supplies the needs of the saints; it goes much further than that by
13 reason of the many expressions of gratitude to God. And as a result
of the proof furnished by this service, they glorify God for your
submission to the same profession of Christ's gospel, and for all the
simple generosity with which you share with them and with all.
14 They in turn in their prayers give vent to the affection for you
15 elicited by God's surpassing grace bestowed on you. Thanks be to
God for his unutterable gift!

THE APOSTLE DEFENDS HIS COMMISSION

CHAPTER 10

A WARNING TO THE CORINTHIANS

1   As for myself, I, Paul, personally appeal to you by the meekness
and gentleness of Christ — I who to your face am "very lowly among
2 you," but, when absent, "am fearless toward you"! Yes, I beseech
you that, when I come, I may not have to be bold with that assurance
I count on showing against those who regard us as acting according

9:9. Ps. 111:9.

to human motives. Human though we are, we do not wage war 3
with human resources; the weapons of our warfare are not human 4
but powerful enough in the service of God to demolish strongholds.
We demolish human calculations, yes, every fortified height that 5
rears itself against the knowledge of God. We bring every thought
into captivity under obedience to Christ, and we shall make quick 6
work of punishing every act of disobedience, once your own obedience is complete.

PAUL'S AUTHORITY

Look at what is right before your eyes. If anyone is confident 7
that he is Christ's, let him take further thought within himself that
even as he is Christ's, so too are we. Yes, when I boast a little too 8
much about our authority which the Lord has given for your upbuilding and not for your destruction, I shall not have to blush. But 9
I must not seem to terrify you by letters. It is actually said, "His 10
letters are weighty and emphatic, but his bodily presence is weak and
his speech is worthless." If anyone believes this, let him understand 11
that we are in word by letters when absent exactly what we are in
deed when bodily present.

Of course, we do not have the audacity to class or compare 12
ourselves with certain individuals, who commend themselves. But
they, when they measure themselves by themselves, and compare
themselves with themselves, are not acting intelligently. As to 13
ourselves, we shall not boast beyond bounds, but within the bounds
of the province God has assigned us — a province which extends even
to you. We certainly do not have to strain ourselves excessively, as 14
though we are not reaching you. Why, we were the first to get to
you with the gospel of Christ. We do not boast beyond bounds — 15
of the fatiguing labors of others — but we have the hope that, as your
faith in us increases, our prestige may be greatly enlarged through
you. Then we may hope, while still keeping within our province,
to bring the gospel to countries beyond yours, instead of boasting 16

10:5. *fortified height*: St. Paul is using technical military language to describe
the proud philosophical speculations and pretended knowledge that hoped to
demolish the teachings of the Gospel. Others think that *fortified height* or high
wall refers to the Mosaic Law which, because it was misunderstood, prevented the
clear vision of the truth of the Gospel message.

17 in another man's province about work he has already done. "He who
18 boasts should boast in the Lord," because it is not he who commends himself that is approved, but he whom the Lord commends.

CHAPTER 11

PAUL PREACHES GRATUITOUSLY

1   Would to God you could bear with a little of my foolishness!
2 Please do bear with me! After all I am jealous for you with a divine jealousy. For I betrothed you to one spouse that I might present you
3 a chaste virgin to Christ. But I fear lest, as the serpent seduced Eve by his cleverness, so your thoughts may be corrupted and fall from
4 the single-minded devotion and purity you owe to Christ. Why, if the first one that comes along preaches a Jesus differing from the one we preach, or if you receive a different kind of spirit than you received from us, or a different gospel message than you got from
5 us, you would submit with fine toleration! Now I count myself as
6 not one whit inferior to those super-apostles. Granted that I may be untrained in oratory, I am not so in knowledge, but in every respect and in all things we have made that clear to you.

7   Or did I do wrong when I humbled myself that you might be
8 exalted, preaching the gospel of God to you free of charge? I robbed other congregations, taking pay from them so as to minister to you.
9 And when I was with you and in want, I was a burden to no one, since the brothers that came from Macedonia supplied my needs. Thus, in all things I have kept myself from being a burden to you,
10 and so I intend to keep myself. By the truth of Christ who dwells within me, this boast shall not be taken from me in the district
11 of Achaia. Why so? Because I do not love you? God knows I do.
12 But what I am doing, I will go on doing, that I may cut away the ground from those who are wishing for ground to be considered
13 in their boasting exactly like us. Why, men like those are sham

---

10:17. Cited freely from Jer. 9:22–23.
11:2. *jealous:* Paul is jealous for God with a divine jealousy, which insists on the exclusive love of man.
11:4. *Jesus differing:* i.e., in his message, spirit, teachings.
11:5. *super-apostles:* refers in irony to the spurious apostles who challenged Paul's authority and the accuracy of his teaching.

apostles, fraudulent workers disguised as apostles of Christ. And no 14
wonder, since Satan disguises himself as an angel of light. It is no 15
great thing, then, if his ministers disguise themselves as ministers
of holiness. Their end will be in keeping with their deeds.

PAUL LABORS AND SUFFERS

I repeat, let no one think me foolish. But if so, then regard me 16
even as such, that I may also boast a little. What I am saying with 17
this assurance in boasting, I am not saying in keeping with the Lord's
example, but as a fool. Since many boast for purely human reasons, 18
I too will boast. Having so much common sense, you gladly put up 19
with those that have none! For example, you tolerate it if a man 20
enslaves you, or preys upon you, or makes away with your possessions,
or is overweening, or slaps you in the face! I must confess to my 21
shame: it is to be believed that we have been too weak. But in
whatever respect anyone has shown boldness, I too show the same
boldness. I know that I am speaking foolishly. Are they Hebrews? 22
So am I! Are they Israelites? So am I. Are they the descendants of
Abraham? So am I! Are they ministers of Christ? I — to speak like 23
a man out of his mind — surpass them by reason of fatiguing labors
more abundant, imprisonments more frequent, lashings innumerable,
many threats of death. From the Jews five times I received forty 24
lashes less one. Three times I was scourged, once I was stoned, three 25
times I suffered shipwreck; a night and a day I was adrift on the
high sea; in frequent journeys on foot, in perils from floods, in 26
perils from robbers, in perils from my own nation, in perils from
the Gentiles, in perils in the city, in perils in the wilderness, in
perils on the sea, in perils from false brothers, in fatigue and hard- 27
ship, in many sleepless nights, in hunger and thirst, in fastings, often
in cold and nakedness. Apart from these things, there is my daily 28
pressing anxiety, my solicitude for all the congregations! Who is weak 29 ‑

11:24. *forty lashes less one:* the Law, Deut. 25:3, limited the number of lashes
in scourging to forty, but the casuists of the time stipulated that only thirty-
nine strokes be given, lest by a miscount one might inadvertently go beyond
the legal limit.

11:25. *scourged:* the Roman scourging. At Philippi (Acts 16:22) one of
these whippings was administered; of the others we have no record. He was
stoned at Lystra (Acts 14:19). We have no other record of shipwrecks and
day and night on the sea here mentioned. The shipwreck described in Acts 27
was after the composition of this letter.

without my sympathizing with his weakness? Who is led astray without my burning with indignation?

30   If I must boast, I will boast of the things that show my weakness.
31   The God and Father of our Lord Jesus Christ, who is blessed for
32   evermore, knows that I do not lie. In Damascus the ethnarch of King Aretas had stationed guards about the city with the intention of
33   having me arrested, but I was lowered in a basket through a window in the wall, and escaped his hands.

Chapter 12

PAUL'S REVELATIONS AND INFIRMITIES

1   I am obliged to boast. Although there is nothing to be gained by it, I will proceed to tell of the visions and revelations granted
2   me by the Lord. I know a man in Christ, who fourteen years ago — whether in the body or out of the body I do not know, God knows
3   — this individual was caught up to the third heaven. And I know that this person — whether in the body or out of the body I do not
4   know, God knows — was caught up into paradise and heard unutter-
5   able utterances which no man is permitted to repeat. Of such a man I will boast; but as regards myself I will boast of nothing save
6   my infirmities. If I should wish to boast about myself, I would not be unreasonable, since it is the truth that I am about to tell. But I forbear lest any man should esteem me beyond what he sees me
7   to be or hears from me on the basis of the surpassing grandeur of my revelations.

For this reason, lest I should be puffed up with vanity, there was given me a thorn for the flesh, a messenger of Satan to buffet
8   me. Concerning this I three times besought the Lord that it might

---

12:1. *nothing to be gained*: i.e., according to the Lord. St. Paul seems to have conflicting sentiments, not wishing to boast since it is opposed to humility, yet feeling the necessity of doing so to establish his authority and answer his critics.

12:2. *whether in the body*, etc.: St. Paul probably believed, according to the prevalent notions of the time, that the soul could withdraw from the body without losing its identity or cognitive powers. *third heaven*: i.e., paradise, the abode of the blessed, as distinguished possibly from the sphere of the heavenly luminaries, the second heaven, and from the sky with the clouds immediately above the earth, the first heaven.

leave me. And he said to me, "My grace is sufficient for you, for 9
my power is made perfectly evident in your weakness." Gladly,
therefore, will I boast of my infirmities, that the power of Christ
may spread a sheltering cover over me. For this reason I take delight, 10
for Christ's sake, in infirmities, in insults, in hardships, in persecutions, in distresses. For when I am weak, then I am strong.

WHY PAUL BOASTS TO THEM

I have become foolish! You have forced me. Surely I ought to 11
have been commended by you, since in no way have I fallen short
of those super-apostles, even though I am nothing. Certainly the 12
criteria that distinguish the apostle were produced among you, in
all manner of endurance, in miracles, in wonders, and exhibitions of
power. In what have you been less favored than the other con- 13
gregations — except in this, that I was no burden to you? Pardon
me this wrong!

HIS IMPENDING VISIT

Consider that this is the third time I am ready to come to you. 14
And I will not be a burden to you; I do not seek your possessions
but yourselves. Children should not save for their parents but
parents for their children. But I will most gladly spend myself and 15
be spent to the limit for the sake of your souls, even though the
more I love you the less I am loved.

But be it so. I was no burden to you, but "being clever, I 16
caught you by trickery." Did I take advantage of you through any 17
of those whom I sent you? I urged Titus to go, and I sent our brother 18
to accompany him. Did Titus take advantage of you? Have we not
acted in the same spirit? Have we not followed the same steps?

Are you thinking all this time that we are defending ourselves to 19
you? We speak in the presence of God in Christ, but in all things,
beloved, for your own upbuilding. For I fear lest perhaps when I 20
come I may not find you as I should wish, and lest I may be found
by you not as you would wish. I fear that there may be found among
you some discord, jealousy, hatred, dissension, detraction, gossiping,

---

12:16. *I caught you by trickery:* so St. Paul's enemies accused him of doing.
While refusing support from the Corinthians, St. Paul was accused by his
enemies of getting money under the pretext of a collection for the benefit of
the poor Christians at Jerusalem.

2 CORINTHIANS — 12:21

21 arrogance, disturbance. I fear that when I come again God may humiliate me in your presence, that I may mourn over many who sinned before and have not repented of the uncleanness and immorality and licentiousness which they practiced.

CHAPTER 13

FINAL WARNINGS

1 This is the third time that I am coming to you. "On the word
2 of two or three witnesses, every word shall be confirmed." I have already warned, when present, and now in my absence I again warn those who sinned formerly, and all the rest, that if I come again, I
3 will show no leniency. Do you seek a proof that Christ speaks through me? He is not weak in your regard, but rather powerful
4 among you. True, though he was crucified through weakness, yet he lives through the power of God. Yes, we also are weak in him, yet in your regard we shall live to deal with you through the power of God.
5 It is your own selves that you should test over and over again to see whether you are living up to the faith. It is your own selves you should examine over and over again. Do you not recognize that Christ Jesus is in you, unless perhaps you are incapable of passing
6 the test? But I hope that you will come to realize that we are not
7 incapable of passing the test. And we pray God that you may do no evil at all, not that we may be shown to have passed the test, but that you may do what is good, and we may not be incapable
8 of passing the test. We can do nothing against the truth, but only for the truth.
9 And so we rejoice when we are weak but you are strong. And this is what we pray for, your amendment.
10 For this reason I write these things in my absence that when present I may not act sternly with you, according to the power the Lord has given me for upbuilding and not for tearing down.

13:1. Deut. 19:15. Some commentators refer this to the two or three visits of St. Paul and the testimony to be gathered against the culprits; but it more probably means that St. Paul will follow strictly legal procedure and demand the concordant testimony of at least two witnesses before proceeding to take punitive measures.

468

CONCLUSION

In conclusion, brothers, farewell. Mend your ways, be comforted, *11* ך
live in harmony, be at peace; and the God who is the source of
peace and love will be with you. Greet one another with a holy *12*
kiss. All the saints send you greeting.

The grace of the Lord Jesus Christ, and the love of God, and *13*
the communion of the Holy Spirit be with you all.

13:11. *farewell:* or "rejoice."

THE EPISTLE TO THE GALATIANS

It is not certain when St. Paul brought the glad tidings of Christianity to the Galatians. It may have been during his first missionary journey, briefly summarized in Acts 13:1–14:27. This was about the year 48. Or it may have been during the second journey about 50 or 51, as summarized in Acts 15:36–16:10. The uncertainty is due to the doubt as to just exactly what territory these people occupied and who they were. Was it the old geographical country of Galatia or the later political division that included more territory than the original Galatia, which lay between Bithynia, Paphlagonia, and Pontus on the north and Cappadocia, Lycaonia, and Phrygia to the south? And were the people to whom the Epistle was addressed the racial group of Galatians, immigrants from Gaul, or the inhabitants of the political division, regardless of race?

This uncertainty leads to a second uncertainty. Was the Epistle written about 49 before the epochal decision given at the Jerusalem meeting (Acts 15), or after it? We cannot be sure.

The Epistle is quite generally, if not unanimously, accepted as genuine, and from it we can gather considerable information. It was an attack of sickness that brought St. Paul to the Galatians. This illness was of such a nature that it made the Apostle repulsive to others, yet the Galatians received him with great enthusiasm and joy, and gave wholehearted acceptance to the Christian message. The preaching of St. Paul and the faith of the Galatians were approved by God through miraculous phenomena of one kind or another, and the Galatians congratulated themselves on their good fortune in receiving the gift of faith, in which they found a deep satisfaction.

But after St. Paul's departure, Jewish Christians appeared on the scene and questioned the authority of the Apostle and the correctness of his presentation of the Christian doctrine. They contended

471

that for salvation it was necessary to be circumcised and observe all the Mosaic rites.

News of these attacks on the Apostle and his teaching somehow, somewhere, reached him. He became indignant and wrote this letter in defense of his authority and his teaching.

The theme is the same as that of the Epistle to the Romans, that we are rendered holy by faith in Jesus Christ, that the Mosaic rites and observances have been abrogated and have lost what effectiveness they may have had. They were a temporary arrangement to prepare for the coming of Christ, and with their mission discharged they became outmoded and useless. In the Epistle to the Romans, however, we have a much more fully developed and better ordered treatment than in Galatians. There we find the calm, coolly pondered and carefully worked out treatise, while in Galatians, which obviously was composed under the stress of strong emotion, we have a rather sketchy presentation.

The Galatian Epistle also resembles 2 Corinthians, in that a large portion of this letter is devoted to a defense of St. Paul's authority as an Apostle, which was under attack at Corinth in much the same way as it was in Galatia. These attacks came from Jewish Christians who wanted to retain as necessary for salvation the Mosaic rites, particularly circumcision.

Because of the silence of the Epistle on the point, we do not know where St. Paul was when he wrote to the Galatians.

THE DIVISION OF THE EPISTLE TO THE GALATIANS

Introduction, 1:1–10.
Personal defense, 1:11 to 2:21.
    His apostolate is from Christ, 1:11–24.
    A defense of his teaching, 2:1–21.
Doctrinal part, 3:1 to 4:31.
    Justification comes from faith, 3:1–29.
    Christ freed us from slavery, 4:1–31.
Moral part, 5:1 to 6:10.
    General moral advice, 5:1–26.
    Specific counsels, 6:1–10.
Conclusion, 6:11–18.

THE EPISTLE OF

ST. PAUL THE APOSTLE

TO THE GALATIANS

INTRODUCTION

CHAPTER 1

GREETINGS

Paul, apostle — not one commissioned by man or by any group 1
of men, but one appointed by Jesus Christ and God the Father
who raised him from the dead — and all the brothers who are with 2
me, send greetings to the congregations of Galatia. To you grace 3
and peace from God our Father and the Lord Jesus Christ, who 4
sacrificed himself for our sins, that he might deliver us from this
present wicked world according to the will of our God and Father.
To him be glory for ever and ever. Amen. 5

A STERN REBUKE

I am astounded that for another gospel you are so quickly 6
deserting him, who, thanks to the grace of Christ, has called you.
There is no other gospel; it is merely that some people are upsetting 7
you and wish to distort the gospel of Christ. Let me tell you that 8
if even we ourselves or an angel from heaven should proclaim to
you a gospel other than we have proclaimed, let him be accursed. I 9
repeat what I have said: if anyone proclaims to you a gospel other
than you have received, let him be accursed. Am I now trying to 10
win the favor of men rather than of God? Or am I seeking to please
men? If I were still trying to please men, I should not be Christ's
servant.

1:10. *servant*: literally, *slave*.

473

His Apostolate Is From Christ

11 I give you to understand, brothers, that the gospel which was
12 proclaimed by me is no man-made thing, since it is not from a
human source that I received or learned it. On the contrary I got
13 it by a revelation from Jesus Christ. You have surely heard of my
former life in Judaism: how beyond all measure I persecuted the
14 Church of God and ravaged it. And I advanced in Judaism beyond
many of my own contemporaries in my nation, surpassing them in
15 zeal for the ancestral traditions. But when he who, even before my
16 birth, set me apart and called me by his grace, was pleased to reveal
his Son within me, that I might preach him among the Gentiles,
17 I did not immediately take counsel with human beings, or go to
Jerusalem to those who had been appointed apostles before I was, but
retired into Arabia and again returned to Damascus.
18 Then after three years I went to Jerusalem to pay my respects
19 to Peter and I remained with him for fifteen days. But I saw none
20 of the other apostles, except James, the Lord's brother. Now in what
I am writing to you, be sure that I am not lying. I call God to
21 witness. After that I went into the regions of Syria and Cilicia.
22 However, to the congregations of Judea which are in Christ I was
23 unknown by sight. They had only heard it said, "He who formerly
24 persecuted us, now preaches the faith he once ravaged." And they
glorified God for what he had done within me.

A Defense of His Teaching

Chapter 2

THE APPROVAL BY THE APOSTLES

1 Then after fourteen years I went again to Jerusalem with Barnabas.
2 With his consent I also took Titus with me. I went up in consequence of a revelation, and I laid before the Christians there in

2:1. *With his consent:* seems to be implied in the Greek verb here used.

474

a general assembly the gospel I habitually preach among the Gentiles, and in a private session laid it before those in authority, to make sure that my course of action was not and had not been in vain. But although Titus, my companion, was a Greek, he was not com- 3 pelled to submit to circumcision. The question had arisen on account 4 of the false brothers, who had been brought in on the sly, and had sneaked in to spy on the liberty which we enjoy in Christ Jesus, with the intent of reducing us again to slavery. To these people we made 5 no concession; not even for a moment did we yield, in order that what the true gospel teaches might remain in your possession. Furthermore, the men of authority (what they once were makes no 6 difference to me; God does not take external advantages into account) — the men of authority, I say, laid no further burden on me. On the contrary, when they saw that to me was committed the 7 preaching of the gospel to the uncircumcised, just as to Peter the apostolate to the circumcised (for he who imparted his energy to 8 Peter for the apostolate to the circumcised, imparted his energy to me for the Gentiles) — and when they recognized the grace given 9 to me, James and Cephas and John, who were considered the pillars, extended to me and to Barnabas their right hand in token of perfect accord: we were to go to the Gentiles and they to the circumcised. Only we were to remember their poor, the very thing I was 10 eager to do.

THE INCIDENT AT ANTIOCH

But when Cephas came to Antioch, I resisted him to his face 11 because he was in the wrong. In fact, he used to take his meals with 12 the Gentiles before certain persons came from James. But when these came, he withdrew and held himself aloof for fear of the advocates of circumcision. And with him the rest of the Jews failed 13 to act according to their convictions, with the result that by their

---

2:4. These false brothers were stanch advocates of circumcision as necessary for salvation. St. Paul, in accord with the Christian teaching, promulgated officially by St. Peter in Acts 10 and 11 and solemnly decreed at Jerusalem (Acts 15) held circumcision and the Mosaic rites in general to be now useless. Liberty and slavery here have reference to the Mosaic Law. So Lagrange.

2:9. For Cephas many authorities read "Peter." Also in verse 11.

2:11. he was in the wrong: his error was in conduct, not in teaching, says Tertullian.

14 inconsistency they led astray even Barnabas. But when I saw they
were not acting straightforwardly in keeping with the truth taught
by the gospel, I said to Cephas in the presence of them all, "If
you, though a Jew, adopt the Gentile way of life and not the Jewish,
how is it that you compel the Gentiles to adopt the Jewish way
of life?"

15   We are Jews by birth and not sinners of Gentile ancestry.
16 Yet we know that no man is sanctified by the deeds the Law prescribes, but by faith in Jesus Christ. Hence we believe in Christ
Jesus, that we may be sanctified with faith in Christ Jesus as the
starting point, and not by the deeds the Law prescribes, because
17 by such legal deeds no man is sanctified. Now if, while we are
seeking to be sanctified in Christ, we discover ourselves also grouped
18 with sinners, is not Christ then catering to sin? By no means! Really,
if I reconstruct the things I have destroyed, I make myself a trans-
19 gressor. As for me, by the law of faith I have died to the Law that
20 I may live for God. With Christ I am nailed to the cross. It is now
no longer I who live, but Christ lives in me. The physical life that
I now live, I live by faith in the Son of God, who loved me and
21 sacrificed himself for me. I do not reject as worthless the grace of
God. In fact, if holiness comes by the Law, then Christ's death is
to no purpose.

Justification Comes From Faith

Chapter 3

GALATIANS' EXPERIENCE PROVES THIS

1   Foolish Galatians! Who has bewitched you, before whose very
2 eyes Jesus Christ crucified has been so vividly portrayed? Let me
ask you but one question: did you receive the Spirit because you did
what the Law commands, or because you gave ear to the faith?
3 Are you so foolish? After having been initiated by the Spirit, do
you seek admission to the ranks of the perfect by material rites?

2:19. This translation is based on the Ambrosiaster's interpretation. Others
explain that the believer dies mystically with Christ who by his death on the
cross satisfied all the claims of the Mosaic Law against sinners.

Have you had so many delightful experiences to no purpose if they 4
really were to no purpose. Does he who lavishes the Spirit on you, 5
and works miracles among you, do so because you have observed the
Law, or because you have given ear to the faith? Just so "Abraham 6
believed God, and it was credited to him as holiness."

EXAMPLE OF ABRAHAM SHOWS THIS

Understand well, then, that those who believe are the real sons 7
of Abraham. And the Scriptures, foreseeing that God would sanctify 8
the Gentiles by faith, announced to Abraham beforehand, "In you
shall all nations be blessed." Therefore those who believe shall be 9
blessed with the believing Abraham.

NO MAN SANCTIFIED BY THE LAW

Really, those who rely on the deeds prescribed by the Law are 10
under a curse. The Scripture proves it:

> "Cursed is everyone who does not persevere
> in the practice of all the things
> that are written in the book of the Law."

That by the Law no man is sanctified in the sight of God is evident, 11
because "the just man lives by faith." Now the Law does not rest 12
on faith but on deeds, for "he who does these things shall live by
them." Christ redeemed us from the curse threatened by the Law, 13
when he became the object of a curse for us. The Scripture says,

> "Cursed is everyone that hangs on a gibbet,"

that the blessings bestowed on Abraham might come to the Gentiles 14
through Christ Jesus, that through faith we might receive the
promised gift of the Spirit.

GOD'S PROMISE NOT ANNULLED BY THE LAW

Brothers — I reason as do men in daily life — when even a man's 15

3:6. Gen. 15:6.

3:10. St. Paul's argument is elliptical. He presupposes that no man can
perfectly and at all times observe the precepts of the Law by his own strength.
And although God may supply the necessary aid, the Law itself does not contain
and offer such aid to man. Therefore, left to his own resources and to the mere
Law, man is doomed to fail and thus fall under the curse directed against
transgressors. So Lagrange. The citation is from Deut. 27:26.

3:13. Deut. 21:23.

16 last will has been ratified, no one nullifies or alters it. The promises were made to Abraham and to his descendant. It does not say, "And to his descendants," as if referring to many, but only to one. "And
17 to your descendant," who is Christ. Now I mean this: the Law which was promulgated four hundred and thirty years later does not nullify the covenant which was ratified by God, and thus set aside
18 the promise. For, if the right to inherit comes from the Law, it no longer comes from the promise. But it was by promise that God granted it to Abraham.

THE ROLE OF THE LAW

19   What about the Law, then? It was enacted because of transgressions by the ministry of angels through a mediator, until there
20 should come the descendant to whom the promise was made. Now a mediator does not intervene where there is only one party, and
21 God is One. Is the Law, then, contrary to the promises of God? By no means. For if a law had been enacted that could impart life,
22 holiness would truly be derived from the Law. But it is written that all men are held in bondage to sin, in view of realizing the promise by faith in Jesus Christ in favor of those who believe.

23   Before the faith came, we were in the custody of the Law, held
24 captive while waiting for the faith that was to be revealed. In this way the Law has been our attendant on the way to Christ, that we
25 might be sanctified by faith. But now that the faith has come, we
26 are no longer under the care of the attendant. You are, in fact, all
27 children of God through faith in Jesus Christ, since all of you who have come to Christ by baptism have clothed yourselves with Christ.

3:16. Gen. 12:7; 13:15; 15:18 and elsewhere.

3:19. *because of transgressions:* in view of Rom. 5:20 and 4:15, where St. Paul is more explicit, the meaning is not that the result of the Law was to repress transgressions, but rather to multiply them. God's providential purpose was to bring men to realize their weakness and the need of divine aid. So St. Augustine and others.

3:20. The meaning of this rather obscure verse seems to be that the Law, which came only indirectly from God, is inferior to the promise which came directly from God. This promise was absolute and unconditioned, but the Law and the promises it contained depended for their fulfillment on the people's faithful observance of the Law. Thus the Law is clearly inferior to the promise.

3:22. St. Paul probably had in mind the passage he would cite later in Rom. 3:10–18.

3:23. *Before the faith came:* faith in Jesus Christ is meant, i.e., the system of sanctification which was established by Christ.

No longer is there Jew or Greek; no longer is there slave or freeman; 28
no longer is there male or female. You are all one in Christ Jesus.
And if you are Christ's, then you are the offspring of Abraham, heirs 29
according to the promise.

CHRIST FREED US FROM SLAVERY

CHAPTER 4

YOU ARE NOW SONS

Now I say, as long as the heir is a child, he differs in no way 1
from a slave, though he is the master of the entire estate, but he is 2
under tutors and guardians until the time set by his father. So we 3
too, when we were children, were enslaved under the elementary
notions the world had to offer. But when the designated period of 4
time had elapsed, God sent his Son, born of a woman, born in
subjection to the Law, in order to redeem those who were in sub- 5
jection to the Law, that we might receive the adoption. And because 6
you are sons, God sent the Spirit of his Son into your hearts, crying,
"Abba, Father." You are, then, no longer a slave but a son; and if 7
a son, an heir also through God's grace.

DO NOT BECOME SLAVES AGAIN

But formerly, since you did not know God, you served those who 8
were really not gods, while at present, since you have come to know 9
God, or rather to be known by God, how is it that you turn back
again to the weak and worthless elementary notions, and wish again
to be enslaved to them? You observe days and months and seasons 10
and years. I am fearful for you, lest, perhaps, I have labored among 11
you in vain.

I beseech you, brothers, become like me, since I myself have 12

4:3. *elementary notions:* both Jews and Gentiles prior to their conversion
to Christianity were guided only by the imperfect knowledge which Revelation
supplied or which they deduced, sometimes erroneously, by their unaided reason.
Compared to the fullness of revealed truth, which Christ imparted, the knowledge which the Jewish and Gentile worlds had at their disposal was rudimentary.

4:10. *days and months,* etc.: the Jewish Sabbaths, jubilee years, annual festivals
such as the Pasch, etc.

4:12. *become like me:* St. Paul had forsaken the practices of the Mosaic
Law. He asks the Galatians to do the same.

13 become like you! You have done me no wrong. It was, as you know,
on account of a physical infirmity that I preached the gospel to you,
14 yet my physical condition, which was a sore trial to you, you did
not regard with contempt or loathing. On the contrary you welcomed
15 me as one of God's angels, even as Jesus Christ. What, then, has
become of your mutual congratulations? I can really testify that,
if possible, you would have plucked out your very eyes and given
16 them to me. Have I, then, become your enemy, because I tell you
17 the truth? These men court you from no good motive; they rather
18 seek to shut you out, that you may court them. It is good, however,
to be courted for a good motive, and that at all times, not only when
19 I am present with you. My dear children, I am again suffering the
pangs of childbirth for you, until Christ is formed within you!
20 Yet I wish I could be with you at the present moment, and thus
adjust my words to the situation, because I do not know what to
make of you.

CHILDREN OF THE FREE WOMAN

21 Tell me, you who desire to be subject to the Law, do you under-
22 stand the Law? There it is written that Abraham had two sons, the
23 one by a slave and the other by a free woman. But, whereas the
son of the slave was born according to the laws of nature, the son
24 of the free woman was born in virtue of a promise. These things
have an allegorical meaning, since these women represent the two
covenants: the one given at Sinai, bringing forth children for slavery;
25 this is Agar (for Mount Sinai is situated in Arabia,) and she
corresponds to the Jerusalem now existing. She is in slavery with

---

4.15. *mutual congratulations:* on receiving the Gospel from St. Paul, the
Galatians were elated and found cause for mutual felicitations in their new-
found faith.

4:21–31. St. Paul's argument is based on facts recorded in Gen. 15:21.
He takes it for granted that God proceeds in the spiritual realm in a way
similar to his procedure in the natural realm. Paul finds an analogy between the
facts of Christianity and Judaism on the one hand and the account of Abraham's
two sons on the other. The two situations are parallel. Judaism was a religion
of fear and servitude. Christianity is a religion of sonship and freedom. The
former must yield to the latter just as Agar and her son yielded to Sarah
and Isaac. The same God who ordered the banishment of the slave mother
and child now orders the termination of the old system of slavery and fear
for the new of freedom and sonship. So Lagrange. The citation in verse 27 is
from Isa. 54:1.

her children. But the Jerusalem on high is free, and she is our mother. 26
So it is written, 27
  "Rejoice, you barren one who do not bear,
     burst out into a shout of joy, you who do not travail;
  For the children of the desolate woman are more numerous
     than those of the woman with a husband."
You, brothers, are the children born in virtue of the promise, as 28
was Isaac. Yet, just as at that time the child born according to the 29
laws of nature persecuted the child born through the intervention
of the Spirit, so too is it now. What does the Scripture say? "Get rid 30
of the slave and her son, because the son of the slave shall not be
heir with the son of the free woman." Therefore, brothers, we are 31
not children of the slave but of the free woman.

GENERAL MORAL ADVICE

CHAPTER 5

FAITH, NOT CIRCUMCISION, AVAILS

   Christ has set us free to enjoy freedom. Stand fast, then, and 1
do not be caught again under the yoke of slavery. Take note, it is I, 2
Paul, who tell you that if you have yourselves circumcised, Christ
will be of no advantage to you. Once again I solemnly declare that 3
every man who has himself circumcised is bound to observe the
whole Law. You who would be sanctified by the Law are separated 4
from Christ; you are fallen from grace. On the contrary we who act 5
from the spiritual point of view by faith, wait for the realization of
our hopes based on our sanctification. In fact, in Christ Jesus 6
neither circumcision nor its absence is of any avail. What counts is
faith that expresses itself in love.

JUDGMENT ON FALSE TEACHERS

   You were running the race splendidly. Who has prevented you 7
from continuing to submit to the truth? This persuasion is not 8
from him who calls you. A little leaven leavens all the dough. 9
I have confidence in you in the Lord that you will not entertain 10

any other views. The one, however, who is disturbing you, whoever
11 he may be, will bear the penalty. As for me, brothers, if I still preach
circumcision, why am I still persecuted? Then the stumbling block
12 they find in the cross would be removed! Would that those who are
upsetting you would castrate themselves!

THE CHRISTIAN LIFE

13 Yes, brothers, you have been called to liberty; only do not use
liberty as an occasion for sensuality, but in love serve one another.
14 Why, the whole Law is fulfilled by the observance of the one pre-
15 cept. "You shall love your neighbor as yourself." But if you bite and
devour one another, take heed, or you will be consumed by one
16 another. But I say: conduct yourselves by spiritual ideals, and you
17 will not yield to the cravings of sensuality. The cravings of sensuality are opposed to spiritual ideals, and these spiritual ideals are
opposed to sensuality. These two are arrayed against each other,
18 and so you do not follow your natural tendency. But if you are
19 guided by spiritual ideals, you are not under the Law. Now the
actions prompted by sensuality are manifest. They are fornication,
20 impurity, licentiousness, idolatry, witchcraft, enmity, contention,
21 jealousy, outbursts of anger, quarrels, factions, schisms, envy,
drunkenness, carousings, and other vices similar to these. I warn
you beforehand, as I have already said, that those who do such things
22 will not inherit the kingdom of God. But the fruit of spiritual ideals
23 is love, joy, peace, long-suffering, affability, goodness, fidelity, gentle-
24 ness, self-control. Against such there is no law. Those who belong
25 to Christ have crucified their flesh with its passionate cravings. If we
26 live by spiritual ideals, let us conduct ourselves by these ideals. Let
us not become desirous of vainglory, provoking one another, envying
one another.

5:12. This is sarcasm. If the fanatical advocates of circumcision so wish, let
them imitate the fanatics of the cult of the pagan god, Cybele, and castrate
themselves. So the Greek and Latin Fathers. Some moderns understand the
word as the severing all relations with the Christian Church.

SPECIFIC COUNSELS

CHAPTER 6

GENTLE FRATERNAL CORRECTION

Brothers, if anyone is led by surprise into the commission of a 1
wrong, you who are spiritual should set him right in a spirit of
gentleness. But meanwhile, each one should keep an eye on himself, lest he be tempted. Help bear one another's burdens, and so 2
you will fulfill the law of Christ. If anyone imagines himself to be 3
something, whereas he is nothing, he deceives himself. Let everyone 4
test his own accomplishment, and so he will have grounds for credit
on his own merits, and not by comparison with another. Really 5
each individual has his own load to carry. And let him who is being 6
instructed in the doctrine give a share of all the good things he has
to his teacher.

MAN REAPS WHAT HE SOWS

Be not deceived. God is not mocked. A man reaps just what he 7, 8
sows. Yes, he who sows in his corrupt nature, from that corrupt
nature reaps corruption. But he who plants in the field of the spirit
will reap life everlasting. In doing good let us not be discouraged, 9
because in due time we shall reap if we do not become careless.
Therefore, while we have time, let us do good to all men, especially 10
to those of the household of the faith.

CONCLUSION

See with what large letters I write to you with my own hand! 11
As many as wish to cut a fine figure in outward observance, compel 12
you to be circumcised, simply that they may avoid persecution for
the sake of Christ's cross. Why, not even those who are circumcised 13
keep the Law; yet they desire you to be circumcised that they may

6:11. Many ancient commentators thought that St. Paul wrote this whole
letter with his own hand, but modern interpreters prefer the opinion of St.
Jerome who thought that only at this point does St. Paul begin to write. It
was his regular practice to dictate his letters.

14 make a boast of your subjection to external rites. As for me, God forbid that I should glory except in the cross of our Lord Jesus Christ, through which the world is crucified to me and I to the
15 world. What really counts is not circumcision or its absence, but being a new creature.
16 May peace and mercy rest on all those who follow this principle, and on God's Israel.
17 From now on let no man give me trouble, for I bear the marks
18 of our Lord Jesus in my body. The grace of our Lord Jesus Christ be with your spirit, brothers. Amen.

6:17. marks: literally, "stigmata," a reference to the scars left by St. Paul's scourgings, stonings, etc. The term was used of the brandings put on a person to indicate that he belonged to a certain master, or to the army or that he was a devotee of one or another of the pagan gods.

THE EPISTLE TO THE EPHESIANS

The Epistle to the Ephesians, together with the two that follow, are known as the "captivity" Epistles. This title is due to the fact that they were all written while St. Paul was in prison, as is indicated by allusions to his chains, or something of the kind indicative of imprisonment. These three and Philemon, the fourth captivity letter, were apparently dispatched together as they had the same bearers, Tychicus, Onesimus, and Epaphroditus.

St. Paul's longest known imprisonment began at Jerusalem, probably in the year 58, and continued for four years, two approximately at Caesarea in Palestine and two at Rome (Acts 21:27–28, 31). It is not quite certain whether these Epistles were written while St. Paul was at Caesarea or later while he was a prisoner at Rome. St. Paul may have been imprisoned also at Ephesus, and probably the Epistle to the Philippians was written from Ephesus.

There is considerable disagreement as to the recipients of this Epistle. The words "at Ephesus" are missing from some important manuscripts, and there are indications in the Epistle itself that it could hardly have been written to the Christians at Ephesus. St. Paul had spent several years there, yet in the Epistle itself he writes as though he did not know those whom he is addressing and that he himself has not delivered the Gospel message to them. The personal tone which strongly marks St. Paul's letters to the congregations he established is missing. Various hypotheses have been put forth. One is that the Epistle was originally directed to the Laodiceans (see Col. 4:16), and that subsequently, because of the severe indictment of this church in the Apocalypse (3:14–22), the words "at Laodicea" were omitted as a sort of *damnatio memoriae* and the space left blank in some manuscripts while in others "at Ephesus" was inserted. Another hypothesis is that we have in this Epistle a circular letter which was to be read in various churches and that a space was left blank for the reader to insert the name of the local church.

The doctrine of the Epistle, closely parallel to that of the Epistle to the Colossians but more profound, deals with the Church as the Mystical Body of Christ and with the benefits of Redemption, which are communicated to mankind through the Redeemer's Mystical Body, the Church. St. Paul bases a strong plea on this doctrinal foundation for his readers to lead a holy life, worthy of the sublime vocation and privileges which are theirs as Christians.

The Division of the Epistle to the Ephesians

Introduction, 1:1–14.
Doctrinal part, 1:15 to 3:21.
    The Church is one with Christ, 1:15 to 2:22.
    Paul's task to preach this Mystery, 3:1–13.
    Paul prays for their spiritual growth, 3:14–21.
Moral part, 4:1 to 6:20.
    Counsels for Christians in general, 4:1 to 5:20.
    Christian family life, 5:21 to 6:9.
    Courage and vigilance, 6:10–20.
Conclusion, 6:21–24.

THE EPISTLE OF

ST. PAUL THE APOSTLE

TO THE EPHESIANS

INTRODUCTION

CHAPTER 1

GREETINGS

Paul, by the will of God an apostle of Jesus Christ, to the saints 1
and faithful at Ephesus in Christ Jesus: to you grace and peace 2
from God our Father and the Lord Jesus Christ.

GOD'S ETERNAL DESIGNS

Blessed be the God and Father of our Lord Jesus Christ, who in 3
Christ has blessed us with every manner of spiritual blessing in the
heavenly realm. These blessings correspond to his choice of us in 4
Christ before the foundation of the world, that we should be holy
and without blemish in his sight. Out of love he predestined us for 5
himself to become through Jesus Christ his adopted children, con-
formably to the good pleasure of his will, to the praise of his 6
resplendent grace, with which he has adorned us in his beloved Son.

In him we have our redemption through his blood, the remission 7
of our transgressions, in keeping with the riches of his grace. With 8
this grace he has inundated us, by imparting to us all manner of
wisdom and practical knowledge, making known to us, in keeping 9
with his good pleasure, the mystery of his will. And this good 10
pleasure he decreed to put into effect in Christ when the designated
period of time had elapsed, namely to gather all creation both in
heaven and on earth under one head, Christ.

1:1. *at Ephesus:* some important witnesses omit these words.
1:5. *Out of love:* joined with the preceding words by most translators.

11   In him we have also been joined to the Chosen People, since, in keeping with the decree of him who carries out everything accord-
12   ing to the designs of his will, we have been predestined to be devoted to the praise of his glory — we who before Christ's coming
13   had hoped in him. You, too, were joined to the Chosen People, after you had heard the message of truth, the Good News proclaiming your salvation, and had believed in it, and had been sealed with
14   the promised Holy Spirit, who is the first installment of our inheritance. The final purpose of thus being sealed is that we may be his possession by right of purchase to the praise of his glory.

The Church Is One With Christ

CHRIST IS HEAD OF THE CHURCH

15   For these reasons I for my part, since I have heard of the faith in the Lord Jesus which prevails among you, and of the love you
16   have for all the saints, never cease, while giving thanks to God, to
17   remember you in my prayers, that the God of our Lord Jesus Christ, the author of glory, may grant you spiritual wisdom and revelation.
18   May he give to your hearts, eyes that have been enlightened with a deep knowledge of him, that you may understand of what nature is the hope to which he calls you, what is the wealth of the splendor
19   of his inheritance among the saints, and what is the surpassing great-
20   ness of his power toward us believers. The exercise of the might of this power was shown when he raised Christ from the dead and
21   seated him at his right hand in heaven, high above every Principality and Power and Virtue and Domination, yes, high above every being, no matter by what title it may be called, no matter whether
22   it is in this world or in the world to come. He has subjected every single thing to his authority and has appointed him as universal
23   head of the Church, which is truly his body, the complement of him who fills all the members with all graces.

1:11. *joined to the Chosen People*: literally, "became the inheritance of." But Israel is God's inheritance as his Chosen People. Christians constitute the new Israel. So St. John Chrysostom.

1:14. *first installment*: or "the pledge" — the first part, the beginning, and the pledge of the consummate happiness of heaven. So Voste following SS. Jerome and Thomas.

1:23. *the complement*: that which completes. Just as the head is completed

Chapter 2

WE LIVE WITH THE LIFE OF CHRIST

Once, you were dead by reason of your transgressions and sins, 1
in which you lived in keeping with the ways of this world, in obedi- 2
ence to the prince who exercises his power in the air, the spirit
which is now active in the rebels. In fact we too, all of us, were 3
in the company of such people, when we led lives enslaved to fleshy
cravings, yielding to the desires of our flesh and its aims, and were
by nature objects of wrath, just like the rest. But God, who is rich 4
in mercy, was moved by the intense love with which he loved us,
and when we were dead by reason of our transgressions, he made 5
us live with the life of Christ. By grace you have been saved. ⌣
Together with Christ Jesus and in him, he raised us up and en- 6
throned us in the heavenly realm, that in Christ Jesus he might 7
show throughout the ages to come the overflowing riches of his
grace springing from his goodness to us. Yes, it is by grace that 8
you have been saved through faith; it is the gift of God; it is not 9
the result of anything you did, so that no one has any grounds for
boasting. We are his handiwork, created in Christ Jesus in view of 10
good deeds which God prepared beforehand for us to practice.

CHRIST MADE GENTILE AND JEW ONE

Therefore, bear in mind, that once Gentiles by birth, you were 11
called uncircumcised by those who called themselves circumcised —
a rite administered by human hands. Bear in mind that at that 12
time you were apart from Christ, deprived of the right of citizenship in Israel, and strangers to the covenant which contained the
promise, having no hope and without God in this world. But now 13
in Christ Jesus, you, who were once far off, have been brought near

by the rest of the body, so Christ is completed in his mission as Savior by the
Church which continues and prolongs his work through time and space. He,
in turn, supplies the members with all needed graces. So Voste. Others translate: "the complement of him, who in all things is made complete by means
of us all."

2:3. *by nature*: by the tendency of human nature to evil. This tendency is an
evil inheritance from our first parents.

2:9. *of anything you did*: the gift of grace in the first instance is absolutely
unmerited.

2:10. *prepared*: decreed that we do good voluntarily.

14 through the blood of Christ. For he himself is our peace; he it is who has made both Jews and Gentile one, and has broken down the
15 partition wall of hostility which separated them. The Law with its commandments and decrees he abolished through his human nature, that of the two races he might create in himself one new being, so
16 making peace and reconciling both in one body to God by the cross,
17 since he had killed that hostility. He came and announced the Good News of peace to you who were afar off, and of peace to those who
18 were near, because by one and the same Spirit through him both of
19 us have found entrance to the Father. It follows that you are no longer foreigners and guests; no, you are fellow citizens with the
20 saints, and members of God's household. You are an edifice built on the foundation of the apostles and prophets with Christ Jesus
21 himself as the chief cornerstone. In him the whole structure is being closely fitted together by the Spirit to become God's temple
22 consecrated in the Lord. In him you, too, are being fitted by the Spirit into the edifice to become God's dwelling place.

PAUL'S TASK TO PREACH THIS MYSTERY

CHAPTER 3

THE MYSTERY REVEALED TO PAUL

1   For this reason I, Paul, in prison for the cause of Christ Jesus
2   on behalf of you Gentiles, bow in worship. I take it for granted that you have heard of my office, conferred on me by God's grace,
3   in your regard: how by revelation was made known to me the
4   mystery, as I have just briefly stated. If you read this statement you can perceive how well versed I am in this mystery relative to Christ,
5   which in former ages was not made known to mankind, as it has now been revealed by the Spirit to his holy apostles and spokesmen.
6   The mystery is this, that the Gentiles are joint heirs and fellow members of the same body, and joint partakers in Christ Jesus of the promise by means of the preaching of the Good News.

APPOINTED TO PREACH TO THE GENTILES

7   Of that message I was made a minister by the gift of God's grace,
8   which was granted to me in virtue of the exercise of his power. Yes,

to me, the very least of all the saints, this grace was given to
announce among the Gentiles the Good News of the unfathomable
riches of Christ, and to enlighten all men as to what is the wonder- 9
ful plan, that mystery which has been hidden from eternity in God,
who created all things. The purpose of this plan was that now the 10
manifold wisdom of God, in keeping with his eternally established 11
decree at present realized in Christ Jesus our Lord, may be made
known by the Church to the Principalities and the Powers in heaven.
In Christ we have assurance and, through faith in him, confident 12
entrance to God's presence. Therefore I beseech you not to be dis- 13
couraged by the tribulations I suffer for you, since they are your glory.

PAUL PRAYS FOR THEIR SPIRITUAL GROWTH

For this reason on bended knees, I beseech the Father from 14, 15
whom every family in heaven and on earth derives its origin, that 16
he may grant you, in keeping with his glorious riches, to be
strengthened with power through the Spirit for the development of
your inner selves, and to have Christ dwelling through faith in your 17
hearts, and to be rooted and grounded in love. Thus will you have 18
the power to grasp fully, together with all the saints, what is the
breadth and length and height and depth of this mystery, and to 19
know Christ's love which surpasses knowing, in order that you
may be perfected and bring to realization God's complement.

Now to him who is able beyond all limits to accomplish im- 20
measurably more than we ask or conceive, in keeping with the power
that is at work in us — to him be glory in the Church and in Christ 21
Jesus down through all generations for ever and ever. Amen.

COUNSELS FOR CHRISTIANS IN GENERAL

CHAPTER 4

PRESERVE THE UNITY IN THE MYSTICAL BODY

I, therefore, the prisoner in the Lord, exhort you to conduct 1
yourselves in a manner worthy of the calling to which you have
been called, with all humility and meekness. Have patience and 2

3:19. *which surpasses knowing:* which can never be fully known. *complement:*
the Church. So St. John Damascene.

3 bear lovingly with one another. Strive anxiously to preserve harmony
4 of mind by means of the bond which effects peace. There is one
body and one Spirit, even as you, from the moment you were called,
5 had the one hope your calling imparted. There is one Lord, one
6 faith, one Baptism, one God and Father of all, who rules all things
and pervades all things and sustains all things.

DIVERSITY OF GRACES FOR THE WHOLE BODY

7 But to each one of us grace has been given to the extent to
8 which Christ imparts it. Thus the Scripture says,
"Ascending on high, he led away captives;
he gave gifts to men."
9 Now what does this expression "he ascended" mean, but that he
10 had first descended into the lower parts of the earth? He who
descended is the same one who also ascended above all the heavens,
11 that he might fully impart all graces. He established some men as
apostles, and some as inspired spokesmen, others again as evangelists,
12 and others as pastors and teachers, thus organizing the saints for the
work of the ministry, which consists in building up the body of
13 Christ, until we all attain to unity in faith and deep knowledge of
the Son of God. Thus we attain to perfect manhood, to the mature
14 proportions that befit Christ's complement. Thus we shall no longer
be children tossed to and fro and carried about by every wind of
doctrine, which wicked men devise with the ingenuity and clever-
15 ness that error suggests. Rather by professing the truth, let us grow
up in every respect in love and bring about union with Christ who
16 is the head. The whole body is dependent on him. Harmoniously
joined and knit together, it derives its energy in the measure each
part needs only through contact with the source of supply. In this
way the body grows and builds itself up through love.

RENEW YOURSELVES CONSTANTLY

17 This, therefore, I say and assert in the Lord, that from now on
you are not to conduct yourselves as the Gentiles do, in the empti-

4:8. Ps. 68:19.
4:9. *lower parts of the earth:* either Christ's coming to earth in his Incarnation, or more probably with SS. Jerome and Chrysostom his descent to Limbo.
4:13. *complement:* the Church.
4:16. *source of supply:* Christ.

ness of their minds, with their understanding plunged in darkness, 18
estranged, because of the ignorance that exists among them and the
obstinacy of their hearts, from the life that God imparts. Without 19
remorse they have abandoned themselves to shameful lusts, insati-
able in their indulgence of every kind of impurity. It is not such 20
lessons you have learned from Christ. I take it for granted that you 21
have hearkened to him and have been taught in him, since truth is in   ·
Jesus. You are to put off your old self, with its former habits, which 22
is on the road to ruin as its deceptive lusts deserve. Renew your- 23
selves constantly by spiritual considerations, and put on the new self, 24
created after the image of God in the justice and holiness that come
from truth.

ACT AS MEMBERS OF ONE ANOTHER

Thus, let everyone of you lay aside falsehood and speak the 25
truth to the neighbor, because we are members of one another.
If you become angry, do so without sinning. Do not let the sun 26
go down on your resentment. Do not give the devil a chance. 27
He who is in the habit of stealing, let him steal no longer; rather 28
let him labor with his hands in honest toil, so as to share with those
in need. Let no foul word come from your lips, but rather what- 29
ever is good, as the occasion requires, that your speech may be a
source of grace to those that are listening. And do not grieve the 30
Holy Spirit of God, by whom you have been sealed in preparation
for the day of redemption. Let all bitter resentment, and passion, 31
and anger, and loud abusive speech, in a word every kind of malice,
be banished from your midst. On the contrary be kind to one 32
another, and merciful, generously forgiving one another, as also
God in Christ has generously forgiven you.

CHAPTER 5

Therefore, follow God's example, as his very dear children, 1
and let your conduct be guided by love, as Christ also loved us 2
and delivered himself for us as an offering to God, a sacrifice that
has an agreeable fragrance.

4:30. *day of redemption:* full and complete redemption to be realized at
the end of time with the resurrection of the body.

3   As is quite proper among the saints, let there not so much as
be mention among you of fornication or any kind of impurity
4 or lustful desires. Let there be no shameful conduct, or senseless
talk or suggestive jesting. These are all unbecoming. Rather give
5 thanks. You ought to know well that no fornicator, no impure or
lustful person — these vices are idolatry — has any inheritance in
6 the kingdom of Christ and of God. Let no one lead you astray with
empty arguments, since on account of these sins the wrath of
7 God comes upon the unbelievers. Do not then associate with such
8 people, because, while formerly you were darkness, now in the Lord
9 you are light. Conduct yourselves as children of light. The effects of
10 the light are every kind of goodness and justice and truth. Make
11 sure of what is well pleasing to the Lord. Have no part in deeds
that seek the darkness. They are barren of fruit. Rather expose
12 them by your conduct for it is shameful to speak of what such
13 people are doing in the dark. None but the evil that is openly condemned appears in full light, and whatever so appears becomes light.
14 Thus it is said,

> "Awake, sleeper,
> And arise from the dead,
> And Christ will give you light."

15 So watch your conduct carefully. Do not act as fools, but as
16 sensible men, putting every opportunity to good use in evil times
17 like these. This is why you should not be thoughtless, but con-
18 sider what is the will of the Lord. Do not get drunk on wine, which
19 is a cause of debauchery, but fill yourselves with the Spirit. Recite
among yourselves psalms and hymns and inspired canticles, singing
20 and giving praise to the Lord with all your heart. Give thanks to
God the Father everywhere and for every gift in the name of our
Lord Jesus Christ.

5:3. *lustful desires:* literally, "covetousness." St. Jerome favors the former
sense.
5:5. *lustful person:* literally, "covetous person." St. Jerome favors the former
sense.
5:14. This quotation is found nowhere in these words in any book of Scripture. It may be from an early Christian hymn.

CHRISTIAN FAMILY LIFE

CHRISTIAN WIFE AND HUSBAND

Be subject to one another out of reverence for Christ. Let wives 21, 22
be subject to their husbands who are representatives of the Lord,
because the husband is head of the wife just as Christ is the head 23
of the Church and also the savior of that body. Thus, just as the 24
Church is subject to Christ, so also let wives be subject to their
husbands in all things.

Husbands, love your wives, just as Christ loved the Church, and 25
delivered himself for her, that he might sanctify her by cleansing 26
her in the bath of water with the accompanying word, in order to 27
present to himself the Church in all her glory, devoid of blemish
or wrinkle or anything of the kind, but that she may be holy and
flawless. Even so ought husbands to love their wives as their own 28
bodies. He who loves his wife, loves himself. Now no one ever hates 29
his own flesh; on the contrary, he nourishes and cherishes it, as
Christ does the Church, because we are members of his Body. 30
"For this cause a man shall leave his father and mother, 31
    and cling to his wife;
    and the two shall become one flesh."
This is a great mystery — I mean in regard to Christ and the 32
Church. Meanwhile, let each of you love his wife just as he loves 33
himself, and let the wife reverence her husband.

CHAPTER 6

CHRISTIAN CHILDREN AND PARENTS

Children, yield obedience in the Lord to your parents, for that 1
is right. "Honor your father and your mother." So reads the first 2
commandment with a promise, "that it may be well with you and 3
that you may be long-lived on the earth."

5:24. *in all things:* i.e., that pertain to the right relationship of husband
and wife. If the husband follows the Apostle's ideal and has a profound love
for his wife, this subjection can never become slavish submission to a tyrant.
5:26. *the bath of water:* Baptism.
5:31. Gen. 2:24.
6:2. Exod. 20:12.

4   You who are fathers, do not provoke your children to anger, but rear them by training them and instructing them in the Lord.

CHRISTIAN SLAVES AND MASTERS

5   You who are slaves, obey your human masters with reverence
6 and respect and heartfelt sincerity as you would Christ. Serve not
in the hope of being seen, to win human approval, but as Christ's
7 slaves who with all their heart do the will of God. Render your service heartily and willingly in view of the fact that you are serving
8 the Lord and not men, in the conviction that, whether a man is free or slave, he will be repaid by the Lord for whatever good he does.
9   You who are masters, act in the same spirit toward them. Give up threatening. You know well that your Lord and theirs is in heaven, and that he knows no partiality.

COURAGE AND VIGILANCE

THE ARMOR OF GOD

10   In conclusion, brothers, find strength in the Lord and in his
11 almighty power. Put on all the armor that God has forged, that you may be able to make a stand against the devil's cunning tricks.
12 Our wrestling is not against weak human nature, but against the Principalities and the Powers, against those that rule the world of darkness, the wicked spirits that belong to an order higher than
13 ours. For this reason take up all the armor that God has forged, that you may be able to resist in the evil day, and, when it is all
14 finished, still be on your feet. Stand, then, ready for battle, with the belt of truth about your waist, wearing the breastplate of
15 holiness, and the shoes of preparedness furnished by the gospel of
16 peace. With all this take up the shield of faith, with which you will be enabled to put out all the flaming arrows of the wicked

6:5. St. Paul by this advice does not intend to approve of slavery. Christian teaching promulgated the principles whose application would lead to the disappearance of slavery. But its abolition must be gradual, else there would have been a terrific upheaval of society which would have greatly prejudiced the cause of Christianity.

6:15. *shoes of preparedness*: readiness to engage in the struggle. Both the motives and means for undertaking this struggle are supplied by the Gospel, which holds out the promise and the means of peace between man and man and between man and God. Others interpret: "readiness to preach the gospel."

enemy. Finally take the helmet of salvation and the sword supplied   17
by the Spirit, that is, the word of God.

PERSEVERE IN PRAYER

Pray always with the mind, using every kind of entreaty and   18
petition. Be on the alert in this matter and persevere. Pray for
all the saints, and particularly for me that I may be given words to   19
speak with bold confidence and to make known the mystery of the
gospel. To proclaim that mystery I am an ambassador in spite of my   20
chains. Pray that for its sake I may have the courage to speak as
I ought.

Conclusion

That you may know my circumstances and what I am doing,   21
Tychicus, our dear brother and faithful minister in the Lord, will
tell you everything. I have sent him to you for this very purpose   22
that you may learn our circumstances, and that he may comfort
your hearts.

Peace be to the brothers and love with faith from God the   23
Father and the Lord Jesus Christ. Grace be with all those who have   24
a love undying for our Lord Jesus Christ. Amen.

6:18. *with the mind*: or "in the Holy Spirit."

The Diocese of the Epistle to the Philippians

THE EPISTLE TO THE PHILIPPIANS

Philippi in Macedonia was the first city in Europe to be evan-
gelized by St. Paul. The converts were very fervent and very
devoted to St. Paul. They came to his assistance by financial support more than once, and when he was in prison at Rome or possibly
at Ephesus, they sent Epaphroditus with gifts of money and instructions to stay and assist the Apostle during his imprisonment. It is
evident from this Epistle that St. Paul returned their devotion;
the Epistle itself contains several expressions of the Apostle's deep
and tender love for the Philippians.

The account of St. Paul's first visit there and of the establishment
of his first local church or congregation on European soil is sum-
marily recorded in Acts 16:6-40. We are told that a Macedonian
appeared in a vision to St. Paul, and pleaded with him to come and
help his compatriots. The vision spurred St. Paul to go as quickly
as possible to Macedonia. He chose Philippi as the first field of
his evangelical labors, and made numerous converts. He freed a girl
from diabolic possession. This infuriated her masters who had made
no small profit from her fortunetelling. They contrived to have St.
Paul and Silas arrested, scourged, and thrown into prison. A midnight earthquake so terrified the jailer that he asked for instruction
in the faith and was baptized with his family. Subsequently the
magistrates of the city wished to send St. Paul away secretly, but
he objected, pleading that his rights as a Roman citizen had been
flagrantly violated. The magistrates then made amends to St. Paul
and he departed from the city.

Twice subsequently he visited the Christians at Philippi and
finally when he was a prisoner at Rome or Ephesus, he addressed
this letter to them. St. Paul expresses his gratitude in the Epistle
and takes occasion to exhort them to the practice of various Chris-

tian virtues. He also warns them against that element who pretended that the observance of the Mosaic Law, particularly of circumcision, was necessary for salvation.

There is no doubt that the Epistle is genuinely Pauline. It was probably written from Rome in A.D. 62 or 63 or possibly from Ephesus in 56 or 57.

THE DIVISION OF THE EPISTLE TO THE PHILIPPIANS

Introduction, 1:1–11.
Personal news, 1:12–26.
Exhortation to perfection, 1:27 to 2:18.
News about Timothy and Epaphroditus, 2:19–30.
Do not follow false teachers, 3:1 to 4:1.
Conclusion, 4:2–23.

THE EPISTLE OF

ST. PAUL THE APOSTLE

TO THE PHILIPPIANS

INTRODUCTION

CHAPTER 1

GREETINGS

Paul and Timothy, servants of Christ Jesus, to all the saints in *1*
Christ Jesus that are at Philippi, with their bishops and deacons:
to you grace and peace from God our Father and from the Lord *2*
Jesus Christ.

A THANKFUL PRAYER

I give thanks to my God for your participation in the spreading *3, 5*
of the gospel from the first day it reached you until now. This I do *4*
in my every remembrance of you, always in all my prayers praying
joyfully for all of you. I am convinced of this, that he who has *6*
begun this good work in you, will continue to perfect it until the
day of Christ Jesus. I have a right to feel so about all of you, *7*
because I have you in my heart, all of you who during my imprisonment are partakers with me in my apostolic office, and in the defense
and confirmation of the gospel. God is my witness how I long for *8*
all of you with the tender affection of Christ Jesus. The object of *9*
my prayer is that your love may become richer and richer and be
accompanied with a full knowledge and a keen practical insight, so *10*
that you may appreciate true values. I pray, too, that you may continue to be upright and blameless until the day of Christ, and be *11*

1:3. The order of words and phrases has been inverted in the translation.
The order of the original is: "I give thanks to my God in every remembrance
of you, always in my every prayer for you, (4) with joy making prayer for
you for your sharing in the gospel from the first day until now."

1:6. day of Christ Jesus: Christ's coming at the end of the world to preside
at the general judgment. So Medebielle.

501

filled with the fruit that springs from holiness through the aid of
Jesus Christ to the glory and praise of God.

Personal News

THE PROGRESS OF THE GOSPEL

12 Now I wish you to know, brothers, that my experiences have
13 turned out rather to the advancement of the gospel, so that it has
become well known throughout the praetorium and everywhere else
14 that I bear my chains for the sake of Christ. And the majority of
the brothers in Christ, who have gained courage from my imprisonment, have shown great boldness in speaking the word of God
15 fearlessly. It is true that some men proclaim Christ from motives
16 of jealousy and rivalry, but others have a good intention. These,
knowing that I am appointed for the defense of the gospel, pro-
17 claim Christ out of love. But the others proclaim Christ out of
rivalry, not disinterestedly, with a view to increase the anguish of
18 my imprisonment. But what of it, provided only that, in every way,
whether insincerely or sincerely, Christ is being proclaimed? Over
19 this I rejoice, yes, and I shall continue to rejoice. For I know that
this shall turn out to my salvation, thanks to your prayers and the
20 assistance afforded me by the Spirit of Jesus Christ. This is in
accord with my eager longing and hope that I shall never be put
to shame, but that always with bold assurance, as before, so now,
Christ will be glorified by this body of mine, whether it lives or dies.

PAUL'S DEVOTEDNESS TO THEM

21 In fact for me to live means Christ and to die means gain.
22 Suppose I continue to live in the flesh? Well, that means for me
23 fruitful labor. And yet I do not know which to choose. In fact I am
hard pressed from both sides, desiring to depart and be with Christ,
24 a lot by far the better, yet to stay on in the flesh is more necessary

---

1:13. *praetorium:* either the imperial palace or the soldiers who guarded St.
Paul.

1:17. *anguish of my imprisonment:* they imagined that their success would
sadden St. Paul, and thus add to his sufferings.

1:21. *to live means Christ:* Paul's life was dedicated entirely to the service
of Christ, yet death would be a gain, since it would unite him more closely
and forever to his beloved Lord. "That is not to be feared which frees us
from all fear" (Tertullian).

for your sake. And with this conviction I know that I shall remain 25
and continue side by side with you for your progress and joy in the
faith. Thus, you will have additional reason in Christ Jesus to be 26
proud of me, when I come again to visit you.

EXHORTATION TO PERFECTION

BE COURAGEOUS

Only let your lives be worthy of the gospel of Christ, so that, 27
whether I come and see you or am absent, I may hear that you stand
with unity of mind and heart, fighting together to maintain the faith
of the gospel. Do not be terrified in any way by your adversaries. 28
Your steadfastness, a gift of God, is a sign to them of their destruction, but to you of your salvation. For you have been given the 29
favor on Christ's behalf, not only of having faith in him but also
of suffering for him. Your struggle is the same as mine. You 30
formerly saw me engaged in it, and now hear how I continue that
struggle.

CHAPTER 2

BE OF THE SAME MIND AS CHRIST

If, therefore, you would give me any comfort in Christ, and any 1
encouragement such as love imparts, if you have any spiritual communion with me, and if you would show me some affection and
compassion, make my joy complete by unanimity of sentiments 2
and of love springing from one soul and a unity of thought. Never 3
act out of rivalry or vainglory, but in humility deem others as better
than yourselves. Look not to your personal interests, but rather to 4
those of others. Be of the same mind as Christ Jesus, who, though 5, 6
he is by nature God, did not consider his equality with God a
condition to be clung to, but emptied himself by taking the nature 7
of a slave, fashioned as he was to the likeness of men and recognized
by outward appearance as man. He humbled himself and became 8

2:7. *emptied himself:* not by giving up the divine nature — an utter impossi-
bility — but by foregoing the outward glory attaching to it. *fashioned* . . .
outward appearance: Jesus Christ was true man, but he was also God. In outward appearance he was man and nothing more. His divine nature lay concealed. So St. John Chrysostom.

9 obedient to death; yes, to death on a cross. This is why God has
10 exalted him and given him the name above all names, so that at
   the name Jesus everyone in heaven, on earth, and beneath the
11 earth should bend the knee and should publicly acknowledge to
   the glory of God the Father that Jesus Christ is Lord.

BE CHILDREN OF GOD

12 So then, my beloved, obedient as you have always been, work
    out your salvation with fear and trembling, not only as you did
13 when I was present, but still more now that I am absent. Really it
 ⌄ is God who of his good pleasure accomplishes in you both the will
14 and the attainment. Do all things without murmuring and without
15 questioning, so as to be blameless and guileless, children of God
    without blemish in the midst of a depraved and perverse generation.
    Among these you shine like heavenly luminaries in the world.
16 Cling to the life-giving doctrine; it will be to my credit on the day
    of Christ that I did not enter the lists and weary myself in toilsome
17 labor for nothing. But even if I am made a libation upon the
    sacrificial offering which is your faith, I am glad and rejoice with
18 you. And in the same way do you also be glad and rejoice with me.

News About Timothy and Epaphroditus

19 Now I hope in the Lord Jesus soon to send Timothy to you,
20 that I may be encouraged when I learn the news about you. I really
    have no one so like-minded, none so genuinely solicitous for your
21 interests. They all seek their own interests, not those of Jesus Christ.
22 Recognize his worth; as a child serves father, so he has served me in
23 spreading the gospel. He then is the one I hope to send to you as
24 soon as I see how things stand with me. But I also trust in the Lord
    that I myself shall very soon come to you.
25 I think it necessary to send to you Epaphroditus, my brother and
    companion in labor and in combat, whom you have sent officially

---

2:16. *lists:* the arena of the world where St. Paul strove so valiantly against
terrific odds to bring the Gospel to the Gentiles.
    2:17. St. Paul thinks of the Philippians' faith as a sacrifice. Their faith
makes their lives a worship that is acceptable to God, a continued act of
adoration. Foreseeing the possibility of his martyrdom, St. Paul thinks of his
blood as the wine of libation which was a part of ancient pagan sacrifices.
So St. John Chrysostom.

to me to minister to my needs. I send him because he is yearning 26
for all of you, and is distressed that you have learned of his illness.
Yes, he was so sick that he almost died. God, however, had mercy 27
on him, and not only on him but on me also, that I might be spared
sorrow upon sorrow. For this reason I send him the more eagerly, 28
that seeing him again you may rejoice and that my own anxiety
might be lessened. Welcome him, then, in the Lord, with complete 29
joy. Hold men of such worth in honor, because it was for the sake 30
of Christ's work that he was so near death, risking his life to make
up for the services which you were not here to render to me.

Do Not Follow False Teachers

Chapter 3

PAUL RENOUNCED HIS JEWISH PRESTIGE

Now, then, my brothers, rejoice in the Lord. To be constantly 1
writing the same things to you is certainly not irksome to me; it
is necessary for your safety. Beware of the dogs; beware of the evil- 2
doers, beware of their mutilation. Really we are the genuinely cir- 3
cumcised, we who render worship with the aid of God's Spirit, we
who glory in Christ Jesus and have no confidence in fleshy observances, though I should have every right to rely on them. If anyone 4
else thinks he has a right to confidence in fleshy observances, still
more have I. I was circumcised the eighth day; I am sprung from 5
Israel, from the tribe of Benjamin. I am a Hebrew born of Hebrew
parents. As to the Law, I was a Pharisee; as to my zeal for it, I 6
carried it to the point of persecuting the Church. As to conformity
to the Law's requirements, I was blameless.

RENUNCIATION FOR LOVE OF CHRIST

But the things that were an advantage to me, these for the sake 7
of Christ I have counted loss. More than that, I count everything 8
loss in comparison with the supreme advantage of knowing Christ

---

3:2. dogs: those who advocated the observance of the Mosaic enactments as
necessary for salvation. Their rite of circumcision with the advent of Christianity
became a meaningless observance, nothing more than a mutilation.

Jesus, my Lord. For his sake I have suffered the loss of all things,
9 and I count them as rubbish that I may gain Christ, and be found
united to him, not with a holiness of my own derived from the
Law, but with that which is obtained by faith in Christ, the holiness
10 which God imparts on condition of faith. I would know Christ
and what his resurrection can do. I would also share in his sufferings,
11 in the hope that, if I resemble him in death, I may somehow attain
12 to the resurrection from the dead. Not that I have already attained
this ideal, or have already been made perfect but I press on, hoping
13 that I may lay hold of it, since Christ has laid hold of me. Brothers
I do not consider that I have reached it. But one thing I do: for-
14 getting what is past, I strain toward what is ahead. With my eyes
fixed on the goal, I press on to the prize in store for those who have
received from above God's call in Jesus Christ.
15   All of us, then, who have reached maturity must agree, and if
16 in any point you disagree, in this God will enlighten you. Meanwhile,
whatever the point we have reached, let us continue to advance in
orderly fashion.

FOLLOW HIS EXAMPLE

17   Brothers, vie with one another in following my example, and
18 mark those who live after the pattern you have in us. As I have
often said to you, and now repeat with tears, there are many who
19 conduct themselves as enemies of the cross of Christ. Their end
is ruin, their god is their belly, their glory is in their shame, they
20 are earthly minded. As for us, our commonwealth is in heaven, and
it is from there that we eagerly await our Savior, the Lord Jesus
21 Christ. It is he who by an exercise of the power which enables him
even to subject the universe to himself will refashion our lowly
bodies, conforming them to his glorious body.

CHAPTER 4

1   So then, my brothers, beloved and longed for, my joy and my
crown, stand firm in the Lord, beloved.

3:10. *resurrection can do*: it proves Christ's divinity, elevates him to the
glory of the Father, and is the exemplary cause and pledge of the resurrection
of our bodies.

CONCLUSION

CONCORD

I beg Evodia and I beg Syntyche to come to a mutual under- 2
standing in the Lord. And I ask you, also, my loyal comrade, help 3
them, for they have toiled with me in spreading the gospel, as have
Clement and the rest of my fellow workers. Their names are in the
book of life.

PEACE AND JOY

Rejoice in the Lord always; I repeat, rejoice. Let your forbearance 4, 5
be known to all men. The Lord is near. Have no anxiety, but in 6
every concern by prayer and supplication with thanksgiving let your
petitions be made known in your communing with God. Then the 7
peace of God which surpasses all understanding will guard your
hearts and your thoughts in Christ Jesus.

In conclusion, brothers, whatever is true, whatever is honorable, 8
whatever just, whatever pure, whatever lovable, whatever merits
praise — if there be any virtue, if anything worthy of praise — such
are the things you should keep in mind. And whatever you have 9
learned and received and heard and seen in me, let such things shape
your conduct. And the God who imparts peace will be with you.

PHILIPPIANS' GENEROSITY

I rejoice greatly in the Lord that now at last your concern for 10
me has blossomed out again. In fact you have always had concern
for me, but lacked the opportunity to show it. Not that I say this 11
because I am in want, for in whatever circumstances I am, I have
learned to be content. I know how to live in privation, and I know 12
how to live in abundance. I have been initiated into each and every
condition: of satiety and of hunger, of abundance and of want. I 13
can do all things in him who strengthens me. Still you have done 14
well by sharing in my affliction. But, Philippians, you yourselves 15
know that after I had in the early days preached the gospel to you
and had left Macedonia, no congregation, excepting you, went into

4:3. *loyal comrade:* possibly a proper name, "loyal Syzyge." *book of life:*
a figure expressive of God's knowledge of his faithful servants, whom he will
welcome to his heavenly kingdom of eternal life when they pass to eternity.

16 partnership with me in the matter of giving and receiving, since
even when I was in Thessalonica, not merely once but twice you
17 sent something for my need. Not that I am eager for the gift, but
18 I am eager for the profit accumulating to your account. I have all
and more than enough. I am fully supplied now that I have received
from Epaphroditus what you sent. It was a sweet aroma, a sacrifice
19 acceptable and well pleasing to God. My God will, in Christ Jesus,
20 gloriously supply your needs in keeping with his riches. To our God
and Father be glory for endless ages. Amen.

FAREWELL

21, 22   Greet every saint in Christ Jesus. The brothers here with me
greet you. All the saints greet you, especially those of Caesar's house-
23 hold. The grace of our Lord Jesus Christ be with your spirit. Amen.

4:22. *Caesar's household:* i.e., government employees, whether slaves or
freedmen.

THE EPISTLE TO THE COLOSSIANS

Colossae was a city of Phrygia, about one hundred miles east of Ephesus in the Lycus valley. St. Paul never visited this city in person. It is very probable that during the Apostle's stay at Ephesus from about A.D. 53 to 56, one of Paul's converts, Epaphras, carried the Christian faith to Colossae and established a congregation there (Col. 1:7). The converts there were fervent and strong in the faith.

During St. Paul's imprisonment at Rome, or possibly at Ephesus, Epaphras visited him and gave a very favorable report on the condition of the Church at Colossae. There were, however, certain dangers: false teachers had made their appearance and threatened to corrupt the purity of the faith. They assigned an exaggerated dignity to angels, and thus obscured or denied the supreme dignity of Christ over all creatures, human and angelic. They claimed to have a deeper knowledge of the faith and insisted on Mosaic observances and certain practices of false asceticism. It would seem that Epaphras requested St. Paul to write to the Colossians and combat the errors taught by these false teachers. This letter is an answer to that request.

St. Paul emphatically states, in passages of great dogmatic importance, the pre-eminence of Christ to all creatures because he is himself the divine Creator of all creatures. The Apostle vigorously warns against false teachers and the doctrines and practices they advocated and sets forth rules for the ideal Christian life.

There is a striking similarity in content and phraseology between this Epistle and that to the Ephesians. They were both written at the same time to congregations made up of the same type of converts and faced with the same dangers. The two Epistles should be studied together.

THE EPISTLE OF

ST. PAUL THE APOSTLE

TO THE COLOSSIANS

Introduction

Chapter 1

GREETINGS

Paul, by the will of God an apostle of Christ Jesus, and our 1
brother Timothy to the saints and faithful at Colossae, our brothers 2
in Christ: to you grace and peace from God our Father.

THANKSGIVING

We always give thanks to the God and Father of our Lord Jesus 3
Christ for you in our prayers, ever since we heard of your faith in 4
Christ Jesus and of the love you have for all the saints, in view of the 5
hoped for blessings reserved for you in heaven. Of these blessings
you heard long ago when the true message of the gospel came to 6
you. This gospel continues to bear fruit and gain ground among
you, as it does throughout the world. It has done so among you from
the moment you heard it and came truly to appreciate the grace
of God, in the way you have learned from Epaphras, our beloved 7
fellow servant. He it is, a faithful minister of Christ in your behalf,
who brought us word of your spiritual love. 8

PRAYER FOR THEIR SPIRITUAL PROGRESS

This is why we too have been praying for you unceasingly, since 9
the day we heard this. We ask that you may be filled with a deep
knowledge of God's will through perfect spiritual wisdom and
insight. Thus your life will be a credit to the Lord and will please 10
him in every respect; you will be fruitful in every kind of good deed
and grow in deep knowledge of God; you will in every way be 11
strengthened through his glorious power, and brought to perfect

12 patience and long-suffering; you will give thanks joyfully to the
Father. He it is who has qualified you for a share in the lot of the
13 saints in the light, and who has rescued us from the power of
darkness and transferred us into the kingdom of his beloved Son,
14 in whom we have our redemption, the remission of our sins.

THE PRE-EMINENT DIGNITY OF CHRIST

CHRIST AND HIS FATHER, THE WORLD, THE CHURCH

15   He is the image of the invisible God, begotten before every
16 creature, because in him were created all creatures in the heavens and
on the earth, both visible and invisible, whether Thrones, or Domina-
tions, or Principalities, or Powers. All have been created through him
17 and for him. He exists prior to all creatures, and in him they are all
18 preserved in being. Further, he is the head of his body, the Church,
in that he is the beginning, the first to rise from the dead, so that
19 he may have pre-eminence over every creature. For it pleased God
20 the Father that in him all fullness should dwell, and that through
him God should reconcile to himself every being, and make peace
both on earth and in heaven through the blood shed on the cross.

CHRIST THE CONCILIATOR

21   You yourselves were at one time estranged and in your evil deeds
22 you were of hostile mind. But now he has reconciled you by his
death in his human body, to present you holy and without blemish
23 or blame in God's presence. Only you must remain firmly founded
and steadfast in the faith, and not be easily moved from the hope
that comes from the gospel you have heard — that gospel which
has been preached to every creature under heaven, and of which I,
Paul, have become a minister.

WORK OF CHRIST CONTINUED IN PAUL

24   I rejoice now in the sufferings I bear for your sake, and what is
lacking to the sufferings of Christ I supply in my flesh for the
25 benefit of his body, which is the Church. Of this Church I have

---

1:15. *image:* "Implies exact likeness" (St. Chrysostom).
1:24. *lacking:* either the sufferings Christ's missionaries must undergo to
bring the fruits of Redemption to mankind, or the sufferings of the members of
Christ's body, the Church, which they must undergo to be like their Head.

been made a minister in virtue of the commission given me by God
for your benefit, to proclaim without stint the word of God, the 26
mystery hidden for ages and generations, but now clearly shown to
his saints. To them God willed to make known how rich in glory 27
is this mystery among the Gentiles — Christ in you, your hope of
glory. Him we preach, admonishing every man and teaching every 28
man in all wisdom, that we may present every man perfect in Christ
Jesus. For this I also labor strenuously, according to the power 29
which he mightily exerts in me.

CHAPTER 2

I wish you to know what a great struggle I carry on for you and 1
the Laodiceans, and for so many who do not know me personally.
I strive to bring consolation to their hearts, and by strengthening 2
their love, to enrich them with the fullness of understanding, and
to bring them to the deep knowledge of the divine mystery, Christ.
In him are to be found hidden all the treasures of wisdom and 3
knowledge.

BEWARE OF FALSE TEACHERS

A GENERAL ADMONITION TO THEM

Now I say this that no one may deceive you with specious argu- 4
ments. For though I am absent in body, yet in spirit, I am with 5
you, and rejoice at seeing your orderly array and the steadfastness
of your faith in Christ. Therefore, lead your life in union with the 6
Christ who is Jesus, the Lord, in the way you have received him.
Be rooted in him and built up on him, and strengthened in the 7
faith precisely as you have learned it, and make progress in it with
thanksgiving.

SPECULATIVE ERRORS TO BE REJECTED

See to it that no one makes you a victim of "philosophy" which 8
is but an empty conceit resting on human tradition, on the rudimentary notions which the world has to offer, and not on Christ.

2:8. *rudimentary notions:* the very imperfect and sometimes false ideas which
were known to both Jewish and Gentile peoples, very **rudimentary** in comparison
to the Christian revelation. So St. Jerome.

9. For in him is embodied and dwells the fullness of the Godhead.
10 In union with him who is the head of every Principality and Power
11 you have been made complete. In union with him you have received
the circumcision of Christ, not a circumcision administered by hand,
12 but that which consists in cutting away our sinful nature. Buried
with him by Baptism, you also rose with him by your faith in the
13 power of God who raised him from the dead. At that time when
death had come to you from your sins and your lack of physical
circumcision, God brought you to life with Jesus, when he forgave
14 you all your sins, and canceled the bond with its decrees that was
15 against us. He did away with it when he nailed it to the cross. God
disarmed the Principalities and Powers; he exposed them publicly
to derision and displayed them in Christ's triumphant cortege.

AVOID ERRONEOUS PRACTICES

16   Let no one, then, call you to account for what you eat or drink
or for the observance of a festival or a new moon or a Sabbath.
17 These are but shadows of the realities which were to come, but
18 the reality is Christ. Let no one cheat you of the prize by affecting
humiliation and the worship of angels. Such are the ideas of vision-
aries who have crossed forbidden thresholds and are vainly conceited
19 with their merely human thoughts. Such men fail to hold fast
to the head from whom the whole body is supplied with nourishment and strength by the joints and ligaments, thus growing with a
growth that is divine.

20   If you have died with Christ to the rudimentary notions which
this world has to offer, why do you act as though you still belonged
21 to the world by submitting to such rules as "Do not touch; do not
22 taste; do not handle!" These are formulated according to merely
human precepts and doctrines about things that must perish in their

---

2:9. *dwells:* not as a statue in a temple but by a personal union of the
human and divine natures.
2:10. *complete:* supplied with all necessary grace.
2:14. *bond:* either the natural law and the debt contracted by mankind
through its violation, or the Mosaic Law.
2:18. *humiliation:* a feeling of the unworthiness necessitating recourse to the
angels as mediators. "Some maintained that we must be brought to God by
angels rather than by Christ. This latter would be too great an honor for us, they
say" (St. Chrysostom). *forbidden thresholds:* attempting to explore mysteries
which were beyond their grasp.

very use. To be sure, these rules have a show of wisdom with their 23
self-imposed worship, their practices of humiliation and unsparing
treatment of the body, but they are not to be held in esteem since
they lead to the mere gratification of our lower nature.

CHAPTER 3

LIFE IS HIDDEN WITH CHRIST

If, then, you have risen with Christ, seek the things that are   1
above, where Christ is seated at the right hand of God. Set your   2
mind on the things that are above, not on the things that are on
earth. For you have died and your life is hidden with Christ in God.   3
When Christ, your life, appears, then you shall appear with him   4
in glory.

THE IDEAL CHRISTIAN LIFE

RENOUNCE THESE VICES

Therefore put to death the passions which belong to earth;   5
immorality, uncleanness, lust, evil desires, and avarice, which is a
form of idol-worship. The wrath of God comes upon the unbelievers   6
because of these vices. They were once your norms of conduct when   7
your lives were under their control. But now rid yourselves of all   8
these vices: angry and passionate outbursts, malice, abusive language,
and foul-mouthed utterances. Do not lie to one another. Strip off   9
the old self with its deeds and put on the new, which is being   10
progressively remolded after the image of its Creator and brought
to deep knowledge. Here there is no Gentile, no Jew, no circumcised,   11
no uncircumcised, no barbarian, no Scythian, no slave, no free man,
but Christ is everything in each of us.

2:23. *gratification of our lower nature:* through vain complacency and conceit. Other interpretations of this difficult passage: "since they are worthless for
subduing the insolence of the flesh" (Benoit); "since they refuse to honor
the body by providing for its legitimate needs" (Estius following St. Augustine).
3:11. *Here:* in real Christians as members of the Body of Christ. *everything:*
everything worth while in the Christian comes from the presence of Christ
in him. All other advantages are as nothing when compared to union with
Christ. "Christ will be all things to you, both rank and descent" (St. Chrysostom).

PRACTICE VIRTUE, ESPECIALLY LOVE

12 Therefore, as God's chosen ones, holy and well beloved, clothe yourselves with sentiments of compassion, kindness, humility, meek-
13 ness, long-suffering. Bear with one another and forgive whatever grievances you have against each other. Just as the Lord has forgiven
14 you, so you must forgive. But over all these virtues clothe yourselves with love; it is the bond that perfects and binds them together.
15 Let the ruling principle of your hearts be the peace of Christ, to which you were called as members of one body; and be thankful.
16 Let Christ's message with all its wealth of meaning abide in you; with fullness of wisdom teach and admonish one another, and from the bottom of your hearts gratefully sing psalms, hymns, and spiritual
17 songs to God. Whatever you do or say, let it always be in the name of the Lord Jesus, while you give thanks to God the Father through him.

THE CHRISTIAN HOME

18 Wives, be submissive to your husbands, as is becoming for those
19 who are in the Lord. Husbands, love your wives and do not be bitter
20 toward them. Children, obey your parents in all things, since this
21 is pleasing to the Lord. Fathers, do not provoke your children to anger, lest they become discouraged.

SLAVES AND MASTERS

22 Slaves, obey your human masters in all things, not only when you are under their eyes to win human approval, but with singleness
23 of purpose because you fear the Lord. Whatever you do, work at it
24 heartily, as for the Lord and not for men, in the realization that from the Lord you will receive the inheritance as your reward. Be
25 the slaves of Christ, your Master. For he who does a wrong will receive without partiality the penalty for the wrong he did.

CHAPTER 4

1 Masters, treat your slaves with justice and fairness in the realiza-
2 tion that you too have a Master in heaven. Be assiduous and attentive
3 in prayer with thanksgiving. At the same time pray for us too, that

God may give us an opportunity to preach and announce the mystery
of Christ, for which I am indeed a prisoner. Then I shall make it 4
known as it is my duty to do so. Conduct yourselves wisely as regards 5
outsiders, making the most of the opportunity. Let your speech, 6
while always attractive, be seasoned with salt, that you may know
how to answer everyone.

CONCLUSION

TYCHICUS AND ONESIMUS ARE COMING

Tychicus, our dearest brother and faithful minister and fellow 7
servant in the Lord, will tell you all the news about me. I have 8
sent him to you for this very purpose, that he may make known the
news about us and comfort your hearts. With him is Onesimus, our 9
dear and faithful brother, your countryman. They will tell you all
that is going on here.

GREETINGS FROM PAUL'S CO-WORKERS

Aristarchus, my fellow prisoner, sends you greetings. So does 10
Mark, Barnabas' cousin. Concerning Mark you have received instructions. If he comes to you, welcome him. Jesus, called Justus, sends 11
you greetings. Of the Jewish converts they alone are working with
me for the upbuilding of the kingdom of God. They have become a
comfort to me. Epaphras, your countryman, sends greetings. He is a 12
servant of Jesus Christ and is ever solicitous for you in his prayers,
that you may be steadfast in perfection and in full accord with all
God wills. Yes, I bear him witness that he labors much for you 13
and for those who are at Laodicea and Hierapolis. Luke, our most 14
dear physician, and Demas send you greetings.

A MESSAGE FOR THE LAODICEANS

Greetings to the brothers who are at Laodicea and to Nympha 15

4:5. *making the most of the opportunity*: to impress non-Catholics and thus
dispose them favorably toward the faith.
4:6. *seasoned with salt*: the supernatural wisdom that grace and faith impart.
4:9. *Onesimus*: see the Epistle to Philemon.
4:14. *Luke*: the author of the Third Gospel.

16 and the congregation that meets in her house. And when this letter has been read among you, see that it is read in the congregation at Laodicea also, and that you too read the letter that will come to you 17 from Laodicea. Give this message to Archippus, "Look to the discharge 18 of the ministry which you have received in the Lord." I, Paul, greet you with my own hand. Remember my chains. Grace be with you, Amen.

4:16. *letter . . . from Laodicea*: some think this is the Epistle which is now known as the Epistle to the Ephesians (Voste); others, that it is a circular letter which was passed from one church to another, and now appears in our New Testament as the Epistle to the Ephesians.

THE FIRST EPISTLE TO THE THESSALONIANS

Thessalonica, the present-day Greek city of Saloniki, was, when St. Paul established a Christian community there, a prosperous commercial center, capital of Macedonia, and enjoyed the status of a free city. It was governed by two magistrates whose technical title was politarchs, or city managers. It had a large Jewish colony.

St. Paul first reached Thessalonica about A.D. 51, and remained there for a considerable time. As was his custom, he first preached in the synagogue, and after three successive Sabbaths succeeded in inducing a few Jews to embrace the faith. But the majority of his compatriots, moved by jealousy at the large number of converts St. Paul won from the ranks of the Gentiles, raised a persecution against him, so that he left for Beroea. From there he went on to Athens and Corinth (Acts 17:1–18:1).

At Athens St. Paul was beset with anxiety about his converts at Thessalonica, and sent Timothy to strengthen and comfort them in the persecutions which their faith occasioned (1 Thess. 3:1 ff.). Timothy brought back to St. Paul, who meanwhile had gone to Corinth, glowing reports of the fervor of the Thessalonian Christians. There were, however, certain difficulties. There was some misunderstanding about the glorious return of Jesus. Some thought that those who died before this great event would not share in the Lord's triumph, while others, thinking that it was imminent, gave up working and in idleness were living on the generosity of others.

Timothy's report led to St. Paul's writing the first letter to the Thessalonians. He pays glowing tribute to their goodness, further enlightens them as to the return of the Lord, admonishes the delinquent, and gives general directions as to the proper ordering of their lives in keeping with Christian ideals.

519

THE FIRST EPISTLE TO THE THESSALONIANS

The letter was written about A.D. 52 from Corinth, and with the possible exception of the Epistle to the Galatians, is the earliest extant Epistle of St. Paul.

THE DIVISION OF THE FIRST EPISTLE TO THE THESSALONIANS

Introduction, 1:1–10.
Paul and the Thessalonians, 2:1 to 4:12.
The second coming of Christ, 4:13 to 5:22.
Conclusion, 5:23–28.

THE FIRST EPISTLE OF

ST. PAUL THE APOSTLE

TO THE THESSALONIANS

Introduction

Chapter 1

GREETINGS

Paul, Silvanus, and Timothy to the congregation of the Thes- *1*
salonians assembled in God the Father and in the Lord Jesus Christ:
grace and peace be to you.

THANKSGIVING FOR THEIR FAITH

We give thanks to God always for all of you. We never cease *2*
remembering you in our prayers because we are mindful in the *3*
presence of our God and Father of the deeds in which your faith
finds expression, and of the labors which your love inspires, and of
your enduring hope in our Lord Jesus Christ.

We know, brothers, beloved of God, how you were chosen. *4*
We were not satisfied with preaching the gospel to you in mere *5*
words; it was accompanied also with power, with the blessing of
the Holy Spirit, and with full conviction. You know full well what
kind of men we showed ourselves for your good while we were
with you. You also followed our example and the Lord's, when, *6*
in spite of great affliction, you welcomed the message and experienced
the joy the Holy Spirit imparts. Thus you became a model to all *7*
the believers in Macedonia and Achaia. Yes, the message of the *8*
Lord sounded forth from you not only throughout Macedonia
and Achaia, but everywhere your faith in God has gone forth, so
that I need not say a word about it. They actually report about us *9*
the welcome we got from you, and how you turned to God from
idols to serve the living and true God, and to await his Son from *10*
heaven, whom he raised from the dead, Jesus, our Savior from the
wrath to come.

PAUL AND THE THESSALONIANS

CHAPTER 2

HIS CONDUCT AMONG THEM

1 You yourselves know, brothers, that our coming among you was
2 not in vain. On the contrary, in spite of the sufferings and indignities
we had just experienced at Philippi, as you are aware, we derived
the courage from God to preach to you God's Good News amid
3 much struggle. Our appeal was not based on error or on the promise
4 of indulgence; neither did it use fraud. But we speak as ministers
whom God has tested and then entrusted with his gospel, not as
5 those who seek to please men but God, who tests our hearts. You
are well aware that at no time did we have recourse to flattery or
6 to pretexts for enriching ourselves. God knows! We did not seek
7 human praise from you or anybody else, although we could have
stood on our dignity as apostles of Christ. But in your midst we
8 became as gentle as a nursing mother fondling her children. Such
was our tender love for you that not only would we gladly have
shared the gospel with you but even ourselves, because you had
9 become so dear to us. You recall, brothers, our fatiguing labor and
toil, when we worked night and day so as not to burden any of
10 you to whom we preached the gospel of God. You are witnesses, and
so too is God, how holy and just and blameless was our conduct
11 toward you believers. You are aware of how we entreated and
12 encouraged and adjured you, as does a father his children, to live
lives worthy of the God who calls you to his kingdom and glory.

ADMIRATION OF THEIR CONSTANCY

13 For this too we give unceasing thanks to God, that when you
received the word of God's message from us, you welcomed it,
not as a human message, but, as it truly is, the message of God
14 which is doing its work in you believers, because you, brothers,

---

2:3. *promise of indulgence:* oriental religions often appealed to sensual indulgence, a part of their ritual observance.
2:7. *stood on our dignity:* by demanding support instead of working to support ourselves. "Not hankerng for honors, or boasting, or demanding the attendance of guards" (St. Chrysostom).

followed the example of the congregations of God in Christ Jesus that are in Judea, in that you suffered the same indignities from your own countrymen as they did from the Jews, who killed the 15 Lord Jesus and the prophets, and have persecuted us. They are displeasing to God and hostile to all men, since they hinder us 16 from speaking to the Gentiles that they may be saved. Thus they are continually filling up the measure of their sins, and God's wrath has come upon them to the utmost.

We, brothers, since we found ourselves separated from you for 17 a very short time, in person, not in heart, have made more than ordinary efforts to hasten to see you, so great has been our longing for you. For this reason we proposed to visit you — I myself, Paul, 18 did so over and over again, but Satan hindered us. For what is our 19 hope or joy or crown to be proud of in the presence of our Lord Jesus Christ at his coming? Is it not yourselves, our pride and joy? 20

CHAPTER 3

THE VISIT OF TIMOTHY

And so when we could bear it no longer we decided to be left 1 behind all alone at Athens, and we sent Timothy, our brother and 2 God's minister in preaching the Good News about Christ, to strengthen and encourage you, so that not a single one of you 3 might waver in faith because of these afflictions. You know well that such is our appointed lot. Yes, even when we were with you, 4 we used to tell you beforehand that we should suffer afflictions, just as it has come to pass, as you know. Consequently when I 5 could bear it no longer, I sent to make sure of your faith, lest the tempter might have tempted you and our labor come to naught.

But now Timothy has come back to us from you, and has brought 6 us the good news about your faith and love and your kindly remembrance of us at all times. He told us that you long to see us just as we long to see you. Your faith has accordingly brought us 7 encouragement in the midst of all our trials and afflictions. For now 8 we really live, since you persevere in the Lord. What thanks can 9 we give to God on your behalf in return for all the joy we experience

---

2:16. utmost: or "at last" or "forever."

10 on your account before God? Night and day we pray more and
more earnestly that we may see you again face to face and make good
whatever may be wanting in your faith.

11   May God himself, our Father and our Lord Jesus smooth our way
12 to you. May the Lord make your love toward one another and
toward everyone increase till it overflows, as does ours toward you.
13 Then he will confirm your hearts in irreproachable holiness, in the
presence of God our Father, when our Lord Jesus Christ comes with
all his saints.

CHAPTER 4

PAUL URGES CHASTITY AND CHARITY

1   Further, brothers, as you have learned from us how you ought
to conduct yourselves to win God's approval, so you do conduct
yourselves; yet we beg and entreat you in the Lord Jesus to make
2 even greater progress. You know what instructions I have given you
3 by the authority of the Lord Jesus. What God wills is your sancti-
4 fication. He wills that you abstain from immorality, that each one
of you know how to acquire a wife for himself chastely and honor-
5 ably, not impelled by the fire of passion like the Gentiles who do
6 not know God. Let no one by lust injure his brother in this matter,
since the Lord will avenge all these things, as we have told you
7 before and have solemnly testified. God has not called us to unclean-
8 ness but to holiness. So, he who rejects these teachings rejects not
man but the God who has given you his Holy Spirit.
9   Concerning brotherly love, you need not have anyone write to you
since you yourselves have learned from God to love one another.
10 You certainly practice it toward all the brothers throughout
Macedonia. Still we entreat you, brothers, to make even greater
11 progress. Make it a point of honor quietly to mind your own
12 affairs, and work with your own hands, as we charged you. In this
way your conduct will win the respect of outsiders and you will
depend on no one for support.

4:4. *wife*: literally, "vessel," which some understand on one's own body
whose unruly inclinations are to be controlled.
4:6. Or: "Let no one transgress or wrong his brother in business." St.
Chrysostom: "To each man God has permitted one wife, and has set bounds
to nature. Relations are licit only with one's wife. To have relations with any
other is transgression and robbery."

THE SECOND COMING OF CHRIST

THE DEAD WILL SEE IT

We do not want you to be ignorant, brothers, concerning those 13
who are asleep, lest you should grieve, as the rest who have no hope.
Since we believe that Jesus died and rose again, so God will bring 14
with Jesus those who have fallen asleep in his faith. We say this on 15
the authority of the Lord: we who are alive, who survive until the
coming of the Lord, shall not take precedence over those who have
fallen asleep. At the given signal, at the summons of the archangel, 16
at the blast of God's trumpet, the Lord in person will come down
from heaven and the dead who are in Christ will rise first. After- 17
wards we who are alive, who survive, shall be caught up with them
on clouds into the air to meet the Lord, and so we shall continue
in the Lord's company forever. Therefore encourage one another 18
with these words.

CHAPTER 5

TIME OF CHRIST'S COMING IS UNKNOWN

There is no need, brothers, to write you about times and dates, 1
since you know full well that the day of the Lord is to come like a 2
thief in the night. Just at the moment when men are saying, "Peace, 3
all is well," sudden destruction will come upon them, as birth pangs
upon the expectant mother; and there shall be no escape.

BE ALWAYS PREPARED FOR HIS COMING

But you, brothers, are not living in darkness, and so the day 4
will not like a thief take you by surprise. No, but you have all 5
been born to the light, to noonday brightness. We belong neither
to night nor to darkness. And so we are not to sleep as do the rest 6
of men, but to be vigilant and alert. Sleepers sleep at night and 7
drunkards are drunk at night. But let us, who belong to the day, 8
be alert. Let us put on the breastplate of faith and love, and for a
helmet the hope of salvation. For God has not destined us to incur 9

4:15. survive: this does not mean that St. Paul was convinced that he personally
would live to see the second coming of Christ, but merely that some human
beings would be alive at the end of the world.

10 wrath, but to gain salvation through our Lord Jesus Christ, who died for us in order that, whether we are awake or asleep, we may
11 find life in union with him. Therefore continue to encourage and edify one another, as you are doing.

VARIOUS COUNSELS

12 We beseech you, brothers, to appreciate those who toil among you and have authority over you in the Lord and admonish you.
13 Esteem them with a more abundant love on account of their work.
14 Be at peace among yourselves. We exhort you, brothers, reprove the idle, encourage the fainthearted, support the weak, be patient
15 with all men. See that no one returns evil for evil to any man, but always strive to do what is good both to one another and to everybody.
16–18 Always be joyful. Never cease praying. Always be grateful. Such
19 sentiments God wills you to have in Christ Jesus. Do not extinguish
20, 21 the Spirit. Do not despise the utterances he inspires, yet test them
22 all. Hold on to that which is good, and have nothing to do with any kind of evil.

Conclusion

23 May God himself, the author of peace, make you perfect in holiness. May every part of your being, spirit, soul and body be preserved blameless for the day when our Lord Jesus Christ shall
24 come. He who called you is faithful and will do this.
25 Brothers, pray for us.
26, 27 Greet all the brothers with a holy kiss. I adjure you by the authority of our Lord Jesus Christ to have this epistle read to all the brothers.
28 The grace of our Lord Jesus Christ be with you.

THE SECOND EPISTLE TO THE THESSALONIANS

Shortly after St. Paul had written the first letter to the Thessalonians, he received some disturbing reports concerning them. They may have misunderstood what the Apostle had to say in his first letter about the return of the Lord, or they may have been misled by ill-informed Christians who unintentionally misquoted the Apostle, or it may be that a forged letter or letters were circulating at Thessalonica under the name of St. Paul.

Whatever the cause, the erroneous impression was widely shared at Thessalonica that the Lord would return at any moment in glory and take off the elect with him to heaven. If such is the case, the Thessalonians argued, there is no sense in working for a living. Thus some of the faithful sat around in dreamy-eyed expectation and idleness, and unsettled the people by word and example.

St. Paul wrote this second letter to the Thessalonians to set them right on these points.

THE DIVISION OF THE SECOND EPISTLE TO THE THESSALONIANS

Introduction, 1:1–12.
The signs of the second coming of Christ, 2:1–12.
Thanks, prayers, and exhortations, 2:13 to 3:15.
Conclusion, 3:16–18.

THE SECOND EPISTLE OF

ST. PAUL THE APOSTLE

TO THE THESSALONIANS

INTRODUCTION

CHAPTER 1

GREETINGS

Paul, Silvanus, and Timothy, to the congregation of the Thes- 1
salonians assembled in God our Father and the Lord Jesus
Christ: grace be to you and peace from God the Father and the 2
Lord Jesus Christ.

WORDS OF ENCOURAGEMENT

We owe continual thanks to God for you, brothers. It is a just 3
debt because your faith knows no bounds and the mutual love all
of you have is steadily increasing. Consequently we ourselves are 4
proud of you throughout the congregations of God on account of
your patience and faith in the midst of all the persecutions and
afflictions you are enduring. This fact is a clear indication of the 5
just judgment of God, that is, that you will be judged worthy of
the kingdom of God, since you suffer for its sake. It is certainly 6
just for God to requite with affliction those that afflict you, and to 7
reward with rest in our company you that are being afflicted. This
will come to pass when the Lord Jesus is revealed in the sky amid 8
flaming fire with his angels, heralds of his power. Then will he
execute vengeance on those who know not God and submit not
to the gospel of our Lord Jesus Christ. These will be punished with 9
eternal ruin, far removed from the Lord's presence and the majesty
of his might on that day when he comes to communicate his glory 10

1:10. *to communicate*: St. Thomas writes: "To be glorified in his saints who
are his members, in whom he dwells and will be glorified when his glory
passes to his members." Others translate: "to be glorified" in his saints.

to all his saints and become the wonderment of all believers because of the faith you gave to the testimony we presented to you.

PRAYER FOR THEIR SPIRITUAL ADVANCEMENT

11   To this end we pray always for you that our God may make you worthy of his call, and by his power accomplish all your yearning for moral goodness, and bring to perfection the actions your faith
12   prompts. In this way the name of our Lord Jesus will be glorified in you, and you will be glorified in him by the grace of our God and Lord Jesus Christ.

SIGNS OF THE SECOND COMING OF CHRIST

CHAPTER 2

1   In regard to the coming of our Lord Jesus Christ and our being
2   gathered together to meet him, we beseech you, brothers, not to let your mind be readily unsettled or agitated either by spiritual manifestations or by any word or letter allegedly coming from us,
3   to the effect that the day of the Lord is already here. Let no one deceive you in any way, because the following events must precede the day of the Lord: the apostasy (from God); the revelation of
4   the man wholly given to sin and destined to destruction, the adversary who exalts himself above whatever is called or worshiped as God, who goes so far as to enthrone himself in God's temple and
5   proclaim himself God. Do you not remember that while I was still
6   with you, I used to tell you about these things? And you know what is holding him back now, that he may be revealed at his
7   appointed time. Already the force of evil is actually at work, but in
8   secret until he who holds it back is gotten out of the way. And then the wicked one will be brought to light, but the Lord Jesus will destroy him with the breath of his mouth and reduce him to
9   naught by the splendor of his coming. This other's coming will

2:6. *holding him*: what this restraining force was and who wields it the Thessalonians knew but we can only conjecture. It may be the force of orderly government that recognizes and protects the rights of men, or it may be the Church which, through the powers of hell will never overcome her, will suffer a temporary eclipse as foretold in Apoc. 11:4–12.

be accompanied by all manner of counterfeit miracles, signs, and
wonders, effected with the aid of Satan's powerful activity, and by 10
all the seductiveness of evil in regard to those who by refusing to
embrace the love of the truth which would save them are on the road
to destruction. This is precisely why God sends them a powerful 11
seductive force so that they may put faith in that falsehood.
Ultimately all who refuse to put faith in the truth, and, instead, 12
delight in wickedness will be condemned.

THANKS, PRAYERS, EXHORTATIONS

THANKSGIVING

We, however, owe continual thanks to God for you, brothers, 13
beloved of the Lord, because God has selected you from eternity
to be saved through the sanctification which the Spirit effects and
through belief in the truth. To this he has called you by our 14
preaching, namely, to gain the glory of our Lord Jesus Christ. So 15
then, brothers, stand firm and hold fast to the traditions which you
have learned from us by word or letter. Our Lord Jesus Christ him- 16
self and God our Father, who has loved us and by grace given us
everlasting encouragement and good hope, will encourage your 17
hearts and make you steadfast in every good deed and good word.

CHAPTER 3

REQUEST FOR PRAYERS

In conclusion, brothers, pray for us that the Lord's message may 1
spread rapidly and be accorded honor, as it was in your case, and 2
that we may be rescued from troublesome and wicked men. Not
all men, alas, have the faith! But the Lord keeps faith and he will 3
make you steadfast and will guard you from the wicked one. We 4
rely in the Lord on you, brothers, that you are doing and will continue to do what we command. And may the Lord direct your hearts 5
to the love of God and to patient waiting for Christ.

2:13. *from eternity*: literally, "from the beginning." According to another
reading: "as first fruits."

IDLENESS CONDEMNED

6   We command you, brothers, by the authority of our Lord Jesus Christ, to hold yourselves aloof from every brother who is leading an idle life, not in keeping with the instructions they received from
7   us. You yourselves certainly know how you are in duty bound to
8   follow our example. We did not lead an idle life among you, neither did we eat anybody's food free of charge. On the contrary we worked day and night in fatiguing labor and struggle to avoid being a burden
9   to any of you. It is not that we have not the right. Our purpose
10 was to give you a model in our conduct for your imitation. Even when we were with you, we gave you the command: If anyone is
11 unwilling to work, do not let him eat. And now we hear that some among you live in idleness and do no work but meddle in the work
12 of others. Such people we command and exhort by the authority of the Lord Jesus Christ quietly to earn their own living.
13, 14   But you, brothers, must not grow tired of doing good, if anyone refuses to obey the directions we give in this letter, note him
15 and do not associate with him. Thus he will be put to shame. Yet do not treat him as an enemy but admonish him like a brother.

CONCLUSION

16 May the Lord himself, the source of peace, grant you peace at all times and in every way. May the Lord be with all of you.
17 This greeting is in my own hand — Paul's the signature in every letter of mine. This is my handwriting.
18 The grace of our Lord Jesus Christ be with you all!

THE FIRST EPISTLE TO TIMOTHY

The Division of the First Epistle to Timothy

Re...
Pastoral Recommendations, 1:3...

THE FIRST EPISTLE TO TIMOTHY

The Epistles to Timothy and Titus are aptly called the pastoral Epistles, because they set forth the duties of pastors or shepherds of souls. Whereas the other Pauline Epistles, except that to Philemon, were directed to local congregations, these were addressed to individuals.

These individuals were loyal and devoted disciples of the Apostle; Timothy in particular was a sort of vicar-general whom St. Paul sent on sundry important missions, and who, when this letter was addressed to him, was presiding over the congregation at Ephesus.

The situation which these Epistles reflect was rather serious. The purity of the faith was threatened by false teachers who proposed new and strange doctrines, at variance with the revealed message of our Lord. These false teachers appealed to Jewish genealogies and fables of one kind or another, and advocated a false asceticism in regard to marriage, food, and drink. St. Paul urgently requests Timothy and even pleads with him to condemn these teachings and to insist on the genuine message of salvation taught by our Lord and to defend it to the utmost. This anxiety of St. Paul to have the revealed truth preserved intact strongly emphasizes the importance of sound doctrine. The Apostle urges Timothy to be very careful in the selection of deacons and bishops or presbyters who would be the leaders of the local congregations, and sets forth the requisite qualifications for the office.

The Acts of the Apostles tells us nothing of the activity of St. Paul after his release from prison in Rome. The Acts does not even tell us that he was set free, although it insinuates as much. It was some time after this release that the Apostle wrote the pastoral Epistles — that is, between the years A.D. 63 and 67.

These Epistles are of great importance doctrinally, as they em-

533

phasize the hierarchical character of the Church, and bring out the teaching and disciplinary powers inherent in "the house of God, which is the Church of the living God, the pillar and bulwark of truth."

THE DIVISION OF THE FIRST EPISTLE TO TIMOTHY

Introduction, 1:1–2.
Restrain false teachers, 1:3–20.
Pastoral recommendations, 2:1 to 3:13.
Oppose false doctrine, 3:14 to 4:16.
Precepts for various classes, 5:1 to 6:19.
Conclusion, 6:20–21.

THE FIRST EPISTLE OF

ST. PAUL THE APOSTLE

TO TIMOTHY

CHAPTER 1

GREETINGS

Paul, an apostle of Christ Jesus by the command of God our 1
Savior and of Christ Jesus our hope, to Timothy, my true son in 2
the faith: grace, mercy, and peace from God the Father and from
Christ Jesus our Lord.

RESTRAIN FALSE TEACHERS

TIMOTHY'S TASK AT EPHESUS

As I urged you when I was leaving for Macedonia, stay on at 3
Ephesus to charge certain persons not to teach erroneous doctrines,
nor to devote themselves to fables and endless genealogies. Such 4
studies promote controversies rather than the divine plan of salvation
which rests on faith. Now the end to be achieved by this charge 5
is love that springs from a pure heart, a good conscience, and an
unfeigned faith. Some people have failed to hit the mark, and have 6
turned to vain babbling. They crave to be teachers of the Law, 7
when they understand neither what they say nor the points on
which they put so much stress.

TRUE ROLE OF THE LAW

We are fully aware that the Law is good, if a man uses it lawfully, 8
in the knowledge that the Law is enacted not for the just but for 9

1:4. *fables and endless genealogies*: the *fables*, whatever they were, did not
harmonize with revealed truth, and the genealogies were probably more or less
fictitious family trees of the more illustrious heroes of the Old Testament.
"They reckoned their fathers and grandfathers that they might enjoy a reputation
for historical knowledge and research" (St. Chrysostom).

the lawless and rebellious, for the ungodly and sinners, for the
irreverent and profane, for parricides and matricides, for murderers,
10 for immoral people, for homosexualists, for kidnapers, for liars and
perjurers, and against any other crime contrary to sound doctrine
11 as set forth in the gospel which has been committed to my trust
and tells of the glory of the blessed God.

MEMORIES OF HIS OWN LIFE AND CONVERSION

12 I am grateful to Christ Jesus our Lord, who has strengthened me,
because he counted me trustworthy when he made me his minister,
13 although formerly I defamed, persecuted, and insulted him. Still
I obtained the mercy of God because I acted ignorantly in unbelief.
14 Surely the grace of our Lord was lavished superabundantly on me
along with faith and the love that results from union with Christ
15 Jesus. Trustworthy and deserving of wholehearted acceptance is the
saying, "Christ Jesus came into the world to save sinners." Of these
16 I am at the head of the list. Yet I obtained mercy for this reason,
that in me first Christ Jesus might display his perfect patience as an
example to those who are to rest their faith on him and thus attain
17 eternal life. To the King of the ages, the immortal, invisible, and
only God, be honor and glory for ever and ever. Amen.

PAUL URGES TIMOTHY TO BE FAITHFUL

18 I commit to you this charge, my son Timothy, according to the
inspired utterances which pointed to you, that relying on them,
19 you may fight the noble fight, holding fast to faith and a good
conscience. This some have abandoned and thus have made ship-
20 wreck of their faith. Among such are Hymeneus and Alexander,
whom I have delivered to Satan that they may learn not to
blaspheme.

1:18. *inspired utterances:* these indicated Timothy's fitness and unusual
qualifications for the ministry. The same matter is referred to in 4:14. "As if
he had said, 'It is not I that charge you, but he who chose you'" (St.
Chrysostom).
1:20. *delivered to Satan:* see 1 Cor. 5:5.

Pastoral Recommendations

Chapter 2

HE RECOMMENDS PRAYER

I urge, then, first of all, that supplications, prayers, intercessions, 1
and thanksgivings be offered for all men: for kings and for all who 2
are in authority, that we may lead a quiet and tranquil life, adorned
with perfect piety and dignity. Thus to pray is good and acceptable 3
in the sight of God our Savior, who wills that all men be saved and 4
come to the knowledge of the truth. For there is but one God 5
and one Mediator between God and men, Christ Jesus, himself
man, who gave himself a ransom for all, a fact attested at the 6
proper time. Of this fact I have been appointed a herald and an 7
apostle, to teach the Gentiles faith and truth. I am telling the truth;
I am not lying.

WOMANLY DECORUM IN PUBLIC ASSEMBLIES

It is my will, then, that the men pray everywhere. Let them lift 8
up hands that are pure and be free from resentment and strife.
So too, women are to pray, decently attired, adorning themselves 9
with modesty and restraint, not with braided hair, gold, pearls, or
expensive clothing, but with good deeds, as befits women who make 10
profession of worshiping God. Woman is to be a silent and perfectly 11
submissive pupil. I do not allow a woman to teach or to exercise 12
authority over men; rather she is to keep quiet. A reason for this is 13
that Adam was formed first, then Eve; and Adam was not deceived, 14
but the woman, after being deceived, fell into transgression.
Woman's salvation is in childbearing, if she perseveres in faith and 15
love and holiness with modesty.

2:15. St. Paul's meaning is that as a general rule the mission of woman in
life is that of wife and mother, and that in accepting this role which God
has assigned her, she will work out her salvation, provided she is adorned with
Christian virtue. In the Greek the last phrase is in the plural. St. Paul thinks of
the singular "woman" as a class, and so passes to the plural. Or possibly the
plural refers to the children. Accordingly the rank and file of women will work
out their salvation in accepting their providential role as mothers, whose function
is not merely to bear children but to educate them to the Christian life.

CHAPTER 3

QUALITIES NEEDED IN A BISHOP

↓ 1   Trustworthy is the saying: "If anyone is eager for the office of
2 bishop, he desires a noble post." A bishop, then, must be blameless,
married only once, reserved, prudent, of good conduct, hospitable,
3 capable of teaching, not a drinker or brawler, but considerate, not
4 quarrelsome, not avaricious. He should manage well his own household, keeping his children under control and perfectly respectful.
5 For if a man cannot manage his own household, how can he take
6 care of one of God's congregations? He must not be a recent convert,
or he will be puffed up with pride and incur the condemnation
7 pronounced against the devil. Besides, he must have a good reputation with outsiders, lest he should fall into disgrace which the devil
may use as a snare.

QUALITIES NEEDED IN A DEACON

8   In the same way deacons must be honorable, not double-tongued,
9 not given to much wine, not greedy for base gain, but holding the
10 mystery of faith with a pure conscience. And let them first be tried,
and if found without reproach, let them be allowed to serve as
11 deacons. In the same way let their wives be honorable, not slanderers,
12 but reserved, trustworthy in every respect. Deacons should not be
married more than once, and should manage well their children
13 and their own household. Those who have discharged well the
↑   deacon's office, will win a fine position for themselves and much
bold assurance in preaching the faith which is in Christ Jesus.

3:2. married only once: St. Paul here does not wish to make marriage a
prerequisite for a bishop or deacon. His meaning is that if a candidate for the
office is married, he should have been so but once. A second marriage after
the death of the first spouse was considered an imperfection, although it was
allowed in the case of those who did not aspire to ecclesiastical office. St.
Chrysostom comments: "He does not prescribe this as a rule, as if a bishop
must be married, but as forbidding his having more than one wife."

3:13. a fine position: perhaps the idea of promotion to the rank of presbyter
or bishop is what St. Paul had in mind. So St. Chrysostom explains it.

OPPOSE FALSE DOCTRINE

THE CHURCH IS THE PILLAR OF TRUTH

I hope to come to you shortly, but I write these instructions to 14
you, so that if I am delayed, you may know what your conduct 15
should be in the house of God which is the Church of the living
God, the pillar and bulwark of truth. And by common acknowl- 16
edgment great is the mystery of the true religion:

> He was made visible in his human nature,
> vindicated in his spiritual nature,
> seen by angels,
> preached among the Gentiles,
> accorded faith in the world,
> taken up in glory.

CHAPTER 4

SOME ERRONEOUS DOCTRINES

Now the Spirit expressly says that in later times men will depart 1
from the faith, by giving heed to deceitful spirits and doctrines of
diabolical origin, propagated through the dissembling of liars who 2
have a seared conscience. They will forbid marriage, and enjoin 3
abstinence from foods which God has created to be partaken of
with thanksgiving by those who believe and know the truth. For 4
every creature of God is good, and nothing is to be rejected that is
received with thanksgiving; for it is sanctified by the word of God 5
and prayer.

VALUE OF TRUE PIETY

By recommending these instructions to the brothers, you will be 6
a good minister of Christ Jesus, nourished on the words of faith
and of the good doctrine which you have carefully followed. But 7

3:16. The mystery of the true religion is the God-Man. What follows was
probably part of an ancient liturgical hymn.

4:5. *word of God:* perhaps the creative word of God which called things
into being, or more probably the words of Scripture which the Christians used
to give expression to their prayers and thanksgiving. So Bardy.

avoid foolish fables and old wives' tales, and train yourself in piety.
8 Bodily training is of little profit, while piety is profitable in all
respects, since it holds promise for the present life as well as for
9 the next. That saying is trustworthy and deserving of wholehearted
10 acceptance, for we work and struggle to this end, because we hope
in the living God, who is the Savior of all men, especially of
believers.

BE DEVOTED TO YOUR WORK

11, 12   Command and teach these things. Let no man despise your
youth, but be an example to the faithful in speech, in conduct, in
13 love, in faith, in chastity. Until I come, attend to public reading,
14 to exhorting, and to teaching. Do not neglect the grace of office you
have, which was granted to you by inspired designation with the
15 imposition of the presbyter's hands. Meditate on these things, give
yourself entirely to them, that your progress may be manifest to all.
16 Take heed to yourself and to your teaching. Persevere in it because
by so doing you will save both yourself and those who hear you.

PRECEPTS FOR VARIOUS CLASSES

CHAPTER 5

A RÉSUMÉ

1   Be not harsh in rebuking an elderly man, but exhort him as you
2 would a father. Treat younger men as brothers, elderly women
as mothers, younger women as sisters with perfect chastity.

CONCERNING WIDOWS

3, 4   Honor widows who are truly widows. If a widow has children
or grandchildren, let these first learn to practice filial piety toward
their own family and thus make suitable return to their forebearers,
5 since this is pleasing to God. But she who is truly a widow, that is,
one left utterly alone, has set her hope on God and continues in
6 supplications and prayers night and day, whereas she who gives
7 herself up to pleasure is dead while she is still alive. Command
8 these things, so that they may be without blame. But if anyone does
not take care of his own relatives, and especially of his immediate

family, he has denied the faith and is worse than an unbeliever.

A widow may be enrolled if she is not less than sixty years old   9
and has had but one husband. She should have a reputation for   10
good deeds, such as bringing up her children well, practicing hospitality, washing the saints' feet, helping those in trouble, and taking
part in every good movement. But refuse to enroll younger widows,   11
because when they wantonly turn away from Christ, they wish to
marry; thus they incur condemnation because they have broken their   12
prior pledge. And further, they get used to idleness and go about   13
from house to house. Not only are they idle but gossipers as well
and busybodies, saying what they ought not. I desire, therefore,   14
that the younger widows should marry, bear children, manage their
households, and thus give the adversary no occasion to criticize
them. For already some have strayed after Satan. If any believing   15, 16
woman has widowed relatives, let her provide for them and do not
let the congregation be burdened, so that it may provide for those
who are truly widows.

CONCERNING PRESBYTERS

Let the presbyters who rule well be held worthy of double honor,   17
especially those who labor in preaching and teaching. As the Scrip-   18
ture says, "Do not muzzle the ox when it treads out the grain,"
and "The laborer is entitled to his support." Do not listen to an   19
accusation against a presbyter unless it is supported by two or three
witnesses. Rebuke habitual sinners in the presence of all, that the   20
rest may stand in fear. I charge you in the presence of God and   21
Christ Jesus and the elect angels to observe these points impartially,
in no way favoring either side. Do not hastily impose hands on any   22
one, and do not be a partner in other men's sins. Keep yourself chaste.

Stop drinking water only, and use a little wine for your stomach's   23
sake and your frequent ailments.

5:9. *enrolled:* there was a confraternity of consecrated widows who dedicated
their lives in chaste widowhood to works of Christian charity.

5:12. *prior pledge:* to devote their lives to the service of the Church in
chaste widowhood.

5:17. *double honor:* possibly: "double remuneration." "The honor here
spoken of is attention to them, and providing for their necessities" (St.
Chrysostom).

5:18. Deut. 25:14; 24:4.

541

24   Some men's sins are manifest before investigation, and other men's
25 only after it. In the same way good deeds are manifest, and those
that are not good cannot remain hidden.

CHAPTER 6

CONCERNING SLAVES

1   Let those who are under the yoke of slavery account their masters
deserving of all honor, that the name of the Lord and his teaching
2 may not be defamed. And when their masters are believers, the
slaves should not despise them on the ground that they are brothers,
but should serve them all the more faithfully because they who
partake of their services are believers and beloved. Teach and urge
these things.

CONCERNING LYING TEACHERS

3   If anyone teaches otherwise and does not agree with the sound
instruction of our Lord Jesus Christ and that doctrine which makes
4 for piety, he is swollen with pride, has no expert knowledge, but
dotes on controversies and disputes about words. These give rise to
5 envy, quarreling, slander, base suspicions, wrangling among men
whose minds are corrupt and deprived of the truth, and who believe
6 that religion is a source of gain. A great source of gain is religion
7 which brings contentment with our lot, for we brought nothing
8 into this world, and certainly we can take nothing out of it. But
9 let us be content if we have food and clothing. Those who seek to
become rich fall into temptation and a snare and many senseless
and harmful desires, which plunge men into ruin and destruction.
10 The love of money is the root of all evils, and some in their eagerness to get rich have strayed from the faith and have found themselves pierced with many a pang of sorrow.

FINAL PLEA TO TIMOTHY

11   But you, O man of God, flee these things; rather pursue holiness,
12 piety, faith, love, patience, mildness. Fight the noble fight that the

5:24-25. The translation of these verses is difficult and the meaning obscure.
The investigation is probably that of God in the judgment after death, when
even the most secret sins of men will be brought to light.

faith inspires, lay hold of eternal life to which you have been
called, when you made that splendid profession in the presence of
many witnesses. In the presence of God, who gives life to all things   13
and in the presence of Jesus Christ, who made that splendid profession at the bar of Pontius Pilate, I charge you to be faithful to   14
your duties, and thus continue unstained and without reproach until
our Lord Jesus Christ appears. This appearance will be made manifest   15
in his own time by him who is the blessed and only Sovereign,
the King of Kings and the Lord of Lords; who alone has immortality   16
and dwells in light inaccessible, whom no man has seen or can
see. To him be honor and everlasting dominion. Amen.

CONCERNING THE RICH

Charge those blessed with the riches of this world not to be   17
proud, or to trust in the uncertainty of riches, but in God, who
provides all things in rich abundance for our enjoyment. Let them   18
do good and be rich in good deeds; let them be liberal in sharing
their goods with others, and thus provide for themselves a good   19
foundation for the time to come, in order that they may lay hold
on the true life.

Conclusion

O Timothy, guard what has been entrusted to you, and keep   20
free from profane novelties in speech and the contradictions that
come from so-called knowledge. This some have professed and have   21
fallen away from the faith.

Grace be with you.

THE SECOND EPISTLE TO TIMOTHY

This Epistle is St. Paul's last will and testament, his farewell to Timothy and through him to all his beloved converts everywhere. There is a tone of sadness running through the letter, yet the Apostle's trust in God remains unshaken. At the time of writing this Epistle, St. Paul was a prisoner at Rome. Of his faithful disciples Luke alone is with him; all the others have left him for one reason or another. He is lonely and most anxious to have Timothy, his most beloved and faithful co-worker, come to him and bring Mark. At one time St. Paul had been rather keenly disappointed in Mark (Acts 15:36-39), but since then Mark had mended his ways and found his way back into the circle of St. Paul's dearest friends. The Apostle no doubt wished the comfort of these friends' companionship, but he also wished to deliver some stirring final exhortations to them to carry on with great zeal the work of spreading the Gospel, and to guard with the utmost care the integrity of the Christian message. False teachers were threatening it.

St. Paul seems convinced that his death is near. His blood is about to be poured out as a sacrificial libation. He has kept the faith, he has run the course, and in trustful humility he is awaiting the reward of a holy life, which the just Judge will give him.

The date of this Epistle depends on the date of the Apostle's martyrdom which took place sometime between A.D. 64 and 67.

THE DIVISION OF THE SECOND EPISTLE TO TIMOTHY

Introduction, 1:1–5.
Pastoral recommendations, 1:6 to 2:13.
Fidelity to his duties, 2:14 to 4:8.
Conclusion, 4:9–22.

THE SECOND EPISTLE OF

ST. PAUL THE APOSTLE

TO TIMOTHY

INTRODUCTION

CHAPTER 1

GREETINGS

Paul, an apostle of Christ Jesus, by the will of God to proclaim *1*
the promise of life in Christ Jesus: to Timothy, my beloved son: *2*
grace, mercy, and peace from God the Father and from Christ Jesus
our Lord.

HIS DESIRE TO SEE TIMOTHY

As I remember you without ceasing in my prayers night and day, *3*
I am grateful to God, whom I serve with a clear conscience, as did
my forefathers. When I recall your tears, I long fervently to see *4*
you, that I may be filled with joy. I remember that unfeigned faith *5*
of yours, which dwelt first in your grandmother Lois and in your
mother Eunice, and dwells, I am certain, in you also.

PASTORAL RECOMMENDATIONS

BE COURAGEOUS

For this reason I remind you to stir up God's grace of office which *6*
you have through the laying on of my hands. God has not given *7*
us a spirit of cowardice, but of courage and love and self-control.
Do not, therefore, be ashamed of testifying to our Lord, nor of me, *8*
his prisoner, but in reliance on the power of God, engage in painful
labors with me for the gospel. He has saved us and called us with *9*
a holy calling, not in virtue of our deeds, but in virtue of his own

---

1:4. The occasion of Timothy's tears was probably the Apostle's departure,
or his imprisonment.

purpose and grace which was granted to us in Christ Jesus before
10 this world existed, and is now manifested through the appearance
of our Savior Christ Jesus. He has destroyed death and brought life
11 and immortality to light through the gospel, of which I have been
12 appointed a herald, an apostle, and a teacher. That is why I am
V suffering these trials; yet I am not ashamed. For I know whom I
have believed, and I am certain that he is able to guard until that
13 day the trust committed to me. In the faith and love that are in
Christ Jesus, hold to the form of sound teaching which you have
14 heard from me. Guard that noble trust with the aid of the Holy
Spirit, who dwells in us.

LOYALTY OF ONESIPHORUS

15   This you know that all in the province of Asia have turned away
16 from me, among them, Phygelus and Hermogenes. May the Lord
grant mercy to the household of Onesiphorus, because he often
17 comforted me. He was not ashamed of my chains, but when he
18 reached Rome, he diligently sought me out and found me. May the
Lord grant him the favor of finding mercy in the Lord's presence
on that day. You know very well the many services he rendered me
at Ephesus.

CHAPTER 2

DEVOTE YOURSELF TO YOUR WORK

1   Therefore, my son, be strengthened by the grace which is in
2 Christ Jesus, and what you have heard from me in the presence of
many witnesses, commend to trustworthy men who will be com-
3 petent in turn to teach others. Like a good soldier of Christ Jesus,
4 join the ranks of those who bear hardship. No one serving as a

---

1:12. The trust committed to St. Paul is the revealed message. There was
an ever present threat that it would be distorted by false teachers. Some interpreters would understand the trust as referring to the Apostle's labors for
the Gospel, which he entrusted to God, while he awaited the heavenly reward
which God will grant him for them. St. Chrysostom says, "What is the committed trust? The faith, the preaching of the gospel. He who committed it to
him, he says, will preserve it unimpaired. . . . Or he refers to the faithful as
the charge which God committed to him, or which he committed to God."
1:16. The way in which St. Paul speaks of Onesiphorus indicates that this
official of the congregation at Ephesus was now dead.

soldier entangles himself with the affairs of daily life, that he may
win the approval of the officer who enlisted him. And again, one   5
who enters a contest is not declared the winner unless he competes
according to the rules. The hard-working farmer should be the first   6
to get his share of the crops. Take in what I tell you; the Lord will   7
give you a ready understanding in everything.

THE THOUGHT OF CHRIST GIVES COURAGE

Remember Jesus Christ, risen from the dead, descendant of   8
David. This is what I preach. For this gospel I suffer ills and even   9
fetters like a criminal. But the word of God is not fettered. For its   10
sake I endure all manner of suffering on behalf of the elect, that
they also may attain salvation and eternal glory which are in Christ
Jesus. Trustworthy is the saying,   11

>   "If we have died with him,
>   we shall also live with him.
>   If we endure,   12
>   we shall also reign with him.
>   If we disown him,
>   he in turn will disown us.
>   Though we be faithless,   13
>   he remains faithful,
>   since he cannot disown himself."

FIDELITY TO HIS DUTIES

CORRECT HANDLING OF TEACHERS

Recall these things to the minds of the faithful, charging them   14
in the presence of the Lord not to dispute about words. That is
useless; it leads to the ruin of the listeners. Use all care to present   15
yourself to God as a man approved, a worker that cannot be ashamed,
rightly handling the word of truth. But avoid profane and empty   16
babblings, for those who engage in such talk will contribute much
to impiety and their doctrine will spread like gangrene. Of this sort   17
are Hymenaeus and Philetus, who have wandered from the truth   18

2:11–13. This is probably a fragment of an ancient liturgical hymn.
2:14. Many manuscripts read "God" instead of Lord.

by saying that the resurrection has already taken place. They are
19 destroying the faith of some. But the sure foundation which God
has laid stands firm, bearing this seal: "The Lord knows who are
his"; and, "Let everyone who names the name of the Lord depart
from iniquity."

THE FAITHFUL SERVANT

20   In a large house there are vessels not only of gold and silver,
but also of wood and clay. Some are for noble, but some for ignoble
21 uses. If, therefore, anyone cleanses himself from what is ignoble,
he will be a vessel for noble use, sanctified and useful to the Master,
ready for every good undertaking.
22   Flee the passions of youth and pursue holiness, faith, love, and
peace, together with those who call on the Lord with a pure heart.
23 Avoid also foolish and stupid controversies, knowing that they breed
24 quarrels. The Lord's servant must not quarrel, but be gentle toward
25 all, qualified to teach, patient, gently admonishing those who resist.
God may perhaps give them repentance and lead them to the knowl-
26 edge of the truth. In this way they will escape the snare of the devil
who has subjected them to his will.

CHAPTER 3

FUTURE DANGERS

1   Know this, that in the last days dangerous times will come.
2 Men will be lovers of self, lovers of money, vain, proud, abusive,
3 disobedient to parents, ungrateful, unholy, lacking affection, pledge-
breakers, slanderers, incontinent, undisciplined, haters of what is
4 good, treacherous, reckless, swollen with pride, loving pleasure more
5 than God. They will have a semblance of religion, it is true, but
6 will disown its power. Avoid these. Among them are those who
make their way into homes and captivate silly women who are sin-
7 laden and led astray by various cravings, seeking information from
every source yet powerless to attain to genuine knowledge of the
8 truth. Just as Jannes and Jambres resisted Moses, so these men resist

---

3:8. Jannes and Jambres: ("Mambres" in the Vulgate), according to Jewish
tradition, were the magicians who opposed Moses at the court of Pharao.

the truth, because they are corrupt in mind, reprobate as regards the
faith. But they will make no further progress, for their folly will be 9
obvious to all, as was that of these two men.

COMFORT FROM PAUL'S EXPERIENCE

But you have closely followed my doctrine, my conduct, my 10
purpose, my faith, my long-suffering, my love, and my patience.
You have kept in touch with my persecutions, my afflictions, such 11
as befell me at Antioch, Iconium, and Lystra. What persecutions
I suffered! Yet the Lord delivered me from all of them. Certainly 12
all who want to live piously in Christ Jesus will suffer persecutions.
But the wicked and impostors will go from bad to worse, deceivers 13
and deceived. But see that you continue in the truths you have 14
learned, of which you are convinced, well aware from whom you
have learned them and that from your infancy you have known 15
the Sacred Writings. They can instruct you for salvation through
the faith which is in Christ Jesus. All Scripture is inspired by God 16
and useful for teaching, for reproving, for correcting, for instructing
in holiness, that the man of God may be perfect, fully equipped 17
for every good deed.

CHAPTER 4

PREACH SOUND DOCTRINE AT ALL TIMES

In the presence of God and Christ Jesus who will come to judge 1
the living and the dead, I solemnly charge you by his appearing
and his royal authority: preach the word, be urgent in season, out 2
of season. Convince, rebuke, exhort people with perfect patience and
teaching, for a time will come when they will not endure sound 3
doctrines, but according to their own whims they will multiply for
themselves teachers who will tickle their ears. They will turn away 4
from hearing the truth and rather go astray after fables. But as for 5
yourself, you should be self-controlled in all things, bear trials
patiently, work as a preacher of the gospel, discharge your ministry.

As for me, I am already being poured out in sacrifice, and the 6

3:11. Acts 13, 14, and 19 have an account of some of these persecutions.
4:6. St. Paul sees his imminent martyrdom and refers to it in sacrificial
language. His blood, like the wine poured out in honor of pagan gods at a
sacrifice, was about to be shed in defense of Christianity.

7 time of my departure is at hand. I have fought the good fight, I
8 have finished the course, I have kept the faith. What remains is
the crown due to holiness which the Lord, the just Judge, will give
me on that day, and not only to me but also to those who love his
brilliant coming.

CONCLUSION

PAUL'S LONELINESS

9, 10   Make every effort to speed your coming to me, for Demas, in love
with the present world, has deserted me and gone to Thessalonica,
11 Crescens to Galatia, Titus to Dalmatia. Luke alone is with me. Get
12 Mark and bring him with you, for he is very helpful to me for the
13 ministry. I have sent Tychicus to Ephesus. When you come, bring
the cloak I left at Troas with Carpus, and the books, especially the
14 parchments. Alexander, the coppersmith, has done me much harm;
15 the Lord will render to him according to his deeds. Avoid him
yourself, for he has vehemently opposed our words.

HIS TRIAL

16   At my first defense no one came to my support, but all deserted
17 me. May it not be laid to their charge. The Lord, however, stood
by me and strengthened me, that through me the preaching of the
gospel might be completed, and that all the Gentiles might hear
18 it. I was delivered from the lion's mouth. The Lord will deliver me
from every assault of evil, and will save and bring me to his
heavenly kingdom. To him be the glory for ever and ever. Amen.

GREETINGS

19   Greet Prisca and Aquila and the household of Onesiphorus.
20 Erastus stayed at Corinth; Trophimus I left sick at Miletus.
21 Make every effort to come before winter. Eubulus, Pudens, Linus,
and Claudia and all the brothers greet you.
22   The Lord Jesus be with your spirit. Grace be with you.

4:10. There is considerable evidence in favor of reading "Gaul" instead of
Galatia.

4:13. The books St. Paul requested were probably papyri containing Old
Testament writings. The parchments were probably not blank but also contained
portions of the Old Testament.

4:14. This *Alexander* cannot be identified with certainty. A man of this name
is mentioned in 1 Tim. 1:20 and in Acts 19:33.

THE EPISTLE TO TITUS

St. Titus, one of St. Paul's most beloved and trusted disciples, was born of Greek parents. He accompanied Paul and Barnabas to Jerusalem where the Christian party, which advocated the necessity of circumcision, tried to force this rite on Titus. St. Paul refused to give in to them (Gal. 2:1 ff.). Since St. Paul in this Epistle addresses Titus as "son," it is thought that the Apostle had baptized him, or at least converted him to the faith. He was sent by St. Paul on several important missions during the third missionary journey. Twice Titus was sent by the Apostle to Corinth (from Ephesus, 2 Cor. 2:12; 7:6 f., and from Macedonia, 2 Cor. 8:16 f.). After this we lose sight of Titus; there is no reference to him in the Epistles of the captivity. Our subsequent information concerning him is derived from the pastoral Epistles. When St. Paul wrote this letter to him, Titus was in Crete, where he had been appointed a sort of auxiliary bishop by the Apostle (1:5). He was summoned to meet the Apostle at Epirus (3:12), and during St. Paul's final imprisonment at Rome Titus was sent on a mission to Dalmatia (2 Tim. 4:10). Tradition tells us that he spent his last days exercising his episcopal office in Crete and there he died.

We cannot definitely determine from our recorded sources of information when St. Paul visited the island of Crete and preached the Gospel there. He touched this island during his voyage as a prisoner to Rome (Acts 27:12), but had no opportunity at that time to do any extensive missionary work. It can only be after St. Paul was freed from his first Roman imprisonment that he visited the island of Crete, probably after his journey to Spain.

The Epistle to Titus was written about the same time as the first to Timothy.

The situation was in general the same as that which confronted

Timothy at Ephesus. Leaders of the Christian community were to be chosen; various practices which fell short of the Christian ideal had to be condemned, and false teachers had to be repressed. The Apostle deals with these various points in this Epistle.

THE DIVISION OF THE EPISTLE TO TITUS

Introduction, 1:1–4.
The mission of Titus, 1:5–16.
Teach the Christian ideal, 2:1 to 3:11.
Conclusion, 3:12–15.

THE EPISTLE OF

ST. PAUL THE APOSTLE

TO TITUS

CHAPTER 1

GREETINGS

Paul, a servant of God and an apostle of Jesus Christ, to proclaim 1
the faith for God's elect and the full knowledge of the truth dealing
with genuine religion based on the hope of everlasting life. This 2
hope the God who cannot lie promised before the world existed, and 3
at the proper time made his message known through the preaching
entrusted to me by order of God our Savior.

To Titus, my true son in virtue of the faith which we have in 4
common: grace and peace from God the Father and from Christ
Jesus our Savior.

THE MISSION OF TITUS

APPOINT WORTHY MINISTERS

The reason why I left you behind in Crete was to set right 5
what was defective and appoint presbyters from city to city, as I
directed you. They must be blameless, married only once, men 6
whose children have the faith and are free from the charge of
being dissolute or disobedient. Obviously a bishop must be blame- 7
less, since he is God's steward, not arrogant, or ill-tempered, or a
drinker, or a brawler, or greedy for base gain; but hospitable, a lover 8
of what is good, prudent, just, holy, and continent. He must cling 9
to the trustworthy message which corresponds to what has been
taught. So, he will be able to encourage others with sound doctrine
and to confute opponents.

1:6. See the note on 1 Tim. 3:2.

CHECK ERROR AND EVIL

10 There are many disobedient men, vain babblers and deceivers,
11 especially of the circumcision party. These must be silenced, since
they upset whole households by teaching for the sake of base gain
12 what they ought not. One of their own, an oracle in their eyes,
13 said, "Cretans are always liars, evil beasts, lazy gluttons." This testimony is true. Therefore rebuke them sharply that they may be sound
14 in faith, and not listen to Jewish fables and commandments coming
15 from men who turn their backs on the truth. To the clean all things
are clean, but to the defiled and unbelieving nothing is clean. Their
16 very minds and consciences are unclean. They profess to know God
but by their deeds they disown him. They are abominable and disobedient and worthless for any good enterprise.

TEACH THE CHRISTIAN IDEAL

CHAPTER 2

INSTRUCT THE DIFFERENT CLASSES

1,2 As for you, speak what befits sound doctrine. Urge elderly men
to be reserved, honorable, prudent, sound in faith, love, and patience.
3 Urge the elderly women likewise to be marked by holiness of
behavior, not to be slanderers, or enslaved to excessive wine drinking.
4 Urge them to teach what is right, that they may train the younger
5 women to be prudent, to love their husbands and children, to be
reserved, chaste, homemakers, gentle, obedient to their husbands, so
6 that the word of God may not be reviled. Exhort the younger men
7 in like manner to be prudent. Show yourself in every respect an
example of good deeds. In teaching, manifest integrity and dignity.
8 Let your speech be sound and blameless, so that an opponent may
9 be put to shame at having nothing bad to say of us. Exhort slaves
to obey their masters, to please them in every respect, not to oppose

1:12. St. Jerome says that this quotation is from the poet Epimenedes of
the sixth century B.C. and is found in the oracles. Theodoret ascribes it to
Callimachus.
2:5. homemakers: literally, those who work at or have an interest in providing
a good home; "good housekeepers" expresses the idea very well.

them, not to pilfer, but to show utter and heartfelt fidelity. Thus 10
in all their actions they will reflect credit on the doctrine of God
our Savior.

MOTIVES FOR THEIR CHANGED LIFE

The grace of God, which is the means of salvation for all men, 11
has made its appearance and instructed us to reject irreligion and 12
worldly lusts and to live prudent, just, and religious lives in this
world, while we await the realization of our blessed hope, the brilliant 13
coming of our great God and Savior Jesus Christ. He gave himself 14
for us, to redeem us from every kind of iniquity and cleanse a people
for his very own, zealous for good deeds. Speak these truths; exhort 15
too and reprove with full authority. Do not allow anyone to
despise you.

CHAPTER 3

Remind the faithful to be subject to rulers and authorities, to 1
be obedient to commands, to be ready for any good undertaking.
Remind them to speak evil of no one, to avoid quarreling, to be 2
considerate and show perfect gentleness to all men. For we ourselves 3
were once without understanding, without obedience, deceived, slaves
to various lusts and pleasures. We lived in malice and envy; we were
hateful and hating one another. But when the goodness and kindness 4
of God our Savior toward all mankind appeared, then, not because 5
of deeds we ourselves had done in a state of holiness, but in virtue
of his mercy, he saved us through the bath in which the Holy
Spirit regenerates and renews us. This Spirit God has richly poured 6
out on us through Jesus Christ our Savior, in order that, made holy 7
by his grace, we may in hope become heirs of life everlasting.

LAST EXHORTATION

What I have just said is trustworthy, and I desire you to insist 8
on these things so that those who have faith in God may be anxious
to excel in good deeds. These counsels are excellent and useful to
men. But avoid foolish controversies and genealogies and quarrels 9
and disputes about the Law, for they are useless and futile. A factious 10

3:5. *bath:* i.e., the sacrament of Baptism.

11 man avoid after a first and second admonition, fully aware that such
a one is perverted and will go on sinning; he is self-condemned.

CONCLUSION

12 When I send Artemas or Tychicus to you, make every effort to
come to me at Nicopolis, for there I have decided to spend the
13 winter. Be eager to help Zenas the lawyer and Apollos on their way;
14 take care that they lack nothing. Let our people also learn to excel
in good deeds, so as to care for urgent cases. In this way they will
not be destitute of good deeds.
15 All my companions greet you. Greet those who love us in the
faith. Grace be with all of you.

3:12. Nicopolis was in Epirus.
3:13. Zenas . . . Apollos: probably the bearers of this letter to Titus.

THE EPISTLE TO PHILEMON

Onesimus, whose name means "useful," was a fugitive slave who had been lazy and had stolen from his master, Philemon. The fugitive found his way probably to Rome, and, perhaps fearing lest his master apprehend him, had recourse to St. Paul, his master's friend, to intercede for him. St. Paul instructed and baptized Onesimus. The Apostle seems to have recognized many good qualities in the converted slave, and wished to make him one of his assistants in the work of evangelizing the world. But he would first get the approval of Philemon as well as his forgiveness of the fugitive.

Such is the occasion of the Epistle to Philemon. This little note has an importance far beyond its length. We see in it the practical application of the principles of Christianity relative to the equality of all men. In Christ, St. Paul had written to the Galatians and to others, there is no longer slave or free man; we are all one. St. Paul could appeal to these principles in the case of a Christian slave owner, and even insist on their application, as he tells Philemon. But in the case of pagan slave owners and in a society where perhaps more people were slaves than free, such principles could not be generally preached and insisted on, without leading to a great social upheaval that would have been worse than the un-Christian institution of slavery. The leaven of Christianity would in the course of time permeate society and gradually lead to the abolition of slavery without violence or bloodshed.

Everyone agrees that this little Epistle is one of the world's literary masterpieces, and also that it is a genuine Pauline Epistle. It was written from Rome, most probably, about A.D. 62 or 63. It is one of the "Captivity Epistles." (See the introduction to the Epistle to the Ephesians.)

THE EPISTLE OF

ST. PAUL THE APOSTLE

TO PHILEMON

INTRODUCTION

Paul, a prisoner of Christ Jesus, and our brother Timothy, to 1
Philemon, our beloved fellow worker, to Appia, our sister, to 2
Archippus, our fellow soldier, and to the congregation that meets
in your house: to you grace and peace from God our Father and 3
from the Lord Jesus Christ.

When I remember you at my prayers, I always give thanks to 4
my God, because I hear of the love and faith which you have 5
toward the Lord Jesus and exercise in behalf of all the saints.
I pray that the generosity which springs from your faith may be 6
made effective to the glory of Christ by the deep knowledge of all
the blessings which you and yours possess. I derived much joy 7
and comfort, brother, in your love, hearing that you have refreshed
the hearts of the saints.

PLEA FOR ONESIMUS

For this reason, although in Christ I have ample boldness to 8
command you to do your duty, I prefer in the interests of love to 9
plead with you. I, Paul, an old man, and also at present a prisoner
for Christ Jesus, plead with you for my child, whose father I became 10

---

1. Philemon had been converted to the faith by St. Paul; this is the debt
(verse 19) that Philemon owes the Apostle.

6. Philemon's generous Christian conduct would manifest to nonbelievers
what fine conduct the faith inspires, and thus give them a knowledge of the
splendid social implications of the teachings of Christ. This could easily lead
to their conversion and redound to the glory of Christ. An alternative translation:
"that the sharing of your faith may promote the deep knowledge of all the
good you enjoy. . . ."

9. old man: or "ambassador."

11 during my imprisonment. I mean Onesimus. Once he was useless
12 to you, but now he is quite useful both for you and for me. I am
sending him back to you, that is, I am sending my very heart.
13 I would have preferred to keep him with me to serve me in your
14 stead during my imprisonment for the gospel; but I would do
nothing without consulting you, so that your goodness may not be
forced but spontaneous.

15 Perhaps this is why he was briefly separated from you, that he
16 might be restored to you forever, no longer as a slave, but much
more than a slave, as a beloved brother. Such he is to me in the
highest degree, and such he ought to be with greater reason to you
17 both as a man and as a Christian. If, then, I have any share in your
18 affection, welcome him as you would myself. And if he did you any
19 injury or owes you anything, charge it to my account. I, Paul, am
writing this with my own hand. I will make payment, not to mention
20 that you are indebted to me for your very self. Yes, brother, do me
this favor in the Lord. Comfort my heart in Christ.

CONCLUSION

21 Confident of your compliance, I am writing you, knowing full
22 well that you will do more than I ask. At the same time make ready
to welcome me as a guest, for I have hopes through your prayers of
being restored to you.
23, 24 Epaphras, my fellow prisoner in Christ Jesus, Mark, Aristarchus,
Demas, Luke, my fellow workers, greet you.
25 The grace of the Lord Jesus Christ be with your spirit. Amen.

11. The name Onesimus means "useful."
12. Some important witnesses here add: "Welcome him."

THE EPISTLE TO THE HEBREWS

Apart from some doubts expressed unofficially in the West before the fourth century, the traditional Catholic view has always maintained the Pauline authorship of the Epistle to the Hebrews, at least in the sense that it was conceived by St. Paul and written under his direction. Its thought is Pauline and much of its phraseology is also distinctly Pauline. The style, however, is definitely superior to that of St. Paul

The prevailing view of present-day Catholic critics is that expressed in the third century by Origen: "This is my opinion: the views expressed are those of St. Paul, but the choice and arrangement of words are the work of someone else who wished to recall and edit as in a commentary what he had heard from his teacher. . . . But who actually wrote it is, I think, something that is known to God alone."

The Epistle was probably written at Rome about A.D. 63, shortly after St. Paul's release from his first Roman imprisonment. The Epistle was directed to the Jewish Christians of Palestine, who under the stress of trials were in danger of relapsing into Judaism.

To strengthen the Christians against this temptation and to deepen their attachment to their faith, the author describes most eloquently the eminent superiority of the new dispensation over the old. Inaugurated by the Son of God himself, this new dispensation was God's final public revelation to man. It completed the message of the prophets, and brought to perfection all that was of permanent value in the Mosaic covenant. Such considerations were designed to strengthen the sorely tried Christians of Jewish origin in Palestine.

The death and martyrdom of St. James, beloved bishop of Jerusalem, was a severe blow to the faithful. A certain Theobouthis, according to Eusebius, disappointed that he had not become St.

563

James's successor, troubled the Christian community of Palestine with heretical doctrines. The rebels, known as *sicarii* (cutthroats), roamed abroad in the land and terrified the people with their ruthless murders.

In such circumstances the Christians became discouraged and some were tempted to abandon their Christian faith. They needed a moving and convincing presentation of the splendor of their faith and its superiority to the old Jewish religion. Such is the thesis of this Epistle.

The old dispensation was given by the ministry of angels through the medium of Moses, but the new came directly from Jesus Christ, who, as the Son of God, is superior to the angels (1:4–2:18) and to Moses (3:1–4:13). The priesthood of Christ is more excellent than that of the old dispensation and the sacrifice which Christ offered once for all is incomparably more excellent than that of the Old Law.

Interspersed with these arguments are pleas to cling to the Christian faith and warnings against apostasy. The author concludes with a strong plea for faith in imitation of the Old Testament heroes and with other practical exhortations.

THE DIVISION OF THE EPISTLE TO THE HEBREWS

The superiority of the new dispensation over the old, 1:1 to 10:18.
    Christ is a superior mediator, 1:1 to 4:13.
    Christ is a superior high priest, 4:14 to 7:28.
    We have a superior covenant, 8:1–13.
    The superiority of Christ's sacrifice, 9:1 to 10:18.
Exhortations, 10:19 to 13:17.
    Exhortation to persevere in the faith, 10:19 to 11:40.
    Exhortation to other virtues, 12:1 to 13:17.
Conclusion, 13:18–25.

THE EPISTLE OF

ST. PAUL THE APOSTLE

TO THE HEBREWS

CHRIST IS A SUPERIOR MEDIATOR

CHAPTER 1

CHRIST IS SUPERIOR TO THE ANGELS

In many fragmentary and varying utterances, God spoke of old 1
to our ancestors through the prophets; at the present time, the 2
final epoch, he has spoken to us through his Son, whom he has
appointed heir of the universe. Through him, too, he made the
world. This Son is the radiant reflection of God's glory, and the 3
express image of his nature, conserving all things by his mighty
command. After he had cleansed us from sin, he took his seat at the
right hand of the Majesty on high, since he had become superior 4
to the angels in that he had inherited a rank surpassing theirs. To 5
which of the angels, in fact, did God ever say,

>"You are my son,
>   today have I become your Father?"

or again,

>   "I will be to him a Father
>   and he shall be to me a Son?"

Further, when he introduced his first-born into the world, he says, 6

>"And let all God's angels adore him."

1:2. *final epoch:* the birth of Christ divided all time into two periods, that
of expectation, the former epoch, and that of fulfillment, the final epoch lasting
until the end of the world. Ps. 2:7; 2 Kings 7:14.

1:3. *conserving:* literally, "carrying" or "supporting." St. Chrysostom: "governing"; St. Gregory of Nyssa: "bringing into existence"; others: "carrying along
and directing."

1:6. Deut. 32:43. (LXX); Ps. 96:7.

7 Of the angels he says,
> "He makes his angels winds
> and his ministers flames of fire."

8 But of the Son,
> "Your throne, O God, stands for ever and ever,
> and the scepter of your kingdom
> is a scepter wielded in equity.
9 You have loved justice and hated iniquity;
> therefore God, your God, has anointed you
> in preference to your associates
> with the oil that brings gladness."

10 And,
> "You, O Lord, in the beginning established
> the earth,
> and the heavens are the work of your hands.
11 They will perish, but you remain;
> And they will all grow old like a cloak;
12 like a mantle you will roll them up,
> and they will be changed.
> But you continue the same
> and your years will have no end."

13 Did he ever say to anyone of the angels,
> "Sit at my right hand,
> until I make your enemies the stool
> of your feet?"

14 Are they not all spirits in the divine service, commissioned to serve those who are to inherit salvation?

CHAPTER 2

EXHORTATION TO FIDELITY

1 Therefore we must give the closest attention to the teachings

---

1:7. God makes the angels winds and flames of fire either in the sense that he has put them in charge of these elements, or as St. Augustine and St. Gregory the Great say, that he has given to these pure spirits the subtlety of wind and the ardor of fire.
1:8 f. Ps. 44:7 f.
1:10–12. Ps. 101:26–28.
1:13. Ps. 109:1.

we have heard, lest perhaps we should drift away. Surely if the 2
message transmitted by angels proved valid, and every transgression
and disobedience received a just punishment, how shall we escape 3
if we neglect such a wonderful salvation? It was first announced by
the Lord and later guaranteed to us by those who heard him. God 4
also gave added testimony in signs and wonders and various miracles
and gifts which the Holy Spirit distributed as he wished.

CHRIST, THE HEAD, SUFFERED FOR HIS BROTHERS

Certainly it was not to angels that God subjected the world to 5
come, of which we are speaking. Rather, someone has testified 6
somewhere.

"What is man that you are mindful of him,
    or the son of man that you have regard for him?
For a little while you have made him lower than the angels, 7
    you have crowned him with glory and honor,
    you have subjected all things under his feet." 8
Now in subjecting all things to him, he left nothing outside his
authority. But at the present time we do not as yet see all things
subject to him. Yet we do see Jesus — who for a little while was 9
made lower than the angels — crowned with glory and honor because
he suffered death so that he might by God's gracious bounty experience the throes of death for the sake of every human being.
In bringing many sons to glory it was fitting that he for whom and 10
by whom all things exist should by suffering raise to the heights
of perfection the author of their salvation. In fact both he who 11
sanctifies and they who are sanctified have a common origin. This is
why he is not ashamed to call them brothers, when he says,

2:2. *message:* the revelation made at Sinai. So Estius. According to Jewish
tradition, God made use of angels to communicate with Moses.

2:5. *world to come:* the Christian dispensation or Messianic period, so called
because of the long period of hopeful waiting for Christ's coming, and also because
the perfect fulfillment of the Messianic promises will be realized only in the
next life. So Medebielle.

2:6. Ps. 8:5–8.

2:7. Some Greek manuscripts add: "And have set him over the works of
your hands."

2:9. Another possible translation: "We do see Jesus, who for a little while
was made lower than the angels in order to suffer death that he might by
God's gracious bounty taste death for everyone."

2:11. *have a common origin:* i.e., probably, in the father of the human race,

12   "I will declare your name to my brothers;
          in the midst of the assembly I will sing your praises."
13   And again,
          "I will put my trust in him";
      And again,
          "Here am I, and my children whom God has given me."
14   Therefore, because his children have blood and flesh in common, he
      in like manner partook of these that through death he might destroy
15   him who had control over death, that is, the devil, and deliver
      those whom throughout their lives the fear of death held in bondage.
16   Now, of course, it is not to angels that he is extending a helping
      hand, but it is to the offspring of Abraham that he extends this
17   helping hand. That is why he should in every respect become like
      his brothers, that he might become a merciful and faithful high
      priest in matters pertaining to God and so expiate the sins of the
18   people. Since he himself has suffered and been tempted, he is able
      to bring aid to those that are tempted.

CHAPTER 3

CHRIST IS SUPERIOR TO MOSES

1   Therefore, holy brothers, partakers of a heavenly calling, consider
2   Jesus, the apostle and high priest of the faith we profess. How
      faithful he was to him who appointed him, as was Moses in every
3   part of God's household. Yet Jesus was deemed worthy of greater
      glory than Moses, just as the builder of a house has greater honor
4   than the house. Every house is built by someone, but God is the
5   builder of the universe. Now Moses was faithful in every part of
      God's household as a servant, destined to bear witness to what was to
6   be spoken later; Christ, however, is faithful as Son over his own

---

Adam. So Estius. The statement refers to Christ's human nature only. According
to St. Chrysostom this common origin is in God, the father of all.
   2:12. Ps. 21:23.
   2:13. 2 Kings 22:3; Ps. 17:3; Isa. 8:18.
   3:1. *apostle:* i.e., delegate or envoy sent by God.
   3:2. God's household was in pre-Christian times the Israelite nation. Now
it is the new Israel, the historical development of the synagogue, the Church
which includes all the faithful, whether they are Jews or Gentiles.
   3:6. *to the end we hold fast:* omitted in some important manuscripts.

household. We are that household, provided that to the end we hold
fast to our confidence and the hope in which we glory.

Therefore, as the Holy Spirit says, 7
"If today you hear his voice,
  do not harden your hearts 8
  as when your fathers provoked me
  on the day of tempting in the desert,
where they put me to the test, 9
although they had seen for forty years 10
  what I had done.
For this reason I was very angered with that generation,
  and said, 'always their hearts go astray,
  since they have not understood my ways.'
As I have sworn in my wrath, 11
They shall never enter my Rest."

Beware, brothers, lest perhaps there should be in any of you an 12
evil, unbelieving heart, leading you to apostatize from the living
God. Therefore exhort one another every day, while it is still Today, 13
that none of you may be hardened by sin's deceitfulness. For we 14
have been made partakers of Christ, provided we hold fast our first
confidence in him to the end, as long as the appeal is made. 15
"Today if you hear his voice,
  Do not harden your hearts as when
   they provoked me."

Who was it, I ask, that heard and yet gave provocation? Was it not 16
all that came from Egypt under Moses' leadership? With whom was 17
God very angered for forty years? Was it not with those that sinned,
whose corpses fell in the desert? To whom did he swear that they 18
should not enter his Rest, but to those who were unbelieving? So 19
we see that they could not enter because of unbelief.

CHAPTER 4

OUR HEAVENLY REST

As long, therefore, as the promise of entering his Rest still holds 1

3:7. Num. 14:21–23; Ps. 94:8, 11.
3:8. Literally, "in the contradiction, on the day of tempting." The Hebrew:
"at Meriba, on the day of Massa."
3:13. Today: The present life as contrasted with the tomorrow of eternity.

2 good, let us fear lest any of you should be judged a failure. The
Good News, you know, was given to us just as to them. But the
message they heard was of no use to them, because those that heard
3 put no faith in it. We believers certainly enter that Rest, as he
has said,

> "As I have sworn in my wrath,
> They shall not enter my Rest."

Yet his works were completed as soon as the world was established.
4 What he has spoken somewhere of the seventh day proves it,

> "God rested the seventh day from all his works";

5 and again in this passage,

> "They shall not enter my Rest."

6 Since, therefore, it remains for some to enter it, and those who first
received the Good News did not enter on account of disobedience,
7 God designates a new day, Today, when he says a long time later
in the psalm of David, as already quoted,

> "Today, if you hear his voice,
> do not harden your hearts."

8 Certainly if Josue had given them rest, God would not speak after-
9 wards of another day. So then, there is reserved a Sabbath Rest for
10 the people of God. In fact, whoever enters God's Rest, also rests from
11 his labors as did God from his. Let us, therefore, make every effort
to enter that Rest, in order that no one may fall by giving the same
12 example of disobedience. For the word God speaks is living and
effective and sharper than any two-edged sword. It penetrates to the
division of soul and spirit, of joints and marrow, and discerns the
13 thoughts and intentions of the heart. And no creature is hidden
from him: all things are laid bare and are uncovered to the eyes
of him to whom we have to render account.

4:3. Ps. 94:11.
4:4. Gen. 2:2.
4:12. The divine word (*logos*) or decrees are irresistible and infallibly produce
their effect. They penetrate the inmost recesses of our being, described as soul
(the sensitive part) and spirit (the spiritual faculties, intellect and will of man),
joints and marrow, a figurative way of expressing the all-pervasive force of the
divine will. So Estius. This word discerns and judges because it is one with
the divine knowledge. Some of the Fathers thought that the *logos* here described
is the same as in the prologue of the Fourth Gospel. But the context does
not well suit that explanation.
4:13. *we have to render account*: or "concerning whom we speak" or "with
whom we have to do."

CHRIST IS A SUPERIOR HIGH PRIEST

CONFIDENCE IN OUR HIGH PRIEST

Since then we have a great high priest, who has penetrated the 14
heavens, Jesus, the Son of God, let us hold fast to the faith we
profess. We do not have a high priest incapable of sympathizing with 15
our weaknesses. He has experienced them all, just as we, yet without
sinning. Let us, therefore, confidently draw near to God's throne, 16
the source of grace, that we may obtain mercy and find grace to
aid us when we need it.

CHAPTER 5

CHRIST IS OUR HIGH PRIEST

In fact every high priest is chosen from among men and appointed 1
to serve men in what concerns the worship of God. He is to offer
gifts and sacrifices in expiation of sins. He knows how to deal 2
gently and bear with the ignorant and wayward, since he too is
enveloped with weakness. For this very reason he is bound to offer 3
sacrifices in expiation of his own sins as well as of those of the
people. Moreover a man does not arrogate to himself this dignity, 4
but is called to it like Aaron. Similarly Christ did not seek for 5
himself the glory of becoming the high priest, but God said to him:

> "You are my Son;
>
> today have I become your Father."

So too he says in another place, 6

> "You are a priest forever
>
> after the manner of Melchisedech."

Jesus, when he had a mortal body, offered prayers and supplications 7
with piercing cries and tears to him who was able to save him from
death, and he was heard because of his reverent piety. Son though 8
he was, he learned obedience through what he suffered, and after 9
he had been raised to the heights of perfection, he became to all

---

5:5. Ps. 2:7.

5:7. The object of Christ's prayer was not to be delivered from death, but
rather to accomplish the divine will, even though it should require death to
which the sensitive appetite of Christ had a strong aversion. St. Thomas refers
this prayer to Christ's word on the cross: "My God, why have you forsaken me?"

5:9. *heights of perfection*: i.e., moral perfection attained through his heroism;
perfection as priest, since he merited all grace for mankind and gives us the

10 who obey him the cause of eternal salvation, since God had proclaimed him a high priest after the manner of Melchisedech.

THEIR DULLNESS OF PERCEPTION

11 On this point we have much to say, and it is difficult to explain,
12 because you have grown dull of perception. Whereas by this time you ought to be teachers, you need someone to instruct you in the rudiments of God's oracles. You have become such as have need of
13 milk instead of solid food. Whoever is fed on milk is unskilled
14 in the doctrine that teaches holiness; he is but a child. Solid food is for full grown men.

CHAPTER 6

GO FORWARD

1 Therefore, let us leave the elementary teaching concerning Christ and advance to things more perfect. Let us not again lay a foundation which consists in repentance from lifeless deeds, in faith in God,
2 in the teaching on various kinds of baptism, in the laying on of
3 hands, in the resurrection of the dead and eternal judgment. And this advance we will make if God permits.

DO NOT SLIP BACK INTO APOSTASY

4 Really it is impossible to bring back to a state that leads to repentance those who were once enlightened, who have relished the
5 heavenly gift, and have become partakers of the Holy Spirit, who have relished the sweetness of God's word, and the marvelous powers
6 of the messianic era, and then have become apostates. Why? Because as far as lies in their power they again crucify the Son of God
7 and expose him to mockery. For example, ground that drinks in the frequent rainfalls, and produces useful vegetation for those by
8 whom it is cultivated, shares in God's blessing. But land that produces thorns and thistles is worthless; a curse hangs over it; it is destined finally to be destroyed by fire.

---

assurance of sympathetic understanding of our difficulties; perfection of glory in his Ascension and position at the right hand of the Father in heaven. So Medebielle.

6:1. *lifeless deeds:* i.e., serious sins, devoid of merit and incompatible with the supernatural life of grace. So St. Thomas.

6:4. *impossible:* because the apostate in discarding the faith removes the only basis on which repentance can rest.

HAVE COURAGE

Although we speak in this strain, yet in your case, dearly beloved, 9 we are convinced that there will be better results that give promise of salvation. God is not unjust, he will not forget what you have 10 done, and the love you have shown for his sake in the services you have rendered and continue to render to the saints. But we 11 ardently long for everyone of you to show the same earnestness toward the full development of your hope until the end. Thus you 12 will not become sluggish, but will imitate those who through faith and patience come into the possession of the promised blessings.

CERTAINTY OF OUR HOPE

In fact, when God gave his promise to Abraham, he swore by 13 himself — there was none greater by whom to swear —

"Surely I will bless you, 14
Surely I will multiply you."

Thus encouraged, Abraham, after a long period of patient waiting 15 obtained the fulfillment of the promise. Men swear by one who is 16 greater than themselves, and an oath is a guarantee for them that puts an end to all controversy. In this way God wished to show 17 more convincingly to the heirs of the promised blessings the irrevocable character of his plan; he intervened with an oath. Thus by 18 two irrevocable assurances, where deceit on the part of God is impossible, we have great encouragement to take refuge in a firm grasp on the hope set before us. It is an anchor for the soul. Sure 19 and steadfast it passes beyond the inner veil, where Jesus has entered 20 as a forerunner on our behalf, having become forever a high priest after the manner of Melchisedech.

CHAPTER 7

MELCHISEDECH WAS GREATER THAN ABRAHAM

It was this Melchisedech, king of Salem, priest of the most high 1 God, who met Abraham as he returned from the slaughter of the

---

6:14. Gen. 22:16.
6:18. *two irrevocable assurances:* i.e., the promise and the oath.
7:1. Gen. 14:17–20.

2 kings, and blessed him. To him Abraham gave a tenth part of all the spoils. Melchisedech was, in the first place, as his name means, King of Justice, and in the second place, King of Salem, that is, 3 King of Peace. He had no father, no mother, no genealogy. He had neither beginning of days nor end of life. He was the perfect type of the Son of God, and continues a priest forever.

MELCHISEDECH WAS SUPERIOR TO LEVI

4 Now consider how great this man is. To him even Abraham, the 5 Patriarch, gave a tenth of his choice spoils. Those of the sons of Levi who receive the priestly office have, according to the Law, an order to levy tithes on the people, that is, on their brothers, 6 although these also are descendants of Abraham. But this man, who was not a member of their race, received tithes from Abraham, and 7 blessed him who had received the promise. Now it cannot be denied 8 that the inferior is blessed by the superior. Moreover, here mortal men receive tithes, but there is one who, as it is testified, continues 9 to live. Finally if I may so speak, even Levi, the recipient of tithes, 10 has them levied against him in the person of Abraham, since he was yet unborn when Melchisedech met his father.

LEVITICAL PRIESTHOOD WAS IMPERFECT

11 If then perfection had been realized by means of the Levitical priesthood — in dependence on which the people received the Law — what further need would there have been for another priest after the manner of Melchisedech to appear on the scene? And what need would there have been to say that he is not 12 after the manner of Aaron? Now a change of priesthood necessarily 13 involves a change of law also. In fact he to whom these words were addressed belongs to another tribe, from which no member has ever 14 served at the altar. It is quite obvious that our Lord took his origin from Juda, a tribe about which Moses spoke not a single word

---

7:3. *no father*, etc.: Melchisedech is introduced in Genesis abruptly with no mention of his birth, parentage, or death. As far as Genesis' testimony goes, he was eternal. This literary eternity makes him an apt figure of Christ who was in the real order all that Melchisedech was in the purely literary order. Our Lord was without father as man, without mother as God, without beginning or end of days, and without genealogy as God. So Estius.

7:8. *testified*: only negatively, as Genesis makes no mention of his birth or death.

relative to priests. This becomes even more obvious, if, after the 15
pattern of Melchisedech, another priest appears on the scene, who 16
has become a priest not in virtue of a law of carnal descent, but in
virtue of an imperishable life. The following testimony proves it, 17

> "You are a priest forever
> after the manner of Melchisedech."

THE PRIESTHOOD OF CHRIST REPLACED IT

On the one hand an earlier code is set aside because it was weak 18
and useless, since the Law made nothing perfect. On the other hand, 19
there is introduced a better hope, which brings us near to God.

CHRIST IS A PRIEST BY DIVINE OATH

To the extent that this transaction was made with an oath, 20
to that extent Jesus became surety of a superior covenant. The others 22
in fact were made priests without any oath; in the case of Jesus 21
there intervened the oath of him who said to him,

> "The Lord has sworn
> and will not change his mind,
> 'You are a priest forever.'"

Furthermore, the other priests were numerous, because death pre- 23
vented their continuing in office, but he, because he continues 24
forever, has an imperishable priesthood. Consequently he is able 25
at all times to save those that come to God through him, living
always, as he does, to make intercession on their behalf.

CHRIST IS A SINLESS AND PERFECT HIGH PRIEST

Such was certainly the high priest that fitted our needs, holy, 26
innocent, undefiled, set apart from sinners, and exalted higher than
the heavens. He has no need of offering sacrifice day by day, as do 27
the other high priests, first for their own and then for the people's
sins. He did this once for all, when he offered himself. The Law in 28
fact appoints men subject to weakness as high priests, while the

---

7:17. Ps. 109:4.

7:21. Ps. 109:4. For a better translation, verse 22 has been put before verse 21.

7:27. *once for all:* the sacrifice of the Mass is the same sacrifice as that offered by Christ on Calvary, in that there is the same victim and the same priest. The Mass externalizes and renders visible the eternally enduring sacrifice of the cross; only the manner of offering is different.

oath, coming after the Law, is so worded that it appoints the Son
who has attained everlasting perfection.

We Have a Superior Covenant

Chapter 8

1   Now the main point in what we are saying is this: we have
just that kind of high priest. He has taken his seat at the right
2   hand of the divine Majesty's throne in heaven. There in the sanctuary
and the true tabernacle, which the Lord, and not man, has erected,
3   he carries on priestly functions. To this every high priest is appointed
— to offer gifts and sacrifices. He too then must have something to
4   offer. Now if he were still on earth, he would be no priest at all,
since there are already those who offer gifts according to the Law.
5   Such priests' worship is a mere shadowy outline of the heavenly
realities, according to the oracle addressed to Moses when he was
about to finish the tabernacle: "See," said God, "that you make
everything according to the model shown you on the mountain."

CHRIST IS MEDIATOR OF A SUPERIOR COVENANT

6   But now he has obtained a superior priestly function, inasmuch
as he is mediator of a more excellent covenant, enacted on the basis
7   of more excellent promises. In fact, if that first covenant had been
8   faultless, no place would have been sought for a second. But God
really finds fault with the Israelites when he says,
"See, days are coming, says the Lord,
when I will conclude a new covenant with the
house of Israel
and with the house of Juda,
9   Not like the covenant I made with their fathers
the day I took them by the hand
to lead them out of the land of Egypt.
Since they did not remain faithful to my covenant,
I, for my part, neglected them, says the Lord.

8:5. Exod. 25:40.
8:8 ff. Jer. 31:31–34; Hebr. 10:16.

576

This is the covenant that I will make 10
   with the house of Israel
   after those days, says the Lord;
I will put my laws into their minds
   and write them on their hearts;
   I will be their God,
   and they shall be my people.
No longer will fellow citizens have to teach one another, 11
   or brother his brother, saying 'Know the Lord,'
Because all, from the least to the greatest,
   shall know me.
I will forgive their iniquities 12
   and I will no longer remember their sins."
By speaking of "a new covenant" God declares the former obsolete; 13
and what is obsolete and old is on the verge of disappearing.

SUPERIORITY OF CHRIST'S SACRIFICE

CHAPTER 9

THE EARTHLY TABERNACLE

Of course the former covenant had regulations for worship and 1
the earthly sanctuary. A tabernacle was arranged in the front part 2
of which were the lampstand, the table, and the showbread; this
is called the Holy Place. Behind the second veil was the part called 3
the Holy of Holies. It had a golden altar of incense and the ark 4

8:10. *I will put,* etc.: the new covenant or religion will be interior and spiritual, although outwardly expressed in rites and symbols; it will introduce into the soul the light of faith and sanctifying grace, the source of holy living and union with God. So Medebielle.

8:11. *No longer:* the idea is that the new religion will diffuse supernatural knowledge far and wide; it will be readily available to all who desire it. This, however, does not dispense with the necessity of an official body of teachers, entrusted with the office of speaking authoritatively in the name of God.

9:2. *showbread:* literally, "the presentation of the loaves." Twelve loaves of freshly baked bread, especially prepared and renewed every Sabbath, were kept constantly before the Holy of Holies to symbolize the consecration of the twelve tribes to the Lord, and to indicate that they were to live constantly in his presence.

9:4. *It had:* the altar of incense was not actually behind the veil in the Holy of Holies. The author does not say so. His language, which is somewhat vague, can be interpreted to mean that the altar of incense was connected

of the covenant completely covered with gold. In the ark was a golden urn which contained the manna, the rod of Aaron which had
5 budded, and the tablets of the covenant. Above the ark there were the cherubim, ministering to the Glory and overshadowing the mercy-seat. At present there is no reason to speak of these things in detail.

A TYPE OF THE HEAVENLY SANCTUARY

6   Such then were the arrangements. The priests enter at all times
7 into the front part of the tabernacle to perform their ritual, but into the rear part the high priest alone enters but once each year, and that with blood which he offers for his own and the people's
8 sins of ignorance. The Holy Spirit signifies by this that the way into the Holy Place is not open as long as the first tabernacle main-
9 tains its standing. This is a figure of the present time, in that the gifts and sacrifices offered are incapable of perfecting the conscience
10 of the worshipers. These offerings with their foods and drinks and various ablutions are but outward regulations temporarily imposed until the time of reformation.

CHRIST THE HIGH PRIEST AND VICTIM

11   But when Christ, high priest of the messianic blessings, appeared, he entered once for all through the greater and more perfect tabernacle not made by human hands, that is, not of earthly origin.
12 It was not the blood of goats and calves but his own blood that was the means of his entering the Holy Place and securing eternal
13 redemption. Now if the blood of goats and calves and the sprinkled ashes of a red cow sanctifies the defiled and results in outward
14 cleansing, how much more will the blood of Christ — he who through his eternal spirit offered himself unblemished to God —

---

closely with the ark (cf. 3 Kings 6:22; Exod. 40:5) as an integral part of the liturgical furnishings. The best sources place this altar outside the Holy of Holies.
   9:5. *ministering to the Glory:* literally, "of the Glory." The two figures of cherubim with their wings outstretched above the ark formed what was regarded as the throne of God, here designated as *Glory.*
   9:8. *Holy Place,* i.e., heaven. The *present time* (verse 9) probably designates the pre-Messianic epoch when the closed Holy of Holies, symbol of heaven, indicated that the Mosaic sacrifices were powerless to win entrance into heaven for mankind.
   9:11. *Messianic blessings:* literally, "blessings to come." Other ancient authorities: "Blessings that have come."

cleanse our own conscience from lifeless deeds and fit it for the worship of the living God?

REDEMPTION FROM TRANSGRESSIONS

And this is why he is the mediator of a new covenant and died *15* for redemption from the transgressions committed under the former covenant, in order that those who have been called may receive the eternal inheritance which had been promised. Now when there *16* is a will, the death of the testator must be established, since a will *17* takes effect only in case of death; it has no force as long as the testator lives.

THE BLOOD OF VICTIMS IN THE OLD COVENANT

This is why even the first covenant was not inaugurated without *18* bloodshed. When all the commandments contained in the Law had *19* been proclaimed by Moses to all the people, he took the blood of calves and goats with water and scarlet wool and hyssop and sprinkled the book itself and all the people. At the same time he said,   *20*
> "This is the blood of the covenant,
>   which God has made obligatory for you."

In the same way he also sprinkled the tabernacle and all the vessels *21* used in worship. In a word, the Law would have all things purified *22* with blood; unless blood is shed there is no remission.

CHRIST WAS OFFERED ONCE

It was therefore necessary that the copies of the heavenly realities *23* should be cleansed by these means, but the heavenly realities themselves by sacrifices superior to these. Why? Because it is not into a *24* Holy Place made by human hands, a mere type of the genuine, that Christ has entered, but into heaven itself, where he now presents himself in the presence of God on our behalf. And it was not that *25* he might offer himself many times, as does the high priest with blood other than his own. Why, in that case Jesus must have *26*

9:20. Exod. 24:3–8.

9:23. cleansed: in speaking of the cleansing of heavenly realities, the author does not imply that heaven had been defiled by sin. It was affected, however, by sin to the extent that sin had closed its gates to mankind. The effectiveness of Christ's sacrifice reached even to heaven and opened its gates to mankind. So St. Thomas.

suffered over and over again from the time of the world's foundation.
But now once and for all in the final epoch he has presented
27 himself to abolish sin by his sacrifice. And just as it is appointed
28 for men to die once and then to undergo judgment, so also was
Christ offered only once to bear the sins of the multitude; at his
second appearance he will not deal with sin, but will bring salvation
to those who await him.

CHAPTER 10

EFFICACY OF CHRIST'S ONE SACRIFICE

1   In fact, the Law by means of the same sacrifices offered year by
year has no power whatever to bestow lasting perfection on those
who have recourse to it. Why? Because it possesses merely the
shadow of the messianic blessings, not the full expression of their
2 reality. Otherwise the worshipers would have given up offering
them, since they would have been once and for all cleansed, and
3 would no longer have the least consciousness of sin. Yet in these
4 sacrifices there is year after year a reminder of sin. Clearly it is
5 impossible for the blood of bulls and goats to take away sins. For
this reason at his entrance into the world Christ says,
> "Sacrifice and oblation you did not wish,
>> but you have fitted together a body for me.
6 >> You took no pleasure in burnt offerings
>> and sin offerings.
7 >> Then I said, 'Here I am; I have come
>> to do your will, O God,'
>> as it is written in the roll of the book."
8 After he had said, "Sacrifices and oblations and burnt offerings and
sin offerings you did not wish, and took no pleasure in them" —
9 offerings prescribed by the Law — he then said, "Here am I; I
have come to do your will." He thus abolishes the former to
10 establish the latter. It is in virtue of this "will" that we have been
sanctified through the offering once for all of the body of Jesus Christ.

9:28. *offered only once:* the offering endures eternally and is renewed and
made visible in the Mass.
10:5. Ps. 39:7 f.

ITS ETERNAL EFFECTS

Moreover, every other priest stands day after day performing 11
his priestly functions and offering over and over again the same
sacrifices which are powerless ever to take away sins. But this priest 12
offered but one sacrifice for sins, takes his seat forever at the right
hand of God, and from then on waits for his enemies to be made 13
the stool under his feet. By a single offering he has perfected for- 14
ever those who are sanctified. Such too is the testimony of the 15
Holy Spirit, for after saying,

> "This is the covenant that I will make with them   16
>   after those days, says the Lord:
> I will put my laws into their hearts,
>   and I will engrave them on their minds."

he adds,

> "Their sins and their iniquities I will   17
>   remember no longer."

But when these have been remitted, no longer is there need of an 18
offering for sin.

EXHORTATION TO PERSEVERE IN THE FAITH

FIRST MOTIVE: THE JUDGMENT TO COME

Therefore, brothers, we have confident access to the Holy Place, 19
thanks to the blood of Jesus, by following the new and living path 20
which he has opened for us through the veil — I mean his flesh; and 21
we have a high priest in charge of the house of God. So let us 22
draw near with a sincere heart, in full assurance of faith, with our
hearts purified from an evil conscience, and with our bodies washed
in pure water. Let us cling without faltering to the hope which we 23
profess, for he who has given us the promise is faithful. And let 24
us take thought for one another in view of rousing one another to
acts of love and good deeds. Let us not forsake our own assembly, 25
as some are in the habit of doing, but encourage one another, all
the more as you see the Day drawing near.

10:20. *living path:* the path of grace, the life of the soul. *through the veil:*
the humanity of Christ by its immolation opened heaven, the real holy place,
to all mankind. This opening of heaven was symbolized by the rending of the
veil which shut off the typical Holy Place in the temple at Jerusalem. See Mt.
27:51.

26 Why? Because if we go on sinning willfully after having received
the full knowledge of the truth, no longer is there in reserve a sacri-
27 fice for sins. Nothing is left but a dreadful expectation of judgment,
28 a fierce fire which will devour God's adversaries. A person who sets
at naught the Law of Moses is shown no pity and is put to death
29 on the testimony of two or three witnesses. Of how much more
severe punishment, do you not think, will he be judged worthy who
tramples underfoot the Son of God, deems profane the sanctifying
blood of the covenant, and outrages the Spirit who bestows grace.
30 We surely know who has said,
                "Vengeance is mine, I will repay,"
And again,
                "The Lord will judge his people."
31 It is a dreadful thing to fall into the hands of the living God.

SECOND MOTIVE: MEMORIES OF THEIR PAST

32 Call to mind the early days when, after you had been enlightened,
33 you had so much to combat and endure, now being exposed as a
public spectacle to reproaches and afflictions, again making common
34 cause with those so treated. For example, you had compassion on
prisoners and gladly welcomed the plundering of your property,
realizing that you had a better possession, and that too an abiding
35 one. Do not therefore throw away your confidence, since it has a
36 great reward. Of patience, indeed, you have need, that, having
done the will of God, you may receive the promised reward:
37   "For yet a very little while,
                and he who is to come will come,
                and will not delay.
38   But my holy one shall live by faith.
                But if he shrinks back,
                my soul has no pleasure in him."
39 As for us we are not of those who shrink back and thus go to
destruction, but of those who keep the faith and thus save our souls.

10:26. *sinning willfully*: by rejecting the faith. The first step toward this
apostasy consists in forsaking the assembly, i.e., the public worship held in the
Christian churches.

CHAPTER 11

THIRD MOTIVE: FROM THE OLD TESTAMENT

Faith is the foundation of the blessings for which we hope, the 1
proof of the realities which we do not see. It is because they had 2
this faith that the men of old won a favorable testimony. By faith 3
we understand that the world was fashioned by God's word in such
a way that what is visible has an invisible cause.

By faith Abel offered to God a sacrifice richer than Cain's. 4
Through that faith he received testimony that he was holy, since
God bore testimony in favor of his gifts. And through his faith,
dead though he is, he still speaks.

By faith Henoch was taken up so that he did not see death; and 5
he was not found because God had taken him. Indeed, before he
was taken it had been attested that he pleased God. Without faith 6
it is impossible to please God, since whoever comes to God must
believe that he exists and rewards those that seek him.

By faith, Noe, after he had been divinely warned about dangers 7
as yet unseen, reverently prepared the ark for the safety of his family.
By faith he condemned the world, and was made heir of the holiness
that is won by faith.

By faith Abraham obeyed the divine call, and departed for a 8
country which he was to receive as his property; moreover, he
departed without knowing where he was going. By faith he so- 9
journed in the Promised Land as in a foreign country, where he
lived in tents, as did Isaac and Jacob, heirs with him of the same
promise. Why? Because he was awaiting the city with foundations 10
whose architect and builder is God.

11:1. foundation: or "substance" or "firm expectation." The preferable rendering seems to be that of the text above. Faith is that which supplies an unshakable
foundation to those things for which we hope, such as the resurrection of the
body and an eternity of happiness in the vision of God. So St. Chrysostom.

11:3. invisible cause: i.e., God. Other renderings: "so that visible things
were not made from visible things," i.e., the world did not cause itself; "visible
things were made from invisible things," the invisible things being, according
to St. Thomas and others, the ideas or plans of created things which existed
from eternity in the divine mind.

11:4–38. The records of the heroes of Israelite history here alluded to will
be found in the books of Genesis, Exodus, Josue, Judges, Kings, and Machabees.

11   By faith Sara, too, received the power to conceive, in spite of
having passed the time of life for it, because she deemed him
12   faithful who had made the promise. And so from one man, as good
as dead, sprang issue as numerous as the stars of heaven, and as
countless grains of sand along the seashore.

13   It was in faith that these people died without realizing the
fulfillment of the promise. They only saw and greeted from afar
the promised blessings, while admitting that they were but foreigners
14   and travelers on earth. Those that so speak show clearly that they
15   are in search of a homeland. Surely if they had in mind the country
16   they had left, they would have had means to return to it. But, as
it is, all their yearnings are directed to a better, a heavenly homeland.
This is why God is not ashamed to be called their God; he has
prepared a city for them.

17   By faith Abraham, when he was put to the test, offered Isaac. He
18   who had received the promise, he to whom it had been said, "Of
Isaac issue will be born to you," was on the point of sacrificing his
19   only-begotten. He reasoned that God has power to raise men from
the dead. Thus Abraham got back his son, who was to serve as
a type.

20   By faith Isaac blessed Jacob and Esau concerning even messianic
21   blessings. By faith Jacob on his deathbed blessed each of Joseph's
sons and bowed in worship, supporting himself on the top of his
22   staff. By faith Joseph at the end of his life made mention of
the departure of the sons of Israel and gave orders concerning
his burial.

23   By faith Moses' parents because of the child's beauty kept him
hid for three months after his birth without fearing the king's edict.

24   By faith Moses when he had grown up renounced the title of the
25   son of Pharao's daughter. He preferred a share in the hardships of
God's people to the enjoyment of the fleeting pleasures of sin.
26   With his eyes fixed on the reward he held reproaches suffered for
the anointed greater riches than all the treasures of the Egyptians.
27   By faith he left Egypt with no fear of the king's wrath. Like one
28   seeing the unseen, he did not flinch. By faith he observed the

11:19. Isaac was a type foreshadowing Christ immolated on Calvary and then
rising from the dead. So, many of the Fathers.
11:26. *the anointed*: i.e., God's Chosen People, Israel.

Passover and the sprinkling of blood, that the destroyer of the
first-born might not touch his first-born.

By faith the Israelites crossed through the Red Sea, as through   29
dry land, although the Egyptians who attempted to cross were
drowned. By faith the walls of Jericho collapsed after they had been   30
encircled for seven days.

By faith Rahab the harlot escaped from perishing with the rebels   31
because she gave a peaceful welcome to the spies.

And what more shall I say? Time would fail me to tell of   32
Gedeon, Barac, Samson, Jepthe, David, and Samuel, and the
prophets, who by faith conquered kingdoms, enforced justice, had   33
promises realized, stopped the mouths of lions, put out raging fires,   34
escaped the edge of the sword, became strong when they were weak,
grew valiant in battle, routed invading armies. Women recovered   35
their dead children brought back to life. Others in the hope of rising
to a better life were beaten to death rather than accept release.
Others endured bitter mockery and scourging, yes, even chains and   36
imprisonment. They were stoned, they were sawed asunder, they   37
were put to death by the sword. They went from place to place,
clothed in sheepskins and goatskins, destitute, distressed, mistreated.
The world was not worthy of them. They wandered about seeking   38
refuge in deserts, hills, caves, and holes in the ground.

These all, to whom their faith had borne favorable testimony,   39
did not receive the promised blessings, because God, holding better   40
blessings in reserve for us, would not have them reach perfection
apart from us.

EXHORTATION TO OTHER VIRTUES

CHAPTER 12

THEIR HEROISM INVITES US TO PERSEVERE

This is why we too, surrounded as we are by such a throng of   1

11:37. *sawed asunder:* after these words many ancient authorities add: "they
were tempted."

11:40. *perfection:* probably a reference to the perfection which will come
to the elect at the end of the world when glorified body and soul will be
forever reunited.

witnesses, should cast off every encumbrance that weighs us down, especially sin, which so easily entangles us. Let us eagerly throw ourselves into the struggle before us, and persevere, with our gaze fixed on Jesus, the pioneer and perfect embodiment of confidence. He, in view of the joy offered him, underwent crucifixion with contempt of its disgrace, and has taken his seat at the right hand of God's throne. Meditate on him who in his own person endured such great opposition at the hands of sinners; then your souls will not be overwhelmed with discouragement.

4 Your resistance in the struggle against sin has not yet gone as
5 far as bloodshed, and have you forgotten the exhortation addressed to you as sons?

"My son, do not make light of the Lord's discipline,
      and do not get discouraged when he reprimands you.
6   Why, the man whom he loves the Lord disciplines,
      and everyone whom he accepts as his son he chastises."

7   It is to discipline you that you are exposed to suffering. God treats you as sons. Is there a son that is not disciplined by his father?
8   If then you were without discipline, the common lot of all, you
9   would be illegitimate children and not genuine sons. If we respected our earthly fathers when they disciplined us, shall we not much more willingly submit to the Father of our spiritual selves and so have life?
10 They disciplined us for a short time as they saw fit, but he disciplines
11 us for our benefit that we may share his holiness. All discipline, it is true, for the moment seems painful rather than joyful, but later it produces the fruit of serenity in an upright life for those who have been trained by it.

12, 13 So stiffen your slack hands and tottering knees. Make straight paths for your feet. Then lame joints will not be dislocated, but rather healed.

14 Strive for peace with all men, and for that holiness without which
15 no one will see the Lord. Watch carefully that no one lose aught of

---

12:1. *easily entangles*: the meaning of the Greek word, which occurs nowhere else in Scripture, is doubtful. The sense here given is suggested by St. John Chrysostom who also proposes the alternative: "is so easily avoided." Others render: "clings so closely."

12:2. *confidence*: our Lord gives us the perfect example of trust in God. He was sure that God would deliver him as man from his executioners and bring him back in triumph to life and glory.

12:5. Prov. 3:11.

God's grace, that no bitter root spring up, cause trouble, and defile
the majority of you. Watch that no impure or irreligious person 16
like Esau arise who for a single meal sold his birthright. You know 17
well that afterward when he sought to have the blessing allotted to
him, he was rejected and had no chance for a change of heart,
although he had sought the blessing with tears.

FOR OURS IS A SUPERIOR COVENANT

You have not come to a mountain that may be touched, to a 18
flaming fire, to black clouds and a thunderstorm, to a resounding 19
trumpet and to a voice so speaking that those who heard it begged
that it speak no further word to them. Why? Because they could 20
not stand the order given, "If even a beast touches the mountain,
it is to be stoned." The spectacle was indeed so terrifying that 21
Moses said, "I am overcome with fear and trembling." But you have 22
come to Mount Sion, to the city of the living God, the heavenly
Jerusalem, to countless angels, to the festive gathering and assembly 23
of the first-born who are enrolled in heaven, to God, the judge of
all men, to the spirits of just men made perfect, to Jesus the 24
Mediator of the new covenant, to the sprinkled blood that speaks
more eloquently than Abel's. Be on guard that you do not resist him 25
that speaks, because if they did not escape who resisted him that
spoke oracles on earth, much less shall we escape if we reject him
that speaks oracles to us from heaven. Then his voice shook the 26
earth but now he has given his promise,

"Yet once again I will shake
not only the earth but heaven also."

These words "yet once again" announce the removal of what has 27
been shaken since it is but created, and so what is unshaken will
remain. Therefore let us hold fast to grace because we are on the 28
point of receiving an unshakable kingdom. By means of that grace

---

12:15. *bitter root:* i.e., any person who would have a bad influence.
12:17. *change of heart:* i.e., either on the part of Esau who could not bring
himself to the dispositions which genuine repentance demands, or on the part
of Isaac, who refused to retract the blessings already bestowed on Jacob.
12:18. *mountain:* omitted by many authorities.
12:22. *to countless angels:* or "to the festive gathering of countless angels."
12:26. Agg. 2:7.
12:28. *grace:* or "gratitude."

we offer to God acceptable worship, blended with piety and rever-
29 ence. Our God, you know, is a consuming fire.

CHAPTER 13

CHARITY AND CHASTITY

1, 2   Persevere in brotherly love. Do not forget the duties of hospitality.
In its exercise some have entertained angels without knowing it.
3   Be mindful of prisoners, as though you were prisoners with them,
and of those who are ill-treated, since you too continue liable to
4   ill-treatment. Let marriage be held in the fullest honor and let the
marriage bed be undefiled, because God will condemn those that are
immoral and adulterous.
5   Keep your manner of life free from avarice; be content with what
you have. Has not God said,
"I will never abandon or forsake you?"
6   In complete trust then we can say,
"The Lord is my helper;
I have nothing to fear
What can man do to me?"

LOYALTY TO CHRIST AND SUPERIORS

7   Remember your superiors, since it was they who spoke the word
of God to you. Consider closely the happy issue of their lives, and
8   imitate their faith. Jesus Christ is the same yesterday, today, and
9   forever. Do not be led astray by various strange doctrines. It is better
to make the heart steadfast by grace than by foods which failed to
10 profit those that used them. We have an altar from which those in
11 the service of the tabernacle have no right to eat. In fact the bodies
of the expiatory victims whose blood is carried by the high priest into
12 the sanctuary, are burned outside the camp. It is for the same
reason that Jesus whose blood was to sanctify the people, suffered
13 outside the gate. Therefore, let us go to him outside the camp,
14 bearing the same reproaches as he. Here indeed we have no lasting
15 city; but we are in search of the city that is to come. Through him

---

13:3. *liable to ill-treatment:* literally, "in the body" and therefore subject to
ill-treatment.
13:6. Ps. 117:6.

then let us continually offer to God a sacrifice of praise, that is, the
fruit of lips that acknowledge his name. Do not forget to do 16
good and to share what you have, since God is well pleased with
such sacrifices.

Obey your superiors and be subject to them, since they keep 17
watch over your souls, mindful that they will have to render account.
Then they will do this joyfully and not with deep sighs. This would
not be advantageous for you.

Conclusion

Pray for us. Assuredly we are confident that we have a good 18
conscience, and are resolved to act uprightly in every respect. But 19
I especially beg your prayers that I may be restored to you the sooner.

May God, the source of peace, who by the blood of the eternal 20
covenant has brought back from the dead the great Shepherd of
the sheep, our Lord Jesus, fit you for the fulfillment of his will 21
through the performance of every kind of good deed, by effecting
in us through Jesus Christ what is well pleasing in his sight. To him
be glory for ever and ever. Amen.

I exhort you, brothers, to bear with these words of exhortation. It 22
is but a short letter I have written you. I must let you know that 23
Timothy has been set free. If he comes soon, he and I together
shall see you. Greet all your superiors and all the saints. The 24
brothers from Italy send you greetings. Grace be with all of you. 25
Amen.

13:24. *from Italy:* may mean either that the brothers' place of origin from
which they are now absent is Italy, or that the brothers send greetings from Italy.

THE EPISTLE OF ST. JAMES

This and the six Epistles following it in the New Testament are known as *Catholic*, i.e., universal. This name has been traced back to early ecclesiastical writers such as Eusebius, Origen, and St. Jerome. The explanation of this name is found in the fact that these Epistles, except 2 and 3 John, are addressed to a much wider circle of readers than are the Pauline Epistles. St. Paul's letters are addressed to individuals or to particular congregations, whereas the Catholic Epistles are in the nature of encyclicals addressed to the whole Church.

St. James the Less, the author of the first Catholic Epistle, was the son of Alphaeus or Cleophas (Mt. 10:3). His mother Mary was a sister or close relative of the Blessed Virgin, and for that reason according to the usage of the day, St. James was called a brother, i.e., a relative, of the Lord. St. James held a prominent position in the early Church. He was a witness of the Resurrection of Christ (1 Cor. 15:7); St. Paul (Gal. 2:9) describes him as a "pillar" of the Church. He was present and played a prominent part in the meeting at Jerusalem about A.D. 49 (Acts 15:4). He held the post of Bishop of Jerusalem and was martyred for the faith in the year 62.

The theme of the Epistle is that the faith must be lived, not merely believed in a theoretic way. The faith is not a speculative creed; it is also a code of conduct. Faith that fails to regulate the conduct of the believer is sterile, dead, worthless. This main idea underlies all the teaching of the Epistle. The advice on putting faith into practice (1:22–25), on the nature of true religion (1:26–27), on partiality (2:1–3), on the control of the tongue (3:1–12), on the exercise of brotherly love (4:11; 5:9), and on zeal for the conversion of sinners (5:19–20) presents so many practical applications of faith to daily life.

St. James also wished to encourage his readers in their trials by proposing the hope of recompense in the life to come for the good and of adequate punishment for the wicked.

The Epistle was written from Jerusalem sometime before 62 and was addressed to Jewish Christians in various parts of the world.

THE DIVISION OF THE EPISTLE OF ST. JAMES

Introduction, 1:1.
Exhortation to patience in trials, 1:2–18.
The need of a living and active faith, 1:19 to 2:26.
The dangers of teaching, 3:1–18.
Concord among Christians, 4:1–17.
Final admonitions, 5:1–20.

THE EPISTLE OF

ST. JAMES THE APOSTLE

CHAPTER 1

GREETINGS

James, servant of God and of the Lord Jesus Christ, to the 1
Jewish Christians dispersed throughout the world: greetings.

EXHORTATION TO PATIENCE IN TRIALS

Consider it genuine joy, my brothers, when you are engulfed by 2
trials of various kinds, since you know that the trying of your faith 3
makes for patience. And let patience accomplish a perfect work, 4
that you may be perfect, flawless, and without shortcoming.

If, however, any of you lacks wisdom, he should ask it of God, who 5
gives to all simply and with never a word of reproach, and wisdom
will be given to him. But he should ask with faith, with no hesita- 6
tion. He who hesitates is like a wave of the sea that is driven and
tossed to and fro by the wind. Certainly such a person, double 7, 8
minded as he is and fickle in his whole conduct, should never imagine
that he will have a single request granted by the Lord.

The brother in a lowly condition should glory in his exaltation, 9
and the rich man in his lowliness, because he will pass away as the 10
bloom of a plant. The sun rises with a scorching wind and parches 11
the plant. Its bloom droops and its beautiful appearance is ruined.
So too will the rich man vanish with his pursuits.

1:1. *Jewish Christians:* literally, "the twelve tribes of the Dispersion." Commentators commonly agree that the phrase refers to Jewish Christians outside
the Holy Land. The New Testament basis for this interpretation is the statement that the Christian Church constitutes the new Israel. Gal. 3:7–9; 1 Pet.
2:9–10; Gal. 4:26–29.

1:2. *trials:* principally the persecutions to which the Jewish converts were
subjected by their fellow countrymen.

1:9. *in his exaltation:* in the dignity to which faith has raised him, like
Paul "in the Lord" (2 Cor. 10:17). *in his lowliness:* in his own nothingness
before God, like Paul (2 Cor. 12:9).

1:11. *with a scorching wind:* others translate "with burning heat."

12   Blessed is the man who patiently endures trial, because after he
has withstood the trial, he will receive the life-giving crown, which
the Lord has promised to those that love him.

THE WORK OF THE PASSIONS AND THAT OF GOD

13   No one should say when he is tempted, "I am tempted by God."
It is a fact that God cannot be tempted by evil, and that he tempts
14   no one. Rather each individual is tempted by his own passion,
15   inasmuch as he is allured and enticed by it. Then passion conceives
and gives birth to sin; and when sin has grown to maturity, it brings
forth death.

16, 17   Do not be deceived, my beloved brothers. None but a good gift,
none but a perfect donation comes from above. It comes down from
the Creator of the heavenly luminaries. With him there is no varia-
18   tion or shadow resulting from movement. Of his own free will he
begot us by the true teaching, that we might, so to speak, be the
first fruits of his creatures.

NEED OF A LIVING AND ACTIVE FAITH

HEARING AND KEEPING GOD'S WORD

19   You know this, my beloved brothers. Everyone should be quick
20   to listen, slow to speak, slow to get angry. By anger man does not
21   achieve the holiness that God requires. For this reason you should
forsake every trace of defilement, every remnant of malice. Meekly
embrace the teaching planted within you; it has the power to save
22   your souls. Carry it into action; do not be a mere listener. Other-
23   wise you deceive yourselves. If anyone listens to the doctrine and
does not carry it into action, he is like a man who looks into a mirror
24   at the face nature gave him. He looks at himself, yes, but then goes
25   his way, and at once forgets what he looks like. But he who has
looked carefully into the perfect law that imparts liberty, and

---

1:13. In the preceding verses, St. James speaks of the trials of Christians
which come from without. Now he begins to discuss those that arise from
within us, either from the temptations of the devil or from our fallen nature.
So St. Bede.
1:17. *shadow:* produced by the movement of the heavenly luminaries.
These shadows are night and eclipses. God, the eternal light, knows no setting,
no eclipse. He is always the same. So Chaine.

observes it, who is not one that listens and forgets, but puts it into practice, this type of person is to be congratulated for observing it.

If anyone thinks himself religious without controlling his tongue, 26 he deceives himself. That man's religion is worthless. Religious prac- 27 tice pure and undefiled before God our Father is this: to care for orphans and widows in their affliction, and to keep oneself from being tainted by the world.

Chapter 2

NO PARTIALITY TOWARD THE RICH

My brothers, do not practice your faith in our glorious Lord Jesus 1 Christ with partiality. For instance, suppose a man in fine clothes 2 and wearing a gold ring on his finger enters your assembly, and then a poor man in shabby clothes enters. Now if you show deference to 3 the one dressed in fine clothes and say, "Take this place of honor," but say to the poor man, "Stand there," or "Sit by my footstool," are 4 you not inconsistent with yourselves, and are you not judging on bad principles?

Listen, my beloved brothers. Has not God chosen those who are 5 poor in the eyes of the world to be rich in faith and heirs of the kingdom which he promised to those that love him? You, however, 6 dishonor the poor man. Is it not the rich that oppress you, and drag you before courts? Is it not they that heap abuse on the noble 7 name to which you are dedicated?

But if you fulfill the royal law, which according to the Scriptures 8 reads, "Love your neighbor as yourself," you do well. If, however, 9 you show partiality, you commit a sin, and are convicted by the law as transgressors. Why, whoever observes the whole law, but errs in 10 one point, becomes blameworthy in regard to its every precept. Why? 11 Because he who said, "Do not commit adultery," also said, "Do not kill." Now if you do not commit adultery but kill, you have become a transgressor of the law.

2:4. *inconsistent:* literally, "judge," by preferring one to another on trivial, purely extrinsic grounds. The meaning should be determined in the light of 1:6, where the same word is translated "hesitate." Here the person hesitates between the principles of the world and those of the faith. He gives preference to worldly principles, and thus is inconsistent with his religious principles.

12 Speak and act as men who are to be judged by the law that
13 imparts liberty. In fact judgment without mercy will be meted out
to him who has shown no mercy. The merciful man will exult victoriously when he is judged.

TRUE FAITH IS A PRACTICAL FAITH

14 Of what good is it, my brothers, if a man says he has faith but
15 has no corresponding deeds? Can such faith save him? If a brother
16 or a sister has no clothes or daily food, and one of you says to them,
"Go and be at peace; warm yourselves and eat plenty," yet does not
give them the things that are necessary for the body, of what good
17 is it? So too faith if it does not express itself in deeds, has no
life in it.
18 Someone may argue, "You have faith, and I have deeds." Prove
to me your faith without deeds, and I shall prove to you my faith
19 by the evidence of my deeds. Do you believe that there is one God?
In that you do well. Even the demons believe, yet they tremble
in terror.
20 But do you wish to know, senseless man, that faith without deeds
21 is useless? Was not Abraham justified by deeds when he offered up
22 Isaac, his son, on the altar? You see that faith worked together
23 with his deeds; his faith was made perfect by his deeds. And so
the Scripture was fulfilled which says, "Abraham believed God, and
it was reckoned to him as holiness, and he was called 'God's
24 friend.'" You see, a man is justified by deeds, and not merely by
25 faith. So also, was not even Rahab, the harlot, justified by deeds,
when she extended hospitality to the messengers and sent them out
26 by another way? Really, just as the body without the soul is lifeless, so also faith without deeds is lifeless.

2:13. *will exult victoriously when he is judged:* literally, "will boast greatly
over judgment." This statement is based on the promise of our Lord (Mt.
7:1-3).

2:14-18. In this section St. James insists that faith alone without the good
deeds it dictates is insufficient for salvation. He does not contradict St. Paul,
who insists that the deeds prescribed by the Mosaic Law will not make a man
holy. St. Paul himself repeatedly demands holy living in addition to faith.

2:18. It is impossible, argues St. James, to prove that a man has faith unless
it produces corresponding deeds. The existence of faith without deeds is not
denied, but such a sterile faith is not merely valueless; it is impossible even
to prove its existence. So Chaine.

The Dangers of Teaching

Chapter 3

CONTROL OF THE TONGUE

Not many of you should set yourselves up as teachers, my *1*
brothers, since you know that we shall undergo a more severe
scrutiny. We all commit many faults. If a person does not com- 2
mit faults in speech, he is perfect and capable of controlling his
whole body. Now if we put bits into horses' mouths to make them 3
obey us, we direct their whole bodies. Consider ships also. Large 4
as they are and driven by strong winds, yet by means of a very
small rudder they are steered wherever the will of the pilot deter-
mines. So too the tongue is a small member, yet it can boast of 5
great achievements. See how great a forest is set ablaze by a very
small fire. The tongue is a fire; it makes wickedness attractive. 6
Among our members it is the tongue that defiles the entire body and
sets on fire the whole course of our life, as the tongue in turn is
set on fire by hell.

Human ingenuity is able to tame and has tamed every kind of 7
wild beast and bird, reptile and sea animal; but no man can tame 8
that restless evil, full of deadly poison, the tongue! With it we 9
bless the Lord and Father, and with it we curse men who are made
in the image of God! Out of the same mouth come blessing and 10
cursing. It is not right, my brothers, that it should be so. Does the 11
spring gush forth fresh and bitter water from the same outlet?
Can a fig tree, my brothers, produce olives, or a grapevine, figs? 12
Neither can salt water produce fresh water.

3:6. *it makes wickedness attractive*: literally, "ornament of wickedness." The
tongue, i.e., the human speech, directed by a perverse mind, seeks to excuse
sin, to make it alluring. Isidore of Pelusium mentions this as a possible interpretation. Others translate: "world of iniquity," which Zorell explains, "the
instrument and occasion of all kinds of evil." Others explain: "the perverse
world . . ." The tongue is so harmful that it represents in an eminent degree
the world, that force of wickedness which is opposed to the conquests of
Christian sanctity. So Charue. *the whole course of our life*: literally, "the wheel
of our nature (or birth)," a symbol of life's constant rotation of joy and sorrow,
of good and bad fortune.

597

DANGER OF FALSE WISDOM

13 Who among you is wise and experienced? He should prove by his conduct that his deeds are done in meekness proper to wisdom.
14 But if you have bitter jealousy and a spirit of strife in your hearts,
15 do not boast and so prove false to the truth. Such is not the wisdom that comes from above. On the contrary it is earthly,
16 animal, devilish. Wherever jealousy and a spirit of strife exist, there
17 is disorder and every vile practice. On the other hand, the wisdom from above is especially guileless, but also peaceable, indulgent, docile. It is merciful to the highest degree and fruitful in good deeds.
18 It is devoid of partiality and hypocrisy. The holiness that wisdom brings forth works in peaceful conditions and is planted by peacemakers.

CONCORD AMONG CHRISTIANS

CHAPTER 4

THE PASSIONS CAUSE DISCORD

1 What is the source of quarrels and disputes among you? Is it not sinful pleasures continually battling in your bodily members?
2 You desire something but you do not get it; so you commit murder. You are jealous but cannot obtain what you covet, so you quarrel and fight. You do not attain what you desire, because you do not
3 pray. And if you do pray, you do not receive what you request because you pray with the wrong intention, namely, of squandering
4 what you receive on sinful pleasures. You disloyal people, do you not know that friendship with the world means enmity with God? Whoever, therefore, wishes to be a friend of the world makes himself
5 an enemy of God. Or do you suppose that the Scripture utters empty words when it says that the soul which God made to dwell

---

3:17. *partiality:* the meaning of the Greek word is doubtful. Other possible translations: "not judging," "without dissimulation," "without remorse of conscience."

4:4. *disloyal:* literally, "adulterers." The union between God and his people is in a familiar biblical image compared to a marriage. Infidelity or disloyalty to God in keeping with this image is called adultery.

4:5. St. James probably cites freely from memory, and so it is difficult to determine what passage of Scripture he has in mind. Perhaps Gen. 6:5. Other translations proposed for this passage are: "The Spirit whom God has

in us has jealous desires? But he gives greater grace. For this reason 6
the Scripture says, "God resists the proud, but gives grace to the
humble." Submit, therefore, to God; but resist the Devil, and he 7
will flee from you. Draw near to God, and he will draw near to you. 8
Wash your hands, you sinners, and purify your hearts, you double-
minded people. Afflict yourselves and mourn and weep. Turn your 9
laughter into mourning, and your gaiety into gloom. Humble your- 10
selves before the Lord, and he will exalt you.

AVOID PRESUMPTION

Do not talk against one another, brothers. He who talks against 11
a brother or passes judgment against him, talks against the law and
passes judgment against the law. But if you are a judge of the law,
you are not an observer of it. There is one Lawgiver and Judge, 12
he who can save and destroy. But you who judge your neighbor,
who are you?

Come now, you who say, "Today, or tomorrow, we will go and 13
spend a year in such and such a city, carry on business, and make
money," when you do not know what tomorrow will bring. 14
Why, what is your life? You are but a puff of smoke that appears for
a little while and then disappears. You should rather say, "If it is 15
the Lord's will, we shall be alive and do this or that." As it is, you 16
are complacent in your boasting. All such complacency is evil.
Whoever, therefore, knows how to do good but leaves it undone is 17
guilty of sin.

FINAL ADMONITIONS

CHAPTER 5

WARNING TO THE UNJUST RICH

Come now, men of wealth, weep and howl over your impending 1
afflictions. Your wealth has rotted; your clothes are moth-eaten. 2

---

made dwell in us loves us jealously" or "God yearns jealously for the soul
which he has made dwell within us." The translation in the text above is
preferred by Estius and others. The first alternative is that of St. Bede and
others; the second is that of the majority of commentators. Old Testament
passages which St. James may have had in mind are Gen. 20:8 or Gen. 2:7;
4:6; Prov. 3:34.

3 Your gold and silver have rusted, and their rust will give evidence
against you and will feed on your flesh as does fire. You have laid
4 up treasures for the last days. Mark my words: the wages of which
you have defrauded the workmen who mowed your fields cry aloud,
and the cries of the reapers have reached the ears of the Lord of
5 Hosts. You have led a soft life on earth and have indulged in
pleasure. You have fed yourselves well for the day of slaughter.
6 You have condemned, you have murdered the innocent man, even
though he is not your adversary.

COUNSELS FOR THE AFFLICTED

7 Be patient, then, brothers, until the coming of the Lord. Think
how the farmer waits for the precious crop of the land. He is patient
8 with it until the fall and spring rains come. You, too, should be
patient; strengthen your hearts, because the coming of the Lord is
9 near. Do not complain against one another, brothers, that you may
10 not be judged. Remember the Judge stands at your gates. Brothers,
take as models of patience in hardships the prophets who spoke
11 in the name of the Lord. See how we call them blessed for having
remained patient. You have heard of Job's patience, and you know
the outcome brought about by the Lord, because the Lord is full
12 of mercy and compassion. But above all, my brothers, do not swear,
either by heaven or by earth, or by any other oath. Rather let your
Yes really be Yes, and your No really No, that you may not fall
under condemnation.

LAST ANOINTING, CONFESSION, PRAYER

13 Is anyone of you in trouble? He should pray. Is anyone cheerful?
14 He should sing a psalm. Is anyone of you sick? He should call in the
presbyters of the Church, and have them pray over him, while they
15 anoint him with oil in the name of the Lord. That prayer, said
with faith, will save the sick person, and the Lord will restore him

---

5:4. *Lord of Hosts:* or "armies," i.e., the heavenly luminaries and perhaps
also the angelic spirits.
5:6. *the innocent man:* St. Bede and others refer this to the passion and
death of our Lord. Others, more probably in view of the context, refer it
to any poor man unjustly oppressed by the rich.
5:7. *fall and spring rains:* literally, "the early and later rains."
5:14. According to the Council of Trent, St. James here promulgates the
sacrament of Extreme Unction.

600

to health. If he has committed sins, they will be forgiven him.
So confess your sins to one another, and pray for one another that   16
you may be healed. The fervent prayer of a holy person is very
powerful. Elias was a man like us, subject to the same weaknesses.   17
He said an earnest prayer that it might not rain upon the land, and
it did not rain for three years and six months. He prayed again, and   18 ↑
rain fell from heaven, and the land brought forth its crops.

CONVERT THE SINNER

My brothers, if any of you strays from the true rule of conduct   19
and someone brings him back, let him know that whoever brings   20
a sinner back from his erroneous way, will save the sinner's soul
and will win the forgiveness of many sins.

5:20. *will win the forgiveness*: literally, "will cover," a Hebrew idiom meaning
forgiveness. The sins forgiven may well be those of both the converted sinner
and of the one who leads him to conversion. So St. Bede.

THE FIRST EPISTLE OF
ST. PETER THE APOSTLE

St. Peter, originally called Simon, was a native of Bethsaida in Galilee (Jn. 1:42–44), but he had settled in Capharnaum (Mk. 1:21). He was married (Mk. 1:30) and plied the trade of fisherman (Mt. 4:18). He and Andrew, his brother, had been drawn to the lower Jordan valley by the Baptist's preaching. There he was introduced to Jesus the Messias. Jesus looked with favor on his future vicar and changed his name to Peter (Rock). Peter then followed Jesus into Galilee (Jn. 1:42–43) and was present for the wedding at Cana (Jn. 2:2). Later he became a disciple of Jesus (Lk. 5:1 ff.) and was chosen as an Apostle (Lk. 6:12–16). Jesus promised to make him his vicar (Mt. 16:17–19). More than once he was signally honored by our Lord (see especially Mk. 5:37 f.; 9:1 f.; 14:33 f.). More than once he acted as spokesman for the other Apostles (Mt. 15:15; 16:18; Lk. 12:41; Jn. 6:69). After the Resurrection, Jesus solemnly made Peter the head of his Church on earth (Jn. 21:15–17), and after the Ascension Peter immediately took over as Primate of the Church and Vicar of Christ (Acts 1:15 f.; 2:14–41; 3:1–5, 12 ff.; 10:1–18; 15:1 f.). After the martyrdom of James the Great, he miraculously escaped from prison and left for some unnamed place (Acts 12:17), possibly Rome. But he returned to Jerusalem and presided at the meeting in 49/50 (Acts 15). Then he spent some time in Antioch (Gal. 2:11 f.). It is historically certain that St. Peter also was in Rome where he endured martyrdom, either in A.D. 64 or 67, during the reign of Nero.

This Epistle was written from "Babylon" (5:13), which according to the Fathers and nearly all commentators is a symbolic name for Rome. It was addressed to Gentile Christians in Asia Minor, who were being persecuted and oppressed by their pagan neighbors (2:12; 3:6; 4:4; 4:14) and had fallen into a number of un-Christian practices (2:11 f.; 4:2 f.). They were in danger of relapsing into paganism (1:7; 3:14; 4:12; 5:7, 12). When St. Peter learned of this situation, he wrote them the present letter of encouragement in their trials, of warning against the dangers to which their faith was exposed, and of exhortation to remain steadfast in their hope of heavenly reward.

THE DIVISION OF THE FIRST EPISTLE OF ST. PETER

Introduction, 1:1–12.
General counsels for holiness, 1:13 to 2:10.
Particular counsels for conduct, 2:11 to 4:19.
Counsels for the community, 5:1–11.
Conclusion, 5:12–14.

THE FIRST EPISTLE OF

ST. PETER THE APOSTLE

INTRODUCTION

CHAPTER 1

GREETINGS

Peter, apostle of Jesus Christ, to those who dwell as strangers 1
scattered throughout Galatia, Cappadocia, Asia, and Bithynia. You 2
have been chosen according to the foreknowledge of God the Father
to be brought by the sanctifying action of the Spirit to submission to
Jesus Christ, and to be sprinkled with his blood. Grace and peace be
yours in abundance.

THANKSGIVING FOR GOD'S MERCY

Blessed be God the Father of our Lord Jesus Christ! Through 3
his great mercy he has begotten us anew to a living hope through
the resurrection of Jesus Christ from the dead. This hope is directed 4
to the inheritance imperishable, flawless, unfading, reserved for you
in heaven. God's power guards you through your faith for the 5
salvation that is held in readiness to be revealed at the end of time.
Because of this you experience steadfast happiness, even though now 6
for a little while you must be afflicted by various trials, that your 7
faith more precious than perishable, fire-tried gold, after it has withstood the test, may be found worthy of praise, glory, and honor at
the moment of Jesus Christ's manifestation. You love him though 8

1:2. *sprinkled:* by this figurative expression St. Peter declares that the believer is through Baptism made a partaker of the merits of Christ which he
won for us by the shedding of his blood on the cross. The expression is taken
from Exod. 24:8, where we read that the Sinaitic covenant was sealed by the
sprinkling of the blood of the sacrificial victims.

1:3. *living hope:* i.e., solidly grounded and therefore exercising a vital influence on those who have it. So Holzmeister. Or hope is living because it is
directed to the full and perfect life of heaven. So Charue.

1:5. *salvation:* the Christian already possesses salvation in germ. Its full
effects will be realized only at the end of time with the resurrection of the body.

you have not seen him. If you go on believing in him, though at present you do not see him, you will exult with unspeakable and
9   heavenly joy when you attain the reward of your faith, the salvation of your souls.
10   Into this salvation the prophets, who prophesied of the grace
11   which was meant for you, inquired and examined. They examined as to what date and what circumstances the Spirit of Christ within them was indicating, when he predicted the sufferings reserved for Christ
12   and the manifold glory which would follow. It was revealed to them that not for themselves but for you they received the mission to foretell these things. They have now been proclaimed to you by those who announced the Good News to you through the heaven-sent Holy Spirit. The angels long to pore over the realization of these predictions.

GENERAL COUNSELS FOR HOLINESS

EXHORTATION TO HOLINESS AND REVERENCE

13   For this reason, keeping your minds clear of distractions and living austerely, place your hope entirely in the grace that is to be
14   brought to you when Jesus Christ will be manifested. As obedient children do not conform yourselves to the evil desires which ruled
15   you when you were in ignorance. On the contrary, after the model of the Holy One who called you, become yourselves holy in your
16   entire conduct. So it is written, "You shall be holy, because I am holy."
17   And if you call upon him as Father who judges each one impartially according to his deeds, let your conduct during the time
18   of your sojourn be motivated by reverence. You know well that not with perishable things, such as silver or gold, were you redeemed from the worthless manner of living you inherited from your fathers,
19   but with the precious blood of Christ, that unblemished and spotless
20   Lamb. He was foreknown, indeed, before the foundation of the

---

1:13. *keeping your minds clear:* literally, "keeping your mental loins girded." The long, flowing garments of St. Peter's time were gathered up and held by a belt so as not to impede travel or work. Progress in the spiritual life requires a similar mental discipline by which distracting thoughts are held in check, so that the mind may remain fixed on our eternal goal.
1:16. Lev. 11:4; 19:2; 20:7.

world, but appeared in the final period of the world for your sake. Through him you are believers in God who raised him from the 21 dead and gave him glory, so that your faith and hope are centered in God.

EXHORTATION TO BROTHERLY LOVE

You have purified your souls by submission to the truth that 22 you might have a sincere brotherly love. Therefore, fervently and unaffectedly love one another from the bottom of your heart, because 23 you have been born anew, not from a perishable, but from an imperishable life-germ, through the living and eternal word of God. In contrast, all things human are like a plant, and all their glory 24 like the bloom of a plant. The plant withers, and its bloom droops, but the Lord's word endures forever. Such is the Good News which 25 was announced to you.

CHAPTER 2

EXHORTATION TO PROGRESS

Put away, then, all malice, all deceit, hypocrisy and envy, and 1 all slander. As newborn babes long for the unadulterated spiritual 2 milk, so that you may grow up to salvation in the Lord. You have 3 already tasted how sweet he is. Draw near to him, the living stone, 4 rejected indeed by men, but chosen and honored by God. You 5 also, as living stones, are being built into a spiritual edifice, so as to be a holy priesthood to offer up spiritual sacrifices which will be

---

1:23. *life-germ:* sanctifying grace, imparted to the soul by the saving and eternal word of God, in other words by Christianity which is the power of God to save every believer.

2:2. *spiritual milk:* the doctrine of Christ. The better it is known, the more perfect is the neophyte's assimilation and union with Christ.

2:3. *tasted:* experienced the delights of life in union with Christ and of all the blessings that come with that union. They may be a reference to Holy Communion.

2:5. *a holy priesthood:* Adam says: "There are three sacraments which give the Christian his fixed and definite place within the body of Christ, his fundamental relation to the whole body, and thereby to the high-priesthood of Christ which supports and pervades the whole. They are the sacraments of Baptism, Confirmation, and Holy Orders. Each of these imparts . . . an abiding religious character, whereby the soul is incorporated in the high-priesthood of Christ in a greater or less degree according to the nature and substance of the sacrament. The highest form of this sacramental incorporation . . . is the

6 acceptable to God through Jesus Christ. Because of that the following stands in Scripture:
        "See, I place a cornerstone in Sion, chosen, honored.
        He who believes in him shall not be put to shame."
7 This honor, therefore, is for you who believe; but for those who
   do not believe he is
        "a stone which the builders rejected.
        It has been made the chief cornerstone.
8   Over it men stumble and trip."
   Such indeed is the destiny of those who stumble in unbelief of the
9 message. You, however, are a chosen race, a royal priesthood, a holy
   nation, a people that is God's possession, that you may proclaim the
   excellence of him who called you out of darkness into his marvelous
10 light. You who had not obtained mercy have now obtained mercy.

PARTICULAR COUNSELS FOR CONDUCT

APOSTOLATE OF GOOD EXAMPLE

11   Beloved, I exhort you as strangers and pilgrims to abstain from
12 carnal cravings that war against the soul. See that your conduct
   among the pagans is praiseworthy, so that, as to the points on which
   they slander you as evildoers, they may come to a better appreciation
   of your praiseworthy deeds and glorify God when he grants them
   the grace of conversion.

DUTIES OF CITIZENS

13   Be submissive to every human authority for the Lord's sake;
14 whether to the king since he is supreme, or to governors since they
   are delegated by him to punish those who do evil and to praise those
15 who do good. The will of God is precisely that your virtuous lives
16 should silence foolish men who do not know true worth. Live as free
   men, yet not as those who make freedom a cloak for malice. No!

---

sacrament of Holy Orders." The priesthood of the laity comprises only a limited
number of priestly powers. Baptism and Confirmation give the Christian a
genuine participation in the priesthood of Christ, set him apart from the world,
and consecrate him for those most general acts of worship which belong to
the vocation of a child of God.
   2:6. Ps. 117:22.
   2:12. grants them: literally, "on the day of visitation," which some authorities
refer to the Day of Judgment.

Live as servants of God. Honor all men; love all the brothers; 17
reverence God; honor the king.

DUTIES OF SLAVES

Slaves should be subject and show their masters every mark 18
of respect, not only those masters who are kind and considerate, but
even those who are unreasonably exacting. In fact it is pleasing to 19
God if, mindful of him, one endures the pain of unjust suffering.
What glory is there if you patiently take a beating for having sinned? 20
But to endure suffering for having done good earns a claim on
God's favor. Really, you have been called to suffer, because Christ 21
on his part suffered for you, leaving you his example that you
might follow in his footsteps.

"He committed no sin,   22
      and no deceit was found on his lips."

When he was insulted, he did not return the insult; when he was 23
mistreated, he did not threaten, but entrusted himself to him who
judges justly. He bore our sins in his own body on the cross that 24
we, having died to our sins, might live for holiness. By his wounds
you were healed. Till then you had been straying sheep, but now you 25
have come back to the Shepherd and Guardian of your souls.

CHAPTER 3

DUTIES OF WIFE AND HUSBAND

So also, wives, be submissive to your husbands, so that, if there 1
are some husbands who refuse to obey the message, they may be won
over without the message by the conduct of their wives, when they 2
observe your chaste conduct inspired by reverence. Let not yours 3
be the outward adornment of an artistic coiffure, or of wearing gold
jewelry or putting on dresses; rather let it be the inner self, hidden 4
in the depths of the heart, that is adorned with the incorruptible

---

2:18. *Slaves:* literally, "household servants," who were nearly always slaves.
Although Christianity taught the principles whose logical application would
lead to the emancipation of slaves, a too sudden enforcement of these principles
would have brought about a disastrous social upheaval. The Apostles preferred
to wait for the leaven of Christianity gradually to permeate society and in due
time and orderly fashion to effect emancipation.
2:22 f. Isa. 53:7–9.

adornment of gentleness and tranquillity of mind. This is very
5 precious in the sight of God. In fact in this way the holy women
of old used to make themselves beautiful, by hoping in God and
6 obeying their husbands. For example, Sara obeyed Abraham and
called him lord. You are children of hers if you do what is good
and rid yourselves of every anxiety.

7   Similarly, you husbands, under the guidance of wisdom lead the
common life with your wives, the weaker sex, and honor them as
joint heirs of the blessings the Christian life imparts, so that nothing
may diminish the efficacy of your prayers.

MUTUAL DUTIES OF ALL

8 Finally, all of you should be like-minded, sympathetic, brotherly
9 in affection, full of mercy, humble. Do not return evil for evil, or
insult for insult; on the contrary, bless, because you have been called
to inherit a blessing.

10   "He who wishes to love life
                     and see happy days,
                        must keep his tongue from evil,
                        and his lips from speaking deceit.
11   He must turn away from evil and do good;
                     he must seek peace and strive for it.
12   For the eyes of the Lord are on the holy,
                     and his ears attentive to their prayers;
                     but the Lord's angry look is directed against
                        evildoers."

FAITHFULNESS IN PERSECUTION

13   And who is there that will harm you if you are zealous for what
14 is good? Even if you should suffer for justice' sake, you are blessed.
15 So neither fear threats, nor be troubled; rather reverence Christ the
Lord in your hearts. Be ready always to give an answer to everyone
16 who asks you the basis of the hope you cherish. Do this, however,
with meekness and reserve, keeping your conscience clear, so that

---

3:7. *the Christian life:* literally, "life," which is commonly understood of
the life of grace on earth or of glory in heaven. The two views differ only
slightly as the life of grace on earth is the beginning, the indispensable preparation for the life of glory.
3:10–12. Ps. 33:13–17.

when you are calumniated, those who insult your good conduct in
Christ may be put to shame. Indeed, it is better, if such be God's   17
will, to suffer for doing good than for doing evil. Christ died once   18
for sins, the Holy One in behalf of the wicked. He was put to death
as his human nature permitted, but brought back to life, as his
divine nature required, that he might lead us to God. In this divine   19
nature he went to bring the Good News in turn to the spirits that
were in prison. They had formerly been disobedient when, in the   20
days of Noe, God in his long-suffering waited while the ark was being
prepared. In that ark a few, that is, eight persons passed over the
water to safety. This water prefigured Baptism which at present   21
saves you too, not by removing filth from the body, but by asking
of God a good conscience. This request is made effective through
the resurrection of Jesus Christ, who has returned to heaven and is   22
seated at the right hand of God with the Angels, Powers, and Virtues
subject to him.

CHAPTER 4

HOLINESS THROUGH SUFFERING

Because, then, Christ suffered in his body, you on your part   1
should arm yourselves with the same ideal, namely that he who has
suffered in his body has broken with sin, so that during the time   2
left for him in this life he no longer should live according to the
lusts of men but according to the will of God. In the past you   3
wasted enough time acting after the pagan pattern, living as you did
in licentiousness, lusts, drunkenness, revelings, carousings, and immoral idolatrous practices. They think it strange that you do not   4
rush into the same cesspool of dissipation, and so they insult you.
They will render an account to him who is ready to judge the living   5
and the dead. This is why the Good News was proclaimed even   6
to the dead, that, although condemned to death in their bodies, as
is the lot of men, they might live in their souls according to God.

3:18. *divine nature:* literally, "the Spirit."
3:21. *by asking,* etc.: Baptism is a request for the cleansing of the soul from
sin and the introduction of sanctifying grace. This request derives from Jesus
Christ an intrinsic efficacy, which can only be impeded by the lack of proper
disposition on the part of the recipient or of the proper intention on the part
of the minister.

CHRISTIAN VIRTUES, ESPECIALLY CHARITY

7 The end of all things is at hand. Be prudent, then, and on the
8 alert, the better to devote yourselves to prayer. Above all things
practice constant love among yourselves; it wins forgiveness for
9, 10 many sins. Show ungrudging hospitality to one another. Each of
you should use what endowments he has received in the service of
11 others, as good stewards of the manifold bounty of God. If anyone's
endowment is eloquence, he should employ it in keeping with the
divine utterances. If anyone exercises a function of the ministry, he
should be mindful that it is effective in virtue of God's concurrence.
Thus in all things God will be glorified through Jesus Christ, to
whom belong glory and power for ever and ever. Amen.

BLESSINGS OF PERSECUTION

12 Beloved, do not be startled at the fiery ordeal which befalls
you to test you, as though something unusual were happening to
13 you. No, but rejoice to the extent that you share in the sufferings
of Christ, so that you may also rejoice and exult when his glory
14 will be revealed. Happy are you if you are reproached for the name
of Christ, for the Spirit who imparts glory, the Spirit of God, rests
15 on you. See to it that none of you suffers for being a murderer or
16 a thief or an evildoer or a meddler in others' affairs. On the other
hand, if anyone suffers for being a Christian, he should not be
17 ashamed; rather he should glorify God for that very title. The time
is here for judgment to begin with the household of God. But
if it begins with us, what will be the outcome for those who do
18 not obey the Good News that God has announced. And
"If the holy man is saved only with difficulty,
what will become of the godless and sinful man?"
19 Those, then, who suffer according to God's will in the performance
of good should entrust themselves to the Creator. He will never
fail them.

4:8. *wins forgiveness:* literally, "covers." The sins of the one who exercises
love and perhaps too of the one to whom the love is directed are forgiven.
4:11. *in keeping,* etc.: mindful of the respect the divinely revealed message
demands and of the fact that it must be the norm of orthodoxy.
4:12. *fiery ordeal:* a figure designating severe trials in general, as Holzmeister
thinks, rather than a reference to martyrdom by fire.
4:18. Prov. 11:31.

COUNSELS FOR THE COMMUNITY

CHAPTER 5

TO PASTORS

I, therefore, exhort the presbyters in your company. I myself am 1
a fellow presbyter and a witness of the sufferings of the Christ, a
partaker too in the future glory which will be revealed. Be shepherds 2
to the flock that God has entrusted to you, governing not by con-
straint but willingly, as God would have it; not for sordid gain,
but out of a sense of duty. Do not lord it over those allotted to you, 3
but be models to your flock. And when the Chief Shepherd appears, 4
you will come into unfading glory as your reward.

TO ALL

Similarly, you who are younger, should be subject to the pres- 5
byters. And all of you should clothe yourselves with humility in
your mutual dealings. As you know,
>   "God resists the proud
>   but gives his grace to the humble."

Humble yourselves, then, under the mighty hand of God, that he 6
may exalt you in due time. Cast all your anxiety on him, because 7
he takes care of you. Be sober, watchful! Your adversary, the devil, 8
like a roaring lion, prowls about looking for someone to devour.
Resist him with a firm faith, in the knowledge that you are experienc- 9
ing the same sufferings as befall your brothers all over the world.
God, the source of all grace, who has called you to his eternal glory 10
in Christ, will himself, after you have suffered a little while, perfect,
steady, strengthen, and firmly establish you. To him belongs power 11
for ever and ever. Amen.

5:1. *presbyters*: those who ruled the Church, priests in all probability. When
St. Peter calls himself a *presbyter*, he simply states that he shared the government
of the Church with them, without wishing to insinuate that he was in no way
superior to them. It is clear from many other passages in the New Testament
that he was the primate and leader of the Church's government.
5:5. Prov. 3:34.

Conclusion

12   Through Sylvanus, whom I esteem as your faithful brother, I
am sending you these few lines to encourage you and to testify that
what I have written is the true favor imparted by God. Stand fast
13 in it. The congregation that is in Babylon, chosen together with
14 you, sends you greetings, as does my son Mark. Greet one another
with a loving kiss. Peace be to all of you who are in Christ.

5:12. *true favor*: i.e., the glory of heaven and the hope which assures us of
attaining it is a result of God's gratuitous bounty.

THE SECOND EPISTLE OF
ST. PETER THE APOSTLE

This Epistle is St. Peter's farewell to his flock. It contains a fervent plea to them to cling to their precious faith and a stern warning against false teachers.

The faithful have received from God's impartial justice the gift of faith as precious as that of the Apostles. As a result of that boon, provided it is accompanied with the virtues it calls for, we are enabled to escape from the corruption of the world and become partakers of the divine nature.

St. Peter insists especially on the importance of knowing Jesus Christ, his example, and his teaching. Fully aware that his life is near its end, St. Peter would to the last call to the attention of his flock how precious is the faith that is theirs, and how they should zealously guard and strengthen it.

The Prince of the Apostles recalls what must have been one of the greatest thrills of his life, the Transfiguration, when he caught a fleeting glimpse of the glory of Christ and heard the Father from heaven attesting to the divine sonship of Jesus. That testimony is reinforced by the writings of the prophets who were God's own mouthpiece.

The faith is threatened by false teachers. St. Peter warns the faithful against them, and denounces them roundly. Among these false teachers are those who distort the meaning of St. Paul's writings, as they do the rest of Scripture.

St. Peter recalls the return of the Lord at the end of time and the destruction of the world. In view of this the faithful have every reason to lead spotless and blameless lives so that at the coming of the great Judge they may have a good and peaceful conscience.

THE SECOND EPISTLE OF ST. PETER THE APOSTLE

The Epistle was written at Rome shortly before the Apostle's martyrdom, and was addressed to the same groups to whom the first Epistle had been written.

THE DIVISION OF THE SECOND EPISTLE OF ST. PETER

Introduction, 1:1–2.
Christian virtue: its necessity and motives, 1:3–21.
Against false teachers, 2:1–22.
The second coming of Christ, 3:1–18.

THE SECOND EPISTLE OF

ST. PETER THE APOSTLE

CHAPTER 1

GREETINGS

Symeon Peter, servant and apostle of Jesus Christ, to those who 1
have received the gift of faith as precious as ours, by reason of the
impartial justice of our Lord and Savior Jesus Christ. Grace and 2
peace be yours in a measure ever increasing in proportion to your
deep knowledge of our Lord.

CHRISTIAN VIRTUE

CO-OPERATE WITH GRACE

It is a fact that his divine power has bestowed on us all needed 3
aid for our spiritual life and piety, by imparting the deep knowledge
of him who called us by his own glory and power. Through these 4
manifestations he has bestowed on us precious and very great
promises, to enable us to escape the corruption which lust causes
in the world, and become partakers of the divine nature. For this 5
reason, make every effort to supplement faith with moral courage,
moral courage with knowledge, knowledge with self-control, self- 6
control with patience, patience with piety, piety with brotherly 7
affection, brotherly affection with love.

1:1. Here as in Acts 15:14 the Hebrew name Symeon is used instead of the
Greek form Simon.

1:2. *of our Lord:* other manuscripts read: "of God and our Lord Jesus
Christ." The reading here preferred seems to be required by the singular pronoun in the next verse, and has good support in ancient versions. The more
deeply we come through meditation and contemplation to know Jesus Christ,
the greater measure of grace and peace will be ours. See Jn. 17:3.

1:3. *glory:* manifestation of Christ's glory through his miracles, especially the
Transfiguration and Resurrection. *power:* or "virtue" in the sense of moral
goodness.

1:4. *partakers:* grace so transforms our fallen natures that we share in the
divine life. Life is thought, affections, desires, acts, etc. Grace enables us to
think, love, desire, and act as does God.

1:5. If we are partakers of the divine nature, we must live accordingly and
practice the virtues here mentioned.

617

STRIVE FOR VIRTUE

8　　If you have these virtues in abundance, they will make you both active and fruitful, and bring you to the deep knowledge of our
9　Lord Jesus Christ. He who does not have these virtues is practically blind in his nearsightedness and forgetful that he has been cleansed
10　from his former sins. Consequently, brothers, strive even more to make your calling and election secure, because if you do this you
11　will never stumble. Indeed, in this way ample provision will be made for your entrance into the eternal kingdom of our Lord and
12　Savior Jesus Christ. Hence, I tried again and again to remind you of these things, even though you know them and are firmly grounded
13　in the truth you now possess. I consider it my duty to arouse you
14　by way of reminder as long as I am in this tent. I know that the time is near at hand for the removal of my tent, as also our Lord Jesus
15　Christ indicated to me. But I will also take care that after my death you may at all times have the means to recall these instructions.

CERTAINTY OF CHRIST'S RETURN

16　　We were certainly not following cunningly devised myths when we made known to you the power and coming of our Lord Jesus Christ. On the contrary, we were eyewitnesses of his majesty.
17　The fact is, he received from God the Father honor and glory when out of majestic splendor there came this voice:

"This is my beloved Son,
　　with him I am well pleased."

18　We ourselves heard this very voice as it came from heaven when we were with him on that holy mountain.

19　　We have besides the more firmly established message of the prophets. You do well to be attentive to it. It is like a lamp shining in a dark place until the day dawns and the morning star rises in

---

1:9. *cleansed:* generally understood of Baptism.

1:13. *tent:* i.e., the body, an image taken from nomad life and suggestive of the brevity of our sojourn on earth.

1:15. *means to recall:* some see here an allusion to the Gospel according to St. Mark, which contains St. Peter's instructions, but more probably the reference is to the contents of this letter.

1:17. St. Peter recalls the Transfiguration. See the account in Mt. 17:1–8.

1:19. *more firmly established:* the reference is probably to what St. Peter writes in the second chapter. To warn against false teachers and the dire

your hearts. Above all else you must realize that no prophecy of *20*
Scripture is matter for private interpretation, because no prophecy *21*
was ever produced by man's will. On the contrary, men with a
message from God spoke as they were moved to do so by the
Holy Spirit.

AGAINST FALSE TEACHERS

CHAPTER 2

THREAT OF PUNISHMENT

As there were false prophets among the people of Israel, so among *1*
you there will be false teachers, who will secretly introduce destructive errors. These teachers will go so far as to deny even the Master
who redeemed them. In this way they will bring down on themselves
swift destruction. Many will follow them in their acts of debauchery. *2*
They will draw down vile abuse on the true religion. In their greed *3*
they will exploit you with glib catchwords. Their sentence of condemnation, long since pronounced, is not meaningless, and destruction stalks them night and day.

Certainly God did not spare the angels that sinned, but hurled *4*
them into hell and committed them to dark dungeons to be guarded
until judgment. He did not spare the ancient world, yet he preserved *5*
Noe, a herald of holiness, and seven others with him, when he
brought the deluge on the world of godless men. He condemned *6*
to destruction and reduced to ashes the cities of Sodom and
Gomorrah, and set them up as an example for future godless
generations, yet he rescued holy Lot, who was weighed down by *7*
the debauched living of those lawless men. This holy man, while *8*
dwelling among them, saw and heard their lawless deeds. Day after
day this was a torment for his holy soul. The Lord, therefore, knows *9*
how to rescue the God-fearing from trial and keep the godless for
the Day of Judgment, chastising them in the meantime, but *10*

consequences of incredulity, the message of the Old Testament prophecies is
stronger than the evidence of the Transfiguration.

1:20. *matter:* a possible translation: "No prophecy of Scripture is produced
by human efforts." The prophet does not give his own but God's thoughts.

2:3. From this verse to the end of the chapter there is a very close parallel
to the Epistle of St. Jude.

especially those who live lustful lives in the defilement of passion, and who despise authority.

VICES OF THE HERETICS

11   Daring and arrogant, these men are not afraid of reviling the spirits fallen from glory, whereas their fellow angels, though greater in might and power, do not place before the Lord a reviling charge
12   against them. These men, however, like irrational animals, by nature born to be captured and destroyed, revile what they do not under-
13   stand. They too shall perish as do these animals and thus receive what their wickedness deserves. They count our daylight joy mere vulgar pleasure. They are blotches and blemishes, yielding as they do to mere sensual enjoyment when they banquet with you in their
14   love feasts. They never look on a woman except with lustful desires, and sin continually. They ensnare unsteady souls. They have hearts
15   that are trained in greed. An accursed brood! They have left the right way and have gone astray. They have followed the way of Balaam, the son of Beor, who loved the wages earned by wickedness,
16   but was rebuked for his transgressions when a dumb beast of burden, speaking with a man's voice, checked the prophet's madness.
17   These men are springs without water and clouds driven by wild
18   winds. For them the blackest darkness has been reserved, because with their pompous and meaningless discourses, by means of lustful desires and debaucheries, they ensnare persons who had barely
19   escaped from those who live in error. They promise them freedom while they themselves are slaves to corruption. The fact is, a man is the slave of whatever overcomes him.
20   If, after escaping the defilements of the world in virtue of the deep knowledge of our Lord and Savior Jesus Christ, they are again

---

2:10. *spirits fallen from glory:* literally, "glories." In the light of Jude 9, the reference is to fallen angels.

2:13. *They count,* etc.: this verse is difficult. In the translation given above, *daylight joy* is understood of the Lord's Supper which was concluded before dark. Other proposed translations: "They count it pleasure to revel in the daytime" (Spencer); "To live in luxury while the day lasts is all their pleasure" (Knox); "They look for happiness in the sensual indulgence of the moment" (Charue). *love feasts:* i.e., the *agape,* the Lord's Supper. Many manuscripts read instead, "in their deceits."

2:14. *They never look,* etc.: literally, "Their eyes are full of an adulterous woman."

2:15-16. Num. 22:17-22.

entangled and overcome by them, this latter state is worse than the
first. Really, it would have been better for them not to have known 21
our holy way of life than having had this deep knowledge, to turn
back from the holy program of life which has been handed down to
them. What the proverb says turned out to be true of them, 22

"A dog goes back to his vomit,"

and

"A sow that has been washed goes back to wallow in
the mire."

The Second Coming of Christ

Chapter 3

WARNING

This, beloved, is now the second letter that I write to you. 1
In both of them what I recall to you is designed to arouse your
sober thoughts, that you may be mindful of the words formerly 2
uttered by the holy prophets, and of the program of life which
our Lord and Savior proposed to you through your apostles.
You must realize above all else that in the last days there will come 3
inveterate scoffers, men living according to their lusts. "Where is 4
his promised coming?" they will ask. "Why, ever since our forefathers fell asleep, all things have remained as they were from the
beginning of creation." They willfully overlook the fact that the 5
heavens existed long ago, and the earth, at God's command, emerged
out of the water and was surrounded by water. By these same 6
waters, too, the world of that time perished when the flood came.
But the present heavens and the earth, in virtue of the same word, 7
are held in reserve for fire, kept until the day of judgment and of
destruction for godless people.

At least keep this in mind, beloved: With the Lord one day 8
is as a thousand years, and a thousand years as one day. The Lord 9
does not delay fulfilling his promise, as some estimate delay, but he

---

2:22. Prov. 2:22.
3:5. surrounded by: or "rested on" or "made from." The author has in mind
the account of creation in Gen. 1.
3:6. By these same waters: a slight textual change will give, "by the same
command."

is long-suffering toward you, not wishing a single soul to perish, but that every last one should have a change of heart and mind. 10 The day of the Lord will come as a thief. Then the heavens will pass away in a roaring flame and its elements will burn up and be dissolved. The earth and all the deeds performed on it will be sought 11 out and found. Since all these elements are to be dissolved in this 12 way, what holy and pious lives you ought to lead, as you await and hasten the coming of God's day. By that coming the heavens will be set afire and dissolved, and the elements will be burned up and 13 melted. Yet, in keeping with his promise we look for new heavens and a new earth, in which holiness dwells.

EXHORTATION

14 Therefore, beloved, since you await these events, make every effort to be spotless and blameless, so that God may find you with 15 a peaceful conscience. And regard the long-suffering delay of our Lord's coming as a means of salvation. Paul, our dear brother, wrote 16 the same things to you according to the wisdom granted him, just as he did in all his letters when speaking of these matters. In his letters there are some passages hard to understand. The unlearned and unsteady twist the meaning of these to their own destruction, as they do also the other Scriptures.

17 You, therefore, beloved, informed beforehand as you are, should be on your guard lest, carried away by the error of lawless men, and along with them, you should fall from your steadfast founda-18 tion. Moreover, grow in grace and in the knowledge of our Lord and Savior Jesus Christ. To him belongs glory both now and unto the day of eternity. Amen.

3:10. *in a roaring flame:* the Greek word means "a loud noise," which could be the whistling sound of falling stars, but the translation given above seems to fit the context better as we are told of the conflagration which is to destroy the world.

3:12. *hasten:* the day of the Lord will be hastened through conversion, as the delay is to allow sinners time to repent.

THE FIRST EPISTLE OF
ST. JOHN THE APOSTLE

This Epistle partakes to some extent of the nature of a theological treatise, yet has some of the characteristics of a letter. Although it has neither initial salutation nor farewell greeting, the author alludes frequently to the spiritual condition of those to whom he writes and frequently addresses them in endearing and affectionate terms.

The similarity of ideas and expressions makes it certain that the Epistle comes from the same pen that wrote the Fourth Gospel, that of St. John, the beloved disciple.

His purpose is to exhort his beloved children to a fuller appreciation of the precious treasure that is theirs in the Christian Revelation and of the obligations it places on them. He warns them of the dangers which false teachers offer to their faith, and although he refutes these heretics, his primary purpose is rather to exhort the faithful to cling to the faith and discharge its obligations, principally that of the love of God and of neighbor.

The error which he seems to have in mind is the false teaching of Cerinthus, who, according to St. Irenaeus, held that Christ came down upon the man Jesus at his baptism, dwelt in him by some sort of accidental union, spoke and worked miracles, and then returned to heaven, prior to the crucifixion, so that the Jesus who suffered and died was a mere man. St. John is concerned with showing that Jesus and Christ, or the Son of God, is but one divine Person united in two natures, the human and the divine.

The Epistle was addressed to Christians of Asia Minor or possibly of Syria who had been pagans before their conversion, as is indicated in the warning to beware of idols. Some few manuscripts and fathers have the address: *to the Parthians.*

The Epistle was most probably written at Ephesus either shortly

before or shortly after the Gospel according to St. John. The tone
and content of both are too closely allied for their composition to
have been separated by a long interval of time. The Epistle is more
probably a sort of postscript to the Gospel, rather than a forerunner
and introduction to it.

THE DIVISION OF THE FIRST EPISTLE OF ST. JOHN

Introduction, 1:1–4.
God is light, 1:5 to 2:27.
God is justice, 2:28 to 4:6.
God is love, 4:7 to 5:12.
Conclusion, 5:13–21.

THE FIRST EPISTLE OF

ST. JOHN THE APOSTLE

CHAPTER 1

WITNESS TO THE WORD OF LIFE

We proclaim what was from the beginning, what we have heard, 1
what we have seen with our own eyes, what we have gazed upon,
and what we have embraced with our own hands. I refer to the
Word who is and who imparts life. Indeed, this Life has manifested 2
himself. We ourselves have seen and testify and proclaim that
Eternal Life which was with the Father and has manifested himself.
To you we proclaim what we have seen and heard, that you may 3
share our treasure with us. That treasure is union with the Father
and his Son, Jesus Christ. I write this to you that we may have joy 4
in the fullest measure.

GOD IS LIGHT

LIVE IN THE LIGHT

Here is the message we have heard from him and proclaim to 5
you: God is light, and in him there is not the faintest shadow of
darkness. If we should say that we are united with him while we 6
continue to shape our conduct in an atmosphere of darkness, we
are liars; we fail to live up to the truth. But if we shape our conduct 7
in the atmosphere of his light, as he himself is in light, we have
union with one another, and the blood of Jesus, his Son, cleanses
us from every stain of sin.

If we should say that we are not guilty of sin, we deceive our- 8
selves, and the light of truth is not within us. If we openly confess 9
our sins, God, true to his promises and just, forgives us our sins

---

1:1. The opening words of this Epistle are parallel to the opening words
of the Fourth Gospel. Note the same ideas predicated of the Eternal Word:
light, life, and existence prior to the world's beginning.

1:6. *in an atmosphere of darkness*: i.e., to act without the benefit of revealed
truth and, therefore, in a pagan manner, sinfully.

1:9. *openly confess*: literally, "confess." The term, however, is used in the

10 and cleanses us from every stain of iniquity. If we should say that we have never been guilty of sin, we make him a liar, and his message does not dwell within us.

CHAPTER 2

1 My little children, I write this letter to you to keep you from sin. Yet if anyone should commit a sin, we have an advocate with
2 the Father, Jesus Christ, the Holy One. He himself is the propitiation for our sins; indeed not only for ours, but for those of the whole world.

OBSERVE THE COMMANDMENTS

3 By this we can be sure that we know God, if we keep his
4 commandments. He who says, "I know him," but does not keep his commandments, is a liar, and the truth does not dwell in him.
5 But whoever keeps God's word, truly that man's love for God is
6 perfect. By that sign we are sure that we are in him. He who says he abides in him, ought to model his life on that of Jesus.

ESPECIALLY CHARITY

7 Beloved, I am not writing you a new commandment, but the old one, which you have heard from the beginning. The old
8 commandment is the message which you have heard. And yet, it

New Testament of an external confession, not merely of acknowledging one's guilt in the secrecy of one's conscience to God. The reference is more probably to the liturgical confession, such as we are familiar with today in the Mass. St. John, however, knew of the Sacrament of Penance. See Jn. 20:23. St. Augustine writes: "If you do not tell God what you are, God will condemn what he finds in you. You do not wish, do you, to have God condemn you? Then condemn yourself. Do you wish him to pardon you? Then, acknowledge your sins."

2:2. for those of: literally, "for the whole world."

2:7. St. John says that the commandment is not new; then he says that it is. His meaning is that it is not newly proclaimed, since the faithful had been instructed in it from the beginning of their conversion. But in another sense it is new both for Christ and for the faithful. It is new for Christ since he announced it as a new commandment (Jn. 13:34). Its novelty consists in the extent of this love to all mankind, even enemies, and in its motive and intensity. The Christian is to love his fellows as Christ loved and because Christ's love imparts a new dignity to all men and makes them brothers. It is a new commandment for the faithful, because this Christian law of love was a novelty to any convert either from paganism or from Judaism.

is a new commandment I write to you, new in regard to him and in regard to you, because the darkness is passing away, and the true light is already shining. He who says that he is in the light, yet 9 hates his brother, is still in darkness. He who loves his brother abides 10 in the light, and so he has no cause for stumbling. But he who hates 11 his brother is in darkness and walks in it. He has no idea where he is going, because the darkness has blinded his eyes.

HIS CONFIDENCE IN THEM

I write to you, little children, because your sins are forgiven 12 through his name. I write to you, fathers, because you know him 13 who was from the beginning. I write to you, young men, because you have overcome the evil one. I write to you little ones because 14 you know the Father. I write to you, fathers, because you know him who was from the beginning. I write to you, young men, because you are strong, and the message which God has revealed abides in you, and you have overcome the evil one.

GUARD AGAINST THE SPIRIT OF THE WORLD

Do not love the world or what the world has to offer. If anyone 15 loves the world, he has no love for the Father, because all that the 16 world has to offer is the cravings that arise from our animal nature, the cravings that arise from what we see and a vain display in one's mode of life. These come not from the Father, but from the world. Besides, the world with its cravings passes away, but he who does 17 the will of God abides forever.

GUARD AGAINST FALSE TEACHERS

Little ones, the last epoch is here. You have heard that the 18 Antichrist is coming. Well, there are many antichrists now. By that fact we know that the last epoch is here. They took their leave 19 of us but they did not really belong to us. If they had, they would have stayed with us. On the contrary, they took their leave, so that it might be quite evident that none of them really belonged

---

2:15. The world here designates sinners and their false principles.

2:18. the Antichrist: we cannot be quite sure whether the Antichrist is a person or a movement hostile to Christ, and whether there is to be but one antichrist or many. At any rate the author here styles anyone who opposes Christ and his work in any way whatever an antichrist, at least in a loose sense.

20 to us. You, however, have been anointed by the Holy One, as you
21 all know. I write to you, not because you do not know the truth, but because you do know the truth. You know, too, that a lie never springs from the truth.

22 Who is a liar, but he who denies that Jesus is the Christ? The
23 Antichrist is he who denies the Father and the Son. No one who denies the Son is in union with the Father; one who acknowledges
24 the Son is in union with the Father also. As for you, let what you have heard from the beginning abide with you. If what you have heard from the beginning abides with you, you too will abide in the
25 Son and in the Father. And this is what he has promised us, life eternal.

26, 27 I write this about those who attempt to mislead you. As for you, the anointing which you have received from him abides in you, so you need no one to teach you. Rather, just as the anointing by him who is truthful and not deceitful teaches and has taught you all things, so abide in it.

GOD IS JUSTICE

BE GOD'S CHILDREN IN REALITY

28 And now, little children, abide in him, so that when he appears, you may have assurance and not shy away from him in shame when
29 he comes. Since you know that he is holy, you are also well aware that everyone who lives a holy life is a child of God.

2:20. *You, however, have been anointed:* literally, "You have an anointing from the Holy One." This anointing probably designates the Holy Spirit whom our Lord imparts at the Baptism and Confirmation of the new convert. Perhaps St. John is here playing on words. The Greek for "anointing" is *Chrisma*, from the same root as "Christ," which means "anointing."

2:27. *you need no one to teach you:* St. John supposes that the faithful hear and learn the traditional teaching proposed by the Apostles and their successors. But to accept it and understand it there is need of the light of the Holy Spirit. St. Augustine says: "The sound of our words strikes the ear, but the teacher is within you. Do not think that anybody learns anything from man. We can give admonitions in a loud voice. But if he is not within you to teach you, the loud tones are in vain." It should be noted too that the doctrine of this Epistle coincides with that of the Fourth Gospel, which, however, has one of the most forceful texts in favor of the teaching authority and primacy of St. Peter (Jn. 21:15–17).

CHAPTER 3

See what kind of love the Father has bestowed on us that we 1
should be children not merely in name but in reality. The world
does not recognize us, because it has not recognized him. Beloved, 2
now we are children of God, and what we shall be has not yet been
manifested. We know that when he appears, we shall be like him,
because we shall see him just as he is. Everyone who cherishes this 3
hope in God strives to be holy, just as he is holy. Everyone who 4
commits sin, commits also an act of lawlessness. That is precisely
what sin is. You know that he made himself manifest to take away 5
our sins — he who himself is free from sin. No one who abides in 6
him sins; no one who sins has either appreciated or understood him.

SINNERS ARE THE DEVIL'S CHILDREN

Little children, let no one mislead you. He who lives a holy life 7
is holy, just as God is holy. He who commits sin springs from the 8
devil, because the devil has been sinning from the beginning. The
Son of God made his appearance for the purpose of destroying sin,
the work of the devil. No one who is a child of God sins, because 9
the life-germ implanted by God abides in him, and so, he cannot
sin. He is a child of God. Here is the sign which reveals who are 10
God's children and who are the devil's: Whoever fails to lead a
holy life is no child of God, neither is he who fails to love his brother.

This is precisely the message which you have heard from the 11
beginning — that we should love one another. Be not like Cain who 12
was a child of the evil one and murdered his brother. Why did he
murder him? Because his own life was wicked, whereas his brother's

---

3:1. *not merely in name:* mere adoption may confer the name and certain
extrinsic legal effects on the adopted child, but the Christian in Baptism is born
again, and receives not merely the name of a child of God, but also a share,
in a certain sense, in the nature of our adopting Father, God. See 2 Pet. 1:4.

3:2. *we shall be like him:* on earth the faithful have a very imperfect resemblance to God, but in the face-to-face vision of heaven the mind will be so
elevated by grace as to see God in direct vision. This is a peculiarly godlike
activity.

3:6. *No one who abides in him sins:* i.e., maliciously and habitually.

3:9. *he cannot sin:* this is to be understood relatively. In 1:8 above St. John
admits the possibility of the faithful sinning. St. Augustine explains: As long
as one abides in Christ, one does not sin.

13 was holy. Do not be surprised, brothers, if the world hates you.
14 We know that we have passed from death to life, because we love
15 our brothers. He who does not love abides in death. Everyone who
hates his brother is a murderer, and you know that no murderer
has eternal life abiding in him.

TRUE LOVE

16 We know what love is from the fact that Jesus Christ laid down
his life for us. We, too, ought to lay down our lives for our brothers.
17 How, then, can the love of God abide in him who possesses worldly
18 goods, and, seeing his brother in need, closes his heart to him? Little
children, let us not love merely in word or with the tongue, but in
action, in reality.

CONFIDENCE IN GOD

19 By that we shall know that we are born of the truth, and we
20 shall calm our conscience in his presence, no matter what our
conscience may reproach us with, because God is greater than our
21 conscience, and knows everything. Beloved, if our conscience does
22 not reproach us, we have assurance in God's presence. We also
receive from him whatever we ask, because we keep his command-
23 ments and do what is pleasing in his sight. His commandment is
this, that we should believe in the name of his Son, Jesus Christ,
24 and love one another, as he commanded us. He who keeps his
commandments abides in God and God in him. It is the Spirit
abiding in us who gives us the assurance that God abides in us.

CHAPTER 4

TRUE AND FALSE SPIRITUAL MANIFESTATIONS

1 Beloved, do not believe every spiritual manifestation, but test
them to see whether they are of divine origin, because many,

3:20. *God is greater*: God's knowledge is more penetrating than ours, and
he sees not only the failings with which we reproach ourselves but also the
deep-seated love there is in the individual's soul.

4:1. *spiritual manifestation*: literally, "spirit," i.e., a gift of eloquence or of
tongues or something of the kind, supposedly coming from the Holy Spirit,
and called *charismata* in the Epistles of St. Paul. These could be of divine
origin, but they could also be merely human and, therefore, not genuine, or
even of diabolical origin.

equipped with counterfeit gifts have gone forth into the world. You 2
can recognize such manifestations as of divine origin by this test:
Every manifestation that acknowledges Jesus Christ incarnate is of ⌣
divine origin. No manifestation that denies Jesus is of divine origin. 3
On the contrary it is a manifestation that originates with the Antichrist. You have heard he is on the way. Well, at this moment he
is already in the world.

You, little children, are born of God, and you have overcome the 4
false teachers, because God who is in you is greater than the devil
who is in the world. They are born of the world. That is why they 5
speak the language of the world, and the world listens to them.
We are born of God. He who knows God listens to us; he who is 6
not born of God does not listen to us. By this test we distinguish
the spiritual manifestation that is inspired by the truth from the
spiritual manifestation that is inspired by the deceiver.

God Is Love

LOVE UNITES US WITH GOD

Beloved, let us love one another, because love takes its origin 7
in God, and everyone that loves is a child of God and knows God. He 8
who has no love does not know God, because God is love. God's 9
love was made manifest among us by the fact that God sent his
only-begotten Son into the world that we might have life through
him. This love consists not in our having loved God but in his 10
having loved us and his having sent his Son as a propitiation for
our sins. Beloved, if God so loved us, we in turn ought to love 11
one another.

No one has ever seen God, yet if we love one another, God 12
abides in us and our love for him reaches perfection. We know that 13
we abide in him and he in us by the fact that he has made us
partakers of his Spirit. And we ourselves have seen and now testify 14
that the Father has sent his Son to save the world. When anyone 15
acknowledges that Jesus is the Son of God, God abides in him ⌣

4:3. *denies:* a well-attested reading has "dissolves." This would refer to those
who would disassociate Jesus and the Incarnate Word and deny the substantial
union of the divine and human natures in the Second Person of the Blessed
Trinity. *already in the world:* in the sense of false teachers and false doctrines.

16 and he in God. And we ourselves know and believe in God's enduring love at work among us. God is love, and he who abides in love
abides in God and God in him.

17 This love has become perfect through our co-operation, in that
we have confidence against the day of judgment, because we in this
18 world resemble Christ (in heaven). There is no fear in love; rather
perfect love drives out fear, because fear implies chastisement, and
19 he who fears has not reached the perfection of love. We exercise
20 mutual love because he first loved us. If anyone says, "I love God,"
yet hates his brother, he is a liar. Why? Because he who does not
love his brother whom he sees, cannot love God whom he does
21 not see. Besides, we have received this commandment from God:
He who loves God must love his brother also.

CHAPTER 5

BASIS OF LOVE IS FAITH

1 Everyone who believes that Jesus is the Christ is born of God.
2 Everyone who loves the parent loves his child also. We know by
this sign that we love the children of God: when we love God and
3 keep his commandments. Yes, to love God means to keep his
4 commandments. They are not burdensome, because every child of
God has enough strength to become a victor over the world. And
5 this is the victory that has conquered the world, our faith. Now,
who is it that is a victor over the world, if not he that believes that
Jesus is the Son of God.

6 He it is who came to make us victors by purifying and redeeming
us, and by the effusion of the Spirit. He made victory possible for us
not merely by the water of baptism but both by the water and by
his blood. The Spirit also continually bears reliable witness, because

4:16. *at work among us:* literally, "in us."
4:17. *through our co-operation:* literally, "with us." *Christ (in heaven):* our
resemblance to Christ consists in our fraternal love. Christ showed his love by
his death for us, and he continues to show that love in heaven in that he is
the permanent propitiation for our sins.
5:6. An alternative meaning: "He it is who fulfilled his mission by his
baptism (the inauguration of our Lord's public life), by his passion and by
sending his Spirit." Literally, "This is he who came by water and blood, etc."
The words "by the Spirit" are of doubtful authenticity. According to St. Augustine, St. John seeks to prove the reality of the Incarnation, and refers to the

the Spirit is Truth. And so, we have three reliable witnesses of 7
victory: the Spirit, the water, and the blood, and these three are 8
in agreement. We accept the testimony of men, but the testimony 9
of God has much greater authority. This is, in fact, the testimony
of God: He has testified concerning his Son. He who believes in 10
the Son has within himself the testimony of God. He who refuses
to believe God treats him as a liar, because he does not believe the
testimony that God has given concerning his Son. Now this testi- 11
mony is to the effect that God has given us eternal life, and that
the Son has this life. He, then, who partakes of the Son partakes 12
of that life; he who does not partake of the Son does not partake
of that life.

CONCLUSION

I write this to you, that you, believing as you do in the name 13
of the Son of God, may know that you have eternal life.

CONFIDENCE IN PRAYER

This is the extent of our confidence in him: No matter what 14
we ask, provided it is in keeping with his will, he hears us. Now if 15
we know that he hears us in regard to whatever we ask, we know
that we have already obtained the requests we have made of him.

If anyone sees his brother committing a sin that does not spell 16
death, he should pray for that sinner, and God will give the sinner
life, that is, if he belongs to that class who do not commit the sin
that spells death. There is a sin that spells death. Concerning this

---

water and blood which issued from Christ's side when it was pierced (Jn. 19:34).
Others see a reference to Baptism and the Eucharist. The Venerable Bede com-
bines the two interpretations: "He came by water and blood, namely, the water
of baptism and the blood of his passion. He deigned not only to be baptized
that he might consecrate and give to us the sacrament of Baptism, but he also
gave his blood for us, redeeming us by his passion, and being always refreshed
with the sacraments we are nourished with unto salvation."

5:7. witnesses of victory: or "witnesses to his divinity."

5:16. The two sins here mentioned could both be grievous, but the one
that spells death is the sin of completely rejecting Jesus as Christ and God.
The distinction St. John here has in mind is not that which today holds such
a prominent place in the technical language of moral theology. We are reminded of the unforgivable sin in Mk. 3:29; Mt. 12:31; and Lk. 12:10; also of
Hebr. 6:4–8. St. John does not forbid prayer for the apostate but judges the
sin so grave that prayer for him becomes almost useless.

17 I do not say that one should pray. Every act of evil is sin, but there is a special kind of sin that leads not to death.

AVOID SIN

18 We know that no child of God commits sin. On the contrary, the child of God guards himself, and so the evil one does not touch
19 him. We know that we are born of God, but the whole world is
20 under the influence of the evil one. We know, moreover, that the Son of God has come and has given us understanding that we may
ᘐ know the True One. In fact we are incorporated into this True One, God's Son, Jesus Christ. He is the true God and Eternal Life.
21 Little children, guard yourselves from idols.

THE SECOND EPISTLE OF ST. JOHN THE APOSTLE

This brief letter is addressed to the Lady Elect. Efforts have been made to prove that this title designates an individual, but the prevailing and more probable opinion is that reference is made to a local congregation.

The author, St. John the Apostle, stresses his favorite theme of fraternal love, and warns against certain false teachers who denied the reality of our Lord's Incarnation.

The Epistle was probably written from Ephesus some time after the year A.D. 90. The local congregation, styled Lady Elect, was probably located in Asia Minor.

THE SECOND EPISTLE OF

ST. JOHN THE APOSTLE

GREETINGS

The presbyter, to the Lady Elect and to her children, whom I, 1
and not only I, but all those who have come to know the truth, love
according to the dictates of truth.

I love them because of the truth which abides in us, and which 2
will be with us forever. Grace, peace, and mercy will be with us 3
from God the Father and from Jesus Christ, the Father's Son, provided we persevere in truth and love.

EXHORTATION TO BROTHERLY LOVE

It was a great joy for me to find some of your children living in 4
accord with the dictates of the truth, just as we have been commanded by the Father. And now I beg you, Lady, let us love one 5
another. This is not a new commandment that I write, but the one
that we have had from the beginning. Now love means that we live 6
according to his commandments. The commandment, as you have
heard from the beginning, is that you make love the rule of
your life.

PERSEVERE IN THE FAITH

I beg this of you, because many deceivers have gone forth into 7
the world, men who do not acknowledge the coming of Jesus Christ
in the flesh. Here you have the deceiver and the Antichrist. Look 8
to yourselves, so that you do not lose what we have gained, but that
you may receive a full reward. Anyone who forges ahead of Christ's 9
doctrine and fails to remain true to it, does not hold on to God.

---

1. *presbyter:* see the note on 1 Pet. 5:1. Here the title is used more in its
original meaning "elder," without excluding the added meaning of priest and
even bishop. Since St. John calls himself "the elder," the title was most probably
conferred on him by the Christians at Asia Minor because of his advanced age
and their high regard for him.

8. *we have gained:* many manuscripts read: "you have gained."

9. The sense is that these men are ambitiously progressive, under pretext
of a higher knowledge, but they exceeded the limits of genuine truth.

10 He who remains true to this doctrine holds on to both the Father
    and the Son. If anyone comes to you and does not bring with him
    this doctrine, do not receive him into your home. Do not even
11 speak words of greeting to him, for he who does so shares in his
    wicked deeds.

CONCLUSION

12   Though I have much to write you, I do not wish to do so with
    paper and ink. But I hope to be with you and have a heart to heart
    talk with you that your joy may be complete.
13   The children of your Elect Sister send you greetings.

THE THIRD EPISTLE OF
ST. JOHN THE APOSTLE

The Gaius to whom this Epistle is directed is otherwise unknown to us. Attempts to identify him with one or another Gaius mentioned in other parts of the New Testament or in the writings of early commentators are all largely conjectural.

The Apostle tells Gaius how happy he is to hear that Gaius is leading a truly Christian life, and praises him for the hospitality he extended to a group of missionaries.

The Apostle has some harsh words to say about a certain Diotrephes who was ambitious and seems to have shown some contempt for the Apostle John. Diotrephes was not a heretic, but rather an ambitious ecclesiastic who resented and resisted the authority which St. John rightly sought to exercise over the congregation where Diotrephes held the leading position. Nothing further is known of this Diotrephes.

Demetrius, who cannot successfully be identified, receives words of high praise.

The Epistle was written some time after the year A.D. 90 from Ephesus or some place nearby.

THE THIRD EPISTLE OF

ST. JOHN THE APOSTLE

GREETINGS

The presbyter, to the beloved Gaius, whom I love according to 1
the dictates of truth.

PRAISE OF GAIUS

Beloved, I pray that all goes well with you, and that you are 2
in good health, just as all is well with your soul. Really, it was a 3
great joy for me when some brothers came and spoke favorably of
your fidelity to the truth, that is, that you live in accord with the
truth. Nothing gives me greater joy than to hear that my children 4
are living in accord with the truth.

Beloved, you act like a true believer when you render service to 5
the brothers, even though they are strangers. They themselves spoke 6
favorably in an assembly of the faithful about your love. You will
do well to send them on their journey in a manner worthy of God.
For they have gone forth for the sake of his name, without accepting 7
anything from the pagans. So we ought to welcome such men, and 8
thus become fellow workers for the truth.

DIOTREPHES AND DEMETRIUS

I wrote a message to the congregation, but Diotrephes, who likes 9
to have the first place among them, does not acknowledge us. For 10
this reason, if I come, I will remind him of his conduct, how he
indulges in malicious gossip against us. And not content with that,
he himself does not admit the brothers and even hinders those who
wish to do so, and expels them from the congregation.

Beloved, do not imitate what is evil, but what is good. He who 11
does good is of God; he who does evil has no idea of God.

---

9. *I wrote:* the Vulgate and some Greek manuscripts: "I would have written."
The letter here referred to was most probably addressed to the congregation
of which Gaius was a member; the letter has been lost.

12   Everybody speaks favorably of Demetrius, even truth itself. We ourselves speak favorably of him, and you know that our testimony is true.

CONCLUSION

13   I have much to write you, but I do not wish to write you with
14   pen and ink. I hope to see you soon, and we will have a heart to
⌣   heart talk.
15   Peace be to you. Your friends send you greetings. Extend personal greetings to my friends.

---

12. *even truth itself*: the truth of the Christian revelation testified in favor of Demetrius, in that his conduct was obviously such as the ideals of Christianity proposed.

THE EPISTLE OF ST. JUDE, THE APOSTLE

The date of composition is placed by Catholic authorities between 62 and 67, and the inspiration of the Epistle has been a dogma of faith in the Catholic Church ever since the Council of Trent.

THE EPISTLE OF
ST. JUDE THE APOSTLE

The author of this Epistle identifies himself as the brother of James. His only reason for so doing was that James must have been an illustrious person, whose memory was held in benediction. Consequently it is generally held that the James referred to is James the Less, Bishop of Jerusalem, who was martyred about 62. Similarly it is quite probable that Jude was the son of Alpheus and an Apostle.

Jude had been quite eager to write a letter to a group of Jewish Christians, but had not got around to it, when some circumstance — probably the activities of the false teachers he so severely condemns in this letter — made it imperative for him to write an urgent appeal to his correspondents to do battle for the holy faith once and for all delivered to them. We can readily gather from this brief Epistle what the activities of these false teachers were. They evidently advocated certain licentious practices, perhaps under the false pretext of Christian liberty; they denied our Lord Jesus Christ more probably by their scandalous conduct than by the theoretical rejection of his divinity.

St. Jude appeals to the Old Testament for terrifying examples of God's punishment on sinners, and declares that the same punishment is in store for these scandalous men.

He then urges the faithful Christians to cling to their faith, to pray fervently, and to cherish the hope of eternal life. He gives some practical advice as to how to deal with these heretics, and ends with a doxology in praise of our Lord Jesus Christ.

There is a close parallel between this Epistle and 2 Peter and consequently there must be dependence of one on the other. Authorities disagree as to which Epistle borrows from the other.

The date of composition is placed by Catholic authorities between 62 and 67, and the inspiration of the Epistle has been a dogma of faith in the Catholic Church ever since the Council of Trent.

644

THE EPISTLE OF

ST. JUDE THE APOSTLE

INTRODUCTION

ADDRESS AND PURPOSE

Jude, servant of Jesus Christ and brother of James, to those who 1
have been called, who have been loved by God the Father and
guarded for Jesus Christ. May mercy, peace, and love be extended 2
to you in abundance.

Beloved, while I was very much concerned about writing to you 3
relative to our common salvation, I found myself constrained to
write and exhort you to do battle for the faith which has been once
for all entrusted to the saints. For certain men have gained admis- 4
sion among you by stealth, men who long ago were marked out
for the well-known judgment. They are ungodly persons who pervert
the grace of our Lord God and turn it into licentiousness, and deny
our only Master and Lord, Jesus Christ.

WARNING AGAINST FALSE TEACHERS

I wish to remind you, even though you were once for all informed 5
about every point, that the Lord, though he saved the people from
the land of Egypt, later destroyed those who did not believe.
Even the angels who did not keep their pre-eminence, but who 6
abandoned their high estate, have been kept everlastingly enchained
by God in darkness until the judgment of the great day. In the 7
same way, too, Sodom and Gomorrah, and the surrounding cities
which like these committed fornication and lusted after things
forbidden, serve as a lasting warning, as they suffer the punishment
of eternal fire.

---

1. *loved by God*: literally, "loved in God."
3. *constrained*: some circumstance arose which made the letter imperative.
once for all: this phrase indicates the immutability of a divinely revealed body
of doctrine, without however excluding the possibility of its being added to.
4. *long ago*: or "recently" or "already." Verses 4 to 18 are closely paralleled
by 2 Pet. 2:1–3:3.
7. *lusted after things forbidden*: we understand this of homosexuality.

8   In the same way, nevertheless, these men also, dreamers that they are, defile the body, reject authority, and vilify glorious spirits.

9   Even Michael the archangel, when he contended and disputed with the devil over the body of Moses, did not dare to make an

10 abusive charge, but merely said, "May the Lord rebuke you!" These men, however, speak injuriously of things they do not understand; but the things they know by instinct, like irrational creatures, they

11 use as the means of destruction. Perdition awaits them because they have gone astray in the way of Cain, and have hurled themselves into the error of Balaam for the sake of gain, and have

12 perished in a rebellion like that of Core. These men are stains on your love feasts, where they banquet together irreverently, and set their heart on feeding themselves alone. They are clouds without water, driven by the winds; they are autumn trees, fruitless, twice

13 dead, uprooted. They are raging waves of the sea which cast up their disgrace as foam; they are wandering stars, to whom the densest darkness has been reserved forever.

14   Of these very people Enoch, who was the seventh in line from Adam, prophesied. "See," he said, "the Lord came amid thousands

15 of his holy ones to institute trial against all and convict all the godless people of their godless deeds that they had committed in so godless a manner, and of the insolent things that godless sinners

16 have spoken against him." These people are discontented grumblers, who follow their own passions, whose mouth utters arrogant words.

17 They flatter people to serve their own ends. You, beloved, keep in mind the words that have been spoken to you beforehand by the

18 apostles of our Lord Jesus Christ. They used to say, "In the last epoch there will be scoffers who will indulge their own passions

---

8. *glorious spirits:* literally, "glories," i.e., angels.

9. This example is not drawn from Scripture but rather from Jewish tradition or from the *Assumption of Moses,* a noninspired Jewish book.

12. *love feasts:* most probably the Eucharistic feast, so designated in the Pauline Epistles.

14. A citation, most probably from the noninspired book of Henoch. An inspired writer may use an example from a noninspired source, or quote words not formerly being inspired. In this case the citation states a religious truth acknowledged by both Jews and Christians, the punishment by God of sinners.

17. *spoken:* not necessarily a reference to spoken, as distinguished from written, words. Warnings like this are found in Acts 20:29; 1 Tim. 4:1; 2 Tim. 3:1–5; and 2 Pet. 3:2.

in wicked deeds." It is these who cause divisions, since they are *19*
slaves to their senses, and devoid of the Spirit.

Admonitions for Christians

You, beloved, build yourselves up on the foundation of your *20*
most holy faith; pray with the aid of the Holy Spirit. Keep yourselves *21*
in the love of God, while you await the mercy of our Lord Jesus
Christ, which will bring you to eternal life.

Reprove those who are judged to be wrong; save others by *22, 23*
snatching them out of the fire. To still others show mercy tempered
with fear, hating even the garment soiled by carnal passions.

Conclusion

To him then, who is powerful enough to keep you from stumbling *24*
and to bring you blameless and exultant to the presence of his
glory, to this only God, our Savior through Jesus Christ our Lord, *25*
belong glory, majesty, dominion, and authority before all time and
now and throughout all ages. Amen.

22, 23. There are considerable textual variants in these verses.

THE APOCALYPSE OF
ST. JOHN THE APOSTLE

"Apocalypse" means unveiling or revelation. It is an apt title for the last book of the New Testament, which unveils for us the future of the Church on earth and in heaven.

The book was written by the Apostle St. John, the beloved disciple, about the year 96, when he was in exile on Patmos, a small island in the Aegean Sea near the coast of Asia Minor.

The purpose of the author was to encourage the Christians. Our Lord had predicted his return and had given some signs which would precede it. All these signs were apparently realized at the end of the first century, and in the midst of savage persecution the Christians were in need of strong encouragement. Buffeted by persecution and assailed by doubt, they are told by St. John in the Apocalypse that the final triumph of Christ and those who remain loyal to him is assured, but before the dawn of that blessed day of victory there must needs come atrocious struggles between the powers of darkness and the forces of light. The story of the Apocalypse is accordingly that of the dramatic struggle between the contending forces of good and evil, culminating in the complete triumph of our Lord and his followers over Satan and his cohorts.

The characteristic tone of the Apocalypse is, then, one of triumph and exultant joy, although there appears from time to time the minor chord of atrocious combat and fierce persecution against the faithful. But these violent encounters will never harm the elect who have been signed and sealed with the mark of identification imprinted by God. The book terminates on the triumphant note of the heavenly Jerusalem, the city of peace and glory, where there shall be no more tears, no more pangs, no more struggles. The whole

649

Church, uniting its voice with that of the Spirit, implores God for the speedy realization of Christ's final triumph: "Come Lord, Jesus!" and his reply is: "I am coming, quickly."

It must be remembered that the Apocalypse is written in symbolic language, and that each series of seven symbols repeats or recapitulates its predecessors, giving a general picture of the whole history of the Church on earth. Although many of the symbols were taken from contemporary history and from the Roman Empire, yet these contemporary events are but symbols of all similar events down through the centuries.

THE DIVISION OF THE APOCALYPSE
Prologue, 1:1–8.
Vision of the seven letters, 1:9 to 3:22.
    Preparatory vision, 1:9–20.
    The seven letters, 2:1 to 3:22.
Vision of the seven seals, 4:1 to 8:1.
    Reception of the sealed book, 4:1 to 5:14.
    The breaking of the seals, 6:1 to 8:1.
Vision of the seven trumpets, 8:2 to 11:18.
Vision of the seven signs, 11:19 to 15:4.
Vision of the seven bowls, 15:5 to 16:21.
The fate of Babylon the Great, 17:1 to 19:10.
The fate of the beast and Satan, 19:11 to 20:15.
The new world and the new Jerusalem, 21:1 to 22:5.
Epilogue, 22:6–21.

THE APOCALYPSE OF

ST. JOHN THE APOSTLE

PROLOGUE

CHAPTER 1

SOURCES AND CONTENT

A revelation received from Jesus Christ which God gave him 1
to reveal to his servants. These revelations deal with what must
soon take place. He made them known by sending his angel to his
servant John, who attests that whatever he perceived is the word 2
of God and the testimony of Jesus Christ. Blessed is he who reads 3
in public the words of this prophecy, and blessed are those who
hear them and observe what is written here, for the time is near.

GREETINGS

John to the seven congregations that are in Asia. Grace be to 4
you and peace from him whose name is "He is," "He was," and
"He is coming," and from the seven Spirits who are before his
throne, and from Jesus Christ, the trustworthy witness, the first to 5
rise from the dead, and the sovereign of the kings of the earth.
To him who loves us and has freed us from our sins through his
own blood and has made us a kingdom, priests for his God and 6
Father, belong glory and power for ever and ever. Amen.

CHRIST'S COMING

Take note. He is coming amid the clouds, and every eye will 7

1:1. *received from:* or "concerning." *angel:* this could be a designation of
Christ, but more probably it refers to the angel or angels who frequently served
as intermediaries to communicate God's message to St. John, as in 7:1; 8:2,
and elsewhere.

1:4. This threefold title of Christ expresses his eternity and divinity. The
seven Spirits more probably stand for the Holy Spirit with his sevenfold gifts.

1:6. *priests:* see 1 Pet. 2:9. *Amen:* often translated "So be it" or "So it is."
It indicates assent of the many to the statement or prayer made by one
spokesman.

see him, even of those who pierced him. And all the tribes of the
8 earth will lament over him. "Yes, Amen. I am the Alpha and the
Omega," says the Lord God, "whose name is 'He is,' and 'He was'
and 'He is coming,' the Almighty."

PREPARATORY VISION

ORDER TO WRITE THE VISION

9 I, John, your brother who shares your affliction and royalty
and perseverance in union with Jesus, found myself on the island
called Patmos, because I preached the word of God and testified
10 to Jesus. I found myself in prophetic ecstasy on the Lord's day,
11 and heard behind me a voice as resounding as a trumpet. "Write
in a book what you see," it said, "and send it to the seven congregations: at Ephesus, at Smyrna, at Pergamum, at Thyatira, at
Sardis, at Philadelphia, and at Laodicea."

THE VISION OF THE SON OF MAN

12 Then I turned to see whose voice was speaking to me. When I
13 turned, I saw seven golden lampstands, and in their midst one like
the Son of Man, clothed in a long robe and girded around the breast
14 with a golden cincture. The hair of his head was as white as snow-
15 white wool; his eyes were like a flame of fire; his feet were like
burnished bronze smelted in a furnace; his voice was like the sound
16 of many waters. And in his right hand he held seven stars. From his
mouth there came forth a sharp two-edged sword, and his face was
like the sun shining in full splendor.

17 When I saw him, I fell down at his feet as if dead, but he laid
his right hand on me and said, "Do not be afraid. I am the First
18 and the Last and the Living One. I was dead, but how wonderful,
I live for ever and ever, and have the keys of death and of the
19 nether world. Write, then, what you saw, both what now is and

---

1:8. *Alpha, Omega*: the first and last letters of the Greek alphabet, and
probably correspond to the first and last letters of the Hebrew alphabet. The
idea is that of totality. God is the totality of being.

1:9. *Patmos*: a small island in the Aegean Sea not far from Ephesus.

1:10. *Lord's day*: the first day of the week, Sunday. Perhaps an indication
that this day of the week was then observed as a holy day.

1:18. *keys*: a symbol of absolute power.

what will take place later. As for the mystery of the seven stars 20
you saw in my right hand and the seven golden lampstands: the
seven stars are the angels of the seven congregations, and the seven
lampstands are the seven congregations."

THE SEVEN LETTERS

CHAPTER 2

TO THE CONGREGATION AT EPHESUS

"To the angel of the congregation at Ephesus write: 1
'He who holds the seven stars in his right hand and walks among
the seven golden lampstands has this to say: I know your conduct, 2
your toil, and your patience. I know how you cannot bear evil men,
how you put to the test those who claim to be apostles, though they
are not, and how you have found them false. I know that you have 3
patience, and have borne up for my name's sake, and have not grown
weary. Nevertheless I hold this against you that you have given up 4
the love you had at first. Remember, then, the state from which 5
you have fallen, repent, and return to your former ways. Else I
will come to you to move your lampstand from its place, unless
you repent. This, however, is in your favor that you hate the doings 6
of the Nicolaites, just as I also do. Let him who has ears listen 7
to what the Spirit says to the congregations: To him who is victorious
I will grant the privilege of eating of the tree of life, which is in
the paradise of God!' "

TO THE CONGREGATION AT SMYRNA

"To the angel of the congregation at Smyrna write: 8
'The First and the Last, he who was dead but lives, has this

1:20. angels: these are rather the bishops of the local Christian communities
than their guardian angels.
2:5. move your lampstand: this is a threat from our Lord to take away from
Ephesus the position of pre-eminence it had in the district of Asia Minor among
the Christian communities.
2:6. Nicolaites: a group of heretics, headed by a certain Nicholas of whom
we have no certain information. We gather from the Apocalypse that this
sect approved of a certain participation in pagan worship, such as sharing in
pagan sacrificial banquets and in religious orgies which included a ritualistic
prostitution.

9 to say: I know your affliction and your poverty, still you are rich;
and the slander from those who assert that they are Jews, though
10 they are not, but are a synagogue of Satan. Do not fear what you
are about to suffer. See, the devil is about to throw some of you
into prison that you may be tried, and for ten days you will be
afflicted. Be faithful even till death, and I will give you the crown
11 which belongs to life. Let him who has ears listen to what the Spirit
says to the congregations: He who is victorious will not be hurt at
all by the second death.' "

TO THE CONGREGATION AT PERGAMUM

12   "To the angel of the congregation at Pergamum write:
13   'He who has the sharp two-edged sword has this to say: I know
where you dwell, in the place where Satan has his throne. Still you
hold fast to my name and you did not deny faith in me even in the
days of Antipas, my trustworthy witness who was killed in your
14 midst, where Satan dwells. Nevertheless I hold a few things against
you. You have some there holding the doctrine of Balaam who
taught Balac to place a stumbling block in the way of Israel, so
that they might eat food sacrificed to idols and commit fornication.
15 Thus, you too have some who hold the doctrine of the Nicolaites.
16 Repent, then, or else I will come to you quickly to fight against
17 them with the sword that is in my mouth. Let him who has ears
listen to what the Spirit says to the congregations: To him who is
victorious I will give the hidden manna, and I will give him a white
stone, and on this stone is a new name written, which no one knows
except he who receives it.' "

TO THE CONGREGATION AT THYATIRA

18   "To the angel of the congregation at Thyatira write:
'The Son of God, who has eyes like a flame of fire, and whose

---

2:10. *ten days:* a very short period.
2:11. *second death:* condemnation forever to hell.
2:13. *where Satan,* etc.: because Pergamum had many temples and shrines
dedicated to pagan deities, as well as the famous pilgrimage place dedicated to
Asklepios, and more probably because there was a temple dedicated to the
worship of the Roman Emperor.
2:17. *white stone:* the source of this symbol is much in dispute, but the
name on it is that of God or of our Lord. It serves as a mark of dedication to
God and entitles its holder to admission to the heavenly kingdom. The manna
according to Origen, St. Bede, and others symbolizes the Eucharist.

feet are like burnished bronze, has this to say: I know your achieve- 19
ments, your faith, love, service, and patience. I know, too, your
latest achievements which outnumber the early ones. Nevertheless 20
I hold it against you that you tolerate that woman Jezebel who
calls herself a prophetess and teaches and seduces my servants to
commit fornication and to eat food sacrificed to idols. I gave her 21
time to repent, but she does not wish to repent of her immorality.
Mark well, I will hurl her on a sick bed, and those who commit 22
adultery with her I will hurl into great affliction, unless they repent
of the sins she leads them to commit. Her children I will strike 23
dead, and so, all the congregations will know that I am the one who
searches consciences and hearts, and rewards each of you according
to your deeds. But to the rest of you at Thyatira who do not hold 24
this doctrine and who have no knowledge of the profound mysteries
of Satan, as they call them — to you I say, I am laying on you no
other burden. Only hold fast what you have until I come. 25
To him who is victorious and follows my ways until the end, I will 26
give power over the nations. And he will rule with an iron staff, and 27
like earthenware they will be crushed to pieces, just as I have received 28
power from my Father. I will give him the morning star. Let him 29
who has ears listen to what the Spirit says to the congregations.' "

CHAPTER 3

TO THE CONGREGATON AT SARDIS

"To the angel of the congregation at Sardis write: 1
'He who has the seven spirits of God and the seven stars has
this to say: I know your conduct. You have the name of being alive,
but you are dead. Be watchful and strengthen the rest who are 2
about to die. For I do not find your conduct perfect in the sight
of my God. Remember, then, how you have received and heard 3
the message. Observe it and repent. If you will not be watchful, I
will come as a thief, and you will not have the least idea of the
hour when I will come to you. On the other hand, you have a few 4

2:20. *Jezebel:* a symbolic name, but most probably designating a real woman,
a bad Christian who was promoting the errors of the Nicolaites.

2:28. *the morning star:* St. Bede says: "Christ is the morning star, who after
the night of this life has passed, as he had promised will shed the eternal light
of life on his saints."

persons at Sardis who have not soiled their garments. Clothed in
5 white they will walk with me, because they deserve to do so. He
who is victorious shall be dressed in white garments, and I will not
erase his name from the book of life, but I will acknowledge his
6 name before my Father and before his angels. Let him who has
ears listen to what the Spirit says to the congregations.' "

TO THE CONGREGATION AT PHILADELPHIA

7   "To the angel of the congregation at Philadelphia write:
'He who is holy and true, who has the key of David, who opens
and no one can shut, who shuts and no one can open, has this
8 to say: I know your conduct. Take notice. I have placed before you
a door which has been opened, and which no one can shut. I know
that you have little strength, though you have kept my word and
9 have not denied my name. Mark well, I will bring some of the
synagogue of Satan, who say they are Jews, though they are not,
but are lying. I say that I will make them come and lie prostrate
10 at your feet, and they will know that I have loved you. Because
you have followed the example of my patient suffering, I in turn
will preserve you from the hour of trial that is about to come upon
11 the whole world to test those who dwell on the earth. I am coming
quickly. Hold fast what you have that no one may snatch away
12 your crown. Him who is victorious I will make a pillar in the temple
of my God, and he shall never leave it again. And I will write on him
the name of my God, and the name of the city of my God, the new
Jerusalem that comes down out of heaven from my God, and my
13 own name. Let him who has ears listen to what the Spirit says
to the congregations.' "

TO THE CONGREGATION AT LAODICEA

14   "To the angel of the congregation at Laodicea write:
'He who is absolutely faithful, the trustworthy and true witness,
15 the beginning of God's creation, has this to say: I know your
conduct. You are not cold; you are not hot. Would that you were
16 cold or hot! And so, because you are lukewarm and neither cold

---

3:7. *key of David*: a symbol of absolute authority over the new Jerusalem, the new Israel.
3:8. *a door*: this designates an opportunity for making converts to Christianity.
3:14. *absolutely faithful*: literally, "Amen."

nor hot, I am going to vomit you out of my mouth. You say, I am 17
rich and have become wealthy and have no need of anything, but
you do not know that you are wretched and pitiable and poor and
blind and naked. I counsel you to buy from me gold refined by fire, 18
that you may be wealthy, and buy white garments that you may be
clothed and the shame of your nakedness may not be manifest.
Buy salve, too, that you may anoint your eyes and see. As for me, 19
I reprove and chastise those whom I love. So be zealous and repent.
Here I am standing at the door and knocking. If anyone listens to 20
my call and opens the door, I will come in to him and have supper
with him and he with me. To him who is victorious, I will grant 21
the favor of being seated beside me on my throne, as I too was
victorious and am seated beside my Father on his throne. Let him 22
who has ears listen to what the Spirit says to the congregations.' "

RECEPTION OF THE SEALED BOOK

CHAPTER 4

THE SCENE IN HEAVEN

After this I had a vision. There was a door in heaven standing 1
open, and the voice like a trumpet, which I had previously heard,
spoke to me, "Come up here, and I will show you what must take
place later." Suddenly I was thrown into an ecstasy. To my surprise, 2
there was a throne set up in heaven, and someone was seated on
the throne. The occupant of the throne looked like jasper and 3
cornelian, and around the throne was a rainbow like a vision of
emerald.

Surrounding this throne were twenty-four thrones, and seated 4
on them were twenty-four elders clothed in white robes, and on their
heads were golden crowns. From the throne came forth flashes of 5

3:18. *gold . . . white garments . . . salve:* these symbols are taken from the
city's commercial and industrial activities. It was a well-known banking center.
It manufactured woolen cloth and eye powder. The gold, etc., designate faith
and the other Christian virtues, whose source is the grace of Christ.

4:2. *someone:* to add to the mystery of the scene, St. John does not mention
the name of the occupant of the throne. It is God.

4:4. *twenty-four elders:* these represent angels who preside over the unfolding
of history as God's ministers.

lightning, rumblings, and peals of thunder. There were seven torches burning before the throne. They are the seven spirits of God.

6 Before the throne there was something like a sea of glass, resembling crystal. In front of and around the throne were four living beings,

7 full of eyes in front and behind. The first living being was like a lion; the second was like an ox; the third had the face of a man;

8 and the fourth was like a flying eagle. Each of the four living beings had six wings; all around and within they were full of eyes. Day and night they continually repeat,

"Holy, holy, holy, is the Lord God Almighty
whose name is 'He was' and 'He is' and 'He is coming.'"

9 Whenever these living beings give honor and glory and thanks to him who is seated on the throne and lives for ever and ever,

10 the twenty-four elders prostrate before the occupant of the throne and worship him who lives for ever and ever and cast their crowns before the throne. They chant,

11 "Worthy are you, O Lord our God,
to reserve for yourself glory and honor and power,
because you created all things,
and by your will they came into being and were created."

Chapter 5

THE SCROLL AND THE LAMB

1 I saw in the right hand of him who was seated on the throne a scroll with writing on the inside and the outside, sealed with seven

2 seals. I saw a mighty angel proclaiming with a loud voice, "Who

3 is worthy to open the scroll and break its seals?" But no one in heaven or on earth or under the earth could open the scroll or look

4 into it. So I wept much because no one was found worthy to open

5 the scroll or to look into it. Then one of the elders said to me, "Do not weep. See, the lion of the tribe of Juda, the root of David, has

---

4:6. *four living beings:* these represent angels, who gather into their nature all that is most excellent in the created universe, the strength of the bull, the majesty of the lion, the swiftness of the eagle, and the intelligence of man. The eyes symbolize their far-reaching knowledge.

5:3. *no one:* the inability of any creature to open the scroll indicates that only God knows the secrets of the future and can reveal them to us.

conquered and so he can open the scroll and its seven seals." Then 6
I saw standing in front of the throne and in the midst of the four
living beings and of the elders, a Lamb as if slain, having seven
horns and seven eyes, which are the seven spirits of God who were
given a mission to the whole earth. The Lamb came and took the 7
scroll out of the right hand of him who was seated on the throne.
When the Lamb took the scroll, the four living beings and the 8
twenty-four elders prostrated themselves before him, each having
a harp and golden vials filled with perfumes, which symbolize the
prayers of the saints.

THE SONG OF PRAISE

They sang a new canticle: 9
"You are worthy to take the scroll and to open its seals,
Because you were slain, and with your blood you redeemed
    for God
Men of every tribe and tongue and people and nation,
And you made of them a kingdom and priests for our God;   10
And they shall reign over the earth."
In my vision I heard a chorus of many angels and of the living 11
beings and elders who encircled the throne. Their number was
myriads on myriads and thousands on thousands. In a loud voice 12
they said,
"Worthy is the Lamb who has been slain
    to receive power and wealth and wisdom and strength
    and honor and glory and blessing."
In the same way every creature that was in heaven and on the earth 13
and under the earth and in the sea, yes, all the beings that dwell in
them, I heard saying,
"To him who is seated on the throne and to the Lamb
    blessing and honor and glory and dominion for ever
    and ever."
The four living beings said, "May it be so." But the elders prostrated 14
themselves and worshiped him who lives for ever and ever.

5:6. *seven horns:* symbol of the plenitude of power and jurisdiction. The seven
eyes indicate the fullness of his knowledge. The seven spirits represent the Holy
Spirit, who was given a mission by the Father and the Son to the world.

The Breaking of the Seals

Chapter 6

THE FIRST SEAL: VICTORY

1   In my vision, when the Lamb had opened the first of the seven
seals, I heard one of the four living beings say with a thunderous
2   voice, "Come." And suddenly I saw a white horse. Its rider had a
bow, and a crown had been given him. He went forth a victor to
further increase his victory.

THE SECOND SEAL: WAR

3   When the Lamb opened the second seal, I heard the second
4   living being say, "Come." Then another horse came out, a red one.
Its rider was commissioned to take away peace from the earth, so
that men would kill one another. A great sword was handed to him.

THE THIRD SEAL: FAMINE

5   When the Lamb opened the third seal, I heard the third living
being say, "Come." And suddenly I saw a black horse. Its rider
6   had a pair of scales in his hand. I heard a voice in the midst of the
four living beings say, "A quart of wheat for a silver piece, and
three quarts of barley for a silver piece; but do not harm oil
and wine."

THE FOURTH SEAL: PESTILENCE

7   When the Lamb had opened the fourth seal, I heard the voice

---

6:1. The various visions that follow do not give the history of the Church
by epochs in chronological order. They rather contain a résumé of the same
series of aspects in the struggle against the worldly powers. Their principal
object is the triumph of the Lord over the idolatry and persecution of the
Roman Empire, which in turn is a symbol of all opposition to the Church,
offered by all subsequent governments to the end of time.

6:2. The white horse and rider symbolize the victorious course of Christianity
over the world. The red horse symbolizes war, the third famine, and the fourth
pestilence and death.

6:5. During famine the necessities of life, wheat and barley, would be very
costly. The silver piece, or denarius, was the average daily wage of the working-
man. The order to spare the wine and oil is an indication that the famine would
not be absolute. This order probably came from God or the Lamb.

of the fourth living being say, "Come." And suddenly I saw a pale 8
yellow horse. Its rider's name was Death. The nether world was
following him. Power over one fourth of the earth was given them
to kill with sword, famine, and death, and by means of beasts.

THE FIFTH SEAL: THE MARTYRS

When he had opened the fifth seal, I saw under the altar the 9
souls of those who had been slain on account of the revelation made
and attested by God and received by them. They cried out with 10
a loud voice: "How long, O holy and true Sovereign, before you
will judge and avenge our blood on those who dwell on earth?"
To each of them was given a white robe, and they were told to 11
wait patiently a little longer until the number of their fellow servants
and their brothers who were to be slain, just as they had been,
would be complete.

THE SIXTH SEAL: SIGNS ON EARTH AND IN HEAVEN

When the Lamb had opened the sixth seal, I had a vision of a 12
great earthquake. The sun became black as haircloth; the moon in
its entirety became red as blood, and the stars in the sky fell on the 13
earth, just as the unripe winter figs fall from the fig tree when it is
swept by a gale. The sky receded as a scroll that is rolled up, and 14
every mountain and island was dislodged. The kings of the earth, 15
the nobles and the captains, the rich and the powerful, every slave
and free man, hid themselves in the caves and rocks of the mountains. They said to the mountains and to the rocks, "Fall on us 16
and hide us from the face of him who is seated on the throne and
from the anger of the Lamb, because the great day of their anger 17
has come, and who can stand his ground?"

6:8. *nether world*: the abode of departed souls, not necessarily a place of
punishment.

6:9. *revelation*: this might mean the preaching of Revelation by missionaries
but more probably the reference is to their acceptance of the revealed message.
under the altar: the souls of Christian martyrs are here, perhaps, because the
blood of sacrificial victims flows down to the base of the altar, and according to
the Jewish idea the soul was in the blood. Or, perhaps, the souls of the martyrs
are thus represented as being close to God, and, therefore, enjoy already the
happiness of heaven.

Chapter 7

SEALING OF THE SERVANTS OF GOD

1 After this I saw four angels standing at the four corners of the earth, holding back the four winds of the earth, that no wind should

2 blow over the land or the sea or on any tree. Then I saw another angel arise from the east, holding the seal of the living God. He cried in a loud voice to the four angels who were empowered to

3 harm the earth and the sea, "Do not harm the earth or the sea or the trees till we have sealed the servants of our God on their fore-

4 heads." And I heard the number of those who were sealed. One hundred and forty-four thousand were sealed with representatives from every tribe of the sons of Israel:

5   Of the tribe of Juda twelve thousand were sealed,
      of the tribe of Ruben twelve thousand,
      of the tribe of Gad twelve thousand,
6   of the tribe of Aser twelve thousand,
      of the tribe of Nephtali twelve thousand,
      of the tribe of Manasses twelve thousand,
7   of the tribe of Simeon twelve thousand,
      of the tribe of Levi twelve thousand,
      of the tribe of Issachar twelve thousand,
8   of the tribe of Zabulon twelve thousand,
      of the tribe of Joseph twelve thousand,
      of the tribe of Benjamin twelve thousand.

THE SONG OF THE SEALED

9 After this I had a vision. Suddenly there appeared a great multitude that no one could number, from all nations and tribes and peoples and tongues, standing before the throne and before the Lamb, clothed in white robes with palm branches in their hands.

10 They were crying out in a loud voice and said, "Our salvation is caused by our God, who is seated on the throne, and by the Lamb."

7:4. The number 144,000 is symbolic of a very great multitude. Dan is not mentioned, perhaps, because according to Jewish tradition the Antichrist was to come from that tribe. Both Manasses and Joseph are mentioned. Ephraim is not mentioned.

All the angels stood encircling the throne and the elders and the 11
four living beings. They prostrated on their faces before the throne
and worshiped God. "So it is," they said. "Blessing, glory, wisdom, 12
thanksgiving, honor, power and strength are due to our God for ever
and ever. Amen."

THE SEVENTH SEAL

Then one of the elders addressed me. "Who are these clothed 13
in white robes," he asked, "and from where did they come?" "My 14
Lord," I answered, "you yourself know." Then he explained to me,
"Those are they who have come out of great tribulation and have
washed their robes and made them white in the blood of the Lamb.
Therefore they are before the throne of God and serve him day and 15
night in his temple, and he who is seated on the throne will diffuse
his glory on them. No longer will they thirst or hunger. No longer 16
will the sun or any heat strike them. For the Lamb before the 17
throne will be their shepherd and will guide them to the springs
of living waters, and God will wipe away every tear from their eyes."

CHAPTER 8

When he had opened the seventh seal, there was silence in 1
heaven for about half an hour.

THE VISION OF THE SEVEN TRUMPETS

THE SEVEN ANGELS WITH TRUMPETS

I saw the seven angels who stood in the presence of God, and 2
seven trumpets were given to them. Another angel came and stood 3
by the altar, carrying a golden censer, and a great quantity of incense

---

7:12. So it is: literally, "Amen." They give assent to the prayer of the
martyrs in verse 10.

8:1. The period of silence, some think, is indicative of the anxious suspense
of the angels awaiting the future revelations to be made. According to others,
the angel's hymns of praise are interrupted for the sake of the prayers of the
martyrs.

8:2. In Scripture trumpets often serve to herald God's intervention in world
affairs.

8:3. The incense, according to St. Bede, represents Christ; it is by union
with his intercession that our prayers are made worthy.

was given to him that he might offer it with the prayers of the saints
4 on the golden altar before the throne. The smoke of the incense, together with the prayers of the saints, ascended from the angel's
5 hand to the presence of God. The angel took the censer and filled it with live coals from the altar and hurled it to the earth, and there were peals of thunder, rumblings, flashes of lightning, and an earth-
6 quake. Now the seven angels with seven trumpets prepared themselves to sound the trumpets.

THE FIRST FOUR TRUMPETS SOUND

7 The first angel sounded his trumpet. Then there was a hailstorm and fire mixed with blood, and it was hurled to the earth. A third of the earth was burned up, and a third of the woods and all of the green grass were destroyed by fire.
8 The second angel sounded his trumpet. Then it seemed a great
9 mountain was all afire and was hurled into the sea. A third of the living creatures in the sea died, and a third of the ships were wrecked.
10 The third angel sounded his trumpet. Then there fell from the sky a great star, burning like a torch. It fell on a third of the rivers
11 and on the springs of water. The name of the star was Wormwood. A third of the waters became wormwood, and many people died from the waters, because they were made bitter.
12 The fourth angel sounded his trumpet. Then a third of the sun was struck, and a third of the moon, and a third of the stars so that a third of them lost their light. The day lost a third of its light, as also the night.

THE CRY OF AN EAGLE

13 In a vision I heard an eagle, as it flew in the middle of the sky, cry out in a loud voice, "Perdition, perdition, perdition to the inhabitants of the earth, because of the rest of the trumpet blasts of the three angels who are going to sound their trumpets."

8:5. The fact that the same instrument serves to carry the prayers of the saints to the throne of God and to visit punishment on sinful men seems clearly to indicate a connection; the punishment is in answer to the prayers of the saints.

8:7–12. The physical catastrophes here mentioned are but symbols of various punishments visited on them to induce them to repentance, such as disease, remorse of conscience, disillusionment, and despair.

CHAPTER 9

THE FIFTH TRUMPET SOUNDS

The fifth angel sounded his trumpet. Then I saw a star that 1
had fallen from the sky to the earth. The key to the bottomless
pit was given to him, and he opened the bottomless pit. Smoke 2
rose out of the pit like the smoke of a great furnace; the sun and
the air were darkened by the smoke from the pit. From the smoke 3
came forth locusts on the earth, and they were given power like that
of earthly scorpions. But they were told not to hurt the grass or 4
any green plant or tree, but only the human beings who did not
have God's seal on their foreheads. They were commissioned only 5
to torture, not to kill these people during a period of five months.
Their torture was like the torture of a scorpion when it stings a
man. In those days men will seek death and will not find it; they 6
will long to die, but death will flee from them.

In appearance the locusts were like horses prepared for battle. 7
On their heads were what seemed to be crowns of gold. Their faces
were like the faces of men. They had hair like a woman's, teeth like 8
a lion's, breastplates as of iron. The noise of their wings was like that 9
of many horses with chariots rushing into battle. Like scorpions, 10
they had tails and stings, and in their tails they had the power to
harm human beings for a period of five months. They had as 11
their king the angel of the bottomless pit, whose name in Hebrew
is Abaddon and in Greek Apollyon. The first woe is past. Take note, 12
two more woes are to come after this.

THE SIXTH TRUMPET SOUNDS

The sixth angel sounded his trumpet. Then I heard a voice from 13

9:1. *star:* an evil angel, most probably the "Abaddon" of verse 11, and the
Satan of Chapter 20.

9:2. *smoke:* a symbol of error and falsehood. The darkened sun symbolizes
the obscuring of truth by error.

9:3. *locusts:* diabolic influences.

9:5. *only to torture:* this may indicate that the suffering was designed to
recall its victims to repentance. *five months:* some think this covers symbolically
the whole period from Christ to the end of time, but others think it stands for
a limited time.

9:11. *Abaddon:* Hebrew for "destroyer." Some commentators think there is
a play on the word *Apollyon* and the Greek god "Apollo."

14 the four corners of the golden altar before God. The voice said to
the sixth angel with the trumpet, "Release the four angels who are
15 bound at the great river Euphrates." Now the four angels who had
been held ready for this hour, day, month, and year were released,
16 that they might kill a third of mankind. The number of the troops
of horseman was twenty thousand times ten thousand. I heard
their number.

17 This is how the horses appeared in my vision. The riders wore
breastplates of fire, hyacinth, and sulphur. The horses' heads were
like those of lions, and from their mouths came forth fire, smoke,
18 and sulphur. By these three plagues a third of mankind was killed,
that is, by the fire, the smoke, and the sulphur that came forth from
19 their mouths. The power of the horses was in their mouths and tails;
their tails, with which they caused harm, were like snakes and
had heads.

20 The rest of mankind, who had not been killed by these plagues,
did not repent of the idols that their hands had made or cease
worshiping them — demons of gold, silver, brass, stone, and wood,
21 which can neither see nor hear nor walk. Nor did they repent of
their murders, their sorceries, their immorality, or their thefts.

CHAPTER 10

THE ANGEL WITH THE OPEN SCROLL

1 I saw another strong angel coming down from heaven, clothed
in a cloud and a rainbow was over his head. His face was like the
2 sun, and his legs like pillars of fire. He held a little scroll open in
his hand. He set his right foot on the sea and his left on the earth.
3 Then he cried out in a loud voice, just as a lion roars. When he
4 had cried out, the seven thunders gave forth their sound. When

---

9:14. *angels . . . Euphrates:* these angels are wicked spirits permitted when
they are unbound to unleash war. According to St. Bede and many others, the
Euphrates is a symbol for world empire which makes war.
10:2. *right foot . . . left:* the angel's stature indicates the importance of his
mission, and his posture shows that his mission is universal in extent, including
both land and sea. *little scroll:* as contrasted with the great scroll which only
the Lamb could open, this little book contained relatively unimportant and
restricted revelations.
10:4. *Seal up:* St. John was to keep certain revelations to himself, perhaps
because they were like St. Paul's "unutterable utterances, which no man is permitted to repeat" (2 Cor. 12:4).

the seven thunders had sounded, I was about to write, but I heard a voice from heaven say, "Seal up the things the seven thunders have uttered, and do not write them down."

Now the angel whom I saw standing on the sea and the earth 5 raised his hand to heaven and swore by him who lives for ever and 6 ever, who created heaven and the things in it, that there should no longer be any delay, but that at the time when the seventh angel 7 sends out his call, at the sound of his trumpet, the mystery of God will be accomplished, just as he proclaimed by his servants, the prophets.

The voice that I had heard from heaven, I heard again speaking 8 to me. "Go," it said, "take the scroll that is open in the hand of the angel who is standing on the sea and the earth." I went to the 9 angel, telling him to give me the little scroll. "Take it," he said, "and eat it. It will make your stomach bitter, but in your mouth it will be sweet as honey." So I took the little scroll from the angel's 10 hand and ate it. In my mouth it was sweet as honey, but when I had eaten it, my stomach was made bitter. And they said to 11 me. "You must prophesy again about many nations, peoples, tongues, and kings."

CHAPTER 11

THE COMMAND TO MEASURE THE TEMPLE

A reed like a staff was given to me with the message: "Rise, 1 measure the temple of God and the altar, and count those who worship there. But exclude the court outside the temple from your 2 measuring, because it has been given over to the nations, who will trample underfoot the holy city for forty-two months. I will em- 3 power my two witnesses, clothed in sackcloth, to be my spokesmen for a thousand two hundred and sixty days.

10:9. *bitter . . . sweet:* bitter because they foretold God's punishment on his unrelenting enemies, and sweet because they foretold his mercy on the faithful and on repentant sinners.

11:1. It is probably the Lamb, the Son of God, who gives John the reed and the order to measure the temple. The temple is a symbol of the inner sanctuary of the Church, and the Holy City and exterior court stand for the external life of the Church which must needs be carried on in this world. Measuring was a means of protecting the inner life of the Church from harm.

11:3. *my two witnesses:* represent the Church's mission to preach and defend

THE TWO WITNESSES

4 These are symbolized by the two olive trees and the two lamp-
5 stands present before the Lord of the earth. Fire will come out of
the witnesses' mouths to consume their enemies who seek to harm
them. In just that way anyone who wishes to harm them will be
6 killed. These witnesses are empowered to close up the sky so that
no rain will fall during the days of their prophetic mission. The
witnesses have power over the waters to turn them into blood, and
to strike at will the earth with every kind of plague.
7 When they have finished their testimony, the beast arising out
of the bottomless pit will make war on them, conquer and kill
8 them. Their corpses will lie in the streets of the great city, called
in prophecy Sodom and Egypt, where their Lord was crucified.
9 Men from every tribe, people, tongue, and nation will look on their
corpses three days and a half, and will not allow them to be laid
10 in tombs. The inhabitants of the earth will rejoice over them and
make merry, and will exchange presents, because these two spokes-

revealed truth. They are two because of the deuteronomic law that two
witnesses are requisite to establish a truth in court. Their garb of sackcloth
symbolizes that the Church's attitude here below as long as it is fighting evil
must be that of penitence and not of triumph. The period of the Church's
activity is forty-two months, or twelve hundred and sixty days, or three and a
half years. This designates the whole period from the birthday of the Church
on the first Pentecost until the end of time. The numbers are Messianic.
Forty-two is the equivalent of the name David, three and a half corresponds
to the three and a half years which St. John in his Gospel assigns to the
public life of our Lord. Just as his life of preaching and healing lasted three
and a half years, so the life of his mystic body on earth would last for three
and a half divisions of time. Just as there were forty-two generations before the
advent of Christ, so after his return to heaven there will be forty-two periods
of time until his return at the end of the world. The figure twelve hundred and
sixty was probably employed simply as a variant expression, but perhaps too,
St. John wished to emphasize the contrast between the length of the witnesses' activities and the brevity of their cessation, three and one-half days, a
ratio of one to three hundred and sixty. Probably the cessation of the witnesses'
activities is what St. Paul referred to in 2 Thess. 2:5, where he speaks of a
restraining force which delays the advent of the Antichrist.
11:4-5. The witnesses are compared to olive trees which furnish the oil for
lighting and the stands which hold up the light to the world, an apt symbol
of the mission of the Church to proclaim the light of revealed truth.
11:6. The defensive and punitive measures here mentioned rather symbolize
the power of the Church's prayers to win from God whatever defense and
whatever punishment of her enemies Providence may see fit to send. It will be
impossible for the Church's enemies to stop her activity until her mission is
accomplished.

men of God had tormented the inhabitants of the earth.

But after three days and a half the breath of life from God 11 entered them. They stood on their feet, and great fear fell on those who saw them. They heard a loud voice from heaven say to them, 12 "Come up here." Then they ascended into heaven in a cloud, while their enemies looked on. At that hour there was a great 13 earthquake and a tenth of the city fell, and seven thousand persons were killed in the earthquake, and the rest, who were overcome with fright, gave glory to the God of heaven. Now the second woe is 14 past. I warn you, the third is coming quickly.

THE SEVENTH TRUMPET SOUNDS

The seventh angel sounded his trumpet. Then there were loud 15 voices in heaven saying, "The reign over this world has passed to our Lord and to his Christ, and he will reign for ever and ever." The twenty-four elders who were seated on their thrones before 16 God prostrated themselves and worshiped God. "We give you 17 thanks, O Lord God Almighty," they said, "whose name is 'He is' and 'He was,' because you have taken possession of your great power and have begun to reign. The nations had aroused themselves 18 to anger. Then the day of your anger came, the time to judge the dead and to reward your servants — the prophets, the saints, and those who revere your name, little or great. The time has come to destroy the destroyers of the earth."

The Vision of the Seven Signs

THE VISION OF THE WOMAN AND THE DRAGON

Then the temple of God in heaven was opened, and the ark of 19 his covenant was seen in his temple. There were flashes of lightning, rumblings, peals of thunder, and earthquakes, and large hailstones.

Chapter 12

A great sign appeared in the sky: a woman clothed with the sun, 1 with the moon under her feet, and on her head a crown of twelve

12:1. *a woman:* the spiritual Israel which gave birth to Christ in his real and in his mystic body, or as St. Augustine and many other Fathers put it, the

2   stars. She was with child and cried out because of the pain and
    anguish of childbirth.

3   Another sign was seen in the sky. Suddenly there appeared a
    huge red dragon having seven heads and ten horns, and on his head
4   were seven diadems. His tail swept away a third of the stars in the
    sky and hurled them to the earth. Then the dragon stood before
    the woman on the point of childbirth, that he might devour her
5   son as soon as she had been delivered of him. She gave birth to a
    male child who is destined to rule all nations with an iron rod. The
6   child was caught up to God and to his throne. Then the woman
    fled into the wilderness, where she had a place prepared by God.
    Here she would be nourished for a thousand two hundred and
    sixty days.

THE DRAGON IS HURLED DOWN

7   Then war broke out in heaven. Michael and his angels had to
8   fight the dragon; the dragon fought, and so did his angels. But they
    were defeated, and a place was no longer found for them in heaven.
9   That huge dragon, the ancient serpent, was hurled down, he who is
    called the devil and Satan, he who leads the whole world astray.
    He was hurled down to earth, and his angels were hurled down
    with him.

THE SONG OF TRIUMPH

10   Then I heard a loud voice in heaven. "Now the salvation which
    God brings about," it said, "his power and royalty, and the authority
    of his Christ have been established because the accuser of our
    brothers has been hurled down, he who accused them before our
11 God day and night. But they conquered him by means of the blood

city of God, which, of course, includes the Blessed Virgin Mary. Her clothing
is indicative of her grandeur.
    12:4. *dragon:* the devil, whose immense power and opposition to the light of
Revelation is symbolized by his sweeping a third of the stars from heaven. Some
see in these stars a reference to fallen angels.
    12:6. *the wilderness:* the inner life of the Church, consisting in prayer and
contemplation. The other phase of the Church's activity is symbolized by the
two witnesses. These two will continue on, the Church's life of prayer and
contemplation, and its active ministry in defense of revealed truth, until Christ's
definitive victory at the end of time.
    12:7. *war . . . in heaven:* perhaps an attempt on the part of Satan and his
forces to unseat the triumphant Christ or at least to undo his work on earth.

of the Lamb and the word of their testimony, and because they
despised life even to the point of being willing to die. Therefore, 12
be glad, O heaven, and you who dwell there. Perdition to you,
O earth and sea, because the devil has gone down to you in a great
rage, since he knows how brief is the time he has."

THE DRAGON PERSECUTES THE WOMAN

When the dragon saw that he was hurled down to the earth, he 13
pursued the woman who had given birth to the male child. The 14
two wings of the great eagle were given to the woman that she
might fly to her dwelling in the wilderness, where, far from the
serpent, she was nourished for a time and times and half a time.
The serpent poured out of his mouth water like a river after the 15
woman. Then the earth came to her aid by opening its mouth and 16
swallowing up the river that the dragon had poured out of his mouth.
Now the dragon was angered at the woman and went away to make 17
war on the rest of her offspring who kept the commandments of
God and held fast the testimony concerning Jesus. And he stood on 18
the sand by the sea.

CHAPTER 13

THE WILD BEAST FROM THE SEA

I saw coming out of the sea a beast, having seven heads and 1
ten horns. On the horns were ten diadems and on its heads
blasphemous names. The beast of my vision was like a leopard. 2
Its feet were like those of a bear, and its mouth like that of a

---

12:14. *two wings:* may designate prayer and contemplation by which the
Church withdraws spiritually from the turmoil of the world. *time and times,*
etc.: the same period as forty-two months, twelve hundred and sixty days, three
and one-half years.

12:15. *water:* symbol of persecutions. Their being absorbed symbolizes the
fact that nations at war with the Church are often distracted by internal strife,
or they collapse or engage in conflict with other nations.

13:1. The sea is an apt symbol of restless humanity from which rises secular
governments. Although St. John probably had the Roman Empire in mind,
he would not restrict the symbol to that power. He had in mind any secular
government which resists God and his Church. Such governments combine the
massive strength of the bear, the feline vigilance and cunning of the leopard,
and the roar of the lion. The wounding and healing of the beast symbolizes
the fact that governments fall but others rise to take their place.

lion. The dragon gave to it its own power and throne and great
3 authority. Then one of the heads received a fatal wound, but when
the fatal wound was healed, all the earth followed the beast in
4 admiration. They worshiped the dragon because he had given power
to the beast, which they also worshiped. "Who is like the beast,"
they said, "and who can fight against it?"
5 It was given a mouth to utter haughty words and blasphemies.
It was also given authority to carry on its activities forty-two months.
6 It opened its mouth to utter blasphemies against God, to blaspheme
7 his name and his tabernacle and those who dwell in heaven. It was
8 empowered to make war on all the saints and to conquer them. All
the inhabitants of the earth will worship it, that is, those whose
names have not been written in the book of life of the Lamb that
was slain from the foundation of the world.
9, 10 If anyone has ears, let him listen. If anyone leads others into
captivity, into captivity he goes. If anyone kills with the sword, with
the sword he must be killed. This calls for the patience and the faith
of the saints.

THE WILD BEAST FROM THE LAND

11 I saw another beast coming up out of the earth; it had two
horns like those of a lamb, but it was wont to speak like a dragon.
12 It exercised all the power of the former beast in its presence and
made the earth and its inhabitants worship the former beast, whose
13 fatal wound was healed. It worked great wonders; it even made fire
14 come down from heaven to earth in the sight of men. It led astray
the inhabitants of the earth because of the wonders that it was
empowered to work in the presence of the beast, telling the inhabitants of the earth to make a statue of the beast which had been
15 wounded by the sword, and yet lived. It was enabled to give life
to the statue of the beast so that it even spoke and had everyone
16 who refuses to worship it put to death. It had a mark put on the
right hand or on the forehead of the little and the great, of the rich
17 and the poor, of the free and the slave. It also prevented all, except
those who had the mark, either the name of the beast or the number
of its name, from buying or selling.

13:11. The other beast is a parody on the Lamb of God, and symbolizes
false religions and false philosophies which abet the secular power in its opposition to the Church or Kingdom of God on earth.

Wisdom is needed for the following. Let him who has under- 18
standing calculate the number of the beast, which really is the
number of a man. The number is six hundred and sixty-six.

CHAPTER 14

THE LAMB AND THE VIRGINS

I had a vision. I saw the Lamb standing on Mount Sion, and 1
with him a hundred and forty-four thousand who had his name and
the name of his Father written on their foreheads. Then I heard 2
a sound from heaven like the sound of many waters and like the
sound of loud peals of thunder. The sound I heard was like that of
harpists playing on their harps. They sang a new song before the 3
throne and before the four living beings and the elders. No one
could learn the song except those one hundred and forty-four thousand who have been purchased from the earth. They are those who 4
preserved complete virginity, because they are celibates. They follow
the Lamb wherever he goes. They are purchased from among men,
first fruits for God and for the Lamb. No lie was found on their 5
lips; they are without blemish.

I saw another angel flying in midheaven, having everlasting 6
good news to proclaim to those who dwell on the earth and to every
nation, tribe, tongue, and people. "Fear God," he said with a loud 7
voice, "and give glory to him, because the hour of his judgment
has come. Worship him who made the heaven and the earth, the
sea and the springs of water." Another angel followed. "She has 8
fallen," he cried, "she has fallen, Babylon the great, she who gave
all nations to drink of her immorality, which merits God's anger."
And another, a third angel followed them. "If anyone worships the 9
beast and its statue," he cried in a loud voice, "and receives their

---

13:18. *six hundred and sixty-six:* the numerical value of the letters in Hebrew
of Caesar Nero is equal to this sum, but Nero is merely a symbol of all subsequent
rulers who resist the kingdom of God.

14:4. *preserved complete virginity:* literally, "have not defiled themselves with
women." The reference is to those who have fully observed the evangelical
counsels. It is to be noted that there is nothing defiling about the honorable
relations of the sexes in lawful marriage. The union of marriage is only relatively
defiling in that it detracts from the higher merit of the celibate life, entered
into for the love of God and the desire for the higher perfection.

10 mark on his forehead or on his hand, he shall drink of the wine of God's anger, and shall be tormented with fire and brimstone in
11 the sight of the holy angels and of the Lamb. The smoke of their torments shall rise for ever and ever, and they who worship the beast and its statue, and whoever receives the mark of its name,
12 shall have no rest day or night." In this situation the saints who faithfully keep God's commandments and their faith in Jesus have
13 the opportunity for patient endurance. I heard a voice from heaven. "Write," it said, "From now on, blessed are the dead who die in the Lord." "Yes," says the Spirit, "they are to have rest from their toils, for their deeds accompany them."

THE VISION OF THE JUDGMENT

14 I had a vision. I saw a white cloud, and one like the Son of Man was seated on the cloud, having on his head a golden crown and
15 in his hand a sharp sickle. Then another angel came from the temple. He cried in a loud voice to him who was seated on the cloud, "Put your sickle to use, for the hour to reap has come because
16 the earth's harvest is ripe." Then he who was seated on the cloud swung his sickle on the earth, and the earth was reaped.
17 Now another angel came forth from the temple that is in heaven.
18 He too had a sharp sickle. Still another angel who had power over fire came forth from the altar, and he called in a loud voice to him who had the sharp sickle. "Put your sharp sickle to use," he said, "and gather the clusters of the earth's vine, for its grapes are ripe."
19 The angel swung his sickle on the earth and gathered the vintage of the earth and threw it into the great wine press of God's anger.
20 The wine press was trodden outside the city, and blood flowed from the wine press as high as the horses' bridles for a distance of a thousand and six hundred stadia.

CHAPTER 15

THE SEVEN ANGELS AND THE SEVEN PLAGUES

1 I saw another sign in heaven, great and wonderful, seven angels with the seven plagues which are final, inasmuch as with them God's anger reaches its climax.
2 I saw something that resembled a sea of glass glowing with fire.

I saw standing on this sea of glass those who as victors escape from the grasp of the beast, its statue, and its numerical name, and who hold the harps of God. They sing the song of Moses, God's servant, 3 and the song of the Lamb:

"Great and wonderful are your deeds, O Lord God Almighty.

Just and true are your ways, O King of the nations.

Who will not fear you, O Lord, and glorify your name? 4

For you alone are holy, and all nations will come to worship you,

Because your judgments have been made manifest."

The Vision of the Seven Bowls

THE ANGEL WITH THE BOWLS

After this I had a vision. The temple of the tabernacle of the 5 testimony was opened in heaven, and the seven angels with the 6 seven plagues came forth from the temple. They were clothed in clean white linen, and their breasts were encircled with golden sashes. One of the four living beings gave the seven angels seven 7 golden bowls full of the anger of God, who lives for ever and ever. The temple was filled with smoke because of God's glory and power, 8 and no one could enter the temple till the seven plagues of the seven angels were ended.

CHAPTER 16

THE FIRST THREE BOWLS ARE POURED OUT

I heard a loud voice from the temple. "Go," it said to the seven 1 angels, "and pour out the seven bowls of God's anger on the earth." The first went and poured out his bowl on the earth, and a malig- 2 nant and pernicious ulcer attacked those who had the beast's mark and worshiped its statue. Then the second poured out his bowl 3 on the sea. It became like the blood of a dead man, and every living thing in the sea died. Next the third poured out his bowl on the 4 rivers and springs, and they became blood. I then heard the angel 5

16:2. The plagues represented by the seven bowls are a recapitulation of the plagues symbolized by the seven trumpets. These plagues represent various afflictions in the form of disease and natural catastrophes visited on sinners by God to induce them to repentance.

of the waters say, "O Lord, whose name is 'He is' and 'He was,'

6 O holy One, you are just in pronouncing these judgments. Because they have shed the blood of the saints and the prophets, you have

7 given them blood to drink; they deserve it." I heard the altar too saying, "Yes, O Lord God Almighty, true and just are your judgments."

THE SECOND THREE BOWLS ARE POURED OUT

8 Then the fourth poured out his bowl on the sun, and it was

9 strengthened to scorch men with fire. So men were scorched with great heat, and they blasphemed the name of God, who has power over these plagues. But they did not repent and give glory to him.

10 Now the fifth poured out his bowl on the throne of the beast, and its kingdom was darkened. Men kept gnawing their tongues because

11 of the pain. They blasphemed the God of heaven because of their

12 pains and sores. But they did not repent of their deeds. After this the sixth poured out his bowl on the great river Euphrates, and it was dried up so that a way was made ready for the kings from the East.

THE UNCLEAN SPIRITS OF DEMONS

13 I saw three unclean spirits like frogs coming out of the mouths

14 of the dragon, the beast, and the false prophet. They were spirits of demons working wonders. They went to the kings of the whole earth to gather them together for the battle on the great day of God

15 Almighty. ("Mark well, I come as a thief! Blessed is he who is vigilant and retains possession of his clothes, so that he does not

16 have to walk about naked and be put to shame.") So they gathered them together in a place that in Hebrew is called Harmagedon.

THE SEVENTH BOWL IS POURED OUT

17 Lastly, the seventh poured out his bowl on the air, and a loud

---

16:12. *river Euphrates:* the barrier that held the warlike kings of the East from attacking was the river Euphrates. Its drying up symbolizes the unleashing of the war lords.

16:13. *unclean spirits:* these symbolize the ceaseless bickerings between nations, suspicions, charges, and countercharges which ultimately lead to war.

16:16. *Harmagedon:* a Hebrew word, really two words (*Har-Megiddo*), which means "mountain of Megiddo." Here it stands for the plains of Esdraelon, which are adjacent to Megiddo. This plain was the great battlefield of Palestine. It is a symbol of the divine struggle against Satan and his forces.

voice came from the throne in the temple. "It is done," it said.
Then there were flashes of lightning, rumblings, peals of thunder, 18
and a great earthquake such as has never been since men were on
this earth, so great an earthquake was it. The great city broke 19
into three pieces, and the cities of the nations fell. God was
mindful of Babylon the great to give her the cup of wine of
his fierce anger. Every island fled away, and mountains could not 20
be found. Large hailstones, heavy as talents, came down from 21
heaven on the men, who blasphemed God because of the plague
of hail. It was very grievous.

The Fate of Babylon the Great

Chapter 17

"BABYLON THE GREAT"

One of the seven angels with the seven bowls came and spoke 1
to me, "Come, I will show you the judgments on the great harlot
seated on many waters. The kings of the earth have committed 2
fornication with her, and she has made the inhabitants of the earth
drunk with the wine of her immorality." The angel carried me 3
away in ecstasy into a wilderness. There I saw a woman seated on a
scarlet beast covered with blasphemous names. It had seven heads
and ten horns. The woman was clothed in purple and scarlet, and 4
glittered with gold, precious stones, and pearls. She held in her
hand a cup full of the abominations and impurities of her immorality, and on her forehead a mysterious name was written, 5
"Babylon the Great, the mother of harlots and of the abominations
of the earth." I saw the woman drunk with the blood of the saints 6
and with the blood of the martyrs of Jesus.

THE EXPLANATION BY THE ANGEL

When I saw her, I was filled with great wonder. The angel 7
said to me, "Why do you wonder? I will tell you the mystery of

16:21. *talents:* the weight of the talent was from 100 to 130 pounds.
17:1. *the great harlot:* later identified as Babylon represents pagan Rome
and all other imperial cities which oppose the kingdom of God on earth.
17:3. *wilderness:* a symbol of life without God.

the woman and of the seven-headed and ten-horned beast on which
8 she is riding. The beast that you saw existed once, now has
ceased to be. Yet it is about to come up from the bottomless pit
to go to destruction. And the inhabitants of the earth whose names
have not been written in the book of life from the foundation of
the world will wonder when they see the beast, because it existed,
9 then ceased to be, yet will come back to life. A wise mind is
needed to interpret this. The seven heads are seven mountains
10 upon which the woman is seated. They are also seven kings. Five
of them have fallen, one still exists, and the other has not yet made
11 his appearance. When he does, his stay must be short. The beast that
existed, then ceased to be, is himself an eighth king, though he
belongs to the seven and must go to destruction.

12   "The ten horns that you saw are ten kings who have not yet
received a kingdom, but they, together with the beast, will receive
13 authority as kings for one hour. They have one purpose, and they
14 give their power and authority to the beast. They will fight against
the Lamb, and the Lamb will conquer them, for he is the Lord of
Lords and the King of Kings. They who are with him are called and
chosen and faithful."

15   He also said to me, "The waters that you saw where the harlot
16 is seated are the people, multitudes, nations, and tongues. The ten
horns that you saw as well as the beasts will hate the harlot, make
17 her desolate and naked, eat her flesh, and consume her with fire. For
God has put it into their hearts to carry out his purpose. Consequently they have but one purpose, to give their dominion to the
18 beast until God's orders are carried out. The woman whom you saw
is the great city that has dominion over the kings of the earth."

CHAPTER 18

THE FALL OF BABYLON THE GREAT

1   After this I saw coming down from heaven another angel
invested with great authority, and the earth was lighted up by his

---

17:9–11. *seven mountains:* seem to be an unmistakable allusion to the seven
hills of Rome, and the kings are the Roman emperors. Domitian is the eighth,
but he also belongs to *the seven* because he was looked upon as a reincarnation
of Nero.

glory. He cried out in a loud voice, "She has fallen, she has fallen, 2
Babylon the great, and has become a dwelling of demons and a
stronghold of every unclean spirit and of every unclean bird, because 3
all the nations have drunk of the wine of her immorality that
deserves God's anger, and the kings of the earth have committed
fornication with her, and the merchants of the earth have grown
rich with the wealth of her wantonness."

PUNISHMENT FOR HER SINS

I heard another voice from heaven say, "Go out from her, my 4
people, that you may not be accomplices in her sins, and that you
may not share in her plagues along with her. Her sins have reached 5
heaven, and the Lord has remembered her iniquities. Render to her 6
in the same way that she has rendered to others. Give her double
in keeping with her deeds. Mix a double portion in the cup that
she has mixed. Visit on her torment and grief to the extent that she 7
has glorified herself and has given herself up to wantonness, because
in her heart she says, 'I am enthroned as a queen. I am no widow, and
I shall see no grief.' Therefore, her plagues, death, mourning, and 8
famine shall come in one day, and she shall be burned by fire, for
the Lord God who will judge her is mighty."

THE KINGS WEEP OVER HER

The kings of the earth who committed fornication and lived 9
wantonly with her will weep and mourn over her when they see the
smoke as she is burning. Standing afar off for fear of her torment 10
they will say, "Woe, woe, great city, Babylon, strong city, because
in a moment your judgment has come!"

THE MERCHANTS MOURN OVER HER

The merchants of the earth will weep and mourn over her 11
because no one will any longer buy their merchandise. This included 12
gold and silver, precious stones and pearls, fine linen, purple, silk
and scarlet, every kind of thyine wood, every kind of ivory product,
every kind of most costly products in wood, brass, iron and marble,
cinnamon too and amomum, incense, myrrh and frankincense, wine, 13
oil, fine flour and wheat, beasts of burden and sheep, horses and
chariots, and slaves, even human lives. The profit which your soul 14

coveted is gone from you. All the dainties and splendor are lost to
15 you, and men will never find them again. Dealers in these com-
modities who grew rich from her will stand far off for fear of her
16 torment. They will weep and mourn. "Woe, woe, great city, that
was clothed in fine linen, purple and scarlet, and glittered in gold,
17 precious stones and pearls, because in a moment these great riches
were laid waste!"

THE MARINERS CRY OUT

Every shipmaster and everyone who makes journeys, the mariners
18 and all the men who work at sea, stood afar off. They cried out
when they saw the smoke as the city was burning. "What city is
19 like this great city?" they asked. They threw dust on their heads,
and weeping and mourning they cried out, "Woe, woe, the great
city in which all who had ships at sea grew rich out of her wealth,
20 because in a moment she has been laid waste!" Make merry over
her, O heaven, and you, the saints and prophets, because God
judged your case against her.

THE ANGEL'S PROMISE

21 A strong angel took up a stone as great as a millstone and
threw it into the sea, saying, "With this violence will Babylon,
22 that great city, be thrown down and will never be found again. No
longer will the sound of harpists and musicians and flutists and
trumpeters be heard in you. No longer will all the craftsmen of
whatever craft be found in you. No longer will the sound of the
23 millstone be heard in you. No longer will the light of lamp shine in
you. No longer will bridegroom and bride be heard in you, because
your merchants were the great men of the earth, because by your
24 sorcery all the nations have been led astray. In her was found the
blood of prophets and saints and of all who had been slain on
the earth."

CHAPTER 19

THE ANGELIC SONG

1 After these things I heard what sounded like a loud voice of

a great crowd in heaven. It said, "Alleluja! Salvation and glory and power come from our God. His judgments are true and just; he has judged the great harlot who corrupted the earth with her immorality, and has avenged his servants' blood which her hands have shed." Again they said, "Alleluja! Smoke from her rises for ever and ever." The twenty-four elders and the four living beings prostrated and worshiped God, who was seated on the throne, and said, "Amen. Alleluja!" A voice came from the throne, "Praise our God, all you, his servants, and revere him, small and great."

THE VICTORY SONG

Then I heard a voice like that of a great crowd, and of many waters, and of mighty thunders, saying, "Alleluja! Now the Lord our God Almighty reigns! Let us rejoice and exult and give glory to him, for the time of the marriage of the Lamb has come. His bride made herself ready. Hers was the privilege of clothing herself in fine linen, bright and clean." The fine linen is the holy deeds of her saints.

He said to me, "Write: Blessed are they who are invited to the marriage feast of the Lamb." Again he said to me, "These are the true words of God." I prostrated before his feet to worship him, but he said to me, "Do not do that. I am a fellow servant of yours and of your brothers who hold fast the testimony concerning Jesus. Worship God, for the testimony concerning Jesus is a sure mark of the prophetic spirit."

THE FATE OF THE BEAST AND SATAN

THE KING OF KINGS

I saw heaven opened. I saw a white horse, and its rider is called Faithful and True. He judges and wages war justly. His eyes are like a flame of fire, and on his head are many diadems. He has a name inscribed that no one but he knows. He is clothed in a garment sprinkled with blood, and his name is "The Word of

---

19:1. *Alleluja:* a Hebrew word meaning "Praise you Ja" (Jehovah).
19:10. In his enthusiasm John wished to show especial homage to the angel, who, however, reminded John that an Apostle is almost the equal at least in

14 God." The armies of heaven, clothed in fine linen white and clean,
15 were following him on white horses. From his mouth comes a sharp
sword with which to strike the nations. He will rule them with an
iron rod, and he treads the wine press of the fierce anger of God
16 Almighty. He has on his garment and on his thigh a name inscribed,
"King of Kings and Lord of Lords."

DEFEAT OF THE BEAST AND OF THE FALSE PROPHET

17 I saw an angel standing on the sun. He cried in a loud voice
to all the birds that fly in midheaven, "Come, assemble for the
18 great supper God has prepared, in order to eat the flesh of kings,
of captains; of mighty men, of horses and of their riders, the flesh
of all men, free and slave, small and great."
19 I saw the beast and the kings of the earth and their armies
assembled to wage war against him who was riding the horse and
20 against his army. The beast was captured and with it the false
prophet who worked wonders in its presence, and thus deceived
those who accepted the mark of the beast and worshiped its
statue. These two were hurled alive into the lake of fire that burns
21 with brimstone. The rest were killed with the sword of the rider
of the horse, the sword that comes from his mouth. All the birds
were glutted with their flesh.

CHAPTER 20

SATAN IS BOUND

1 I saw an angel coming down from heaven, having the key of
2 the bottomless pit in his hand. He seized the dragon, the ancient
serpent, that is, the devil and Satan, and bound him for a thousand
3 years. He hurled him into the bottomless pit and closed and sealed
it over that Satan might no longer mislead the nations until the end
of the thousand years. After that he is to be released for a short time.

functions if not in nature of an angel. Everyone who testifies to Jesus' divinity
and redemptive work is a prophet or has the spirit of true prophecy.
20:2. a thousand years: this is generally interpreted by Catholic scholars as
referring to the whole period from the founding of the Church down to near
the end of time. Satan's power will be greatly curtailed; his work of seduction
will be done for him by individual men, false teachers, and irreligious governments opposed to the Church.

REIGN OF THE SAINTS WITH CHRIST

I saw thrones, and men seated on them who were given the 4 authority to exercise judgment. I saw also the souls of those who had been beheaded because of their testimony to Jesus and because of the word of God. They did not worship the beast or its statue; they did not accept its mark on their foreheads or on their hands. They came to life again and reigned with Christ a thousand years. The rest of the dead did not come to life until the thousand years 5 were ended. This is the first resurrection. Blessed and holy is he 6 who shares in this first resurrection. Over them the second death has no power, but they will be priests of God and Christ, and will reign with him a thousand years.

SATAN IS LOOSED

When the thousand years are ended, Satan will be released from 7 his prison, and will go out to mislead the nations that are at the 8 four corners of the earth, Gog and Magog. He will assemble them for battle. Their number will be as the sand of the sea.

They went up over the broad plain of the earth and surrounded 9 the camp of the saints and the beloved city, but fire came down from heaven and devoured them. Then the devil who misled them 10 was hurled into the lake of fire and brimstone, where the beast and the false prophet will be tormented day and night for ever and ever.

THE LAST JUDGMENT OF ALL

I saw a great white throne and the one who was seated on it. 11 From his presence earth and heaven fled, and no place was found for them. I also saw the dead, the great and small, standing before 12 the throne as scrolls were opened. Another scroll, the book of life, was opened, and the dead were judged according to their deeds as recorded on the scrolls. The sea gave up the dead that were in it, 13

20:4. *They came to life:* i.e., the blessed life of heaven. The first resurrection is the resurrection to the life of grace through faith and Baptism.

20:5. *The rest of the dead:* sinners, those who died without faith and Baptism. They too will experience a corporal resurrection at the end of time, but not a resurrection to glory.

20:8. *Gog and Magog:* probably the Scythians, a ferocious, warlike people who here become a symbol of all the nations who will make war on the Church.

and death and the nether world gave up the dead they imprisoned.
14 Each of them was judged according to his deeds. The nether world
and death were hurled into the lake of fire, which is the second
15 death. Whoever was not found recorded in the book of life, was
hurled into this lake of fire.

THE NEW WORLD AND THE NEW JERUSALEM

CHAPTER 21

THE NEW JERUSALEM

1   I saw a new heaven and a new earth, for the first heaven and
2 the first earth had passed away, and the sea was no more. I also
saw the holy city, New Jerusalem, coming down out of heaven from
3 God, prepared as a bride adorned for her husband. I heard a loud
voice from the throne say,

>   "How wonderful! God's dwelling place is among men;
>   he shall make his home among them.
>   They shall be his people,
>   and God himself shall abide in their midst.
4   He shall wipe away every tear from their eyes.
>   No longer will there be death.
>   No longer will there be mourning
>   or cry of anguish or pain,
>   Because the former things have passed away."

THE PROMISE AND THREAT

5   He who was seated on the throne said, "See I make all things
new." Then he added, "Write, because these words are trustworthy
6 and true." He said to me,

>   "It is done. I am the Alpha and the Omega,
>   the beginning and the end.
>   To him who thirsts I will give of the water of life
>   free of charge from the fountain.

21:2. New Jerusalem: i.e., the Church, considered both in its earthly, temporal aspects, as well as those which are heavenly and eternal. Cities and nations
in the Old Testament are sometimes figuratively represented as brides.

He who is victorious shall possess these blessings,   7
    and I will be his God, and he shall be my son.
But as for the cowardly, unfaithful, and abominable peoples,   8
    the murderers, immoral persons, and sorcerers,
    the idolaters and liars,
    their portion shall be in the lake
    that burns with fire and brimstone.
    This is the second death."

THE HEAVENLY JERUSALEM

One of the seven angels who had the bowls full of the seven   9
last plagues came and spoke to me. "Come, I will show you the
bride, the spouse of the Lamb." Then he took me in ecstasy up   10
to a large and high mountain, and he showed me the city of
Jerusalem, coming down out of heaven from God, surrounded with   11
the divine glory. Its radiance was like a most precious stone, like
jasper, clear as crystal. It had a massive and high wall with twelve   12
gates, and twelve angels at the gates. Names were inscribed on
them, names of the twelve tribes of the sons of Israel. On the east   13
were three gates, on the north three, on the south three, and on
the west three. The city walls had twelve foundation stones, and   14
on them were the twelve names of the Lamb's twelve apostles.

He who spoke to me had a measuring rod of gold to measure   15
the city, its gates and its wall. The city was square, that is, its length   16
was as great as its breadth. He measured the city with the rod —
twelve thousand stadia. Its length and breadth and height were
equal. He measured its wall — a hundred and forty cubits by man's   17
standard, which the angel used. The material of its walls was jasper,   18
but the city itself was pure gold, like clear glass. The foundation   19
stones of the city walls were adorned with every kind of precious
stone. The first foundation stone was jasper, the second sapphire,

---

21:8. *second death:* i.e., eternal damnation.

21:10. *coming . . . from God:* this indicates the heavenly origin of the Church.

21:11. *radiance:* the glory of the Church consists in its doctrine, its means of sanctification, and the holiness of its saints.

21:12–14. The names of the twelve tribes and of the Apostles symbolize the historical continuity of the Church with the synagogue. The gates on all sides indicate the universality of the Church which opens wide its portals on all sides for whoever wishes to enter.

20 the third agate, the fourth emerald, the fifth sardonyx, the sixth
    sardius, the seventh chrysolite, the eighth beryl, the ninth topaz,
    the tenth chrysoprase, the eleventh jacinth, the twelfth amethyst.
21 The twelve gates were twelve pearls, that is, each gate was of a single
    pearl. The avenues of the city were pure gold, transparent as glass.

ITS LIGHT IS GOD AND THE LAMB

22   I saw no temple in it, for the Lord God Almighty and the Lamb
23 are its temple. The city has no need of the sun or moon to shine
    on it, because the glory of God lights it up, and the Lamb is its
24 lamp. The nations will walk by its light, and the kings of the earth
25 will offer their tribute of recognition to it. Its gates will be wide
    open all the day long, which will never be brought to an end by
26 night. The nations will lay at its feet all that is estimable and
27 precious. But nothing defiled will enter it. No one that practices
    abomination or falsehood will ever gain entrance but only those
    who are recorded in the Lamb's book of life.

CHAPTER 22

THE RIVER AND THE TREE OF LIFE

1   The angel showed me a river with the water of life clear as crystal,
2   coming from the throne of God and of the Lamb. In the center,
    between the avenues and the river, was the tree of life, bearing
    fruit twelve times each year, that is, one crop each month. The leaves
    of the tree had a healing power for the nations.

THE THRONE OF GOD AND OF THE LAMB

3   No longer will any person or thing deserving of execration be

---

21:24–26. Here is foretold the world-wide recognition to be accorded the
Church on earth, as also its holiness.
    22:1. The river represents the waters of Baptism, through which the Holy
Spirit is communicated to the baptized.
    22:2. The tree of life, whose fruit, symbolic of the Eucharist, ripens through-
out the whole extent of time and eternity, represents Jesus who gives himself
as nourishment to the faithful. The curative powers of the leaves represents
the sacrament of Penance.
    22:3–5. St. John passes from the consideration of the Church on earth
(verses 1–2) to the Church in heaven, where there will no longer be the night
of sin, and where God will impart the light of glory to the elect.

found there, but the throne of God and of the Lamb shall be established in that city, and his servants will minister to him. They 4 will see his face, and his name will be on their foreheads. Night 5 will be no more, and so they will have no need of the light of lamp or of sun, because the Lord will shine on them, and they will reign for ever and ever.

Epilogue

THESE WORDS ARE TRUE

He said to me, "These words are trustworthy and true, for the 6 Lord, the God from whom prophetic gifts come, has sent his angel to show to his servants what must soon happen. Mark well, I am 7 coming soon. Blessed is he who keeps the words of the prophecy contained in this book." It is I, John, who heard and saw these 8 things. When I heard and saw, I fell down to worship at the feet of the angel who showed me these things. But he said to me, "Do 9 not do that. I am a fellow servant of yours and of your brothers, the prophets, and of those who keep the words of this book. Worship God."

DO NOT SEAL UP THE WORDS

Then he said to me, "Do not seal up the words of the prophecy 10 in this book, because the time is near. Let him who does harm, 11 continue to do so. Let him who is filthy, continue to be so. Let him who is just, continue to be so, and let him who is holy, continue to be so. Mark my word, I am coming soon. I bring my reward to 12 requite each one according to his deeds. I am the Alpha and the 13 Omega, the first and the last, the beginning and the end." Blessed 14 are they who wash their robes that they may have the right to the tree of life, and that they may enter the city by the gates. Outside 15 are dogs, the sorcerers, the immoral persons, the murderers, the idolaters, and everyone who loves and practices falsehood.

FINAL ATTESTATION

"I, Jesus, sent my angel to testify to you these things concerning 16

22:10. *Do not seal:* the book is to be left open, available for all to read as it has precious instruction for all peoples of all times.

the congregations. I am the root and the offspring of David, the
17 bright morning star." The Spirit and the bride say, "Come." So,
let him who hears it, say, "Come." Let him who thirsts, come, and
18 let him who wishes, receive the water of life as a free gift. I testify
to everyone who hears the words of the prophecy in this book. If
anyone adds anything to it, God will inflict on him the plagues that
19 are described in this book. If anyone takes away from the words of
this prophetic book, he will be deprived by God of his share in the
20 tree of life and in the holy city, which this book describes. He who
testifies to these things says, "Indeed, I am coming soon."
21   "Amen! Come, Lord Jesus." The grace of our Lord Jesus Christ
be with all. Amen.

EPISTLES AND GOSPELS

FOR SUNDAYS AND HOLYDAYS OF OBLIGATION

Day	Epistle	Gospel
First Sunday of Advent	Rom. 13:11–14	Lk. 21:25–33
Immaculate Conception	Prov. 8:22–35	Lk. 1:26–28
Second Sunday of Advent	Rom. 15:4–13	Mt. 11:2–10
Third Sunday of Advent	Phil. 4:4–7	Jn. 1:19–28
Fourth Sunday of Advent	1 Cor. 4:1–5	Lk. 3:1–6
Christmas (first Mass)	Tit. 2:11–15	Lk. 2:1–14
Christmas (second Mass)	Tit. 3:4–7	Lk. 2:15–20
Christmas (third Mass)	Hebr. 1:1–12	Jn. 1:1–14
Sunday within Octave of Christmas	Gal. 4:1–7	Lk. 2:33–40
Circumcision	Tit. 2:11–15	Lk. 2:21
The Holy Name	Acts 4:8–12	Lk. 2:21
Epiphany	Isa. 60:1–6	Mt. 2:1–12
The Holy Family	Col. 3:12–17	Lk. 2:42–52
Second Sunday after Epiphany	Rom. 12:6–16	Jn. 2:1–11
Third Sunday after Epiphany	Rom. 12:16–21	Mt. 8:1–13
Fourth Sunday after Epiphany	Rom. 13:8–10	Mt. 8:23–27
Fifth Sunday after Epiphany	Col. 3:12–17	Mt. 13:24–30
Sixth Sunday after Epiphany	1 Thess. 1:2–10	Mt. 13:31–35
Septuagesima Sunday	1 Cor. 9:24–27, 10:1–5	Mt. 20:1–16
Sexagesima Sunday	2 Cor. 11:19–33, 12:1–9	Lk. 8:4–15
Quinquagesima Sunday	1 Cor. 13:1–13	Lk.18:31–43
First Sunday of Lent	2 Cor. 6:1–10	Mt. 4:1–11
Second Sunday of Lent	1 Thess. 4:1–7	Mt. 17:1–9
Saint Joseph	Ecclus. 45:1–6	Mt. 1:18–21
Third Sunday of Lent	Eph. 5:1–9	Lk. 11:14–28
Fourth Sunday of Lent	Gal. 4:22–31	Jn. 6:1–15
Passion Sunday	Hebr. 9:11–15	Jn. 8:46–59
Palm Sunday	Phil. 2:5–11	Mt. Chapters 26 and 27
Easter Sunday	1 Cor. 5:7 f	Mk. 16:1–7
Low Sunday	1 Jn. 5:4–10	Jn. 20:19–31
Second Sunday after Easter	1 Pet. 2:21–25	Jn. 10:11–16
Third Sunday after Easter	1 Pet. 2:11–19	Jn. 16:16–22
Fourth Sunday after Easter	James 1:17–21	Jn. 16:5–14
Fifth Sunday after Easter	James 1:22–27	Jn. 16:23–30
Ascension Thursday	Acts 1:1–11	Mk. 16:14–20
Sunday within Octave of Ascension	1 Pet. 4:7–11	Jn. 15:26 f, 16:1–14
Pentecost	Acts 2:1–11	Jn. 14:23–31
Trinity Sunday	Rom. 11:33–36	Mt. 28:18–20
First Sunday after Pentecost	1 Jn. 4:8–21	Lk. 6:36–42
Corpus Christi	1 Cor. 11:23–29	Jn. 6:56–59
Second Sunday after Pentecost	1 Jn. 3:13–18	Lk. 14:16–24
Third Sunday after Pentecost	1 Pet. 5:6–11	Lk. 15:1–10

689

Day	Epistle	Gospel
Saints Peter and Paul	Acts 12:1–11 . .	Mt. 16:13–19
Fourth Sunday after Pentecost	Rom. 8:18–23 . .	Lk. 5:1–11
Fifth Sunday after Pentecost	1 Pet. 3:8–15 . .	Mt. 5:20–24
Sixth Sunday after Pentecost	Rom. 6:3–11 . . .	Mk. 8:1–9
Seventh Sunday after Pentecost . . .	Rom. 6:19–23 . .	Mt. 7:15–21
Eighth Sunday after Pentecost	Rom. 8:12–17 . .	Lk. 16:1–9
Ninth Sunday after Pentecost	1 Cor. 10:6–13 . .	Lk. 19:41–47
Assumption of the Blessed Virgin . . .	Ecclus. 24:11–13, 15–20	Lk. 10:38–42
Tenth Sunday after Pentecost	1 Cor. 12:2–11 . .	Lk. 18:9–14
Eleventh Sunday after Pentecost . . .	1 Cor. 15:1–10 . .	Mk. 7:31–37
Twelfth Sunday after Pentecost . . .	2 Cor. 3:4–9 . . .	Lk. 10:23–37
Thirteenth Sunday after Pentecost . .	Gal. 3:16–22 . . .	Lk. 17:11–19
Fourteenth Sunday after Pentecost . .	Gal. 5:16–24 . . .	Mt. 6:24–33
Fifteenth Sunday after Pentecost . . .	Gal. 5:25 f, 6:1–10	Lk. 7:11–16
Sixteenth Sunday after Pentecost . . .	Eph. 3:13–21 . . .	Lk. 14:1–11
Seventeenth Sunday after Pentecost . .	Eph. 4:1–6 . . .	Mt. 22:34–46
Eighteenth Sunday after Pentecost . .	1 Cor. 1:4–8 . . .	Mt. 9:1–8
Nineteenth Sunday after Pentecost . .	Eph. 4:23–28 . . .	Mt. 22:1–14
Twentieth Sunday after Pentecost . . .	Eph. 5:15–21 . . .	Jn. 4:46–53
Twenty-First Sunday after Pentecost . .	Eph. 6:10–17 . . .	Mt. 18:23–35
All Saints	Apoc. 7:2–12 . . .	Mt. 5:1–12
Twenty-Second Sunday after Pentecost .	Phil. 1:6–11 . . .	Mt. 22:15–21
Twenty-Third Sunday after Pentecost . .	Phil. 3:17–21, 4:1–3	Mt. 9:18–26
Twenty-Fourth Sunday after Pentecost .	Col. 1:9–14 . . .	Mt. 24:15–35